Mecca of Revolution

OXFORD STUDIES IN INTERNATIONAL HISTORY

JAMES J. SHEEHAN, SERIES ADVISOR

The Wilsonian Moment
Self-Determination and the International Origins of Anticolonial Nationalism
EREZ MANELA

In War's Wake
Europe's Displaced Persons in the Postwar Order
GERARD DANIEL COHEN

Grounds of Judgment
Extraterritoriality and Imperial Power in Nineteenth-Century China and Japan
PÄR KRISTOFFER CASSEL

The Acadian Diaspora
An Eighteenth-Century History
CHRISTOPHER HODSON

Gordian Knot
Apartheid and the Unmaking of the Liberal World Order
RYAN IRWIN

The Global Offensive
The United States, the Palestine Liberation Organization, and the Making of the Post–Cold War Order
PAUL THOMAS CHAMBERLIN

Mecca of Revolution
Algeria, Decolonization, and the Third World Order
JEFFREY JAMES BYRNE

Mecca of Revolution

Algeria, Decolonization, and the Third World Order

JEFFREY JAMES BYRNE

Oxford University Press is a department of the University of Oxford. It furthers
the University's objective of excellence in research, scholarship, and education
by publishing worldwide. Oxford is a registered trade mark of Oxford University
Press in the UK and certain other countries.

Published in the United States of America by Oxford University Press
198 Madison Avenue, New York, NY 10016, United States of America.

© Oxford University Press 2016

First issued as an Oxford University Press paperback, 2019

All rights reserved. No part of this publication may be reproduced, stored in
a retrieval system, or transmitted, in any form or by any means, without the
prior permission in writing of Oxford University Press, or as expressly permitted
by law, by license, or under terms agreed with the appropriate reproduction
rights organization. Inquiries concerning reproduction outside the scope of the
above should be sent to the Rights Department, Oxford University Press, at the
address above.

You must not circulate this work in any other form
and you must impose this same condition on any acquirer.

Library of Congress Cataloging-in-Publication Data
Byrne, Jeffrey James, author.
Mecca of revolution : Algeria, decolonization, and the Third World order / Jeffrey James Byrne.
pages cm
Includes bibliographical references and index.
ISBN 978–0–19–989914–2 (hardcover : alk. paper); ISBN 978–0–19–005377–2 (paperback : alk. paper)
1. Algeria—History—Revolution, 1954–1962.   2. Algeria—History—Autonomy and
independence movements.   3. Jabhat al-Tahrir al-Qawmi—History.   4. Algeria—Politics
and government.   5. Algeria—Foreign relations.   I. Title.
DT295.B96 2016
962.046—dc23
2015035929

For my parents

CONTENTS

Acknowledgments ix
Abbreviations xiii

Introduction 1

1. Method Men: The Praxis of Anticolonial Resistance 14

2. Our Friends Today: Algeria Joins the Third World 68

3. Real Existing Third Worldism: National Development in the Age of Ideologies 113

4. The Allure of Globalism: Continents, Colors, and the Cold War 172

5. Mecca of Impatience and Anxiety: Globalizations and the Third World Order 227

Conclusion 286

Notes 299
Bibliography 347
Index 365

ACKNOWLEDGMENTS

When asked how he went bankrupt, a character in Ernest Hemingway's *The Sun Also Rises* replies, "Two ways: gradually, then suddenly." I wrote this book in similar fashion. I have left a trail of gratitude across space and time, from the impecunious early days to the thrilling denouement, from Algiers all the way to Vancouver.

First of all, it would have been impossible for me to pursue my research in various locations without the help of others. In London, I am grateful to Tiha Franulovic for all sorts of logistical and bureaucratic support, and also to all the staff and inhabitants of the Ideas Centre at London School of Economics (LSE), formerly the Cold War Studies Centre. No less important, my brother picked up the tab for morale-boosting evenings on countless occasions. Svetozar Rajak, of the LSE Ideas Centre, additionally provided invaluable assistance that enabled my research in the Serbian and former Yugoslavian archives, as did Jovan Čavoški. Vladimir Unkovski-Korica was a genial guide through Belgrade's nightlife. In Paris, I am very grateful to the Tilquins and to the Frankels for their boundless hospitality. My sincere thanks also to Anne Liskenne, conservateur en chef du Patrimoine at the archives of the French foreign ministry, for the benefit of her expertise and generously granting access to Algeria-related material that was still in the process of classification. Terah Maher provided hospitality and entertainment in Boston, as did the Blevinses and Fuvarskies in Washington DC.

In Algiers, I will always cherish the support, hospitality, and camaraderie afforded to me by Père Thierry Becker and the other residents of "Les Glycines." I benefited in particular from Clement Hervé's keen sense of the mot juste in multiple languages. Down the road in Oran, Bob Parks and Karim Ouaras of the Centre d'Etudes Maghrébines en Algérie provided vital logistical support, as did Krimat Abderrahmane back in the capital. I am also grateful to Daho Djerbal of NAQD and Fouad Soufi, now of CRASC, for their time and advice. My research in Algiers would simply not have been successful without the help, insight, and advice generously granted to me by Ryme Seferdjeli, Aissa Seferdjeli, Ahmed Laïdi, Nourredine Djoudi, and Slimane Shikh. Furthermore, *Mecca of Revolution* would have been profoundly different (and less fulfilling for me) were it not for the cooperation, support, and patience granted to me by the direction and staff of the Archives Nationales d'Algérie.

During the graduate studies that produced the first draft of this book, Melvyn P. Leffler, Odd Arne Westad, and the Harry S. Truman Library granted me an invaluable intellectual opportunity and financial support through the Cambridge History of the Cold War project. I also received financial support from the John F. Kennedy Library, the Lyndon Baines Johnson Library. A multi-year grant from the Canadian Social Sciences and Humanities Research Council made it possible for me to achieve my research goals, pursue new directions, and share my work.

My intellectual debts are almost impossible to catalogue. First and foremost, however, this book is a testament to the mentorship of Odd Arne Westad, my thesis supervisor at the LSE and an irreplaceable source of guidance ever since. He is as great a teacher as he is a scholar, always pushing his students to pursue their inquiries to the end, wherever the destination. As befits a supporter of Arsenal FC, he never lost faith in the face of inconsistent performances. Astute readers will likely detect Arne's influence in all the book's good bits and regret its absence elsewhere.

I am also grateful to Matt Connelly who has been a generous source of both practical and intellectual support over the years. Although his *Diplomatic Revolution* bestrides the field of Algerian international history like a colossus, he has always been commendably open to competing interpretations and willing to share his own research. James McDougall and Fawaz Gerges were wonderful examiners for my viva at LSE: this "exam" was a very rewarding experience, and their extensive reports and comments on the doctoral thesis exemplified how that process can guide the creation of a first monograph. Likewise, I offer my thanks to the anonymous readers selected by Oxford University Press for their considered and constructive feedback and to Vijay Prashad, Bob Vitalis, Julia Clancy-Smith, and Matt Connelly for reading and commenting on the manuscript before publication.

I am equally grateful to Paul Kennedy and John Gaddis, directors of International Security Studies at Yale, for bringing me into their fecund intellectual community. My time at ISS was crucial not only to this particular project's development but, more importantly, also to my growth as a scholar in the purest sense. In addition to being associate director of ISS during this time, Ryan Irwin has been a perennial intellectual companion at conferences and seminars. *Mecca of Revolution* is better for our discussions. More recently, the National History Center's International Seminar on Decolonization was another hugely rewarding experience that has shaped my thoughts. Every participant taught me new things, but I would particularly like to thank the seminar's leaders, Wm. Roger Lewis, Jason Parker, Marilyn Young, Dane Kennedy, and Philippa Levine.

A great many people have given me opportunities to present, disseminate, and refine my work, directly contributing to this book's evolution. In that respect, in no particular order, I extend my sincere thanks to Gil-li Vardi, Rob Rakove, David Holloway, Professor Maurice Vaïsse, Tanya Harmer, Victoria de Grazia, Massimiliano Trentin, Bob McMahon, Federico Romero, Elisabetta Bini, Giuliano Garavini, Brad Simpson, Bob Vitalis, Todd Shepard, Malika Rahal, the direction of the Centre de Recherche en Anthropologie sociale et Culturelle in Oran, Bob Brower, Jessica Chapman, Mark Lawrence, Benjamin Brower, Sandra Bott, Jussi Hanhimäki, Janick Schaufelbuehl, and Marco Wyss. Lien-Hang Nguyen, Paul Chamberlin, Artemy Kalinovsky, Jessica Wang, and John Roosa also stand out as intellectual interlocutors whose insights have helped to shape this project, although this list is certainly inadequate.

I could not imagine simultaneously completing a book and mastering professorhood anywhere other than the History Department at the University of British Columbia, where my colleagues generate an uncommonly convivial and considerate environment. I am grateful also to my students for asking the questions I did not know that I did not know the answer to, even while wishing that this were a less frequent occurrence. Susan Ferber, Molly Morrison, and the team at OUP took a chance on me and have been wonderful to work with. Thanks especially, Susan, for pretending that I haven't been difficult.

Lastly, I simply owe it all to my parents and to Sasie. What can I say? It's finished now, folks, really finished. Welllll, maybe just one small change . . .

ABBREVIATIONS

AAPC	All-African Peoples' Conference
AAPSO	Afro-Asian Peoples' Solidarity Organization
ALN	Armée de Libération Nationale (National Liberation Army, Algeria)
ANC	African National Congress
ANP	Armée Nationale Populaire (People's National Army, Algeria)
CIAS	Conference of Independent African States
CNL	Conseil National de Libération (National Liberation Council, Congo)
CNRA	Conseil National de la Révolution Algérienne (National Council of the Algerian Revolution)
CPSU	Communist Party of the Soviet Union
EMG	Etat Majeur-Général (General Staff of ALN)
ENA	Etoile Nord Africain (North African Star)
FFS	Front des Forces Socialistes (Socialist Forces Front, Algeria)
FLN	Front de Libération Nationale (National Liberation Front, Algeria)
FNLA	Frente Nacional de Libertaçao de Angola (National Front for the Liberation of Angola)
FRELIMO	Frente de Libertação de Moçambique (Mozambique Liberation Front)
GPRA	Gouvernement Provisoire de la République Algérienne (Provisional Government of the Algerian Republic)
GPRA-MAE	Ministère aux Affaires Extérieures, GPRA (Ministry of External Affairs, Algerian GPRA)
MAE	Ministère des Affaires Etrangères (Ministry of Foreign Affairs, France and Algeria)

MK	Umkhonto we Sizwe (Spear of the Nation, South Africa)
MNA	Mouvement National Algérien (Algerian National Movement)
MNC	Mouvement National Congolais (Congolese National Movement)
MPLA	Movimento Popular de Libertação de Angola (Popular Movement for the Liberation of Angola)
MTLD	Mouvement pour le Triomphe des Libértés Démocratiques (Movement for the Triumph of Democratic Liberties, Algeria)
NAM	Non-Aligned Movement
NATO	North Atlantic Treaty Organization
NLF	National Liberation Front (South Vietnam)
OAS	Organisation Armée Secrète (Secret Armed Organization, Algeria)
OAU	Organization of African Unity
OCAM	Organisation Commune Africaine et Malgache (African and Malagasy Common Organization)
ONRA	Office National de la Reforme Agraire (National Office for Agrarian Reform, Algeria)
OS	Organisation Spéciale (Special Organization, Algeria)
PAIGC	Partido Africano da Independência da Guiné e Cabo Verde (African Party for the Independence of Guinea and Cape Verde)
PCA	Parti Communiste Algérien (Algerian Communist Party)
PCF	Parti Communiste Français (French Communist Party)
PLO	Palestinian Liberation Organization
PPA	Parti du Peuple Algérien (Algerian People's Party)
RDA	Rassemblement Démocratique Africain (Democratic African Rally)
RADP	République Algérienne Démocratique et Populaire (People's Democratic Republic of Algeria)
SAS	Sections Administratives Spécialisées (Special Administrative Sections)
SWAPO	South West African People's Organization
UAR	United Arab Republic
UDMA	Union Démocratique du Manifeste Algérien (Democratic Union of the Algerian Manifesto)
UGEMA	Union Générale des Etudiants Musulmans Algériens (General Union of Muslim Algerian Students)
UNCTAD	United Nations Conference on Trade and Development

UNFP	Union Nationale des Forces Populaires (National Union of Popular Forces, Morocco)
UPC	Union des Populations du Cameroun (Union of Cameroonian Peoples)
ZAPU	Zimbabwe African People's Union

Mecca of Revolution

Introduction

It was an exemplary coup d'état. Trusted military units, prepositioned near the capital, moved into the city in the dead of night. Confused locals awoke to find tanks and soldiers of their own nation's army occupying major intersections and vital locations, such as the government buildings, the state radio and television broadcaster, and the airport. By then, the president had already been spirited away to an unknown fate. The plotters had captured him in his bed, the depth of his defeat demonstrated by the fact that the group that came for him included the very man he had been counting on to prevent this turn of events. Presented with a fait accompli, perhaps not so attached to their president as he had hoped, few members of the public offered overt criticism or protest. Indeed, the foreign minister, who was one of the coup's primary orchestrators, bragged that they would have killed their former leader if they had known how little resistance they would face. It was false bravado. As he well knew, in June 1965 Algeria was subject to intense international scrutiny.

In fact, the coup initially provoked greater consternation abroad. Charismatic and dynamic, President Ahmed Ben Bella managed in his brief tenure, beginning at Algeria's independence three years earlier, to establish himself as one of the most prominent statesmen in the Southern Hemisphere. His erstwhile colleagues and usurpers, chief among them the minister of defense, Houari Boumedienne, therefore now faced a crisis of legitimacy in Africa, the Middle East, Latin America, and Asia. Egyptian president Gamal Abdel Nasser, the most powerful man in the Arab world, demanded that his friend be released into his care. Several African heads of state, including Ghana's Kwame Nkrumah and Julius Nyerere of Tanzania, declared that Ben Bella's fate was a matter of concern for the whole continent and insisted on an investigation. From the far side of the Atlantic Ocean, Cuba's Fidel Castro thundered blistering denunciations with characteristic vigor. More contemplative was the response of Castro's counterpart from British Guiana, Cheddi Jagan, who penned a mournful ode to the man he had so admired: "Where is he now / Ben Bella / What dark prison holds him / away from his people?"[1] While neither poetry nor petitions sprang Ben Bella, such demonstrations of international concern may well have spared his life: hidden from the world for a decade and a half, he was eventually released, in the wake of Boumedienne's premature death, in December 1978. By that time, an era had passed for Algeria and the postcolonial world as a whole.

Of course, Ben Bella's considerable individual charm notwithstanding, this outpouring of concern reflected the considerable prestige that Algeria as a whole enjoyed throughout the "Third World." The North African country had accumulated many sympathizers in the course of its long and brutal war of independence from France, 1954–1962, which claimed as many as one million lives and hastened the dismantling of Europe's great empires. This costly struggle granted its people a heroic image elsewhere in the postcolonial world, where liberation through force of arms was the exception rather than the rule. For its part, the embattled Algerian Front de Libération Nationale (National Liberation Front, FLN) reciprocated Asia and Africa's admiration. Its leaders greatly prized the support of those countries that were already independent. They credited their participation in the two meetings that laid the foundations for postcolonial international affairs—the April 1955 Summit of Asian-African Heads of State in Bandung, Indonesia and the September 1961 founding conference of the Non-Aligned Movement (NAM) in Belgrade, Yugoslavia—with changing the fortunes of their campaign.[2] The symbiosis of Third World internationalism and Algerian nationalism was personified in Frantz Fanon, the psychiatrist from French Martinique who happened to be working in an Algerian hospital when the nationalist rebellion began, embraced the FLN's cause as his own, and became arguably the single most influential ideological voice of both the Algerian Revolution specifically and revolutionary anticolonialism in the more general, global sense.

Moreover, with independence achieved in July 1962, the new République Algérienne Démocratique et Populaire (People's Democratic Republic of Algeria, RADP) continued to express its identity and pursue its ambitions through those relationships and international initiatives that its diplomats referred to as "this Third World project." Forged in the crucible of the FLN's pioneering international campaign, that unusually capable diplomatic team allowed Algeria to assume disproportionate responsibility, in relation to its size, for the maintenance of globe-spanning coalitions like NAM and the Group of 77 (G77) that maximized the developing countries' influence in world affairs. In the same spirit, the Algerians played a central role in the founding of the Organization of African Unity (OAU) in April 1963, which they considered the prototype for a postcolonial order free of systemic Western interference. At the same time, portraying their country as a "pilot state," Ben Bella and his colleagues presented Algeria's socialist experiment as an example for others to follow. They accepted an influx of foreign anarchists, Trotskyists, and other assorted fellow travelers who were eager to build a new utopia amid the wreckage of colonialism. In the words of a French diplomat posted to the embassy in Algiers in the early 1960s, the atmosphere there was "simultaneously convivial, revolutionary, disorganized, and generous." Moreover,

> Trotskyites, anarchists, internationalists from France and elsewhere lavished the young president with often confusing advice.... Dissidents from every authoritarian regime in the Southern Hemisphere flocked to Algiers to devise the ideology that came to be known as "Third Worldism." It... rejected the inertia of Western civilization and counted on the new youth of the world, who sought to liberate themselves once and for all.[3]

For those disillusioned with both the Western and Eastern examples, Algeria seemed set to fulfill the Third World's promise of a third way, a better way.

In addition to these bold diplomatic and economic endeavors, this poor and war-ravaged country received even greater recognition for its wholehearted commitment to the principle of anticolonial solidarity. Algeria offered support and hospitality to a panoply of national liberation movements, guerrilla armies, and insurrectionary exiles from every corner of the globe. As a result, Algiers quickly became an entrepôt of subversion, where rebels from such places as Palestine, Angola, Argentina, and Vietnam, among many others (including, in time, the Western countries Britain, the United States, and Canada) lived together, conspired together, and vowed to die together. It was this policy that inspired the nationalist rebel from "Portuguese" Guinea-Bissau, Amilcar Cabral, to approvingly dub the Algerian capital the "Mecca of Revolution."[4]

However, it was no coincidence that Boumedienne and his allies chose to overthrow Ben Bella on 19 June 1965, mere days before Algiers was scheduled to host the long-awaited Second Summit of Afro-Asian Heads of State, or "Bandung 2." Hosting Bandung 2, the sequel to the 1955 conference that had by this time achieved mythical status in the Southern Hemisphere, should have been the culmination of Algeria's efforts to become a guiding force in Third World affairs. It was only fitting, enthused one senior diplomat, that the meeting should take place in a country "whose exploits and sacrifices ... epitomize ... the anticolonial struggle."[5] With Egyptian, Chinese, and (somewhat ironically) French assistance, Ben Bella's government had overseen the construction at breakneck pace of a grand new conference venue and luxury hotel complex being built expressly for this occasion. That decision was typical of Third Worldist diplomacy in that era. The Ethiopian government had built gleaming new headquarters for the OAU two years before, while Nkrumah had ordered the construction of yet another grand complex from scratch in the Ghanaian capita, Accra, in order to hold an African summit in the autumn of 1965. Critics might charge that such schemes were hubristic excesses for poor countries, that even allowing for foreign benefactors covering much of the expense, these showpiece projects amounted to a sort of postcolonial Potemkinism intended to conceal grim socioeconomic realities that might otherwise make a mockery of new elites' grandiose rhetoric. Yet, they also reflected the genuine spirit of optimism and possibility that characterized the early years of independence, a period all too easily obscured by subsequent disappointments and the contemporary era's dominant narratives of postcolonial disillusionment.[6]

Indeed, if the Algerian coup blemished this optimistic era and possibly augured its closure, it was also oddly indicative of it. For Ben Bella's rivals feared that, if he were permitted to preside over Bandung 2, he would so thoroughly attach himself to the universal yearnings of the age that his political position, at home and abroad, would become unassailable. Better than most, they understood the reciprocity of international and domestic legitimacy in the postcolonial context. Hence their decision to act, even as the first of thousands of expected dignitaries were already descending on Algiers. But if it was true, as the country's leaders insisted, that Algeria's individual fate was inseparable from that of the global anti-imperialist struggle, what, then, did tanks in the streets of the Mecca of Revolution portend for the Third World project?

Mecca of Revolution uses its Maghribi vantage to examine decolonization and the phenomenon of Third World internationalism on a larger scale. Algeria is ideally suited to the task. In addition to being an exemplary and prominent participant in the Third World movement, it is also an unusually interconnected place. Positioned at the interstices of North and South, Europe and the "Orient," Africa and the Arab world, this expansive land (the largest country on the African continent following the secession of South Sudan) has long been a crossroads between cultures and civilizations. In the first half of the twentieth century, its inhabitants defied the French authorities' increasingly determined efforts to isolate them from forces of change afoot in the world, so that Muslim Algerian society and politics reflected the dynamism and diversity of thought that characterized the late colonial era as a whole. Arab nationalism, Islamic modernism, liberalism, communism—these influences and others left their mark. Defying Western categories and the prevailing "area studies" mentality that deemed Algeria peripheral to various regional units, the country's new leaders saw their interstitial status as a source of strength.[7] They believed that they could maximize their influence by acting as an interface between political spheres and regions.[8]

Non-Algerians also hoped to harness the country's interstitial position and international prestige. Fanon dreamt of "carrying Algeria to the four corners of

Africa"; Palestinian nationalist Yaser Arafat described it as "the window through which we appear to the West," while a French policymaker deemed it "the 'narrow doorway' through which we enter the Third World."⁹ The Cuban and Yugoslavian governments saw Algeria as their bridge to Africa, while African revolutionaries traveled between continents on Algerian passports.¹⁰ Dubbed the *pieds rouges* (red feet) in sarcastic reference to the enigmatic nickname for colonial Algeria's European inhabitants, *pieds noirs* (black feet), the European leftists who flocked to Ben Bella's government, saw the postcolonial world as a blank slate or conceptual space on which to build the new societies rejected in their own lands. Such notions validated the Algerians' ambitions and reveal that the desire to escape one's geographical fate was widespread. To that effect, the unconventional internal organization of the new Algerian foreign ministry—which segmented the world into "Latin America and Asia," "the West," "socialist countries," "Arab countries," and so on—is a reminder that geography is a social and ideological construction, susceptible to alteration during primordial periods such as the era of decolonization.¹¹

If Algeria could be many things to many people, the "Third World" continues to be a slippery concept and a challenging subject of inquiry, for reasons beyond that of sheer geographical scale.¹² Was it a place, an economic category, or a political movement? Does it still exist? On the one hand, an identifiable body of widely read literature and common ideological references gives the impression of a fairly cohesive and coherent "Third Worldist" perspective. Early cornerstones of the canon included the writings of Lenin, Mao Zedong, Mohandas Gandhi, and Michael Collins, while the likes of Ernesto "Che" Guevara, India's Jawaharlal Nehru, Fanon, and Nkrumah also became popular inspirations by the 1960s. Yet Third Worldism was still far from being a codified or formalized ideology, and scholars have often used words like "trend," "vogue." or "mentalité" to convey its fuzziness as a mobilizing idea.¹³ Perhaps, though, that fuzziness was key to its undeniable popularity and power. While the French economist Alfred Sauvey first coined the term *tiers monde* in 1952 to describe poor countries with tremendous population growth and revolutionary potential, the new leaders of the Southern Hemisphere then quickly appropriated it to convey their intent to rapidly transform their own societies and international society, too. The Third World signified an alternative to the discredited philosophies of Western and communist civilization, accused of inveterate militarism and despotism. Anticolonialism, world peace, and global economic equality were the dominant themes of this transformative impulse. President Sukarno of Indonesia declared at the 1955 Bandung conference, generally considered the beginning of the Third World as a diplomatic and rhetorical phenomenon, that "we can inject the voice of reason into world affairs[, w]e can mobilize all the spiritual, all the moral, all the political strength of Asia and Africa on the side of peace."¹⁴

The Third Worldist trend should be understood in this spirit: an application of the optimism of decolonization to the international sphere.[15]

Taking its cue from its central Algerian protagonists, as well as from historians such as Vijay Prasad and Odd Arne Westad, *Mecca of Revolution* examines the Third World as a political project—active cooperation between political elites in the developing world to achieve an extremely ambitious, yet not wholly unrealistic, agenda of political and economic reordering on a global scale.[16] This cooperation began well before decolonization, its internationalist spirit evolving symbiotically with localized anticolonial trends as a result of the inherently cosmopolitan character of Europe's empires in the post–World War I era.[17] Growing numbers of students, low-level administrators, workers, and soldiers from the colonies mingled in metropolitan universities and factories or, alternatively, served in one another's homelands. For example, Gandhi worked as a lawyer in South Africa, numerous influential Caribbean activists and future African national leaders mingled in London in the 1930s and 1940s, and Arab Maghribi conscripts fought for France on battlefields from Italy to Indochina. These experiences inspired political awakenings, instilled a sense of shared suffering, and encouraged colonials to look at imperialism as a massive integrated system that could only be defeated through collective resistance. This spirit of solidarity and globalist perspective often implanted itself at an early stage in the evolution of local nationalist movements, so that the Third Worldist instinct was inextricable from many postcolonial identities. Following Bandung, Third Worldist diplomacy placed great emphasis on a constant stream of international meetings that popularized diverse expressions of internationalist solidarity like "positive neutralism," "nonalignment," "Afro-Asianism," "tricontinentalism," pan-Africanism, Arab unity, and in reference to North Africa specifically, Maghribi unity. Such terms riddled the discourse of international affairs the Southern Hemisphere. By the early 1960s, organizations such as the G77 and the United Nations Conference on Trade and Development (UNCTAD) gave concrete form to the desire to restructure the world economy, to the benefit of poor countries, in parallel to the political transformations already taking place.

Nevertheless, the luster of these initiatives has faded to such a degree that "Third World" is often thought to be a pejorative expression, at least in wealthy English-speaking countries. If the prolonged economic and political difficulties of so many former colonies were the most proximate cause of the Third World's sullied reputation, that reputation is also the product of a rich vein of skepticism on the part of many Western observers and policymakers, dating back to the original Bandung conference.[18] American, British, and French diplomats had obvious reasons to dislike strident, open criticism of their imperial policies, military activities in the Southern Hemisphere, and, indeed, the simple suggestion that the Cold War between the United States and Soviet Union was not the most important issue in world affairs for all people. Secretary of State John Foster Dulles famously, or notoriously, stated in 1956 than nonalignment was "immoral and short-sighted."[19] Subsequently, in light of the obvious disconnect between the grandiosity of Third Worldist rhetoric and the meager resources of the participating countries, as well as the increasingly despotic character of their regimes, it became easier to dismiss the movement as either deluded or cynical, or both. Nor have its proponents and defenders always been effective, since they tend to share the critics' preoccupation with a public discourse that was noble but, in itself, insubstantial.[20] A related problem is the corruption of history: major inaccuracies, such as the claim that Nkrumah attended the Bandung conference, have been repeated in print so many times over the years that it is difficult for diligent scholars to be certain of the facts, because retracing citations so often leads to dead ends. Similarly, there is a tendency toward ahistoricity in the literature on the subject. A mythologized Bandung casts too heavy a shadow, speeches from 1955 often dubiously quoted to explain events occurring two decades later, while terms like Afro-Asian and nonalignment are often mistakenly treated as synonyms.[21] On the whole, admirable exceptions to the rule notwithstanding, the Third World phenomenon does not boast a literature commensurate with its import to modern history.[22]

In this light, Algeria is a particularly useful locus of investigation because its leaders and cadres were themselves gravely concerned by the Third World's supposed ideological deficiencies and recognized the need to translate rhetoric into practicable policies. Happily, the country is also rich in a rare commodity in postcolonial history: evidence from state archives.[23] In addition to interviews with key figures, such as Ben Bella himself, this book makes extensive use of the Algerian archives, including those of both the FLN liberation movement and the independent Algerian state. The archives of another prominent participant in Third World affairs, Yugoslavia, as well as a variety of powerful states, such as France, Britain, and the United States, complement the Algerian perspective and reveal the bigger picture. This evidence makes it possible to look behind the thick layers of rhetoric and bombast that shield the Third World movement from insightful inquiry. It reveals, for example, that terms like "Afro-Asianism" and "nonalignment" were not mere expressions of sentiment or interchangeable slogans, but distinct geopolitical trends that shaped international affairs in the Southern Hemisphere and were even, at times, in direct conflict with one another. Likewise, this new evidence shows how, owing to the widespread popular sentiment in the postcolonial world that diplomacy should be a reflection of a nation's cultural and religious identities, the leaders of countries like Algeria tended to obscure the very real practical foreign policy ramifications of solidarity themes, such as Arab unity and pan-Africanism, which they deliberated and prioritized in a manner not so different from, say, a British Foreign Office official contemplating European integration and the Commonwealth. In short, with the demystification of Third Worldism, the affairs of Africa, the Middle East, and the Southern Hemisphere as a whole are revealed from a new, insider's perspective.

This alternative perspective's first notable contribution to our understanding of modern international and global history is to further situate the Cold War in the larger context of decolonization.[24] *Mecca of Revolution* is not so much a book about the Cold War in the Third World as one about the Third World's Cold War. National liberation movements like the FLN and poor countries like Algeria were active and willing participants in the geopolitical turbulence of their time. In the same manner that historians have argued that the Western European countries "invited" American empire in the 1940s and 1950s, the comparatively weak state and nonstate actors of the developing world frequently pulled the United States and the Soviet Union into their affairs to their own (presumed) advantage.[25] To be sure, it can be trite to observe that such-and-such weak actor had more influence in international affairs than hitherto recognized, and the fact is that the yawning disparity of power between Third World forces and the superpowers ensured that the former's miscalculation often ended in disaster. Nevertheless, aware of the risks, the Algerians and their likeminded peers across the Southern Hemisphere practiced a doctrine of nonalignment that, contrary to their harmonious public rhetoric, actively sought to incite international tensions to their own advantage. The FLN and the state it created were insurgents that traveled the globe but also insurgents with respect to global order. Moreover, their maneuvers reveal a world far more complex than that allowed for in traditional Cold War narratives. In the dimming light of empire, secondary powers, such as France and communist China, emerged as credible competitors against the United States and the Soviet Union for the friendship of Africans and Asians. Third World actors tried to pit the superpowers against these second tier powers as much as against one another, exposing a multipolar Cold War well before the period of detente and Richard Nixon's visit to China, in the early 1970s.[26]

More profoundly perhaps, the emergent elites of the Third World chose to replicate the multiple dimensions of the Cold War at the local regional level and within their own societies, geopolitics being only one of those dimensions. Rival states and national liberation movements, such as those in Morocco and Algeria, say, or the competing Angolan nationalist groups, also frequently hurled themselves into the global battle between "ways of life" and theories of socioeconomic organization. Only rarely did Third World forces fully embrace Western or communist ideologies, but they accepted the premise that they were living in an age of ideology that necessitated having one of one's own—typically, a hybrid of various outside ideological influences with supposedly authentic indigenous identifiers. As nationalist identities merged with socioeconomic identities, local contests over territory and cultural legitimacy, such as that between independent

Morocco and Algeria, expressed themselves as economic contests akin to that between the two Germanies (a comparison sometimes made by the antagonists themselves). In other words, the convergence of the Cold War and the processes of decolonization had the effect of imbuing national identities with a functional rationale: the purpose of the nation was development.

No less significantly, the Third World replicated the Cold War's vertical hierarchies of power, from the international level to the subnational level, as a means of replicating the European sovereign state model.[27] A vital mechanism for doing so was the adoption of the Cold War's competing practices of political organization.[28] Liberal internationalist diplomacy in the tradition of Woodrow Wilson's Fourteen Points, on the one hand, and the communist world's proven methods of subversive organization and revolutionary war, on the other, put the opponents of the imperial order on the path toward building sovereign states. Indeed, for all of the attention paid to the colonial world's reception of Wilson's and Vladimir Lenin's ideas, modes of action were more appealing than ideologies to many anticolonial militants, because they were impatient to begin their assault on the status quo.[29] It is because of this underrecognized dynamic that the superpowers managed to fuel so much internal disorder in supposedly fragile Third World states lacking innate territorial logic, yet only very rarely altered postcolonial borders or threatened the integrity of state sovereignty.

Many readers will know Algeria best from Matthew Connelly's history of the war of independence, *A Diplomatic Revolution*, which showed how the FLN was a herald of globalization, a transnational movement that defied the prerogatives of state sovereignty by leveraging the new normative and institutionalized framework of international affairs.[30] Happily, Algeria has more wisdom to share. This book pillages Connelly's insights even as its differing analytical focus leads in almost the opposite interpretive direction. Above all, by extending its analysis beyond independence into the postcolonial era, and by placing greater emphasis on "South-South" international relations, it argues that the net result of decolonization was a dramatically more state-centric world order than had been true of even the very late colonial post–World War II years. That is to say, the onset of globalization and the proliferation of transnational phenomena—meaning human interactions of all kinds outside of state channels—indisputably happened, but neither the relative nor the absolute power of sovereign states declined as a result. Indeed, it seems likely that transnational phenomena have become more visible to historians precisely because states have been multiplying and monitoring ever more aspects of life. It is perhaps against trend to thrust the state back into the center of historical analysis, as it is to focus on political elites and diplomacy, but intellectual trends that primarily reflect the preoccupations of Western societies have kept essential aspects of Third World history underexamined.

The chapters ahead chart the evolution of the Third World project from its interwar beginnings to the crucial inflection point of 1965. A crucial aspect of this story is the manner in which Third Worldism transformed from a transnational mode of cooperation that evaded and subverted the authority of the colonial state into an international collaboration that legitimized and zealously defended the authority of the postcolonial state. In other words, Third Worldism imposed order and structural uniformity on the process of decolonization. After all, the nationalist endpoint to the evolution of anticolonialist thought and mobilization should not be taken for granted. Decolonization's state-based outcome was neither self-evident nor inevitable, arguably even as late as the mid-1950s in Africa, when both the imperial powers and anticolonial groups were still experimenting with different notions of limited autonomy, transnational "interdependence" between the metropole and the colony or regional confederations that combined multiple territories. After Bandung, the great Algerian Islamic intellectual Malek Bennabi, reflecting this period of hopeful experimentation, predicted the onset of nothing less than "a wholly new era in the evolution of international society and civilization . . . a veritable transfiguration of international relations through the slow but steady progression from a 'closed' society of states to an 'open' international society."[31]

But this transfiguration did not come to pass. Instead, entities such as NAM and the OAU came to serve as mutual recognition societies for the participating governments, which also pledged to respect the inviolability of one another's borders and internal affairs. Recognizing that their successful mediation between the international and imperial spheres had been vital to their political ascendance, the Third World's new leaders made sure to control and monitor interactions between their national domains and the outside world. For better or for worse, the postcolonial order quickly became an emphatically "closed" one.

Chapter 1, "Method Men," follows the evolution of the Algerian nationalist project from the end of World War I to 1959/1960, just after the midpoint of the Algerian War. During the 1920s and 1930s especially, Algerian nationalism evolved in the context of mounting politicization throughout the colonial world, and Algerian activists were fully integrated in the global exchange of ideas among their African, Arab, and Asian peers. Within this rich and complex late-colonial political environment, the chapter argues, the dueling dogmas of Wilsonianism and Leninism played a decisive role in the creation of the FLN. Vitally, however, the import of these two influences was much less ideological than practical. The young militants who founded the FLN were impatient for action, and for them the liberal internationalism of Woodrow Wilson suggested one means to achieve their goals—diplomacy—while Lenin's genius at revolutionary organization demonstrated another. The resultant combination of diplomacy and revolutionary nation-building then drove the FLN in an increasingly state-oriented conception of "liberation," a trend that reached its logical conclusion in the movement's effort to completely control Algerian political life and its founding of the Gouvernement Provisoire de la République Algérienne (Provisional Government of the Algerian Republic, GPRA) in 1958.

Chapter 2, "Our Friends Today," examines the FLN's embrace of the Third World concept during the latter years of the War of Independence. Its diplomatic cadres and the officers of the Armée de Libération Nationale (National Liberation Army, ALN) were especially attracted to the charismatic Cuban Revolution, and they responded to the accelerating decolonization of sub-Saharan Africa by seeking to play the same "vanguard" role on that continent as Fidel Castro claimed for Cuba in Latin America. The FLN expanded into West Africa, with Fanon as one of its most important representatives in the region, and even began supporting smaller independence movements from such places as Angola and Cameroon. The Algerians epitomized the confused condition of the African international system during decolonization: while insisting on their own quest for sovereignty, they undermined the sovereignty of their neighbors Morocco and Tunisia. The FLN's leaders and cadres also began to subscribe to the transformative dreams of Third Worldism, advocating increasingly bold visions of a new society to be constructed after independence. Yet, with the leadership now mostly based outside Algeria, the movement ran the risk of becoming too transnational, of existing more as an idea beamed from radio stations throughout North Africa than a tangible force among the populace.

Chapter 3, "Real Existing Third Worldism," traverses the precolonial and postcolonial threshold in order to highlight the ambiguous and variable nature of "independence." The driving narrative of this chapter recounts the negotiations between the FLN and the French government: initially, the negotiations that began in early 1961 and culminated in the Evian Accords of March 1962, which ended the war and granted Algeria its independence, and then the next round of negotiations between Algiers and Paris from late 1962 through 1963. Believing their independence to be incomplete on account of the concessions granted to France in the Evian settlement, which notably helped perpetuate France's preponderant economic position in their country, independent Algeria's new leaders initiated the "second stage" of their national revolution, in the form of socialism. They also had to brave the Cold War's heated ideological contentions as they sought out alternative sources of commerce and development assistance, Ben Bella notably embroiling himself in the Cuban Missile Crisis while seeking American aid. The Algerians' experiences epitomized the challenges of underdevelopment and state-building in an era when differing political and economic philosophies could be the cause of nuclear war.

How Algiers earned the nickname "Mecca of Revolution" is the subject of chapter 4, "The Allure of Globalism." Many important aspects of independent

Algeria's foreign policy were simply continuations of the wartime FLN's numerous international relationships. Notably, Algeria greatly expanded the FLN's policy of supporting nationalists and rebels from around the world, giving succor not only to African and Middle Eastern groups but also to ones from Asia, Latin America, Europe, and North America. Simultaneously, Algeria sought to maximize its international influence by positioning itself as the interface between regions—introducing Palestine to Africa and African nationalists to potential Cuban, Yugoslav, and Chinese supporters. The founding of the OAU in early 1963 also served as the prototypical Third Worldist project for Algeria, exemplifying the creation of international institutions that were independent of Western participation. Yet just as Algeria's globe-spanning ambitions seemed on the point of fruition, the constraints of territoriality reasserted themselves in late 1963, when Morocco launched a military offensive to claim a resource-rich region of the Sahara. The so-called Sands War highlighted the contradiction between the FLN's transnational habits and the prerogatives of statehood.

The final chapter, "Mecca of Impatience and Anxiety," continues to explore the fundamental tension between internationalism and the nation-state project. To a certain degree, the divergence between these two agendas was manifest in the rivalry between Ben Bella, who practiced the wartime GPRA's method of using diplomacy to win domestic legitimacy, and his minister of defense, Boumedienne, who had always been very much focused on national interests and the construction of the state apparatus. In 1964, Boumedienne used the conflict with Morocco to stir nationalist passions and justify a military buildup that strengthened his position. His political "clan" also capitalized on growing popular resentment, channeled by conservative religious elements, of the substantial foreign presence in Algiers and in Ben Bella's government. This local resistance to globalism converged with the increasingly polarized dynamics within the Third World coalition. Algeria hoped to harmonize the disparate trends of Afro-Asianism, nonalignment, African unity, and so on. Instead, regional rivalries and communist infighting—the Sino-Soviet split in particular—rent the Southern Hemisphere. Such divisions paralyzed the Third World project and Algerian diplomacy with it, so that mere days before the Bandung 2 conference was scheduled to begin in June 1965, nobody knew whether Ben Bella would defy China by inviting the Soviets. Ultimately, the pressure of managing these disputes contributed to Boumedienne's coup d'état on 19 June, which toppled Ben Bella and resulted in the cancellation of the Afro-Asian summit altogether.

Despite the tumultuous nature of many of these events, this book is not a eulogy for the Third World. On the contrary, its writing has been motivated by the conviction that the tenets of Third Worldism and the normative framework of South-South international relations at the height of the Cold War are more influential in the early twenty-first century than ever before. On the one hand, certain countries steeped in that diplomatic heritage have acquired greater sway in international affairs. On the other, the US-centric unipolarity of the post–Cold War world provides the motivation to rekindle the provocative nonalignment (though not necessarily under the aegis of the still-extant NAM) that is described in the following chapters. Meanwhile, subversive forces in the Middle East and elsewhere recall some of the traits of the left-wing, Third Worldist revolutionary trend of the 1960s and 1970s, even when they renounce these antecedents. The evidence mounts: the postcolonial world is our world.

1

Method Men

The Praxis of Anticolonial Resistance

> How useful it would be for the Annamese to know how their Hindu brothers are organizing against English imperialism, or how the Japanese workers united to fight capitalist exploitation, or how the Egyptians have made sublime sacrifices to demand their liberty.
>
> Ho Chi Minh, May 1920

> Oh Algerians, my brothers,
> It is time to wake up
> Look around you
> At what your neighbors are doing
>
> Song lyrics by Mahieddine Bachtarzi, 1919

When the Front de Libération Nationale (FLN) declared war on the French colonial order on 1 November 1954, it seemed a dubious endeavor. Though some had been active in politics, most of its young founders were totally unknown to the Algerian public. Most Muslims were baffled when Cairo's Voice of the Arabs radio station broadcast the first proclamation of this mysterious organization, which claimed to have instigated a revolution in their name and insisted on their loyalty. Nevertheless, within two years this upstart revolution had engulfed Algeria. By the beginning of 1957, the FLN's armed wing, the Armée de Libération Nationale (ALN), had grown into a potent guerrilla force of 40,000 mujahideen (freedom fighters), *djounoud* (soldiers), and active supporters. That January, it carried out 4,000 attacks and acts of sabotage, flaunting its ability to operate in every region and town. Determined to restore control, by that time France had mobilized a massive counterinsurgency army of more than half a million men, including professional and conscript soldiers, troops from the sub-Saharan African colonies, and pro-French Algerian Muslim militias known as the *harkis*. Elite commandos pursued the mujahideen across sizable expanses of the *bled* (countryside) that had been designated "free fire" zones following the forced resettlement of the local inhabitants into guarded camps—a policy that eventually encompassed nearly a third of the rural population, or about 2 million people. French soldiers torched their abandoned homes, fields, and livestock in order to deny the rebels shelter and sustenance. Terror had polarized Algeria's society and flattened its politics; communities across the land lived in daily fear of one side or the other inflicting a brutal collective punishment for suspected disloyalty. In short, the FLN's founders could hardly have expected to destroy the status quo any more quickly or thoroughly.[1]

Of course, theirs was not a purely destructive purpose. An illuminating episode from that same month, January 1957, shows how their movement also endeavored to build a new Algeria amid the ashes of the old. On the night of 25 January, an informant confided to French intelligence, eight rebel fighters stole into the village of Attatla in the mountainous Kabylia region, to the east of Algiers. After posting lookouts in all directions, they called the settlement's adult males to a meeting. There, a particularly impressive young man, fluent in French and Arabic, took charge of the proceedings by instructing his audience on the FLN's efforts on their behalf as well as its expectations of them, as Algerian patriots. Evidently his unit's political commissar, the young mujahid showed little deference to age or to Attatla's *djemâa*, the traditional council of elders and local authorities that had been a cornerstone of rural life in the Maghrib for centuries. If accurate in the main, the informant's account of the political commissar's comments provides a useful view of the methods used by the FLN's cadres to overthrow the old order—as well as some of the far-reaching, unintended consequences of those methods.

The rebel started with practical matters, reflecting his vital role in the front's efforts to create its own subversive administrative and governance structure among Algeria's Muslim Arab population. Inspired largely by communist precedents and the writings of Lenin, Mao Zedong, and Ho Chi Minh—though the Irish War of Independence was also an important reference point for the Algerian nationalists—the movement hoped to supplant the colonial system in the provision of medical services, education, justice, and civil ceremonies. According to one set of instructions to the ALN's political commissars, issued six months earlier, their role was "judge, tax collector, supply manager, head of propaganda, . . . health services, [and] the press."[2] Accordingly, the FLN's man in Attatla chastised its residents for not paying the "taxes" that they owed to the revolution. He peremptorily levied duties on each in accordance with his occupation. In this fashion, he and his brothers (*frère* or *yakhuya*, "my brother" in Algerian dialectal Arabic, was the standard form of address among FLN members) attempted to construct a new national reality under the feet of France's settlers and soldiers.

Meeting no objections, he moved on to international affairs. By this time, the front's "external delegation" had already managed to gain some foreign allies and stoke contentious discussion of the Algerian question at the United Nations in New York, where the movement had even set up a public relations office. The political commissar explained that the primary objective was the passage of a resolution in the General Assembly that supported Algeria's independence, which was an accurate portrayal of the FLN's strategy at that time. Its leaders believed that only international pressure—above all American pressure—could actually compel Paris to let go of Algeria. Intriguingly, however, the political commissar then departed from the official script by suggesting that France's Western allies might block that route to victory. In that event, he declared, "The USSR is our great hope: it helps Egypt and all the Arab countries. It is more powerful than America." Furthermore, he continued, "We can't achieve our independence straightaway and all alone . . . [so] the Russians will help us little by little, until we are capable of living by ourselves." At this point, perhaps resenting the late hour, one of his listeners raised a surly protest that if the young mujahid's predictions were true, they would simply exchange one set of foreign masters for another. But the rebels had not risked the journey for a debate, and they brusquely told this brave dissenter to hold his peace.[3]

The political commissar's comments in Attatla that cold January night in 1957 are one small piece of evidence pointing toward a highly consequential yet underappreciated trait of the FLN's liberation struggle: namely, the movement's highly effective methods of revolutionary organization and diplomatic agitation induced a certain ideological progression in the cadres that implemented them. On the ground, the ALN's commanders and commissars imitated the Leninist-Maoist doctrine of underground organization and guerrilla warfare by trying to create a sort of shadow state under the noses of the French, binding the Muslim population to its subversive authority. In the international arena, the external delegation's intrepid young guerrilla diplomats (some plucked directly from their studies) worked the angles of the liberal internationalist order established in 1945, with the United Nations at its heart. The FLN's internal records show how, in the course of the long struggle, these two groups in particular underwent an inconsistent but discernible evolution in their political orientation. Collectively, they identified increasingly with the communist countries in geopolitical terms, while also becoming more consciously left-wing in their socioeconomic views. So while his comments on the Soviet Union certainly contradicted the front's public propaganda at that time, this particular political commissar was not alone among his brothers in seeing the communist superpower as more than just a potential ally of convenience, but rather as a sort of mentor to Algeria. This chapter aims to show that this generalized reorientation was only partly a consequence of pragmatic calculus. More fundamentally, strategic calculus was subtly channeled by the internal logic of the revolutionary methods that the Algerian nationalists already practiced.

In a century defined by the clash of ideologies, the Algerian revolutionaries were notable for putting praxis before theory and valuing actions more than ideas. Their two methods of struggle—guerrilla-revolutionary and diplomatic—were actually the FLN's raison d'être, since its leaders explicitly defined their "revolution" in terms of means rather than ends. Fed up with the late-colonial era's vibrant debates between differing critiques of the imperial status quo, they began their assault on the colonial order on 1 November 1954 with practically no preliminary discussion of goals or political orientation. As one later explained, "The only possible option presented to the Algerian people [at that time] was to instigate the armed revolution without waiting to engage in minute and precise study, without waiting for the full elaboration of a program of action and coordination at every level."[4] Subsequently, the leadership tried to avoid ideological contagion, diligently excising overtly Maxist-Leninist terminology from the communist manuals they copied, for example, in order to maintain a unified coalition at home and a policy of neutrality in the international arena.[5] Nevertheless, somewhere along the way the means began to shape the ends. In time, the hidden ideological underpinnings of their chosen methods did begin to influence the deferred discussion of the revolution's basic principles and objectives. The result was a gradual recasting of the Algerian nationalist project in terms of socioeconomic outcomes familiar to any Cold Warrior—a marked re-evaluation of the Algerian revolution's position on the global ideological spectrum.

Thus, while highlighting the influence of communist and liberal internationalist methods of political mobilization, this chapter is not an effort to crudely impose the Cold War framework on the intellectual and cultural vibrancy of late-colonial Algeria (much less an effort to rehabilitate French efforts to brand the FLN as communist during the war). Instead, it argues that the front was, in effect, a brilliantly effective nation-building mechanism whose revolutionary internal strategy created a new Algeria from the ground up at the same time that its external diplomatic campaign asserted Algerian sovereignty from the outside in. Because its methods were its raison d'être, the FLN was able to incorporate such a diversity of constituencies in the revolution's early years, including such hitherto antagonistic groups as bourgeois Francophiles and stridently arabophone Islamic ulema (religious scholars). As a consequence, however, the deferred task of defining Algeria in cultural, linguistic, and religious terms would be inflected by the exigencies of the guerrilla and diplomatic campaigns. For this reason, significant symbolic advances in the Algerian national project, such as the founding the FLN's Gouvernement Provisoire de la République Algérienne (GPRA) in September 1958, also precipitated significant leftward shifts in the movement's ideological and geopolitical orientation.

Tools of History: The Methodological Origins of the FLN

While it was the combination of guerrilla and diplomatic warfare that assured the FLN's eventual success, it won its first major battle on the field of history. After all, at the time of its founding, in 1954, its leaders were mostly unknown figures in a vibrant political milieu that featured numerous well-established parties and popular personalities. As was the case elsewhere in the late-colonial world, during the first half of the twentieth century Algeria experienced systemic change in the form of rapid population growth, industrialization, and integration into an unstable global economy—all of which encouraged questioning of the status quo. At the same time, multiplying opportunities for travel and long-distance communication (notably radio technology) granted Algerian Muslims access to a great number of complementary discourses of change, such as France's imperial *mission civilisatrice* (civilizing mission), Salafi Islamic reformism (or Islamic modernism), pan-Arabism, Bolshevism, fascism, Irish nationalism, Ataturkism, and liberal internationalism. Participants in a global anticolonial conversation, Algerians contemplated hybrid, oscillating, perhaps sometimes even contradictory identities and goals. Thus faced with the challenge of competing against the battle-hardened organizations and influential figures that had emerged from these oft-contentious debates, the FLN's founders condemned the entire scene as petty and ineffectual. In their initial proclamation, broadcast on Egyptian radio on 1 November 1954, they described themselves as "a group of responsible young people and dedicated militants" who had decided to "take the National Movement out of the impasse into which is has been led by the conflicts of individuals and influence, and to launch itself into the truly revolutionary struggle." Declaring 1954 to be "Year Zero," the front's propaganda tried to draw a line under what it considered to be the old elites' history of pointless, endless debate and misguided "reformist" politicking.

Consequently, any analysis of the FLN's origins must take account of the many disfavored concerns and individuals that would continue to shape the country's future during and after the revolution, in spite of the revolutionaries' concerted efforts to obscure or omit them from the narrative. The following discussion highlights some of the more important trends in this regard, situating Algerian dynamics within the stream of global history in the post–World War I era. However, for all the variety of anticolonial thought in this era—or perhaps because of it—the FLN's revolutionary lineage is clearest in the domain of political methodologies rather than ideologies. Indeed, especially in the first half of the Algeria's War of Independence, the movement's own leaders distinguished "revolutionary" from "reformist" in terms of means, not ends. Declared one pamphlet on the front's origins, probably produced in 1955 or 1956, "None of the Algerian political parties measured up to their responsibility to give the Algerian people the tool [*outil*] of their liberation. The FLN arose from their rubble, just in time to nip their vague notions of reform in the bud."[6] In fact, the action-oriented revolutionaries did not even take the time to develop a clear program or political apparatus before starting their struggle in 1954, such was their aversion to discussing theory. Therefore, in the place of an ideological evolution, two praxes of anticolonial action—the diplomatic and the revolutionary— began in Algeria in response to the pronouncements of Woodrow Wilson and Vladimir Lenin in 1918, were then practiced in parallel for three decades by a succession of movements, and finally converged in 1954 in the founding of the FLN.

Of course, just as Algeria would begin anew neither in 1954 nor in 1962, the transformations of the post–World War I era did themselves occur in the wake of nearly a century of traumatic colonization. Attributed variously to a dispute over debt repayments to Algerian merchants, the Hussein Dey's (the Ottoman governor) alleged lashing of the French consul with his fly swatter, or the unpopular King Charles X's need for an impressive foreign adventure, France's conquest began in 1830 with the swift defeat of the Ottoman regency in Algiers. Initially lacking any long-term purpose, by the time the subjugation of the full territory of present-day Algeria was completed in 1870, France's colonial project had taken on a totalizing scope. French armies met significant resistance, most famously that of the charismatic young religious leader, the emir 'Abd el-Qadir, who spearheaded a successful guerrilla-style campaign until 1847. The remnants of Ottoman power also held out in the high Kabylia region, in the northeast, for another ten years, with the ravine-straddling town of Constantine posing a particularly difficult challenge to the invaders. Likewise, the perennially unyielding communities of the Atlas and pre-Sahara regions, where the fertile north meets the desert, generated several sizable rebellions until the 1860s. Algeria's last mass rebellion before 1954 occurred in Kabylia in 1871. Epitomized by the ruthless Marshall Thomas-Robert Bugeaud, whose tactics inspired the expression "scorched earth campaign," the imposition of French rule was therefore a bloody business. All told, about 1 million Algerian inhabitants died between 1830 and 1870 as a result of war, sickness, and famine—one-third of the total precolonial population. Consequently, despite Algeria's seeming quiescence, memories of defiance and subjugation were still raw in the twentieth century. For example, one scholar has recently shown how village *djemâa* councils, such as the one at Attatla, helped sustain an oral-institutional culture of rebellion among the peasantry into which the FLN could later tap.[7]

In terms of its basic political and economic characteristics, *l'Algérie française* proper began in 1870, when the growing number of white settlers, or *colons*, insisted that civilian governance take over from the military. Immigration accelerated as the *colons* set about buying up most of Algeria's prime farmland and building a society whose raison d'être was the exploitation of the original Muslim population and their descendents. In 1881, the government in Paris declared Algeria an integral part of sovereign French territory, in accordance with the constitution of the Third Republic. From that point, the *colons* in Algeria were "normal" French citizens who just happened to live in three *départements* (France's basic administrative regions) that were located across the Mediterranean but legally identical to, say, Normandy or Provence. Like their compatriots on the mainland, the Algerian French elected their local deputies to the National Assembly in Paris, where they formed an uncompromising, united bloc on settler-colonial issues. At the same time, however, the 1881 Code de l'indigénat (Native Code) relegated Algeria's Muslims to an entirely separate and repressive legal framework that sharply curtailed personal freedoms, neglected due process for criminal matters, and placed domestic matters under the auspices of Islamic courts. Subjects not citizens, most Muslim Algerians lived in the *communes mixtes* (mixed communities), areas whose administrators and judges (cadis) were appointed by the colonial authorities. Therefore, the defining division of colonial Algerian society was that between Muslim and non-Muslim—a truth made explicit in the 1870 Crémieux Decrees that extended French citizenship to Algeria's 25,000 Jews (a community that boasted many centuries of history in that land) and stipulated that those very few Muslim *évolués* (literally, "evolved") who were deemed worthy of French citizenship had to renounce Islam first. In social terms, some of the old elites did integrate into the colonial system, while a thin strata of middle- and working-class Arabs gradually emerged in the larger towns and cities in the twentieth century, but the vast majority of Algeria's Muslims belonged to either the near-destitute peasantry or the pool of cheap labor that served *colon* farms and *colon* homes.

Given that all the evidence indicates that Khaled was a convinced assimilationist to that point, his response to the so-called Wilsonian Moment in 1919 is all the more noteworthy. In the closing stages of World War I, the American president, Woodrow Wilson, publicized a sweeping vision for a new international order based on "liberal internationalist" principles. In his famous "Fourteen Points" speech to the US Congress in January 1918, Wilson called for the creation of an international organization, a "league of nations," that would maintain the peace by regulating disputes between countries, great or small. He stressed the principle of "national self-determination," arguing that every people had the right to choose their own government, citing specifically his desire to see an independent Poland and independent Turkey emerge from the debris of the Russian and Ottoman Empires, respectively. Wilson deliberately disseminated his ideas through the international press and by means of increasingly powerful radio technology, in order to raise widespread support for his agenda before he arrived at the momentous peace conference convened at the Palace of Versailles, in January 1919. In the magnificent mirrored hall at Versailles, the leaders of Britain, France, Italy, and the United States would decide the fate of their defeated foes—as well as huge swaths of the globe and its inhabitants.[8] Yet, exhibiting the prejudices common to southern American gentlemen in that era, Wilson was thinking principally of east-central Europe, not "the Orient", in his advocacy of self-determination and equality between nations. Unintentionally, his ideas also energized politics in many parts of the colonial world, where activists in places as far apart and diverse as Syria, Korea, Ireland, China, and India championed the Fourteen Points. Rather awkwardly from a diplomatic perspective, crowds of "colonials" shouted the American president's name in mass protests against their British and French overlords. One of the largest such commotions occurred in Egypt, where massive unrest broke out across the country in early 1919 in response to Britain's tightening control. The initial spark for the uprising came when the British rejected the demand of an otherwise moderate establishment politician, Sa'd Zaghlul, to send a *wafd* (delegation) to Versailles to make the case for Egyptian independence. When repression alone failed to quell the unrest, the colonial authorities did finally try to placate the protesters by allowing the *wafd* to proceed to the conference in April—but only after ensuring that neither Wilson nor anyone else of consequence would receive them.[9]

The American president's rebuff would live in infamy in Cairo. "Here was the man of the Fourteen Points . . . denying the Egyptian people its right to self-determination and recognizing the British protectorate over Egypt," wrote the famous journalist Mohammed Haykal. "Is this not the ugliest of treacheries?! Is it not the most profound repudiation of principles?!"[10] Nevertheless, Wilson still played a vital symbolic role in Egypt's 1919 Revolution, which proved to be a momentous event in the progression of the country's nationalist consciousness. Zaghlul's Wafd Party, named after the failed mission to Versailles, would play a central role in Egyptian politics until the 1950s. Crucially, though, given Egypt's own rich intellectual culture and decades of intensive exposure to European thought, Wilson made less of an ideological impression than a geopolitical one. He did not suggest new possibilities of what independence might be. Rather, he opened up new practical avenues of achieving it by positioning the Anglo-Egyptian power relationship in a wider international context.

Engaged Muslim Algerians, who held Cairo to be the capital of the Arab world, certainly followed Egyptian developments (an early Young Algerian newspaper, *El Hack*, or "truth," was subtitled "The Young Egyptian").[11] The war's end brought increased instability in Algeria, too. By 1918, a full third of working-age Muslim Algerian men were employed in France as either soldiers or laborers, and they returned home with a new perspective on the world as well as expectations of reward for their service. German and Turkish propaganda had also tried to stir up anticolonial sentiment in French North Africa during the war, and the Algerian Arab public enthusiastically cheered on Kemal Atatürk's forces in their war with Greece, which broke out in May 1919, because they viewed it as a national struggle against Franco-British imperialism. In this light, the modest political reforms that Georges Clemenceau's government implemented in February 1919—increasing to 500,000 the number of Muslims allowed to vote in a dual-college system that gave Arabs very limited say over their own affairs without challenging the pieds noirs' supremacy—were an inadequate response to rising discontent and a surge in directionless, uncoordinated violence.

Yet even in these circumstances it was very surprising that the emir Khaled, the committed Francophile assimilationist, demanded in January 1919 that an Algerian delegation be allowed to attend the Versailles conference in a capacity similar to the representatives of Britain's dominions. Like Zaghlul, he set out for Paris with four companions in May, though he too managed only to deliver a letter to Woodrow Wilson's staff. Addressed to "the honorable President of American Liberty," it asked that an investigatory delegation be dispatched to Algeria in order to "decide our future fate, under the aegis of the Society of Nations."[12] Naturally, the letter made no impact on the Versailles proceedings, and there is no evidence that the American president actually read it. Nevertheless, the endeavor incensed the pied noir community, who branded Khaled a dangerous subversive in thrall to foreign designs and succeeded in having him exiled to Damascus in 1924.[13]

The substance of Khaled's appeal to Wilson, undeniably at least proto-nationalist in its implications, was so discordant with his otherwise impeccable record as a Francophile assimilationist that scholars believed for many years that the pied noir lobby had simply made the story up. In vain, Khaled insisted on his loyalty to France, declaring in 1922 that "the people of Algeria are all, without distinction as to religion or race, equally children of France and have an equal right in her home." Similarly, a Young Algerian newspaper swore after his exile that "we will always remain apart from any movement impregnated by nationalist or religious ideology. We are definitively French." Yet eminent French historian Charles-Robert Ageron was eventually stunned to find a copy of the letter to Wilson in the American archives, prompting him to completely re-evaluate Khaled as the budding nationalist.[14] Revealingly, the FLN's "official" history also came to treat him as such, reflecting the legitimacy conferred posthumously by this fleeting diplomatic initiative in spite of the rest of Khaled's recorded positions being so anathema to the nationalist narrative. Even if he did sincerely renounce the letter's implications, his having written it demonstrates how new methods of political action could radicalize the goals those methods were meant to serve.[15]

The ambiguity of Khaled's position reflects the fact that Algeria was a land of change and uncertainty. First of all, the Young Algerians could still dream of assimilation at a time when it was not at all self-evident that empire was entering its twilight years. Algeria's industry and agriculture grew rapidly, particularly in the viticulture and mining sectors. Wealthier *colons* bought up land to reap economies of scale with larger farms and new agricultural technologies, thereby fueling construction in the cities as smaller white farmers relocated there. Consequently, much of Algeria's extensive modern transportation infrastructure and urban landscape dated to the late-colonial era, testifying to the prevailing sense of permanence among Algeria's European community and many of their compatriots on the mainland. In the spirit of the times, the pieds noirs and the metropolitan colonial lobby orchestrated a boisterous, yearlong celebration of the centenary of the conquest of Algeria in 1930, while the more generalized Colonial Exposition in Paris the following year drew an impressive 35 million visitors.

Yet the French Algerian historian Jacques Berque dubbed this triumphal moment the "false apogee" of *l'Algérie française* on account of the ominous changes afoot within Muslim society, which outnumbered the Europeans by roughly 9 million to 1 million by 1954.[16] Most striking was the "pauperization" of the peasantry: agricultural consolidation forced the fast-growing rural population to subsist on less and less land so that, by one historian's estimation, the period 1930–1960 saw the number of Muslim landowners fall by 40 percent even as the size of the rural population increased by 45 percent, from 4.5 million to 7 million people.[17] With mechanization also cutting the demand for farming laborers, hundreds of thousands of Algerian peasants migrated to the cities and to France in search of work, provoking disquiet on the parts of many colonial officials who justifiable fretted about the dangerous ideas factory life might instill in them.[18] The Muslim share of the growing workers' population jumped from 1 percent on the eve of the First World War to 10 percent in 1930, but then even more dizzyingly to 30 percent by 1940, while approximately 2 million Algerians lived in France by 1954. As occurred elsewhere in Africa, the railways and mines were important sites of employment and politicization, but the picture is complicated by the very sizable pied noir workers' movement, which encouraged activism but did so within the context of French unions, French parties (an intercommunal Parti Communiste Algérien [PCA] split off from the metropolitan party in the mid-1930s), and not inconsequently the French language.[19]

Consequently, despite the bravado of the centenary celebrations, a sense of alienation was mounting among the pieds noirs. European farmers in the *bled* found themselves increasingly isolated, while their counterparts in the cities occasionally resorted to bulldozing the metastasizing bidonvilles (shantytowns) that swelled with destitute peasants—a desperate bid to preserve the existing order.[20] Thus did the former governor, Maurice Viollette, publish a cry of alarm in 1931 titled *L'Algérie, vivra-t-elle?* (Algeria, will it survive?).[21] Yet the Europeans' disorientation was mild compared to that of the Muslim majority. A changing land was ripe for definition.

By the late 1930s, the pieds noirs' stubborn opposition to any reforms proposed by Paris had all but killed off the Young Algerians' notion of an Algeria fully integrated into France with equal rights for its Muslim inhabitants. A coalition of *élus*, those elected to a separate Muslim assembly with narrowly limited powers, pressed this cause, but repeatedly found that public office and their relatively privileged, well-integrated position in society offered little real influence or respite from the colonial lobby's suspicions and vitriol. When these Francophile parliamentarians dispatched a delegation to Paris in 1933 to lobby for reform, the authorities in Algiers branded them as anti-French Bolshevik stooges.[22] Ferhat Abbas, a pharmacist from the important regional town of Setif, was one of the most prominent figures in the assimilationist movement and typified its professional, petit bourgeois demographic. In February 1936 he penned an oft-quoted article in which he insisted that if such a thing as an Algerian nation existed, then he would be a proud nationalist, but that he had failed to find any evidence in history of an Algerian *patrie*. Shortly afterward he and his colleagues experienced a devastating setback when Léon Blum's Popular Front government abandoned a package of reforms known as the Blum-Viollette bill. The bill merely proposed to grant citizenship to 25,000 *évolués*, so most Algerians cautiously supported it only as a step in the right direction. But what hope was there for assimilation when even a government that consisted largely of supposedly anti-imperialist socialists and communists caved before the pied noirs' obstinacy?

The failure of the 1936 Blum-Viollette reforms came at a time of particularly acute unrest in Algeria. For the first time, large numbers of lower- and working-class Muslims began to mobilize, march, strike, and protest alongside the political elites. Voter turnout increased to the benefit of reformist candidates rather than the so-called *beni-oui-ouis* (pliant "yes-men"), activists organized boycotts of European and Jewish merchants, and riots and violence occasionally broke out—most notably when a Muslim mob killed twenty-three Jews in the eastern city of Constantine in August 1934. Although not too much significance should be attributed to some marchers' provocative chanting of "Vive les Soviets!" or "Vive les fascistes!," there was an international context to this important upsurge in popular activism. As was the case in numerous British African colonies at this time, the unrest was partly due to the global economic crisis, which put pressure on jobs and wages in all those new industries the authorities had encouraged in recent years. There was also growing public awareness of events elsewhere in the Arab world, such as the failed Syrian Revolt against French colonialism in 1925 and the deteriorating situation in "British" Palestine that led to a similarly large-scale Arab revolt there in 1936. Numerous Algerians traveled to the eastern Arab countries, the Mashriq, for the hajj pilgrimage to Mecca or to be educated in the great centers of Islamic learning. Regional conversations about pan-Islamism or pan-Arabism also reached North Africa via radio and by a transnational newspaper network that linked Algiers, Cairo, Tunis, and even Zanzibar, allowing local organizations with common interests to exchange information and opinions. Thus the notable—but by no means universal—deterioration in relations between Algeria's Muslims and its small but centuries-old Jewish community was due not only to the fact that the French had elevated the latter by granting them full citizenship but also to popular outrage at the Zionist project in Palestine.

A movement of reformist ulema, or religious scholars, was one of the most important vectors for this Arabist current. The two most prominent figures among the ulema, Sheikh 'Abd al-Hamid Ben Badis and Bachir Ibrahimi, typified the movement's origins in that they both came from established patrician families but received traditional Koranic educations and spent long periods of time in centers of Islamic scholarship outside Algeria. The ulema were reformist in the sense of being greatly influenced by the Islamic modernist thinkers of the late nineteenth century and by the Salafi movement, which advocated a return to "original" or "orthodox" Islam. Their primary mission was therefore educational and cultural: they founded schools for Arabic instruction and criticized the Maghrib's indigenous "unorthodox" Islamic institutions such as marabout preachers, Sufi brotherhoods, and the frequent worship of local saints. But in the colonial context, such concerns had inherent political ramifications. Many in the existing religious establishment, for example, were technically French civil servants since the authorities sought to monitor and control what transpired in mosques and Koranic schools. The ulema also taught a nationalist history that directly contradicted the French curriculum's argument that no Algerian nation had ever existed; Ahmad Tewfik al Madani, who later became an important FLN diplomatic operative, published the first nationalist history book in 1932, *Kitab al Jaza'ir* (The book of Algeria). Accordingly, Ben Badis publicly responded to Ferhat Abbas's aforementioned antinationalist article in 1936 by asserting categorically that "this Muslim population is not part of France, cannot be part of France, and does not want to be part of France."[23]

It should be noted that the ulema did found schools with official sanction, such as the Progress Club in downtown Algiers, which served as a venue for discussion and debate among the Muslim elite, Europeans, representatives of the Jewish community, and so on.[24] Bashir Ibrahimi also strove to build a Muslim cultural organization that would straddle both sides of the Mediterranean, suggesting that political separation of Algeria and France was not his paramount concern.[25] But on the whole, one progressively minded French education official was justified in his mournful observation that "the reformist ulema will end up being the only masters of Arabic in Algeria, alas they will teach Arabic as the language of liberation and resistance!"[26] Notably, Tewfik al Madani and Ben Badis each maintained an active correspondence with the prominent Syrian Arab nationalist thinker the emir Shakib Arslan and with the Grand Mufti of Jerusalem, Sheikh Amin al-Husayn, a Palestinian nationalist and religious leader who fled the British Mandate after the failure of the Arab revolt there in 1936–1939. As early as 1932, the ulema journal, *Al Chihâb* (The meteor), called for a boycott of Jewish merchants in Algeria to protest Zionism in Palestine.[27] In the 1930s a teenage Mostefa Lacheraf, later the FLN's leading intellectual light, attended both a French lycée in the morning and an ulema school afterward. In his memoirs, he described the latter as a rich site of political imagination and exchange, or "a kind of sociological cell in full cultural bloom and [where] the contrasting currents of nationalism in the Algeria of those days awoke together."[28]

While the political foment in Algeria gathered pace, the movement that was the most direct antecedent of the FLN had been gaining strength across the sea, in France, since the early 1920s. Founded among the metropole's working-class Arab immigrant community, the Etoile Nord Africain (North African Star, ENA) party was a precursor to the FLN in a philosophical and organizational sense, for which it owed a great debt to Marxist tutelage. For many, Wilson's refusal to support anticolonial causes in 1919 left a bitter taste—the influential Egyptian journalist Mohamed Haykal judged it "the ugliest of treacheries . . . the most profound repudiation of principles!"—and this disillusionment helped propel some nationalists toward the Soviet Union in their search for guidance and support.[29] The epitome of this trend was an Indochinese nationalist called Nguyen Tat Thanh, then making his living in France as a photo retoucher, but whose real vocation was disseminating anticolonial pamphlets under the name of Nguyen Ai Quoc (Nguyen the Patriot). Turned away unceremoniously from Versailles, the future Ho Chi Minh ("Enlightened Will") experienced a Damascene conversion on reading Lenin's "Thesis on the National and Colonial Questions," in which the Bolshevik leader argued that communists had a duty to assist colonial subjects in their struggle against imperialism.[30] Ho joined those urging the Communist International, or Comintern, to train anticolonials in political methodology and to help activists from different parts of the world share experiences and strategies.[31]

The Comintern directed national parties to teach the colonials in the ways of modern political organization and mobilization, and to that effect the Parti Communiste Français (French Communist Party, PCF) ordered its pied noir members to return to Algeria "to become propagandists in colonial *milieux* and ensure liaison with revolutionary groups [since] propaganda methods used by the natives sometimes attain astonishing results."[32] Indeed Messali Hadj, who quickly became the ENA's recognized leader after helping to found the party in Paris in 1926, later credited the efforts of pied noir communists for his initial political awakening, and the PCF closely assisted the party's development. At that time he was a shop boy and his cofounders were factory workers, and like many other such anticolonial groups, the ENA was intimately enmeshed in the French left-wing milieu.[33] Messali actually married a PCF militant, and a 1929 Paris police report claimed sixteen of the twenty-eight members of the ENA's central committee were also members of the communist party. Moreover, communist mentorship undoubtedly influenced the ENA's doctrine. Not only was the ENA the first Algerian group to advocate consistently for outright independence, but its official party program for 1933 also called for "the complete transfer to the Algerian State of the banks, mines, railroads, ports and public services monopolized by the conquerors; the confiscation of the large estates monopolized by the feudal allies of the conquerors, the colonizers and the financial firms; and the transfer of this seized land to the peasants."[34] Messali and his comrades had internalized Lenin's argument that imperialism was the product of European capitalism.

The ENA also participated in anticolonial transnational forums such as the 1927 Anti-imperialism Congress in Belgium, where future national leaders like India's Jawaharlal Nehru and Léopold Sédar Senghor of Senegal formed the League against Imperialism, a short-lived Comintern-sponsored initiative that nevertheless created many durable relations between far-flung activists.[35] Other intercolonial exchanges happened outside the communist umbrella, though usually with some connection to the diverse left wing of French politics. For example, the ENA cooperated with the Ligue de Défense de la Race Nègre (Negro Race Defense League), a black African movement founded by Senghor and the French Sudanese (Mali today) activist Tiemoko Garan Kouyaté, to protest the Italian conquest of Ethiopia in 1935–1936. The January 1935 issue of the party's newspaper *El Ouma* (Nation, or Community) urged that "Algerians, Moroccans, Tunisians, Annamese [i.e., Vietnamese], Malagasy, Senegalese, etc., get together, find common ground . . . and work together closely, shoulder to shoulder with the French intellectual and manual proletariat for their economic, political and social independence. Oppressed people from the colonies, unite to protect your interests."[36]

By the mid-1930s, however, there were clear divergences between the communist and anticolonial agendas, and Messali's movement experienced a particularly angry parting of the ways with former comrades in the Marxist mainstream. The immediate cause was geopolitical: obeying Stalin's orders, the PCF and its new Algerian offshoot, the PCA, deprecated the anticolonial cause to focus on forging an anti-Fascist coalition in Europe, and to keep Léon Blum's Popular Front government in power in Paris. Thus the ENA condemned the Blum-Viollette reform bill of 1936, which would have further expanded the Muslim franchise in Algeria and "assimilated" thousands of *évolués*, as a colonialist project that betrayed socialist principles.[37] Worse still, the government ultimately caved to pied noir outrage on the matter. In January 1937, Messali penned a recriminatory letter to *L'Humanité*, the main French communist newspaper, accusing the PCF of turning its back on a decade of friendship, shared adventures, and shared imprisonments.[38]

Philosophically, however, Messali and communism were already drifting apart because he prioritized national liberation over proletarian revolution. While the ENA had participated in various inter-Arab and pan-Islamic initiatives, its leader experienced a revelation when he spent six months in 1935–1936 hiding from the French police in Geneva, where he kept close company with the influential Arab nationalist figure Shakib Arslan. "Certainly, I am Syrian," Shakib told the star-struck Algerian, "but above all I am an Arab, a Muslim, and a combatant."[39] He encouraged Messali to reconcile with the Islamic reformist movement in his homeland, which the latter had seen as an elitist project of Algeria's haughty ulema, because jihad was a powerful means to national liberation. Likewise, the Tunisian nationalist (and future president) Habib Bourguiba recommended combining modern political mobilization with the expression of national cultural identity: "Both elements are indispensable: the first to spread the Arabic language, history, and religion, the other to organize and struggle."[40] Messali saw the wisdom of their counsel. When he returned to Algeria in 1936 to join the surging political ferment there, he sought to combine the political methods and message of social justice that he had developed in France with a new emphasis on cultural "authenticity"—starting with the long flowing beard and robes of a traditional Maghribi sheikh.[41]

Once on home soil, Messali founded a new party, the Parti du Peuple Algérien (Algerian People's Party, PPA), which quickly established an impressive base of support among the desperate peasantry—more so, notably, than was the case for Algeria's vibrant and growing urban workers' movement that might have seemed his most natural constituency. But with his original populist message and new appearance, Messali seemed to evoke the millenarian traditions of the marabout, religious figures often linked to rebellions in the nineteenth century, or even that of the Mahdi, the prophesied savior that so many rural folk still hoped for. Accompanying Messali during one visit to the destitute villages of Kabylia in the late 1940s, a PPA militant from that region called Hocine Aït Ahmed saw men, women, and children line the streets to greet him, often having traveled dozens of kilometers on foot to do so. Recognizing that Messali owed his popularity to a powerful charisma and terrific stage presence as much as to the substance of his message, Aït Ahmed described him with ambivalent admiration as "Orson Welles in the land of Islam, performing Shakespeare with Wagnerian stylings and intonations."[42] Born in 1926 to a once-prominent religious family, Aït Ahmed was also a key member of a younger generation beginning to chafe under Messali's "cult of personality" and domineering leadership. Privileged, but not of the true elite, issuing from smaller towns in the countryside and therefore closer to the peasantry than to the big cities, men such as Aït Ahmed later formed the core of new, self-avowed "revolutionary" group within the PPA in the late 1940s.

As had the 1914–1918 war before it, World War II weakened the colonial status quo in Algeria and permanently altered the political dynamics there. Indeed, around the globe, this great conflagration undermined the basic foundations of Europe's empires in multiple ways. First, in the realm of ideas and ideologies, President Franklin Delano Roosevelt re-energized the liberal internationalist project by agreeing on a formal list of war aims with the British prime minister, Winston Churchill, on a ship off the coast of Newfoundland in August 1941. In calling for the creation of a new community of free nations, dubbed the "United Nations," and the establishment of an international system based on national self-determination and other democratic principles, the so-called Atlantic Charter revived the excitement of 1919's Wilsonian Moment. The United States was, once again, promising to create a world that rendered imperialism obsolete (a consequence that Churchill unhappily foresaw). Second, more prosaically, the relentless succession of German and Japanese victories in the war's early stages weakened Europe's empires through the conquest of both colonies (such as Indochina, Singapore, and Indonesia) and imperial metropoles (France and Belgium).[43] The British, French, and Dutch, for example, would never manage to convincingly re-establish their authority in East Asia once the Japanese army had swept away their apparatuses of control in 1941–1942. In other cases, such as much of Africa, imperial authority suffered simply from having the colonizer's aura of military supremacy so thoroughly dispelled. Finally, the imperialists depended more than ever before on their colonial subjects to win the war: not only did many thousands of Indians, North Africans, and sub-Saharan Africans fight to defeat "despotism" and defend "liberty," but colonial populations as a whole were induced to work harder and earn less in exchange for vague promises of future reforms.

Algeria was a good example of all of these dynamics. In addition to tens of thousands of Algerians and Moroccans fighting in the French army for the liberation of Europe, North Africa itself was a theater of war. An interesting twist in the Maghrib was that it was an Anglo-American invasion, not an Axis one, that toppled the colonial administration in 1942, since Algeria, like many colonies, had pledged its loyalty to the fascist Vichy regime in southern France after the fall of Paris. Although General Charles de Gaulle then made Algiers the temporary capital of his defiant government in exile, his "Free French" forces ruled only on the sufferance and largesse of their American allies. Messali's newspaper had celebrated the spectacle of American military might, breezily brushing aside Vichyite defenders as "the first serious defeat for the French colonial army since 1830," while Algerian Muslims were in awe of the GIs' unconscious demonstrations of wealth, such as sharing their cigarettes with whomever happened to be standing nearby, as well as the sheer quantity of their advanced military hardware.[44] Moreover, the US military presence was substantial in North Africa until the conquest of Italy. So even though Roosevelt's personal envoy, Robert Murphy, assured the authorities in Algiers that Washington's policy was to respect and support the restoration of France's sovereignty "throughout all the territory, metropolitan and colonial, over which flew the French flag in 1939," Algeria's Muslim politicians could not help but be excited by the presence of so close an assistant to the author of the Atlantic Charter.[45]

Indeed, after agreeing to meet with Ferhat Abbas and other representatives of the Arab community, Murphy reported to Washington that the locals could talk about little else but the charter. Rather like the emir Khaled's effort to get a letter to Wilson in 1919, Abbas first infuriated the French authorities by addressing a petition for social and political reforms to the "Responsible Authorities in Algiers."[46] Then, in the summer of 1943, he oversaw the drafting of a public "Manifesto of the Algerian People" that explicitly called for limited political autonomy. Perhaps most remarkably, the manifesto initiative briefly united the Salafi ulema, Messali's PPA, and the Algerian Communist Party; it also stoked considerable popular enthusiasm. In short, the combined impact of the Atlantic Charter and the American presence in North Africa facilitated a new period in Muslim Algerian politics, with all parties agreeing on limited autonomy as their minimal goal. Abbas's progression from pro-colonial assimilationism to proto-nationalism was particularly significant. While progressive disillusionment in the face of pied noir intransigence was certainly a factor, Abbas—like Khaled in 1919—also appears to have experienced a political radicalization in response to a new opportunity to effect political change by going beyond the French context.

However, Washington prioritized the exigencies of war over anticolonial principles. As the British historian Martin Thomas has pointed out, instead of fomenting unrest, American officials actually worked closely with their European allies, in Algeria and elsewhere, to maintain a steady flow of strategic commodities from the colonies to the United States and Britain.[47] Moreover, in spite of French officials' somewhat conciliatory reception of the Algerian Manifesto in 1943 and de Gaulle's widely noted speech in Brazzaville the following year, where the future French president told colonial administrators that reforms were forthcoming, the return to peace in 1945 saw both the French and British governments quickly retreat from such language. Their reversal collided with the expectations of a great many Africans, especially those veterans returning home with new perspectives. Recalled Waruhiu Itote of his service in the British army in Burma:

> Among the shells and bullets there had been no pride, no air of superiority from our European comrades-in-arms.... The white heat of battle had blistered all that away and left only our common humanity and our common fate.... I had become conscious of myself as a Kenyan African, one among millions whose destinies were still in the hands of foreigners, yet also one who could see the need and the possibility of changing that situation.[48]

However, on finding British officialdom and the Kenyan white settler population determined to return to the prewar "normalcy," Itote subsequently became a leader of Kenya's "Mau Mau" rebellion in the early 1950s. Across the continent, disgruntled veterans rallied to newly coalescing nationalist movements.

Similarly, in Algeria, Krim Belkacem and Ahmed Ben Bella both served with some distinction in the French army before becoming two of the FLN's "Historic Nine" founders, nearly a decade later. In fact, Ben Bella always boasted that de Gaulle himself had decorated him after the Battle of Monte Cassino, in Italy. Yet the two veterans' disillusionment occurred more swiftly than was the case elsewhere in Africa, in the form of the notorious Sétif massacre. In the large provincial town of that name, thousands of Muslims demonstrated on V-E Day, 8 May 1945, to demand social and political reforms as a reward for Algeria's wartime loyalty. But when rioting broke out, the French military and security services responded with brutal and indiscriminate force. Soldiers fired repeatedly into massed crowds of protesters, aircraft bombarded nearby villages, and by some accounts naval vessels shelled the interior from the coast. An estimated 5,000 to 10,000 Muslims were killed, their bodies filling Sétif's soccer field. The massacre was a turning point, convincing Krim Belkacem, Ben Bella, and many other young men that peaceful change could never happen in Algeria. The general who carried out this dirty business presciently informed Paris, "I have given you peace for ten years. But don't deceive yourselves."[49]

In the wake of the war and the Sétif massacre, Algerian anticolonialism entered a new phase. "Self-determination" was now the rallying cry across the political spectrum, from Abbas to the communists, though in most cases that did not yet signify full independence from France. The concept of total independence was difficult to envision for many Algerian Muslims, so intimate and multifaceted were the ties between their territory and the mainland. But in 1947 a younger generation of militants in Messali's PPA began to assert themselves, calling for the party to reform along more "revolutionary" lines and to use more confrontational, possibly even violent, methods to achieve Algeria's independence. Although the polls that year were blatantly manipulated to favor *beni-oui-oui* candidates, international events seemed to inspire this new revolutionary faction at least as much as those closer to home. Hocine Aït Ahmed, the young Kabyle son of a cadi (local administrator), presented a report calling for the complete reform of the PPA at a clamorous party congress in a warehouse in Belcourt, a working-class quarter of Algiers, which he later compared to a "Dublin brasserie" throbbing with patriotic conspiracy and heated debate. In fact, Ireland was the main precedent highlighted in the report: bearing some resemblance to Algeria as a heavily settled colony located just across the water from the imperial metropole, Ireland had liberated itself through confrontational politics, diplomacy, and armed struggle. Aït Ahmed and his like-minded colleagues called on the PPA to create its own armed wing, an Organisation Spéciale (Special Organization, OS), as the Irish republican party Sinn Féin (We Ourselves) had done.

But the dynamics of the incipient Cold War also weighed heavily on their thinking, especially in the case of Mohamed Lamine Debaghine, a young doctor whose father owned a restaurant in the picturesque seaside town of Cherchelle, west of Algiers. Ever since the Allied invasion in 1942, Debaghine had been convinced that Algeria's independence could only ever result from the "conjunction of internal and external factors," but he had struggled to convince his fellow PPA militants of the necessity or feasibility of a grand diplomatic strategy involving the great powers beyond France. His moment of vindication came on 12 March 1947, when Harry S. Truman's "Truman Doctrine" speech to the US Congress declared America's determination to contain communism on a global scale, starting in the eastern Mediterranean with Greece and Turkey. Suddenly the notion of involving Washington in the Algerian question no longer seemed a fantasy, and the PPA leadership in Algiers immediately instructed Debaghine and Aït Ahmed, among others, to begin preparations for a revolutionary struggle. From this point forward, the belief that the Cold War could be a boon to the anticolonial cause would be a staple of the Algerian conception of international politics.

At the same time, the young radicals' ardent espousal of "revolution" was all the more noteworthy for its vagueness. Armed struggle was only one aspect of revolution, but one clearly influenced by Bolshevism and current events in East Asia: in drawing up the initial plans for the OS, Aït Ahmed relied heavily on the latest analyses of the war in Indochina, extracts of Marx and Engels, and diverse material on guerrilla warfare. More fundamentally, however, they were attracted to the notion of a dramatic break with the past and, in time, the usurpation of the existing Muslim elite—including Messali—by the collective authority of a disciplined, committed organization. An FLN pamphlet later portrayed their exasperation with traditional politics and their intoxication with the idea of revolution by saying of the 1947 congress that "it was at this time that a revolutionary tendency appeared within the national movement, certainly still young, but firmly determined to go to the limits.... [While] one [tendency] insisted on the liberation struggle by all possible means (political, military, economic and social etc.), the other slowly diverged from this path to eventually get mired in demagogic, sterile, paper-pushing bureaucracy."[50] Yet even at this early stage, at least some of the advocates of revolutionary methods consciously valued the potential for means to redefine goals. "The key idea," Aït Ahmed explained in his memoirs, "was the notion of revolution being simultaneously the goal and the means of struggle, and that the whole nationalist doctrine must refocus on this."[51]

As an organization, the OS was actually a dismal failure—the security services were able to quickly penetrate and roll up the group in early 1950—but it proved to be merely the trial run for the FLN. Numerous participants in the OS regrouped to found the front four years later. Ahmed Ben Bella, born in 1918, was the son of a small farmer near the town of Maghnia in western Algeria who managed to complete secondary school before distinguishing himself as a noncommissioned officer in the Free French army during the war, and later claimed to have received a medal from de Gaulle himself for his performance in the notorious Battle of Monte Cassino. Mohamed Khider was an autodidact born of humble origins in Algiers in 1912, and also the brother-in-law of Aït Ahmed. These three—Aït Ahmed, Khider, and Ben Bella—all participated in a failed attempt to hold up the Oran post office in 1950 and had to flee Algeria. Ben Bella was actually arrested but escaped from jail in 1952, rejoining Aït Ahmed and Khider in Cairo in the wake of the Free Officers' Coup that summer, when a conspiracy of nationalist and revolutionary-minded officers led by the charismatic Colonel Gamal Abdel Nasser overthrew the Egyptian monarchy. The three Algerians set themselves up as the "external delegation" of the PPA-MTLD in order to win the support of the new regime, which declared itself profoundly Arab nationalist and anti-imperialist in outlook. Ben Bella in particular impressed the Egyptians with his militancy and open disdain for regular politicians, and he secured from Nasser the promise of armaments for a new rebellion.

Meanwhile, by 1954 the PPA-MTLD had fallen into paralyzing schisms, most notably between Messali loyalists—he had recently proclaimed himself president of the party for life—and those advocating a more collective leadership (known as the "Centralists"). Consequently, the trio in Cairo found common cause with other OS veterans still in Algeria who shared their frustration with the existing nationalist leadership. These included another French army veteran turned rebel called Belkacem Krim, the Kabyle son of a cemetery guard born in 1922, who went up to the maquis (the underground, or rebellion) in the high mountains of Kabylia after being accused of murder in 1947. Other outlaws evading conviction were Rabah Bitat, born in 1925 in the eastern city of Constantine, and Mohamed Boudiaf from the Hodna, a region on the edges of the Sahara. Though they did not all evade capture during the coming revolution, each continued to wield considerable authority within the FLN, at least until 1962. Completing the Historic Nine were Mohamed Larbi Ben M'Hidi, the son of a peasant family near Biskra in the southeastern fringes of northern Algeria, Mostefa Ben Boulaid, a small merchant's son and former soldier from the same general part of the country, and Mourad Didouche, who was the youngest of the nine and the only true city boy among them, being born in Algiers in 1927. These last three—Ben M'Hidi, Ben Boulaid, and Didouche—would all die relatively early in the war for Algeria's independence.

On the whole, therefore, the FLN's founders had relatively modest rural backgrounds, and though they were all reasonably educated (or self-educated, in Khider's case), only a few could truly be considered intellectuals. As a consequence, they identified first and foremost with the peasantry. On the other hand, while several of them came from once-prominent Sufi marabout families that had fallen on harder times in the colonial era, they were not especially religious as a group. Indeed, only Aït Ahmed and Khider were proficient in formal Arabic—as opposed to an Algerian dialect largely incomprehensible beyond the Maghrib—giving their movement a distinctly francophone character. Notable also was the fact that only Ben Bella hailed from western Algeria, and the northeastern part of the country, where the terrain was better suited to guerrilla warfare, would be the epicenter of the revolution. In time, all of these somewhat accidental aspects of the FLN's founding would prove highly consequential in terms of the linguistic, regional, and religious tensions that characterize Algerian society to the present day.

What united these conspirators in the spring and summer of 1954 was their mutual contempt for traditional politics, which they saw as divisive, timid, and ineffective. They also feared that while the politicians bickered, Algeria risked missing a global window of opportunity signified by the Vietnamese victory at Dien Bien Phu, the subsequent Geneva Accords between the four great powers that ratified North Vietnam's independence, and the more advanced nationalist movements in neighboring Morocco and Tunisia. An internal tract subsequently distributed among the FLN's militants justified the need for the front's founders to take matters into their own hands on the basis that "hesitation was impermissible. The struggle of the fraternal Tunisian and Moroccan peoples had reached an advanced stage, and the international environment was characterized by postwar anticolonialism. The situation had become more favorable than ever."[52] Before settling at the last minute on Front de Libération Nationale, they initially called themselves the Comité Révolutionnaire pour l'Unité et l'Action (Revolutionary Committee for Unity and Action, CRUA), a label that neatly encapsulated their three guiding mantras.

The commencement of the FLN's revolution, on the night of 31 October–1 November 1954, was extraordinary in its the audacity. The plotters had progressed from initial discussions to all-out war in a mere six months, without waiting even to create a proper political apparatus. As one participant later explained, they believed that there was no time "to engage in minute and precise study . . . [or] the full elaboration of a program of action and coordination at every level."[53] In theory they could call on a few thousand rebel fighters, mostly on the run in Kabylia, though at best half of them possessed any kind of firearm, and their attachment to the FLN would depend on the movement quickly establishing some degree of momentum. Yet while the French security services were quite well informed of the plans of, in the words of one intelligence report, "some impatient young militants" to form a "super-clandestine terrorist group" that would bring Algeria to the attention of the UN and the Arab League, the FLN's founders were relative nobodies in the larger context of the diverse Algerian political scene.[54] Consequently, most listeners were bemused by this hitherto unheard of group's grandiose proclamation on 1 November, broadcast on Cairo's Voice of the Arabs radio station, that declared war on French colonialism and demanded the loyalty of all Algerians. Moreover, the decidedly unimpressive results of a series of coordinated attacks around the country that same night did little to convince anyone that these so-called revolutionaries could either defeat the French or reshape the political landscape.

That they dared to do so was a testament, first of all, to their courage. As Mohamed Boudiaf confessed to a French journalist eight years later, "We hoped, without being sure, that the masses would come into play. If not, it would be a suicide mission."[55] Yet more important still was their belief in history's calling, or the convergence of irresistible epochal dynamics, and their confidence that the complementary "tools" of revolution and diplomacy would make them masters of Algeria's destiny. In fact, their faith in these tools is all the more striking for the scant thought they put into them beforehand, and in that respect, the founders of the FLN were proof of the dissemination of empowering, utilitarian abstractions of reality. In early 1956, Abbas flew to Cairo and held a press conference to declare, "My role, today, is to stand aside for the chiefs of the armed resistance. The methods that I have upheld for the last fifteen years—cooperation, discussion, persuasion—have shown themselves to be ineffective."[56] While the front's grasp of history certainly ran roughshod over a rich political, social, and cultural legacy—a legacy that could not be long ignored—it also made the movement mighty.

A War of Two Systems

The astounding escalation of the FLN's revolution quickly vindicated its founders' self-belief and their interpretation of historical auspices. In early 1955 an official in Kabylia noted that "not even three months have gone by, and already [the local populace's] vocabulary has changed."[57] The attacks of 1 November 1954, which the authorities breezily dismissed as the actions of fringe criminals, set off the steady expansion of rebel activities and heavy-handed security countermeasures over the next two years, so that by late 1956 the conflict in Algeria had already become one of the largest of the postwar era. Though the French government would never officially recognize the reality of a "war" in North Africa—stubbornly insisting on the use of euphemisms such as "the situation" or "the events" in Algeria—Paris had deployed nearly half a million military personnel there by the close of 1956. These numbers facilitated a resource-intensive counterinsurgency strategy known as *quadrillage* that effectively segmented the whole country into garrisoned grids. Yet despite the army's heavy presence on the ground, or perhaps even because of it, the ALN's capabilities continued to grow; two years after the revolution's start, approximately 50,000 mujahideen were carrying out as many as 4,000 attacks per month in practically every part of Algeria.[58]

Furthermore, the FLN was also forging ahead on the diplomatic and internal nation-building fronts. Its representatives attended the summit of Afro-Asian heads of state in Bandung, Indonesia, in April 1954—the meeting generally considered to have launched the global Third Worldist movement—and attached themselves to friendly delegations, such as that of Saudi Arabia, in the United Nations General Assembly in New York, where they lobbied for the passage of resolutions supporting Algerian independence and condemning French policy. This assertion of nationhood on the international stage—aptly dubbed the "diplomatic revolution" by historian Matthew Connelly—complemented the rebels' efforts to build a revolutionary administrative apparatus from the ground up in every *douar* (village) in Algeria by providing new judicial, educational, and religious services in competition with those of the existing colonial order.[59] An ALN tract from late 1957 explained to the mujahideen's political commissars that "the difference between the French administrative organization (of a bureaucratic nature) and the revolutionary Algerian organization is evident. . . . The former endeavours to preserve itself, whereas the latter struggles to destroy that which exists and to build anew."[60]

In other words, during these largely successful first two years of the revolution, the FLN appeared to be in harmonious accord with its era, epitomizing and profiting from the main dynamics of the early Cold War international system.

On the ground, the revolutionary nation-building project employed communist techniques and methods—to the point that the FLN's leaders even copied communist instructional texts wholesale while simply substituting overtly ideological terms like "proletariat" and "class" for "nation" or "people." In the diplomatic sphere, the nationalist rebels tried to take advantage of France's demotion to a second-rank power by appealing to its NATO partners and embracing the new postwar ethos of "international community" that the superpowers had themselves institutionalized. Nevertheless, real as these accomplishments were, closer examination of the first half of the Algerian War shows that the FLN's seemingly timely strategy soon ran into grave difficulties. Indeed, by late 1957, perilous setbacks on all fronts would compel its leaders to profoundly reappraise their position in the Cold War world, strategically, ideologically, and diplomatically. Nor would it be coincidental, moreover, that their evolution in this respect was consistent with oft-overlooked dynamics within the broader Third Worldist milieu.

The FLN's first great accomplishment was to level Algeria's political landscape, overturning the status quo ante so thoroughly that by 1956 only Messali himself and a relatively small number of his loyalists openly rejected the front's primacy. First, the authorities' heavy-handed response to the rebellion greatly aided the FLN's growth. The security services crudely swept up PPA-MTLD militants and student activists wholesale in early 1955, thereby inadvertently converting many of them to the revolution's cause, only to release them again several months later. In reality, the FLN's founders had so neglected political organization prior to 1 November 1954 that initially there was little substance to the movement beyond its armed wing, but this new wave of adherents that included former PPA-MTLD politicos, university students, and labor organizers gave the revolution a vital injection of political skills and manpower. Noteworthy recruits included Lamine Debaghine—who had originally declined an invitation to join the FLN conspiracy in 1954—and a Kabyle MTLD member called Ramdane Abbane, who had been imprisoned since 1950 only to be released serendipitously in early 1955. By dint of his widely acknowledged political acumen and organizational skills, Abbane quickly acquired the informal status of first among equals in the FLN's Algiers group, from where he set about imposing centralized coordination and control, establishing a consistent public message, and liaising with other movements such as the ulema, Ferhat Abbas's reformist politicians, and the communists. In late 1955 and early 1956 the front's communications and propaganda apparatus really got off the ground, including the launch of its primary newspaper, *El Moujahid* (The Mujahid).

Violence was fundamental to the FLN's quick ascendency. Falling instinctively on tried and trusted methods, the police and armed forces swept through suspect neighborhoods and villages with an iron fist, hoping to replicate the swift decapitation of the OS five years earlier. This vigorous response did indeed exact a heavy toll on the mujahideen, thousands of whom were killed or arrested in the revolution's early months. Among the early casualties among the movement's founders were Mourad Didouche, killed in January; Rabah Bitat, caught shortly afterward; and Mostefa Ben Boulaid, who was first captured in early 1955, then escaped only to be blown up by a booby-trapped radio the following year. But, gradually, the FLN recovered from its serious initial setbacks and saw both passive support and active recruitment skyrocket toward the end of the year. The excesses of the French response backfired politically while the very suffering of the underdog mujahideen inspired Algerian sympathies—not unlike the militarily quixotic but historically groundbreaking 1916 Easter Rising in Dublin, a precedent that Abbane, for example, had studied during his imprisonment. Likewise, one of the war's most notorious incidents, the massacre of a hundred pied noir civilians by their Muslim neighbors in a mining town near Philippeville in August 1955, arose from the local ALN commander's recognition that violence had the power to utterly transform sociopolitical dynamics, even at the risk of revulsion and opprobrium. Before egging on the local population to butcher pied noir families in particularly macabre fashion, he argued that "the Revolution is not sufficiently aided by the populace. . . . The fraternisation between the Algerian and French populations . . . must cease."[61] As was his intent, the resultant carnage provoked still more brutality from the security services.

The revolution's founders had wasted no time in pressing ahead with their international strategy. Three of them—Ahmed Ben Bella, Mohamed Khider, and Hocine Aït Ahmed—constituted the movement's external delegation in Cairo when the revolution began, and their first public relations success had been to broadcast their initial proclamation of 1 November 1954 on Egyptian radio, thereby reaching most of the Arab world. The Algerians then quickly used Arab sympathies as a bridgehead to what they believed would be the decisive diplomatic battlefield: the United Nations. By the new year, Khider had already won King Saud's promise to push for a General Assembly resolution in favor of Algerian independence, as well as his agreement to bring FLN spokesmen into the assembly as part of the Saudi delegation, bearing Saudi passports.[62] To this effect the following April, if not earlier, the Cairo office produced its first English-language publicity material with an international and especially an American audience in mind. Titled "What Is Algeria: The Algerian Question in Outline," the pamphlet put particular emphasis on the material deprivation of most Algerian Muslims—an effective line of attack against France in an era in which economic concerns dominated the political discourse at both the national and the international level.[63] Aït Ahmed and a thirty-two-year-old former student militant named M'hamed Yazid traveled to New York to establish the FLN office and coordinate efforts there, resulting in a dramatic early success on 30

September. Perhaps underestimating the resourcefulness of the front's ragamuffin diplomats and the extent of worldwide sympathy for their cause, the French delegation failed by just one vote to prevent a motion empowering the General Assembly to open a dossier on the Algerian question (which the French government insisted was a purely domestic matter beyond the UN's jurisdiction). Aït Ahmed recalled—hopefully in jest—resorting to counting votes on his fingers and toes as the issue went down to the wire, then exulting as the French delegation stormed out of the hall in protest of the motion's passage.[64] It was an important symbolic victory, but Paris would not repeat the error of haughtily ignoring the pro-Algerian campaign: the French embassy in New York quickly threw personnel and money into a slick public relations operation of its own, retaining the services of a prominent American communications firm to polish its message.[65]

The ultimate goal of this war of words and resolutions was to stir Washington. From the beginning, there was little appreciation among American policymakers for French claims that Algeria was as integral a part of France as Normandy or Provence, or that the rebels were the tools of a Nasserite-communist plot to control North Africa. Discreetly, some State Department officials met with Aït Ahmed and Ben Bella in the Libyan capital, Tripoli, in late 1955. The Algerians impressed them with the subtlety of their arguments and the determination of their convictions as they discussed the Franco-American relationship in a realistic way while also playing on Washington's Cold War concerns. With France pulling large numbers of its troops from Western Europe to fight in Algeria, Ben Bella argued that the continuation of the war was weakening NATO's defenses, but he acknowledged that public pressure on Paris would likely be counterproductive. Instead, he suggested, Washington should privately urge France to end the war through direct negotiations with the FLN.[66] In addition to accurately conveying the FLN's envisioned route to victory, the idea of a negotiated change of Algeria's status appealed to the Americans' desire above all for "stability," and their fear that international communism would exploit London, Paris, and Brussels's aversion to evolving or to parting with their imperial possessions in a timely fashion. Yet the fast-changing governments of the Fourth Republic (Edgar Faure replaced his Radical colleague, Pierre Mendès-France, as prime minister in February 1955, before the socialist Guy Mollet succeeded him the following January) expected the full support of their American allies, and for the time being at least they obtained it. Diplomatically, the Eisenhower administration actively defended the French position in the General Assembly, orchestrating the defeat of successive motions on Algeria, and continued to furnish substantial quantities of military materiel under NATO's aegis, much of which was used to hunt mujahideen in Algeria instead of facing down the Red Army in Europe. For the FLN's leaders, therefore, the key was to increase the cost of Washington's support for France so that the Americans would eventually feel compelled to convene an "Algerian Geneva," by which they meant a meeting of the great powers to settle the Algerian question such as they had for Vietnam with the Geneva Accords of May 1954.

It was very fortunate for the FLN, therefore, that the initially Asian-centric effort to create a loose but vast coalition of developing countries coincided so closely with the beginning of the Algerian Revolution. Orchestrated principally by the Indian, Chinese, and Indonesian governments, the Summit of Asian-African Heads of State that took place in Bandung, 18–24 April 1955, brought together the leaders of twenty-nine countries, mostly Asian but also several from the Middle East as well as Africa's Gold Coast. Participants and observers alike declared the Bandung Conference to be a major historical event—the re-emergence of non-Western diplomatic life after centuries of European domination, the unprecedented meeting of the representatives of more than half of the world's inhabitants in all their variety. "I could sense an important junction of history in the making," recorded the African American writer Richard Wright, "Every religion under the sun, almost every race on earth, every shade of political opinion, and one and a half thousand million people from 12,606,938 square miles of the earth's surface were represented here."[67] Certainly many of the attending national leaders rose to the occasion with soaring rhetoric denouncing the Cold War, the superpowers' arms race, and the gross disparity in living conditions between North and South. The likes of Nasser, Nehru, Chinese prime minister Zhou Enlai, and Sukarno did much to enhance their international profile, with the Indonesia president's stirring opening speech immediately bestowing a grandiose, moralizing, almost religious tenor on the proceedings. Condemning the destructive history of the Western order, he asserted that the end of empire heralded a new era by bringing "all the spiritual, all the moral, all the political strength of Asia and Africa on the side of peace."[68] The influence of Nehru's heavily promoted five principles of peaceful relations between peoples, or Panhscheel, was evident throughout the conference and in the attendees' collective final declaration, which pledged fealty to the principles of neutralism and disengagement vis-à-vis the Cold War, noninterference in one another's affairs, the completion of decolonization, and redressing the imbalances in the global economic order.[69]

Bandung was almost too good to be true for the FLN, coming as it did just as the rebels were struggling to gain traction with their diplomatic campaign and to shore up their credibility with the Algerian people. The FLN's experience also offers a useful reminder of the reality of Bandung, an event that has all too often been reduced to the level of symbolism and rhetoric by both admirers and skeptics. But for the statesmen who organized and took part, the conference's essential purpose was geopolitical. The initial impetus was a compact between the Indian and Chinese governments, looking for a way to begin asserting what they saw as their inevitable rise and domination of Asia. "America and some European countries have seen Asian countries becoming strong and are envious," Nehru had told Mao the year before. "They envy China becoming strong, they also envy India becoming strong."[70] Bandung was thus in part communist China's coming-out party onto the world stage, since the mainland was still a pariah state barred from the UN at this time, and much of the rhetorical emphasis on peaceful relations reflected the need to reassure nervous Asian governments that Peking's rise would be a pacific one.[71]

With this original motivation in mind, supported by Nasser and Sukarno, the FLN teamed up with Moroccan and Tunisian nationalists to overcome Nehru's initial reluctance to admit national liberation movements to the Bandung event, with the cautious Indian prime minister explaining to Aït Ahmed that because the conference was threatened by "all sorts of plots," it was imperative that the organizers avoid controversial issues—of which Algeria was most certainly one.[72] In the end, the North Africans gained admission as a combined "observer" delegation that included Aït Ahmed and Khider and were given the opportunity to address the assembly in order to publicize their cause. The assembly's response, a subsequent internal FLN report observed, exceeded even their most optimistic hopes: the inclusion of a firm statement of support for Algerian independence in the final joint communiqué of all the participating governments.[73] Suggesting that words could be turned into deeds, this statement then played a key role in corralling twenty-eight votes in the UN General Assembly that September—the vote that prompted the French walkout. Consequently, for the Algerian rebels at least, Bandung's exuberant announcement of the era of Third World diplomacy was much more than a rhetorical milestone; it produced immediate tangible benefits. Of course, atmospherics mattered too: the FLN's participation in the Asian-African summit provided a much-needed fillip to morale and legitimacy back home.[74] We are not alone, the front's propaganda assured the Algerian people, dubbing Bandung the "international 1 November."[75]

Consequently, the FLN dedicated a substantial portion of its limited resources to the developing world as it continued to build its diplomatic apparatus. In early 1956, a talented young lawyer named Tayeb Boulahrouf became probably its first official "ambassador," in Rome, while a worldly English-speaking journalist, Abdelkader Chanderli, subsequently took charge of the New York office. By the end of 1956, the front had managed to send delegations to tour Latin America, Asia, the Middle East, Southeast Asia, and Europe. Nearly everywhere, local solidarity committees greeted the Algerians warmly and the left-wing press organized press conferences and interviews, and even if the governments of Latin America, Britain, West Germany, and Italy formally kept their distance in deference to French sensitivities, Paris was nevertheless outraged that any of its European allies would allow FLN representatives to operate on their territory at all.[76] At the same time, the front also began recruiting heavily from a student activist group formed in Paris the year before, the Union Générale des Etudiants Musulmans Algériens (General Union of Muslim Algerian Students, UGEMA), leading in time to a close-knit clique of young men forming the backbone of the international campaign. First Mohammed Benyahia, a twenty-four-year-old freshly minted lawyer, and a twenty-two-year-old political science student called Lakhdar Brahimi were dispatched to represent Algeria at an Afro-Asian students' conference in Jakarta, scheduled for April and May 1956 to capitalize on Bandung's momentum. The original plan was for Benyahia to remain as ambassador in the Indonesian capital and for Brahimi, who had quit his university studies to serve the revolution, to take several months to learn English before moving on to New Delhi. But when the former fell terribly ill and had to return to Cairo, it fell instead to Brahimi to remain in Jakarta for close to four years, while also traveling extensively throughout the region in an effort to advance the Algerian cause. Intrepid, resourceful, a firm believer in the power of diplomacy and internationalism—Brahimi offers an example of how the FLN's hardscrabble diplomacy managed to thrive against the odds. "After the *médersa* [high school], I feel that Indonesia has been my second school, an extraordinary school," he later recalled fondly. "Whatever I did not learn in the *médersa*, I learned in Jakarta."[77]

Naturally, atrocities such as Philippeville could be problematic for the FLN's primarily Western-oriented public relations campaign, and Abbane in particular would soon insist on the need to subordinate military operations to the greater diplomatic good. At the same time, and in ways that have perhaps not been fully appreciated before, the FLN's symbolic ties to the wider Third Worldist and anti-colonial movement actually seemed to abet the ruthless separation of Algeria's Muslim and pied noir communities. In one recent documentary film, for example, a former mujahid participant in the Philippeville massacre recounted how when two airplanes appeared in the sky, he cried out that Nasser must have sent them to fight alongside the Algerians. The aircraft were obviously French, and the notion that they had flown from Egypt extremely fanciful, but that evening his unit retreated to hide in quarries up in the hills, where they huddled around a battery-powered radio listening to Cairo's Voice of the Arabs radio recount their exploits.[78] Perhaps such external sources of validation are part of the explanation for how ALN fighters and ordinary Algerian civilians were able to set upon their European neighbors with knives and farming tools, sparing neither infants nor the unborn, for the knowledge that they were part of some great global revolution may have eased the burden of their sins that night. Before he himself joined the FLN, the Martinican psychiatrist Frantz Fanon became intimately familiar with the psychological consequences of the Algerian Revolution while working in a hospital in the important provincial town of Blida. It is notable, therefore, that in the books that quickly established him as possibly the foremost ideologist of Third Worldism, Fanon stressed the importance of both radio and mass violence to the success of anticolonial struggle, arguing that they allowed the colonial subject to overcome a state of internalized subservience.

Intercommunal violence and the excesses of French repression polarized society to such an extent that the old parties had little choice but to rally to the FLN's communal nationalist banner. In early 1956 Ferhat Abbas, once the figurehead of Francophile assimilation, flew to Cairo and held a press conference to declare that "my role, today, is to stand aside for the chiefs of the armed resistance. The methods that I have upheld for the last fifteen years—cooperation, discussion, persuasion—have shown themselves to be ineffective."[79] In addition to Abbas, notable converts outside of the former PPA-MTLD who came to play prominent roles in the revolution included the reformist 'alim Tewfik al Madani and a former general secretary of the PCA, Omar Ouzegane, who remained greatly influenced by communist ideology in spite of falling out with the communist movement. Abbane played the chief role in persuading so many representatives of the old order (the remnants of the PPA-MTLD, Abbas's UDMA, the ulema, and the communist party) to disband their own organizations and join the FLN on an individual basis. The front strictly imposed this principle of individual recruitment, rather than conversion en masse, in order to avoid the importation of preexisting cliques and patronage clans, although it is significant that the PCA in particular quietly managed to preserve its organization even after formally dissolving.[80]

The front also quickly gained a small but consequential number of pied noir and French sympathizers, mostly from leftist and communist milieux. Jean-Paul Sartre became something of a pariah in French intellectual life by coming out in support of Algerian independence, while the pied noir communist Henri Alleg wrote a vivid exposé of the torture he suffered at the hands of French paratroopers, *La Question*, which influenced metropolitan public opinion in the war. From the beginning, the FLN's propaganda deliberately courted Algeria's European and Jewish communities with the vision of an equitable, multicultural future. Of course, while at least the more cosmopolitan cadres based in Algiers sincerely believed in this multicommunal future, developments out in the bloodied *bled* frequently gave cause to question its viability. The inconsistency of the FLN's message on this particular issue was but one manifestation of a greater problem: the hitherto largely autonomous operation of the movement's six *wilayat* (regional commands) and even of subregional units below the *wilaya* level. Some commanders in the field were busily churning out religiously themed motivational material for their troops even as the editors of *El Moujahid* and other "official" representatives strove to deny France's portrayal of the rebels as a gang of bloodthirsty fanatics.[81]

In short, by the summer of 1956 the FLN contained a genuinely comprehensive representation of Muslim Algeria's various sociopolitical tendencies. However, it would be of lasting historical significance that the tricky internal political dynamics of holding together such a broad coalition reinforced the FLN's embrace of "revolutionary" organizational principles. "Democratic centralism" and "collective leadership" became the movement's bywords in internal discussions and public propaganda alike, with equal emphasis placed on condemning the "cult of personality" phenomenon. These concerns stemmed originally from the experience of Messali's domineering hold over the PPA-MTLD, but they continued to be relevant throughout the FLN's development in order to maintain unity in the absence of an undisputed ideological guide along the lines of, say, Mao Zedong or Ho Chi Minh. Similarly, in an environment that insisted on the moral supremacy of the Historic Nine and those who first heeded their call, johnny-come-latelies converting from the old parties had a clear interest in championing the notion of revolutionary rebirth in order to escape their "tarnished" pasts. Lamine Debaghine, for example, argued in his subsequent effort to draft a comprehensive history and doctrine for the FLN that "people who remain marked by their past are less effective than those who have elevated themselves above their past. . . . If the past is forgotten, the FLN will be a humanly homogenous organism."[82] Thus, although the front's ideological character remained ill-defined in terms of long-term goals, or even became murkier as a result of its rapid expansion, there was a very real collective commitment to "revolutionary" practices and habits.

In that same spirit, the high point of Abbane's leadership and the FLN's organizational drive in the war's early years was the so-called Soummam Platform of August 1956. The document was hashed out at a meeting of most of the front's senior leadership, boldly held under French noses by dint of various diversionary operations in an innocuous-appearing farmhouse in the Soummam Valley in Kabylia. So as to alienate neither conservative elements within the movement nor the Western audience that was paramount in Abbane's calculus, the text of the platform said remarkably little about the FLN's long-term goals other than the achievement of independence. Instead the focus was emphatically on hierarchical and organizational concerns. Soummam formalized the principle of collective leadership by declaring that ultimate authority rested in a new body called the Conseil National de la Révolution Algérienne (National Council of the Algerian Revolution, CNRA), a sort of parliament of the FLN that would convene intermittently to set overarching strategic and operational priorities. The senior controlling body on a day-to-day basis would be the Comité de Coordination et d'Éxecution (Coordinating and Executive Committee, CCE). Moreover, Soummam's schema borrowed heavily from the Bolshevik and Maoist doctrines in revolutionary warfare as it described a complete structural hierarchy right down to the local level: *wilaya*s consisted of *mintaqa*s, or zones, which consisted of *nahiyya*s, which consisted in turn of *qism*s (departments or sectors), below which finally lay the *douar*, or individual village. In theory a triumvirate of military commander, liaison-information officer, and political commissar was in charge at every successive level of this hierarchy, thereby enshrining the principles of democratic centralism, collective authority, and full political-military coordination.[83] The front's purpose, Abbane argued, was not simply to fight the French but to mold the Algerian people into a "modern" nation. Earlier in the summer, new instructions to the ALN commanders in one particular region had succinctly summarized this concept: "A double task awaits us: to conquer and to organize.... [The political commissar's] competencies in politics and organization make him play a role as chief of the civilian population: he is thus judge, tax collector, responsible for supplies, head of propaganda, ... of health services, of the press."[84] In short, by endeavoring to distill praxis from theory, the Soummam Platform was an intriguing exercise in nonideological revolution.

The French army and the ALN embarked on competing administrative projects in the name of modernity and organization and, amid a backdrop of terrible violence, thereby brought the long-neglected *bled* into contact with global trends. To begin with, the army's approach was not unlike an updated version of the original nineteenth-century conquest. In 1955 the liberal new governor-delegate, Jacques Soustelle, ordered the formation of an elite corps of Arabic-speaking officers, the Sections Administratives Spécialisées (Special Administrative Sections, SAS). The SAS would live among the peasants and combine military duties with basic social operations in a manner reminiscent of the Bureaux Arabes by which the army had once managed Algeria before authority eventually passed to the growing settler community.[85] Indeed, given how much Algeria had changed in recent decades, the counterinsurgency soon resembled reconquest and, with it, rediscovery. Large farmers had bought out most of the pied noir smallholders who, being closer to the Muslim population, had been the authorities' best eyes and ears on the ground. Numbering 150,000 at their height, 6 out of 7 Europeans had upped and left for the cities as early as 1930.[86] Soustelle called on the SAS to "bridge the yawning gap between the administration and the poorer inhabitants." Their work was supported by anthropologists and social scientists, and they also submitted their own detailed studies of the social structures, customs, and even topology of the local area. They issued identity cards to village residents, but the provision of women's health services and schooling also served as subtler ways of cataloging and monitoring the peasants while courting their loyalty.[87] In sum, to use James C. Scott's formula, a vital purpose of the SAS was to make Algeria legible to the colonial state once again.[88]

The rebels, in contrast, wanted to blind the enemy. The mujahideen's attacks often consisted of sabotaging telephone lines and electricity supplies and blocking roads and rail lines. In late 1957, though, the ALN leadership in the Oran region determined that "the SAS represents the fundamental cell of the enemy's policy. It is [the SAS] that tortures, that creates information networks, that sabotages our revolutionary work. It is the primary objective that we must confront."[89] Because one of the SAS's most basic tasks was to conduct a census and issue identity cards to the local population, the ALN ordered Muslim women not to remove their veils in order to be photographed. This was a clever way to implicate women in the revolution by appealing to their sense of modesty while blurring the line between public morality and support for the revolution.[90] Likewise, the FLN initially tried to ban the consumption of alcohol and tobacco, although it seems to have largely given up this effort later in the war. Not being a notably abstemious bunch themselves, the leadership was not concerned for Algerians' souls so much as cutting off social interactions with Europeans in bars and cafes, describing it as "an opportunity to express your solidarity with Algeria's fighting forces . . . to show the world that you are ready, that you know how to follow orders"—to make it impossible, in other words, for the French to distinguish friend from foe.[91] In March 1956, Muslim high school students obeyed the call to boycott French schools. In September, the front extended the boycott to primary schools, arguing that this gesture would show that "the rupture is ordered [*condamné*] between the Algerian people and French authorities in every domain, up to and including the cultural domain. . . . Even though our desire and our thirst for culture and science are greater than ever, must we forget that every school and *madrasa* in our *douars* and villages has become a military post?"[92]

When these instructions went unheeded, the punishment was severe. In a message to "Brother 25," one ALN captain located near Oran warned that "the officers of the SAS are conscious of the psychological wall which separates them from our population. They are employing more and more Muslim advisers. The latter often make clandestine contact with the People."[93] Therefore no Muslim's collaboration with the colonial occupier could be tolerated. The ALN head in each town was ordered "to form a group of terrorists and lead them into combat. It is necessary to take out [*abattre*] all the *Caïds* [and] village policemen . . . to take out every man and women of poor conduct. . . .. The order is given to burn every village that asks for 'the protection of France' and to take out every man older than 20 years living in those village."[94] Seemingly innocuous places like schools and medical centers became the front lines of a ruthless war. Hence the disquiet of reports such as that from a French officer in the Kabylie in the summer of 1956 who warned that "the population ignores the troops, the SAS, the doctor. There is more than indifference in this attitude, there's also hostility."[95] In effect, the FLN wanted to return French perceptions of Algeria to the racist attitudes of the colonial era, when pied noir settlers and administrators would frequently describe the Muslims as a sea of inscrutable dark faces concealing unknowable opinions and desires. The front's goal was to create an impenetrable nation that would eventually expel the colonial presence from its body.

As this battle escalated through 1956 and into 1957, Abbane in particular was dissatisfied with its direction and concerned that some of his brothers in the field were hopelessly pursuing the war as an end in itself. The combat in the hinterland was transpiring out of sight of the wider world, not least because of French media controls. In the autumn of 1956 he issued "Directive Number 9" instructing that they begin terrorist activities in the cities: "Is it preferable for our cause to kill enemies in some riverbed in Telergma, which no one will talk about, or rather a single one in Algiers, which the American press will report the next day? Though we are taking some risks, we must make our struggle known."[96] The Battle of Algiers was joined, and at its height in January 1957, the FLN called for a general strike of Arab shopkeepers and workers as a show of the unity to coincide with the upcoming meeting of the UN General Assembly. Abbane confidently predicted that "the international repercussions will be very great and will allow the population to demonstrate its power."[97]

Of course, the FLN had already been remarkably successful in bringing international attention to its cause. The support of the April 1955 Bandung Conference had particularly inspired the FLN by seeming to vindicate the vision of transcolonial solidarity rallying to its side. The "spirit of Bandung" was now a propaganda staple, and *El Moudjahid* insisted that "the struggle of the Algerian people is neither isolated nor unique; it is but an episode in the universal struggle ... against European colonialism."[98] In concrete terms, the external delegation devoted much of its meager resources to courting the Afro-Asian constituency. That autumn, the Afro-Asian governments supported a UN motion calling for the peaceful resolution of the Algerian question in accord with the charter's right to self-determination. When it passed by a single vote, the French delegation stormed out of the hall, to the delight of the FLN team present.[99] When Morocco and Tunisia became independent soon after, their governments pledged total fraternal assistance to the Algerians and permitted the ALN to establish base areas on their territory. The goal of forcing France to accept an "Algerian Geneva" seemed at hand.[100]

The external delegation then spread itself thin to tour Latin America, Asia, the Middle East, Southeast Asia, and Europe by the end of 1956. Nearly everywhere, local solidarity committees greeted them warmly, and the left-wing press especially facilitated press conferences and interviews.[101] In the summer the young lawyer Mohammed Benyahia and Lakhdar Brahimi, who had quit his university studies in Paris to join the revolution, established a two-man mission in Jakarta. Learning English on the job, Brahimi also traveled to New Delhi.[102] The front's guerrilla diplomats boasted admirable pluck. Living on a shoestring with the ever-present menace of French operatives, they endeavored to comport themselves as ambassadors as they parlayed with senior officials and even heads of state.

Yet concrete results were hard to come by. Among the Arab states—effusive in expressions of unity—only the Saudis had put their money where their mouth was. One of the FLN's senior diplomats, M'hamed Yazid, noted that many of their Bandung friends had retreated from the confrontational approach used in the UN the previous year in order to avoid the anger of Paris (later on, for example, de Gaulle threatened to aid the Sumatran rebels if Indonesia continued to brazenly abet the FLN).[103] In October 1956, Khider in Cairo urged Yazid and others to attend a socialist convention in Rangoon, where they should take the Indians to task for colluding with France to adjourn an Algerian debate in the General Assembly and remind all the Asian states to fulfill the pledges they had made at Bandung.[104] It soon became obvious that Moroccan and Tunisian independence did not augur Algeria's imminent liberation; instead, France wanted to focus on holding onto that most important colony. Toiling diligently to churn out propaganda and documentary material in New York, the front's UN team noted that the opposition had massively boosted its countereffort with a huge staff and budget dedicated to public relations, even hiring an American communications firm to proselytize France's case in Algeria.[105]

Transnationalism also entailed inherent negative aspects. Under the patina of internationalism, tensions and mutual suspicion were rife between the revolutionaries and the "fraternal" nations that hosted them. Deep resentments also festered between those fighting the French inside Algeria and the external team, many of whom were late additions to the revolutionary leadership—moderate types like Ferhat Abbas pushed forward because they were educated, cultured, and pleasing to a Western audience. A fierce rivalry developed between Abbane in Algiers and Ben Bella in Cairo, whom Abbane accused of developing a "cult of personality" by turning himself into the public face of the revolution ("While we're in the shit up to our necks every day, Monsieur schemes and already takes himself for Gamal Abdel Nasser!").[106] Algiers and Cairo even had rival delegations vying with each other in Tunis, and the Algerians rightly suspected Habib Bourguiba of encouraging such scissions.[107] The military types' feeling that the external delegation never did enough to find and supply them with weapons and support, while living it up abroad themselves, contributed to a divergence in their perceptions of international affairs.

These tensions became more acute as the FLN ran into grave difficulties on both diplomatic and military fronts. Abbane and Larbi Ben M'Hidi, the Algiers chief who died in French custody, had conceived the Battle of Algiers as the ideal convergence of the armed struggle and the international campaign, but it ended very badly for the FLN. Led by Colonel Jacques Massu, whose charismatic brutality was later immortalized in Gillo Pontecorvo's film, French paratroopers ruthlessly unraveled the front's network in the capital and broke the January strike. The surviving leaders fled Algiers for the safety of Tunisia, prompting Ali Mahsas—an ally of Ben Bella and critic of Abbane—to bemoan that "we have risked the dismantling of the revolutionary Organization to make a noise at the United Nations. It's stupid and ridiculous!"[108] Meanwhile, "secret" preliminary discussions between the revolutionaries and the French government had ended abruptly in October 1956, when hard-line senior officers in Algeria unilaterally hijacked a Moroccan jet ferrying Ben Bella, Aït Ahmed, Khider, and others to talks in Tunis. Efforts to restart discussions led nowhere, since the military was now practically running the war itself and hell-bent on victory.[109] The former top commander in Indochina, General Raoul Salan, took charge of both military and civilian affairs in Algeria on 1 December. By the end of 1957, the army had constructed massive barriers of electrified fence, minefields, and artillery along the borders of Morocco and Tunisia. It was a stunningly literal effort to cut Algeria off from the outside world and soon proved very effective at blocking the resupply and reinforcement of the ALN. Inside the country, the French steadily improved their counterinsurgency tactics and began to reverse what was hitherto a pattern of steady growth in the mujdahideen's numbers and operational potential.

By 1957, the war was taking on a globalized significance for both sides. The FLN was not just trying to bring its struggle to the world's attention; they also increasingly saw themselves as one element in a transnational revolutionary wave. Perhaps because of their growing military difficulties, more and more this is how they presented themselves to the Muslim population. In May, the team in Cairo told the leaders inside the country "to prepare Muslim opinion in Algeria for the forthcoming debates in the UN General Assembly. . . . Insist particularly on the current comportment of the USA, which seeks the friendship of Arab states and wants to expand their influence in North Africa on account of Algerian oil and possible military bases."[110] The instructions of an ALN captain near Oran, found by French troops in early 1958, show how this propaganda effort capitalized on every diplomatic coup, in this case particularly the French air bombardment of the Tunisian border town of Sakiet Sidi Youssef, which provoked widespread international condemnation: "The mujahideen and the people must be kept up to date on the international situation that is currently critical for France, who is condemned by the entire world. . . . This is the moment to issue directives, to reorganize, to recontrol and demand of the people that they make a new effort."[111] Around the same time, the FLN propagandists were told to remind the people that "we are not alone," that Asia and Africa had definitively begun the process of decolonization if this did not *yet* take the form of armed struggle in every country. The military and diplomatic combats would support each other, they were reminded, until an Algerian flag flew at the UN.[112]

Yet many on the French side, particularly within the army, also defined their struggle in global terms. The same units often fought in Indochina, Algeria, and Egypt—with the disastrous Suez expedition of October and November 1956 motivated in part to cut off the FLN's lines of support from Cairo. Remembered their experiences in nostalgic memoirs as "those long years of combat in the cold, the snow, the heat, the jungle, the desert," many officers believed that they manned Western civilization's ramparts against a collusion of communist totalitarianism and native fanaticism across the decolonizing world.[113] When General Salan took charge at the close of 1956, he championed the doctrine of "revolutionary war"—*guerre révolutionaire*—whose exponents sought essentially to fight the revolutionaries with their own tools: propaganda, mobile warfare, indoctrination, and "psychological warfare." Salan appointed a former prisoner of the Viet Minh, well exposed to their ideology and "brainwashing" techniques, to head up a special training center for French officers in Algeria. The adherents of this theory sought not just to imitate the revolutionaries on a tactical level—foreign observers noted how like their enemy some French units had become in their lax style of dress and disdain for traditional military hierarchy—but even to defeat them on an ideological level.[114] They noted that, in comparison to the Viet Minh, the Algerians had a very underdeveloped ideological agenda. For example, one intelligence report from early 1957 concluded that, in order "to rally as quickly as possible the large majority of the population and especially the political heads of the old parties," the FLN had sacrificed political depth for breadth at Soummam:

> The various simple themes of the political "program" of the FLN are sure of everybody's agreement and do not consider the future in any detail. . . . [T]he FLN-ALN is not aiming for the ultimate objective of a totalitarian type of revolution, that is to say aiming for a radical transformation of individual or collective structures . . . [but] the methods and practices of combat are those of "totalitarian" revolutionary war.[115]

Thus the most militant elements of the French army co-opted for themselves the modernizing mission typical of Cold War–era anticolonial movements, and some even came to see the FLN and the pieds noirs alike as twin obstacles to France's historic duty to lift the colonial peoples out of the mire. The key theme for their propaganda, one report instructed, should be that the FLN

> pillages, burns, steals, destroys and slows economic development by the fear it instills and by diverting billions of francs for the maintenance of

order.... This transformation [of Algeria] cannot be achieved without outside help (capital—technicians—materials). This help can come neither from Cairo, nor from Morocco, nor from Tunisia ... but only from France who knows Algeria's needs.... Only those who will understand the *Greatness of this Future* will have a place in the New Algeria.[116]

Certainly, not every French commander subscribed to the lofty goals of *guerre révolutionnaire*, and many historians rightly caution that the doctrine's impact was greatly diminished by the pervasive brutality of the counterinsurgency campaign in general.[117] It was perhaps more significant as an intellectual trend than a military doctrine, and it featured heavily in French media and propaganda at least through 1958. The subsequent progression of the FLN's own doctrine and political strategy must be understood in this context: the front felt the need to reassert its credentials as Algeria's revolutionary vanguard.

In December 1957, Abbane was murdered by some of his own colleagues in the senior leadership in Morocco. This rare case of internal assassination was the result of bitter personal rivalries, but it was also a consequence of the failure of the strategy Abbane had championed of risking more visible defiance, in particular the Battle of Algiers. Following the creation of the frontier fortifications, the FLN was entering its period of greatest peril, and the hope of progressing quickly from guerrilla war to open revolt had to be abandoned. In April 1958, an Indochina veteran and ALN officer wrote to the senior command that the Chinese and Vietnamese cases had proven empirically that the revolution must progress to "classical" war only in its final stages. "If [we want] to go against the revolutionary orthodoxy defined by Mao Zedong," he insisted, "I fear that that such speculation will engender for our army sacrifices disproportionate to the objectives we wish to attain."[118] Perhaps having read this report, a few days later the then-chief of the FLN's War Department, Belkacem Krim, echoed its warning: "Taking into account our potential and conditions at the moment ... [it is inconceivable] to move from the guerrilla stage to that of classical war. The enemy is watching and hopes for a change in the methods we have used." Though the international campaign was making progress, the Sakiet crisis being the most encouraging development yet, Krim concluded that "the interior must stay organized for a long and hard war."[119]

Whereas Abbane had subordinated the military effort to international strategy, there was a new recognition that the perpetuation of the ground war underwrote all their political and diplomatic efforts. Even Ferhat Abbas acknowledged that if the ALN were defeated, "there would hardly be any need for a wider policy and to waste time in chancelleries and international events. All will be lost, irredeemably lost. Algeria will become a new Palestine."[120] The urgent need to shore up the ALN's military and political organization inside Algeria prompted a more hardheaded appraisal of the revolution's foreign relations. It is no coincidence that *El Moujdahid* openly criticized US policy for the first time in January 1958, accusing Washington and Bonn of funding the French war effort, and lumping the Western countries together as a monolithic "imperialist" bloc. For all of American officials' handwringing and growing relationship with the FLN representatives in New York, newly effective French counterinsurgency efforts relied more and more on American helicopters and other supplies.[121] A growing chorus of voices, particularly among the ALN chiefs, insisted it was madness to continue to ignore the communist countries as a source of material assistance. At the very least, they argued, an opening to the East might scare the West into a change of policy.[122] Nor were their allies in the Middle East and Asia willing to provide the degree of military or political support they now needed.

In contrast, at the same time another representative, Ibrahim Ghafa, was invited to attend a "day of solidarity" with Algeria in Peking, where he was warmly welcomed by the university's students and professors.[123] There were also substantive discussions with Chinese officials away from the ebullient public relations exercises, as a result of which Ghafa could report excitedly that "People's China is looking by every means to establish permanent and close contacts with us." The Chinese were looking to expand their international reach, and having no relations with France, they were impervious to any retaliation from Paris. It is highly revealing that Ghafa seemed much less concerned with Western opinion than with the likelihood that Egypt would react badly to direct FLN-Chinese contacts. This reflected the sentiment that the West had already picked its side, as well as mounting resentment at Morocco's, Tunisia's, and Egypt's domineering ways.[124]

Indeed, chafing relations with the FLN's main supporters and host nations added greatly to the sense of morass. When Aït Ahmed suggested a declaration of independence and the establishment of a provisional government, the military chief Omar Ouamrane seconded the motion. He wrote to his colleagues in July that the world was getting used to the war in Algeria, offering nothing but platitudinous resolutions at the United Nations, and he too pointed to the potentially decisive role of the communist bloc. His rationale, however, had more than a merely pragmatic basis. Scorning "reformist" methods, he deemed a unilateral declaration of independence to be a properly revolutionary act. One of the more avowedly revolutionary of the senior figures, Ouamrane was arguing for nothing less than a fundamental repositioning of the FLN on the Wilsonian-Leninist continuum that had influenced Algerian nationalism for four decades:

> We have preferred pseudo-revolutionary verbiage to a truly revolutionary politics making a tabula rasa of French institutions and the French constitution, [and] to audacious concrete initiatives to pull the Nation

out of the colonial paradigm. . . . With [the Western] bloc we still appeal to the grand principles of liberty [and] democracy, principles in which we are surely the last to believe. . . . We continue to talk of the past ("Algeria has long constituted a State") or of the present (torture), forgetting that the future alone counts (political projects—economic projects—fate of the European minority).[125]

By 1958, therefore, both practical strategic considerations and a discernible (if only from a historian's distance) leftward drift in the FLN's collective ideology informed a reassessment of the Algerian revolution's rightful place in the Cold War order. A strategy of subordinating the ALN's military struggle to a diplomatic campaign directed primarily at Western capitals and New York had yielded some tangible achievements, but the long-term significance of these early diplomatic accomplishments was not nearly as appreciable to the front's leaders in the midst of a merciless counterinsurgency as it would be many years later for reminiscing revolutionaries and scholars. On the contrary, in 1958 the revolution's outcome was very much in doubt, and the existing diplomatic strategy had failed to find the correct balance between supporting the mujahideen and pursuing the ultimate political objective. But while pragmatism urged that the FLN pursue opportunities for material support in the East, either for its own sake or to put pressure on Washington, the accumulated weight of new evidence from the front's internal communications also proves that a more radical sentiment was gaining momentum, one that took root in the Leninist and Maoist dynamics of an underground battle for the allegiance of the economically oppressed masses and then flourished in the light of sustained American intransigence and communist encouragement. More and more voices were echoing Ouamrane's call to give the nationalist cause more economic and political substance, and all the exigencies of the ground war and the international environment seemed to coalesce in pointing toward a more radical left-wing direction.

Moreover, distinct from any prospective strategic adjustment or political realignment, a subtler change in the FLN's relationship to the outside world was already underway. In an effort to quarantine their own fragile unity and also to avoid alienating any potential allies, the Algerian rebels had tried to keep the contentions of the international sphere at arm's length even as they endeavored to profit from them, but now this imperfect segmentation was breaking down altogether. Already, the external delegation's base in Cairo had exacerbated factionalism within the movement, but with even more of the political and military leadership relocating to Morocco, Tunisia, or even farther afield, the scope for pernicious entanglements of Algerian disputes and foreign agendas was vastly greater. At the same time, the front was showing greater readiness to get its hands dirty in international rivalries at the highest level, between the United States and the Soviet Union, and at the local level between Rabat and Tunis. In sum, by abandoning their strict neutrality in international affairs, and by embracing a more ideological conception of their nationalist project, the Algerian revolutionaries were becoming Cold Warriors.

The Algerian War Joins the Cold War, 1958–1959

Despite the exertions of both sides over the past three years and more, the summer of 1958 was only the midpoint of the Algerian War and the start of a period of fundamental transformation. Charles de Gaulle's return in May began a rejuvenation of France's strategy and political structures. The FLN was likewise changing its organization and methods, as epitomized by the creation of the provisional government, the GPRA, in September. Many scholars consider this to be the beginning of the period in which the FLN declined militarily but conquered diplomatically, but this view neglects the evolving goals of each side. Gradually, de Gaulle tried to transition from the defense of the colonial status quo to justifying France's role in Algeria on the basis of postcolonial partnership. Certainly the revolutionaries needed to counter their deteriorating military position—the numbers of weapons and men successfully crossing into Algeria each month were plummeting—but they also had to respond to the innovations in de Gaulle's political strategy.[126] In the villages of the interior, the political commissars looked increasingly to the mighty and distant Soviet Union for salvation.[127] Indeed, by the close of 1959, the communist world had become the FLN's main source of ordnance and ideology alike.

Rebellious army offices and pied noir hard-liners called for de Gaulle's return in part because they believed that *le général* alone had the determination and stature to defend French Algeria from the predations of the United States. Indeed, Connelly has dubbed 13 May an "anti-American revolt" because of the open fear of a "diplomatic Dien Bien Phu."[128] In his memoirs, de Gaulle stressed his conviction that France alone would determine Algeria's fate, and this claim at least is credible in a work redolent with self-aggrandizement: "We would pay no attention to any overtures from any capital, to any offer of 'good offices,' to any threat of 'agonizing reappraisal' in our foreign relations, to any debate in the United Nations."[129] Indeed, the CIA had begun funneling some money to the FLN's refugee camps through the major American federation of trade unions, the AFL-CIO, while the front's representative in New York, M'hamed Yazid, had established regular contact with State Department officials, including ambassador to the United Nations, Henry Cabot Lodge. However, in the weeks after de Gaulle's return, Yazid's contacts admitted that Washington did not want to put its hand in the "viper's nest" again and would be very circumspect in putting any pressure on de Gaulle vis-à-vis Algeria.[130]

In the face of French diplomatic and economic pressure, the FLN's allies were also moderating the extent of their support. In March 1958, for example, even before de Gaulle's return, Nehru had pled impotence in the face of French intransigence with regard to pushing harder at the UN. "We have done all that we can," he said weakly, "but [if] France won't budge . . . what can we do?"[131] Meanwhile, underneath the veneer of oft-proclaimed fraternal solidarity, relations were deteriorating with the front's most important allies, Morocco and Tunisia, and especially with Habib Bourguiba, who distrusted the Algerian army growing on his territory and cooperated more and more with the United States in impeding the flow of weapons from abroad. On 16 June, Bourguiba angered the FLN leadership by urging them to compromise their goals because de Gaulle's return strengthened Paris's hand in both Washington and Moscow; he warned that "the arrival of de Gaulle is an event in the world. If before de Gaulle the position of France was very weak in the international sphere, things have since changed." To this suggestion, Ferhat Abbas responded defiantly: "For us Algerians, de Gaulle's position means war, whatever support he might receive from the Americans, the Russians, or even the Egyptians."[132] The very next day Kwame Nkrumah met with FLN representatives in Cairo, who assured him that the revolution would not wilt in the face of the long war augured by de Gaulle's policies. Satisfied, the Ghanaian leader insisted that the Algerian cause was vital to Africa—and that he in turn would strive for Africa's support. The striking difference in tone between Nkrumah and Bourguiba presaged the Algerian Revolution's alignment with the emergent radical wing of African politics.[133]

Yet most of Africa was yet to be decolonized, and in August the external delegation in Cairo produced a prognostication on the upcoming session of the UN General Assembly that reflected its discontent with the changing international environment: "[The Western group] is definitively unfavorable to the Algerian cause, and we must not expect any spectacular change in the near future. . . . [The communist group] has been content to offer us support in principle for a propaganda win, pure and simple." There was no use, the report decided, in pushing for a strongly worded resolution that would fail to obtain a majority— "this could be satisfying from a purely propaganda point of view, but such a step is greatly outdated after four years of unpitying war"—and instead they hoped for, at best, the passage of a moderately worded resolution. Results from diplomacy in Latin America and Asia were mixed and unspectacular. The sense of frustration was palpable.

That autumn, both France and the FLN dramatically reformed their political structures, opening a distinct new phase in their struggle. Of the two sides, however, France was the pacesetter. Because the war in Algeria exemplified or exacerbated the diverse crises afflicting France in the postwar world—political instability, declining empire, ebbing international stature, a lost sense of national purpose—de Gaulle's approach to the conflict must be understood as being one key component in an even broader and more complicated effort to redress all those concerns. First, this ruinous conflict—in every sense—had to conclude in a way that confirmed the authority of the civilian government in Paris over mutinous soldiers and pied noir hardliners; second, the war's solution had to be seen as a *French* solution, not one dictated by foreign powers or by the rebels themselves; third, instead of epitomizing the collapse of empire, Algeria should serve as a model for France's postcolonial relations throughout Africa; and finally, tying together all these considerations, the Algerian solution should confirm for the French public that their country still retained a unique purpose in international life, and that French culture and republican values still bettered and ennobled the citizens of its former colonies. Therefore, de Gaulle held a referendum on 28 September 1958 to approve the constitution of the Fifth Republic, which promised a new era of political stability by means of a powerful presidency but also incorporated his proposal for a French Community preserving tight political and economic links with the former African colonies.[134] Although the FLN had ordered a boycott of the referendum, Muslim turnout was high and overwhelmingly approving of the new constitution, appearing to grant de Gaulle license to present his plans for Algeria.[135] Just a week later, in the Eastern city of Constantine, on 3 October, the French president announced an ambitious five-year economic and development program for Algeria and shortly after publicly invited the mujahideen to call a truce, a "peace of the brave," even as he made plans for a redoubled military campaign to quash the insurgency.

For the Algerian nationalists, France's reinvigorated political offensive was at least as dangerous as its counterinsurgency efforts. "A special place is destined for the Algeria of tomorrow," de Gaulle declared, "an Algeria that will be pacified and transformed, developing its personality itself and closely associated with France."[136] The revolutionaries recognized the appeal that this message of compromise and peace would have to a war-weary population; the struggle was entering a new stage in which the FLN would have to discredit and overcome a far more compelling and progressive-sounding message than previously seen from the enemy. "At this moment," one GPRA report argued, "it is essential [for de Gaulle] . . . to extract from the chaos a reasonable, moderate Algeria that would be likely to accept a French Algeria through a 'renovated' neocolonialism. Thus the Constantine Plan which, in the mind of the general, is the antidote and anesthetic for Algerian nationalism."[137]

Ferhat Abbas assumed the GPRA presidency despite—or perhaps because of—his lack of a real power base within the FLN, but also because he was well known abroad as the moderate, cultured face of Algerian nationalism.[138] Yet despite the expectation that their declaration of independence would strengthen the Algerians' case before the international community, initially only thirteen states recognized the provisional government: the Arab states except Lebanon, Indonesia, communist China, North Vietnam, and North Korea. A report written in Cairo at the beginning of December, perhaps by Dr. Lamine Debaghine, the GPRA's first foreign minister, noted that a "very feeble minority" of governments had recognized the GPRA, and the demurral of India and other important Afro-Asian countries meant that "we have to resign ourselves to the idea that any resolution making even a feeble allusion to the GPRA will have no chance of passing in the current session [of the UN General Assembly]."[139] However, this prediction soon proved overly pessimistic, for later that month an Afro-Asian resolution that recognized Algeria's right to independence and called for immediate negotiations between the French government and the FLN failed to achieve a binding two-thirds majority by only a single vote. More important, Ambassador Lodge had registered Washington's abstention on the motion—a dramatic departure from the Americans' established pattern of handwringing support for the French position that cheered the revolutionaries as much as it outraged de Gaulle's government.[140]

Even so, the Algerians were already embarking on a serious exploration of China's advances. A three-man delegation visited Peking as the debate in New York played out. Two members of the delegation, Benyoussef Ben Khedda and Saad Dahlab, would soon rise to positions of influence within the GPRA. French intelligence perceived them to be sympathetic to the communist bloc, and Dahlab's memoirs indicate why this might have been the case.[141] He recalled being greeted at the airport like heads of state and experiencing a wave of emotion on hearing the FLN's national anthem played for the first time, by a Chinese military band. Four years into the revolution, suffering heavy losses in the field, and feeling abandoned by the wider world, the Algerians were profoundly appreciative of such gestures. Mao Zedong expressed his appreciation for the GPRA's recognition of his own government, and his officials readily confirmed their willingness to furnish military supplies as well as aid for the hundreds of thousands of Algerian refugees amassing in Tunisia and Morocco.[142]

In fact, Ben Khedda and Dahlab's trip would prove the beginning of a new era for the FLN's international strategy. Four years after the war's beginning, de Gaulle's return had rejuvenated the enemy, and the creation of the GPRA strengthened the voices of those calling for a bolder engagement with the tensions between the Cold War's antagonists. A report penned under the code name "Mostefai" warned that de Gaulle's strategy would take years to defeat, "again giving the military aspect of our revolution a determinative character." Nor did he fear the collapse of their established diplomatic strategy by pursuing contacts with China, judging that their "half success" at the UN "confirms the correctness of a firm and dynamic international policy." America's abstention, he argued, showed that the trip to Peking had not provoked a violent reaction in the West but had instead raised the prospect of blackmailing the United States with the menace of communist intervention.[143] "If we can manage to isolate France from its allies just a little bit, even without obtaining a radical conversion of US policy in our favor," concurred a second report from the diplomatic wing's Cairo headquarters, "we will achieve a substantial diplomatic victory."[144] It seemed that the irresistible prospect of Chinese military support and the seductive logic of the "blackmail" strategy were finally starting to overcome the rebels' hitherto extreme reluctance to risk alienating the West.

Of course, while Aït Ahmed and other nationalist activists had been advocating the idea of pitting East against West for years, actually putting this gambit into practice was a step in the dark and fraught with risk. Ramdane Abbane, for one, had always opposed the blackmail strategy, dubbing it a "double-edged sword" because of its potential for backfiring and provoking outright American hostility.[145] On the contrary, the FLN's spokesmen had hitherto exhaustively refuted French claims that they colluded communist subversion, and their efforts had been rewarded by John F. Kennedy's speech in support of the Algerian nationalist cause on the Senate floor in 1957. Nor were the communist states of Asia without enemies inside the Afro-Asian group, and in fact by late 1958 the Algerians were perhaps concerned less with American opinion than with the prospect of their blossoming relationship with Peking antagonizing the Egyptian or the Indian government.[146] Moreover, quite apart from any strategic calculus, the history of bad blood between the left wing of Algerian nationalism and the international communist movement stretched back to Messali Hadj's falling-out with the PCF in the early 1930s, and the more religious and conservative elements of the front's broad coalition had a special abhorrence of the godless foreign ideologies of secular socialism. In sum, a reorientation toward the communist world might alienate foreign allies and weaken the FLN's internal unity.

Given this long-standing commitment to ideological and international neutrality, the realization that choosing sides might be a more effective strategy was a profound one. More and more of the Algerian revolutionaries concluded that their travails in the ground war and in the diplomatic battle were both symptoms of the same overly cautious strategy. Defending himself from criticism in January 1959 that the Ministère des Affaires Extérieures (Ministry of External Affairs, MAE) ought to have secured the recognition of more than a dozen-odd countries, Debaghine asserted that their diplomatic efforts were actually of little import in a world riven by ideological divisions. "It is extremely significant to note," he told his colleagues, "that, apart from Indonesia, none of the other Asian countries that have recognized us (People's China, North Vietnam, and Outer

Mongolia) have ever been contacted by us, and conversely that India ... where we have maintained active FLN representation for a long time ... refuses to recognize us still."[147] In the Cold War paradigm, in other words, external relationships were a product of internal politics, and the FLN's studied ideological inoffensiveness was holding the revolution back. However, the full significance of Debaghine's train of thought is that the reverse might also be true: by decrying the revolution's vague nationalist political content as a diplomatic boondoggle, the MAE chief shows how international ideological choices might be a function of international objectives. "A good number of these [foreign] powers will hesitate to recognize the GPRA," he warned, "as long as it avoids taking a clearer position on [its current and future orientation] and is content to be vaguely the friend of everybody and the enemy of no one. ... The difficulties we suffer in our foreign relations proceed from the cruel lack of doctrine that is the main characteristic of the FLN."[148]

Russian historian Evgeniia Obichkina's study of the Soviet archives suggests that Debaghine's argument had merit. At first, the Kremlin was far more interested in pursuing the possibility of driving a wedge between the French government and its NATO allies than in abetting an obscure native rebellion in North Africa. Additionally, open Soviet support for the FLN would have been an electoral calamity for the PCF. One of the GPRA's analysts showed a canny understanding of the situation by arguing that the Soviets were initially ill-served by the PCA's and PCF's forced theoretical explanations of the Algerian problem that justified France's continued presence. "Yet they could not run in the face of facts for long," he wrote. "The failure of the PCA's attempt to join the Revolution while preserving its autonomous structure, the progression of our people's struggle, ... [and] the anti-imperialist elan in the Arab countries following the attack on Suez constituted elements of new significance that the USSR could not ignore."[149] Partly out of consideration for their burgeoning relations with Egypt, the Soviets did start supplying arms from Czechoslovakia for Nasser to pass on to the Algerians, although the FLN leadership could only guess their provenance. Overall, Moscow's limited interest in Algeria had been defined by its policies toward Egypt and France, and the Algerian nationalists had done little to spark the Kremlin's curiosity in their own right.

However, just as American pressure on Tunisia to restrict the FLN's activities was a major cause of the Algerians' growing hostility to Washington, in 1958 Moscow interpreted Algero-Tunisian acrimony as a positive indication of the FLN's shifting position between the two blocs.[150] Accordingly, though Soviet officials had pointedly avoided speaking to two FLN representatives attending an Afro-Asian writers' conference in Tashkent in October that year, Khrushchev's close adviser Anastas Mikoyan then met unofficially with the Ben Khedda–Dahlab delegation as it returned from Peking via Moscow in

December.¹⁵¹ Mikoyan indicated that the Kremlin wished to strengthen its contacts with the Algerians, without going so far as to recognize the GPRA or furnish arms directly. Subsequently, on Christmas Eve the Polish first secretary in Tunis told the FLN diplomat M'hamed Yala that the communist bloc had come to a "collective decision" that only the Asian countries would recognize the provisional government so as to protect the Algerians from the taint of communist subversion.¹⁵² Clearly the Soviets wished to keep the FLN at arm's length, but their level of interest had jumped once the Algerian nationalists seemed to be reaching out to Peking, while making enemies in all the right places.

Though the Soviet opening was much more hesitant than that of the Chinese, the combined effect was to inspire in the Algerians a new enthusiasm for the acute tensions of the Cold War. The following March, a political commissar in Wilaya 4, the region south and west of Algiers that exhibited perhaps the strongest left-wing tendencies within the ALN, claimed that "despite the efforts of certain leaders, the people in its near totality [and] the *djounoud* (fighters) are anti-American and judge that the assistance of the USSR alone can advance the action of the Algerian people toward their total independence: political, economic and social independence."¹⁵³ The leadership was already undertaking initiatives to that effect. On 28 January, Abbas wrote to the North Vietnamese foreign minister to thank him for his government's recognition of the GPRA in September. The timing was significant, since even by the FLN's disorganized standards four months was a long delay on such an important issue.¹⁵⁴ This paved the way for a military team to spend a week in Peking and Hanoi two months later, where the discussions focused on guns and revolutionary strategy in equal measure. In concrete terms, the Chinese provided their first arms shipment to the value of $25 million. Of higher quality and greater firepower than the varied assortment the mujahideen had relied on thus far, the weapons proved their worth by enabling the destruction of a French frontier post in August.¹⁵⁵

But the Eastern bloc's attentions also paid dividends far beyond the battlefield by raising Algeria's import as a point of leverage between the great powers. That summer Abbas wrote that the delegations to China and Vietnam "have opened up the path that leads to Moscow. In this regard let's not forget, not ever forget, that the USSR is the great hope for the colonized peoples in their struggle for independence. Without it the USA would be lined up, as in 1918, on the side of the colonialist nations and they would have abandoned the principles of the San Francisco Charter as readily as they abandoned Wilson's 14 Points in 1918."¹⁵⁶ Partly in response to the American abstention at the UN the previous December, in March de Gaulle showed a strong hand in his own game of blackmail by announcing that the French navy was withdrawing from the NATO command structure. On the other hand, in August the Soviet foreign minister, Andrei Gromyko, warned his French counterpart, Maurice Couve de Murville, that the Kremlin might "drop the restraint" it had shown in its relations with the FLN were the new resident of the Elysée Palace to continue his steadfast backing for Bonn's position in the Berlin Crisis.[157] At a meeting of Arab diplomats in November, Debaghine—who had vacated the foreign minister's office in March but retained diplomatic responsibilities—admitted that he dreaded the possibility of detente and peaceful coexistence between the two blocs.[158] "We cannot continue alone," he argued. "We must enlarge our circle of friends. . . . Currently we have turned toward China. Possibilities exist and they are enormous."[159]

But the ramifications of friendship quickly went beyond the confines of a mutually beneficial partnership. Until 1959, the Algerians had studied the Chinese and Vietnamese examples from books and the insights of veterans of the French expeditionary force. Now they went directly to the source. When the ALN delegation visited Peking and Hanoi in April, Mao's and Ho's generals treated its members to lengthy seminars on the histories of their own campaigns and lessons on revolutionary guerrilla strategy. Though the ALN had long relied on the practical and operational facets of revolutionary war, these discussions highlighted the innate ideological assumptions that had always been at the doctrine's strategic core.[160] For example, in Hanoi, Vo Nguyen Giap counseled patience in dialectical language: "Like any great revolutionary endeavor, the Algerian people's endeavor to liberate their country currently faces temporary difficulties. However, we are living now in the era of a great victory for Socialist Revolution [and] for the National Liberation movement. . . . The Algerian people will surely conquer their total independence." His was a world in which the forces of socialism and national liberation were steadily vanquishing the era of imperialism; "total independence" signified economic as well as political liberation.[161] The next day, the Algerians were advised on the essentiality of the ideological-political dimension of their war: "Victory proceeds from the accuracy of the political line. . . . The army is a political instrument." Though the mujahideen had indeed always been conceived as a political weapon, one of their hosts (it is not clear from the GPRA record of the meeting if this was still Giap talking) insisted on the need for a substantial socioeconomic message in addition to nationalist exhortations. The people, he said, supported the revolution because it promised material happiness and national prosperity, and since the peasants were the majority, it was necessary to promise them the land. "Ideology is the trait of revolutionary armies," he concluded. "The French expeditionary corps [in Indochina] was better armed. . . . But for a man, esprit and ideology are decisive."[162]

The counsel of the Chinese and Vietnamese struck a chord with the Algerians because it coincided with a fundamental reconsideration of the ALN's strategy in light of the worsening military situation and the emergence of a new generation of commanders pushing aside the old. During the previous year, the organization of the ALN had been overhauled by establishing two Military Operational Commands (COMs) in Morocco and Tunisia, and like the formation of the GPRA of the Tunis on the political side of things, this change reflected the reality that the frontier barriers had pushed the front's center of gravity outside Algeria. The capable young Colonel Houari Boumedienne (colonel being the highest rank in the rebel army) made a name for himself by quickly turning COM-West into a paragon of organizational efficiency—in marked contrast to the mess one of Belkacem Krim's protégés made of the Eastern command, which displayed all of the FLN's worst traits of factionalism, indiscipline, and disorder.[163] Consequently, Boumedienne assumed command of both COMs—putting him well on the way to eventually achieving mastery of the entire armed wing of the revolution. Throughout 1959, strategic debates were inflected by the power struggle between Krim and Boumedienne's patron, Abdelhamid Boussouf, formerly chief of the *wilaya* of Oran in the west of Algeria. Because of this subtext, many observers view the Boumedienne clan's advocacy of ideological radicalization as a cynical gambit to outmaneuver his rival, but though no amount of documents can reveal the true nature of his innermost thoughts, the new evidence from the FLN archives proves that Boumedienne was a consistent partisan of revolutionary goals from at least 1959.

It is remarkable how closely the ALN's ruminations matched Giap's advice. First, a high-level strategic report echoed the Vietnamese general's emphasis on ideological clarity to maintain order within the revolutionary army and to counter the enemy's own political project: "Firstly, it is the absence of doctrinal principles in the regulatory, organizational, disciplinary sense . . . that is at the heart of our difficulties and our mistakes." The task of either subverting or destroying the *harkis*, the shock troops of de Gaulle's bid to create a moderate "third force" in Algeria, was the first item in the report's list of strategic imperatives: "The enemy wants to threaten the Revolution with the danger of what we call 'baodaïsation.' The importance of the *harkis* will be a danger to the Revolution if immediate measures are not taken."[164] During an intense discussion of the ALN's long-term goals in September, Boussouf argued for a radical agenda by making an implicit comparison with the supposedly "mercenary" *harkis*. "We told everyone that we were revolutionaries," he said, "that we were for a radical change to the existing state of things and we did not speak [just] of independence. Has the ALN fallen into the role of a gang of mercenaries—so if we are not militants of the revolution, what are we then?"[165]

Second, Giap's emphasis on the peasantry found support in another high-level strategic analysis that stressed that "the peasantry constitutes the most important driving force of the revolution." Consequently, the FLN's long-term goals had to reflect the desires of this portion of the population: "The Algerian peasant is profoundly aware that he participates in a revolution more than a war of liberation. . . . For the peasant, the struggle to liberate the national territory from foreign occupation and [the struggle for] social and economic revolution are one and the same. They do not constitute two distinct stages."[166] To be sure, the peasantry had always been the front's core base of support, but especially in the time of Ramdam Abbane's greatest influence, the movement had tried to appeal to a broad spectrum of constituencies that theoretically included liberal elements in the European and Jewish minorities.

Yet, with the Battle of Algiers a receding memory and the mujahideen pushed deeper underground and farther into the wilderness by French *commandos de chasse*, more than ever the Algerian Revolution stood for the aspirations of the rural masses. Hereafter, the ALN's relationships with Peking, Hanoi, and Belgrade only deepened. Peasant refugees fled from the French army's scorched-earth tactics into the ranks of Boumedienne's growing army on the frontiers, where they were clothed in communist-supplied uniforms, equipped with communist-supplied weapons, and indoctrinated by communist-inspired political commissars. Already, the leadership were beginning to account for their difficulties with the Moroccan and Tunisian regimes on the basis of differing political doctrines: "By its origins, character and eventual prospects, the Algerian revolution worries the bourgeois republic of Tunisia and the neoliberal monarchy of Morocco. The conservative instinct pushes retrograde politics and the denial of the people's deepest aspirations."[167] In sum, thanks to the dispersion of communist models of revolutionary war, the Algerian mujahideen were paradoxically becoming both more essentialist in their conception of Algerian nationhood and more internationalist in their conception of that nation's role in a dialectical world.

Our Friends Today

From the diverse critiques of colonialism that proliferated after the First World War until the founding of the FLN's provisional government in September 1958, the Algerian nationalist movement evolved in tandem with the Third Worldist one. Despite the differences between groups such as the Salafi ulema, the Francophile assimilationists, or Messali Hadj's leftist populist parties, during the interwar years every mobilized element of Muslim society engaged with the world beyond North Africa. Algeria was typical in this regard for, although the specific term "Third World" was not coined until the 1950s, the accumulation of such contacts fostered a genuine sense of solidarity and common purpose across the Southern Hemisphere in the first half of the twentieth century. Yet Algeria's connection to the global anticolonial scene also went beyond exchanging ideas, comparing experiences, and sharing socioeconomic transformations.

Through Messali at first, and then the young revolutionaries who broke away from his party to form the Front de Libération Nationale, certain Algerians were also early participants in the Third World project, a decades-long campaign to coordinate the actions of the emergent nationalist elites in Africa, Asia, and the Middle East. This project arguably began in 1927 with the League against Imperialism conference in Brussels, where Messali met Nehru and other nationalist figures, but it had its "official" unveiling at the summit of Asian-African heads of state in Bandung, in 1955, where the FLN scored its first major diplomatic victory. At that point, the two projects—Algerian nationalism and Third World internationalism—became practically interreliant and nearly inseparable in the minds of many of the front's cadres. With their fates intertwined, the Algerian perspective is particularly revelatory of the anticolonial phenomenon as a whole.

While not the case for every country or territory, Algeria's relationship with the Third World project illuminates the progression of anticolonial thought from reformism or inchoate proto-nationalism with external connections of an inherently transnational nature, roughly during the 1920s–1940s period, to a new consensus on outright nationalism and formalized interstate relations in the middle and late 1950s. After all, until then significant support still existed on both sides of the imperial-colonial divide for a form of decolonization that replaced empire with pseudo-federal and semiautonomous structures, rather than destroying it altogether through the universal application of the sovereign nation-state model. Bandung is best known for popularizing the principles that gained near-instantaneous acceptance as the basis for international relations in the global South—anticolonial solidarity, Cold War neutrality, pacifism, economic development—but perhaps its most significant effect was to hasten the consolidation of this new state-centric consensus. As a naked celebration of diplomatic protocol and the elevated status of its participants, the conference suggested that statesmanship was the ultimate expression of individual and national liberation. The organizers' formalization of Third World relations introduced a new sense of hierarchy to the anti-imperialist scene. Jawaharlal Nehru had initially opposed the participation of any representatives of still-colonized territories, lest their controversies constrain independent countries like India, and the admission of the French North African delegation with "observer" status was simultaneously a great victory for the former and an indication that the transnational era's expectation of equality no longer applied. Therefore, perhaps even more than the rhetorical content of Third Worldist diplomacy, it was its praxis that encouraged the colonial world's new political movers to consider anything other than the achievement of full statehood as a lesser, inferior outcome.

The FLN's political development during the first half of the Algerian War is a testament to the influence of the Third World project. Both at the time and long after the fact, the rebels credited Bandung's imprimatur with saving the revolution in its difficult early days, when the security services threatened to annihilate the front before most Algerians even knew much about it. While the Third World's validation obviously boosted the FLN's international profile and perceived legitimacy in foreign eyes, in the revolution's initial stages it had a far more significant effect inside Algeria itself. By 1958, diplomatic accomplishments constituted the majority of the propaganda that the nationalist rebels aimed at their own population, with the Third World scene generally providing the most enthusiastic and most bountiful opportunities for photographs, handshakes, and speechifying. Quite apart from geopolitical strategic goals, diplomatic *performance* became more central to the FLN's nation-building project. Moreover, the influence of Bandung's formalized, interstate version of Third World internationalism clearly informed the decision to create the GPRA in late 1958, which ruled out any possibility of negotiating with Paris in the near future by setting aside the vague and flexible rhetoric of *autodétermination* (self-determination) for the uncompromising *l'indépendence*. The pursuit of formal diplomatic relations with the governments of Asia and Africa was, therefore, the immediate cause of this watershed in the history of Algerian nationalism.

The effectiveness of both the Third World project and the FLN's revolutionary strategy derived from the fact that they worked with, not against, the new structures of international power in the Cold War era. Anti-imperialist forces, broadly speaking, supported the superpowers' joint reorganization of international society along lines that weakened the colonial system. After all, Bandung's call for the heterogeneity and instability of empire to be replaced everywhere with independent states, all of them invested in the success of the United Nations and the other cornerstones of the post–World War II order, concurred with the superpowers' shared skepticism with regard to Europe's lingering imperial attitudes and highlighted the way that Washington and Moscow—even through competition—combined to reorder global life. In practical terms, this meant that elites in the colonial world frequently "bought into" the Cold War as a structuring of international power because it challenged imperialism in fundamental ways. In the 1940s and 1950s, the most common strategy was to pit the United States against its imperialist allies, such as Ho Chi Minh quoting the preamble to the American Constitution when he declared Vietnam's independence in 1945, Gamal Abdel Nasser persuading Washington to punish Britain and France at Suez in 1956, and as the FLN's leaders hoped to do at the beginning of their revolution. The following chapter explores how, in the late 1950s, some Third World actors then moved to a more provocative strategy of pitting the Soviets directly against the Americans—or the Chinese. Yet, before this more radical approach became widespread, many participants in the Third World project hailed the Cold War's impact on the structures of international society, without feeling constrained by the geopolitical ideological substance of the bilateral conflict. The American secretary of state, John Foster Dulles, could complain that nonalignment was "obsolete, . . . immoral and short-sighted," but the Third World's basic demand for sovereignty still resonated with American officials and the public because it seemed commonsensical and stability-promoting.[168]

Consequently, by late 1958 a decisive segment of the FLN's cadres and diplomats had become Cold Warriors. Although French efforts to portray them as stooges of international communism were crude and rightly failed to convince, the nationalist revolutionaries had now made several conscious decisions, roughly at what proved to be the midpoint of the Algerian War, to more closely enmesh their struggle in the global contest between East and West. The GPRA's first minister of external affairs, Lamine Debaghine, had argued persuasively that the front's original policy of neutrality or nonalignment, which was effectively to steer well clear of the Cold War's geopolitical and ideological contentions, simply resulted in Algeria being ignored by a world preoccupied by those concerns.

More profoundly, however, while the Cold War context does not explain *why* the Algerian Revolution happened—bitter memories of subjugation and the Muslim majority's perennially dire living conditions accounted for that—it did largely determine how. For their methods and their timing, FLN's founders took their cue from the Cold War's first interactions with the end of empire in East Asia, in the late 1940s and early 1950s. They wanted to replicate the Vietnamese nationalists' military victory at Dien Bien Phu and, even more so, their diplomatic victory (at least in the Algerians' view) at the Geneva summit. The FLN's very raison d'être was to pursue without restraint those diplomatic and revolutionary methods of action first presaged, from the anticolonial perspective, by Woodrow Wilson and Vladimir Lenin in 1918. Then with time, as Vo Nguyen Giap had advised them with regard to the Chinese-Vietnamese doctrine of guerrilla war, the innate logic of those methods of political mobilization urged their Algerian practitioners to deepen their socioeconomic program. The ALN's political commissars in the field were already responding to a perceived programmatic deficiency, with one pamphlet distributed in Kabylia in late 1957 assuring that "our administration will replace that of the occupier everywhere and in every domain [of daily life] . . . today the Algerian is liberating himself and expects all that the revolution can give him, [so we] must be conscious of the thirst for a better life and for freedom."[169] Although they were not yet using the loaded term "socialism," by 1958–1959 the front's internal communications regularly stressed the need to understand "national liberation" in social and economic terms as much as in territorial-political ones. Without engaging directly with the Cold War's central ideological contest, the FLN was nonetheless validating Algerian nationalism against the same criteria as its capitalist and communist counterparts.

Perhaps no moment more clearly illustrates how the rebels became Cold Warriors than their riposte to de Gaulle's "*autodétermination* speech" of 16 September 1959. The French president's promise to deliver the "government of Algerians by Algerians, backed up by French help and in close relationship with her, as regards the economy, education, defense and foreign relations," alarmed the rebels as much as it angered the pieds noirs, since they feared that a war-weary Muslim public might embrace its faux-nationalist imitation of independence.[170] In that mindset, the provisional government's senior figures effectively decided to abandon four years of cautious abstention from the Cold War's bloc rivalries and ideological tensions by sending a high-level delegation to Peking for the anniversary celebrations of the Chinese Revolution. Only the publicity of that occasion, with the added possibility of meeting Nikita Khrushchev there, would make an impact equivalent to de Gaulle's bombshell. Ben Khedda predicted that "such a meeting would be a shock for the interior and the exterior," with Krim Belkacem crowing in concurrence that it would "make the West tremble." Even so, others cautioned, "sending our four most senior figures [to Peking] will suggest a [new] orientation." Were they willing to cross a line that neither the Western press, nor American policymakers, nor conservative elements within their own movement could accept without protest? It was a measure of how far Algeria had traveled that it fell to Ferhat Abbas, former figurehead of Francophile assimilationism and supposedly still his country's liberal voice, to recognize that they had in fact already made their decision a long time ago. "A political dictum dictates that one must not sacrifice a friend to an enemy," he sagely observed. "The Chinese are our friends today, and perhaps tomorrow."[171]

2

Our Friends Today

Algeria Joins the Third World

> How can the masses become conscious of themselves, their interests, and their formidable power? . . . [M]obilization of the masses is not possible without armed struggle. We have learnt this not only from the experience of Cuba but also from those of China and Vietnam. . . . As Debray has stressed, "Under present conditions the most important form of propaganda is successful military action."
>
> Mas'oud Amadzadeh, *Armed Struggle*, 1979

> It is this "organisation" of individual actions within a concerted global action, that poses precisely the problem of ideology.
>
> Malek Bennabi, lecture at Algiers University, 1964

In 1958, Dr. Kwame Nkrumah saw himself as the natural leader of a new Africa. Intellectual and worldly, he had studied at the undergraduate and postgraduate levels in the United States, spent years at the heart of London's transnational pan-African scene, and played a leading role the seminal pan-African Congress in Manchester in 1945. He had then returned home to Britain's Gold Coast Colony, where he gradually established himself as its dominant political figure, overcame the authorities' distrust, and pioneered the peaceful transfer of power in sub-Saharan Africa by leading his homeland to independence under the name of Ghana in March 1957. Thrust into the limelight as the prime minister of the first newly independent country south of the Sahara, Nkrumah felt that he had an opportunity—or even a duty—to steer the continent's unfixed politics as it hurtled toward decolonization in exhilarating but confusing fashion. Being so well acquainted, personally or intellectually, with a wide array of anticolonial activists, Marxists, and black intellectuals from several continents, the Ghanaian leader also believed that he had the answers to his fellow Africans' many profound questions about their postcolonial future in cultural, economic, and political terms. Therefore, in early 1958 Nkrumah moved the management of African affairs out of the Ghanaian foreign ministry and into his own offices, and he decided to convene two international conferences that promised to establish Accra as the de facto continental capital: the Conference of Independent African States (CIAS), in April, and December's All-African Peoples' Conference (AAPC), a meeting of liberation movements, political parties, unions, and other nonstate actors.[1]

However, the Ghanaian prime minister and his diplomatic team were disagreeably surprised when representatives of the Algerian Front de Libération Nationale and the Union des Populations du Cameroun (Union of Cameroonian Peoples, UPC) appeared, uninvited, at the opening day of the CIAS and asked to petition the participating heads of state. The arrival of two bellicose liberation movements made a mess of the Ghanaians' deliberate arrangement of separate conferences for independent states and for nonstate entities, in order that they and the delegations from Liberia, Ethiopia, Sudan, Morocco, Tunisia, Libya, and Egypt (officially the United Arab Republic [UAR] at this time) might set a precedent of dignified statesmanship and establish a continental agenda in peaceful isolation from all the controversies and contentions that the likes of the Algerian rebels carried with them. On the one hand, Nkrumah simply did not want the CIAS proceedings hijacked by a side issue because he intended to use the conference as a platform for himself and his main themes of continental unity and a supposed singular "African personality" shared by all the peoples who lived between Cairo and Cape Town, or Dakar and Dar es Salaam. On the other hand, however, the arrival of the FLN and the UPC (which aimed to depose a French Cameroonian elite deferential to Paris) also highlighted the fact that the Ghanaian leader represented the "moderate," pro-Western, and nonviolent wing of African politics. Unfortunately, he was outnumbered by the five Arab countries. As a member of the Ghanaian delegation later recalled, discussion of the "Algerian question" consumed a large part of the CIAS's first two days, and ultimately the participants agreed to express their complete solidarity with the Algerian cause and to dispatch a joint mission to foreign capitals to press the case. To the Ghanaians' relief, the CIAS did at least reject Egypt's proposal to provide material assistance to the FLN's military campaign.[2]

It would be an exaggeration to say that the Algerian rebels derailed Nkrumah's plans for the CIAS altogether, for the event still achieved its primary purpose of symbolically relaunching the pan-African project on African soil, with Ghana as its champion. However, the FLN arguably did steal the limelight at the All-African People's Conference in December. Standing before a banner emblazoned with the warning "Hands off Africa!!" and the image of a burning torch atop a map of the continent, Nkrumah delivered a rousing speech to the diverse crowd of activists, syndicalists, and militants who had traveled to Accra from both sides of Africa's colonial divide. He promised his government's full support for those movements that were still struggling against colonialism and racist white-minority regimes and that shared his dream of creating a continental federation of sovereign states, united in their common pursuit of "Pan-African Socialism." Yet his insistence on the correctness of the nonviolent path to liberation did not satisfy those who were either actively fighting for independence (such as the Algerians and Cameroonians), contemplating the necessity of taking up arms (such as Roberto Holden from "Portuguese" Angola), or simply sympathetic to those who did make that choice. On the key question of supporting armed liberation struggles, Nkrumah and the like-minded conference chairman, Kenyan trade unionist Tom Mboye, quickly lost control of the debate.[3]

First, the FLN's Ahmed Boumendjel seemed to win the room with his insistence that France had shown time and again that it would only be driven from Algeria by force, and that it was every African's duty to assist his people's campaign. But even more memorable was the interjection of his colleague Frantz Fanon, the Martinican psychiatrist who quit his job at an Algerian hospital to join the liberation struggle of a people not his own. In a speech that helped found his reputation as one of the most persuasive and determined voices of the Third World, Fanon tackled Nkrumah's moral qualms head-on. "Africa is at war with colonialism," he thundered, "and she is impatient! . . . In our fight for freedom, we should embark on plans effective enough to touch the pulse of the imperialists—by force of action and, indeed, violence."[4] These arguments carried the day: the AAPC attendees not only concluded by agreeing that armed struggle was legitimate and deserving of inter-African assistance but also called for the formation of an international African Volunteer Brigade to achieve that purpose. In the pages of the front's main newspaper, *El Moudjahid*, Fanon congratulated the Algerian people on having awoken the men and women south of the great desert. "We must return to the Sahara its historical role as the link between Black Africa and North Africa," he declared.[5]

Fanon's exultation reflected a sense that the Southern Hemisphere was really starting to coalesce and assert itself. The two conferences that took place in Accra in 1958 were not the only indications that, following Bandung's declaration of principles, the Third World project was beginning to take more concrete form. The spirit of pan-Arab nationalism seemed every bit as dynamic as pan-Africanism, since Egypt and Syria formed a federation in February 1958 that was optimistically touted as merely the first stage in the creation of a larger UAR, a group of nationalist officers led by Abdelkarim Qassim overthrew Iraq's pro-British Hashemite monarchy in July and withdrew the country from the Western military alliance known as the Baghdad Pact, and, less spectacularly, Morocco and Tunisia also joined the Arab League. In more global terms, Yugoslavia's Josip Broz Tito, India's Jawaharlal Nehru, and Egypt's Gamal Abdel Nasser continued to meet regularly under the rubric of nonalignment, the Afro-Asian Peoples' Solidarity Organization (AAPSO) had been founded in Cairo at the end of

1957, and Fidel Castro's rebels seized power in Cuba in January 1959. This new stage in the Third World's awakening perhaps reached its peak with the transition of fourteen African countries to independence in 1960, the formal founding of the Non-Aligned Movement (NAM) in Belgrade in late 1961, and, fittingly, the publication of Fanon's book *The Wretched of the Earth* that same year.

All of these developments were a boon to the Algerian FLN, which truly began to integrate itself into the Third World movement during this period. Crucially, the opening up of new diplomatic possibilities in the Southern Hemisphere occurred just at the time when the front felt extremely threatened by Charles de Gaulle's return to power and the reinvigoration of France's military and political offensives in Algeria, and when the Algerian nationalists were also growing exasperated by what they perceived as the inadequate levels of support provided by their traditional allies in the Maghrib and the Arab world. The FLN had involuntarily become an even more transnational organization than before because military setbacks since the Battle of Algiers and France's completion of a virtually impenetrable barrier of electric fences and minefields along Algeria's borders, known as the Morice Line, had forced most of the revolution's leaders and military personnel to relocate to Morocco and Tunisia. Sympathetic as they were to the Algerian cause, the FLN's swelling footprint on their territory gravely disquieted Moroccan king Mohammed V and Tunisian president Habib Bourguiba because it invited French reprisals and risked destabilizing their own fragile polities. Consequently, as the Algerians complained bitterly to Tito during one visit to Belgrade, the Moroccans and Tunisians tried to curtail shipments of armaments into their territory and pressured the rebellion's leaders to negotiate with de Gaulle—interferences that the FLN judged intolerable.[6] In July 1958, Krim Belkacem, charged at the time with running the rebellion's logistics and arms transport operations, dramatically asked his colleagues, will "Algeria will once again in her history be abandoned by her neighbours, isolated thus?"[7]

The motivation to further loosen the FLN's geographical bindings was therefore quite clear. So when Krim Belkacem took charge of the GPRA's Ministry of External Affairs (MAE) at the beginning of 1960 as one of the latest consequences of the FLN's constant internal political upheavals and redistribution of leadership positions, perhaps his highest priority was to aggressively pursue new avenues of friendship and support in Africa and Latin America.[8] Saad Dahlab, the experienced political operative appointed to run the MAE for Krim, submitted a report to the FLN's intermittently convening "parliament," the Conseil National de la Révolution Algérienne (CNRA), urging:

> We must respond to the French war effort, which has been able to mobilize its NATO allies, with an equivalent effort. The Arab States, divided and subjugated, cannot provide [the help we need]. We must knock on

other doors. And the only ones that can open for us are those of China [and] the USSR. . . . Two African States, competing with Tunisia and Morocco, can facilitate the passage of arms: Ghana and Guinea. . . . [S]erious investigations can be made in South America, in Venezuela and in Cuba in particular.[9]

Almost as important as the substantial practical dividends of this campaign was the way in which a great many of the front's leaders and cadres came to identify more strongly with the left wing of Third World politics than with their supposedly more natural allies closer to home. "Instead of troubling [Arab governments], instead of demanding sacrifices of our brothers," complained the MAE's report for the January 1960 meeting of the CNRA, "the war in Algeria has become a tool . . . exploited [by them] for strictly egotistical ends to ensure the prosperity not of [their] people, but of the ruling classes, some medieval, others Europeanized in the capitalist sense of the word."[10] In contrast, GPRA leaders visiting Belgrade had previously gushed to the Yugoslavs that "you do everything you can for us," and with the emergence of sympathetic leaders like Guinea's Ahmed Sékou Touré, Mali's Modibo Keita, and Nkrumah (especially after his belated but enthusiastic conversion to guerrilla warfare), Africa was the most promising domain for Algerian ambitions and influence.[11] Yet of all the countries that the Algerian rebels came to see as fellow travelers in the Third World adventure, perhaps their greatest inspiration would be Fidel Castro's distant island. "Under the sky of Cuba, pearl of the Antilles," an FLN visitor waxed lyrical in early 1960, "in this Caribbean Sea lapping the equatorial shores of the South American continent, we have felt the ardent and fraternal hearts of millions of citizens, freed from the yoke of odious dictatorship, beating in unison with the Algerian Revolution."[12] An already transnational movement was becoming truly global in its operations and outlook.

But what of Algerian shores? What did it profit a national liberation movement to gain the world but remain largely trapped outside of its own country by minefields, barbed wire, and half a million French soldiers? Mohammed Dib's brilliant and bewildering novel *Who Remembers the Sea* (1961) described an allegorical Algiers—inescapably labyrinthine, cowed by alien observation, and cut off from the outside world.[13] In the *bled*, the remaining perilously outgunned and outnumbered ALN commanders grew increasingly critical of the external leadership, accusing them of cowardice and living high on the hog while French helicopters closed in on the few remaining mujahideen. De Gaulle openly mocked the GPRA's internationalist pretensions and portrayed the rebels as deluded pawns of foreign conspiracies, and even Saad Dahlab later conceded, "The FLN was becoming very strong in the exterior, it had men, money, arms, allies, but it seemed to look into the interior without the means to intervene."[14]

Ultimately, the GPRA could not will its country into the Third World by diplomacy alone; Algeria itself would have to rise.

Envisioning Algeria as a "Cuba for Africa"

The FLN's diplomatic team had been advocating a new effort to gain friends in Africa and Latin America for some time, observing that apart from Ghana, they had barely made much of an impression yet on either of two continents that between them accounted for a sizable and growing number of potential pro-FLN votes at the General Assembly. After all, the UN had dubbed 1960 the "Year of Africa" because of the number of countries scheduled to gain their independence there, and the French government was already twisting the arms of its former colonies in order to preemptively isolate the Algerian rebels from this alluring array of potential allies south of the Sahara. Across the Atlantic, meanwhile, Fidel Castro had seized power in Cuba on 1 January 1959. Just as the Algerians hoped to use Ghana as a beachhead to conquer the rest of sub-Saharan Africa—their relationship with Nkrumah improved markedly after the initial coolness—might not the revolutionaries in Havana provide a new entry point to a continent that had previously held little promise for them? Initial contacts suggested that the Cubans were extremely sympathetic to the Algerian cause, and they certainly presented themselves as fellow travelers in the Third Worldist, socialist, combative trend that the FLN's cadres increasingly saw as their natural home. Sure enough, Cuba quickly became an extremely important point of reference for the Algerian revolutionaries—but, somewhat ironically, less as a gateway to Latin America than as a conceptual portal through which the Algerians entered their own continent.

The GPRA's records show that the Algerians were extremely interested in the new Cuban regime from the outset. When a Cuban envoy came to Cairo just a week after Castro's group had seized power, one of the members of the MAE's office there went to meet with him at the Brazilian ambassador's residence. Over a series of amicable discussions the Cuban envoy, Armando Rivera, and one of his Brazilian colleagues enticed their guest with descriptions of Latin America as a region where progressive popular sentiment simmered just beneath the hostile welcome that the FLN's previous missions had received from the region's reactionary governments. They predicted that the Algerians could actually make substantial headway there so long as they took care to avoid countries that were too enmeshed in the American economic sphere. Confident that the Cuban government shared his own personal, heartfelt identification with the Algerian cause, Rivera urged the FLN to send a delegation to Havana immediately, in order to best capitalize on the "emotional" postrevolutionary atmosphere.[15] This advice clearly generated great excitement among the Algerians, for Lamine Debagine (the head of the GPRA's diplomatic team at that time, before being succeeded by Krim Belkacem) ordered the front's primary representative in New York, Abdelkader Chanderli, to make his way to Havana as soon as his responsibilities allowed.[16]

Aside from the potential benefits for their diplomatic campaign, the Algerians seem to have been almost as excited by the natural amity and instant sense of rapport that characterized these early encounters. For example, Chanderli emphasized that his own conversations with the Cuban ambassador to the UN were "more than favorable, even *quasi-fraternal*," in tone. He noted that the ambassador, like many members of the new regime, shared the FLN's acquaintance with life in the underground and guerrilla war.[17] The use of the terms "brotherly" and "fraternal" to describe the tenor of FLN-Cuban relations is noteworthy, since up to this point those words were generally used only in the front's internal communications with respect to fellow Arabs, as befitting the Muslim practice of greeting a coreligionist as "brother." "Brother" was also how members of the FLN referred to one another, in the same fashion as communist party members used the word "comrade." Not too much significance should be attached to the extension of the language of brotherhood to the Cubans (and others in the future), since the FLN did not cultivate or enforce the notion of politically correct vocabulary, and usage also varied with individual attitudes. Nevertheless, it does seem to reflect a progression toward a more ideological-political conception of fraternity, rather than an ethno-religious one, on the part of at least a significant portion of FLN cadres and those involved in Third Worldist diplomacy especially.

It should be noted, too, that the instant rapport between the Algerian and Cuban revolutionaries was not necessarily typical of Havana's initial encounters with other important representatives of the Third World. On the one hand, Cuban sympathies for the Algerian cause predated Castro's triumph in January 1959, reflecting a fairly widespread popular identification with the Algerian struggle in the latter days of Fulgencio Batista's regime. The dissident press ran regular stories on the war in North Africa with a pronounced anti-French tenor, often as a way of obliquely criticizing Batista's government and its relationship with the United States.[18] Conversely, the Third World's established luminaries were not always as instinctively charmed by the Castroists pistol- and bandolier-toting flair as the Algerian rebels were. Ernesto "Che" Guevara's tour in the summer of 1959 was a bit of a flop: Josip Broz Tito reputedly found him to be something of a "beatnik," and Gamal Abdel Nasser's initial impression of the Cubans as a "bunch of Errol Flynns" and "theatrical brigands" was not refuted by Guevara's impolitic criticism of Egypt's agricultural reforms on the basis that they had not produced enough bourgeois refugees. When the Argentinian firebrand clumsily raised the issue of Indian-Chinese relations in New Delhi, Jawaharlal Nehru pointedly switched the conversation to gastronomical matters.[19]

In any case, despite Rivera's optimistic prognostications in Cairo, Cuban-FLN relations did not make any substantial progress in the short term. The United Nations being such a crucial post, circumstances prevented Chanderli from making the journey to Havana for more than a year, and in the interim the island became one of the tensest points on the intersection of the Cold War and Third World politics. When he considered Fidel Castro in his combat fatigues, rallying crowds with populist speeches, Dwight D. Eisenhower saw a dangerous anti-American radical and potential communist stooge. The American president refused to receive the new Cuban leader when he visited Washington in the spring of 1959, thereby making officialdom's hostility plain even if plenty of everyday citizens and students in particular showed much greater curiosity. On arriving home, Castro unleashed much more explicit condemnations of the United States' history of interference in Cuban affairs and dominant position in his country's deeply unequal economy, and he instigated sweeping agrarian reforms that included the seizure of land owned by US commercial interests. Tensions across the Florida Straits—a mere ninety miles of sea separated Cuba from the United States—escalated so quickly in the summer of 1959 that by the autumn the Cuban government decided to reach out to the Soviet Union and communist China for economic and military assistance. When the Soviet agent, Aleksandr Alexeev, met Guevara and Castro in October, the former insisted that "the only way to achieve Cuba's full independence was to build a socialist society," while the latter defied his expectations of an ideologically ignorant brigand by quoting Marx and Lenin. Across the waters, meanwhile, the US Central Intelligence Agency had already begun assisting Cuban exile groups' plans to retake the island by force.[20]

The rapid onset of a siege mentality in Havana compelled Cuban officials to pull back on their initial optimism with regard to supporting the Algerian independence struggle. In late June, they explained apologetically to the FLN that they could not now afford to "battle on multiple international fronts" by picking a fight with France, still a vital customer for Cuban sugar. Still insistent on their determination to be the first country in Latin America to recognize the GPRA as the official government of Algeria, they nevertheless admitted that they would not be able to do so in the near future.[21] Yet in stark contrast to their regular grumbling about the inadequacy of Arab governments that had done actually a great deal more for them in concrete terms, the Algerian rebels' initial admiration for Castro and his companions remained undimmed by this disappointment. Instead, many of the front's cadres and international operatives only seemed to grow more enthusiastic about the Cuban Revolution.

Thus, as Havana embraced the language first of socialism and then of communism, an MAE report that appears to have been written in late 1959 approvingly described Cuba's course as "not simply a political change, but a true social [and] economic revolution," reserving particular praise for the pursuit of "economic independence" through the nationalization of foreign assets, rapid industrialization, and the diversification of trading partners.[22] Written in Cairo, that report was based on observations from a great distance, but when Chanderli finally made it to Havana the following March, he emphatically echoed its enthusiastic appraisal of Cuba's economic plans and the personality of its government. "A people at work," he wrote for El Moudjahid, "the Cubans have thrown themselves with total conviction into the construction of the country on new, totally revolutionary lines." He stressed his hosts' effusive expressions of solidarity with the Algerian cause, from the great leader himself—a man "as romantic as the heroes of centuries past"—to crowds of well-wishers in the street. "Everywhere we went, Algeria was cheered," Chanderli assured his compatriots. "Delirious crowds shouted their support for the Algerian fighters."[23] Naturally he was hardly going to suggest in the FLN's primary propaganda outlet that Cuba stood indifferent to Algeria's plight, but the tenor and substance of Chanderli's piece were quite consistent with the majority of the GPRA's internal exchanges on the subject.

It is striking the degree to which Chanderli and others instantly identified with Cuba, seeing the country, its people, its culture, and its economic and political dilemmas as near mirror images of their own. This instinctive Algerian-Cuban amity stands as a particularly vivid example of a pattern at the core of the entire Third Worldist, Afro-Asian, internationalist-anticolonialist phenomenon. The vitality, ambition, and globe-spanning reach of Third Worldism depended on this form of instant mutual recognition and reciprocal identification, repeated hundreds of times over. There was little or no history of exchanges between Cuba and Algeria, and the countries shared essentially no religious, linguistic (some use of Spanish in eastern Algeria notwithstanding), or imperial commonalities. But while Third Worldism primarily expressed a sense of shared political-economic circumstances among the countries of the Southern Hemisphere, with the Algerian revolutionaries in this case seeing Cuba's contentions with the United States as a corollary to their own classically colonial relationship with France, impressionistic and emotional responses were perhaps at least as important to the creation of these bonds as were more coldly rational or intellectual processes. In Chanderli's case, touching down in Havana, it seems to have been as much familiar environmental factors as sociological analysis that prompted him to equate the Cuban campesino with the Algerian fellah. While he was clearly trying to imbue his account of the visit with some color, it is still worth noting how easily he mixed impressionism with rationalism:

[As a] pilot state, [the Cubans] intend to prove that economic prosperity is compatible only with political liberty. They prove in one stroke that there is no real independence without economic independence.... In this their revolution... is inscribed in the gigantic movement for the emancipation of politically and economically exploited peoples. In this their combat is our own.... [W]e have found among them not only the same pure blue sky of our own country, mountains as tough as our own and from which descended, like ours, the first martyrs of freedom... but also the soul of a people for whom to live free or die is, like it is for us, a daily reality.[24]

Chanderli's enthusiasm was clear. However, his knowledge of Cuba being very limited, his inclination to compare and equate everything that he saw there with Algeria suggests, ironically, that there may have been an oversimplifying or perhaps even Orientalist quality to the sentiment of Third Worldist solidarity. After all, many scholars would later criticize contemporaneous American social scientists and Soviet theoreticians for essentializing agrarian societies and portraying all peasant cultures as basically equivalent to one another.[25]

More than identifying with the Cuban revolutionaries, a prominent contingent in the FLN's leadership, and especially many midranking cadres in the provisional government and the military wing, aspired to imitate them. "Cuban chic" reigned among the young officers who constituted the Etat Majeur-Général (General Staff, EMG) of Houari Boumedienne's new army situated on the Moroccan and Tunisian frontiers. Posters and brochures from the Caribbean island proliferated in their headquarters at Ghardimaou, Tunisia. To the irritation of many of their colleagues from other branches of the FLN, they took to wearing combat fatigues, smoking cigars, and even carrying revolvers and hand grenades into meetings.[26]

But a more substantive form of imitation concerned the Algerians' admiration for Castro and Guevara's insistence that Cuba would export revolution to the rest of Latin America through the power of its example as well as more interventionist methods. By June, the new government in Havana had already sponsored two revolutionary expeditions to the Dominican Republic and Guatemala, in addition to expeditions to Haiti and Panama that had set out with the Cuban authorities' permission.[27] Guevara spoke of creating a base in Bolivia, "where if we insert a guerrilla force, we could spread the revolution all over America."[28] If the Algerian and Cuban Revolutions really were one another's closest peers, as many in the FLN liked to think, no doubt with a degree of jealousy at the way that Cuba had so quickly captured the world's attention and an aura of glamour, then it followed that Algeria must have a similar destiny on its own continent. "Algeria and the FLN hold an important position in the African continent's struggle," Krim Belkacem asserted to Dahlab, but he also complained that "with the exception of our participation in certain congresses and conferences, our contacts with the countries of Black Africa are non-existent."[29] There was an increasing tendency to portray Algeria as Africa's liberator in more ideological terms, of propagating a revolutionary socioeconomic program, rather than the more prosaic argument that the fallout from the FLN's war hastened the process of decolonization. In a comprehensive report to the CNRA in January 1960, the GPRA's diplomatic team argued that

> the fundamental problems of the Algerian people's 'right to live,' in the mechanical and interdependent world of the 20th century, can only be resolved in the context of a humanist socialism which it falls to our generation to learn, to teach, and to adapt to our country and to the Maghrib. Historically, our combat places us at a crossroads where we must be in the avant-garde of the African countries.[30]

Although the Algerian nationalist leadership did not really begin to speak openly and explicitly of their country being the "Cuba of Africa" or "Cuba of the Maghrib" until after independence was achieved in June 1962, because to do so sooner would have been to truly abandon all hope of winning Washington's favor, the substance of their discussions shows that the idea enjoyed a fairly substantial constituency almost from the very moment of Castro's seizure of power and the FLN's initial contacts with the new regime. It is clear, however, from the rhetoric of documents like the one just quoted, that the front's admiration for the Cuban Revolution was tied to an increasingly leftist ideological tilt. The Algerians were particularly inspired by Castro and Guevara's justification of encouraging "revolutionary" forces to overthrow "reactionary" governments in their region, and they did not wait for independence to attempt that strategy in countries on both sides of the Sahara.

Continent Games

In 1959, the year that the Parker Brothers company released a popular new board game in the United States called RISK: The Continental Game, the Algerian War also went continental, with FLN and French strategists vying for Africa's newly appearing countries in their own, much more serious zero-sum game.[31] Though the rebels' initial impetus was to secure new sources of diplomatic support and new routes for the infiltration of weapons and fighters into the Algerian interior, their African campaign quickly became far more ambitious in scope.

With the continent's politics still so much in flux, and inspired in part by Cuba's subversive example, it soon occurred to the FLN's leaders that this arena gave them the opportunity to go beyond simply appealing to governments to support their cause in the United Nations and other diplomatic avenues. Instead, in their multiplying and intensifying relationships with other rebel groups and liberation movements from across the continent, they saw a chance to abet the rise of forces favorable to their cause and undermine those regimes that stood in their way. Somewhat remarkably, although Algeria became famous as a hub for subversion after independence, in reality the FLN had already acquired sufficient influence and resources to begin mentoring less-established groups well before then.

The Algerian War was already a central factor in the larger narrative of the French decolonization of Africa, now at a decisive stage. An earlier precedent for France withdrawing from its colonies in a fashion designed to manage the Algerian crisis was the withdrawal of the government of Pierre Mendès-France from Morocco and Tunisia in 1956, although of course the outcome could only be described as, at best, partially successful from Paris's perspective: while the governments in Rabat and Tunis were the FLN's most important allies in practical terms, their support for the Algerian rebels was certainly not without its limits or tensions. On returning to power in 1958, Charles de Gaulle made the decolonization of Africa an integral component of the transformation of France's constitutional order. The so-called French Community framework was so important to the French president, so fundamental to his belief in France's continued relevance in a changing world, that he included it in the new constitution of the Fifth Republic, submitted to the metropole and to the colonies for approval by referendum in September 1958. A much more substantive vision of postcolonial interconnectedness than the British Commonwealth, the Community essentially proposed that France's former African colonies would continue to receive sizable development and economic assistance, in return for Paris retaining authority over matters of defense, foreign policy, and finances.[32] When he addressed the Federal Assembly of Mali the following year, de Gaulle explained that "this state of Mali is going to assume what is called the status of independence, [but] which I prefer to call international sovereignty. . . . [T]he world being what it is, so small, so narrow, so intrusive, that real independence, total independence belongs to no one."[33] Yet, it was no mere side benefit that this bargain would help Paris block the FLN's diplomatic opportunities in Africa, while at the same time also providing a demonstration of the viability of *autodétermination*, or limited autonomy, that de Gaulle then proposed for Algeria in late 1959. He admitted plainly to a Malian politician that "I made the Community for Algeria."[34]

That truth was not lost on the FLN at the time, for in the run-up to the 1958 referendum, *El Moudjahid* had warned black Africa that "every African who votes in the referendum will chain his people and his country a little bit tighter to French colonialism."[35] However, de Gaulle also made it clear that any overseas territory that rejected the terms of the Community would be turning its back on any further economic or development assistance from France: the choice was "interdependence" in the Community's federal framework—or going it totally alone. The referendum therefore provoked a debate about the very purpose and meaning of decolonization. Probably the most militant stance was that taken by the head of the Guinean Democratic Party, Ahmed Sékou Touré, who announced his determination to vote no on the basis that his people preferred "poverty in liberty to wealth in slavery." In contrast, Félix Houphouët-Boigny, until recently Touré's colleague in the Rassemblement Démocratique Africain (Democratic African Rally, RDA), an umbrella anticolonial organization for the whole of the French West Africa territory that became twelve distinct countries, was passionate about the maintenance of tight links to France during a very gradual evolution toward full independence. Many others found the Community's curtailments on their sovereignty highly disagreeable, but they dared not risk de Gaulle's wrath. In the end, when only Touré's Guinea voted no in the referendum, Paris carried through on its threat. French officials immediately terminated all ongoing and future development projects in the country, destroyed administrative records, and even resorted to pulling equipment and wires from the walls in their thorough determination to deny Guinea any benefits of their former presence.[36]

Whereas Guinea under Sékou Touré, who held similar socialist and militantly anti-imperialist convictions as Kwame Nkrumah, immediately became one of the FLN's strongest advocates in sub-Saharan Africa, Houphouet-Boigny's Côte d'Ivoire remained deferential to de Gaulle's insistence on shunning the Algerians. The latter had even favorably compared the French Community's "message of fraternity" to "the hatred [and] spirit of vengeance which was expressed in Bandung against the former colonizing peoples," offering a clear example of how the FLN's practical objectives suddenly seemed to converge on its more radical Third Worldist attitudes and allegiances.[37] Two distinct tendencies were emerging in Africa, the GPRA concluded, "one centered in Accra and Conakry, the other covering the countries of the French Community and certain countries of English Africa." The first tendency, "resolutely committed to the liquidation of neocolonialism," was their natural ally, while the second prioritized cooperation with the former metropole over anticolonial solidarity.[38] Although they did not want to dismiss out of hand half of their potential new allies on the continent, the movement's leaders saw their African campaign as a systemic assault on the philosophy behind schemes like the Community and liberal-capitalist notions of "interdependence."

Facilitated by Nkrumah and Sékou Touré, the Algerians first made the most progress in West Africa. In July 1959, M'hamed Yazid led a delegation to the second Conference of Independent African States in Monrovia, Liberia. Unlike the AAPC in Accra the previous December, this was a meeting of governments rather than parties, and even if the deck was loaded by the favorable roster of participants—Ethiopia, Ghana, Guinea, Liberia, and the Arab countries—the FLN's participation with the status of invited observers constituted an important breach in the diplomatic wall that France had erected around the GPRA. Ghana had already recognized the provisional government several weeks earlier, and Guinea then followed suit in the course of the conference. Nkrumah and Touré both also worked on Liberia's president, William Tubman, during the meeting, and his positive if noncommittal response marked him out as the Algerians' next target.[39] The Ghanaian and Guinean leaders also invited the Algerians to set up permanent offices in their capitals, thereby providing vital beachheads for the expansion of the front's campaign throughout the region. Omar Oussedik, an experienced former PPA militant from a prominent Kabyle family, took charge of the bureau in Conakry, while Fanon opened the Accra office. Combining forces, in the spring and summer of 1960 the two men first managed to wrangle diplomatic recognition as well as a symbolic financial contribution out of Tubman, then won over Togo, and finally reported very encouraging discussions with political figures in Nigeria and elsewhere.[40] The latter were not especially radical countries compared with Ghana and Guinea, so the GPRA men were pushing against Western pressure—increasingly halfhearted, it seemed, on the parts of Britain and the United States—with public appeals to anticolonial solidarity that were difficult for any African politician to ignore in the face of domestic and continental opinion. Their efforts were bearing fruit, as several Africa leaders with good relations with Washington warned President Eisenhower that the West's plainly pro-French position on the Algerian question was becoming a liability to Western credibility on the continent.[41] Reflecting the progress that the FLN had made in gaining acceptance since its uninvited appearance at the first CIAS in Accra in April 1958, when even the Ghanaians had tried to prevent it from addressing the meeting, the GPRA was admitted to the third conference, in Addis Ababa in June 1960, as the recognized government of Algeria.[42]

These activities constituted the overt, diplomatic component of the FLN's push into Africa—although Oussedik and Fanon still had to be on the lookout for French agents and use false identities when traveling on Air France flights in and out of francophone capitals. But the Algerians simultaneously operated on the more "illicit" or subversive side of African politics, increasing their contacts with other underground movements and lending their assistance to those they considered allies in the continent-wide battle against French neocolonialism. The FLN's offices in Conakry and Accra put the front in regular contact with the numerous other groups enjoying the hospitality of the Guinean and Ghanaian governments, and Belkacem Krim assured Sékou Touré in June 1960 that "the Algerian Government is committed to providing any effective assistance whether material, political, or diplomatic to all of the national liberation movements of Africa fighting for their effective independence and the unity of our continent."[43] Indeed the FLN was receiving enough armaments and equipment from the communist bloc, and enough financial support from the Arab countries and the Algerian expatriate community in France that it was in a position of enviable stability and resourcefulness compared with its peers. With Boumedienne's army still essentially stuck on the wrong side of the Morice Line, it was time to put some of those resources to good use. Krim told his GPRA colleagues that "any unrest in the French colonial empire can only help our struggle."[44]

The FLN's first efforts at influencing the internal politics of other countries started in North Africa with Morocco and Tunisia, where the Algerian rebels had lost patience with what they considered to be Rabat and Tunis's halfhearted support and interference in the front's internal matters. Reminiscent of the description of Latin America by Armando Rivera, the Cuban envoy to Cairo in January 1959, the FLN leadership convinced themselves that the "popular masses" in Morocco and Tunisia were much more supportive of the Algerian cause than the Western-leaning Hassan II and Habib Bourguiba and decided to directly target those populations with their print and radio propaganda.[45] The GPRA's Ministry of External Affairs predicted that if "stirred sentimentally and ideologically . . . the Maghrib would support us, even if our Government is established in Conakry, Cairo or Iraq," with the latter suggestion reflecting the fear that the Moroccan and Tunisian regimes might give in to French and American pressure to such a degree that the FLN would be forced to relocate once again.[46] In its own words, therefore, the FLN "intervened massively" with logistical and financial support for the leftist opposition in Morocco's parliamentary elections in May 1960, the country being a constitutional monarchy.[47] Although the left did not win, Hassan saw a need to respond to rising criticism that his government was not militant enough on anticolonial issues, Algeria in particular. After the sultan's unexpected and premature death during surgery in February the next year, his son and heir, Mohammed V, concluded a sort of "status of forces" agreement with the FLN that reduced the number of "incidents" taking place between the thousands of mujahideen on Moroccan territory and the local security services, and also reopened the flow of arms from the Eastern bloc.[48]

Although relations with Morocco then improved, prominent elements of the FLN would continue to dream of overthrowing what they described as reactionary, neocolonial regimes in Rabat and Tunis. As Ahmed Ben Bella, one of the leaders captured in 1956, observed from his French prison cell just before Hassan's death, "A Sékou Touré in Morocco and a Modibo Keita [the president of Mali] in Tunis, that would be perfect for us."[49] To the anger of the Moroccan and Tunisian governments, the FLN maintained extremely close and mutually supportive relations with the people it hoped would be the "Sékou Touré of Morocco," left-wing leader Mehdi Ben Barka, and the Modibo Keita of Tunisia, Bourguiba's longtime rival, Salah Ben Youssef. Both men shared the FLN's more left-wing socioeconomic philosophy and its deep immersion in the Third Worldist scene, traveling to capitals such as Cairo and Beijing, and with Ben Youssef at least enjoying the support of Nasser's military intelligence service, the Mukhabarat.[50] Although Bourguiba orchestrated Ben Youssef's assassination in Frankfurt in August 1961, his comrades would maintain their ties with the Algerians.

So the FLN already had acquired the habit of interfering in the politics of other territories as it began expanding southward. The immediate Saharan region was the focus of these activities at first, as the rebels tried to open up a new front on Algeria's southern flank while the French army and other agents of the French government tried to nip this option in the bud. Time seemed to be moving at a faster pace—de Gaulle's French Community framework quickly proved unviable in the face of overwhelming popular and elite nationalist sentiment in the colonies, further animated by Guinea's and the British colonies' accession to independence. Thirteen territories transitioned to full independence in 1960, for the most part in a tranquil fashion with Paris's cooperation, but the more confrontational transfer of power in French Sudan, as Mali was known until 1960, created an opening for the FLN. That summer, plans for a Malian Federation that combined Senegal and Soudan/Mali were collapsing because of the very different bases of support and political inclinations of the Senegalese leader, Léopold Sédar Senghor, and Mali's Modibo Keita. Keita was a convinced Marxist (albeit still a practicing Mulism) who positioned himself firmly on the "radical" side of the new division in African politics with his calls for socialist revolution and the elimination of the remnants of European influence on the continent. Moreover, representatives of his party, the Union Soudanaise-Rassemblement Démocratique Africain (Soudanese Union-African Democratic Rally, US-RDA), reached out to Fanon in Accra and indicated that an independent Mali would fully support the FLN.[51] Enthusiastic about this prospect, in August Krim Belkacem devised a plan to supply weapons to a Marxist rebel group operating in Senegal, the African Independence Party, in the belief that stoking unrest there would distract France's attention, hasten the breakup of the Senegal-Soudanese federation, and help ensure Keita's ascendance in Bamako.[52]

Although it is unclear what impact this scheme had, it demonstrated the FLN's determination to "export revolution" and its willingness to interfere in the internal politics of other African countries if there was advantage in it. Two more groups that fit the pattern of being revolutionary movements trying to overthrow the government of an already-independent country were the Sawaba party from Niger, which shared long borders with both Algeria and Mali, and the UPC, which had turned its sights on what it saw as the neocolonial, pro-French puppet regime of Ahmadou Ahidjo when French Cameroon gained its independence on 1 January 1960. Similarly, French intervention helped drive Sawaba from power in Niger in 1959, motivated by the leftist party's vocal opposition to the Community framework and strong sympathies with the Algerian FLN, as well as Paris's desire to ensure its access to Niger's uranium deposits. With both groups trying to topple governments deferential to French policy, they were natural allies for the Algerians. As a letter from one of the groups (which one is unclear from the barely legible original document) to the FLN office in Cairo in 1959 argued, fomenting rebellion in another colony would essentially open up a second front against their common French enemy.[53] Krim Belkacem certainly agreed, telling his GPRA colleagues in the summer of 1960 that "it is in our interest to assist all the revolutionary forces in these countries."[54] By the end of the year, the authorities in British Cameroon were able to track UPC recruits traveling to Morocco to be trained in the ALN's camps there by Algerian instructors. The FLN also established close contacts with Sawaba as both movements flocked into Mali with Modibo Keita's blessing, and the Algerians began supplying training and logistical support to the Nigeriens in what proved to the beginning of a lengthy campaign to undermine the government in Niamey.[55]

But these initiatives with Sawaba and the UPC were simply the beginning of a much bigger engagement with the continent's rebellious forces. By dint of their now-permanent presence in Accra, Conakry, and Cairo, which were the first major nexuses of the trans-African support network for liberation movements and revolutionaries, the Algerians quickly developed relationships with groups and individuals hailing from far beyond the immediate Maghrib-Saharan region. "We Algerians," *El Moudjahid* insisted, "do not dissociate the combat we are waging from that of the Rhodesians or the Kenyans."[56] Putting their materiel where their mouthpiece was, by the end of 1960 the Algerians had already provided guns, money, or training—and in at least one case even seconded personnel as political advisers—to nationalist and "anti-neocolonialist" groups from Cameroon, "Belgian" Congo, Senegal, Ivory Coast, Mali, Morocco, Tunisia, and Niger. They had also established contact with groups from as far away as Angola and apartheid South Africa, laying the groundwork for an expansion of this transnational assistance program in the coming year.[57] The ALN's guerrilla training camps in Morocco, Tunisia, and Mali soon hosted an extremely cosmopolitan mixture of African militants and fighters.

For example, in the latter months of 1960, Modibo Keita offered the Algerians the use of the old colonial *burūj* (towers or forts) that lay in the great Saharan emptiness between Timbuktu and Tamanrasset. There the ALN-EMG (the general staff of Houari Boumedienne's border army) established camps that drilled Algerian recruits alongside a small but appreciable number of fighters from across the Sahel, mostly, and even farther south.[58] Fittingly, the two main themes of their relatively rudimentary political instruction were national unity and international solidarity. In this manner, although the multinational African volunteer army mooted at the December 1958 AAPC never came to pass—largely because the governments of independent states feared the destabilizing potential of such a force that could, after all, be unleashed against any of them if more radical elements had their way—the FLN's camps nonetheless helped foster a spirit of combative pan-African internationalism.[59] It is no coincidence that Fanon's literary output reached its zenith during these months. When he led the FLN's first exploratory team into Mali alongside Abdelaziz Bouteflika (one of Boumedienne's closest lieutenants, future foreign minister and president of Algeria, and also reputedly the typist for *The Wretched of the Earth* during this mission), Fanon described their mission in terms both prosaic—"to open up the southern front[,] transport arms and munitions from Bamako [and] stir up the Saharan population"—and lyrical: "What I should like [are] great lines, great navigation channels through the desert . . . [to] assemble Africa, create the continent."[60]

There was an irony in these sun-baked forts, once the remotest outposts of the French empire, being repurposed for the final assault on colonialism by a multinational alliance of guerrillas, united by the Third World's call. The FLN's African campaign was already diplomatically significant, and would be even more so in 1961, but it was its wholehearted engagement with other liberation movements and nonstate actors that truly completed the front's integration with the transnational Third Worldist trend. Without having yet achieved their own independence, the Algerian rebels had established themselves as some of the most important facilitators in the global exchange of ideas, methods, people, and equipment between revolutionary forces. On the one hand, they had discovered their African calling, for their commitment to the ideals of pan-Africanism was sincere and would henceforth be a central component of their internationalist agenda. On the other hand, though, the FLN's cadres were aware of how they were creating a bridge between Africa and other parts of the Third World. Many felt directly inspired by Cuba's example as a (self-appointed) continental motor of revolution, while the ALN's camps were replete with the iconography and intellectual influence of Castro, Ho Chi Minh, Mao, Fanon, and others of their ilk. Speaking in Hanoi in May 1960, Krim Belkacem told the North Vietnamese leaders, "You have showed to every still subjugated people the correct and difficult path to follow against colonialism.... The Indonesian people, the North-African peoples and the Algerian people in particular, as well as Cameroon, Kenya and Oman, have done nothing other than respond faithfully, each in turn, to this call."[61] Driven from its own country by the French army, the FLN had become a many-tentacled entity binding the insurgent tropics together.

A New Crack in the World

It would not be long before Cuba briefly became the epicenter of the Cold War in the developing world—first through the CIA's shambolic effort to overturn Castro's regime by supporting the exiled opposition's invasion at the Bay of Pigs in April 1961, and then by dint of Nikita Khrushchev's even more reckless decision to place nuclear weapons on the island in the summer and autumn of 1962. However, those twin dramas have somewhat overshadowed the chaotic decolonization of the formerly Belgian Congo in 1960, which was arguably at least as important a factor in escalating the American-Soviet confrontation in the Southern Hemisphere to an intensity unseen since the Korean War. After all, it was the crisis in Congo-Léopoldville (to use a common method of distinguishing it from its smaller neighbor and former French colony, also called Congo, whose capital was Brazzaville) that inspired the Kremlin's first cautious steps toward direct intervention in a Third World imbroglio, when Khrushchev responded to Prime Minister Patrice Lumumba's request for aircraft to ferry loyal nationalist troops into the secessionist, Belgian-backed province of Katanga. Moreover, the sorry progression of events in Congo-Léopoldville, including a controversial United Nations peacekeeping operation and the CIA's murky involvement in Lumumba's execution in January 1961, would loom much larger in the Third World community's collective memory as a grievance and cautionary tale than the relatively unique Cuban situation. Certainly the Congo crisis was a formative lesson for the Algerian nationalists, who also benefited from its fallout in various ways, most notably by finally securing Moscow's firm support. For the FLN, Congo rent a fissure between North and South at least as wide as that between the East and the West at Cuba in October 1962.

A vital context to the Congo crisis was the growing willingness within the Third World community in general, and the FLN leadership in particular, to aggressively exploit tensions between the superpowers rather than shy away from the inherent dangers of such a posture. While the participants in the 1955 Bandung Conference had originally described the supposedly unanimous ideal of "positive neutralism" in very pacific terms, in reality many Third World leaders and their advisers were coming to understand "nonalignment" (which was the preferred term by 1960) as an emphatically proactive policy: not an abstention from the Cold War but rather a strategy for weak and poor countries to wage it, indirectly, to their own advantage. The popularity of this interpretation was evident in discussions among Third World figures in the run-up to the quadripartite summit of the heads of government of the Soviet Union, United States, France, and Britain in Paris in May 1960. With Khrushchev openly hoping to advance his vision of "peaceful coexistence" between the communist and capitalist blocs, the Indonesian foreign minister confessed that Sukarno, Nehru, and Nasser had been discussing the prospect of detente, or a reduction of Cold War tensions, and agreed with the Algerian revolutionaries that it would be a dangerous development for the Third World because it would deprive them of leverage and possibly augur a new "spheres of influence" condominium among the great powers.[62] The Third World seemed to rebuke Moscow at the second AAPSO conference, held in Conakry just weeks before the Paris summit, when the attendees pointedly declined to formally endorse the goals of peaceful coexistence and disarmament. Much to the delight of the Chinese government, which was beginning to openly criticize the Soviet Union's pacific stance and present itself as the truer friend of national liberation movements, the conference's final statement focused instead on more confrontational issues such as the Algerian War.[63]

Unlike the Soviet Union, which had long since abandoned the original Bolsheviks' rejection of traditional European diplomacy, the Chinese shared in Asia's and Africa's instinctive mistrust of Western geopolitical horse-trading. After all, from the Southern Hemisphere's perspective, storied summits such as the Versailles Conference in 1919 and the meeting of Franklin Roosevelt, Winston Churchill, and Joseph Stalin at Yalta in 1945 were remembered chiefly as occasions, like the notorious Berlin Conference of 1884–1885 at the height of Europe's "Scramble for Africa," when the great powers announced new international orders that affirmed their superiority at the expense of the "Orient." In spring 1960, the Soviet leadership's evident desire to be accepted as a superpower (albeit one with numerous profound disagreements with the other major industrial countries) jibed disconcertingly well with de Gaulle's dreams of creating a four-power "directorate" that would grant France an overseer's role in its former colonies. But the FLN attached great import to winning Moscow's support and so, concerned by the prospect of "Franco-Soviet rapprochement and an attenuation of the Cold War," Krim Belkacem urged the GPRA's diplomatic team to intensify its lobbying of the Soviet Union before the Paris summit took place.[64]

Much to their frustration, the Algerians continued to be a notable exception to Moscow's growing engagement with the Arab world and Africa. While long-standing strategic considerations were clearly the underlying basis for the Kremlin's interest in the Middle East, and the growing import of the Afro-Asian movement in international affairs made that a constituency worth winning for

Soviet diplomacy, by 1960 Moscow seemed to be becoming genuinely ideologically invested in the fate of the Southern Hemisphere.[65] The monetary value of Soviet technical and economic assistance to developing countries was nearly six times higher in 1961 than in 1957, with the number of recipient countries increasing from five to twenty over the same period. Among the major beneficiaries were many of the FLN's closest allies, including Egypt, Ghana, Guinea, Iraq, Indonesia, and of course Cuba. Addressing the UN General Assembly in late 1959, Khrushchev declared that the Soviet Union shared none of the West's culpability for the developing countries' poverty, but nevertheless considered it its socialist duty to assist them.[66] As he later insisted in his memoirs, "Our attitude toward the national liberation movement . . . flowed logically from the teachings of Lenin."[67]

In fact, Soviet analysts had long deemed the colonial world and sub-Saharan Africa in particular as being much too "feudal" to have any hope of progressing toward socialism in the imaginable future, so the rapid expansion of Moscow's economic development projects in the late 1950s reflected a substantial ideological innovation. Several new think tanks and academic journals sprang up for Soviet experts to address their deficit of knowledge about the developing world, while the instruction of the Third World's new cadres also became a high priority. In January 1960, the Central Committee of the Communist Party called for the expansion of cultural and intellectual links with Africa, and the following month Khrushchev authorized the construction in Moscow of the new Friendship University for students from Africa, Asia, and the Middle East—the first educational institution for foreigners to be created since the early Bolshevik era. Testifying to the rapid implementation of this educational outreach, the number of students from sub-Saharan Africa studying in the Soviet Union rose from 72 in 1959 to more than 500 in 1961 and reached several thousand soon thereafter.[68] However, Moscow's understanding of Africa was still profoundly limited and frequently bedeviled by crude racial prejudices. "In this country there are no classes, no bourgeoisie, all the land belongs to everyone," one Soviet visitor reported from Guinea in 1960. "All these gifts of nature—pineapples, bananas, coconuts—can just be picked and eaten by anyone. Ninety percent of the population is illiterate . . . they are simply big children. . . . Because these people are still pure, [we have the opportunity] to give them a correct and enlightened education."[69] In spite of such "insights" from the field, one of the better-known examples of Soviet officials' cluelessness about their new mentees was the delivery of a fleet of snowplows to Conakry's airport.

Desperate for some sign of Moscow's favor, the FLN's leaders might actually have appreciated the arrival even of entirely useless equipment from the USSR. Yet with Khrushchev conducting a lengthy public relations tour of France in the run-up to the April 1960 summit, the Kremlin continued to keep the Algerian rebels at arm's length as it strove to cultivate Charles de Gaulle's goodwill. Perhaps the single most important goal of Soviet foreign policy at this time was to win France's backing for the neutralization of East and West Germany and to accentuate the divergent priorities of Paris and Washington.[70] The Algerians had sympathetic intermediaries such as Mao Zedong, Raoul Castro, Touré, and Iraqi president Abdul Karim Qasim lobby Moscow on their behalf. The head of the Arab League told the Soviet foreign minister, Andrei Gromyko, that Algeria was "the most fundamental issue for the Arab countries."[71] But because the Soviet position on the Algerian War rested on the pragmatic calculus of key national security interests, these determined efforts to win over Moscow before the Paris summit took place had little chance for success.

Nevertheless, those efforts are notable for the way in which the Algerian nationalists positioned themselves vis-à-vis revolutionary ideology and the Cold War's geopolitical alignments. In the context of Soviet officials' approving statements on Third World radicalism—Khrushchev told the Egyptian ambassador, for example, that he considered Arab nationalism to be a "progressive phenomenon in so far as it consolidates the power of colonial and dependent people"—the GPRA's Ministry of External Affairs believed that the communist countries saw the Algerian Revolution as being "objectively progressive, going in the same direction as their own," and argued therefore that "they are disposed to bringing their moral, political, and material support to our cause." But the FLN's diplomats also argued that communist support that "will always be a function of our positions with regard to imperialism . . . and to the Socialist Camp."[72] In other words, in order to ensure the firm support of the Soviet Union and the Eastern European countries, the Algerians believed they needed to prove that they were ideologically progressive, in communist terms, and anti-Western. Another MAE report specifically on relations with the communist bloc was even more explicit on this point, suggesting that the FLN leadership should consider "denouncing the role of the Western Countries in the Algerian War . . . strengthening our connections with Guinea, Indonesia, Iraq, the UAR, and Afghanistan . . . [and] erasing the distrust that our [previous] pro-Western foreign policy has engendered." Even improving the front's relations with the much-resented French Communist Party (PCF), which had only very belatedly chosen to support the Algerian nationalist cause, would have to be stomached.[73] Accordingly, in early 1960, El Moudjahid's denunciations of NATO and American "neo-imperialism" increased in frequency and vehemence. Visiting the Czechoslovak embassy in Tunis in late May, two MAE representatives made sure to emphasize the "profoundly popular character" of the Algerian Revolution and predicted that "after it liberates the country from foreign dominance, [our revolution] will unveil socialist achievements." They reported that their Czechoslovak interlocutors "showed a great deal of attention to the idea that the Algerian people fight not only for political independence, but also for economic progress and social justice."⁷⁴ The progression of the Cuban Revolution and its rapidly tightening relationship with the USSR, which of course the Algerians were closely monitoring, was an obvious precedent for this rhetorical journey.

However, whatever progress the Algerians were making with this campaign, it was the crisis that engulfed the "Belgian" Congo in July and August 1960 that proved the turning point in FLN-Soviet relations. The front already knew the fiery Congolese nationalist leader, Patrice Lumumba, from various African meetings and their mutual alliance with Nkrumah. Lumumba and Fanon spent so much time in one another's company in Accra during 1959 and early 1960 that he was known to the latter's young son as "daddy's friend."⁷⁵ A convinced pan-Africanist on the left-wing, "radical" side of the continent's political spectrum, Lumumba dared to take a publicly hostile position on the European powers' obvious desire to hold onto as much as possible of their economic interests and political influence in Africa after decolonization. He warned that if Europeans continued to treat Africa as "their possession," then Africans would be forced to see them as "enemies of our emancipation."⁷⁶ He had approached the Soviets for support in early 1959, stressing upon them his progressive, revolutionary goals.⁷⁷ Furthermore, he also earned the Algerians' admiration by promising Congo's full support once it gained its own independence. Speaking in Conakry, Lumumba declared that "we are going to push the colonialists back from our African frontiers . . . starting with Algeria and South Africa and the other countries under foreign domination."⁷⁸

Although loathed and briefly imprisoned by the Belgian authorities, as the head of Congo's most popular and only truly national-scale party, the Mouvement National Congolais (Congolese National Movement, MNC), this former beer salesman was well-positioned to come to power as a result of Brussels's hasty, poorly planned withdrawal from this massive central African territory in late June 1960. Reluctantly, the Belgian government bowed to popular sentiment by releasing Lumumba from jail and permitting him to win the pre-independence elections that made him Congo's first prime minister, but hoped that the more moderate and less confrontational Joseph Kasavubu, the president, would rein in the younger man and cooperate with Belgium's sizable commercial and political interests still operating in the country.⁷⁹ However, Congo descended into chaos just days after independence when black soldiers mutinied against the long-resented authority of their white officers and led angry mobs in attacks against the European civilian community. Luridly reported by the international press, these riots instantly fueled racial anxieties in the West and made Congo the notorious example of decolonization gone awry, while the political situation dramatically deteriorated when, under the pretext of protecting its citizens, Belgian troops blatantly abetted the copper-rich province of Katanga's declaration of secession from Léopoldville. The transparent involvement of the Belgian government and mining concerns in the Katangese secession outraged the Third World.

Railing against neocolonial conspiracies, Lumumba appealed first to the UN secretary general, Dag Hammarskjöld, who duly deployed a multinational peacekeeping force. But when the UN forces refused to attempt to forcibly reintegrate Katanga or force the Belgian troops to leave, which Lumumba considered essential to the defense of Congo's sovereignty, the irate prime minister threatened to turn instead to the Soviet Union for help. As Khrushchev mulled over the proposition, both Hammarskjöld and the American government hardened their appraisals of Lumumba. The Congolese leader's visit to Washington, DC, in August only damned him further in the American government's eyes, with a senior State Department official condescendingly describing him as "irrational, almost psychotic," in his passionate presentation of his case. The director of the CIA, Allen Dulles, ominously concluded that "in Lumumba we were faced with a person who was a Castro or worse," and in early September the White House duly authorized his agency to orchestrate the assassination of both of those troublesome characters. Lumumba had made himself a lightning rod for Cold War tensions; in the wake of the collapse of the Paris summit in May, British prime minister Harold Macmillan worried that the international situation "has a terrible similarity to 1914. Now Congo may play the role of Serbia."[80]

The FLN swam against the tide of international opinion by strengthening its relationship with the besieged Lumumba. Ferhat Abbas and Krim Belkcam apparently concluded that the headstrong Congolese leader could benefit from the FLN's hard-learned experience in the field of international public relations. They dispatched Serge Michel, an FLN operative of European descent who had orchestrated propaganda projects such as shooting films that exposed France's widespread use of napalm in the Algerian interior, to serve as Lumumba's press adviser in Léopoldville.[81] The Algerians' solidarity was not simply motivated by Lumumba's promise to recognize the GPRA: in his struggle to preserve Congo's sovereignty and territorial integrity, they saw the equivalent of their own battle against *autodétermination* and de Gaulle's threatened secession of the oil-rich Sahara from northern Algeria.[82] Thus *El Moudjahid* decried the UN's refusal to actively enforce Léopold's position in its dispute with Katanga as "the demonstration of the existence of a conspiracy of the Western powers to implant neocolonialism in Africa."[83] More passionate still was the analysis of Hocine Aït Ahmed, one of the original architects of the FLN's international strategy, who lingered in a French prison after his capture in 1956. In a lengthy letter that he managed to sneak out to his GPRA colleagues in Tunis, Aït Ahmed insisted that the FLN had to follow Lumumba's example of braving the Cold War maelstrom. "Moments decide a people's future," he argued.

> Sometimes one timely decision by a leader is enough to tip the prevailing balance of forces and assure the success of a revolution.... Without the intelligence [Lumumba] had at this historic moment and without the force of character that allowed him to make without hesitation the great decision to turn to Khrushchev, the combined forces and intrigues of the West would have succeeded in dislocating Congo for years.... Algeria must become a pressure point in the bidding war between the two great powers.... [Khrushchev] must be induced to tell France and the USA, "paws off Algeria."[84]

In contrast, being better apprised than Aït Ahmed of the realities of the situation, in Accra Fanon feared dark consequences for the Congolese leader. Contrary to his reputation as one of the most unflinching and uncompromising opponents of colonialism and neocolonialism, the FLN's famous Martinican recruit reported to the GPRA that he had tried desperately to deter Lumumba from his confrontational instincts during their final conversations before the latter's return to Congo. "I talked with him through the night," he explained,

> but Nkrumah promised him mountains and marvels and even to 'go to Congo and install him by force' if necessary.... [H]e was very reserved with regard to my counsels for prudence. But he is a demagogue.... Kasavubu for his part asked me not to help out Lumumba any more, since he had 'sold out to the Ghanaians and Guineans.'[85]

Fanon's fears were justified. When Lumumba sought a demonstration of continental solidarity by convening an African summit in Léopoldville in August, no heads of state came, and all save the Guinean delegation vainly urged him to reverse his course.[86]

At the end of the month, Soviet aircraft began to ferry Congolese troops into battle against Katanga's separatist forces, bringing events to a head. Days later, in early September, the government in Léopoldville collapsed, with Kasavubu and Lumumba each claiming to have dismissed the other from their position, creating a state of chaos only partially resolved when the army chief, Joseph Mobutu, instigated a coup with CIA support and placed the prime minister under house arrest. Though Washington welcomed the new government, the foundations were laid for civil war as Lumumba fumed in confinement and his supporters rallied in the east of the country, around the city of Stanleyville. Meanwhile, in order to ensure that Lumumba could not return to power, the CIA station in Léopoldville continued to plot his permanent elimination, although it is not clear whether the Americans ever tried to use the poisoned toothpaste one agent had already brought from Paris for this task.[87]

The fracturing of the Congo reverberated throughout the continent, potentially jeopardizing the FLN's already slim hopes of using Africa's now copious representation in the General Assembly to pass a resolution calling for a UN-organized referendum in Algeria.[88] The crisis had such a polarizing impact that the Algerian nationalists feared it would be impossible, at least in the near term, to rally the African caucus in New York around a cause as troublesome as theirs. In Cairo, Krim Belkacem was dismayed that so many African countries had followed the Western lead in supporting Mobutu's coup, an attitude he felt "hurts Congo [and] unity of action in Africa [and] the Algerian cause as a consequence." At the same time, while mourning the demise of continental unity, the front's diplomatic chief was certain where the blame lay: "[The] Congo question merits great attention in view of numerous similarities with our case, [the] Lumumba government [is] incontestably the most nationalist and most anticolonialist.... Kasavubu and Mobutu [are] agents of neocolonialism."[89] On the other hand, with the environment so tense, France's allies were not looking forward to the prospect of another vote on Algeria. As usual, Paris would expect its friends to argue its case and corral votes while its own delegation pretended not to dignify the proceedings. American diplomats recognized the potential cost of assuming yet another unpopular position on an African matter so soon after deposing Lumumba. "Theoretically there should be no carryover from our attitude on Algeria to the UN role in the Congo," one observed, "[but] there is such a potential risk if we alienate the African states by our stand [on Algeria], once more giving the Soviets an opportunity to pose as the real champion of anti-colonialism."[90] Rebels and superpowers both agreed, in other words, that it was no longer possible to discuss contentious issues like Algeria and Congo in isolation.

True to his proclivity for bold gestures and feeling the need to respond to American and Chinese competition in the Third World, Khrushchev elected to attend the opening of the new session of the General Assembly that September in person in order to, as he later put it, show "the peoples who had won their independence and those who were still fighting for independence ... who was their friend and who was their enemy."[91] During a fortnight-long stay in New York that did not lack photogenic moments—such as the notorious shoe-banging incident provoked, on his last day, by accusations that the Soviet Union was an imperial power in Eastern Europe—the Soviet premier solidified his country's credentials as the primary sponsor of anti-imperialist revolution but also accentuated the Third World's polarization. He overreached in his efforts to capitalize on widespread resentment of the UN's role in the Congo, for his ferocious personal criticisms of Hammarskjöld struck many Afro-Asian observers (including the GPRA) as excessive, since they generally attached great value to diplomatic decorum as a demonstration of national dignity. Likewise, despite their belief that the West enjoyed excessive power in a structurally biased United Nations, the leaders of the Third World still depended on that institution as the fundamental guarantor of sovereignty, and they rejected Khrushchev's far-fetched proposal to replace the secretary-general with a troika representing each of the "three worlds" and to relocate its headquarters to a neutral European country.[92] But Khrushchev did win points (and headlines) with the Third World's radical wing by driving up to Castro's hotel in Harlem and flamboyantly embracing the Cuban leader in a lobby jammed with journalists and photographers, thereby providing a succinct metaphor for the protective arm the Soviet Union had thrown around the revolutionary Caribbean island. Also in New York, Nkrumah asked for secret military assistance as well and insisted to Khrushchev that "there is no other path for Africa except socialism."[93]

After years of Moscow's polite rebuffs, the timing was finally right for the Algerians. The GPRA's president and its interior minister, Ferhat Abbas and Lakhdar Bentobbal, made a visit to Peking and Moscow around this time with the deliberate goal of exploiting the fallout from Congo and the intensifying ideological rivalry between the two largest communist countries. In China, which had already recognized the FLN's provisional government, they received an effusive welcome and all the pomp due to a head of state. Zhou Enlai's speech pointedly saluted Algeria's central role in the "current revolutionary movement in the colonies" in order to unsubtly compare his government's unreserved support for anticolonial causes to Moscow's much more cautious policies with regard to Algeria in particular. The Chinese also backed up this rhetoric by announcing a very sizable increase in the scale of their arms deliveries to the ALN, thereby ensuring their undisputed status as the Algerians' primary military benefactor.[94] By contrast, the Soviet government had not yet recognized the GPRA and had always insisted on delivering any materiel via intermediaries—a process that greatly delayed delivery, limited the size and nature of the provisions, and negated any public relations value. Clearly emboldened by Peking's hospitality, on arriving in Moscow Bentobbal felt free to fairly roughly upbraid the Soviet vice-prime minister, Alexei Kosygin, for his country's comparably weak support for Algeria's liberation struggle. When Abbas began to excuse his colleague's lack of education and refinement, Bentobbal unapologetically retorted, "Perhaps I don't know [Alphonse de Lamartine and Victor Hugo], but I know what I'm talking about when I speak for the Revolution!"[95]

It was no coincidence, then, that the day after Peking announced its new arms agreement with the Algerians, Khrushchev signaled a decisive change in Soviet policy by receiving the FLN delegation in New York at the estate he was staying at on Long Island. The Soviet premier jovially hugged Krim Belkacem for the benefit of the cameras, as he had done with Castro in Harlem, and confirmed to the press that they should interpret this meeting as Moscow's de facto recognition of the GPRA. Although this formula was an ambiguous step short of formal diplomatic recognition, it nevertheless plainly demonstrated that Moscow's calculus of its Franco-Algerian dilemma had changed. Khrushchev did not announce the Kremlin's decision to finally supply armaments directly to the Algerian fighters, in substantial quantities, though FLN spokesmen made sure to hint strongly at that revelation in subsequent interviews. The Soviets had agreed in principle to this step months earlier, but it had lingered in limbo on account of their refusal to make the deliveries themselves.[96] Several weeks later, the first of several Soviet vessels duly arrived in Morocco and unloaded its precious cargo into the eager arms of the ALN's logistics teams.[97] With the FLN now in an unconcealed alliance with the USSR, the Algerian rebels had at last secured the greatest international prize, short of being backed by the United States itself.

Unsurprisingly, these developments provoked consternation in Washington. The head of the State Department's Africa desk feared that if Algeria gained its independence as a result of Soviet assistance, Washington should expect to see—"as a minimum"—the creation in the Maghrib of "a vigorous, dynamic state whose national policies would be somewhat comparable to those of Yugoslavia after World War II."[98] The FLN's representatives were notably happy to lend credence to this fear. Ferhat Abbas, the moderate liberal who had once dreamed of making Algeria French and could hardly be considered an ambassador of the front's radical wing, told an Italian newspaper that "the Socialist camp helps us without conditions at a crucial period in our existence [and] I think the Algerian people will take this into account after they have conquered their independence."[99] In reality, the Algerians knew that they were involved in a contest much more complicated than a bipolar zero-sum game between Moscow and Washington. Contemplating the Kremlin's strange compromise formula of announcing its de facto but not de jure recognition of the GPRA, the MAE's strategists concluded that the Soviets wanted to leave open the possibility of once again supporting a French endgame in Algeria, if necessary. "To what should we attribute so many precautions by a country that has otherwise just recognized our government in such a spectacular fashion?" they asked rhetorically. "The Soviet Union has an interest in Algeria being independent but [only] outside the Western order.... [I]f independent Algeria must fall into the American lap and reinforce the main adversary, [then] the Soviet Union would prefer to accept a French solution."[100] Not for the first time, the FLN's small gang of guerrilla diplomats displayed admirable sensitivity to the increasing multipolarity of global affairs.

In that respect, while events in Congo-Léopoldville had certainly increased US-Soviet tensions to the benefit of the FLN, the more profound consequence of the convergence of the Algerian and Congolese crises was to deepen the divisions between Moscow and Peking, between Washington and Paris, and among Third World countries. Chinese competition seems to have been at least as important as the American variety in compelling Khrushchev to embrace the "genuinely revolutionary" armed wing of African politics with far greater trepidation than the outward enthusiasm of his actual bodily embraces of Krim Belkacem and others betrayed. Meanwhile, in order to block the FLN's proposal for a UN-supervised referendum on independence in Algeria, France relied once more on its allies in the West and among the African Community countries to push through an essentially vacuous General Assembly resolution calling for a ceasefire and negotiations, which de Gaulle gave an air of respectability by declaring his intention to carry out a referendum on *autodétermination*, or limited autonomy, without UN involvement. Paris's gambit succeeded, but the political costs of this effort rose each year, and by now even the British and Americans were becoming more flagrant in their contacts with the FLN regardless of their votes in New York. On the other side of the Atlantic, Omar Oussedik, the front's man in Conakry, took to Guinean radio to vilify as neo-imperialist stooges the governments of Senegal, Cameroon, and Niger for supporting the French proposal, and the polarization of African politics was essentially formalized in early January 1961 when the leaders of Morocco, Egypt, Ghana, Guinea, Mali, and the FLN met in Casablanca to forge a pact of revolutionary forces committed to violent resistance against colonialism.[101]

The Casablanca meeting testified to the growing mistrust, in more radical Third World circles, of the UN and the international institutions. Calling for more decisive efforts to resolve the dispute between Katanga and Léopoldville, Jawaharlal Nehru declared that "the future of the United Nations is in doubt" and warned that the crisis "should not be considered by the old Cold War approach in which Asia and Africa are not interested."[102] Egypt and Ghana pulled their troops out of the UN peacekeeping force, feeling that they had been used to undermine Congo instead of defending it. Mohammed Heikal, the editor of Cairo's *Al Ahram* newspaper and unofficial spokesman for Nasser's government, blamed Hammerskjöld and Eisenhower for Congo's "loss of independence and subjugation to Belgian imperialism" and angrily compared the UN intervention force to the French Foreign Legion in Algeria.[103] Unsurprisingly, the FLN epitomized this trend. Saad Dahlab in the MAE told his colleagues that Congo and the Algeria vote showed the weakness of the United Nations, "the limits of [international] support and the need for the Algerian people to count more on the armed struggle."[104] The Algerian rebels would never again seek UN involvement in their war, and in fact a mutual distrust of international "conflict resolution" subsequently became one issue on which they and de Gaulle saw eye to eye, helping smooth their future negotiations.

Despite the disappointing outcome at the General Assembly, the Algerian nationalist leadership held true to their habit of thriving on global discord and seemed on the whole to be energized by Congo's upheavals. Meeting with his lawyer in a French prison on 27 January 1961, Ahmed Ben Bella hailed the Casablanca meeting for bringing black and Arab Africa together. "In two or three generations," he hoped, "Arab civilization and the Arabic language could become the *point commun* of all the countries of Africa." In political terms, he saw the beginning of a new alliance between the "engaged" countries of the continent. "I am convinced," he said, " . . . that [Lumumba] will try to restart a new adventure. . . . If Lumumba returns tomorrow, liquidates all these [neocolonial] forces and establishes a state that aligns with Sékou Touré, Mali, Nasser, . . . I guarantee you that Africa will change."[105] While this provides an invaluable insight into the worldview of the man who would become the first president of independent Algeria, Ben Bella's prediction also unwittingly demonstrated the huge obstacles in the path of the radical Third Worldist dream. Unknown to him, ten days earlier Katangan secessionists, in league with Belgium and the CIA, had summarily executed Lumumba in the woods and buried him in an unmarked grave.

"Algiers Is No More"

For all of the FLN's diplomatic successes and growing stature in African and Third World circles, there remained one glaring shortcoming in the movement's campaign—the near-total collapse of the insurgency inside Algeria itself. By the end of 1960, in spite of the ALN's rapidly increasingly strength in Morocco and Tunisia, the rebels had not found any reliable way to penetrate the fearsome fortifications of the Morice Line and relieve the dwindling numbers of mujahideen in the interior. The political situation was equally concerning, for although the FLN boasted a very extensive radio network that broadcast its propaganda throughout Algeria (and indeed a large swath of northwestern Africa), there was very little information coming from the other direction. The leadership in Tunis was almost blind. De Gaulle mocked the GPRA's globetrotting pretensions, dismissively referring to it as "the rebel leaders installed for six years outside of Algeria, and who to listen to them will be there for a long time more . . . claiming to be the government of the Algerian Republic which will exist one day, but has never before existed!"[106] Despite their outward protestations of confidence, the rebels' internal communications from this period reveal a rising panic. What good did it do to be fêted in Havana and Hanoi if they could barely communicate with their brothers in Algiers?

For this reason the spectacular, unexpected rising of the Muslim residents of the Algiers Kasbah in December 1960 utterly transformed the FLN's fortunes and sense of purpose. The movement had already become a linchpin of the transnational Third Worldist scene, but that demonstration of genuine popular support proved that they could carry their country with them. Rousingly celebrated in the conclusion to Gillo Pontecorvo's film *The Battle of Algiers*, the December 1960 protests also called time on any lingering hopes of reforming the colonial order. For Pontecorvo, the image of massed Maghribi youths was an inspiration—but to the French and other Western publics, with lurid tales of murder and rape in Congo still fresh in their minds, dark-skinned mobs signified a troubling, unmistakably foreign world. After many decades of romantic imperialism and years of debate over the nature and purpose of "decolonization," by 1961 a consensus had suddenly emerged that the "modern counties" and "Third World" were obviously separate and unalike. On the French mainland, public opinion overwhelmingly favored the final withdrawal from North Africa. By dint of the FLN's long diplomatic campaign, Algeria emerged as one of the most visible and closely watched leaders of the Third World pack, and the movement's cadres intensified their study of countries such as Cuba, Ghana, Egypt, and India in order to clarify their own postindependence plans.

Changing social conditions since the war's outbreak were a key factor in confirming the FLN's status as Algeria's new political elite and in encouraging the movement's leaders to look at their country through *tier-mondiste* glasses. Certainly, one million pieds noirs did not desire to partake in the Third World as a political project, nor did they think of their homeland as belonging to some explicitly nonwhite, underdeveloped region. After all, the second quarter of the twentieth century had actually been the highpoint of *l'Algérie française*: the economy was healthy, industrial growth accelerated in the early 1950s, and the FLN's rebellion had not stopped a building spree that featured bold modernist experiences such as the Le Corbusier-esque Aérohabitat, a village in the sky that dominated the slopes above central Algiers. Despite the pitiable conditions in the *bled*, a visitor who stuck to the northern coastal region and the major cities, where most of the European community lived, might indeed have been able to convince herself that she was in an iconoclastic, Mediterranean corner of France, as legal and administrative fictions had long insisted.

But as the war metastasized, this sleepy colonial idyll had been assaulted by unpredictable violence and defaced by checkpoint after checkpoint. Pied noir farmers fleeing the countryside for the safety of the cities spoke of a once-familiar land, tamed by their parents and grandparents, now turned against them. More alarmingly, the *bled* crept into the urban domain as Muslim peasants driven from their homes by a scorched-earth counterinsurgency crowded into swelling slums and shantytowns, or bidonvilles, around the cities. "Algiers is no more," lamented the esteemed historian of the Maghrib Jacques Berque, as he mourned the demise of Alger la blanche (Algiers the wwhite) and its pleasing geometry of bright buildings and shaded avenues, punctuated by Mediterranean verdure. "Everywhere greenery has yielded to the advance of houses [and] the Muslim habitat spills out from the Kasbah," he wrote. "[This is] the Algiers of slums, a topographical assault and social menace to a certain urban order."[107] Moreover, despite the French army's insistence that the insurgency was on the verge of being eradicated, in 1960 urban terrorism returned to Algiers after a prolonged quiet.[108] The authorities recognized that a mutual sense of dread separated the European community from the Muslims. More and more, the pieds noirs feared the specter of Congo and the terror inflicted on the whites there. When, they wondered, would normality return?[109]

As a flurry of books with titles like *Overpopulated Algeria, Africa Topples into the Future*, and *The Uprooting* could attest, the answer to that question was "never." "Like some infernal machine," wrote sociologist Pierre Bourdieu, "the war has made a clean sweep of the social realities."[110] His colleague Germaine Tillion described *l'Algérie française* as an unsustainable anachronism built on blood, gold, and hatred, whose destruction was preordained in the relentless degradation of the Muslim population by late-stage colonialism and then the counterinsurgency campaign.[111] Unfortunately for those in Algeria's European community who wanted as little as possible to change, these were the analyses of two social scientists in the service of the French army, many of whose officers had come to see the pieds noirs as an impediment to their transformative mission. In addition to perhaps a million peasant refugees living in the slums or camps in Morocco and Tunisia, between October 1959 and January 1961 the army had herded nearly twice that number again into guarded *regroupement* camps in order to deprive the ALN's fighters of shelter and support.[112] Most of these *regroupement* sites were little better than squalid concentration camps, but some were the "modern" new villages described by government propaganda that were, in the words of a more objective American observer, "shiny, white, and hygienic, where [the Muslim inhabitants] are watched over by . . . officers, doctors, and teachers." But even in the nicer villages he found that

> [P]sychically [*sic*] their condition, when it can honestly be sounded, is often not so healthy. But beyond all else it is clear that they are never going to be quite the same villagers again that they once were and the longer the *regroupement* continues the more permanently changed will the face of rural Algeria be.[113]

In other words, whatever else might happen, after the war approximately 3 million people, or a third of the population, would not be going back to their homes and would be living a very different existence than the one they knew in 1954. Most likely they would end up in the bidonvilles, completing Algeria's accelerated, traumatizing process of urbanization.

Therein lay the FLN's opportunity. In their efforts to defeat the insurgency, the French had taken Algeria apart. Could the revolutionaries now reconstruct it according to their own goals? After two years of the fearsome counterinsurgency campaign unleashed by de Gaulle on his return to the Élysée palace, the movement's political organization in the interior was not in good condition. Krim Belkacam warned that "in Algeria it is now certain that we have to reconstitute the [revolutionary] infrastructure over a large part of the territory.... [We must] establish a program—political, social and economic—suited to achieving the Nation's prosperity and to mobilizing the People for the construction of the Country."[114] Rebuilding the organization inside Algeria being a slow and dangerous task, at first most of the burden of this renewed political campaign fell on the front's mass communications apparatus. In the summer of 1959, some of the darkest and costliest days for the fighters in the interior, ALN commanders had realized that the Muslim populace was still able to keep up with the GPRA's diplomatic endeavors via Egyptian radio broadcasts, a fact that helped keep the revolution alive even in those areas where the rebels had been eliminated or driven to ground.[115] Therefore, at the beginning of 1960 the FLN's leaders decided that creating their own comprehensive radio broadcasting network was essential to re-establishing contact with the population and "unifying" the nation, by which of course they actually meant dividing Algerian society as it currently existed. "It will be necessary to achieve the division of Algeria's inhabitants into 2 clearly incompatible blocs," explained the provisional government's report on the challenge of reconnecting with the Muslim population.

> On one side [will be] the Europeans and their collaborators, on the other the reliable people supported by the ALN.... The people must always know as soon as possible how to behave themselves, what they must think, and what to do and not to do. The National [Radio Transmission] Post will constitute the essential element of coordination between the Algerian people and the GPRA.[116]

The radio could deliver news to even the most far-flung settlements, it could reach an illiterate audience, and despite French efforts to jam the signals, it could traverse the frontier fortifications and the barbed-wire fences of the *regroupement* camps. It also enabled the different branches of the decentralized movement to communicate instantly and relatively securely with one another, prompting the MAE to beg, borrow, or steal transmitters for its missions abroad. Throwing itself into the task, by April 1961 the front boasted a radio network of sixty-three transmission stations that ringed Algeria in Morocco, Tunisia, the southern desert, and even as far away as Bamako and Conakry.[117] For the first time ever, the Muslims of Algeria were united by a single source of information, a single cognitive map of the world. "The village, the closed microcosm in which the country dweller once lived, was now in contact with the whole of Algeria," Bourdieu observed. "Through the press, through the radio, through wider contacts, through the action of the political commissaries, each Algerian communicated with and was in communion with a wider social unit; he participated in a national existence."[118] Fanon was similarly struck by radio's centrality to the revolution's endurance. Moreover, this same network blanketed wide swaths of North and West Africa with the front's propaganda, constituting the centerpiece of the movement's efforts to radiate its ideology and enhance its influence in the surrounding regions.

As for the content of these broadcasts, as the ALN's military fortunes declined, rebel propaganda focused more and more on diplomatic activities and international events. On taking over the MAE in early 1960, Krim Belkacem insisted that the diplomatic teams submit at least one propaganda piece per month on their region of responsibility.[119] A steady procession of diplomatic events such as AAPSO and AAPC meetings, UN votes, and the Casablanca Group meeting in January 1961 provided a dependable stream of supportive speeches by friendly heads of state. The authorities in Algiers were increasingly alarmed by the impact of these efforts, particularly among the students and youths concentrated in the cities. They believed that the FLN garnered great prestige among the populace by relaying news of the support it received from countries like China and the Soviet Union.[120]

Although the FLN's leaders and diplomats could not be certain for a long time of the impact of this propaganda, the cumulative effect was to infuse Algeria's captive and bewildered audience with a *tier-mondiste* view of the world. In their prescient book, *L'Algérie des bidonvilles: Le Tiers Monde dans la cité* (Algeria of slums: the third world in the city), Robert Descloitres, Claudine Descloitres, and Jean-Claude Reverdy recognized that the frustrated youths of the Kasbah and the bidonvilles were entranced by the FLN's impressive new allies and exotic adventures:

> [This concerns] the movement of people, but also the movement of ideas. . . . Ideologies clash, propagandas succeed one another, the slogans change. . . . The propagation of foreign modes of thought in the rural world has precipitated the withering of traditional structures. The old leaders are gone, strangers have taken their place.[121]

It helped, of course, that so many of the GPRA's intrepid travelers and the ALN's officers had been recruited directly from university or the main Algerian student union, for educational institutions continued to be key sites of politicization. But the front's propaganda also resonated among the much greater numbers of poorly educated, destitute young men and women whom the war had deprived of the traditional figures of patriarchal and religious authority. To those lacking any prospects or status, participation in the revolution offered purpose, social standing, and an end to humiliation. "This debate goes beyond Algiers, Algeria and decolonization," Jacques Berque wrote in the foreword to *Algeria of Slums*. "Before us is the era when everywhere man searches for himself and remakes himself."[122]

Finally, in early December 1960, the new Algeria revealed itself. When de Gaulle decided to spend five days touring the country in order to rally support for the upcoming referendum on *autodétermination*, the pieds noirs came out in protest at every stop, occupying administrative buildings and battling riot police. They wanted to drown out the message he bore, as presented to several hundred officers at an air force base in Blida on 10 December, that Algeria was something alien to France. It was vain to keep pretending, de Gaulle said, that Algeria was just like Lorraine or Provence. Effectively deferring to the FLN's propaganda campaign, the French president conceded that "the population of Algeria, in its great majority Moslem, has developed a consciousness that did not formerly exist.... [The revolt] and everything connected with it is happening in a new world.... This is the Algerian Algeria that every day, by the force of things, will become even more Algerian than the day before."[123] The very next day, the Muslims of Oran and Algiers proved his point by surging out of the Kasbahs and the bidonvilles and invading the European quarters in a powerful display of political consciousness and numerical superiority. Marching under the FLN's flag, they chanted, "Long live the GPRA!," "Long live Arab Algeria!," "Long live Ferhat Abbas!," "Free Ben Bella!," and even "Long live de Gaulle!" in recognition of the French president's gradual recognition of Algeria's separate identity.[124] The protesters' slogans certainly exhibited some mixed and imprecise messaging, but that fact just proved the genuine, unstaged nature of the event, and there was no doubting the overwhelming sentiment that Algeria was not France and that the people had accepted the FLN as their heroes.

The demonstrations of 11 December looked very much like the realization of Fanon's dream of moving "with all of Africa toward African Algeria ... toward Algiers, the continental city."[125] Predictably, however, Africa did not reclaim Algeria peacefully. The pied noir communities in the two cities had themselves been protesting de Gaulle's tour because they suspected the president of harboring plans to eventually leave Algeria—but now, horrified and terrified by the advancing Muslim crowds, they frantically demanded the protection of the same forces of law and order that they had just been harassing and vilifying. The protests quickly deteriorated into riots as the police and protesters clashed and armed groups from both communities seized the opportunity to snipe and settle scores. The police and army opened fire on the crowds, making little distinction between peaceful protesters and violent elements. One regiment fired continuously into the slums on the hills of Algiers for a full hour as European women cheered them on, shouting "Kill them! Kill them!" from their balconies. All told, there were 120 dead and 500 wounded in Algiers and Oran combined, with all but 8 of the fatalities being Muslim.[126] Rarely had the white community's inferior numbers been more evident, especially in its hitherto exclusive enclaves in the city centers.

Regardless of the savagery of the protests' denouement, they had a tremendous impact on public opinion in metropolitan France and the wider world. As three of the young participants subsequently explained to the front's newspaper, *El Moudjahid*, "the youth [of Algiers] above all burned with desire to intervene in the [UN debates].... We heard often that 'the world is watching us!'. . . . I saw youths shouting out to journalists, to photographers, in French, in German, in Italian, in English 'come here!,' 'use that! Take this photo!' "[127] The press coverage of impressively large crowds of Muslim men and women, marching in solidarity and determination, viscerally refuted the underlying premise of French policy that Algeria somehow stood apart from the trends sweeping across the rest of Africa and the Southern Hemisphere. While de Gaulle had gradually come to publicly acknowledge the inevitability of, in his words, an "Algerian Algeria," he still had hundreds of thousands of French soldiers of Muslim auxiliaries battling in the *bled* to impose a solution described variously as *autodétermination*, autonomy, multicommunitarianism, "association," and other ambiguous formulas that signified an outcome somehow different than a fully sovereign Algerian nation-state. Yet the Muslim inhabitants of Algiers and Oran had now emphatically dispelled any lingering doubts that they desired independence or that they saw the FLN as their legitimate representatives in that goal. Why, then, should Algeria's fate be different from the rest of France's African territories? After all, bowing to overwhelming African sentiment and a general indifference in metropolitan France, by 1960 the French Community framework had already evolved from a scheme in which Paris retained control over key dimensions of its colonies' affairs into a league of genuinely independent states more akin to the British Commonwealth.[128] In the same vein, polls in April 1961 showed not only that 78 percent of French voters favored negotiating with the FLN but also that, more significantly, 69 percent of them believed that Algeria would soon be an independent country.[129]

The evolution of French public opinion seems less due to widespread sympathy for the anticolonial cause than to acceptance of the idea—contrary to decades of imperial romanticism—that France and its colonies simply belonged to separate domains and separate historical trajectories. Algeria's advocates among the Parisian intelligentsia, most notably Jean-Paul Sartre, had certainly not won the battle of ideas and continued to represent a minority, controversial point of view.[130] Instead, the public was increasingly aware that the colonies had stopped being a source of national strength, if that were ever true, and had become instead a massive drain on the country's finances and resources. The *fardeau colonial* (colonial burden), France's noble obligation to lift up its colonial wards culturally and materially, increasingly seemed like an anachronism at a time when the post–World War II economic boom was transforming mainland France into a "modern" consumer society. To put it bluntly, by 1960 most people took much greater satisfaction from owning their own home, car, refrigerator, and television than from the knowledge that the tricolor flew over some wretchedly poor village in the Sahel. Furthermore, with the signing of the Treaty of Rome between the first six members of the European Economic Community in 1957, it was clear that France's future prosperity depended on its ties to the industrialized world, not the tropics. Tellingly, a 1962 survey showed that although metropolitan voters overwhelmingly claimed to be "proud" of France's imperial legacy, on average they could name only two of the fifteen francophone African countries, and a quarter of those surveyed could not identify a single one![131] Presumably everybody had heard of Algeria, but hardly anyone from the French mainland ever visited the supposed crown jewel of the empire, so with the events of December 1960 suggesting that the "troubles" there were still far from over, the last bulwarks of the French public's patience collapsed.

The postwar economic miracle strengthened the narrative of a prosperous West diverging from an underdeveloped "Third World," and the December 1960 demonstrations went a long way toward confirming that Algeria properly belonged to the latter designation. Furthermore, the pro-FLN protests in Algiers and Oran fed into metropolitan France's growing fear of infection by an overpopulated, poor, disorderly, and unruly Third World. Even in the early days of his management of the war in North Africa, de Gaulle himself had privately ruled out the notion of properly assimilating Algeria's Muslims into French society, telling a close confidant that one only had to go and look at them "in their turbans and djellabas" to see that "they are not Frenchmen!"[132] He was far from the only white Frenchman to recoil from the thought of a permanent Maghribi presence in mainland France. Immigration from Morocco, Algeria, and Tunisia had increased markedly in the late 1940s, running for a time as high as 100,000 per year, and reached a total of 1 million people by 1954 with signs of only modest abatement to the steady flow of impoverished Arabs and Berbers across the Mediterranean. The slums evident in Algeria's cities were being replicated around Paris, and the authorities there in turn mimicked the colonial administration's methods of dealing with the problem: bulldozers, police sweeps, and the development of an extensive surveillance and control apparatus. Maghribi immigrants became associated in the public's mind with crime and violence— not least because of the bloody feuds between the FLN and its rivals for the loyalty of the emigrant community.¹³³ Might the Arab masses one day invade Paris as they had invaded the unmistakably French quarters of Algiers? Better to separate France and Algeria definitively, ran the thinking, than see the direction of colonization reversed.

The French public's desire to be rid of Algeria and its lack of sympathy for the pieds noirs' desire to keep the territory as an integral part of the French polity explain the dismal failure of the attempted putsch in April 1961, when *l'Algérie française* hard-liners and uncompromising army officers joined forces to overthrow de Gaulle and take charge of the war effort. Having first taken control in Algiers, the rebels then threatened to drop paratroopers over Paris, an action that would have effectively constituted the expansion of a colonial war back into the metropolitan capital. De Gaulle's charismatic address to the nation at the height of the crisis is justly praised as a bravura performance that ensured the loyalty of the army's rank and file, neutered the putsch, and saved French liberty, but it is also clear that the senior officers who led the rebellion had fallen severely out of sync with mainstream French opinion since December 1960. Whereas the pro-FLN demonstrations that month had been the final straw for an exasperated populace on the northern side of the Mediterranean, they had conversely provoked the *jusqu'au boutists* (bitter-enders) on the opposite shore into their most desperate acts. In the wake of the demonstrations, officials in Algiers had warned Paris that

> for the Europeans [of Algeria], the fear of numbers, the huge demonstrations, bode unfavorably for the future: what Algerian government, if independence occurs, will be able to avert this eruption of the masses to which the situation in December was a prelude? . . . Precedents in Tunisia, Morocco, and more recently Congo haunt the thoughts [of Algeria's whites].¹³⁴

After the ignominious failure of their attempted coup in April, the hard-line pieds noirs and disgraced army officers turned to the notorious terrorist group, the Organisation Armée Secrète (Secret Armed Organization, OAS). The OAS took inspiration from such diverse sources as the French Resistance in World War II, the Vietminh, and the Zionist Haganah militia as it uncompromisingly waged what its members believed to be the last stand of white Christian civilization against Islamo-communist fanaticism, although as the hopelessness of their cause became undeniable, the group blindly and pointlessly slaughtered Algerian Muslims throughout the remainder of the war.¹³⁵ The Arab schoolteacher Mouloud Feraoun recorded in his journal that "the rage of the French in Algeria is out of control. Their rage is filled with hatred and fear. . . . They have money, and they use it to pay ruthless commandos to go terrorize the Arabs at night."[136] Caught between the two sides, himself murdered by the OAS on the eve of independence, Feraoun epitomized the bloody severance of *l'Algérie française* from the emergent *l'Algérie tier-mondiste*.

At the same time, being hitherto unable to judge how effective their propaganda was inside Algeria, the FLN's leaders were themselves joyfully stunned by the December 11 protests, which they deemed "so surprising by their energy and maturity." But they now saw the validation of everything they had been saying: after years of incessant invocation of the legitimacy of "the masses," the masses had suddenly appeared, marching under the FLN's flag! The rebels' sense of relief was palpable. A subsequent GPRA interior ministry report confessed that, until the eruptions in Algiers and Oran, they had considered their efforts to rebuild the revolutionary organization in the Algerian interior a failure. But now, the report cheered, "everything became possible again." The protests were nothing less than a "sudden and quasi-miraculous turnabout of the situation . . . [that has] had the best consequences in every area." The FLN's political ascendency within Algeria was indisputable, and French efforts to cultivate a more moderate Muslim "third force" emphatically rejected. There were military advantages, too, from the pieds noirs' renewed sense of insecurity in the cities, since it obliged the French army to pull troops back from the countryside to reoccupy Algeria's urban centers, thereby relaxing its choking grasp on the ALN. A resurgence of guerrilla activity in the ensuing months showed that, close as the mujahideen had come to extinction, France's much ballyhooed "victory on the ground" really depended on the indefinite maintenance of nearly half a million soldiers in the field. In short, the GPRA's report quite correctly assessed December 1960 as decisive turning point in the war, concluding that "a new phase of the struggle was beginning or better yet, a new Algeria revealed itself."[137]

The demonstrations also greatly strengthened the FLN's international standing by eliminating any doubt that the movement enjoyed popular support commensurate with its diplomatic profile or that it would dominate the Algerian political scene after independence. Wavering governments faced a clear choice between displeasing Paris or the future leaders of one of the more important countries in Africa, prompting many to recognize the GPRA or at least elevate their relations with the Algerian nationalists to a new level. "The Algerian People . . . showed that they are behind the FLN," interior minister Bentobbal told the Yugoslav leader, Josip Broz Tito, in April. "There are only two forces in our country: colonialism and the FLN."[138] Although Yugoslavia had initiated unofficial relations with the GPRA in 1959 and even provided material and financial assistance since then, Belgrade delayed until 1961 to offer its formal diplomatic recognition of the provisional government.[139] On the first day of the new year, Khrushchev gave a speech to the Soviet Union's senior ideologues in which he pledged solidarity with the "sacred struggles" for national liberation in the Third

World, offering specific mention of "the bloody events in Algeria, Congo [and] Laos."[140] Following Moscow's lead, Czechoslovakia offered de facto recognition of the GPRA in the spring, in addition to very substantial arms shipments to the ALN.[141] Meanwhile, on the other side of the Cold War divide, John F. Kennedy had barely moved into the White House before his ambassador in Tunis urged that, lest Algeria became a Congo-like debacle, Washington improve its contacts with the GPRA, "whom Asian-Africans, Yugoslavs and even some NATO members see discreetly and Sino-Soviets meet freely on government and ambassadorial level."[142] Recognizing that the FLN "will inevitably play a large role in Algeria['s] future," Secretary of State Dean Rusk authorized American diplomatic personnel in the region to "deal discreetly but positively with Algerian overtures for exchanges of views at other than [the] present levels." Although he was concerned about how to handle the inevitable French complaints once Paris got wind of this new policy, Rusk himself contrived to meet a GPRA representative at a dinner hosted by the Saudi Arabian government.[143]

But the FLN made the greatest progress in the Third World. Saad Dahlab immediately instructed the diplomatic team to capitalize on the December protests, when the Algerian people had demonstrated their "political maturity and unflagging revolutionary potential" to the world, by rallying the Afro-Asian community in opposition to de Gaulle's neo-imperialist designs for Algeria.[144] He led a delegation that toured Southeast Asia in January and February, securing increased financial assistance from Sukarno and the elevation of the GPRA mission in Jakarta to full embassy status.[145] During the following months, the GPRA also opened two new offices in Pakistan and Nigeria and steadily added to the list of states that formally recognized it, including—finally—Cuba.[146] The campaign continued to be particularly successful in Africa, where even countries as poor as Somalia, described by the GPRA representative to the Arab League, Ahmed Tewfik El-Madani, as an "extraordinarily anemic country lacking in even artisanal industry," insisted on making at least a symbolic contribution to the revolution's coffers.[147] On the other hand, the FLN attendees at the World Peace Council in New Delhi in March were less successful, as Nehru continued to be much too reserved in his support for their liking. Overall, concluded a lengthy report by the MAE on the Afro-Asian scene—excluding China and the Asian communist countries—"the political and material help that we receive from Asia remains feeble and, with the exception of Indonesia, timid and sporadic in nature." In contrast, "Due to its Saharan expanses, Algeria is the 'most African' of the North African countries . . . [which in addition to] our Revolution's historical role accords us a prime position in Africa. It is up to us to use it worthily."[148]

In the spirit of the latter, the front also become steadily more influential in Africa's transnational guerrilla network, where the Algerian people's display of solidarity with the FLN offered hope to all the continent's itinerant and exiled would-be national leaders. Boumedienne's border army was also able to take advantage of its very healthy stocks of supplies and armaments to act as a benefactor to less fortunate groups. In the first half of 1961, the ALN received 42,000 tons of war material from Peking, Moscow, and Prague—a quantity so great that its commanders had difficulty coping logistically and had their soldiers working day and night just to transport and stock it all.[149] "This aid can only increase the Algerian Revolution's ability to maintain itself in the avant-garde of the anticolonialist and anti-imperialist struggle," they crowed.[150] Consequently, from its modest beginnings in Mali's desert forts, the ALN's multinational training program grew into a major operation centered in its large, semipermanent camps in Morocco and Tunisia, welcoming visitors from an ever-widening catchment area that soon included even apartheid South Africa and the Portuguese colonies. By the end of the year the camps had received hundreds of such foreign recruits, two of the more notable ones being Nelson Mandela of the African National Congress (ANC), who apparently showed little aptitude for guerrilla warfare, and Angolan nationalist Roberto Holden. In addition to providing material assistance and combat training, they tried to impress on their guests the importance of political organization and international solidarity to the success of any insurgency.[151] The FLN was already an inspiration to other anticolonial movements on account of its accomplishments, but the openness of its assistance program to smaller movements earned it a great deal of additional goodwill and credibility in Third World circles.

However, the front attained the pinnacle of its Third Worldist diplomacy in November 1961, when the GPRA participated in the first nonaligned summit in Belgrade with the status of a sovereign government. Although it was now customary for liberation movements to attend such events as observers, the Algerian nationalists had to lobby intensively for the right to attend the conference on equal terms to the delegations from independent countries like India, Yugoslavia, Egypt, and so on. Nehru in particular was reluctant to admit either the FLN or the rebel government of Congo based in the eastern city of Stanleyville, led by Lumumba's old ally Antoine Gizenga. By this time, the Indian prime minister was trying to distance himself from the "agitational approach" in Third World politics—the more confrontational, subversive trend that the Algerians now embodied. Indeed, Nehru was wary of the proposal for a nonaligned conference in the first place, since he sensed that it would boast a more radical atmosphere than the relatively pacific, evenhanded tenor of Bandung. The chief orchestrators—Nasser, Nkrumah, and Tito—invited Cuba to attend and essentially vetoed invitations for countries that had not taken sufficiently "anti-imperialist" stances on the Congo crisis and other key issues.[152]

But the ascendance of this radical trend in the politics of the Southern Hemisphere strengthened the Algerians' position, and thanks to the enthusiastic advocacy of Nkrumah and Sukarno in particular, the FLN secured its participation in the conference with full status—unlike the nineteen other liberation movements that attended only as observers.[153] A GPRA report enthused that the nonaligned summit would be "practically the first time that Algeria is participating on an equal footing in an international conference of such importance."[154] In the future, the country's diplomats would remember Belgrade as an accomplishment comparable only to their presence at the mythical Bandung Conference itself. So far as the Third World was concerned, Algeria had arrived.

The Last Battle for Civilization

Created in late 1958 in response to the FLN's defeat in the Battle of Algiers, the rebel leadership's flight into Tunisia, and de Gaulle's revitalization of the French war effort, the GPRA owed much of its success in reversing the Algerian Revolution's fortunes by 1961 to the expansion and consolidation of the "Third World project" at this time. Of course, that project was still not a formalized or centralized endeavor, but the late 1950s and early 1960s witnessed numerous important efforts to make real the somewhat vague and lofty agenda of Bandung. The Conferences of Independent African States, the All-African Peoples' Conferences, the Afro-Asian Peoples' Solidarity Organization, and the Non-Aligned Movement were all evidence of a widespread desire to institutionalize and regularize international relations within the Third World community. Although their constituencies, prime movers, and specific purposes differed, in theory these various groupings expressed the same underlying principles, and in practice their cumulative effect was to give the impression of real momentum behind the Third World project. Advantageously situated countries such as Egypt could enhance their international influence by accentuating their role as a link between, say, the Arab League, sub-Saharan African meetings, and the Afro-Asian scene. Conversely, regionally constrained states like Yugoslavia and Cuba were drawn to the NAM as a way to escape their confines.[155] The Algerian nationalists shared the Cubans' sense of isolation and the Egyptians' interregionalism, but they also craved validation. More than anything else, it was the FLN's admission as an equal to this more assertive and newly organized Third World trend that finally discredited French efforts to quarantine Algeria and prevent its accession to full independence. By February 1962, for example, even as stalwart a Western ally as the leader of South Vietnam, Ngo Dinh Diem, informed Paris that he felt compelled to recognize the GPRA "in order not to abandon the terrain to Hanoi."[156]

At the same time, bolstered by the influx of new African states, the Afro-Asian caucus in the United Nations displayed a strong sense of unity and coordination during the 1960–1961 session of the General Assembly. Most important, in December 1960 the General Assembly unanimously passed a forceful anticolonial resolution declaring "alien domination" of any kind to be in violation of the UN Charter and that there were no acceptable justifications for delaying the independence of any territory, including claims of political, social, or economic unpreparedness. The United States, Britain, France, Portugal, South Africa, and four other Western countries dared only to abstain on a resolution that, while having no practical enforcement, unambiguously rebuked their policies in southern Africa and elsewhere.[157] This more assertive Afro-Asian position bridged the caucus's divisions over issues such as Algeria and Congo, since two of the Third World's strongest supporters of Dag Hammarskjöld's handling of the latter crisis, Tunisia's Habib Bourguiba and India's Jawaharlal Nehru, soon invoked the General Assembly resolution to justify their own forceful efforts to reintegrate vestigial European-held territories. In July 1961, Tunisian and French troops clashed when Bourguiba demanded the return of the French naval base at the Tunisian town of Bizerte, and Hammarskjöld's attempt to resolve the situation provoked de Gaulle's opprobrium and scornful dismissal of the Norwegian as a "self-appointed mediator."[158] In December, Nehru surprised the world by successfully deploying the Indian army to occupy the Portuguese-held province of Goa. Though Western governments criticized the "precipitous" nature of such actions, the Third World's uncompromising anticolonialism was clearly in the ascendency with respect to global opinions and norms.[159] Following Hammarskjöld's death in a plane crash in Rhodesia in September 1961, Burma's U Thant succeeded him as the first nonwhite secretary-general. Because he quickly proved to be an outspoken proponent of the Afro-Asian perspective on contentious issues like Algeria, Cuba, Vietnam, and other crises in the Third World, U Thant's time in office saw American policymakers become increasingly fearful that they were losing control of the UN's agenda.[160]

In the same way that the consolidation of the Third World movement at the end of the 1950s is vital to understanding the FLN's recovery from earlier setbacks and state of near-assured triumph by 1961, the Algerian nationalists' experiences have revealed a vivid and rich view of the global anticolonial scene at that time. Noting that the assistance obtained from the "fraternal countries" of Tunisia and Morocco had been "far from the level we rightfully expected," a March 1961 report by the GPRA Ministry of External Affairs observed that the front had been obliged to "open itself audaciously to the outside world [*l'extérieur*]"—first the Arab countries, then Africa, the Afro-Asian scene, and "all the progressive forces in the world that can deliver the means of victory to the Algerian Revolution."[161] The FLN's successes in this endeavor prove that the *tier-mondiste* ideals of solidarity, unity, and mutual support were principles of genuine import and consequence for many influential people around the world. Remarkably, the Algerians did indeed often find more wholehearted support and warmer friendships in distant and diverse cities like Havana, Hanoi, or Accra than in many places that were culturally, linguistically, spiritually, and literally closer to home.

Moreover, the instantaneity of the Cuban-Algerian rapport after Castro's revolution is particularly illustrative of how these connections cannot be understood just in ideological, political, or pragmatic terms, for there was an elusive personal and psychological dimension too. The mutual recognition of those who were willing to fight colonialism or neocolonialism by force of arms was perhaps the most powerful bond: the Cubans and Algerians made frequent reference to their experiences of guerrilla war, and the FLN's training camps that welcomed recruits from Niger, Congo, Angola, and elsewhere in Africa bestowed the movement with immense credibility and many grateful friends. By dint of its multidirectional exchanges of ideas, practices, people, and guns, the transnational guerrilla network was also the most concrete manifestations of Third World internationalism. Generally, the Algerian nationalists had warmer relations and more greatly valued the counsel of those countries that participated in this network, such as China, Vietnam, and Cuba, than those that advocated a more pacific approach such as India and, initially, Ghana. As the FLN's adopted figurehead in Africa and the newest contributor to the guerrilla-revolutionary canon, Frantz Fanon single-handedly personified the movement's cosmopolitanism and warrior ethos, becoming immortalized after his death from leukemia in December 1961 with such dictums as "decolonization is always a violent phenomenon."[162]

As a result of the FLN's immersion in Third World politics, the Algerian people's regular mass demonstrations after December 1960, and the OAS's headline-grabbing, vicious counternationalist terror campaign, Algeria became fixed in the global imagination as an important chapter in the popular new narrative of divergent hemispheres and clashing civilizations. In South Africa, for example, the FLN's endurance offered inspiration to the ANC's new armed wing, Umkhonto we Sizwe (Spear of the Nation, MK), even though one of its members would later recall ambivalently thinking that "in Algeria, the only other country with a large white minority of the settler type, the struggle was swimming in blood and not encouraging."[163] Certainly the grim scenes of intercommunal and racially motivated violence in North Africa and Congo preoccupied South Africa's white elite. A notably sympathetic US State Department report captured their concern in 1962: describing the apartheid state as "a last white stronghold against black invasion from the north and racialist-inspired upheavals from within," its author directly compared the polarization of the country's racial groups to the gulf of hatred and fear that had opened up between Algeria's Muslims and the pieds noirs.[164] The report's language strikingly echoed that of Raoul Salan, the former commander of all French forces in Algeria who joined the OAS after the failed coup of April 1961. Known as "the Mandarin" for his espousal of the Chinese- and Vietnamese-inspired doctrine of revolutionary war, Salan put his skills to use in the vain pursuit of what he called the "last battle for White Christian civilization in the northern part of Africa."[165]

Though Salan's battle would soon be lost, the discourse of civilizational rupture would have lasting consequences for Algeria. By 1961, war and incarceration weighed heavily on the FLN's famous leaders captured five years earlier, perhaps Ben Bella most of all. In a French prison one day in February 1961, Ahmed Ben Bella mourned to his cellmates, "We are soured, it's finished, we're no longer real Algerians!"[166] Years of war and incarceration plainly weighed heavily on the man who had somewhat arbitrarily become the public face of the FLN as a result of his famous capture in 1956, along with five other senior figures in the revolution, when the French army hijacked the Moroccan jet they were traveling in. Naturally, French security services listened in on many of their conversations during their imprisonment, which in Ben Bella's case in particular reveal a nationalist adrift, steeped in the era's battling ideologies, and struggling to recover a sense of identity. "We have a changed nature [now]," he observed on another occasion.

> It will take two or three generations in Algeria for the mentality to return to how it was. We are no longer normal, for me Western civilization is finished, Christian civilization is dead. Marxism has replaced it, it has responded to capitalism, it has responded to something false—it is false itself.[167]

Ben Bella's sense of dislocation and his desire for some sort of profound national reimagining or purpose were widely shared among the FLN's cadres and upper ranks. Their belief in a postcolonial tabula rasa would encourage bold ambitions for social and economic transformation, and they would look above all to their Third World allies for guidance in the pursuit of the "second stage" of the Algerian Revolution.

3

Real Existing Third Worldism

National Development in the Age of Ideologies

> We are not importing a foreign ideology into Tanzania and trying to smother our distinct social patterns with it. . . . Socialism is international; its ideas and beliefs relate to man in society, not just to Tanzanian man in Tanzania, or African man in Africa. But just because it is a universal concept so it must also relate to Tanzanian man in Tanzania.
> Julius K. Nyerere, *Freedom and Socialism: Uhuru na Ujamaa*, 1968

> In the course of seven and a half years of war, very favorable conditions for a socialist revolution were created and all those who stand outside that framework will be condemned by the people as counterrevolutionaries.
> Ahmed Ben Bella, March 1964

Judging by the behavior of the diplomatic community in New York, it seemed as if the whole world cheered when the independent République Algérienne Démocratique et Populaire (People's Democratic Republic of Algeria, RADP) finally joined the United Nations, on 8 October 1962. Indeed, during some of the Algerian Revolution's darkest days, with the French army hunting the mujahideen to the brink of extinction, the FLN's propaganda had tried to inspire its supporters with a vision of the Algerian flag flying on the plaza in front of the UN headquarters in New York, alongside those of all the other independent countries of world. As the human toll of their struggle mounted, this vision constituted a promise from the political commissars to their dying brethren that the gatekeepers of the "international community" would bear witness and give purpose to their sacrifice.[1] So when Prime Minister Ahmed Ben Bella, Secretary-General U Thant, and various other international dignitaries at last gathered on a gray and drizzling Manhattan day to witness the fulfillment of that promise, inclement weather could not detract from the momentousness of the occasion.[2] In addition to the obvious significance of the flag-raising ceremony for Ben Bella and his compatriots, Thant also took deep satisfaction from the admission of the UN's newest member state. Given how the FLN had so publicly valorized the institutions, principles, and symbols of the post-1945 international system—above all the organization that the Burmese secretary-general presided over—Algeria's independence eliminated a perennial stain on the system's legitimacy and credibility. "The admission of Algeria to the United Nations is the end of a long and painful drama," he told the ceremony's attendees, "... [but it] confirms the fact that the United Nations is indeed an effective force in the liberation of all nations from all forms of alien rule. It adds strength to the reality of the United Nations as an organization of the world community, in which every nation can find a tangible expression of its independence."[3] That is, he celebrated Algerian independence not only as the end of a violent conflict but also as a confirmation of the UN's role as arbiter of the new international order. The Algerians had insisted on sovereign statehood that bore that organization's imprimatur.

Of course, the rich and powerful countries that dominated the UN's agenda had deferred to geopolitical expediency and French pressure until the time, roughly two years prior, at which developing countries sympathetic to the FLN's cause had become too numerous in the General Assembly to rebuff. The Ghanaian representative on the Security Council had briefly reminded his colleagues of these contentions on 4 October 1962, observing that "if ... one must talk about a country being ripe for nationhood ... then Algeria is over-ripe and should have been represented here a long time ago."[4] But overwhelmingly, the diplomatic community preferred to overlook recent awkwardness and to celebrate Algeria's independence in the same spirit as the secretary-general. There was almost an audible sigh of relief through their ranks when Ben Bella and his party joined the General Assembly. His speech to that body, on 9 October, was perhaps the most anticipated event of the session. Returning sluggishly from lunch, several excellencies decried the atypical promptness with which the proceedings began, and with the exception of the Israeli delegation that took exception to the Algerian prime minister's bellicose expression of support for Palestinian nationalists, the entire assembly rose in hearty applause at the speech's conclusion. Even the delegates from the Republic of China rather hesitantly deferred to the spirit of the occasion—in spite of Ben Bella's clear advocacy of communist China's admission to the UN.[5] The Algerians continued to enjoy the spotlight over the next week, juggling appearances on televised news programs, invitations to visit countries as varied as Great Britain and the Soviet Union, and meetings with the likes of Dr. Martin Luther King, Cuban president Osvaldo Dorticós, and, in Washington, President Kennedy. Suddenly, after years of struggling to be heard, all doors were open to them. Naturally, this outpouring of warm sentiment had not banished cynicism from the corridors of power. As the British ambassador in New York noted, the Algerians enjoyed widespread sympathy for their terrible experience of war, but their prestige and influence in the Third World also made them valuable potential allies for numerous interests.[6]

Such calculus—which the Algerians welcomed and encouraged—did not detract from the fact that Algeria's independence was a significant step toward the completion of a structurally homogeneous world system, or the replacement of the heterogeneities of the imperial order with nominally equivalent and equal states. Although Algeria was perhaps not the most emphatic demonstration of this process in this period—that probably being those colonial territories that had a largely theoretical statehood thrust upon them in spite of their near-total lack of real-world state functionality or capacity—the FLN had managed to defeat one of the most determined efforts by an imperial power to prevent the emergence of a fully sovereign state in a former colonial territory.[7] In October 1962, the international community hailed Algerian independence as a triumph for France, and for Charles de Gaulle personally. The French foreign minister, Maurice Couve de Murville, flew into New York to make a show of introducing this former colony to the world. "France has now completed her task," he announced grandly, an interpretation of recent events that the American ambassador, Adlai Stevenson, supporting by saluting de Gaulle as "that brave soldier ... whose vision made it possible to cut the chains which held the people of Algeria."[8] In reality, de Gaulle spent the war's final two years fighting a rearguard action against Algerian sovereignty, which he tried to curtail or redefine in a variety of ways. But the Evian Accords of March 1962 that granted Algeria independence, the result of interminable and hostile negotiations between the French government and the GPRA, deferred to the new global consensus. While numerous anticolonial conflicts remained unresolved—Vietnam, South Africa, Portuguese Africa, and so on—there was little further debate about the ideal structural organization of international society. There was near-unanimous sentiment around the world, North and South, that sovereign statehood constituted the most legitimate, or even solely legitimate, vehicle for human emancipation.

Therefore, by 1962 the Third World's structural reformism was shifting from the political realm to the economic one. Postcolonial elites saw rapid industrialization and (typically socialist) economic transformation as an existential imperative: as the Ghanaian president, Kwame Nkrumah, had told an American audience several years prior, "We cannot tell our peoples that material benefits and growth and modern progress are not for them. If we do, they will throw us out and seek other leaders who promise more."[9] Yet, the prevailing view across the Southern Hemisphere was that the international economy was unfair and exploitative by design, simply the continuation of the colonial system by another name. When more than thirty poor countries, mostly former colonies, convened in Cairo in July 1962 for the Conference on the Problems of Economic Development, they decried that their economic progress was being held back by "international factors beyond their control and [by] tendencies which might have the result of *perpetrating past structures* of international economic relations."[10] Capitalizing on the momentum generated by the nonaligned summit in Belgrade the previous year, the Cairo meeting also boasted stronger Latin American participation than Belgrade and enjoyed the approval of the Argentinian economist Raul Prebisch, who was the most influential advocate for the development agenda within the UN. The participants called for that organization to convene a still larger, more representative conference that could begin the process of reforming the patterns of global trade and aid in a comprehensive fashion. That autumn, the poor countries then used their newfound majority in the General Assembly to approve the proposal, despite the opposition of Western governments who feared that the so-called United Nations Conference on Trade and Development (UNCTAD) threatened Bretton Woods, the General Agreement on Tariffs and Trade (GATT), and the European Economic Community (EEC).[11] Increasingly, Third World actors and opinion makers described political independence as merely the precursor to the more important task of "economic decolonization," necessitating at least as profound a confrontation with the status quo as had been achieved in the destruction of the imperial order.

Algeria's new leaders were not simply exemplary of this trend—they hoped to steer it. As they contemplated Algeria's uncertain future in the closing stages of the war, the majority of FLN cadres seemed to agree that political decolonization in itself did not address the root causes of the revolution, which they deemed to be material deprivation and the disparity of modes of life between North and South. At the tempestuous final meeting of the wartime leadership in Tripoli, Libya, early in the summer of 1962, Ben Bella distributed a tract that called for rapid socioeconomic transformation through socialist revolution. Although the Tripoli Program was as vague in its policy prescriptions as it was ardent in its ideological stance, the victors in that summer's brief intra-FLN struggle for power treated it as the rhetorical firmament of postcolonial political life—the "Koran of the Algerian Revolution," according to one tract distributed by the new government.[12] Meanwhile, Algerian workers and peasants began seizing French-owned factories and farms on their own initiative, which further emboldened Ben Bella and his colleagues while also garnering a great deal of sympathetic attention abroad. Trotskyists, anarchists, and fellow travelers of various stripes made their way to Algiers to participate in the construction of a new kind of society, superior to both the Western and communist models, on the ruins of colonialism. Though local wits quickly dubbed the new arrivals the "pieds rouges," their enthusiasm lent credibility to the government's claim that Algeria could be a "pilot state," or an exemplar to the rest of the developing world. As one of the country's diplomats explained at the UN that autumn,

"Political independence opens the way to a new stage of the national project. The transformation of mentalities, accompanying accelerated economic development to the benefit of all of the people, will allow Algeria to make up for a delay accumulated over generations."[13] Algeria's pell-mell pursuit of real existing Third Worldism (to adapt a well-known Soviet expression) was fueled not only by a sense of urgent necessity but also by one of optimism.

This chapter also explores the effects of the Cold War context on Algeria's modernization drive. For the North African country, as for the large majority of Third World states, economic decolonization was an emphatically outward-looking process. Certainly, the Tripoli Program described France's continued economic hegemony as a fundamental barrier to the socialist revolution, with Ben Bella assuring his colleagues that his plan would create "all the conditions to make the French leave and . . . create the conditions for the revision of the [Evian] accords."[14] But the watchword of Algerian economic policy would be diversification—of trading partners and aid donors—rather than autarky. The new country would not lack for opportunities to multiply its international economic relationships, since its influence in foreign affairs as well as its energy resources ensured that an array of would-be benefactors, of every ideological variety, immediately reached out with assistance and advice in the summer of 1962. Thus, in contrast to the clash between Third Worldism and neoliberal globalization that transpired later in the twentieth century, Algeria offers a striking demonstration of how sovereignty was actually a boon, perhaps even a prerequisite, for economic development in the early 1960s, thanks to geopolitical competition and the new institutional mechanisms that privileged it. On the other hand, as we shall see, the country's first postcolonial leaders would quickly find it much more difficult to preserve their ideological autonomy from the relentless doctrinal conflicts of their time.

The Uncertainties of Evian

A curious quality of the Evian Accords of March 1962 is that they were almost as important a milestone for the evolution of the French national identity as they were for the Algerian one. The formal separation of the two territories was perhaps the most profound—and certainly the most difficult—step in the dismantling of the empire and reorientation of France's "national mission" inward and toward Europe. With metropolitan France in the midst of *les trente glorieuses*, or thirty glorious years, a period of unprecedented economic growth and social transformation, the goal of perfecting this new way of life was far more pressing for the French public than that of bringing civilization to the downtrodden of Africa and Asia. By the time that French-FLN negotiations began in earnest in early 1961 (there had been several previous attempts over the years), the *mission civilisatrice* was more commonly described as the *fardeau colonial* (colonial burden), a drain on resources needed at home.[15] By 1961, the editor of the well-read *Paris-Match* magazine, Raymond Cartier, was popularizing the view that the economics of colonialism simply did not add up to France's advantage.[16] Naturally, in the case of Algeria, war-weariness weighed increasingly heavily on public opinion, but that slice of North Africa so recently considered sovereign French territory was also at the center of growing discomfort with immigration from the colonies, fueled by cultural friction as well as economic concerns.[17] In other words, more and more French citizens came to share the FLN's contention that their two lands were fundamentally different and, crucially, divergent. As the affirmation of two separate national identities, one defined by poverty and one by wealth, the Evian Accords would thereby constitute mutual recognition of a global dichotomy between North and South, First World and Third.

In other respects, however, the Evian settlement was not the clarifying historical event that de Gaulle in particular would claim it to be. Not only was practically every fundamental aspect of Algeria's future combatively contested during months of prolonged and acrimonious negotiation, but the concluding agreements offered much less certainty to the inhabitants of Algeria than to those of France, who at that point mostly ceased paying attention to affairs on the southern shore of the Mediterranean. The beginning of serious negotiations, in early 1961, exposed a continued vagueness to the FLN's agenda in addition to significant differences of opinion among its leading cadres and commanders. With the French government and the FLN starting out with contradictory expectations for even the most basic territorial, political, and socioeconomic characteristics of the new Algeria, the nationalist rebels initially found agreement among themselves only on the question of tactics.

Citing Mao's edict to "fight while negotiating, negotiate while fighting," they were determined to maintain their military campaign until the conclusion of a final and comprehensive agreement, while the GPRA's diplomats took an equally combative approach to the talks themselves.[18] Feeling as outgunned at the negotiating table as the mujahideen were in the field, with their comrades watching hawkishly over their shoulders for any signs of compromise, the front's negotiators essentially adopted a defensive, obstructionist posture by which they broke off the talks on more than one occasion to avoid being drawn into debates that they might lose. In the long run, this stubborn approach forced de Gaulle to concede on one issue after another, but it also prejudiced the FLN's attitude toward any negotiated settlement. Ultimately, even the front's own negotiators would distance themselves from the Evian Accords, leaving Algeria without a roadmap.

From the French perspective, apart from the numerous concrete interests at stake (the status of the pieds noirs, substantial business interests, oil and gas, military bases, and the nuclear test sites in the desert), few in the establishment could imagine handing over Algeria wholesale to an organization that many considered little better than a band of trumped-up bandits and killers. "But what was this GPRA?" de Gaulle's main adviser on Algeria, Bernard Tricot, remembered wondering. "This thing that was 'neither one thing nor the other' . . . [t]his revolutionary organism presented itself as a government without ever exercising any territorial authority, and claimed to represent a State that had never existed."[19] As Matthew Connelly has pointed out, it was entirely natural for the French government to begin with the assumption that all of the various zero-sum issues at stake in the separation of France and Algeria would be resolved at the expense of the latter's sovereignty. That is, Algeria's European community should certainly retain political influence disproportionate to its share of the population, as well as its economic interests and property; Algeria would remain tightly integrated with (i.e., subordinate to) the French economy; it probably ought not to have an independent foreign policy; and the Sahara was not to be integrated with the populous northern region, remaining instead under French administration for the benefit of multiple neighboring countries.[20] Strategically, while de Gaulle was impatient to be rid of the "Algerian problem," he also intended to solve it in a manner true to his message of postcolonial "interdependence" and *coopération* for francophone Africa as a whole. Of course, he also had to placate the now twice-mutinous elements among the pieds noirs and the French officer corps.

In contrast, after its initial exchanges with the French negotiators, the FLN's provisional government confessed to feeling greatly outmatched by its opponents' wealth of experience, expertise, and meticulous argumentation. The MAE quickly cobbled together a commission of "brothers with some political and military experience" in order to study vital issues such as the historical identity of the Sahara, but it warned its colleagues that "this situation was not ideal since, as you know, this area is new to us."[21] The danger of this situation was already becoming evident by the early summer of 1961, with the international community saluting General de Gaulle's "constructive" and "courageous" initiatives to end the war while the nationalists still struggled to present a compelling response. For example, the MAE noted that sympathetic governments like that of the USSR continued to ask in vain for the FLN's official position on the Sahara. The diplomatic team admitted that "there is some astonishment in various diplomatic milieux that we have not issued a 'white paper' at a time when this problem has become so crucial."[22] Plainly, the FLN's acclaimed international wing and public relations apparatus were falling short at the vital moment, and the pressure was showing. "After seven years of pitiless war," they told themselves, "we have no right to disgrace a people who have earned the world's admiration." It was imperative that they "assess the situation with rigorous honesty . . . and find the best solutions to the most difficult problems."[23] To that effect, the full collective leadership of the movement, the Conseil National de la Révolution Algérienne (CNRA), convened in a Tripoli hotel that August in order to hash out these problems and unite behind a common platform for the duration of the negotiations.

Unfortunately, the FLN had never excelled at formulating and disseminating a comprehensive political doctrine. Certain branches of the movement had seen a substantial degree of political development and radicalization—most notably the young cadres of the provisional government, the MAE, and the officer corps of the "border army" under the command of Houari Boumedienne in Tunisia and Morocco. But the same fractured and decentralized structure that made the FLN so difficult to destroy also impeded communication and political development, while stoking internecine rivalries among individuals, regional networks, and organizational "clans." With its different branches often resembling compartmentalized fiefdoms, the front's "transnational" nature was simultaneously its greatest strength and its greatest weakness. The younger generation that was gradually asserting itself through the GPRA had begun to rail vocally against this state of affairs, decrying "the nonexistence of a precise general orientation, . . . the subjective interpretations of goals and means, . . . [and] the lack of uniform structures, methods, systems, or rules."[24] Their complaints echoed those of Boumedienne and his lieutenants in the ALN, who had prioritized correcting the perceived deficiency of their troops' political education and also invoked the Leninist mantras of "revolutionary discipline" and "democratic centralism" as solutions to the movement's inconsistencies. The latter proposed replacing the cabinet of the provisional government with the Bureau Politique, or political bureau, supposedly in order to streamline and centralize authority. Such concerns were manifestations of the ideological inadequacy that increasingly pervaded the FLN (or key sections of it, at least) as a result of the original founders' decision to use revolutionary praxis shorn of the theories that inspired it.

Yet, more senior figures still remembered the logic behind that decision: namely, that it was better to avoid discussing fundamental questions about Algeria's identity in order to create the broadest possible coalition. This prioritization of unity over political development was the key distinction between a "front" and a "party." Unfortunately, the Evian talks obliged the FLN to define Algeria in a way that risked alienating certain consistencies. Indeed, many of de Gaulle's proposals that year aimed to sow division among the rebels. For example, his espousal of a *multicommunitaire* (multicommunal) federal system for Algeria had in mind the interests not only of the European community but also of communities within the Muslim population with distinct cultural identities, such as Berbers in Kabylia and the smaller Jewish and Moazabite (in the Sahara) communities. In fact, the GPRA's interior minister, Lakhdar Bentobbal, was so conscious of the danger of schism along religious, linguistic, ethnic, or political lines that he actually warned his comrades against convening the CNRA at all that summer. The effort to agree on a common doctrine, he said, might "conclude in the most unanticipated ways, endangering the Revolution itself [by] igniting certain arguments, leading to very grave, possibly insoluble divergences."[25] In short, the transition from transnational resistance movement to nation-state was fraught with existential challenges.

Bentobbal's warning proved astute. Despite noble intent—"every great friend of our Revolution, President Mao Zedong chief among them," declared one participant, "has insisted a thousand times that 'to win, you must remain united' "—in reality factional politics preoccupied the August 1961 CNRA, at the expense of the meeting's primary purpose of codifying a political platform and a negotiating strategy. Indeed, the first concern for many of the participants was to stop Boumedienne's steady accretion of power through his control of the border army. More numerous, better equipped, and better organized than the ALN mujahideen inside Algeria, at this point, this force boasted approximately 30,000 troops and consumed the large majority of the revolution's total budget. Collectively, the CNRA (which numbered about fifty people in theory, with some unable to attend due to interdiction or incarceration) rejected Boumedienne's proposal to replace the provisional government with the Bureau Politique and instead streamlined the GPRA's cabinet by reducing the number of ministers and trimming the diversity of perspectives represented there.[26] Benyoucef Ben Khedda and Saad Dahlab replaced Ferhat Abbas and Belkacem Krim as president and foreign minister, respectively, thereby demoting one of the best-known figures in Arab Algerian politics (Abbas) as well as the only founder of the FLN to have avoided death or incarceration (Krim). Ben Khedda also took charge of economics and finance at the expense of Ahmed Francis, an ally of Abbas and former parliamentarian in his liberal party, the Union Démocratique du Manifeste Algérien. As a result of these contentious changes, several weighty individuals left Tripoli angry and resentful. In particular, Boumedienne and his allies loathed the leaders of the GPRA.

The promotion of Ben Khedda and Dahlab, combined with the slimming down of the cabinet, gave a somewhat false impression of ideological development. Childhood friends who had both belonged to the more radical wing of Messali Hadj's PPA-MTLD in the prerevolutionary period, Ben Khedda and Dahlab identified strongly with the leftist Third Worldist trend. Already nicknamed "the Chinaman" in some quarters on account of his open admiration for Mao's accomplishments, Ben Khedda made one of his first public statements as president to reconfirm the importance of the FLN's Third Worldist orientation and its friendships in East Asia. The seeming eclipse of socially conservative and liberal factions prompted French intelligence to conclude that the movement had finally completed the transition from nationalist movement to genuinely revolutionary one.²⁷ Rédha Malek, a key member of the provisional government's negotiating team, likewise believed that the new-look GPRA would perform better for being more "homogeneous" than the previous one.²⁸

Yet, in reality, so intense was the maneuvering and politicking in Tripoli that little was accomplished on a doctrinal level. A telling report by the Ministry of External Affairs reveals that the CNRA's instructions to its negotiating team simply ordered it to stick to the two very broad and vague principles of "national unity" and "territorial integrity," and to break off the talks whenever these principles were in danger, rather than risk engaging the French on technicalities or nuanced positions.²⁹ In light of the bad blood created at the Tripoli meeting, with the likes of Boumedienne inveterately critical of the GPRA's handling of the talks with France, these scant instructions ensured that the FLN's negotiators would be extremely cautious and obstructionist. The talks broke down several times in the following months, with the GPRA team recognizing that practically any concession on its part could be condemned as a violation of "national unity" or "territorial integrity."³⁰

Nevertheless, the FLN's negotiating strategy was ultimately very successful because French national unity was crumbling more quickly and more visibly than that of the Algerian rebels. Most notably, de Gaulle managed to quell an attempted coup d'état in April 1961, led by a cabal of bitter-end army officers that included some of the most senior commanders of the Algerian War. The *putschists*' plans to essentially invade the mainland from Algeria, perhaps by dropping parachutists into Paris in order to impose a government committed to winning the war, ultimately fell flat in the face of public and rank-and-file opposition, deftly mobilized by de Gaulle's stirring televised oratory. Given that three-quarters of mainland voters had approved in a January 1961 referendum to grant their president free license to pursue Algeria's self-determination, the plotters were hopelessly out of step with general sentiment.³¹ Many of them went into hiding afterward, some helping to found the notorious new terrorist organization, the Organisation Armée Secrète (OAS), through which diehard soldiers and pieds noirs would brutalize the Muslim inhabitants of Oran and Algiers for the reminder of the war. While the French army in Algeria remained a potent fighting force—a fact that would allow both the military and the political elite to cling to the myth of victory in the years to come—the reality was that the civilian government's decapitation of the command structure constituted a resounding defeat in a war that both the FLN and the French brass had long since acknowledged as being fundamentally *political* in nature.

Additionally, in the latter part of the year, the FLN escalated its battle against Messali's remaining supporters in France's Algerian immigrant community, and the resultant upsurge of violence further eroded the public's patience for the interminable "emergency" in North Africa. Finally, one of the most notorious and controversial episodes of the war occurred on 17 October 1961, when the Parisian police smashed a pro-FLN demonstration in the capital with extreme brutality—shooting, beating, and even drowning in the Seine as many as 200 protesters. In spite of the censors' determined efforts to conceal the extent of the violence (an effort maintained for nearly forty years), the savagery routine to the colonial system had revealed itself in the center of Paris to all those who were willing to see it.[32] Given this litany of dour news, it should be unsurprising that President de Gaulle himself was openly losing patience with the Algerian conflict and the tortuous pace of the Evian talks. He had already told a close adviser that August, "We must free ourselves of this 'box of sorrows' in which we expend all our energies for nothing."[33]

Time now worked in the FLN's favor at the negotiating table. Having already made one decisive concession at the outset of the talks by agreeing to begin negotiations without a ceasefire in place, de Gaulle was now frustrated by the GPRA's stubborn willingness to walk away rather than concede any major points that touched on the FLN's inviolable principles of "national and territorial unity." Consequently, toward the close of 1961, he unilaterally abandoned many of the pillars of the French position simply to hasten the negotiations' conclusion, even if on the FLN's terms. He dropped the effort to cultivate and negotiate in parallel with a "third force" in Algerian politics that would be in competition with the FLN, thereby conceding that the front alone spoke for Algeria. He dropped, too, the related suggestion of a *multicommunitaire* Algeria that would feature communal power-sharing or even federated enclaves of religious and linguistic minorities (primarily the "Europeans" but possibly also Jews and Berbers). Yet the threat of these proposals had already had an effect on the FLN's political philosophy. The front's cadres had condemned these proposals—among themselves as well as to their allies—by drawing on Third Worldist reference points and precedents. For example, one communiqué from the GPRA leadership to the front's militants in Paris described de Gaulle's "desire at any cost to create a puppet state in the style of Israel, . . . [since] major French and international interests want to quickly create a new voice in Algeria, as in China, Korea, Vietnam, the Middle East (Israel), Congo and so on."[34] One implication for Algeria's domestic politics after independence was that subnational constituencies such as Kabyle Berbers risked being perceived and portrayed by the new national authorities as divisive neocolonial stooges if they strongly asserted separate cultural, linguistic, or religious identities. Indeed, through this Third Worldist prism, political pluralism in general appeared to be the tool of neocolonial manipulators. Probably most reluctantly of all, de Gaulle also gave up hope of continuing to administer and exploit the hydrocarbon-rich Sahara under the aegis of the Organisation Commune des Régions Sahariennes (Common Organization of the Saharan Regions, OCRS), which supposedly developed the region for the benefit of all neighboring countries. While the prospect certainly intrigued the governments of Tunisia, Morocco, and Mali, among others, they recognized that it was politically untenable to be seen to collaborate with France in the dismemberment of territory that the GPRA had successfully convinced the wider world was Algerian.[35]

Therefore, with all these fundamental issues resolved, the basic outlines of a final agreement were apparent by January 1962. The entirety of Algerian territory would become a single sovereign state; that state would not be federated; the FLN would agree to uphold the pieds noirs' property rights and grant them the same status as the Muslim citizenry; France would likely continue to use certain military installations—above all the nuclear testing sites in the desert—for a finite period; and the French government would also ensure Algeria's continued development (and its continued adherence to these concessions) through very significant economic assistance.[36] Collectively, these basic parameters of an agreement amounted to an emphatic affirmation of the principles of postcolonial sovereignty and nation-statehood. Even though the FLN obtained a much more comprehensive form of national liberation than that first expressed, for example, in the original declaration of 1 November 1954, an ironic consequence of de Gaulle's negotiating strategy was to make that final settlement far less palatable to the rebels than it would have been if offered earlier.

At the same time, the negotiations spurred an interesting evolution in the front's position on economic questions. On the one hand, one of the goals—arguably the most fundamental goal—of the Algerian Revolution was the destruction of the colonial economy. As the GPRA's ambassador to the Arab countries, Tewfik El Madani, told a Swiss journalist in April 1961, "The existence of a [Muslim] rural and urban proletariat accounts for the violence and tenacity of the Algerian rebellion.... Political independence appears to them as the dawn of a more just social life, an end to their misery."[37] Madani revealed that he was participating in a small working group in Cairo devoted to studying in depth those economic questions long underanalyzed by the FLN, and this former member of Sheikh Ben Badis's reformist ulema in the 1930s had come to accept a functional, economic raison d'être for the Algerian nationalist movement to a striking degree. After all, one might have expected this traditionally educated scion of a noble family, author of the first nationalist history of the country, *Kitab Al-Djazaïr* (1932), to be fully invested in an essentialist Algerian narrative, but here he was attributing the revolution to historic contingency in very "Western," social science–like terms.[38] "Doubtless certain moral factors—the humiliation of being a second-class citizen in one's own country—played an important role in unleashing the Algerian liberation movement," he said, "but the destitution of seven million Algerians ... is the fundamental cause of the 1954 revolution."[39]

As suggested by Madani's reliance on the statistics and analysis of a new left-wing think tank in Paris, the Club Jean Moulin, the front's conception of economic concerns relied at least as much on French perspectives as on Marxist theory. In many ways, the nationalists seem to have accepted and appropriated the insights of those French academics who had been recruited by the counterinsurgency campaign to devise strategies to steer Algerian peasants away from the rebels. Now that independence had come to seem like an inevitability in the near term, certain French economic initiatives stopped being threats to the revolution and instead became prizes of victory. Thus, as early as April 1961, Mohammed Khider could prophesy to Ben Bella, Aït Ahmed, and their other jail mates that "thanks to its modernism and the benefits resulting from the Constantine Plan, the Algerian state will be a pilot state [*état pilote*] for the Arab world of tomorrow."[40] By the end of the year, French officials realized that, where the FLN had previously tried to impose a boycott, the front was now encouraging Algerians to enroll in the plan's projects in order to hasten the day when they could run things themselves.[41]

Of course, there was a more radical component to the FLN's economic plans, which was focused for the most part on the peasant question. The nationalists' main criticism of the Constantine Plan was that it sought to preserve the European grip on the land, and perhaps their one clearly and consistently expressed goal after independence was radical land distribution, with the likelihood of some kind of socialist ownership and management system. Moreover, regardless of the abstract discussions within the GPRA offices in Cairo and Tunis, local reports show that the Algerian peasantry were already taking land redistribution as a given by the end of 1961.[42] Overall, then, the FLN's economic theorizing, such as it was, had been largely spurred by French initiatives and had settled on a hybrid philosophy that happily borrowed from Paris's plans and "pilot country" rhetoric, while proposing more revolutionary solutions in key areas of differentiation.[43]

Two vital developments occurred in parallel in January and February 1962: the conclusion of the Franco-FLN negotiations and the forging of an anti-GPRA and ambiguously anti-Evian alliance within the front, with Boumedienne and Ben Bella at its head. Typically, scholars have judged this alliance in an essentially opportunistic light: united by their desire for power, Ben Bella and Boumedienne complemented each other's strengths. The older man was the most famous public face of the revolution and had moral authority as one of the FLN's founding members, but he lacked a substantial network of clients. In contrast, Boumedienne commanded the front's armed forces yet avoided the limelight, and his rise was much resented by older figures.[44] The GPRA intellectual turned historian Mohammed Harbi has a characteristically caustic appraisal of Boumedienne's motivations. By his reckoning, when the ALN boss sent his trusted lieutenant Abdelaziz Bouteflika to visit the front's imprisoned leaders in January, he pulled the wool over a credulous Ben Bella's eyes, eager as the latter was to discover a genuinely revolutionary younger generation within the nationalist movement. Just twenty-four years old and bursting with Fanonist rhetoric—and reputed stenographer for *Wretched of the Earth*—Bouteflika certainly seemed to fit this description.[45]

However, without denying the role of naked ambition, there was a more substantive ideological basis for this alliance than has been generally acknowledged. The documentary record shows that Boumedienne called for the ALN to implement communist-style organizational reforms and political training as least by late 1959. Ben Bella, meanwhile, admitted to having fallen under the sway of a great deal of communist literature during his long internment, which is amply supported by the French intelligence service's continuous recordings of his conversations. In a conversation from January 1961, for example, he shared aloud his dream of a "complete leveling of the existing social classes" after independence and the institution of five years' collective labor for every citizen. "The State will feed and house them," he suggested, " . . . and this will mobilize the masses to rebuild the country and launch it toward prosperity."[46] Accordingly, the new allies' first action was to reach out to a group of the GPRA's disaffected young intellectuals, mostly in the MAE, who resigned in mid-February in protest of what they deemed the provisional government's perennially unrevolutionary atmosphere of clannishness and personal politics. They responded positively to Ben Bella's offer to "put them to work" on a new ideological platform, extended through a mutual friend, Mohammed Khemisti, a thirty-one-year-old militant in the FLN's student union from the same small town in eastern Algeria.[47]

Thus, at Ben Bella's urging, the authors of what would become the Tripoli Program gathered in Cairo, under the watchful eye of another trusted friend, the Mukhabarat intelligence officer, Fathi Al Dib. The group consisted of Malek, the Evian negotiator; Harbi from the MAE's central office; Mohammed Benyahia, who had represented the FLN at Bandung in 1955; and Mostega Lacheraf, the front's poet-propagandist who later became the establishment historian of Algerian nationalism. In addition, Ben Bella's phone records indicate that two more MAE diplomats had some involvement—Lakhdar Brahimi, who had recently returned from a mission to Havana, and Abdelmalek Benhabylès, whose nom de guerre was Socrates in recognition of his erudition. "What interests us most at the moment," Ben Bella instructed, "are our party, our organizations, and the goals they pursue. . . . Above all a single party is needed, whose directing committee will have supervision over everything, including the government."[48] That said, working from an initial draft drawn up by Ben Bella and Mohammed Khider, who was the only other member of the six imprisoned leaders who joined this coalition, the young intellectuals went far beyond questions of organization and governance and seized the opportunity to air their views on the core purpose and definition of the Algerian Revolution. "The concept of *coopération*," they wrote, " ... constitutes the most typical expression of French neocolonialist policies. ... [*Coopération*] represents a grave danger to the Revolution by assuming the seductive guises of liberalism, and of financial and economic cooperation that only purports to be disinterested."[49] The Tripoli Program was a fine example of leftist, Third Worldist internationalist thought, to which Ben Bella then tacked on a few references to religion and Algeria's Islamic identity.[50]

In late May, the CNRA convened for the last time, once again in a Tripoli hotel. Evian was signed, the FLN's prisoners had all been released, and a Provisional Executive headed by a moderate Muslim politician bore the responsibility of transitioning Algeria to independence, formally scheduled for early July. All was not going smoothly, however. Inside Algeria, the OAS's scorched-earth campaign invited FLN reprisals, and there were already indications of mass exodus by the pieds noirs. Within the nationalist movement, moreover, the choreographed bonhomie of the reunited leadership's first public appearances in March and April had turned to open confrontation in Tripoli, where foreign journalists found the fifty-odd members of the CNRA divided into various factions seated at separate tables in the hotel's dining room.[51] The primary contest, however, pitted the provisional government against the Ben Bella–Boumedienne coalition. Although the latter did not hesitate to exploit personal resentments such as the grudge Ferhat Abbas held against Ben Khedda for deposing him one year earlier, they also used their new ideological platform to discredit the GPRA and seize the initiative.

The minutes indicate that Ben Bella and one of Boumedienne's closest lieutenants, Ahmed Kaïd (also known as "Commander Slimane"), dominated the proceedings (Boumedienne avoided the spotlight himself). Ahmed Kaïd led the call for instituting more disciplined and more revolutionary political structures; decrying the wartime FLN's perennial failings with regard to organization and doctrine, he argued that "it's time to break with the past. ... Three things are required: an ideology, a party, and leadership." As was the case a year earlier, the buzzword of the meeting was "homogeneity," which Ahmed Kaïd insisted required tighter central leadership in the form of the Bureau Politique.[52] On the one hand, his proposal was a naked bid to sideline the GPRA, prompting Ben Khedda and his allies to storm out of Tripoli early and regroup in Tunis. Yet the idea of the Bureau Politique also drew on the suspicion, common in the Third World, that a more open political system would simply allow imperialists to manipulate regional and subnational interest groups at the expense of a fragile nation.

Likewise, Ben Bella's call for social and economic revolution jibed with the general sentiments of those present, but the language of the Tripoli Program also channeled their unformed and disparate opinions into a much more overtly socialist and comprehensive ideological platform. By emphasizing the peasantry above all, and the need for profound agrarian reform, Ben Bella was in sync with the great many figures in the FLN for whom the national struggle was fundamentally about land. "The Algerian Revolution has been driven above all by the fellahs [peasants]," they told a Swiss journalist in early 1961. "French projects for agrarian reform are motivated by the desire to legalize the expropriations of the peasants' land [during colonization]."[53] Although the Evian settlement anticipated some degree of land redistribution, Ben Bella made plain his personal intent to make most of the European settlers leave, and he dubbed the accords a "bottleneck" on the revolution because of the stipulation that the owners of nationalized properties be adequately compensated. If French officials thought that *coopération* could ride out a storm over the peasant question, they underestimated the import of the Tripoli Program's broader schema. "*Coopération* as conceived in French eyes is the maintenance of colonialism in the form of neocolonialism," Ben Bella declared. "The single word 'independence' does not mean anything; it is thus in Cuba, in Mauritania etc. That is why there is an economic and social aspect to the Program."[54]

On subsequent reflection, recalling the manifold contrasts in biography and bearing between France's polished diplomats and the FLN's delegation of ex-guerrillas and self-appointed statesmen, Bernard Tricot had concluded that "if not for a distrust of dichotomies, one would be tempted to say that two opposing worlds met each other at Evian."[55] He perhaps did not appreciate the degree to which this notion inspired his Algerian counterparts, since they believed that the division between North and South was the most fundamental feature of international life. Apart from the obvious zero-sum issues at stake in the Evian negotiations, vital as they were, narratively the impeccably Third Worldist Tripoli Program was fundamentally contradictory to de Gaulle's vision of postcolonial interdependence. In fact, there was more room for compromise in the substantive issues than in the realm of rhetoric and atmospherics, since the FLN basically agreed with the French explanation for the causes of their revolution and welcomed French solutions for Algeria's ills such as the Constantine Plan. Yet the FLN's continued legitimacy as a whole, in addition to Ben Bella's and Boumedienne's personal claims to leadership, depended on the premise of an incomplete revolution. Their goal was to make Algeria into the exemplary Third World country, not just free of French troops and economic domination, but also a model of development and refuge to other revolutionaries. "The Algerian problem is not fully resolved," the MAE warned in the wake of the Evian Accords. "We will have to continue the struggle against foreign domination in a new form. The international impact of our struggle, and our country's dynamism and revolutionary experience give us this choice."[56] As the postcolonial relationship quickly foundered in the months ahead, de Gaulle would find no solace in the ironic fact that the Algerian revolutionaries had inherited almost as many of their ambitions from him as they had from Mao, Castro, or Nasser.

Tabula Rasa

The brief period between the signing of the Evian Accords, in March 1962, and the formation of the first Algerian government that September (with the formal end of French rule on 5 July) did not simply herald the transition from one era to the next—it constituted a consequential historical inflection point in own right. Although the existence of two largely incompatible roadmaps for Algeria's future—the Evian Accords and the Tripoli Program—testified to the gulf between elites old and new, events on the ground that summer soon made a mockery of the careful plans of both factions. Contrary to expectations, the overwhelming majority of Algeria's European community decided that the end of *l'Algérie française* imposed a choice between "the suitcase or the coffin," so they fled the land of their birth in a panicked exodus. With their departure, economic activity practically ground to halt. So, too, was the rest of the Algerian population in a state of flux, since the war had uprooted nearly half of them, pushing them from the scorched countryside into the slums, the French *regroupement* centers, or refugee camps in Tunisia and Morocco. Most people would never return to their prewar lives, moving en masse to the cities instead. Furthermore, Algeria's political situation was equally chaotic and dysfunctional in this period: the transitional authority agreed on at Evian could not cope with the sheer scale of the country's social upheavals and humanitarian needs, yet the FLN was preoccupied with an internal power struggle that threatened to escalate into full-blown civil war. All told, the summer of 1962 was characterized by a profound sense of dislocation and uncertainty, with many of the basic assumptions underlying the recent Evian Accords and Tripoli Program already overtaken by events.

However, that sense of uncertainty proved formative by stoking the myth of Algeria as a tabula rasa, a supposed "blank slate" ripe for ideological experimentation. On the one hand, the sudden departure of most of the country's predominantly pied noir managerial and professional class, as well as the resultant economic collapse, emboldened those who favored rapid and revolutionary changes to Algeria's socioeconomic structures. The following April, for example, an Algerian official visiting Belgrade explained to his hosts that the millions of peasants who had been forced from their land during the war had lost their connection to the idea of private property, creating the ideal conditions for agricultural collectivization.⁵⁷ Indeed, acting on their own initiative during the previous summer's vacuum of governance, many Algerian workers formed "self-management committees" to administer businesses and farms abandoned by their owners. On the other hand, outsiders of diverse ideological and political perspectives generally agreed that Algeria provided an opportunity to break definitively with the old order. On the left, many of the Trotskyists and anarchists flooding into Algiers harbored near-utopian dreams of building the perfect society there, but even the sober analysts of the World Bank concurred that "the past cannot be used as a pattern for the future in reconstructing the [Algerian] economy; instead everything must be viewed as a part of a new system."⁵⁸ With agreement across the ideological spectrum that Algeria would be a bellwether for the future of the Third World as a whole, numerous foreign governments were eager to demonstrate the merits of their patronage and their economic guidance. Nelson Mandela and Yasser Arafat were among the celebratory throngs in Algiers on 5 July—the first of many influential figures who came in search of inspiration and assistance.⁵⁹ As a result, a many-sided contest began in Algeria that summer, initially taking the form of a race to provide humanitarian aid.

This contest began while the country's political future was still unclear, with both the FLN's and the French government's intentions for a smooth transition foundering on schisms within the Algerian nationalist movement. These schisms were complex, reflecting the emergence of distinct organizational "clans" during the war as well as dynamics within the front. But two main factions vied with one another after the fractious final meeting of the CNRA in Tripoli, where Ben Bella had unveiled his socialist program, obliging other constituencies to either choose sides or stay aloof from the main power struggle. On the one hand, the GPRA's political leaders felt empowered for having negotiated the Evian Accords and, with the front's internal politics largely hidden from the outside world, enjoyed the status of being the public face and recognizable leadership of the nationalist movement to Algerians and foreigners alike. Certainly, the provisional government's diplomatic team was making preparations to assume the responsibilities of a proper foreign ministry, indicative of the assumption that the GPRA was to form the nucleus of the new sovereign government. Accordingly, after Tripoli, Benyoucef Ben Khedda, Krim Belkacem, and their allies established themselves in Algiers and in the nearby "capital" of Kabylia, Tizi Ouzou, where they enjoyed the support of many local mujahideen and their commanders. Pitted against this so-called Tizi Ouzou clan was the new alliance that had Ben Bella as its figurehead and Boumedienne's "border army" as the base of its power—this faction dubbed the "Oujda clan" after the Moroccan border town that was one of its loci. When the French army opened Algeria's borders on 3 July, Boumedienne's comparatively well-equipped forces began to advance from Tunisia and Morocco toward Algiers, roughly in the center of the Algerian coastline. With only perhaps half of the internal ALN forces (i.e., those inside Algeria throughout the war) backing the Ben Bella–Boumedienne alliance, the possibility loomed of this rivalry concluding in an armed confrontation in the Algiers and Kabylia regions. In the meantime, the Provisional Executive established at Evian was the nominal authority in Algiers—or, more precisely, the adjacent administrative center at Rocher Noir (now Boumerdès). However, the executive's head, an old school politician called Abderrahmane Farès, was widely condemned in the FLN as a *beni-oui-oui* and seemed destined to have a peripheral role, at best, in Algerian politics. Still, nothing could be taken for granted, so the likes of Ben Bella's protégé, Mohammed Khemisti, took up positions in Farès's short-lived administration in order to be at the temporary center of power.[60]

Naturally, outside forces were tempted to influence the outcome of the struggle between the GPRA and the ALN. Indeed, because of the disposition of FLN elements in various countries, the governments of France, Morocco, and Tunisia were in the position where even inaction was a form of intervention: should they do nothing to delay or impede the ALN's ingress into Algerian territory, they would in all likelihood facilitate that faction's eventual victory. Indeed, Tunisian president Habib Bourguiba was unable to resist the temptation to prevent the triumph of a clique he detested (he sarcastically asked a British journalist whether Ben Bella and his socialism-espousing comrades were "planning to be a lot of Castros and Maos? Or have they just been reading *L'Express* and *France Observateur* too much?"[61] But his clumsy effort to arrest Ben Bella in Tunis that June backfired by forcing the latter to escape to Cairo, thereby reinforcing his alliance with Nasser.[62] The US Central Intelligence Agency reported, in late July, that elements of the ALN were plotting to assassinate Bourguiba because of his involvement in the FLN's internal feud.[63] Conversely, the French government's decision to open Algeria's borders on schedule in early July—which de Gaulle insisted was the only course consistent with a policy of noninterference— was widely interpreted as an indication that Paris preferred the Ben Bella– Boumedienne group. It was impossible, in other words, for these governments to absolve themselves of events in Algeria, even in inaction.

Other interested parties, further afield, were tempted to assess the Algerian crisis with the binary, zero-sum logic inherent to Cold War politics. In early June, American diplomats pondered whether they should act on the GPRA's request that Washington recognize it as the legitimate political authority in Algeria.[64] The theory was that this might spur other governments to do likewise, thereby giving a fillip of uncertain significance to Ben Khedda's group.[65] While Bourguiba's failed gambit demonstrated the risk of backing the wrong side, American officials and other Western observers generally saw the GPRA as the more "moderate" and desirable faction in terms of its attitudes toward the West—most important, its support for the Evian settlement but also because of its perceived political character. Ferhat Abbas, for example, who was emblematic of Algerian liberalism, described the GPRA as the "moderates" of the disintegrating FLN who stood apart from, on the one hand, a loose "Marxist socialist" tendency spearheaded by Mohammed Boudiaf (one of the surviving "historic nine" chiefs who had been incarcerated with Ben Bella, Khider, and Aït Ahmed), and, on the other, Ben Bella's more organized "Arab socialist" coalition that claimed to represent cultural authenticity and enjoyed an informal alliance with Nasserist Egypt.[66] Signatories and defendants of the Evian Accords, the GPRA seemed to better represent Western values in addition to Western interests. The conservative Parisian daily *Le Figaro* pointedly contrasted Ben Khedda's declaration that "independence is achieved, a page is turned … [and] today it's up to the Algerian people to talk and elect their National Constituent Assembly," with Ben Bella's insistence that "independence is only a stage, now we must achieve the revolution. This will only be achieved with toughness and purity [and] the time for democracy has not yet come."[67] Conversely, the Algerian Communist Party (PCA) indicated the Soviet bloc's tentative analysis of the situation by publicly praising the revolutionary proposals of the Tripoli Program and announcing its tilt toward Ben Bella's side in the FLN's unfolding drama.

Nonetheless, these same outside observers also shied away from forcing the Cold War template onto the Algerian situation. After all, Ferhat Abbas himself demonstrated the indeterminacy of his own Marxist socialist/Arab socialist/moderate schema for the FLN by backing the Ben Bella–Boumedienne coalition: it seemed that his lingering resentment at being replaced by Ben Khedda as GPRA president, a year earlier, outweighed considerations of political philosophy or social background. Indeed, prior to the conclusion of the Evian settlement, Western officials had first seen Ben Khedda's clique as more radical and communist bloc–oriented. Most of the FLN cadres that American diplomats knew and liked best maintained their neutrality in the dispute and advised Washington to do likewise. On the other side of the Cold War's ideological divide, several communist countries found themselves invested in a relationship with a faction that suddenly looked, post-Evian, to be the representative of "neocolonial" interests. The KGB station chief in Tunis claimed to have previously concluded an agreement with the GPRA to help create the intelligence services of the new Algerian state, but Ben Bella's and Boumedienne's ascents rendered many such prior understandings obsolete.[68] Likewise, although the Yugoslavian government started off on a strong footing with Ben Bella and his coalition by dint of their common ties to Gamal Abdel Nasser's regime, Belgrade's officials still bemoaned the looming marginalization of the leadership group they knew and respected. The provisional government, they noted, had demonstrated the competence of its personnel and was already influential in the affairs of the Third World and the Non-Aligned Movement. In contrast, Boumedienne's entourage were largely unknown even to Algeria's allies, and a Yugoslav diplomat in Tunis voiced his concern that the Boumedienne clan's habit of questioning the loyalties of more cosmopolitan and well-traveled rivals pointed to a xenophobic streak. Acknowledging that there was much for Belgrade to like in Ben Bella's Tripoli Program, he suggested regretfully that "it is far more likely that this program could be successfully implemented under the GPRA's direction."[69] In that light, it surely speaks well of the GPRA's diplomatic accomplishments during the preceding years that its passing could be mourned simultaneously in Moscow, Belgrade, and Washington.

Ultimately, Washington, Moscow, and other forces that were further removed from Algerian affairs decided against interfering out of deference to French sensitivities and because they accepted Algerian assurances that the FLN's schism was not related to the outside world's ideological and geopolitical divisions. Taking the threat of US involvement seriously, Ben Bella told the Americans that they risked creating a Cold War dynamic where none existed. He claimed to be no less favorably disposed to the Western perspective and interests than Ben Khedda but warned that he could "guarantee nothing" for their future relationship should Washington try to tilt the balance toward the GPRA.[70] Whatever their internal allegiances, representatives of the FLN seem to have maintained a remarkably united front on the subject of foreign intervention throughout the summer. They insisted to interlocutors from both East and West that their factional dispute was not ideological in any meaningful sense, but rather a purely "internal matter" that was unrelated to Cold War dynamics.[71] Consensus still prevailed among the FLN's cadres that, even though the exploitation of international tensions was vital to their foreign policy, to invite those same tensions into Algeria's internal affairs would be catastrophic—the road to "congolization." As Ben Bella argued, in a discussion with other senior figures at the end of the summer, the key to nonalignment was to avoid becoming the direct object or arena of great power confrontations, a "toy in their hands."[72] This sentiment would be a key tenet of Algerian foreign policy in the years ahead.

Another possible legacy of the FLN's external relations, such as they were, during the summer crisis was to reinforce outside impressions that Algerian politics were fundamentally nonideological, driven by the clash of personalities rather than principles. Whether intentional or not, this message arguably played to the Western tendency to see Arab and African leaders as either cynical schemers or wild-eyed fanatics, but not practitioners of coherent political philosophies or doctrines. As de Gaulle reportedly said to some of his close advisers, "Ben Bella is tormented by djinns ... by the demons active among the Arabs these days: wild romanticism, socialism, pan-Arabism."[73] That is, Algerian efforts to convince outsiders that their internal affairs should not be interpreted through the prism of the Cold War encouraged older obscurantist and essentialist biases.

In any case, deterred for the time being from more direct engagement with Algerian politics, numerous foreign governments instead raced to earn goodwill in the country by providing humanitarian assistance to a nation devastated by war. French napalm had incinerated 8,000 villages and countless hectares of forest, much of the precious cultivable land was strewn with landmines, livestock was scarce, and at least 3 million people were displaced as refugees or internees in the *regroupement* camps.[74] To make things worse, normal economic and administrative activities were severely disrupted by the pieds noirs' departure. In short, Algeria was in exactly the sort of socioeconomic crisis that had fueled American fears of communist penetration since the Marshall Plan in the late 1940s. As Robert Komer of the White House national security team argued in late June, frustrated by Paris's intransigence, "I don't think we can wait any longer for the French lead. The Soviets certainly won't.... [W]e too simply have to put ourselves in a position to respond to the Algerian requests [for aid] almost certainly in the offing."[75]

In fact, quite a lengthy list of donors came to the Algerians' assistance that summer. The United States, the Soviet Union, communist China, the two Germanys, Yugoslavia, and various other countries from both sides of the Iron Curtain provided food, humanitarian supplies, or medical teams. American and Yugoslav doctors, for example, found themselves suturing side by side in the trying conditions of hospitals largely abandoned by their former European staff and lacking in supplies, although the Provisional Executive declined a similar Soviet offer.[76] Initially, partly to avoid raising French hackles or instigating a sort of Cold War "humanitarian arms race," Washington opted first to funnel its aid through the UN, the Red Cross, and other such organizations that had already been working in the FLN refugee camps in Morocco and Tunisia for the past few years.[77] Inevitably, however, the foreign diplomats in Algiers paid keen attention to the nature and scale of each country's deliveries, as well as to the response of the local press. When the first Soviet cargo ship arrived on 8 August with 6,500 tons of wheat on board, a British reporter conceded its value "as a propaganda gesture" in the city of shuttered shops and empty shelves that the pieds noirs had left behind.[78]

A public relations battle started to escalate, and while the Americans immediately noted the poor coverage their aid seemed to receive compared with Soviet and Chinese shipments, to a certain degree that reflected the incipient rivalry between "pro-Moscow" and "pro-Peking" editorial teams as well as a general anti-American bias that pervaded the newspaper scene. For example, defying the impotent Provisional Executive—and occasional machine-gun strafing from hostile FLN elements—the intrepid PCA had already managed to get its daily, *Alger Républicain*, up and running in a downtown hotel.[79] Meanwhile, Serge Michel, the French Maoist previously seconded to Patrice Lumumba, took over the FLN's new *Al Chaab* (The people), and a different group of French Trotskyists and fellow travelers would found *Révolution Africaine* several months later. The local media environment was not going to get any more receptive for the Americans, then. In any case, in response to the White House's desire to make a bigger impact and properly compete with the communist countries, and also in consideration of the Algerians' pressing needs, Washington quickly shifted to larger-scale assistance under the aegis of the Public Law 480 (PL-480) food donation program and announced such an allocation valued at $25 million at the end of August.[80]

Yet this early rivalry over humanitarian aid promised to be merely the precursor to the real contest to influence Algeria's future political and economic orientation. Kennedy had put the Third World almost at the top of his foreign policy agenda, and Congress had passed the Foreign Assistance Act of 1961 in order to prevent communists from exploiting the difficulties faced by developing countries. In this spirit, one of the president's advisers noted in mid-August that the State Department "believes we have to do some aggressive planning even before the Algerians are ready to launch a major development program. [The Algerians] don't fully understand the complexities of development economics, and it will be up to us to provide what positive guidance we can."[81] Notably, Moscow observed events in a very similar way, albeit from the opposite ideological perspective that saw capitalist interests as the thieves of history. Though Soviet analysts were heartened by the language of the Tripoli Program and the likelihood of Ben Bella's victory over the "neocolonialist" Ben Khedda, the local TASS correspondent tempered the optimism of his avid readers by cautioning that "foreign political forces, hostile to an independent Algeria, are trying to use its internal difficulties to direct the country's development along a neocolonialist path."[82] Having been disappointed before, the Soviet government was cautious, waiting not least to see whether the PCA would enjoy an influential role in the new order, as was the case in Cuba, or if Algeria's communists would suffer the same repression as their comrades in other radical Arab states.[83]

Of all the intrigues swirling around Algeria in the summer of 1962, the disposition of the French government was ultimately the most pressing concern for the Americans, the Soviets, and the FLN. The exodus of most of Algeria's European community had already smashed many of the assumptions on which the French government had based the Evian Accords. From an original population of around 1 million, French officials estimated that only 200,000 pieds noirs remained in Algeria by September.[84] The government had not planned on their leaving in such great numbers—as evidenced by the lack of preparations for repatriating so many people to the mainland—putting many of Evian's assumptions in doubt. After all, the pieds noirs had constituted nearly the entirety of Algeria's managerial, commercial, professional, and bureaucratic classes, so from a practical point of view, *coopération* was already in grave jeopardy.[85] Furthermore, the pieds noirs had vital symbolic value to Paris as the linchpin of *rayonnement*, the policy of maintaining French cultural influence in France's former colonies. The new ambassador in Algiers, esteemed economist Jean-Marcel Jeanneney, had been told that maintaining a visible French presence was vital to ensuring that Algeria play "its necessary role, that of hinge between Europe and Africa."[86]

De Gaulle indicated his determination to maintain close oversight of the Algerian situation by instructing Jeanneney to call him personally day or night as needed and by keeping open the special wartime inter-ministerial committee on Algerian matters, the Secrétariat d'Etat aux Affaires Algériennes (SEAA).[87] Moreover, the French president maintained some surprising attitudes toward the Algerian situation. First, while Washington and Moscow both still sought to balance their relations with France against those with its former colony, by and large de Gaulle and his officials seemed more concerned with blocking American initiatives than Soviet ones. Having already seen Tunisia and Morocco fall into the orbit of his wealthy, seductive superpower ally, the French president was determined that the same not happen in Algeria. As he wrote to his foreign minister, Maurice Couve de Murville, a year later, France must not yield its established position in Africa from a misguided sense of Western partnership.[88] Thus Quai d'Orsay officials deliberately impeded the Americans' efforts to get their own aid programs off the ground in Algeria, and their records plainly show that they actually only kept up the pretense of regular meetings with their counterparts from the State Department in order to discover and counter their plans.[89]

The second surprising feature of French policy at this time was its neutrality vis-à-vis the FLN power struggle. In fact, de Gaulle may even have assisted Ben Bella's victory in subtle ways. Certainly, he ignored Ben Khedda's pleas to keep Algeria's borders closed on 3 July to prevent the advance of Boumedienne's troops, while in her monograph on Algerian foreign policy, French scholar Nicole Grimaud repeats the rumor that the French army refueled its vehicles on the way toward Algiers, a gesture necessitated by the logistical shortcomings of the operation.[90] In any case, de Gaulle's seeming equanimity in the face of the Tripoli Program's fervent denunciations of the Evian Accords is noteworthy enough. He apparently accepted Ben Bella's new assurances, in August, that he did in fact feel bound to respect the FLN's commitment to the accords and that his conception of *socialisme à l'algérienne* would not threaten the profits or assets of French firms.[91] Although Ben Bella had an obvious interest in averting any possible French actions against him, de Gaulle was probably of a mind to accept such promises because he tended to be dismissive of revolutionary ideological pronouncements in any case, whether they be Soviet or Algerian, and because he felt that *coopération* was inescapably vital to the national interest of whatever sort of regime took power in Algiers. This attitude accounts for Jeanneney's cool instructions to the effect that the Evian Accords "were valid regardless of the vicissitudes of Algeria's internal politics and, moreover, they have not been reneged by any of the Front's leaders."[92] It also worth considering the possibility that de Gaulle or some of his officials actually preferred to deal with a more radical or authoritarian government because it would govern more effectively, or because a genuinely Third Worldist Algerian partner would bolster France's nonaligned credentials and curtail America's influence.[93]

Thus the ambiguity of the Algerian situation was not resolved even after the conclusion of the FLN's internal power struggle at the beginning of September. Several thousand mujahideen died in fratricidal combat as Boumedienne's troops reached Algiers and Kabylia, but an incipient civil war was averted by the intervention of 20,000 or more frustrated civilians, who marched out between the warring factions chanting "*baraka saba'a sanin*" (seven years, that's enough!).[94] Given the balance of forces, the pro-Tripoli group's victory was complete, so Ben Bella and his allies set about founding a government on the revolutionary lines espoused in the Tripoli Program. Mohamed Khider took charge of the FLN with the intention of transforming it into a proper single party to steer the nation's politics, while as defense minister, Boumedienne owned to a similar goal of "reconverting" the ALN into as powerful a political force as a military one in the new Algeria. On 20 September, the people did get to elect a National Constituent Assembly that was supposed to develop a constitution and define the nation's political structures, but they were only given the option of approving or rejecting a predetermined list of 196 candidates, which a large majority of the 6.5 million eligible voters did.[95] With some embarrassment, in Washington Chanderli justified this procedure to American officials on the necessity of rooting out the communists who might infiltrate an open election. While the PCA did fear for its future in a single-party FLN state, this style of referendum-like election was entirely in accordance with the new regime's conception of popular democracy.[96] On 25 September, Ben Bella was confirmed as head of the Bureau Politique and prime minister of the RADP, and when Krim stepped forward to denounce the "supplanting of collective leadership for personal power," Ahmed Kaïd reprised his role at Tripoli by spiritedly defending the need to avoid political division through revolutionary discipline and democratic centralism.[97]

The reality of these different power structures would never manage to live up to their status and functions on paper. Most obviously, Boumedienne was not in the Bureau Politique at first, but there could be little doubt of his weight in the new leadership. Nor did the FLN exist yet as anything like the sort of party envisioned by Khider, and even the nominal relationship between party, government, and Boumedienne's supposed "vanguard" soldiery was extremely vague. Although the presence of people like Ben Khedda and Krim in the National Assembly offered a fig leaf of unity, allies of Ben Bella, Boumedienne, and Khider dominated that body and especially the senior government positions. The assembly's first act was to elect Abbas as its president, and ever the parliamentarian, he used his inaugural speech to extol the virtues of the separation of powers and genuine civilian authority.[98] Yet such terms did not automatically resonate with this assemblage of erstwhile revolutionaries and politicized soldiery in the same way as they would have with a Western audience. Some weeks later, for example, one deputy wondered aloud whether he attended "as a member of parliament [or] as a militant of the party" before unapologetically answering, "I have come to defend the decisions taken by my party, just as I do outside this Assembly or in my contacts abroad. . . . Some say here that the militants are *Beni-oui-ouis* in regard to the party, in regard to its discipline. All right: to this I say Yes, twenty times Yes: I am a *Beni-oui-oui*."[99] In this respect, Algeria provided a vivid demonstration of the tenuous moral authority of liberal democracy in much of the postcolonial world. Many new political elites, such as the former cadres of the FLN, did not offer even a nominal fealty to the rights of the individual—loyalty to the collective was the first principle of many postcolonial political cultures.

That said, all agreed that the first priority was to redress the disastrous state of Algeria's economy. While Ben Bella had spoken at Tripoli of his desire to force the pieds noirs out of Algeria eventually, the sudden departure of most of Algeria's European managers, administrators, technicians, and professionals had come to pass much sooner than anyone might have anticipated. The economy and public services had come to a crashing halt. The collapse of national output was apparent in the factories that sat idle, the crops untended, and the hospitals operating with skeleton crews—often thanks only to foreign volunteers. In the important construction industry, output would fall by about 55 percent between 1962 and 1963, and nearly three-quarters of the 2,000 businesses in that sector simply disappeared.[100] The crisis had left about 70 percent of Algeria's active population unemployed, and privately held bank deposits were at a quarter of their 1961 level.[101] Notably, the World Bank reported that French mining operations seemed largely unaffected by the dire conditions around them, but that fact testifies only to the bifurcated nature of the colonial order, where two separate economies existed side by side.[102] In any case, by October, the French government had to accelerate the separation of its treasury from that of the new Algerian state in order to stop the profuse bleeding of moneys across the Mediterranean.[103]

In short, for all the attention and acclaim it enjoyed in international affairs, independent Algeria emerged in the midst of a profound socioeconomic crisis, and the country looked certain to be dependent on outside support for the foreseeable future. Its combination of prominence and poverty only increased the interest of the numerous powers that desired to enhance their reputation in the developing world, including the two superpowers. While President Kennedy did not want to depend on France to maintain such a potentially important country within the Western sphere, Soviet policymakers were greatly encouraged by Ben Bella's effusive commitment to socialism. The interest of the great powers was such that, noting the impatience on both sides of the ideological divide to strengthen relations with Ben Bella's new government, the *New York Times* correspondent concluded in early October that "the Cold War has begun in independent Algeria."[104] Luckily, he felt, the country's pressing circumstances meant that "for once the West seems to be in a strong position. . . . The basic advantage of the non-Communist world is that Algeria desperately needs French help to solve its economic and technical problems [and] this affects Algeria's relations with other countries too."[105] Yet, in making this prediction, he perhaps neglected the possibility that the country's economic emergency and its social upheavals might instead impel its new leaders to implement more radical solutions than were allowed for in the Evian settlement. For at the same time that Algeria's problems seemed to confirm its external dependencies—notably on France—events on the ground were empowering those who called for a definitive break with the patterns of the past. Che Guevara observed once that he judged the depth of a revolution by the number of refugees it created, and by that standard Algeria had accrued deep stores of revolutionary potential that were yet to be tapped.[106]

Development in the Shadow of the Bomb

While the specter of "congolization" had been a persistent and popular theme during Algeria's turbulent transition to independence, it was the Cuban parallel that dominated discussion of the new Algerian government's first actions in the international and domestic realms, from September 1962 to the following March. Admiration for the Cuban Revolution was widespread and fervent in the ranks of the former FLN, and French officials justly feared that Franco-Algerian relations might replicate the rapid deterioration of the American-Cuban relationship in the wake of Fidel Castro's seizure of power. Indeed, during GPRA envoy Lakhdar Brahimi's visit to Havana in January 1962, in the final stages of the Evian negotiations, Castro confidently counseled the Algerian nationalists that they should agree to whatever concessions were necessary to get the French out of Algeria as soon as possible, since "once peace has returned and you are well established, you can do whatever you want."[107] Moreover, Cuba was probably the single most polarizing Third World country in the Cold War context. From Washington's perspective, Castro's regime represented the worst-case scenario of communist capture of poor nations' aspirations, whereas the Soviet leadership treasured it as proof that the developing world was destined to adopt socialism and communism. Consequently, Ahmed Ben Bella could hardly have chosen a more contentious debut on the international stage when he announced his intention to travel first to the United States, in mid-October, to preside over his country's formal admission to the United Nations and to meet with President Kennedy at the White House, but then subsequently to fly directly to Havana to thank the Cuban people for their support during the independence struggle. Even if he had not thereby unwittingly implicated himself in the missile crisis—an event that significantly raised the stakes of the Cold War in the Third World—the Algerian prime minister's itinerary would have complicated his foreign and domestic agendas. It is no exaggeration to say that the menace of nuclear devastation would exert a decisive influence on the formulation of Algeria's economic model.

Unfortunately, the Algerian archives have thus far yielded comparatively little inside information on the motives and details of the trip, although alternative sources shed light on independent Algeria's first initiative on the world stage, from a variety of angles. In fact, the fragmentary nature of documentary evidence from these early months of the RADP's diplomacy is itself evidence of the rudimentary state of the new foreign ministry. At thirty-two years old, Mohammed Khemisti was the youngest foreign minister in the world, managing a small team of GPRA veterans in a few offices in Algiers's central administration building, the Palais du Gouvernement. The fact that the MAE's earliest records frequently lacked basic identifying information such as dates, provenance, and addressee testifies to an initial shortage of equipment, procedures, and trained personnel. Although the ministry began to expand quickly, it would take nearly two years to establish a formal filing and archiving system, and even longer for senior staff to be fully relieved of the burden of translating from English, let alone less common languages.[108]

Nevertheless, the Algerians possessed an international agenda whose ambition seemed to greatly outstrip their meager resources, for they were determined to champion the Third World's rise as a political and moral force and to advance their own candidacy for a vanguard role. Moreover, many observers were convinced of their capacity to do so. British officials were immensely impressed by the intelligence and competency of the FLN's battle-hardened diplomats, a rare asset for an African country, and concluded that "if the Algerian cat should jump the wrong way . . . the Algerian delegation at New York . . . could make trouble for the West out of all proportion to Algeria's physical size and strength."[109]

Arriving in New York with Khemisti and a team of senior figures from various branches of the regime, including Ahmed Kaïd to represent Boumdienne's military faction, Ben Bella undoubtedly succeeded in the trip's first objective, which was to cement Algeria's reputation as a leading voice on Third World issues. He delivered an impressive address to the General Assembly on 9 October and gave notice that the policy of nonalignment ought not to be mistaken for a muted timidity with regard to international affairs. Any sovereign state, he insisted, had the right and even the duty to speak its mind on matters of war and peace whether they occurred in the Southern Hemisphere or the Northern one. He criticized the rich countries' control over the global economy and institutions such as the UN and vowed to tear up the post–World War II "gentleman's agreement" by which the "old powers" preserved their domination of the new.[110] But he focused his attention and passion above all on the incomplete national liberation struggles in Palestine and southern Africa, to which he promised Algeria's unqualified support. In fact, Ben Bella spoke so vehemently of the continued unrest in Congo that some American officials feared that Algiers was on the verge of committing its own hardy mujahideen to the left-wing Gizenga government's cause.[111]

Such militancy played well to the Algerians' main constituency, as shown by the fawning coverage in the Tunis-based *tier-mondiste* weekly, *Jeune Afrique*, but dignitaries and journalists of all varieties pursued them throughout their stay. Although they were fêted in African and Asian diplomatic circles in particular— the Guinean president, Ahmed Sékou Touré, had flown in merely to bask in their reflected glory—the British and Soviet governments both also invited Ben Bella to visit their countries at his earliest convenience.[112] All this attention seemed to embolden the Algerian prime minister. He appeared on a least two American television programs, one hosted by Adlai Stevenson, where he unnerved French officials by speaking of France's military bases, nuclear testing sites, and economic preponderance in Algeria as undesirable legacies of colonialism. In doing so, he deviated from a polite acquiescence to the narrative of de Gaulle as the great emancipator.[113] Nor did he refrain from commenting on America's internal politics: on emerging from a meeting with the African American civil rights leader Dr. Martin Luther King on 13 October, he told the waiting press that the United States risked losing its "moral and political voice" in the world should it not defeat racial discrimination within its own society.[114]

However, US officials were far more concerned by Ben Bella's pronouncements on Cuba than his opinions on civil rights. Notably, his first meeting on arriving in New York had been with the Cuban president, Osvaldo Dorticos, whom he warmly embraced in a hotel lobby for the benefit of the cameras.[115] Washington took note of every such gesture, for there had already been some debate as to whether Algeria was a lost cause, or whether the president should rescind his invitation to Ben Bella after hearing the latter's full travel plans. In mid-September, Dean Rusk had ordered his staff at the State Department to investigate ways of diminishing Boumedienne's influence in the new regime after hearing a speech in which the defense minister had admired Castro's domestic policies.[116] On the other hand, US diplomats also considered many of the Algerians known best to them from their service in the GPRA, such as Chanderli and Yazid, to be "basically pro-American" and deemed Ben Bella to be an essentially "pragmatic" person who could be weaned away from communism's chimeric temptations.[117] Robert Komer, for example, conceded that the prime minister was under the sway of "a mélange of revolutionary clichés from Marx, Mao, Nasser, and Che Guevara" but urged Kennedy to keep his appointment with him on the basis that "Cuba may [actually] provide a good pretext to get across [to him] the risk of Communist capture of indigenous national revolutions."[118] So as not to give the impression that Cuba was a litmus test for America's relations with the developing world, the president agreed. He also seems to have retained a special sympathy for the country that had helped make his political career—even as Mohammed Khemisti's own speech to the General Assembly on 12 October indicated how much that sympathy would be put to the test. Defending Havana's right to pursue "economic and social liberation," the Algerian foreign minister denounced any "efforts to attack and undermine the political regime chosen by the friendly people of Cuba."[119]

Inevitably, this topic occupied much of the conversation between the two leaders three days later. Ben Bella and his colleagues stayed only a few hours for what was technically an informal meeting, not an official state visit. Nonetheless, the American president went to the trouble of orchestrating a novel welcome, a twenty-gun salute on the White House lawn, that bestowed a genial air of occasion on the proceedings.[120] The minutes of their discussion accord with Ben Bella's recollection of friendly yet feisty debate; although he began by paying homage to Kennedy's sagacity and courage in supporting Algeria's liberation five years earlier, the two men quickly revealed their markedly different understandings of the meaning of "nonalignment" and their varying interpretations of the Cold War in the developing world. Kennedy argued that Castro was a false prophet, that his foreign policy was decidedly aligned, and that he had betrayed the Cuban national cause. "The Cuban people never had a chance to express their will," he said, "but were delivered over to old hard-line Communists and appended to the Soviet Bloc." In turn, Ben Bella was careful to preface his response with an assurance that although Algeria had to experience a "radical and general revolution," his people "wanted to prevent the possible danger of a radical Communist take-over in their country, for their ideology and [our] religion [are] contrary." However, he then proceeded to describe Cuba as a victim of misguided American hostility, likening Castro's reliance on Soviet military support to Nasser's decision to buy Czechoslovak arms in 1955 as a result of the Eisenhower administration's intransigence. "As a brotherly and friendly suggestion," the Algerian advised, "it would be best to avoid nailing Castro to the Communist camp by failing to give him any other choice." Though the tenor of their talk was amiable, it provided a vivid contrast between one worldview preoccupied by the conflict between East and West, and another that considered the disparity between North and South to be the defining characteristic of international life.[121]

Ironically, Kennedy himself had criticized his predecessor for committing exactly the same Manichaean errors he was accused of, and though the Algerians' admiration and gratitude for his stance during the war were sincere, they were beginning to speak of President Kennedy falling short of Senator Kennedy's high principles. Yet while they judged US policy toward Cuba very critically and held decidedly mixed opinions on Washington's attitude toward their own liberation struggle, the Algerian delegation had also traversed the Atlantic with a second, much more concrete goal in mind: namely, securing a promise of substantial economic assistance from the Americans. This objective ran counter to much of their public and private musings—the GPRA's records show an increasing distrust of US economic influence in Africa, and an undated report by the new MAE, seemingly written not long after these events, described the centerpiece of Kennedy's aid policy in Latin America, the Alliance for Progress, as an effort to "economically suffocate the Isle of Liberty [Cuba] and topple its revolutionary government."[122] Moreover, during his speech in New York a few days earlier, Khemisti had explicitly declared that Algeria rejected capitalism, that it would "find its own road, a socialist road," and serve as a revolutionary "laboratory" for the rest of Africa.[123] On the face of things, therefore, the prospects for Algerian-American economic cooperation seemed dim, especially in light of the fact that at this very moment the Kennedy administration was battling a growing lobby in Congress that wanted to cut off assistance to developing countries that pursued radical policies, criticized the United States, or allied themselves to Fidel Castro.

The motivation for seeking American economic assistance lay in the Algerians' compelling desire to diversify their sources of support and trade. While the French government described *coopération* as a charitable act of historic proportions, the FLN considered it an effort to maintain Algeria's colonial economic structures, in which 95 percent of exports were directed toward the metropole. Despite their socialist principles, the Algerians' internal reports show that at this time they estimated that only the Western capitalist countries, above all the United States, had the potential to counterbalance France's heavy grip on their economy in a significant way.[124] In fact, the American food aid program was already gearing up to feed about 2 million people in Algeria over the coming winter, but Ben Bella and his colleagues would not be satisfied by this form of help alone. They desired, and even seemed to expect, that Washington would make a real financial contribution to modernization and development projects in addition to humanitarian aid. Regarding the seeming ideological incompatibility between the two countries, the Algerians sent mixed signals. On the one hand, playing the "pragmatist" card, Ben Bella assured Kennedy that "socialism is something for the distant future. The Algerians are not dreamers; they know socialism cannot be brought about in a hurry, nor can it be brought about by words alone."[125] Yet Khemisti and Yazid, talking to their State Department counterparts, also said that American assistance should reflect Algeria's economic principles, so public moneys would be preferable to private investment.[126] The Americans, naturally, had the opposite opinion and raised the case of a US firm that was currently deliberating developing a petrochemical facility at Arzew, near Oran, but desired guarantees of compensation in the event of future nationalization. Subsequently, an MAE analysis decided that the Americans were pushing this project to test the flexibility of Algeria's principles; the fact that it subsequently foundered over the question of guaranteed indemnities suggests that ideological concerns could affect practical business between the two countries.[127]

However, in one important respect the two sides were in accord. In explaining their desire to diversify Algeria's economic relationships, Khemisti and Yazid told their hosts that *coopération* with France needed to be placed within a new context of "world-wide cooperation" and this notion actually resonated perfectly with the American government's position in its ongoing debates with the French.[128] Whereas US officials argued that Western countries should distribute their aid in a more multilateral fashion, presenting a united front in the different areas of the developing world, Paris insisted on focusing its development assistance on francophone Africa. De Gaulle's concern, of course, was to protect France's influence in its former colonies against American encroachment, but the American position also matched the Algerians' desire to see the Western countries compete with one another, rather than maintaining exclusive "spheres of influence" in the Third World.[129] Later in December—after the commotion about Algeria's involvement in the Cuban drama had died down somewhat—Kennedy would instruct the various branches of American foreign policy to map out their "next steps in this important country," noting specifically that while France should carry most of the West's burden there, he also wanted his nation to invest enough to "be in a position to respond with sufficient dispatch to serve our political interests."[130] However, the president's desire to meet at least some of the Algerians' requests would run into fierce obstruction from State Department officials whose overriding concern was for Washington's relations with Paris, Rabat, or Tunis.

In any case, Ben Bella's controversial journey to Havana lay before the pursuit of any economic agreements between the United States and Algeria. When Ben Bella offered his services as intermediary, Kennedy had asked the prime minister to convey to Castro the message that he need not fear invasion so long as the Soviet Union only installed defensive military installations on the island. Yet even as the two leaders spoke in the White House that morning, 15 October, CIA analysts elsewhere in the city were excitedly studying the reconnaissance photographs that revealed Khrushchev's missiles in Cuba.[131] So unbeknownst to the Algerian delegates, the celebratory atmospherics of their brief stay in Havana, on 16 and 17 October, transpired against the backdrop of an unprecedented sense of crisis within the American government. Boarding a Cuban airplane to depart at New York's Idlewild airport, Ben Bella enthused to the press that "this is the happiest moment of my trip to America, I feel like I am coming home. For me, coming to Cuba is like returning to Algeria."[132] He and his companions were received at the other end by cheering crowds equipped with Algerian flags and giant portraits of the prime minister, while Castro's welcoming speech hailed the significance of their visit, "at a time when *Yanqui* imperialism intends to vanquish the revolution by its threats, blackmail, and criminal economic and commercial blockade."[133] Though the crowds may have been staged, the Algerians' enthusiasm was undoubtedly genuine, and Ben Bella clearly forgot whatever concern he had for American public opinion in the excitement of the moment. "We were only in Cuba for thiry-six hours," he later recalled, "but what a celebration it was! . . . Protocol was forgotten and we talked, talked. . . . Never had thirty-six hours seemed so short!"[134]

Unfortunately, only indirect third-party accounts exist about the substance of these energetic discussions between Ben Bella, Khemisti, Ahmed Kaïd, Guevara, and the Castro brothers. According to Soviet communications intercepted by American signals intelligence, Ben Bella did make an effort to mediate between Havana and Washington. He recounted his conversation with Kennedy fairly faithfully, though perhaps exaggerating the forcefulness with which he took the American president to task for the wrongs inflicted on Cuba. Most important, he passed on Kennedy's promise—or warning—that the United States would take military action only if the Soviets put offensive military capabilities in place, though he appears to have been unaware of the full significance of this message. Ben Bella advised his hosts to avoid provoking their giant neighbor more than was necessary, suggesting specifically that Cuba take more caution in its support of revolution elsewhere in Latin America, though he then also recognized that spreading revolution was Cuba's duty—just as it was Algeria's duty, he said, to spread revolution in Africa. Though firm conclusions cannot be drawn in the absence of a proper transcript of the Ben Bella–Castro conversation, the Algerian prime minister does seem, per his reputation, to have moderated his manner somewhat in order to please both the American and the Cuban heads of state. Notably, he refused the Cubans' offer to drop any reference to Guantanamo Bay from their concluding joint declaration to the press, which was certain to rile Washington.[135] But his difference in tone in the two capitals is not outrageous, nor is there any evidence of a substantive, policy-related inconsistency. Crucially, there is no indication that the Algerians received any hint that Soviet nuclear weapons were present in Cuba, a fact that would be the source of considerable embarrassment and frustration in Algiers in the days ahead.[136]

The mutual expectation was that the Algerians' visit was merely the beginning of a close relationship. The Cuban official who briefed the Soviet embassy on the talks made a point of stating that the Algerian prime minister had been very complimentary of Moscow's assistance to Cuba and the high level of Soviet technical expertise. This detail may have been for the Soviet ambassador's benefit, as it seems likely in light of subsequent developments that Castro agreed (or himself proposed) at this time to convince Moscow of Algeria's revolutionary bona fides and its worthiness as a beneficiary of Soviet support.[137] In return, Ben Bella offered to serve as Cuba's bridge to Africa and the Middle East. The Algerians would take this duty seriously, helping to open up new arenas for Cuban diplomacy and revolutionary subversion. It is not indicated in this account that the Cubans and Algerians discussed assisting one another's subversive campaigns to export revolution into other countries, though it was also almost certainly broached at some point.[138]

French intelligence's account of the Algerian-Cuban discussions (from an "absolutely reliable" source) echoes much of the Soviet account and provides more information on some of the Algerian delegation's other conversations and activities in Havana. In the economic realm, they offered to assist the Cubans in the challenge of obtaining oil from the Soviet Union and Iraq and proposed to begin a bilateral exchange of oil for sugar, although nothing firm was agreed. Meanwhile, of equal significance were the Algerians' speedy efforts to accumulate as much information as possible on the Cuban Revolution's domestic concerns. Junior members of the delegation had been assigned precise areas of study such as the role of the army and militias, agrarian reform, literacy campaigns, tourism, and women, on which they were to prepare reports for the relevant ministries back in Algiers.[139] The visitors were especially interested in the role of the Cuban Communist Party in state affairs, which is noteworthy given that its Algerian equivalent was at that time arguing for its continued existence in a single-party state by citing the Cuban precedent.[140] In short, with so many shared concerns and attitudes between the two sides, these exchanges confirmed Cuba's status as an important reference point for the new Algerian leadership. Ben Bella later wistfully described the trip to Havana as a moment when "the two youngest revolutions in the world met, compared notes, and together envisioned the future."[141] In that spirit, Ben Bella and Castro agreed not only that they ought to exchange ambassadors as soon as possible but also that Castro should visit Algeria as early as the spring.[142]

While the details of the Algerians' conversations in Havana were unknown to the outside world, the trip's celebratory atmosphere and the warmth of their relations with the Cubans were evident to all. Accordingly, when the Algerian prime minister returned to New York for his flight back across the Atlantic, he experienced a much more hostile reception than he had on his first arrival a week earlier. "We don't greatly care," sniffed the *Wall Street Journal* on 19 October, "what this gentleman from Algeria says or how he chooses to pass his time. But we certainly wonder what's wrong with Washington. It must take a powerful streak of masochism to be so loving toward people who are so eager to kick the US in the teeth."[143] Ben Bella met once more in New York with Adlai Stevenson, who warned him that his statements on Guantanamo and US-Cuban relations had convinced many Americans that Algeria was sincere about nonalignment. Ben Bella ruefully observed that nonalignment was proving to be a difficult and uncomfortable path, and conceded that he might have been too accommodating to his hosts' requests in Havana.[144] Even so, the full ramifications of the trip to Cuba were not yet apparent to him, since the escalating missile crisis had not yet exploded publicly. The Algerian government was about to face a very hard choice between its moral and diplomatic compulsion to stand by a Third World ally, on the one hand, and the pressing circumstances at home that made American economic assistance one of its highest priorities, on the other.

Fittingly, then, the missile story broke just when three of the MAE's most experienced diplomatic operatives—Yazid, Mohammed Sahnoun, and Layashi Yaker—arrived in Washington to pursue the aid talks that they believed both countries had agreed on during Ben Bella's visit a week earlier. The fact that American officials subsequently disputed even the premise of the Algerians' journey, claiming that only very preliminary discussions were on the agenda, underscores the complete breakdown of communications between the visitors and their hosts from the State Department and the United States Agency for International Development (USAID). What is clear is that the backdrop of the Cuban crisis frayed tempers and shortened fuses on both sides of the table when they met at Foggy Bottom on 23 October; the night before, Kennedy had appeared on television to inform the world and a horrified American public of the discovery of Soviet missiles on Castro's island. Whether or not the Algerians were mistaken in their expectation of discussing substantial issues and specific development projects, the tenor of the conversation quickly deteriorated when the Americans refused to entertain any such possibilities and insisted that their brief was strictly limited to the preexisting humanitarian and food aid programs. Declaring that this position rendered the meeting pointless in the first place, Yazid, Sahnoun, and Yaker angrily accused the US government of punishing Algeria for its friendship with Cuba, and a heated argument ensued. Ultimately, having initially made arrangements at their hotel for a lengthy stay, the three Algerians found themselves on the train back to New York later that same day, where a furious Khemisti complained bitterly to the French ambassador (who could scarcely hide his glee) that "the United States intended to subject their aid to political conditions."[145]

Although the Americans claimed afterward that mistaken expectations were to blame for the meeting's collapse, this hitherto obscure incident actually made a very significant impression on the Algerian government. Returning to Algiers, Khemisti defended his team's disappointing failure to secure an aid agreement in Washington by arguing that the Americans had chosen to make economic assistance contingent on Algeria distancing itself from Cuba. The MAE's internal reports would still be repeating this interpretation as accepted wisdom several years later. Lakhdar Brahimi, who was not present, recalls the story that circulated among the Algerian diplomatic corps according to which Yazid, Sahnoun, and Yaker found a note waiting for them when they checked into their hotel, advising them to watch Kennedy's television broadcast that evening.[146] Although certainly not official policy, it is plausible that some American officials, already irritated at the Algerians' outspoken views on US-Cuban relations and outraged at Khrushchev and Castro's audacious nuclear gambit, were at the very least content to let their guests leave with the impression of being punished. Notably, the State Department's official denials were in response to coverage in the *New York Times*, reliant on sources inside Foggy Bottom, that supported the Algerians' interpretation of events.[147] On the other hand, as Porter and his colleagues argued, Khemisti had an interest in rebutting criticism for having made a mess of the aid talks, and once Third Worldist opinion makers such as Robert Malley's Tunis-based *Jeune Afrique* picked up the story of plucky Algeria refusing American money in order to stand by Cuba, Ben Bella's government became heavily invested in that storyline, whatever its accuracy.[148]

Therefore, the Algerian government rode out the Cuban Missile Crisis with two contradictory goals in mind. The Bureau Politique issued a public condemnation of American aggression and reaffirmed its solidarity with the "valiant Cuban people." The local press adopted an even more belligerent tone, but in reality the government's official protests were fairly muted, and Ben Bella notably declined the spotlight himself. Moreover, behind the scenes he was decidedly conciliatory in their communications with the United States. Though at first refusing to see Porter, perhaps giving himself time to decide on a course of action, the prime minister then received the American ambassador at his modest residence in order to clarify emphatically that he had no prior knowledge of the Soviet missiles. He assured Porter of his high regard for President Kennedy and his appreciation for the United States' vital concerns in the emergency. He also said that he blamed Khrushchev for the crisis and bemoaned that the Soviet leader had put a fraternal Third World country in danger.[149] Notably, Khemisti offered more or less the same account to the Yugoslav ambassador, Nijaz Dizdarević, to whom he complained that the Soviet and Cuban conspiracy had made the nonaligned countries "look like fools."[150] Vitally, Washington believed that the Algerians had been kept in the dark about the missiles, and in concrete terms, Ben Bella also agreed to cooperate with American efforts to prevent the Soviet Union from obtaining an African refueling stop for an air bridge to Cuba.[151] In other words, while the semiofficial Algerian press vociferously condemned Kennedy's blockade of Cuba, the authorities in Algiers were actually quietly participating in that (ultimately successful) American effort to peacefully defuse the crisis. As a result, even though Algeria would henceforth bear the enmity of a substantial share of the American press and public, quite a few policymakers—including the president—felt that Ben Bella's government had done enough to earn Washington's patience and forgiveness for at least a little while longer.

Even so, during the weeks that followed, both American and French officials were concerned that the Algerian government's piecemeal steps toward socialism pointed to a "Castroist" trajectory for the country. Ben Bella issued several decrees in November that gave the government's belated imprimatur to Muslim and Arab Algerians' occupation of abandoned French and pied noir properties. The decision to grant legal standing to such properties' new occupants irritated Paris, which was pressing the authorities in Algiers to compensate French citizens and businesses for the seizures. American observers seemed to consider the questions of compensation and of guaranteeing property rights as important litmus tests for Algeria's ideological direction.

In reality, the Algerian government's actions were not the product of Cuban inspiration but were instead an effort to assert its relevance and legitimacy by getting out ahead of a broad-based, popular revolutionary surge. In the capital, a cosmopolitan milieu of fellow travelers and local labor activists helped drive the national discourse through their overrepresentation in the local press and trade unions.[152] Autogestion, or workers' self-management, committees were already in control of thousands of farms and businesses. Ben Bella sought to identify himself with this extremely popular grassroots phenomenon, promising in one speech to hand over another 500 factories to their workers and vowing during a heavily publicized tour of an autogestion farm that "there will be no more wretched on *this* earth."[153] Likewise, Omar Ouzegane, the minister of agriculture and a former communist militant, promised the peasants that Algerian socialism would be implemented in their name. Referring to the best-known of the great pied noir landowners, Henri Borgeaud, he assured the rural poor that "Algerian Borgeauds will not replace the French Borgeauds."[154] In short, Algeria's politicians were scurrying to position themselves at the forefront of a genuinely popular and hitherto self-directed revolutionary movement.

It is in this domestic context, as much as the international one, that the Algerian government's determined efforts to maintain Washington's favor in the wake of the controversial trip to Havana must be considered. In the weeks that followed, the country's political elite as a whole continued to be very sympathetic toward Cuba and critical of the United States' longer-term campaign to isolate and undermine Castro's regime. But Ben Bella and his colleagues made the clear decision to temporarily sacrifice their relationship with Cuba in order to pursue American economic and development assistance. After all, their financial position was especially alarming because Paris had cut off the unregulated flow of funds from the French treasury in October, so that Khemisti told Ambassador Porter on 12 November that "there was not one cent in the Algerian treasury." The young foreign minister observed hopefully that "the international atmosphere has quieted and we would like to resume talks with you about possible American aid to Algeria."[155]

Algerian officials recognized that they would need to accommodate Washington's policies and emphatically demonstrate their appreciation of American assistance. For example, Porter warned them that the provision of development assistance would be contingent on a positive assessment of Algeria's wider economic policies, which suggested they might have to sacrifice key aspects of their commitment to socialism. Ben Bella also began to publicly extol the benevolence of the American food shipments, which Porter had suggested in order to improve Algeria's public image. The White House then cited the changed tenor of Ben Bella's speeches, in early January, to persuade protesting American dockworkers to resume loading cargo ships delivering food aid to Algeria.[156]

Meanwhile, this campaign to win American hearts and minds also necessitated putting some distance between Algeria and Cuba. Contrary to Ben Bella and Castro's discussions in Havana, several months passed without an exchange of ambassadors between the two countries or any further discussion of the Cuban leader's proposed trip to North Africa.[157] As one MAE report lately admitted in plain fashion:

> During the Cuban crisis and blockade . . . despite our sympathy for Cuba and that country's level of engagement with the East, we were obliged to maintain some distance from Cuba. The United States' economic positions in our country are a fact, and it is undeniable that the USA intends to use them for political ends.[158]

Algeria's new leaders had made their first conscious decision to put pragmatism before revolutionary principles.

In similar fashion, they also reconciled themselves to the reality of their dependence on French assistance. Although the Ben Bella–Castro joint communiqué had made no explicit reference to France's economic and military interests in its former colony, French officials hardly needed *Jeune Afrique* to point out the apparent similarities between the two countries, as it did in an editorial for its

14–20 October issue. With Cuba situated just 90 miles from Florida and Algeria 470 miles from Marseilles, the paper observed, they epitomized the Third World's confrontation with America and Europe.[159] Ominously for Paris, when Ben Bella's delegation to America returned home, they appeared reinvigorated with revolutionary zeal. The Algerian authorities undertook a spate of provocative nationalizations of landmarks of the pieds noirs' world, such as the Radio Algiers broadcasting station and the capital's main cathedral. Though one Quai d'Orsay analyst anticipated a Nasserite "muslimification" campaign, the cathedral was first converted into a temple to *tier-mondisme* for the 1 November celebrations on the anniversary of the FLN's revolution, which a host of liberation movements attended. Symbolically, the Algerian government's actions looked like a public repudiation of *coopération* that, in addition to the widespread seizures of the pied noirs' homes and businesses, risked discrediting the Evian Accords in the eyes of the French electorate.[160] The commander of the French naval base at Mers-el-Kébir (which France retained the use of per Evian) even had the garrison on high alert for a time, in case the Algerians attempted to seize that installation too.

De Gaulle and his officials observed these developments with alarm. After all, the French president had invested a sizable portion of his personal political capital in the Evian Accords and the myth that he had somehow "won" the Algerian War. On the one hand, Algerian seizures of French citizens' property provoked calls for retaliation in the form of withholding aid. As one official in the French foreign ministry complained, "under the cover of *coopération*, [the Algerians] appeal for aid from France without concealing their intent to use this aid primarily against the very interests of our compatriots in Algeria."[161] On the other hand, even in the absence of provocative actions by Ben Bella's government, the generally calamitous state of the Algerian economy jeopardized the goal of making the country a showpiece, or "shop window," for the benefit of French assistance to developing countries. As they prepared to put the coming year's sizable budget request forward for approval in the National Assembly, concerned officials fretted that "on the occasion of the discussion of Algeria's [aid] budget, the entirety of our policies over the past six months risks being called into question."[162] They were not taking the legislative body's approval for granted.

However, as Khemisti had confessed to Porter, with the separation of the French and Algerian treasuries, the Algerian government was staring into a financial abyss for the coming year, which gave Paris ample leverage to arrest *coopération*'s deterioration. In late November, the young Algerian foreign minister had to come to Paris to negotiate an agreement for a new disbursement of aid in order for his government to continue to function. A report on the matter for the interministerial Council on Algerian Affairs, which de Gaulle himself attended, advised that "consideration of [the Algerian request for urgent funds] will be the occasion for us to demand in return . . . that the Algerian government shows, in a clear fashion by its acts, its willingness to cooperate."[163] This strategy was repeated in the orders for the new ambassador to Algiers, Georges Gorse, who was transferred from Tunis in early January to replace the ineffective and increasingly defeatist Jeanneney. "Do not forget," Gorse was instructed, "that the fundamental guarantee of the Evian Accords rests on France's financial support; consequently you should use this means of financial pressure as often as possible."[164] The implication was obvious, and Algerian officials certainly understood this dynamic. In parallel with their efforts to reassure Washington of their friendly and appreciative orientation, they discovered new depths of enthusiasm and gratitude for Franco-Algerian *coopération*. Like the Americans, the French government required some substantive compromises of Algeria's revolutionary economic model (such as it was) as well as symbolic concessions for public consumption. Once Algiers promised to reimburse French citizens and businesses that had been dispossessed following the pieds noirs' departure—an issue that had gained traction in France—Khemisti's negotiating team managed to secure a new financial assistance package in January.

As a result of such agreements, officials in Washington and Paris believed in the early months of 1963 that they had helped Algeria to move past a dangerous, but understandable, initial phase of revolutionary zeal. The Secrétariat d'Etat aux Affaires Algériennes concluded that, one year after the Evian Accords, Franco-Algerian relations had seen "a clear normalization in recent months" and could be expected to "truly enter a constructive period."[165] Through a combination of patience and pressure, French and American officials told themselves, they had steered the country's leaders away from the radical solutions to socioeconomic problems peddled by countries like Cuba and onto a more "pragmatic" and "realistic" course. In March, for example, Ambassador Gorse explained to Paris that Ben Bella's government "has shown the wisdom to prefer the advantages of the Evian Accords over the romanticism of a new Castroist adventure, [which is] a good thing for Franco-Algerian cooperation."[166] Likewise, when President Kennedy instructed his foreign policy team to draw up an aid plan commensurate with US interests in "this important country," Robert Komer assured him that "the town now understands that you don't want to rely exclusively on French leadership, that you want more than a token US presence, and that you haven't blackballed Ben Bella for his naiveté about Castro."[167] Yet, while most of the officials concerned surely felt that they were truly acting in the best interests of Algeria and its people, communications such as these do exhibit a patronizing and belittling tone similar to that of late-stage, "progressive" imperial bureaucrats. That tone in turn suggests a lack of self-reflection or awareness on their parts, or an inability to sympathize with the politics of economics in the postcolonial context. Congratulating themselves for influencing Algeria's policies, they mistook coercion for conversion.

In reality, the Algerian leaders had adjusted to Paris's and Washington's policy preferences grudgingly, telling themselves that these concessions were merely temporary. From their perspective, those two Western governments had exposed the hollowness of their high-minded rhetoric of economic assistance by wielding that aid like a cudgel, obliging Algeria to abandon its solidarity with Cuba and to compromise a socioeconomic revolution that was, at that time, still more the product of popular propulsion than of executive decree. Not until the International Monetary Fund's controversial policies of 1980s would the concept of "conditionality," or aid with strings attached, become such a commonly recognized issue, but it was immediately evident to Algerian policymakers that this dynamic had the potential to fundamentally shape their country's future. By compromising on some of its most visible and cherished policies in order to secure Western assistance, Ben Bella's government showed flexibility, but blunt quid pro quo deals were not likely to alter deeply held views on such an important—if not *the* most important—issue. American and French officials watching over the country were about to realize that they had compelled change without convincing.

Our Own Special Brand of Socialism

That March, contrary to American and French expectations, Ben Bella's government launched a new phase of Algeria's socialist revolution. The prime minister announced a series of legal decrees that formalized the nationalization of foreign-owned properties, regulated the widespread phenomenon of autogestion (workers' self-management of nationalized enterprises), and once more set Algeria's national economic policy on a collision course with French and Western interests. While the so-called March Decrees were primarily the product of local circumstances, the dissatisfactory state of Algeria's economic relations with France and the United States determined their timing, and they initiated the country's reorientation eastward with respect to global ideological and geopolitical dynamics. Autogestion became the central theme of Ben Bella's domestic political platform—and also an instant cause célèbre with sympathetic governments and leftist circles around the world. However, Algeria's new reputation as a laboratory of Third World socialism brought complications as well as benefits. On the one hand, Ben Bella and his colleagues struggled to avoid the outright collapse of their relations with Paris and Washington, because their country and their people continued to depend on French and American aid for some of their most basic needs. On the other hand, the effort to diversify their economic relations and, in particular, to strengthen their ties to the socialist world increased the risk of falling under the thrall of "foreign ideologies." Preserving Algeria's ideological autonomy and the supposed "authenticity" of its revolution were paramount concerns for its leaders—ones that entailed significant ramifications for policy in spite of their inherent vagueness.

The most proximate cause for the March Decrees was the sense, that January and February, that the Algerian Revolution had lost its momentum. With a sizable portion of the population still lacking adequate food and shelter, in addition to the decline of economic activity, popular enthusiasm was quickly yielding to disenchantment and frustration. The new political and economic elite were starting to fully appreciate just how great their country's problems were and how difficult the daily grind against structural poverty and inequality would be. The government's initial efforts to organize autogestion had made little impression on a chaotic state of affairs, with many self-management committees unable to source needed goods and equipment or get their own produce to market. A nefarious combination of stagnation and speculation fueled the masses' anger, for they watched as the well-positioned and well-connected tightened their grip on large chunks of the old economy. Similarly, the postindependence scramble for positions in the new political and administrative structures was already provoking grumbling about the dangers of "bourgeoisification." As a sympathetic French specialist on the ground warned, "If everybody, from top to bottom, [continues] to command and sometimes profit from the situation, then the gravest economic consequences are to be feared."[168] Meanwhile, the spectacle of Khemisti traveling to Paris with a promise to reimburse rich pieds noirs for their lost property, in exchange for financial aid already promised in the Evian Accords, encouraged those who grumbled that the country had merely seen a change of management, not of its systems of exploitation. Thus, by March, Algerian officials and foreign diplomats were equally aware of a sense of malaise from the top to the bottom of the social hierarchy, and even Khemisti admitted to Gorse that the country and the revolution were in need of a "second wind."[169]

A hot blast of desert air provided that second wind a fortnight later, when *Le Monde* revealed that the France military had just carried out its first atomic test in the Sahara since Algerian independence. The French government plainly did not expect the resultant uproar in Algeria's streets, for while the operations of the test centers were shrouded in secrecy, the Evian Accords unambiguously granted France the right to continue its nuclear program on Algerian territory. Thousands of indignant protesters poured into the main thoroughfares and squares of Algeria's cities to denounce the test, their outrage echoed—or fueled—by political figures and the state press accusing France of perpetrating the worst kind of neocolonial exploitation and despoilment. Jean de Broglie, the senior French official for Algerian affairs, told President de Gaulle that the protests were largely the consequence of unemployment and stagnation, which produced a belligerent "rent-a-mob" situation. "An army of the unemployed and of underpaid *maquisards* [guerrilla fighters] produces battalions of malcontents," he said, "[who are] just waiting [for an opportunity] to take it to the streets."[170] But it quickly became apparent that, while *Le Monde* might have accelerated the timing of events by embarrassing Algeria in front of other Third World countries, Ben Bella's government already had plans in place to recommence its assault on the economic dimensions of the Evian settlement.

To that effect, on 19 March the Algerian prime minister took the stage at a seminar at Algiers University titled "The Algerian Economy: Socialism or Capitalism?" that featured many foreign experts and French *coopérants* in the audience. He caustically declared that he was "happy to see that the university itself is being constructed at the very moment when a bomb has just exploded, and risks destroying what we have undertaken to construct."[171] In the following days, he issued the three March Decrees that constituted the most comprehensive effort yet to address the legal and administrative void that was holding back the country's proto-socialist economy. Effectively, the decrees initiated a very significant expansion and deepening of the socialist revolution, opening up huge new swaths of French-owned agricultural land to autogestion as well as to more centrally directed collectivization. As Omar Ouzegane, the minister of agriculture, explained to Yugoslavian officials the following month, the Algerian government was implementing the first stage of the complete collectivization of agriculture, encompassing 60 percent of the country's arable land and 3 million hectares of pied noir–owned land.[172] The government carried out this program over the next few months, essentially completing agricultural nationalization by the end of the summer, as well as that of numerous other kinds of French-owned businesses such as cinemas and insurance companies. Personally overseeing the nationalization of the estates of Henri Borgeaud, the best known of the great pied noir landowners, Ben Bella belligerently declared, "We want no more Borgeauds in this country. Out with him, and good riddance... If that's contrary to the Evian Accords, I don't care two hoots."[173]

Perhaps surprisingly, Algeria's revolutionary turn in March 1963 did not result in the total breakdown of relations between Algiers and Paris—far from it, in fact. Algeria's leaders were really initiating an extremely confrontational method of negotiation directly with the French president, Charles de Gaulle, by linking issues he cared about deeply (the nuclear test program and the credibility of the Evian Accords) to one that he personally cared little about (pied noir property rights). They correctly calculated that they could win concessions on the latter issue by threatening the former. Additionally, this revolutionary turn coincided with a complete reappraisal and reorientation of Algeria's external economic relations. Algerian policymakers' paramount objective in this regard was "diversification," by which they meant finding new partners willing to compete with France as a source of development assistance and commerce. When the American government unexpectedly declined to play this role, Algeria's leaders no longer saw any compelling reason to hold back their socialist agenda or refrain from pursuing partnerships in the communist world.

Ben Bella and his colleagues had courted US favor intensively in late 1962 and early 1963, stressing to Washington that although they were grateful for the PL-480 food aid, they hoped for a serious contribution to Algeria's development needs. Algiers identified four agricultural recovery projects (irrigation, land reclamation, and so on) that the Americans might finance, at a cost of $10 to $15 million apiece, and indeed on 23 January a *New York Times* report suggested that American officials, as the Algerians hoped, considered the Four Areas project to be the "first step toward converting an emergency relief program . . . into a more normal American aid program."[174] So when George Mennen Williams, the assistant secretary of state for African affairs, announced that he would visit Algiers on his upcoming tour of Africa, in February, the Algerian authorities persuaded themselves that the Kennedy administration was about to announce a dramatic new contribution to the country's economic development.

Yet Algerian expectations and American intentions had become seriously misaligned, and Washington's attendant representatives might well have fiddled nervously during Ben Bella's welcoming speech for Mennen Williams, in which the prime minister pointedly gushed about American generosity in plain anticipation of new largesse.[175] In reality, the Americans had come prepared only to offer modest assistance. Most significantly, instead of picking up the tab for some of the preidentified, high-priority development projects, Washington trumpeted a rural rehabilitation scheme known as the Four Areas project that anticipated paying Algerian laborers with food rather than in cash.[176] The lack of any real financial component damned the scheme in the eyes of the Algerians, who saw it—with some justification—simply as food aid masquerading as a development program.[177] In addition, the Americans rebuffed Ben Bella's personal request for Peace Corps volunteers, fobbing the Algerians off instead with some scholarships to study in America, and a limited degree of technical and medical assistance.[178] Though much less consequential than the issue of financing development projects, this second matter almost seemed to represent a more categorical rejection on Washington's part, given the symbolic import of the Peace Corps to Kennedy's overall Third World policy and relatively trivial expenditure of resources involved. All in all, Mennen Williams's visit proved to be an awkward occasion, for the Algerians did not hesitate to express their disappointment with its substance, and Ben Bella sent the American diplomat away with a letter expressing the hope that more aid might be forthcoming in the future.

The British ambassador in Algiers expressed the consensus opinion of locals and foreigners alike by concluding that "the Americans were not inclined to do anything very big here and did not want to queer the pitch for the French."[179]

This outcome was all the more significant in light of the fact that Kennedy's prior instructions to his diplomatic apparatus concerning Algeria had expressly stated his intent to avoid giving the impression of deferring to French interests. His intentions seem to have been stymied by bureaucratic factors: the Peace Corps protested that it was already having difficulty meeting the demand for volunteers in francophone countries, while AID officials argued that they simply did not have any additional funds to spare to finance development projects in Algeria.[180] Apart from a natural tendency toward bureaucratic inertia, the Algerian cause had its opponents within American foreign policy circles on account of the Cuban connection, the French desk's opposition to an aggressive aid policy that might antagonize Paris, and a preexisting bias toward the preferences of Washington's existing allies in the region, Morocco and Tunisia. But there were some voices within the State Department and the White House, notably Komer, who argued that it was absurd to have allocated a $2 million aid budget for Algeria (excluding the nominal value of PL-480 aid) while its two North African neighbors received more than ten times that amount each.[181] At their urging, in the wake of Mennen Williams's trip, at the end of February Kennedy issued another memorandum advising that "all concerned should bear in mind the need for a program commensurate with our policy interests in this key North African country. . . . While we want France to shoulder the lion's share of the burden, we also want to increase our own influence."[182] The battles lines were drawn between USAID and most of the other branches of American diplomacy, the latter fighting to have Algeria's budget for the following year, 1964, raised to $15 million—but even this amount would have paid for only one of the Algerians' irrigation or land reclamation schemes.[183]

The disappointment of Mennen Williams's visit and Washington's refusal to properly compete with France in terms of genuine development assistance were precursors to the March Decrees and the Algerian government's new economic course. Certainly, planning for the reinvigoration of the socialist revolution was already underway, but at the very least, Washington's position removed many of the shackles, in terms of both domestic policies and foreign relations, that Algeria's leaders had placed on themselves. The tone of the Algerian-American relationship deteriorated through the summer of 1963. On the one hand, Algiers sought to strengthen its relations with communist countries, including Cuba, while at the same time, Algerian political figures began to speak more disdainfully of American food aid. "Important assistance has been provided to us [by the United States], notably in the provision of hundreds of thousands of tons of surplus foodstuffs," Yaker acknowledged in an MAE report in September, " . . .

but it's with financial assistance and investments that the US shows itself reticent."[184] The symbolism of the food-for-work scheme was atrocious, for the sight of Algerian laborers queuing up to be paid in bread and milk only served to validate the popular view that the capitalist system simply perpetuated the Third World's underdevelopment. Ben Bella even began to speak publicly of America's "poisoned bread."[185] Naturally, most American officials began to look at Algeria's leaders as an ungrateful bunch who did not show sufficient appreciation for American charity—the PL-480 aid was, after all, feeding up to 2 million Algerian citizens. But as the Algerian foreign ministry's economics desk argued, American food deliveries also undermined efforts to develop Algeria's own agricultural sector by flooding the market with free produce. Moreover, the recipient nation had no say over the type of food provided; not only were some American cereals alien to local tastes, but the PL-480 deliveries also included foodstuffs that Algeria was already obliged by treaty to buy from France. Ultimately, the report's author grumbled, the food aid program benefited the United States because "it maintained the price of cereals, reabsorbed America's food surpluses, and also has appreciable propaganda value."[186]

Whatever the merits of these complaints, Algerian officials concluded that the strategic ramifications of Washington's position were clear. In their view, the Americans' refusal to compete meaningfully with France proved that the old imperialist "spheres of influence" mentality was still in effect in Western capitals, by which they meant a conspiracy to divide the developing world into exclusive hegemonic zones. Consequently, they reasoned, the imperative of economic diversification obliged them to look beyond the West for assistance and trade.[187]

The most obvious potential source of economic assistance, outside of the Western countries, was the Soviet Union. Although the FLN had never been particularly impressed by Moscow's hesitant, ultimately modest support for their national liberation struggle, the communist superpower boasted not just deep pockets, comparatively speaking, but perhaps the world's most impressive example of rapid industrialization. In just two generations, the Soviet Union had progressed from a predominantly agricultural society to a pioneer of space exploration. Several of Algeria's Third World peers were already beneficiaries of Soviet advice and support, including India, Indonesia, Ghana, and, as the Algerians had so recently seen firsthand, Cuba. However, the road to a strong Soviet-Algerian partnership was far from smooth, with the main initial stumbling block being the decision by Ben Bella's new government, in November 1962, to ban the Algerian Communist Party. Over the next twelve months, Algeria's political leaders strove to convince their skeptical Soviet counterparts that they were natural ideological allies, despite the many ways in which Algeria's own interpretation of socialism departed from Marxist-Leninist orthodoxy.

Even though Ben Bella and his circle would stridently insist on the uniqueness of Algerian socialism, they were still unable to define it very well. They highlighted the genuinely mass-based and peasant-focused character of their national revolution, which certainly appealed to the anarchists and anti-Stalinist communists who flooded in from abroad, but their religious and cultural agenda was probably the more obvious differentiating factor. Reflecting the cosmopolitan and outward-looking atmosphere in Algiers, the state-controlled newspapers devoted copious column inches to coverage of socialist systems elsewhere, and nearly every week seemed to herald the arrival of agronomists or industrial technicians from some "fraternal country," most frequently Eastern European. At the same time, political figures also stressed that the revolution was true to Algeria's supposed Arab-Islamic identity. Efforts to fuse the two potential conflicting inspirations of religious nationalism and socialist internationalism were emphatic, yet vague. Reportedly, it was only at the last minute that Ben Bella had added fleeting references to Islam to the text of the Tripoli Program, whose authors were decidedly secular and Trotskyist in outlook.[188] Shortly after independence, the minister of religious affairs declared with more conviction that "Islam is a socialist religion, it is a religion of equity"—a statement as infuriating to certain conservative Algerians as it was puzzling to left-wing atheists and communist onlookers.[189] To his credit, Ben Bella openly acknowledged the imprecision of the revolution he championed so enthusiastically. "We have only a program, but no ideology," the prime minister told an audience of university students the following August. "The debate is also an ideological one, [and] you must help outline the central tenets of the ideology of the Algerian Revolution."[190]

Still, while not totally unexpected, the prohibition of the PCA was something of an unwelcome surprise for Soviet observers, given that initial contacts with the new regime had been positive and the latter had demonstrated its admiration for Cuba in such dramatic fashion. Indeed, Cuba's progression toward communism was contributing to significant ideological innovation and re-evaluation in Moscow, with the party's primary ideological organ, *Kommunist*, declaring that September that local variations of socialism could, after all, evolve into proper Marxist-Leninist communism. The paper praised the Cuban and Indonesian communist parties for providing the example of how to play a peaceful and constructive role alongside nationalist ruling parties in the Third World.[191] The Soviets clearly hoped that the well-organized PCA could perform a similar function vis-à-vis the FLN ruling party in independent Algeria. A Soviet representative came to Ben Bella in late September, before his departure to the United States and Cuba, to stress that his country was willing to offer all kinds of assistance to Algeria, including armaments.[192] The sizable economic and military support provided to the two countries Ben Bella seemed to admire most—Egypt and Cuba—left the latter with no doubt as to the potential benefits of Soviet patronage. Consequently, Moscow interpreted the decision to ban the PCA in early November as a clear rebuff, especially as Algiers proceeded to court French and American favor in the following weeks. Unimpressed by Ben Bella's insistence that the PCA was not being singled out for interdiction in the creation of Algeria's single-party state, the Soviet foreign ministry quickly decelerated their relations, delaying the ambassadorial appointment that had previously seemed imminent.[193] The Soviet press now unequivocally castigated the country it had been showering with praise, accusing its leaders of selling out to neocolonial interests.[194]

For their part, the small staff of the new Algerian foreign ministry understood the Soviet point of view. As a subsequent report by the MAE's Socialist Countries Division explained, experience had taught the Soviets "that a liberation movement, for obvious tactical reasons, often made approaches to the Socialist states during the period of struggle. [But] with independence achieved, this movement might retreat and develop on a conservative path."[195] The Algerians recognized that Moscow had not only the Cuban example in mind but also the recent cases of communists being brutally repressed in other Arab countries, including supposed allied countries.[196] "The interdiction of the PCA was seen [in Moscow] as an ideological alignment with the Ba'ath and the UAR," the MAE's analysts judged, "with the primary consequence being the internal repression of any person suspected of communist loyalties."[197] Even so, the FLN's political culture had always been one of extremely hostility toward alternative political forces, so Algeria's leadership was outraged by Moscow's continued association with the now-illegal PCA. In February, Khrushchev and Boris Ponomarev, another Politburo member and the most senior voice on ideological affairs, openly received the Algerian Communist Party's leaders in Moscow and urged them to continue their work on the behalf of the Algerian people.[198] At that point, the leaders of the Soviet Union and Algeria reciprocated one another's suspicions.

It quickly became apparent, however, that Ben Bellist Algeria was in fact very receptive to communists and their ideas. Although the PCA was formally banned, its members were not ruthlessly suppressed. In fact, not only were they free to meet and collaborate, but the prime minister himself invited them to serve the state and help shape the country's future. There were already a good number of communists and former communists playing prominent roles in Algeria's government—many of them Trotskyites rather than Soviet loyalists, many of them foreign. Like many other anticolonial nationalists and postcolonial leaders of the time, Ben Bella had much admiration for communists because, as he told his biographer, "they are ready to sacrifice everything at a moment's notice for the sake of their political ideals . . . [and] I also admit the force of their economic reasoning."[199] Moreover, that spring he made a point of publicly expressing his admiration of communism and the Soviet Union, using language and terminology that had specific relevance and appeal to Soviet officials, such as "scientific socialism," to indicate that Algeria's leaders understood what "proper" socialism was.[200] Indeed, at a socialist conference in Paris in March, the head of the PCA, Bachir Hadj Ali, declared a state of doctrinal harmony, or compatibility, between communism and the Algerian Revolution. "There is *de facto* agreement," he said, "... between us Communists and our FLN brothers on essential objectives and political orientation. In fact, the PCA program has in its present stage the same aims and orientation as the Tripoli Program."[201] Furthermore, the March Decrees were largely the product of two Trotskyites who were among Ben Bella's closest advisers: the former GPRA diplomat, Mohammed Harbi, and a Greek intellectual, Michel Raptis. So while self-management was a much more decentralized conception of economic management than the Soviet model, it was nevertheless recognizably a product of the European Marxist tradition.

That same month, the Algerians began a concerted campaign to win Soviet support. Ideological factors were only a secondary consideration: Ben Bella and his team feared that the French government would respond to their new wave of nationalizations with the outright termination of France's financial and economic assistance. Essentially, the Algerians were gambling that de Gaulle had too much invested in their relationship to take that step, which would have totally discredited the supposedly epoch-defining Evian Accords. But in the event of a cessation or significant reduction of French aid, the Algerians needed another partner to pick up the slack, and it was clear that the United States would not do so. Pragmatism outweighed FLN veterans' coolness toward the Soviet Union.[202] In a speech that April, Ben Bella declared,

> If the Russians did not exist, we would have to invent them because capitalism exists. We are neither communists nor Marxists, but we must respond to the needs of our country, which is a small country of 10 million people, and we do not want to be erased by the huge machines, the monsters, that constitute the great powers.[203]

Several weeks later, the prime minister offered the Soviet ambassador a powerful rationale for the USSR to support Algeria. He argued that Algeria's socialist orientation could no longer be doubted, that the success of this socialist revolution could affect the whole of Africa, and that his willingness to drop the PCA issue meant that there were no other outstanding disagreements between their two governments. In light of these facts, he said, nobody would understand if the Soviets continued to remain aloof from his country's widely observed revolution. The merit of the case was evident to Dizdarević, the Yugoslavian ambassador who was already becoming a confidant of Ben Bella. Of the latter, he told Belgrade, "He is not a communist, but every Marxist can see the truth in these conclusions."[204] Visiting Moscow that spring, Fidel Castro also forcefully vouched for Algeria in the same terms.[205]

The Soviets were convinced. Analysts in the International Department of the Communist Party of the Soviet Union (CPSU) and Moscow's new think tanks scrutinized autogestion and liked what they saw.[206] *Pravda* and *Isvestiia* stopped harping on about the PCA and recommenced laudable coverage of the FLN government's policies. Instead of describing Algeria as a "country that struggles against imperialism to consolidate its independence," the Soviet press spoke instead of a "people who fight for their revolutionary gains"—an indication that the Kremlin was recategorizing the country as "revolutionary" rather than just nationalist and anticolonial.[207] The first concrete forms of Soviet aid actually came in the military realm, starting with the provision, in April, of equipment and specialized personnel for demining operations in the frontier regions that the French army had so heavily fortified (reportedly, at least some of the Algerian army's own efforts to that point had included forcing ranks of *harkis*, the militias who fought for France, to march through minefields).[208] Because Moscow's primary regional ally, Egypt, was already providing Soviet weaponry of all kinds to the Algerians with the understanding that these donations would be restocked, much of the groundwork for direct military assistance was already in place. Strategically, the Soviets were also interested in the possibility of friendly airbases and ports in the western Mediterranean, and they might also have recognized that the French government was actually much less bothered by the prospect of a Soviet-Algerian military relationship than an economic one. Even so, arguably the more significant story was the commencement of economic and, surprisingly, ideological cooperation in the summer of 1963.

By that time, the MAE's Division des Pays Socialistes correctly concluded, the Soviet leadership had set aside its initial reservations about Algeria and begun a profound re-evaluation of the country's political evolution.[209] At the beginning of July, a sizable Soviet delegation traveled to Algiers that consisted, notably, of subdelegations for both governmental and party-to-party discussions. The CPSU was recognizing the Algerian FLN as a peer with compatible goals and similar perspectives, and there was no longer any mention of the PCA that Moscow had so recently championed. The two parties discussed questions of party organization, the FLN's role in politics, and the nature of a socialist revolution that claimed to be true to Algerian society's Arab-Islamic identity. In this sense, Algeria featured prominently in Moscow's ongoing ideological explorations at that time, as Soviet experts and diplomats struggled to account for the massive popularity of socialism in the overwhelmingly agricultural countries of the Third World. After all, how should a communist evaluate the declaration by one Algerian minister that "Islam is a socialist religion"?[210] In the spring, Ben

Bella had complained to Dizdarević that the personnel of the Soviet embassy were not able to understand Algeria's circumstances or its revolution. Later in the year, in contrast, Soviet analysts were starting to publish substantial articles on the county, concluding that while the Tripoli Program differed from Soviet doctrine in several ways, it did "serve the interests of the Algerian people and will enable the creation of objective conditions for the building of socialism."[211] At a time when the countries of Asia, Africa, and Latin America faced a profound choice, the Soviets were confident that Algeria had chosen the noncapitalist road to development.

The Soviet visitors told their hosts that they intended to make Algeria a showpiece for Soviet assistance, including financial aid, technical advice, bilateral trade agreements, and the construction of large-scale industrial and infrastructure projects that should kick-start real development. To that effect, a team of economic and agricultural experts stayed on in Algeria for two months in order to evaluate the country's needs and prepare their government's aid package. Among the projects they identified were the completion of several French initiatives to build steel mills and other heavy industrial plants, the construction of dams to regulate agricultural production, and the provision of 10,000 prefabricated homes and rebuilding 100 villages destroyed in the war to alleviate Algeria's severe housing shortage.[212] After being recalled to Moscow for consultations, Ambassador Aleksandr Nikitich Abramov returned to Algiers in September to present his government's impressive aid package that was valued at $200 million in total, including a loan of $100 million.[213] France's support was still substantially larger, but the Soviet Union had instantly become Algeria's second most important source of aid and also made an appreciable political investment in the success of Algerian socialism.

The Soviet Union was not the only communist country that Algeria turned to, nor was the Cold War competition between East and West the sole fault line that could be profitably exploited by a small and poor Third World country. Just as the first objective of the new Algerian government had been to engender some sense of economic-ideological competition between the United States and France, the backup plan to turn eastward also required playing supposed allies against one another. Of course, the communist world already had its own significant fissures. In particular, by the summer of 1963, the Sino-Soviet split had escalated into public view, with representatives of both countries hurling vicious diatribes at one another at Third World diplomatic events such as the AAPSO meeting in Nicosia, Cyprus, that September. Additionally, Yugoslavia had poor relations with China and troubled ones with the Soviet Union. The embassies of various communist countries waged open propaganda war in Algiers, flooding offices and bookstores with recriminatory propaganda leaflets (as a US diplomat in Algiers noted, "The Communists here are inclined to squabble over Algerian favor, the Russians vying with the Chinese, the Yugoslavs with both, while all except the Chicoms kick and cuff the miserable Albanian").[214] Multipolar competition between the communist powers would have practical benefits for the Third World countries if it spurred each to offer more aid to poor countries than they might have otherwise, but Algerian policymakers also saw benefits of an ideological nature. They reasoned that greater diversification of their economic partnerships would allow the various ideological influences to counterbalance one another, minimizing the potential for Algeria to lose its own ideological autonomy.

The alliance between the FLN and China, during the Algerian War, provided a stronger basis for the two countries' relationship than was the case for the Soviet Union. After all, Mao Zedong was possibly the most important single inspiration for the front's guerrilla strategy. Additionally, Peking did not make an issue of the PCA's dissolution, since the Algerian party was loyal to Moscow. In 1963, however, China's leaders were struggling to adjust to the postcolonial era in the Third World, with economic development supplanting anticolonial resistance as the paramount concern for African and Asian elites.[215] So while independent Algeria's support for violent nationalist rebellions in places like Angola provided a firm basis for continued cooperation between the two countries, Chinese officials also mimicked their Soviet rivals' efforts to reorient the conversation around socioeconomic questions. In fact, by hailing Algeria's socialist experiment as a genuinely revolutionary endeavor, Mao's regime gave its imprimatur to a noncommunist economic project for the first time.[216] Responding to the obvious improvement in Soviet-Algerian relations in the summer of 1963, the Chinese government held an economic exposition in Algiers in September that attracted more than 150,000 visitors, eager to learn more about the country's agricultural and industrial achievements. Jealous of the exposition's success, Soviet and Yugoslav diplomats circulated among the crowd, audibly sniggering at the exhibits and cracking that "Made in the Soviet Union" stickers had been ripped off all of the most impressive machinery on display.[217]

But the Soviets held several advantages over the Chinese communists in the economic domain. First, as those jibes crudely pointed out, the Soviet Union was visibly more industrialized and more technologically advanced than its great Asian rival. Mao and his comrades were correct in thinking that their predominantly peasant society was a point of recognition and sympathy between China and the rest of the Third World, but Algeria's leaders were typical in their desire to leave that reality behind as soon as possible.[218] Best to learn about industrialization from the industrialized, they reasoned, even if they were very grateful for China's support during the liberation struggle.[219] A second, decisive Soviet advantage was that they simply had more resources and more money to throw around. When Peking responded to the hefty $200 million Soviet aid package that autumn by extending its own loan worth $50 million, the gesture was simultaneously a testament to the Algerians' successful diversification strategy and to China's fundamentally disadvantaged competitive position. Tellingly, although Mohammed Benyahia, the MAE's expert on the socialist bloc (and coauthor of the Tripoli Program), opened the Algerian embassy in Moscow in mid-July, it took several more months for the Algerian government to dispatch an ambassador to Peking. Ben Bella confided to Dizdarević that he knew well that Algeria was benefiting from Sino-Soviet tensions, but that he was also mindful of the risks for a small country of becoming too enmeshed in the schemes of the great powers, as Cuba had done.[220]

That consideration explains the appeal of dealing with smaller countries, notably Yugoslavia, whenever possible. Here were two countries that had much to offer one another in both practical and ideological terms. According to the account of the future ambassador to Belgrade, Rédha Malek, a senior Yugoslav diplomat visited Algeria shortly after independence as part of a fact-finding tour of Africa and came away "very impressed by Algeria's economic potential and by the Algerians' degree of evolution, compared to the black Africans."[221] The Yugoslavs quickly made an important gesture to aid the recovery of Algeria's agricultural sector by providing 500 tractors, technicians, mechanics, and public works engineers. Then, early in the new year, they extended a loan worth $10 million for the Algerian government to buy their manufactures and industrial goods.[222] The strong rapport between the two countries was reflected in the selection of Malek, one of the most accomplished of the former GPRA diplomats, for the Belgrade post. He was included in the new MAE's first big wave of ambassadorial appointments in July, which included such high-priority destinations as Moscow, Washington, London, Accra, and Havana (only Paris and Rabat preceded these appointments).[223] There was a prospect for consequential, mutually beneficial trade between Algeria and Yugoslavia—a rarity for two socialist countries outside the communist bloc. "The Yugoslavs have been struck by the current and potential magnitude of Algeria's natural resources," Malek argued in his first major report from Belgrade. "In this light, during the recent negotiations in Algiers [in July 1963], the Yugoslav government hastened to renew the credit . . . that they extended to us at the beginning of the year. It is to be expected, therefore, that Yugoslavia will continually develop its economic relations with us."[224]

Vitally, the countries' business dealings were all the more appealing for their mutually beneficial ideological component. Having escaped Soviet dominance over their affairs, the Yugoslavs betrayed no hint of being bothered by the PCA's interdiction. To the contrary, Algeria had the potential to become the greatest success in Tito's campaign to export his country's own model of socialist development.[225] The authors of the March Decrees were openly admiring of the Yugoslav system, and Ben Bella memorably told a French journalist, "To me, Castro is a brother, Nasser is a teacher, but Tito is an example."[226] Nijaz Dizdarević, a Bosnian reputed to be close to Tito and cousin to the Yugoslav ambassador in Cairo, was appointed to the embassy in Algiers almost immediately after the formation of Ben Bella's government. He very quickly became one of the Algerian prime minister's closest confidants and remained so until the latter's fall from power.[227] In Malek's view, "Our experiment constitutes the striking confirmation of an idea among Yugoslav officials, by which formerly colonized countries can direct themselves toward socialism through an entirely new process, unforeseen by and not conforming to the classic Stalinist schema." At the same time, he acknowledged, the Yugoslav example was important to Algeria, "not, of course, as a model to copy or imitate slavishly, but only as a social, political, and human experiment to study up close . . . so that we in turn can freely create our own model." In his opinion there was little risk of one of their two revolutions falling too much under the influence of the other, since "this danger [which] is very possible when a great power is involved, is less likely with Yugoslavia, a small country that is still underdeveloped in vital areas."[228] For its part, the Yugoslavian leadership was very conscious of the Algerians' ideological wariness. Tito assured a visiting Algerian dignitary, in the summer of 1963, that while his people were happy to share their experiences in the hope that they might be useful, they had no expectation that the Algerians would copy their example wholesale.[229]

In short, by late 1963 Algeria's initial efforts to diversify its economic relationships were paying dividends. In addition to securing new sources of aid and commerce, even if some were relatively minor, Ben Bella and his colleagues believed that they were successfully maintaining the unique identity of Algeria's socialist revolution. They had even succeeded in winning the ideological approval of the two most powerful communist countries, the Soviet Union and China, that had hitherto shown little tolerance for deviations from orthodoxy (the clash of their two "orthodoxies" notwithstanding). As the Algerian prime minister confidently declared, in his opening speech for the Chinese economic exposition in September 1963: "Our own special brand of socialism . . . has confounded those who would like to teach us lessons in socialism. [Yet] we have decided to go as fast along the path of socialism as any other revolution . . . anywhere else in the world."[230]

But perhaps the most successful aspect of the turn to the communist countries was to dissuade the French government from punishing Algeria more heavily for the nationalizations and other measures that violated the Evian Accords. Certainly, in the wake of the March Decrees, Paris stalled on negotiations and held back a portion of its aid funds in an effort to modify Algiers's behavior, but the need for discretion ensured that actions were comparatively minor in their severity. The problem for French officials was that, having invested so much prestige in Franco-Algerian cooperation, which was supposed to be the exemplar of a new relationship between the Northern and Southern Hemispheres, they could not afford to admit the Evian settlement's obsolescence. Domestic criticism of the cost of France's external aid programs was already increasing, and rather awkwardly, de Gaulle's original choice for the ambassadorship in Algiers, Jean-Marcel Jeanneney, penned a damning public report of *coopération* on his return.[231] The secretary for Algerian affairs, Jean de Broglie, assured the French public that, "if [*coopération*] succeeds, the countries of the third world will have the proof that they can depend on an advanced liberal economy for their economic and political promotion. But if it fails, they will look elsewhere."[232] Behind closed doors, however, he himself questioned the rationale of, essentially, paying for a socialist revolution whose purpose was to undermine French interests. He asked his colleagues whether *coopération* was "a rearguard action or a vision for the future? The real problem is that of the viability of cooperation between a socialist country and a capitalist country."[233] Understandably, his associates had no clear answer to this question.

The Country Is the Project

The FLN's emphatic refocus on socioeconomic issues in the closing stages of the Algerian War, after such sparing contemplation of those questions throughout the preceding years, was indicative of a more widespread trend in which Third World leaders advanced surprisingly utilitarian rationales for decolonization. For all their nationalist certitude, rhetoric of historical inevitability, and celebrations of cultural emancipation, most of the new postcolonial elites staked their legitimacy on an appeal to the material self-interest of their citizens. For some, indeed, an equitable and redistributive form of economic development was the very point of independence, placing the legitimacy of the nation-state project itself in jeopardy. As Ben Bella put it, speaking to an admiring biographer in 1963, "Political power was [now] in the hands of the Algerians; but economic power, including the land itself, was still in the hands of the Europeans." So long as the big landowners remained in place, he insisted, "the words 'Independence' and 'Revolution' made no sense."[234] No mere hyperbole, his claim that independence was meaningless without socialist revolution was fully consistent with the commonly held opinion within the FLN that the French authorities could have defeated or even prevented the Algerian Revolution by implementing socioeconomic reforms earlier and with more conviction. By the end, the front's propaganda basically agreed with the French prescription for Algeria's economic transformation but argued that France could not be trusted to carry it out to its fullest extent. In that sense, Algeria's new leaders were typical of those postcolonial elites who, in the final analysis, governed in accordance with the proposition that poverty and economic inequality were the fundamental drivers of decolonization and rebellion in the Third World—rather than whichever irresistible forces of national, cultural, or divine will they claimed to represent.

Moreover, Algeria's experience of independence showed that the global economic system of the early 1960s rewarded sovereignty. On the one hand, industrialized countries' economic relations with the Third World were largely subordinate to geopolitical considerations. This reality was demonstrated by the large number of countries that began to provide Algeria with aid in the summer of 1962, even before the formation of a government in Algiers. Less favorably, it was also evident in the Algerians' failure to secure significant assistance from the United States; despite the demonstrated sympathy of President Kennedy, the relevant Washington bureaucracies judged Algeria's case through the prism of established policies regarding France and Cuba. On the whole, though, the first year and a half of Algerian independence demonstrated the viability of the Third Worldist strategy of increasing aid and trade by playing on the sense of competition between rich countries. Indeed, the Soviet aid announcement in September 1963 prompted a rethink in Washington. "I question whether we could or should enter a major competition with the East," Robert Komer wrote in a memorandum to his National Security Council colleague McGeorge Bundy, "but I don't see our present effort as enough either. . . . [Algeria is] the key to the Maghreb on the one really important coast of Africa. It's worth a larger investment than [we are making] at present."[235] In light of geopolitical realities, namely, the competition for client states, independence and sovereignty did favor development.

On the other hand, the new institutional apparatuses of the postwar world also valorized sovereignty. While the Bretton Woods institutions are more typically understood as forces of global integration that weakened the power of states, it was highly significant in the context of decolonization that statehood was a requirement of membership. That criterion made membership in the World Bank and International Monetary Fund (IMF) valuable in its own right to postcolonial elites—for the same reason that they prized membership in the UN. The Algerian government secured membership in both in 1963, despite its ideological misgivings, and would be able to effectively chastise the bank's leadership, in the years to come, for neglecting its obligations to a member state in good standing because of French pressure. As they proceeded to establish their own state-centric international economic institutions, such as the African Bank for Development in 1964, developing countries tended to reject proposals to deal directly with Western financiers, without recourse to official channels.[236] The new UNCTAD initiative reflected the Third World's ideal solution of fully subordinating the international economy to sovereign oversight. In other words, statehood was a requirement to interface with the global economy, even in the case of institutions that would, in time, be seen to undermine the sovereignty of poor countries. For its part, the World Bank embraced the concept of "national development" in the early 1960s. Its incoming president, George Woods, announced in 1962 that, rather being project-oriented, it was time to recognize that "the *country* is the project."[237]

At the same time, while fundamentally nationalist in its inspiration, Algeria's economic strategy was very much extroverted and outward-looking, rather than isolationist or autarkic. Aside from believing that their country should set an example for others in the Third World, Algerian officials recognized that international trade had to be central to any realistic development strategy. Naturally, an export-oriented strategy could easily end up resembling the perpetuation of the colonial economic order. As Belaïd Abdessalem advised Ben Bella in late 1963, they needed to strike a balance between, on the one hand, simply maximizing oil and gas revenues and, on the other, using Algeria's hydrocarbon resources to fuel its own development, industrialization, and socialist programs.[238] Algerian officials settled on an understanding of "economic independence" that did not aspire to self-reliance but, on the contrary, the diversification and intensification of their international economic exchanges in order to reduce their dependency on any single partner—France especially. Even the communist newspaper *Révolution Africaine* discontentedly accepted the reality of Western-driven economic integration. "There are no isolated problems anymore. Everything has global resonance now," argued an editorial that celebrated the anniversary of the March Decrees:

> This globalization must be taken with all its implications.... The contradiction [between rich and poor countries] will worsen not only because of the unprecedented increase in wealth at one end of the world, but also because of tightening communications and increased information [that] homogenize needs and desires, revealing to those dying of hunger ... the lifestyle of those who rot from indigestion, suffer from cholesterol, and choke on "gadgets."[239]

So while claiming the moral high ground of austerity and self-sacrifice in the short term, the authorities also promised to eventually catch up with the decadent industrialized countries. The challenge was to avail of the forces of global commerce without being subsumed in them. Taking a wider view, while there were certainly elements in the Third World that championed more autarkic goals, by and large, postcolonial national development strategies joined in the processes of economic globalization precisely in order to strengthen their states.

So far as Algeria's ties to France were concerned, although Ben Bella's government had made very little progress by late 1963 in reducing its dependence on the former colonial power in quantitative terms, the quality of that relationship had already started to evolve in the desired direction. President de Gaulle ensured that French officials continued to publicly insist on the viability of *coopération* and the Evian Accords, but they admitted behind closed doors that the supposedly pathbreaking trans-Mediterranean relationship was quickly devolving into bilateral haggling between two self-interested states. Shedding the pretense that there was something visionary about the Evian settlement, de Gaulle himself had observed to a close adviser in the autumn of 1962, "Now that nearly all of the pieds noirs are gone, only the petrol and the [atomic] tests count."[240] Conversely, a year later the Algerian government transmitted an aide-memoire to Paris attesting to its dissatisfaction with the terms of trade between them. Noting that "Algeria has been independent now for more than a year and enjoys full sovereignty internally and externally," the letter argued that "a large portion of its resources continue to be exploited according to a system created before independence."[241] Although Algeria's share of hydrocarbon revenues was the most important issue, the country's economic stewards were also gravely concerned by France's failure to buy Algerian wine in the promised quantities, and they began linking the two issues in their discussions with their French counterparts. In these circumstances, it would become increasingly difficult for de Gaulle to defend *coopération* to his own officials (at least one of whom grumbled that they were throwing money into a bottomless pit) and to the French public.[242] Rebutting skepticism in the National Assembly, Jean de Broglie, the head of the Secretariat of State for Algerian Affairs, conceded that "we are heading toward a simple state-to-state cooperation, with more structural definition and more concern for France's [own] economic problems."[243] In short, the myth of postcolonial "interdependence" was collapsing from both sides; it existed now only rhetorically.

Yet with the second, economic stage of the Algerian Revolution now underway, the country's leaders also insisted that there was still another, ideological dimension to their independence. Ben Bella and his colleagues strove to define their "own special brand of socialism" in the belief that, if they were not operating in accordance with their own ideology, then they would perforce be practicing somebody else's. Despite the vagueness of this quest for ideological autonomy, its sincerity and significance were borne out in practical measures. Algerian officials deliberately cultivated a multitude of foreign influences in order that each would counterbalance the others: with Soviet, American, Chinese, Eastern European, Cuban, and French advisers all running about the countryside, in other words, the Algerians could judge the merits of each country's system without being beholden to any single one of them. They also preferred to deal with smaller countries, like Yugoslavia, on the basis that they were less aggressive ideological proselytizers. Ben Bella was happy to admit that the Algerian Revolution was a hybrid and frequently reeled off a list of influences in his public appearances. As a result, although independent Algeria's external and internal policies inspired as much criticism as admiration around the world, by the close of 1963, observers from both camps generally agreed that Ben Bella's government was at least maintaining a distinctive identity amid the tremendous ideological contestations of their time.

Moreover, the claim that autogestion represented a more "authentic" form of socialism—one that was more humane and somehow truer to local cultures and society—was central to the pioneering mystique that brought so many to Algiers from foreign climes. For example, the pied noir poet Jean Sénac was so inspired by the spectacle of Che Guevara visiting an Algerian cooperative in the summer of 1963 that he penned the immortal couplet to his lover, "you are as beautiful as a rose / you are as beautiful as a self-management committee."[244] However, there were other voices, albeit still few in number, that did not share Sénac's infatuation and resented the prominence of outsiders in Ben Bellist Algeria. That same summer, the army's newspaper, *Al Djeich* (The army), published a letter that railed against "this cosmopolitan fauna that regularly lands on our soil, these beards and intellectuals in turtlenecks, socialism's heroic Saint-Bernards," and bemoaned that Algiers was simply a convenient and accessible "voyage into revolutionary exoticism for all these nauseating Saint-Michel types."[245] This current of discontent would strengthen in the months ahead, challenging the premise that the Algerian Revolution harmoniously fused its external influences with its national heritage.

4

The Allure of Globalism

Continents, Colors, and the Cold War

> When I told [the Algerian ambassador in Ghana] that my political, social, and economic philosophy was Black nationalism, he asked me very frankly: Well, where did that leave him? Because he was white. He was an African, but he was Algerian, and to all appearances, he was a white man. . . . Where does that leave revolutionaries in Morocco, Egypt, Iraq, Mauritania? So he showed me where I was alienating people who were true revolutionaries dedicated to overturning the system of exploitation that exists on this earth by any means necessary.
> Malcolm X, January 1965

> Do you not get it, lads? The Irish are the blacks of Europe. And Dubliners are the blacks of Ireland. And the Northside Dubliners are the blacks of Dublin. So say it once, say it loud: I'm black and I'm proud.
> Jimmy Rabbitte, in Alan Parker's *The Commitments*, 1991

No one who listened to independent Algeria's new leaders could doubt their ambition in the realm of international affairs. When he spoke to the UN General Assembly on 9 October 1962, Prime Minister Ben Bella promised that "for every concrete decision concerning major international problems of peace and global security, we are ready to play the role of a responsible country."[1] His list of problems was as extensive as his assessment of Algeria's responsibilities was expansive. He pledged his country's unqualified support for the black liberation movements of southern Africa, even suggesting that Algerian "volunteers" might join the fight against white minority rule in that region, and expressed his solidarity with the Palestinian nationalist movement in similar terms. But if the Algerians were expected to take strong positions on Afro-Asian questions, Ben Bella's plan to visit Cuba showed that he and his colleagues saw no geographical limits to their responsibilities. Indeed, pointing to communist China's continued absence from the United Nations as an example of structural inequality and Western prejudice, he asserted that Algeria would seek to reform the very foundations of the post-1945 international order, economic as well as political. Nor did the Algerian prime minister shy away from commenting on America's domestic affairs. In a meeting with Dr. Martin Luther King Jr. a few days later, he suggested that the United States was losing its moral authority abroad by failing to address its own racial tensions.[2] In contrast, he told the General Assembly, "Algeria is allied with an ensemble of spiritual families who, for the first time at Bandung, recognized the shared destiny that unites them. The Algerian Republic comes from a liberation struggle that has surpassed its national context." His country might well have been poor and feeble by the traditional measures of geopolitical might, but in the moral sphere, Ben Bella believed, Algeria was a superpower.[3]

Many Western observers were instinctively skeptical of such bold talk emanating from the leader of an objectively weak and war-ravaged country. After all, Ben Bella's sweeping "globalism" was becoming increasingly de rigueur in the diplomacy of the age, when the proliferation of new transportation and communication technologies continued to expand the horizons of clerisies everywhere. Additionally, some American and British officials rather patronizingly opined, the Algerians were understandably still under the influence of the intoxicating—and transitory—thrills of victory, independence, and power. The British ambassador in New York suggested that Ben Bella and his entourage were responding to the "spotlight of Afro-Asian attention" with a show of militancy that the harsh realities of Algeria's domestic troubles would likely soon quell.[4] Yet, as the political scientist Robert Mortimer has previously noted, one of the distinguishing characteristics of Algerian foreign policy was that it sincerely hewed to the radical exhortations of Frantz Fanon and other Third World thinkers.[5] Moreover, by dint of the expertise and experience accumulated during the wartime FLN's diplomatic campaign, Algeria was better equipped than most to implement those designs. As one GPRA veteran told his fellow deputies in the new National Assembly, their diplomacy espoused certain principles, but "it does not consist solely of principles," and even if Algeria had "only entered the concert of nations several weeks ago, we cannot say that we are novices at foreign policy."[6] In the months ahead, Algeria would make real progress in implementing the Third World project, across several continents, in both the exalted diplomatic realm and the underground, subversive one. Refuting both skeptics and cynics, Algeria's leaders were about to put their praxis—and guns, and money, and training camps—where their theory was.

Consequently, the archives of the Algerian foreign ministry—which are in fairly sparse and crude condition for the first twelve to sixteen months after independence—reveal not only the construction of a newly independent country's diplomatic apparatus but also a largely successful effort to translate lofty Third Worldist rhetoric into a practicable foreign policy doctrine. The country's diplomats urged that the increasingly numerous and frequent international meetings flying the banner of one expression of solidarity or another (Afro-Asian Peoples' Solidarity Organization, Afro-Asian economics seminars, Afro-Asian preparatory conferences, nonaligned summits, pan-African summits, Arab League meetings, and so on) must produce concrete results and substantive initiatives. "For it to be effective and positive," Ben Bella told the National Assembly, "neutralism must not be limited simply to statements of principle. The nonaligned countries must establish and develop a real solidarity between them, as much in the political domain as in the economic domain."[7] As a general rule, therefore, his government advocated the formalization and institutionalization of the Third World's various organizing principles. To that purpose, one of Algeria's first major diplomatic accomplishments was its vital contribution to the founding of the Organization of African Unity (OAU) in Addis Ababa in April 1963. Describing that achievement as "both means and ends," the county's leaders strove to replicate this early success and vindication of their vision.[8]

Even so, while it was generally easier to build substantive alliances and structures between fewer parties, a pragmatic Third Worldist doctrine was not necessarily limited in ambition, scale, or daring. On the contrary, the lesson that Algerian policymakers took from their war of national liberation was that the weak were obliged to take risks and look for allies even in the farthest corners of the globe. They believed that stasis in international affairs was as deleterious to the interests of poor countries as it was to liberation movements: instability created opportunity, and provocation was the cure for anonymity. Experience had taught the Algerian elite that it was typically necessary to aggravate the great powers in order to achieve their goals—sometimes even when their goal was to gain the support of the very power that they were irritating. Even with the achievement of independence and statehood, therefore, they would continue to exacerbate Cold War tensions to their own purposes and intensify their support for armed groups and revolutionary forces in other countries. Algerian nonalignment was the neutrality of the insurgents: subversive, provocative, combative.

The third linchpin of Algerian diplomacy was globalism, in the sense of surpassing traditional regional and cultural identities. The Algerians consistently advocated the expansion of the Third World coalition, most obviously to encompass Latin America but also sympathetic forces in Europe like Yugoslavia. On the one hand, this priority simply reflected the calculation that with greater scale came greater influence, but most of Algeria's leaders also believed that their geographically interstitial position was a vital strategic asset. Their country was not especially populous nor a recognized cultural mecca, but they felt that they could multiply their influence in international affairs by serving as the intersection of the Arab world, Africa, Europe, Latin America, and in some cases, even farther afield. Almost immediately, Algeria became a vital gateway for Cuba and

Yugoslavia into black Africa, which was a promising field of opportunity for two countries isolated in their own regions. The Algerians encouraged the numerous liberation movements they supported to coordinate with one another and facilitated voyages to Belgrade, Peking, and the capitals of other potential benefactors around the world. They called on African countries to support the Palestinian cause and put Angola, Congo, and South Africa on the agenda of the Arab League. Through such initiatives, Algeria quickly gained influence disproportionate to its more tangible resources. That said, it is essential to recognize that most of the country's political leaders and diplomatic personnel also sincerely believed in the Third Worldist principles they championed: they thought that their foreign policy benefited Algeria, but it incurred significant costs as well, costs that they could have minimized were they not heartfelt in their commitment to anticolonial solidarity.

This chapter examines independent Algeria's largely successful efforts to express Third Worldist ideals as an operable foreign policy, but it also explores the significant challenges, in some cases insurmountable, that its practitioners faced. They quickly found, for example, that a sovereign state lacked the agility of a transnational revolutionary movement: while the GPRA had often gotten away with presenting different faces to different capitals, the government in Algiers could not escape the ramifications of its actions and statements. A related problem was the fact that, even with the Algerians' practiced skill at manipulating great power rivalries, by 1963 some of these rivalries were becoming more deleterious than beneficial—especially those between the Soviet Union, China, and India, which threatened to rip the Third World coalition apart. Potentially still more problematic was the effect of foreign affairs on Algeria's fragile social equilibrium. The practical necessity of prioritizing between the multiple expressions of solidarity that Ben Bella's team publicly espoused—pan-Africanism, Arabism, and so on—highlighted the contested nature of Algeria's national identity. In particular, the early decision to prioritize African unity over its Arab or Maghribi analogs rankled those who felt that a francophone clique was turning its back on its cultural heritage. The interaction between foreign and domestic affairs is a universal phenomenon, but it is an especially powerful dynamic in the postcolonial context, where the symbolism and ritual of diplomacy can be an essential component of the new elite's legitimacy.

Nevertheless, the most direct threat to Algeria's international agenda was of a very traditional nature. In October 1963, Morocco launched a limited military campaign to seize a disputed section of the Algerian Sahara. The so-called Sands War had more significant consequences than its remoteness and relatively small scale would suggest. In time, Ben Bella's government would turn the situation to its advantage, but in the short term, this battle for the most tangible of resources—land—brought Algerian globalism crashing back to earth.

Maghribi and Arab Unity: Too Close for Comfort

On the anniversary of the FLN's liberation struggle, 1 November 1962, a boisterous crowd gathered in Algiers's central square, the recently renamed Place des Martyrs, to listen to their new prime minister's vision for the future. Numerous foreign dignitaries also assembled to hear more of Ben Bella's agenda, with curious visitors from near and far swelling the sizable diplomatic corps already present in the capital. Adjacent to the speechifying, the city's main cathedral, redesignated a mosque, was adorned instead for the occasion as a temple to Third Worldist solidarity, festooned with paraphernalia saluting Algeria's commitment to Maghribi, Arab, African, and global anticolonial solidarity. In that spirit, before a throng of his compatriots and the eyes and ears of the global community, Ben Bella declared that "joining together with our North African brothers is more than necessary, it is vital, and it will be only a step toward Arab unity, and finally toward African unity."[9] Seemingly bold, this declaration was likely rather comforting to his local audience. After all, that order of progression—Maghrib, Arab world, Africa—concurred with most Algerians' sense of their place in the wider world. In contrast to the many cultural and social bonds between Algeria and its neighbors, and most Algerians' identification with Arab and Islamic civilization, the themes of pan-African and Afro-Asian solidarity were recent introductions to the popular imagination. So it was only to be expected that, if Algeria's new leaders were serious about pursuing transnational or supranational "unity" in a substantive way, they would commence with the Maghreb and proceed to the wider Arab world. However, contrary to his assertions that day, Ben Bella's government quickly declined opportunities for political and economic integration with Morocco, Tunisia, and the radical countries in the Mashriq in order to focus its energies on black Africa instead. Moreover, this choice was not simply the result of political rationale or geopolitical expediency overriding cultural sentiment and historical ties. Rather, those ties proved to be the obstacle to integration. That is to say, it was precisely because Algeria's cultural, religious, and human connections with the Maghreb and the Arab world were so profound that its new leaders judged them too dangerous to handle.

Despite Ben Bella's prediction that Maghrebi unity would be a step toward Arab unity, independent Algeria's relations with its immediate neighbors are best understood in the context of the wider Arab world. Initial indications suggested that Algeria's new leaders intended to play an active role in the region's affairs. On a personal level, Ben Bella was very close to Gamal Abdel Nasser. Houari Boumedienne had received a classical Islamic education in his youth and was widely seen as a pillar of the "Arabist" wing of the FLN, as was Mohamed Khider, secretary-general of the FLN party organization and the third political heavyweight in the new ruling coalition. By dint of its famous liberation struggle, Algeria enjoyed significant public admiration in most Arab countries that could potentially translate into diplomatic influence. By dint of its prime minister's close association with the Egyptian president, Algeria was also expected to back Cairo in the two main contentions in Arab affairs at the time: first, the already intense "Arab Cold War" between conservative and radical states (Algeria and Egypt belonging to the latter category), and second, the troubled Egyptian-Syrian-Iraqi efforts to form the United Arab Republic (UAR)—the moniker that Egypt officially still maintained, alone, after the collapse of the Syrian-Egyptian federation. Additionally, Algeria seemed destined to weigh in on the major issue that, theoretically, united the Arab countries: Israel. In the spring and summer before taking power, Ben Bella had made several bellicose public statements in support of the Palestinians' nationalist cause, urging them to imitate the FLN's strategy and even suggesting to one Lebanese journalist that he was prepared to commit Algerian "volunteers" to the Palestinian struggle.[10]

At first, the latter issue seemed likely to command Algeria's full engagement. Although some in Israel had once hoped that an independent, socialist, and multinational Algeria would be a kindred spirit and ally, in practice the Israeli security services had assisted France's counterinsurgency against the FLN and encouraged Algerian Jews to emigrate. On hearing Ben Bella denounce her country as a colonial enterprise to the UN General Assembly in October 1962, foreign minister Golda Meir concluded that the French withdrawal from North Africa had completed the Arab encirclement of her country.[11] Indeed, the FLN's leaders and cadres had come to perceive Israel through a Third Worldist prism, describing it as an enemy outpost in the global struggle against imperialism, akin to South Africa or South Vietnam, that could only be defeated through collective action. Said one typical report of the Algerian MAE, "Certain islands of [imperialist] resistance remain in areas where nationalism has recent origins and where the petroleum and military interests of Western imperialism demand [it].... The Arab world must confront international Zionism's schemes [which are] backed by its allies in Europe and America."[12] The necessity of Arab unity in the face of neo-imperialism, in the guise of Israel, quickly became the core message of Algeria's relations with other Arab countries.

Moreover, a new Palestinian nationalist group committed to armed resistance, Fateh, drew inspiration from the FLN's example and Fanon's writings. One of its founders, Khalil Wazir, hailed the idea that revolution was not "the outcome of a particular political ideology or social philosophy, but an expression of independent will, a proof of existence."[13] His comrade-in-arms, Yasser Arafat, came to Algiers in the summer of 1962 to witness the independence celebrations and to ask the Algerians for the same kind of assistance they were already providing to numerous African liberation movements. By Arafat's account, Ben Bella told him: "My dear brother Yasser, we made that promise and we will honour it. In the coming days we will sit together and discuss how we can help your revolution."[14] Toward the end of year, Ben Bella's partner in power and FLN secretary-general, Mohamed Khider, visited Cairo and apparently formed a particularly strong bond with Arafat's brother on the basis of their mutual appreciation for Islam's role in politics and society. After first providing them with Algerian passports, Khider brought a Fateh delegation back with him to Algiers, where they were invited to open their first office abroad.[15]

However, Khider's involvement may have been an impediment to Algeria proceeding further with the Palestinians—and perhaps also to intensifying Algeria's involvement in Arab affairs more generally. After these promising early contacts, Algiers seemed to unexpectedly put Fateh on hold for six or seven months, which was quite a marked pause in comparison to the rapid escalation of support for equivalent groups from sub-Saharan Africa. One explanation for this pause is that it came at Nasser's request, so that he could better strengthen Cairo's own influence with the Palestinian nationalists.[16] Alternatively, Lakhdar Brahimi, the GPRA veteran subsequently appointed ambassador to Cairo, suggested in an interview with the author that the Palestinians were simply too disorganized at first for Algeria to provide much practical assistance, although this argument is not entirely persuasive given similar levels of disorganization among early African beneficiaries of Algerian aid.[17] But while Nasser's interests and Palestinian disorder no doubt weighed on Algerian-Palestinian relations, it is likely that Ben Bella's intensifying rivalry with Khider was also a factor. Because Khider was a champion of the Palestinian cause within the Algerian government, the prime minister may have slowed down relations with Fateh in order to deny him a prominent victory.

The rivalry between Ben Bella and Khider reflected concerns that foreign policy should speak to the nation's identity. Unlike Khider, the prime minister was literate only in French and spoke the Algerian dialect of Arabic that was nearly incomprehensible outside of the Maghrib. Arabic was long held sacred as the language of the Koran, its formal written form, or *fusha*, connected the economic and political elites of numerous countries, and the idea of linguistic-cultural unity was as vital to the transnational spirit of Arab nationhood in the 1960s as it had been to its German equivalent a century earlier. The embarrassment that Ben Bella felt when delivering a speech in Cairo that spring, by means of a translator, demonstrated the limitations on his ability to conduct public diplomacy in the Arab world. Indeed, mastery of *fusha* was a relatively rare skill throughout the ranks of Algerian officialdom, which delayed the appointment of ambassadors and staffing the foreign ministry's department of Arab affairs. As one internal report on the MAE's bureaucratic development indicated, the problem was not simply one of finding qualified ambassadors: Arabic-literate secretaries and support personnel were arguably an even rarer commodity, as were Arabic typewriters.[18] The fact that the Algerian government operated almost entirely in French strengthened the impression among Arab visitors and interlocutors that the country was an outlier in more senses than just the geographical.

Khider sought to profit from this situation by touring several Arab countries in December 1962 and January 1963, when there was still no permanent Algerian representation in the region. He hoped to commit Algeria to a nonrevolutionary profile in Arab affairs and establish relationships that would support his efforts at home to steer social policy in a more religious and culturally conservative direction. Therefore, in addition to making contact with the Palestinian nationalists, he discussed commercial and loan agreements with the conservative Kuwaiti and Saudi governments, while the representatives of radical left-wing and socialist parties were reportedly shocked to hear him inveigh at length on the Islamic character of the Algerian Revolution. These initiatives clashed with the agenda of the generally francophone, leftist, and cosmopolitan circle of advisers around Ben Bella and senior staff of the foreign ministry, who intended to ally Algeria with the Arab world's "progressive" forces.[19] Khider's fulminations on Algerian radio against the growing influence of "atheists and enemies of Islam" who did not "hide their vices" also threatened the country's internationalist reputation.[20]

Because Khider was out of step with his colleagues and exceeding his purview, Ben Bella managed to isolate and then eject him from the political scene in April 1963. It was no coincidence that his government's engagement in Arab affairs increased around this same time. Ambassadors were appointed to several capitals, such as the "old" GPRA hand, Lakhdar Brahimi, in Cairo, while Fateh officially opened its Algiers office with great fanfare that September. However, Ben Bella and his advisers seem to have acquired from the experience a fear of unleashing domestic forces, conservative and religious, that they were ill-equipped to lead. Speaking to the author fifty years later, Ben Bella took warranted pride in having subsequently mastered formal Arabic; but in 1963, with diplomacy such a decisive fundament of legitimacy in Algerian political culture, he was wary of making the Arab world a focus of his foreign policy.[21]

That said, neither the prime minister nor other senior figures would publicly admit to deprioritizing Arab affairs, since that might antagonize and energize the very arabophone elements they wanted to keep quiet. Moreover, supporting the Palestinian nationalist cause was still a moral imperative for the Algerians. From September 1963, the Algiers office permitted the Palestinians to make contact with sympathizers around like the world like the South Vietnamese National Liberation Front and Che Guevara. "We had turned the first page in the story of our struggle for recognition as a people who were being denied their rights," Wazir recalled. "The fact that we were seen to have Algeria as our friend gave us a revolutionary credibility that was worth more than gold and guns at the time."²² Even so, gold and guns were soon forthcoming. In the following months, Boumedienne agreed to deliver arms to Fateh via Syria and to train its fighters in the camps of the Armée Nationale Populaire (People's National Army, ANP).²³ At the same time, however, Ben Bella and his colleagues saw Israel as just one problem in the global struggle against imperialism and seemed to examine the Jewish state in more dispassionate and less urgent terms than "front-line" states like Syria or Egypt. "Our views in relation to Israel are not entirely identical to the views of other Arab countries," Ben Bella later admitted to the Yugoslav leader, Josip Broz Tito. Israel was a real political challenge, he said, but not an existential peril, and unlike some other Arab governments, "we do not need Israel to keep the masses under our influence."²⁴

That last comment speaks to another factor limiting Algiers's interest in Middle Eastern affairs, namely, its leaders' quick disillusionment with many of their counterparts in the other capitals of the Arab world. Surprisingly, this was even true of the leaders of the "radical" countries in whose camp Algeria seemed to firmly belong. Algeria gained its independence at a time when the so-called Arab Cold War between radical/progressive governments and reactionary/conservative ones was at its most explosive. Fears of subversion were particularly acute after revolutionary army officers overthrew Yemen's autocratic ruler in September 1962 and declared themselves acolytes of Nasserite Arab socialism. The Egyptian president vowed to defend Yemen's revolution from "reactionary" rebels who, in turn, obtained Saudi Arabia's backing. Within a year, Egypt would have 20,000 troops deployed in the deepening Yemeni quagmire, a number that would double again in 1964. Meanwhile, even though the Syrian-Egyptian United Arab Republic had collapsed acrimoniously in 1961, Egypt nominally maintained the UAR's existence while the Syrian and Iraqi wings of the Arab socialist Ba'th Party continued to advocate the revival and expansion of their revolutionary federation. The radical wing of Arab politics therefore contained its own ideological clash: that between transnational Arab nationalism, or *al-qawmiya*, and nation-statism, or *al-wataniya*.²⁵ In short, Algeria gained its sovereignty at a time when state authorities on both sides of the Arab Cold War warily guarded their turf.²⁶

Initially, it appeared that Algeria might commit to the revolutionary Arab nationalist project. Nasser was determined to consolidate Egypt's ties to Algeria's new leaders. As soon as Ben Bella and Boumedienne formed their government, the Egyptian president provided the genesis of a navy and air force by donating two warships, which steamed into the Bay of Algiers in full view of the foreign dignitaries attending the 1 November 1962 celebrations, and a squadron of Soviet-made MiG fighter jets. The scope of Cairo's military assistance continued to expand in the new year, including training large numbers of Algerian officers. While Ben Bella valued these demonstrations of Nasser's commitment to his regime, there were plenty of local and foreign voices disquieted by the prospect of Algeria becoming an Egyptian client state.²⁷ In light of current events, the Moroccan and Tunisian governments—staunch opponents of Nasser—understandably dreaded an Egyptian plot to foment "another Yemen" in the Maghrib.²⁸ Meanwhile, events in spring 1963, raised the prospect that the Algerians might also support and participate in the ongoing discussions toward recreating the UAR. Algeria joined Egypt and Yemen in extending immediate recognition to the governments produced by Ba'thist coups in Damascus and Baghdad. Algiers's haste in this matter was particularly notable because the deposed Iraqi president, Abdul Karim Qassim, whom the Ba'thists ruthlessly executed on television, had been one of the FLN's most steadfast allies during its war of independence. The young Algerian foreign minister, Mohammed Khemisti, explained in a televised appearance of his own that the decision to recognize the new Ba'th regimes reflected his government's commitment to Arab unity.²⁹ Moreover, Algeria's leaders undertook their first major regional diplomatic initiative by dispatching a high-powered delegation to attend unity discussions in the Egyptian capital and to visit Damascus, Baghdad, and certain other capitals.³⁰ With Boumedienne, Khemisti, and tourism minister Abdelaziz Bouteflika at its head, this delegation certainly boasted the stature to commit Algeria to deeper involvement in the Arab unity project. On 17 April, the Egyptian, Syrian, and Iraqi governments agreed to found a new federal state, with its capital in Cairo, and centralized foreign and defense policies.

However, Algeria's new political elite was not at all interested in joining the UAR scheme because its underlying ideological rationale was quite incompatible with their own political program. While the FLN and Ba'th both championed socialism and an Arab national identity, the Algerian Revolution was also the embodiment of *al-wataniya* that the Ba'th Party condemned as "fragmentation." In the parlance of the latter, places like Algeria or Egypt were not "states" or "countries" but "regions of the Arab homeland."³¹ The party's official "theoretical principles" of October 1963 unambiguously declared that "the desired [unified] Arab state will not resemble the traditional national states established on a purely national basis," with the additional stipulation that even that unified state's constituent subdivisions "need not necessarily be based on the present map of the Arab countries."³² On these questions, the Ba'thist program clearly diverged from that of the Algerian nationalists, who had, after all, significantly prolonged their war of independence and the Evian negotiations to prevent compromising their future state's sovereignty or territorial borders. Consequently, during their visits to Cairo, Damascus, and Baghdad in late March, Boumedienne, Bouteflika, and Khemisti expressed their effusive support for any attempt to create a unified "Arab socialist community" but also clarified that they would be supporting the project from the outside. Algeria's overriding concern at the present time, they said, was the consolidation of its own national independence.³³

Even had they been willing to pursue some form of integration with the socialist countries in the Mashriq, Khemisti and his colleagues thought the project's success unlikely.³⁴ Ba'thist ideology notwithstanding, the previous Syrian-Egyptian federation had failed because of the unavoidable clashes of interests between each country's political elite, and the same tensions were still evident in 1963. The founders of the Syrian Ba'th Party, Salah al-Din Bitat and Michel Aflaq, came to Algiers in April in the hope of persuading Ben Bella to intercede with Nasser to support some of their positions in discussions over the future shape of the UAR.³⁵ Not only did they fail, but the attempt to implicate Algeria in internecine bickering, possibly jeopardizing its relationship with Egypt, did not impress their hosts. To the extent that Algerian diplomacy already had an institutional memory, the GPRA's experiences had instilled mistrust of the petty politicking and infighting between Arab governments. Pridefully, Algerian cadres favorably compared their "authentic" popular revolution, which had the participation of the masses, to the "top-down" elite-driven revolutions of the other supposedly progressive Arab regimes. In that light, Khemisti quite damningly described Bitat as "honest, progressive, but not a militant"—a parliamentarian rather than a proper revolutionary like Nasser who was a "major force able to turn ideas into reality."³⁶

Following the acrimonious collapse that summer of the new UAR project that the Syrian, Iraqi, and Egyptian governments had agreed to in April, Ben Bella felt free to express the Algerian position in forthright fashion.³⁷ Speaking in Cairo the following September, he laid the blame squarely on the Ba'thists:

> As for you, men of Ba'th, having known your writings and doctrines, I have been unable to formulate a clear idea of what you want to achieve in the national and socialist domains. You need Abdel Nasser and I fear that in the event of a division in your ranks, you will again find yourselves obliged to align with imperialism.³⁸

While one might well wonder how the targets of Ben Bella's criticism felt about being lectured in French on the correct way to pursue Arab unity, from the Algerians' perspective, the miring of the UAR project that summer confirmed their skeptical appraisal of the endeavor's feasibility in the foreseeable future. For the time being, Algiers's contribution would be limited to playing the role of an interested observer who dependably backed Egypt's positions in disputes among the radical Arab states.

That said, Algeria did not become an Egyptian client state (as French officials in particular seemed to have feared). While other members of the government, including Boumedienne, feared that Ben Bella's undisguised personal admiration for Nasser could induce the prime minister to follow such a course, their alertness to the possibility also ensured against it. For example, they demonstrated their geopolitical independence early on by rejecting the suggestion that they might contribute troops to the war in Yemen.[39] But neither did Algeria's leaders see themselves as ideological or philosophical protégés of the Egyptian raïs. On the contrary, describing the Egyptian revolution as a "small group of people that represented a progressive force operat[ing] an action from above," Ben Bella later told Tito that, together, Algeria and Yugoslavia had much to teach Nasser and his colleagues about creating a revolution based on the masses.[40] Likewise, in the international realm, the Algerians made Africa, rather than the Arab world, the focal point of their alliance with Egypt. Not only was their partnership much more equal in the African context, but the Algerians were at least partly justified in thinking that they enjoyed greater familiarity and political capital across the Sahara.

As a result of these factors, as well as more than a little bad luck, Nasser's long-awaited, supposedly triumphal visit to the Algerian capital in May 1963 proved to be a surprisingly insubstantial event. Even the trip's theatrical aspects and the public's genuinely rapturous welcome went awry. Nasser had chosen to arrive in grand style, with Ben Bella and his comrades greeting the president's yacht at Algiers's picturesque waterfront. However, the surging crowds quickly overwhelmed the security cordons and forced the two heads of state, with their entourages, to clamber atop a fire engine in order to escape. This exit did not comport with Nasser's assiduous aura of dignity, and his opinion of Algerian organizational prowess fell further when news came from the harbor that one of the two warships that Egypt had donated had somehow crashed into a pier and sunk.[41] Nasser reportedly already wore a grim demeanor that first evening, but the second day brought worse news that eventually overshadowed his visit.[42]

That morning the young foreign minister, Mohammed Khemisti, who had been in a coma for several weeks, succumbed to the gunshot wounds inflicted, apparently, by a rival for his wife's affections. Although Ben Bella sometimes suggested that there was a foreign plot behind Khemisti's death, there is no evidence to support such suspicions, and if there really was a political motive for his murder, then the likeliest culprits were surely to be found within the upper ranks of the FLN elite.[43] The Algerian foreign ministry and associated offices still being a close-knit operation, the funeral and tributes to the fallen diplomat unavoidably affected both behind-closed-doors discussions and public appearances for the remainder of Nasser's trip. Khemisti had managed to achieve a fairly high international profile in his brief time, in part because of the youthfulness that made him and other members of his team popular subjects for Third Worldist publications such as *Jeune Afrique*.[44]

Still, disruption on the Algerian side does not fully account for the lack of real substance to Nasser's visit, which seems to have surprised and disappointed the Egyptian president and his team. Algiers's recent decision to keep out of the ongoing UAR discussions eliminated one entire subject of discussion and rendered much of the Arab nationalist rhetoric manifestly hollow. At one event, Ben Bella had even pointed dramatically to the UAR flag and declared that "the flag of this Republic, on which three stars shine, will wave over other Arab countries, and other stars will come to shine on that flag—notably the Algerian star."[45] However, his official script, which more accurately reflected the Algerian authorities' collective stance, vaguely suggested only that Algeria might pursue some kind of "affiliation" with the UAR after "a considerable period of time" had passed.[46] Conversely, the Yugoslav embassy, which enjoyed excellent contacts with both parties, concluded that the Egyptians and the Algerians seemed equally disappointed in one another. Ben Bella and Nasser's final joint communiqué seemed to skip over a lot of themes that the Yugoslavians had expected to see, and they suspected that the document had been more or less entirely drafted by the Egyptian side, though this is perhaps attributable to Khemisti's death and the resultant disruption among the Algerian diplomatic team.[47]

In a sense, Nasser's visit was a bit of a flop precisely because of the strong connections between the two countries. In its determination to avoid looking like an Egyptian client state, the Algerian side left little in the way of substantive proposals to discuss. Arguably, the Algerians overcompensated in placing so much rhetorical and symbolic emphasis on their connections with sub-Saharan Africa: although Cairo and Algiers largely agreed and cooperated on African affairs, Nasser could hardly celebrate Egypt's African calling while his government was in the midst of negotiating an Arab nationalist federation. More generally, the Algerian government's tacit deprioritization of Arab affairs shortly after independence was the somewhat counterintuitive consequence of the real strength of its people's ties to the region. The Arab world was too close: it was difficult to engage deeply with it without, in the process, stoking contentious debates about the Algerian nation's social and cultural identity that the authorities preferred to avoid. The tensions between Arabists and religious conservatives, on the one hand, and left-wing, internationalist francophone elements, on the other, suggested that too much history impeded the cause of Arab unity.

The ideal of "Maghrib unity" also quickly foundered after Algeria's independence for similar reasons. Though bound by culture and history, in 1962 Algeria, Morocco, and Tunisia were nevertheless divided by territorial disputes, the differing natures of their regimes, and geopolitics. Hassan II, who succeeded his father early in the year, and Habib Bourguiba both resented Algeria's possession of the Sahara's spoils and feared the FLN's relations with Nasser and the leftist opposition in their own countries. But Mohammed V had been cannier than the Tunisian president: although Morocco's participation in the Casablanca Group of radical African states was increasingly anachronistic, the two kings had remained on good terms with the victorious Ben Bella–Boumedienne faction during the FLN's internal crisis. Bourguiba, in contrast, had long irritated the Algerian nationalists by playing favorites among them, culminating in a hapless attempt to arrest Ben Bella in Tunis in June, and important figures in the FLN and the new Algerian government subsequently spoke openly of one day making the Tunisian leader pay for his scheming.[48] Neither regime could rest easy, however, given the open participation of numerous opposition figures at the 1 November celebrations in Algiers, and Ben Bella's assertion that the socialist revolution had a duty to expand beyond Algeria's borders.[49] "Maghrib unity will exist," he predicted, "once the countries of the Maghrib have made the same choices in the domestic and external domains."[50]

Although the Maghrib was a good example of how the inherently cosmopolitan and transnational nature of the modern anticolonial movement inspired notions of regional integration in the first place, the messy aftermath of French empire doomed the project by engendering a strong sense of vulnerable national sovereignties. Morocco was the first to test the new Algerian leadership by raising the prospect of armed conflict over an iron-rich area of the southwest Sahara with a series of small skirmishes between pro-Moroccan and pro-Algerian militias and tribes near Tindouf. But Rabat's real target seemed to be the substantial numbers of Algerians residing in Morrocan territory and the nature of their contacts with Mehdi Ben Barka's left-wing National Union of Populist Forces. In the summer, the local security services began monitoring the Algerian population and arresting those suspected of spreading "subversive" propaganda, while the FLN's extensive radio network continued to blanket the region with propaganda extolling land redistribution and revolutionary politics.[51] However, the Algerian government was in no position to handle even a small-scale military confrontation—their armed forces had barely any presence in the Sahara—and duly took placating measures. Khider and Ferhat Abbas each visited Morocco in October and November, keeping their distance from the opposition and effusively lauding the old king's support for the independence struggle (a gesture that itself testified to the Algerians' ability to confer legitimacy beyond their own borders). When the FLN reversed previous plans to publish an opposition newspaper in Algiers and agreed to end its provocative radio propaganda, the fighting in the south died down.[52]

A failed attempt on Bourguiba's life in late December, dubbed the "Christmas Plot," sparked a similar crisis with Tunisia. Like Ben Barka, Bourguiba's old political rival Salah Ben Youssef had drifted leftward and grown close to Egyptian military intelligence and the FLN during the war. After Ben Youssef's assassination in August 1961, one of his supporters promised to return one day to seize power in Tunis "on an FLN tank," and in autumn 1962 an opposition group installed itself in one of Algiers's fancier hotels, where senior FLN figures openly visited and dined with them on a regular basis, and others operated near the border at least with the tolerance of Boumedienne's local commanders.[53] Thus, on learning that one of the Christmas Plotters had received an Algerian visa and escaped across the border, in January Bourguiba accused Ben Bella personally of harboring a "gang of assassins," insisting that "if elements in the plot have managed to regroup and reinforce themselves, they owe it to the foreign encouragement they find in Algeria."[54]

Indeed, though denying any direct involvement in the plot, Ben Bella freely admitted even to the American ambassador that "it is true he wishes to influence Tunisia[,] but only showing her an example of what could be done for the people. He did not approve, he said, of 'Bourguiba living in Palaces while Tunisians go hungry.'"[55] The Tunisian government broke relations with Algiers, and their negotiators stormed away from the table amid discussions to regulate the movement of people and goods between the two countries—a pressing issue for the Algerians given the large numbers of refugees who had fled across the border during the war. Tunis hinted that their status might be resolved simply by expelling them all, and the Algerian consul was roughed up to underscore the point.[56] Yet, privately, the departing Tunisian ambassador admitted that his government was simply leveraging the complex legacies of decolonization in order to persuade the Algerians to give up the Youssefists.[57]

Playing peacemaker, Hassan convened a meeting of the three countries' foreign ministers in Rabat in mid-February. Although this meeting restored relations between Algiers and Tunis, and initiated discussions on regional integration under the rubric of "the glorious task of unifying the great Arab Maghrib," the evidence from the Algerian side reveals the hollowness of the endeavor. The three sides agreed that economic and cultural cooperation should be pursued without waiting on the resolution of all their political differences, and the talks ended with the expectation that the three ministers would reconvene in April to discuss coordinating their economic relations with the EEC.[58] With all three countries so dependent on their exports to Europe, this subject was of real importance. However, the Algerians' main goal for these discussions was actually to prevent Morocco and Tunisia from jointly concluding a trade agreement with Europe; an agreement with Europe that excluded Algeria would jeopardize its own exports, whereas one that included Algeria could impose undesirable restraints on its socialist development model.[59]

Indeed, one revealing document from the Algerian foreign ministry explained that the government's overarching strategy in the Maghrib was to avoid a military confrontation with Morocco by "[digging] a ditch between Tunisia and Morocco on the basis of Tunisia's recognition of Mauritania, [and playing] the

Maghrib conference game for as long as possible [through] concrete and attractive propositions for economic cooperation."⁶⁰ In other words, the Algerians would pit their neighbors against each other by dangling the carrot of access to the Sahara's profit streams: Bourguiba coveted an agreement to transport oil and gas to the coast through Tunisia, while the Moroccans hoped to negotiate a settlement to the Tindouf question.⁶¹ Although any agreements that resulted from these discussions might look like a form of regional integration, the key for the Algerians was to minimize their scope and to keep their hand on the throttle of the process. For example, their foreign policy team recognized the eventual necessity of placating Morocco by "activating our relations with the EEC, so long as that does not obligate some kind of [ideological] choice."⁶² It also minimized any sense of regional integration by preferring separate bilateral deals with each neighbor; because this balancing strategy could break down with the introduction of a fourth party, Algiers rejected Moroccan suggestions to include Libya in their dialogue.⁶³

A second important aspect of the Algerian strategy was to submit inter-Maghribi relations to larger-scale contexts and normative frameworks that were supportive of Algiers's positions.⁶⁴ In theory, the Non-Aligned Movement or the Arab League could serve this function, but in particular, the Algerians hoped to "delay Algerian-Moroccan confrontation . . . [by] entangling the Moroccans" in continental, Africa-wide commitments to respect the sanctity of postcolonial borders.⁶⁵ For this reason, Ben Bella risked irritating King Hassan by unilaterally canceling an upcoming meeting of the so-called Casablanca Group of radical African states that was to take place in Morocco in spring 1963. Conservative and Western-leaning Morocco had always been an awkward fit among the revisionist and subversive members of the Casablanca Group, but Rabat had hoped to win support for its territorial claims to Mauritania there. Instead, the Algerian prime minister threw his energy into preparations for the conference that would found the OAU in Addis Ababa in April.⁶⁶ Although Morocco should have felt more comfortable in that larger and collectively more moderate association, the continental consensus on the nonviolability of postcolonial borders was so firm that Hassan eventually chose to be the only head of an independent African country who stayed away from Addis Ababa.

In that respect, the border dispute with Morocco was one of several factors pushing Algeria's leaders to focus their foreign policy southward, in spite of their people's historically closer ties to the Maghrib and the rest of the Arab world. Operatively, Algiers's North Africa strategy was very different than the one it practiced in the wider Arab world: the avoidance of institutional commitments or entangling engagements in the latter arena, as opposed to the pursuit of continual negotiation with its Maghribi neighbors. But the purpose and outcome were largely the same in both cases: the effective, if unacknowledged, deprioritization of "Arab unity" or "North African unity" in favor of more promising terrain beyond Algeria's traditional regional contexts. Curiously, therefore, Ben Bella and his colleagues simultaneously valorized state sovereignty and an unbounded, geography-defying globalism. By repeatedly asserting that Arab or Maghribi unity could only be achieved once progressive regimes had taken power in all the countries concerned, they also implicitly valued Algeria's ideological identity over its cultural, social, or religious affiliations. As Ben Bella explained to his Yugoslavian counterpart on one occasion, "We have added a new content to the older form. We said that for us Arabism is not a matter of blood, but rather a culture, a way of life, and emotions. We consider it something much wider, a constitutive part that is open to other constitutive parts."[67] It was a confession that would surely have provoked consternation had he voiced it to an audience of his compatriots.

Algeria in Africa: A Fanonist Foreign Policy

Algerian political figures and foreign analysts were of the same mind: at independence, they all agreed, the Maghribi country was already well-positioned to exert significant influence in African affairs. While the process of decolonization was already close to completion (in the political sense at least), the continuation of Angolan colonialism and white minority rule in southern Africa was a source of growing instability. Many of the continent's new polities were vulnerable to internal dissent and external interference, yet millions of people had still not reconciled competing national, local, and pan-African loyalties in their own hearts and minds. Inter-African cooperation, unknown for almost a century, was inhibited by communications and transport networks that were still directed toward Europe. Meanwhile, Africa's Cold War continued to intensify in spite of the Algerian War's conclusion and the abatement of the ongoing Congo crisis, thanks in part to the Sino-Soviet rivalry. Consequently, with the continent's political structures at a formative and malleable stage, an official from the British Foreign Office concluded that "a country with the prestige, brains, and energy of Algeria is going to have a very considerable influence in developments throughout Africa."[68] The Tunisian foreign minister pinpointed another Algerian asset: watching troops and military equipment trundle through Algiers for the 1 November 1962 celebrations, he observed that "there are arms enough in this country . . . to supply all of Africa."[69] Algeria's own diplomats and leaders certainly thought so. They were convinced that theirs was a "vanguard role": leading the fight against imperialism by supporting national liberation movements to their utmost, leading the struggle against *neo*-imperialism by propagating socialist revolution.

While their preferred course of action in Africa therefore would have looked much like the realization of Frantz Fanon's most passionate writings, Algerian officials also made canny tactical compromises that Fanon the pragmatic FLN diplomat would have approved of, too. The first choice that confronted them was that between ideological purity and unity. In particular, their support for like-minded left-wing revolutionaries in countries that were already independent, such as Niger and Cameroon, exacerbated the polarization of the political landscape and thereby threatened to derail the creation of a continental intergovernmental institution, the OAU. Spearheaded by Ben Bella and Khemisti, Algerian diplomats therefore waged a peacemaking campaign for the first year of their African policy, reaching out to wary Western-oriented states like Côte d'Ivoire and reining in some controversial revolutionary groups (but not national liberation movements). In bridging Africa's political divide, they then played a significant and reputation-boosting role in the successful founding of the OAU at Addis Ababa on 25 May 1963. In return, Algeria secured the OAU's backing for armed anticolonial movements and won the continent's support for its positions in its territorial dispute with Morocco. Furthermore, by assisting in the consolidation of the African state system, the Algerians' temporary ideological truce also helped to create some lasting stability in the continent.

Supporting armed nationalist and revolutionary groups was the foundation for Algeria's relations with the rest of Africa. The FLN had already begun to cooperate with and support other movements well before Algeria gained its own independence; the ALN had trained and equipped recruits from several countries in its camps in Tunisia, Morocco, and Mali. Even so, it was not a given that independent Algeria would continue to assist these movements to the same extent. Few other African states were as unrestrained in their support for subversive transnational groups—especially in terms of military assistance—because they feared diplomatic reprisals or even, as the Moroccan and Tunisian governments had feared when the ALN was on their territory, undermining their own sovereignty. So when Ben Bella declared to the UN General Assembly that "Algeria will not forget her brothers in South Africa and Angola, and will give them her unconditional support," a representative of the multiple nationalist groups in the Portuguese colonies enthused that Algeria had distinguished itself from those governments whose support was "more moral than material."[70] He predicated that "by taking a categorical stance, the first Algerian government will facilitate the polarization of revolutionary African forces in support for the Portuguese colonies."[71] So uncompromising was Algerian prime minister's stance that officials from the US State Department worried that he was about to send Algerian troops directly to join up with Angolan and Congolese guerrillas.

Ultimately, Algeria set a policy of sending its own military personnel into such situations only for training and liaison purposes. But Ben Bella's government quickly proved that it not only was willing to provide any military assistance short of its own troops, but also was intent on preaching the gospel of armed revolution to those who preferred nonviolent forms of resistance. When the African National Congress (ANC) opened an office in Algiers in late June 1963, Ben Bella gave a combative speech in which he pointed out that his country was already training officers from several other African groups so that they could imitate Algeria's example. "We know colonialism," he told the South Africans, "it understands only [the] language of force and violence. We tell our South African brothers [that] hunger strikes and demonstrations will get you nowhere."[72] Of course, the FLN had previously given basic combat training to a rather dubious Nelson Mandela, before his capture and incarceration, at one of its camps in Morocco.[73] Immediately after forming their government, Ben Bella and Boumedienne relocated these camps and their foreign guests inside Algeria proper and set about expanding the program. French lawyer Jacques Verges, who had defended Djamila Bouhired for planting bombs for the FLN, was the first head of a new office created to liaise with national liberation movements. By mid-November, the Algerians were already offering refuge, money, arms, and training to rebels from at least eight countries and colonial territories: Angola, Cameroon, Congo-Léopoldville (as opposed to the smaller, neighboring Congo whose capital was Brazzaville), Mozambique, Niger, Portuguese Guinea, South Africa, and Southwest Africa (Namibia).[74] The breadth and scale of the program began to ramp up. In January 1963, for example, fifty fighters from the Mozambican Liberation Front arrived for training.[75] Nor did the Algerian authorities attempt to hide their assistance program. On the contrary, the prime minister advertised it. "I say it frankly, publicly here," Ben Bella declared in a speech that same month, "as soon as [the Angolans] ask us for arms, we will give them to them within 48 hours."[76]

However, Angola was the early focus of Algeria's anticolonial campaign—and an early demonstration of Algiers's decision to prioritize unity over ideological preference in its dealings with Africa. Two rival Angolan groups, Roberto Holden's Frente Nacional de Libertaçao de Angola (National Front for the Liberation of Angola, FNLA) and the more left-wing Movimento Popular de Libertação de Angola (Popular Movement for the Liberation of Angola, MPLA), had already looked to Algiers for support and inspiration by the end of 1962. Holden's party enjoyed murky ties to the CIA and Israeli Mossad, as well as the support of the Congolese-Léopoldville government, led by Cyrille Adoula, that the Algerians deemed to be the continent's worst collaborator with Western "neocolonialism." At the same time, the FNLA sought to emulate the Algerian FLN: in addition to pursuing a guerrilla war against the Portuguese army, it formed a provisional government modeled on the GPRA, the Govêrno revolucionário de Angola no exílio (Revolutionary Government of Angola in

Exile, GRAE). While the FNLA's origins and base of support lay deep in the poor Angolan interior, bordering Congo, the MPLA's leadership consisted largely of intellectuals from the comparatively cosmopolitan colonial capital, Luanda, with many of them being of mixed racial heritage. The FNLA denounced its rivals as privileged "half castes and '*assimilados*'" who were disconnected from the downtrodden peasant masses, but there was a strong Marxist influence on the MPLA, and the movement's socialist rhetoric aligned it ideologically with the Algerian government.[77] In addition to political factors, it is perhaps also the case that some Algerian officials identified more closely with the MPLA cadres' deeper immersion in the colonizer's culture and language, or felt less constrained by racial dynamics in their company. It was clear in any case that, from the prime minister down, the Algerians preferred the MPLA to the FNLA. Nevertheless, they were careful to support both Angolan factions equitably and urged them to join forces. When Ben Bella introduced Holden to the attendees of an Algerian trade union congress on 17 January 1963, Dr. Eduardo dos Santos of the MPLA stormed the stage to protest that his group was the only authentic voice of the Angolan people.[78] With the audience boisterously chanting for "unity," Ben Bella suggested optimistically that "this is perhaps the first time that two representatives of the Angolan movement can speak to an assembly so frankly" and reassured the crowd that "I have asked them, in the interests of Angola, to unite their efforts in a liberation front."[79]

Urging the formation of united national fronts became a central tenet of Algeria's relations with liberation movements. After all, the FLN strategy had proved essential to Algeria's own liberation, even if that reading of history elided the FLN's ruthless elimination of its own rivals, such as Messali Hadj's Mouvement National Algérien. By 1963, the Algerians were rightly conscious of the fact that the changing pattern of the Cold War in Africa exposed the Angolans and others to much more powerful, external fractious influences than they themselves had experienced. Indeed, Angola was fast becoming a cautionary tale of the Cold War's divisive effect: that summer, Algiers helped put yet another Angolan nationalist leader, Jonas Savimbi, in touch with the Chinese government, whose support subsequently enabled him to compete with both the MPLA and the FNLA.[80] This factionalism ultimately contributed to the protraction of the Angolan liberation struggle, which did not conclude until 1975, when an even longer civil war commenced. So Ben Bella was justified in warning in January 1963 that, "if we do not aid these parties despite their dissensions, I fear that the fascists would regain some success that would harm all of Africa. . . . [We hope], by this aid, to be the artisan of unity."[81] Ahmed Kaïd (aka Si Slimane), who was at this point the Algerian military's primary liaison with liberation movements, and Lakhdar Brahimi, the diplomat, went down to Congo that February with the goal of mediating unity talks between the Angolan nationalists. Their effort proved futile, but Algeria continued to increase its support to both Angolan groups anyway.[82] In May, the MPLA's Mario de Andrade claimed that Boumedienne's training camps had already received 250 of his movement's recruits, while Algeria, in cooperation with Tunisia and Yugoslavia, shipped seventy tons of armaments in the other direction in August.[83]

Furthermore, Algeria's message of national unity was an effort to prevent the controversial subject of supporting armed liberation movements from becoming further enmeshed in Africa's political polarization. Some governments were wary of abetting guerrilla warfare at all, in part because it earned the United States' ire, but the decisive opinion probably lay with those who were worried primarily about subversive, left-wing groups that saw many African governments as "neocolonial" in their policies. The Léopoldville government, for example, was hostile to the MPLA, which had ideological similarities and some contact with Congolese leftists, or "Lumumbists," like Antoine Gizenga and Christophe Gbenye, who hoped to overthrow Adoula. The Congolese authorities impeded the flow of armaments to the group, forcing it to limit its guerrilla campaign (such as it was) to the enclave of Cabinda, north of Angola proper.[84] During their trip to the Angolan camps in February, Slimane and Brahimi were able to assess just how influential Congo and other "front-line states" were in southern Africa because they could provide shelter to rebels and facilitate the movement of materiel and personnel. "Congo is becoming the linchpin of the African Revolution [for] political and strategic reasons," a report by the MAE's Africa desk subsequently argued. "[It will be] decisive for the future of the progressive regimes and for the whole of Africa. The battles for Angola, for 'Portuguese' Guinea and other dominated countries will be won or lost there."[85] Angola was but one dimension of a steadily intensifying Algerian-Congolese rivalry, but Algiers could not afford to antagonize more members of the "moderate," or Western-oriented, wing of African politics. On the one hand, there were plans to open Algerian-run camps closer to the action, in a front-line state like Tanganyika.[86] On the other hand, throughout the spring of 1963, Ben Bella was determined to win a continental consensus on the question of supporting armed liberation movements at the upcoming African unity conference in Addis Ababa. To that purpose, by insisting that the Angolans were all fighting for the same cause and treating both parties equitably, Algiers demonstrated that its policy of anticolonial solidarity was not a cover for revolutionary subversion.

Of course, rather awkwardly, the Algerian leadership *was* abetting revolutionary subversion. For example, when the president of Niger, Hamani Diori, pressured Ghana and Guinea to eject the opposition Sawaba party from their territory in the summer of 1962, the group had found a new home in Algiers.[87] The next February, Sawaba's leader published a defiant and widely noticed article in the Algerian *tier-mondiste* newspaper, *Révolution Africaine*, in which he warned that, in reference to the Addis Ababa heads of state summit, "in no way must African unity become a sort of trade union of men in power who will seek to support one another to resist popular currents."[88] Consequently, the Algerian authorities had to reassure the African continent's unruly underground as well as its new establishment. For the benefit of the latter, Ben Bella's government quieted down groups like Sawaba and gave the appearance of distancing itself from them—as was also the case with Amilcar Cabral's communist nationalist party from Portuguese Guinea, the Partido Africano da Independência da Guiné e Cabo Verde (African Party for the Independence of Guinea and Cape Verde, PAIGC), which the Senegalese government loathed.[89] Conversely, the Algerians reassured these groups that they would defend their interests at the Addis Ababa meeting.[90]

Somewhat separate from the issue of nonstate movements, the staff of the MAE recognized that African governments that generally maintained colonial economic structures and cooperated with Western economic interests were also fearful of "Algerian socialism's contagious example."[91] Côte d'Ivoire was the clearest demonstration of Algiers's charm offensive on such governments in the run-up to Addis Ababa. Even though the FLN had long since vilified the Ivorian president, Félix Houphouët-Boigny, as a pawn of French neo-imperialism, Ben Bella and his diplomatic team strove successfully to make him the first head of state from sub-Saharan Africa to come to Algiers, in late April (it was additionally significant that Houphouët-Boigny's visit preceded Nasser's).[92] The official rationale for the occasion, not entirely spurious, was that Côte d'Ivoire and Algeria were a rare example of two African states that might actually enjoy mutually fruitful commerce, but the trip's political value was more important to both leaders. Houphouët-Boigny received assurances that the Algerians would not aid his domestic opposition, and received heroic Algeria's imprimatur at a time when he was comparatively isolated. Algiers's ambassador in Abidjan believed that the Ivorian president was "conscious of the debt he owes Algeria, and the fact that we took the initiative to establish official diplomatic relations."[93] While that statement sounds somewhat self-aggrandizing, Algeria's public appeal in Africa at that time was a real phenomenon, and even the performative aspects of diplomacy were valued by postcolonial elites as affirmations of their status. In return, the Algerians gained a good amount of diplomatic capital by demonstrably putting the spirit of African unity ahead of any ideological differences.

At the same time, Ben Bella also strove to bring other radical countries around to the Algerian perspective on African unity. He had two main arguments in his communications with two of Algeria's "traditional" allies on the continent, Guinea's Ahmed Sékou Touré and Ghana's Kwame Nkrumah. First, he urged them to set aside their more radical objectives, at least in the short term, to improve the chance of successfully creating an organization that included all of the continent's governments. In a letter to Sékou Touré, he argued that, together, the radical countries could then ensure that this institutionalization of African unity would include a universal commitment to assist national liberation movements. "This will have the simultaneous effect of demonstrating everyone's attachment to the long-awaited construction of Africa," he wrote. "This measure can also take concrete form as an Africa-wide alliance, in which each nation must commit unreservedly to a shared battle for liberation."[94] That is, Ben Bella argued that it was worth working with "neocolonial" governments in order to establish the principle of assisting armed liberation movements as a fundamental norm of African affairs. In Nkrumah's case, there was the additional challenge of convincing the Ghanaian president, who considered himself the political and philosophical fulcrum of the continent, to abandon his own conception of African unity that practically no other national leaders subscribed to. He gave each head of state a copy of his manifesto, *Africa Must Unite*, which argued for the creation of a single continent-wide federation, rather than a mere intergovernmental organization.[95] Unsurprisingly, there was no support in other capitals for a scheme that would have significantly limited national sovereignty.[96] "The goal that Nkrumah was set on," an Algerian foreign ministry report later explained, "was to create an axiomatically Nkrumist continental government . . . and his insistence on achieving his aims irritated almost all the African countries." For his part, Nkrumah was little impressed by Ben Bella's suggestion that a real measure of cooperation, in the pan-Africanist spirit, could be achieved through overlapping commercial and cultural exchanges.[97]

Nkrumah's stance also reflected the reality that, in spite of Ghana and Guinea's earlier support for the FLN and their membership in the informal alliance of "radical" African countries, relations between the three countries could be prickly and competitive. Indeed, while he still seemed as committed as before to supporting liberation movements, such as the PAIGC, Sékou Touré's recent geopolitical reorientation was concerning to the Algerians. Suspecting his domestic opponents had communist ties, he had dramatically broken with the Soviet Union in December and expelled Moscow's ambassador. The leader who had famously rejected Charles de Gaulle's invitation to join the French Community in 1958 was now in the process of reorienting his country's economy once again, replacing Soviet advisers and aid with American and French assistance.[98] Meanwhile, Algerian diplomats found Nkrumah increasingly difficult and obstreperous on account, they believed, of his resentment of their rising stature in African affairs. Wrote one of the Ghanaian president, "Believing himself chosen by Providence to lead Africa to greatness, [Nkrumah] has always gone it alone even when other African countries share his points of view and have the same goals."[99] For this reason, the second thrust of Ben Bella's efforts to ensure their cooperation at Addis Ababa was to convince them that Algeria itself was not seeking to win important offices in the new continental organization, nor to throw its weight around in a more general sense.[100]

In short, while Algeria's contribution to the founding of the OAU was only one part of a multinational endeavor, its diplomatic efforts in the run-up to the May meeting did earn widespread recognition. Aside from wanting the conference to succeed for its own sake, Ben Bella and his colleagues desired to build on their grassroots popularity by demonstrating their reasonableness to those governments that had reason to fear their politics, and they accomplished this goal. Furthermore, as Nasser and Ben Bella agreed in their discussions prior to the Addis Ababa meeting, African solidarity could achieve anything substantive by taking achievable steps toward concrete forms of cooperation, rather than the pursuit of improbable proposals such as Nkrumah's federalism (the Egyptian president's recent experiences of Arab unity surely informed his thinking on these issues).[101] As a result, the Algerians were in a position to exert real influence on the proceedings of the conference.[102]

For Haile Selassie, the seventy-one-year-old emperor of Ethiopia, the long-awaited heads of state meeting, on 22–25 May 1963, was a momentous event. Africa, he said in his opening comments, was "in transition from the Africa of Yesterday to the Africa of Tomorrow. . . . [W]e move from the past into the future."[103] He had taken the opportunity to showcase his country as the exemplar of that journey. The summit was taking place in an impressive, newly built complex whose central assembly space, Africa Hall, apparently cost $2 million. Envisaged by Selassie as a "symbol of the noble aspirations of the African people," the venue credibly supported Addis Ababa's candidacy for the role of continental capital. The city itself, appropriately situated at an altitude of 8,300 feet, had been thoroughly scrubbed and polished along every route that the visiting dignitaries and world press could be expected to travel. Those inhabitants who might also wander into view were bedecked in fresh, white cotton robes. Even the lions roaming the imperial palace's grounds were shampooed and manicured.[104] These Potemkin village–like aspects of the event did perhaps support the aforementioned Sawaba leader's fear that the new OAU would resemble a "trade union of men in power," isolated from the masses. But the thirty heads of state and government—only Morocco's Hassan II was absent—did nevertheless manage to get partway toward justifying the emperor's vaulting rhetoric. He urged them to overcome their differences to create "a single institution to which we will all belong, based on principles to which we all subscribe," and where their decisions "will be dictated by Africans and only by Africans."[105] If not the herald of the glorious future Selassie foresaw, the OAU did at least meet those laudable specifications.[106]

In certain respects a regional complement to the United Nations and its related institutions, the new organization featured a permanent secretariat, led by a secretary-general, as well as several permanent committees to facilitate cooperation in areas such as communications infrastructure, economic development, and scientific research. While the staff of these entities were initially almost entirely Ethiopian, Algeria's diplomats were recognized for taking on much of the unglamorous labor that went into their creation prior to the arrival of the heads of state. One of them, Layachi Yaker, wrote much of the first draft of the OAU's charter.[107] These tasks presented an opportunity to give Third Worldist ideals concrete, practical form.[108] "We think we have a leadership role in Africa," one Algerian diplomat told an American journalist, "but we cannot do anything just by shouting slogans. Our leadership must come from what we do, not through propaganda or self-congratulation."[109] In that spirit, the OAU's charter granted it responsibility for representing Africa collectively to the outside world. Noteworthy early accomplishments in this area included lobbying for greater African representation in the UN's bureaucracies and committees, and a mostly successful campaign to sever all of independent Africa's economic and transportation connections to Portugal and South Africa.[110]

However, it was the formation of the Liberation Committee to coordinate support for the continent's national liberation movements that garnered the most attention, the initiative in which Algeria's participation was most evident. Even among so many dominating personalities, Ben Bella stood out as one of the event's stars. His impassioned speech on behalf of those still colonized and racially oppressed on their continent brought the entire hall to its feet. "Pushing his notes aside, pounding the podium with both hands, very pale," one attending journalist recorded, "the Algerian leader made an impassioned appeal in a breathless voice for aid to the Angolan rebels.... I do not think that I have ever had such a profound sense of African unity as when I listened to Ben Bella, tears in his eyes, visibly moved, urge his listeners to rush to the assistance of the men dying south of the equator."[111] Likewise, although the Algerian prime minister's oration had deleterious implications for Western and British policies regarding the Portuguese colonies, South Africa, and Rhodesia, a Foreign Office official watching the proceedings had to concede that Ben Bella had "cut a world figure" and shown "fire in his guts."[112] Displaying the blunt and restless attitude of a revolutionary, he warned his peers against self-congratulation and complacency:

> It is my duty to say that the Charter that we are going to adopt [here] will resemble all the other Charters that all the other assemblies in the world have adopted. It is my duty to say that all the fine speeches that we have heard will be the best weapon against our unity. We have

spoken of a Development Bank. Why haven't we spoken of a bank of blood to come to the aid of those who are fighting in Angola and elsewhere in Africa?[113]

In combination with the moral authority that the Algerians carried on the subject, Ben Bella's forceful and charismatic performance helped move the assembly to adopt a more radical position than most had probably intended prior to the summit. After all, apart from Ethiopia, only Algeria had won its freedom through bloody conflict, and with the international press attentively watching, even the most reluctant heads of state were anxious to demonstrate their support for the brave freedom fighters. They approved the creation of a Liberation Committee expressly intended to support national liberation movements by military means, including weapons procurement and training. They also agreed to the committee being financed through a fund separate from the OAU's general fund, and to mandatory annual contributions to that fund by every member state. The first seats on the committee were assigned to Algeria, Ethiopia, Guinea, Congo-Léopoldville, Nigeria, Senegal, Tanzania, the UAR, and Uganda, so the "radical" states were amply represented. Although the Algerians and their allies had valid doubts as to whether the other countries would actually live up to these commitments, the Liberation Committee nevertheless constituted a decisive political victory.[114] In the African sphere at least, it was those countries that opposed the radicals' support of violent anticolonial resistance that were now transgressing international norms.

Consequently, following the Addis Ababa meeting, these countries set up several camps in "front-line" Tanganyika, principally to train Mozambican and Rhodesian rebels. The ANC's armed wing, Umkhonto we Sizwe, also quickly joined.[115] Noureddine Djoudi, a former ALN officer fluent in English, opened the Algerian embassy in Dar-es-Salaam, where anticolonial operations would be his primary concern.[116] Algiers instructed him "not to delay in sending us any nationalists for training until the Liberation Committee is able to handle it" and to start planning for the training and equipping of up to 2,000 Tanganyikan soldiers in order to strengthen that country's own defenses.[117] The Liberation Committee convened in Dar-es-Salaam in late June to set general guidelines for relations between nationalist movements and their host countries. Notably, its members agreed that their assistance had to be "conditional on the creation of a unified Front in each territory," and they dispatched a reconciliation mission to Conakry to mediate between Cabral's PAIGC and a rival organization.[118] The MPLA was an early casualty of this policy: Congo and the FNLA obliged the OAU to recognize Holden's provisional government as the valid representative of the Angolan people, and the Adoula government then had the justification it needed to eject the MPLA from its territory.[119]

Despite their friendship with the leftist Angolan group, the Algerians concurred with the committee's decision (though they would continue to support the MPLA unilaterally). They did so in part because they wanted the new entity to succeed, and it was undeniable that the FNLA's guerrilla campaign was more impressive than their rival's at that time. Additionally, it was still in Algeria's interest to maintain its newfound reputation for compromise and consensus-building in Africa. The question of liberation movements aside, the OAU's founding had greatly strengthened Algeria's position in the ongoing border dispute with Morocco. The organization's charter insisted on the permanence of the continent's current political boundaries and forbade any effort to change those borders by force. The ramifications of this principle for Morocco's claims to some Algerian territory and to the whole of Mauritania had persuaded Hassan II to stay away from Addis Ababa in the first place, so Rabat stood alone on this issue.

The Algerian-Moroccan dispute was just one facet of a systemic phenomenon: the consolidation of Africa's postcolonial international order that valued state sovereignty and national integrity over all other considerations. At Addis Ababa, the continent's new political elite had chosen to further protect the legitimacy of the nation, which was the basis of their power, from potential challengers above or below it. By rejecting Nkrumah's proposals for a more profound form of political integration, Africa's heads of state ensured that they were not beholden to any supranational authority either. The Ghanaian leader had to concede the point: in a speech the following year, he tried to repackage his proposal for a government of Africa as something that "does not mean loss of sovereignty . . . [but] will rather strengthen the sovereignty of the individual states."[120] Furthermore, just as the United Arab Republic project was foundering in the Middle East, various notions of regional federation in Africa were also losing what remained of their momentum. For example, in addition to the North African unity project, the proposal to create an East African Federation of Kenya, Uganda, and Tanganyika quietly fizzled out in the wake of Addis Ababa.[121]

On the other hand, the OAU charter also firmly gave the principle of noninterference in another state's domestic affairs precedence over concepts like human rights and minority rights, which could be used to justify outside interventions and secessionism. The January 1963 announcement that the breakaway province of Katanga was rejoining Congo-Léopoldville had ended the most significant subnational challenge to the new African order, but the continent's governments remained hypervigilant to the threat. Algeria was a prime example: tensions with Morocco were simmering throughout the year, in part, because of the protests of people on the ground who felt that the border between the two countries had left them on the wrong side, and Algiers's fear of Kabyle Berber separatism also reached new heights during the brief Sands War in October.[122] Algeria also cooperated fully with its neighbor to the south, Mali, whose government battled to suppress a separatist movement among the Tuareg people inhabiting the northern desert regions. As Ben Bella told Josip Broz Tito,

> [The Tuaregs] want to be incorporated into Algeria, but we are forced to capture them and send them back to Mali. We handed over one of their leaders who had come to us. We are ready to do all that is needed to help our Malian brothers because it is a difficult problem. Tuaregs are found in Algeria, Mali, and Niger. . . . If we are not careful, we know that we might have to face a dangerous problem.[123]

Discussing the same issue with another Yugoslavian official, the Algerian ambassador, Rédha Malek, said that the problem stemmed from nomadic tribes moving across the Sahara's invisible borders. The government in Bamako was trying to bind the tribes to specific territories, he explained, and Algiers was doing its best to make that task easier.[124] He could hardly have offered a more pithy summation of the state-centrism of the postcolonial order.

It is worth pointing out as well that Algeria's support for liberation movements and revolutionary groups did not contradict the rest of its diplomatic agenda. Granted, abetting leftist rebels in countries like Niger and Congo was a clear violation of the principle of noninterference, which Algerian officials justified on the basis that "neo-imperialist" regimes were not legitimately independent, but the transnational operational methods of Algeria's rebel support network did nonetheless work toward an emphatically nation-statist purpose. The Liberation Committee regulated relations between states and nonstate groups, while the policy of "national unity" purposefully discredited movements that represented subnational or ethnic identities. In effect, Algeria and the other supportive African governments asserted that it was only legitimate to fight for "Angola" or "Mozambique," rather than for a province or particular population within those territories.

In the summer and autumn, the Algerians consolidated their diplomatic position. Ben Bella accelerated the appointment of ambassadors and toured West Africa for himself in August, visiting Mali, Liberia, and Ghana.[125] He also received a series of African leaders in his own capital, including Julius Nyerere from Tanganyika, Touré, Mali's Modibo Keita, and Alphonse Massamba-Débat, who had led a left-wing coup against the president of the Republic of Congo in August. The Algerian authorities made a special effort to give these guests a grand, celebratory welcome and to impress upon them their country's genuinely African identity. Ambassador Djoudi reported from Dar-es-Salaam that Nyerere's visit to Algiers had generated a lot of positive sentiment toward Algeria among Tanganyika's political class.[126] The rapport between Ben Bella and Keita became especially warm, the Algerian assuring his Malian counterpart of the great joy his trip to Bamako had brought him and of his "firm conviction that close cooperation between our two Governments will meet the aspirations of our people" and produce solutions to the profound challenges that their countries, and their continent, faced.[127] In short, by the end of the year, Algeria—and Ben Bella personally—was a prominent and dynamic actor in African affairs, enjoying particularly friendly ties with a number of countries.

All told, Algeria's embrace of African unity brought appreciable benefits, but it also contributed to the solidification of the continent's postcolonial political structures. For all the changes and instability in African affairs at that time, the May 1963 Addis Ababa meeting did manage to fix in place the continent's political map, giving it greater durability over the next half-century than it had known for a long time. For their part, Ben Bella and the Algerian diplomatic team had shown an ability to give Third Worldism pragmatic substance: anticolonial solidarity and African unity were institutionalized and active phenomena. However, while the Algerians did defer some aspects of their revolutionary agenda in order to reach across Africa's ideological divide, they did so in the hope that they might subsequently pull all of the continent's governments, together, in a more "progressive" direction. By the end of 1963, the MAE's African department was proposing a change in strategy. A sweeping analysis, presumably for the attention of the new foreign minister, Abdelaziz Bouteflika, argued that being "composed of differing economic, social and political regimes, the OAU could only exist based on compromise." While that compromise had been logical at that time, it continued, "we must [now] ask ourselves whether countries with different political and economic orientations can coexist for long, and whether African unity should be achieved at any price and to the detriment of the revolution and progress."[128] Bouteflika, a onetime comrade-in-arms and unabashed admirer of Fanon, understood that the question was a purely rhetorical one. In contrast to the policies its government had pursued since first achieving independence, Algeria, in the year ahead, would become one of the most polarizing forces in Africa affairs.

Between Continents, Between Blocs

Algeria's leaders were more active in Africa than in any other region, but their activities there were also fully consistent with their desire to expand and consolidate the Third World project on a global scale. In that respect, they frequently spoke of their activities in Africa as being less an expression of an innate identity than the application of a universal political program to one particularly receptive region. As Ben Bella explained to Tito, in March 1964, "Algeria wants to focus on Africa in its policies. Not because of skin color—we are white like you, maybe a little more brown—but because we have problems identical to problems of other nations on the continent and because our problems are intertwined."[129] In this respect, Ben Bella and his colleagues considered the OAU to be a component and prototype for the Third World project as a whole. Just as they had worked toward African unity, they hoped to forge a coalition of all "progressive forces" around the world, regardless of race or geography, and to this purpose offered Algeria as a bridge and intermediary between regions. Likewise, arguing that the countries of NAM "see themselves as the successors and maintainers of the Bandung principles" and that "the interaction between the two movements is so deep that we can say that Non-Alignment is the adopted child of Afro-Asianism," they encouraged a convergence of the Third World's distinct organizing themes.[130] Yet, while this globalist strategy—which Algeria did not pursue alone—did achieve some early successes, it also collided head-on with the great powers' own world-shaping agendas. Moreover, by 1963, it was not so much the established pattern of the Soviet-American contest but instead the newer dynamics of Cold War detente and Sino-Soviet antipathy that posed the greatest danger to the Third World project.

Algeria's function as a gateway between regions was most apparent in its support of nonstate movements. With Algiers and the ANP's training camps being hubs of subversive activity, the Algerians were in a position to facilitate liberation movements' acquaintance with each other and with potential sponsors elsewhere in the world. Examples of such contacts are practically innumerable. Algeria and the other northern African countries tried to persuade black Africa to support the Palestinian nationalist cause, while the Algerians were also particularly active in trying to persuade the Arab states, in return, to support the Angolan and other African nationalists. During their tour of Arab capitals in the spring of 1963, Boumedienne and Khemisti had tried to convince their friends in the Middle East not to get locked into "Arab chauvinism," since, "just as Algeria supports the liberation of Palestine, they would like to see the Arab countries support African liberation, in particular Angola, and favor them with attention and aid."[131] In February, the National Liberation Front of South Vietnam opened a permanent office in Algiers, one of only two the movement maintained in a noncommunist country.[132] Arafat and his comrade Khalil al-Wazir were able to meet the foreign minister of the South Vietnamese FLN as well as Che Guevara, before being included in an Algerian governmental delegation that visited China the following year.[133] Similarly, Ben Bella and Lakhdar Brahimi also helped the Angolan Jonas Savimbi travel to Peking in search of support.[134] Almost immediately, the Algerian network also extended to Latin America: in January, Ben Bella and Boumedienne agreed to take in a small group of Argentinian guerrillas-in-training who had overstayed their welcome in Prague, and shortly after also received a delegation of the Venezuelan National Liberation Front and agreed to ship armaments across to the Atlantic to them.[135] In short, the Algerians systemically acted as a logistical and diplomatic gateway for the movements they ponsored, with their network of contacts stretching across multiple continents just months after the formation of Ben Bella's government. It was for this reason that Amilcar Cabral dubbed Algiers the "Mecca of revolutionaries," while the cofounder of Fateh, Yassir Arafat, highlighted the Algerian capital's usefulness as a diplomatic and public relations base of operations by describing it as the "window through which we appear to the West."[136]

At the same time, in the spirit of the French official Jean de Broglie, who hoped that Algeria might be France's "narrow doorway" to the Third World, the Maghribi country also served as a bridge to Africa, and beyond, for certain other sovereign states. Perhaps most notably, being convinced from their October 1962 trip to Havana that Cuba was isolated in Latin America, Ben Bella and others in the Algerian leadership elected to provide Castro's regime with an outlet to the outside world. Following the temporary lull in Cuban-Algerian contacts in the immediate wake of the Cuban Missile Crisis, the first concrete example of cooperation between the two governments was Algeria's aforementioned assistance, at Havana's request, to the Argentinian and Venezuelan revolutionaries. Operating under the aegis of various shell companies, the Algerian cargo vessel *Ibn Khaldoun* provided a circuitous yet effective supply line to Venezuela, thereby bypassing the United States' close surveillance of Cuba's efforts to export revolution.[137] In May, a grateful Castro sent a team of more than fifty doctors and nurses to help alleviate Algeria's severe health crisis and shortage of medical personnel. Algiers then took further tangible action to alleviate Cuba's isolation by agreeing, in June, to serve as a refueling stop for Soviet aircraft bound for the Caribbean, which necessitated the enlargement of several runways with Moscow's assistance.[138] Accordingly, the Cuban-Algerian relationship was quickly becoming very close in both substantive and atmospheric terms. Fidel had appointed Jorge Serguera to the new embassy in Algiers in February 1963, and the latter arrived proclaiming loudly that his role was not that of a traditional ambassador but instead of a revolutionary ally and "extra combatant in the service of Algeria."[139] When Guevara spent three weeks in Algeria in July, he received a rapturous reception in public and political circles alike. Essentially given license to wander at his leisure, the Argentinian enthused that "each time I see something new in Algeria, I am reminded of Cuba: there's the same esprit, the same enthusiasm, the same inexperience too."[140] It was a testament to the rather improvisational and unapologetic nature of the Cuban-Algerian friendship that the United States' Senate majority leader, who was also visiting Algeria at that time, unwittingly found himself attending a state function on 5 July, the anniversary of Algerian independence, that featured Guevara and Egypt's Marshal Abdel Hakim Amer as joint guests of honor. Unsurprisingly, the senator was rather irate to see his hosts fête the poster child of a revolution that, scarcely half a year prior, had threatened to obliterate his country.[141]

By provoking Washington's ire, the Algerian government showed that it was willing to pay a significant price for its friendship with Cuba. On more than one occasion, State Department analysts confessed to being baffled by the Algerians' motivations, for they could see little benefit for Algeria in meddling in controversies half a world away.[142] Nevertheless, the Algerians' motivations do seem to have stemmed from the principles of revolutionary and anti-imperialist solidarity that American officials found hard to accept at face value; their internal records do not contradict their public statements in this regard. To the extent that cooperation with Cuba was pragmatic, the leaders of both governments believed that they could defend themselves best from American hostility by encouraging revolution elsewhere in Africa and in Latin America, which distracted Washington and created new allies for them. In any case, Algeria's friendship opened up new vistas for Castro and his comrades. If Serguera was perhaps exaggerating the significance of the initial Cuban-Algerian subversive collaboration in Latin America by describing it as a breakthrough for the Afro-Asian world and a pioneering example of anti-imperialist solidarity, this unquestionably bold decision by Ben Bella's government would lead to more cooperative ventures of a similar nature in the near future.[143] Likewise, as historian Piero Gleijeses has noted, besides strengthening the two countries' alliance, the medical mission in Algeria proved to be important to the history of Cuba's international relations because it was the first actual implementation of Havana's rhetorical commitment to humanitarian internationalism—the beginning of a long and proud tradition of providing assistance to other developing countries.[144]

Yugoslavia was the other key ally that Algeria could introduce to Africa. In the same way that Cuba's opportunities were limited in Latin America, the Belgrade regime was an ideological outlier and geopolitically independent in a Europe that was otherwise quite solidly divided into two camps, and the search for new horizons had been a central motivator for Tito's collaboration with Nasser and Nehru to create NAM.[145] The leaders of Algeria and Yugoslavia shared very similar opinions and objectives in the international sphere, such as the expansion of NAM, in addition to having much to offer one another in terms of economic and ideological exchanges. Therefore, Ben Bella was not simply mouthing platitudes when he told a Yugoslavian journalist in December 1962 that "we are inspired by the principles announced at the Belgrade Conference ... our foreign policy correlates particularly with Yugoslavian policy [because] we have the same positions as you on all the important questions."[146] An embassy in Belgrade was near the top of the list of priorities for the new Algerian foreign ministry, which was struggling to build out its diplomatic apparatus, and the eventual appointment of the highly regarded Rédha Malek, one of the GPRA's negotiators at Evian, in the early summer of 1963 was a further reflection of the weight the Algerians placed on this relationship. Malek's task was to forge an "Algiers-Belgrade axis similar and complementary to the Cairo-Belgrade axis" on the basis of "multiplying exchanges of viewpoints, consultations, and conferences at the highest levels."[147] Appropriately, the Yugoslavian ambassador in Algiers, Dizdarević, was a cousin to Belgrade's representative in Cairo. He became a trusted confidant of Ben Bella so quickly that the latter described him as "not an ambassador, but a brother," which was very reminiscent of the way Serguera had described his own relationship with the Algerian leadership—a revolutionary among revolutionaries.[148]

Indeed, the Yugoslavian government was eager to increase its involvement in decolonizing Africa and collaborated closely with Algiers as it expanded both its diplomatic and its subversive activities on the continent.[149] "Conscious of Algeria's weight in Africa and the Arab world," Malek accurately observed, "through their good relations with us, the Yugoslavians would like to strengthen their own cooperation with African and Arab countries. For this reason they are especially interested in Algeria developing a close rapport with African countries south of the Sahara."[150] Algerian-Yugoslav cooperation was mutually beneficial: while the Algerians had strong relationships and credibility in Africa, their comparatively wealthy European partners had greater practical resources. Belgrade furnished much of the military materiel and logistical support to the revolutionary governments and movements that Algiers befriended. For example, when Ben Bella expressed his gratitude to Tito for providing the ship that transported weapons to the Angolan nationalists in August 1963, he acknowledged that "since we do not have ships, those weapons would have stayed in Tunisia had we not intervened with our Yugoslav brothers."[151] In fact, Yugoslavia quickly became so involved in supporting armed movements in Africa that it was the sole non-African financial contributor to the OAU's Liberation Committee.[152] Additionally, in the diplomatic realm, the Algerian foreign ministry itself relied on Yugoslavian shipping to establish and maintain its new missions in the southern regions of the continent, at least in the early days.[153] In other words, Yugoslavia was a relatively powerful, industrialized partner that could assist the likes of Algeria, Egypt, and Ghana in their conception of the Third World project, without bringing its own conflicting agenda to bear as China and the Soviet Union did.

At the same time, if the first pillar of Algeria's Third Worldist diplomacy was bridge-building, the Yugoslavians' enthusiasm for the OAU suggested that they also shared their allies' enthusiasm for building coalitions—at least as far as the Non-Aligned Movement was concerned. Speaking to Nasser just a couple of weeks before the Addis Ababa conference of May 1963, Tito was quite giddy about the prospect of leveraging African unity in order to strengthen and expand NAM. That was indeed the intention of the Algerian and Egyptian governments, and Nasser reassured his Balkan friend that preliminary conversations were already promising. He was confident, for example, that he could convince Nigerian prime minister Abubakar Tafawa Balewa, who had declined to attend the 1961 Belgrade Conference, of NAM's merit once he had the chance to speak to him in person in the Ethiopian capital. More generally, Nasser felt, achieving "a larger conference of the nonaligned will depend a lot on the personal contacts that we will have" at Addis Ababa.[154]

Consequently, those African governments that had participated at Belgrade were gratified to ensure that the OAU's charter committed the signatories to a policy of "non-alignment with regard to all blocs." Granted, the charter's repudiation of military alliances with outside powers and its call to eliminate foreign bases on the continent contradicted glaringly African realities, since the majority of governments had military relationships of some kind with their former colonial power, one of the superpowers, or both. But the Egyptian legal scholar Boutros Boutros-Ghali optimistically claimed that "although the application of this policy may not be feasible in the near future, it is an objective not to be lost to view, for neutralism is one of the surest means of strengthening African unity. It serves as a framework for a united foreign policy and also discourages the intrusion of the [C]old [W]ar into Africa."[155] Furthermore, because nearly all extra-African military alliances involved Britain, France, or the United States, the enshrinement of nonalignment was a victory nonetheless for those, like the Algerians, who saw the West as the greatest threat to their continent's independence, prosperity, and security. One report from the Algerian MAE crowed that "the Americans and their friends had encouraged the Ethiopian emperor to hold the Addis Ababa conference. [But] [t]hey could not predict that a limited number of countries who are beyond their control would manage to impose their point of view."[156] The fact that the logic of the NATO alliance compelled Britain and France to abet Portugal's efforts to hold onto its Guinean, Angolan, and Mozambican colonies helped persuade the African heads of state of the merits of nonalignment, in principle.

The Algerians also valued the OAU as a demonstration of the feasibility of giving Third Worldist internationalism (broadly speaking) real institutional substance—and of doing so without any Western involvement. From their perspective, the opposite example was the Organization of American States that the United States dominated and from which Cuba was expelled, later that year, for pursuing policies very similar to those of Algeria and the other so-called radical African states. For the MAE's African team, Addis Ababa was the happy culmination of all those African unity meetings and people's conferences, starting with the GPRA mission that Fanon had led to Accra in December 1958, that had striven to create a new form of international community, free from the tools of Western oversight and manipulation. Those meetings, said one report, had allowed the participants to liberate themselves from the pervasive and pernicious structures of neocolonialism in Africa, namely,

> the [diplomatic] missions that serve as nerve centers for espionage and pressure points on governments; the representatives of imperialist and colonialist states who agitate under cover of religion, rearmament, cultural organizations, philanthropic organizations and peace corps; the press and radio that are under imperialist control in most of Africa.[157]

It was in that respect that Algeria's international operatives saw the OAU as a prototype for the Third World project as a whole. They believed that while it was vitally important for poor countries to participate in entities like the United Nations, the Southern Hemisphere also needed to replicate for itself the general global trend toward institutionalization and transnational integration, lest it have integration-as-subordination imposed on it by the North. As the Algerian ambassador to China, M'hammed Yala, told Zhou Enlai the following year, "We want to create a permanent and frequent structure [for the Afro-Asian movement]," which, he suggested, should be "easy [to establish] since the African Organization also has one." The Chinese statesman seemed to agree with the proposal and the comparison, which boded well for a *tier-mondiste* version of globalization.[158] In practical terms, it would be very difficult for the Third World to create its own autonomous international society so long as every letter and phone call was routed through the North, and all the broadcasting and news networks were centered in the rich world, which is why much of the business of meetings such as the one at Addis Ababa concerned seemingly dull efforts to foster communications and transportation link between poor countries.

However, the greatest impediment to the Third World project, in the near term, seemed to come from the contrary objectives of the world's great powers and, from the Algerian perspective, the United States above all. While the two countries had divergent views on many issues in international affairs, in 1963 Algeria's aggressive posture against white minority rule in southern Africa drove its leaders into more direct opposition to US foreign policy. With his government having lobbied against the OAU's imposition of an embargo of Portugal because it was "not consistent [with] our NATO interests and commitments," Secretary of State Dean Rusk recognized after Addis Ababa that the Algerians would not be very sympathetic toward his government's (supposed) efforts to encourage "evolutionary," rather than revolutionary, change in Portuguese Africa.[159] Indeed, when another senior State Department official visited Algiers that summer, Ben Bella and Bouteflika chided him on the disparity between America's good intentions and high-minded rhetoric, on the one hand, and its amoral pursuit of a superpower's geopolitical interests, on the other. The question was a simple one, Bouteflika said: "It was for a great nation like [the] US to choose between friendship with 'Salazar and Franco' and friendship [with] 200 million Africans."[160] For the time being, the tenor of Algerian-American discussions continued to be outwardly friendly, so US officials believed that they could maintain a "constructive dialogue" with Ben Bella's government on African questions. But they perhaps underestimated just how poisonous their government's position was to their standing on the continent.

Moreover, although Ben Bella and others continued to hold President Kennedy personally in high esteem, the prevailing view in Algerian foreign policy circles was that supporting Portugal was just the most egregious example of the United States' systematically damaging influence in African affairs. Warning that "American financial groups have penetrated the continent with their neocolonial machinations," the young Fanonites of the MAE's Africa desk argued, "It would be a mistake to think that imperialism is not real and virulent in Africa.... Only [Africa's] revolutionary parties and organizations, and the national liberation movements, are capable of confronting imperialism directly."[161] By this logic, which was very similar to the Cuban government's "defensive" strategy of promoting revolution elsewhere, Algiers began to commit itself to an indirect conflict with the United States across the continent. The challenge was to encourage the growth of like-minded, left-wing forces in African politics without sacrificing the diplomatic gains that Ben Bella's government had achieved by reaching across the continent's ideological divide. As Ben Bella confided to Sékou Touré following left-wing revolutions in Congo-Brazzaville and Dahomey (Benin) later that year, "Sometimes it's necessary to hope for coups d'état without publicly saying so."[162] Gradually, though, the Algerians were stepping up their support for opposition movements once again, having tempered the policy around the time of the OAU's founding. These movements included the left-wing opposition in Morocco, Niger's Sawaba party, the Ivory Coast's secessionist Sanwi government, Cameroon's UPC, Congo-Léopoldville's CNL, and, toward the end of the year, revolutionaries plotting a coup against the pro-British king of Zanzibar. Algiers's goal, one MAE report plainly stated, was to "maintain the struggle against neocolonialism and imperialism by helping progressive groups gain power."[163] This revolutionary escalation occurred in the context of the Algerians' deepening cooperation with Cuba and Yugoslavia, and the concomitant framing of African affairs as an international struggle against the United States.

Meanwhile, majority opinion in Washington was also increasingly hostile toward Algeria, although it was the Algerian government's open rejection of American policies on matters far beyond Africa that accounted for most of this ill will. On the one hand, to American observers, the "Mecca of revolutionaries" looked more like a pirate's cove of disreputable troublemakers, deluded fellow travelers, and willing and unwitting tools of Soviet penetration. Indeed, in late

1963, Algiers offered welcome to opposition groups from Portugal and Spain, in addition to the numerous Marxists and anarchists traveling to the Maghrib on an individual basis.[164] As a result, the American embassy reported, a generally anti-American atmosphere prevailed in the Algerian capital, not least among the editorial staff of the official and ambiguously semiofficial press. "Neither [the] regime nor information media ever pay any real compliments to [the] [W]est," the Americans complained. "By contrast [there is] much favorable attention given to advances of 'Socialist' countries . . . [and a] Western newcomer is likely to be dismayed by 'third world' and Marxist leaning line of press, radio and television."[165] More specifically, Washington objected to the opening of a South Vietnamese NLF office as well as North Vietnamese and North Korean embassies—one of only three Pyongyang maintained beyond the communist world.[166] In fact, by the summer of 1963, the only communist country that did not have representation in the Algerian capital was East Germany, and by Ambassador Porter's reckoning, "Bloc" diplomats outnumbered their NATO rivals seventy to fifty-one (although this count did not include the sizable French contingent).[167] Once Algerian-Soviet relations started to improve markedly that autumn, following the dispute over the Algerian Communist Party, Porter could console himself only with the fact that the communist diplomats in Algiers seemed far more interested in criticizing one another than the United States.

The deteriorating relationship with Washington was an indication that Algerian diplomacy was not as flexible or as unaccountable as it had been in the time of the GPRA. Ben Bella (who held the title of president rather than prime minister from September 1963) intended to speak to the UN General Assembly that autumn and expressed his desire to visit the White House again during his trip, in order to clear the air between their two governments. However, Kennedy categorically rejected this suggestion: among other considerations, the American president was particularly concerned by persistent rumors that Castro might visit Algeria.[168] With the announcement of the large Soviet aid package in September, he had recalled Ambassador Porter to discuss the bilateral relationship, pondering aloud whether he should cut off all aid to the Algerians in order to dissuade them from inviting Castro.[169] Algeria's globe-spanning, activist foreign policy evidently entailed costs as well as benefits—as its practitioners recognized.

Ben Bella also put too much faith in the power of personal relations, and perhaps his own charisma, for while Kennedy continued to retain some sympathy for the Algerian perspective, he was decidedly in the minority in that regard, even among his own staff. Indeed, Robert Komer, on the National Security Council, seems to have been practically the only person left in Washington—though certainly an influential one—arguing for maintaining a positive relationship with Algiers. He told one colleague that he felt they had not made enough of an effort with Algeria, and his president that he felt "duty bound" to make the case for inviting Ben Bella to the White House, so long as Castro did not visit Algiers.[170] "Like Nasser and Sukarno, he's also toying with the Bloc," he argued, " . . . [and] our cold shoulder could lead Ben Bella to lean even further East." The domestic political costs, Komer pleaded, would be "outweighed by prolonging the advantage your special interest in Algeria has given us."[171] Of course, while this argument seems to have worked, the Oval Office's "special interest" in Algeria was about to cease tragically sooner than anyone in either capital expected.[172] Many years later, Ben Bella admiringly described Kennedy to the author as "a man too good to be president of the United States." It was a description that implicitly acknowledged that, even had Kennedy not been assassinated that November, the deterioration in Algerian-American relations was too multifaceted and public for even a president to prevent.[173]

American officials began to express skepticism that Algeria was truly a nonaligned state, but in truth there had long been a tendency among Algeria's cadres and international experts to interpret "nonalignment" as a much more provocative foreign policy doctrine than its original proponents, Jawaharlal Nehru especially, had intended. Washington's understanding of the term correlated more with the neutralism advocated at the Bandung Conference, which sounded more like a sort of abstention from the Cold War, with a pronounced strain of Gandhi-esque pacifism. In contrast, the Algerians' difficult struggle for independence had convinced them of the necessity of both violence and the deliberate destabilization of international affairs. As Ben Bella told Tito in March 1964:

> The idea of nonalignment is for us strongly linked to the fight of African people for liberation and the fight against colonialism, which is found in its crudest form on the African continent. That is why the red telephone between Moscow and Washington should not be connecting only those two countries. Its wires should pass by Angola and all other countries where people are fighting for freedom.[174]

Indeed, just a few months prior, at the turn of the year, even the reputedly CIA-supported Holden Roberto publicly abandoned any hope that the United States would significantly assist the cause of Angolan independence. Announcing that he did not want to "go on fighting another twenty years," the FNLA leader turned instead to China and the Soviet Union for support—thereby repeating the decision that the Algerian FLN had taken a half decade earlier.[175]

For that reason, by late 1963, Algerian diplomats felt that their policy of nonalignment was jeopardized less by American hostility than by the Soviet Union's desire to reduce Cold War tensions. Citing the mantra of "peaceful coexistence," Khrushchev sought to de-escalate geopolitical confrontations with the United States and limit superpower competition to the economic realm. He achieved a real measure of detente that August, when the US, Soviet, and British governments signed the Partial Test Ban Treaty, or Treaty of Moscow, which promised to be a first step toward the mutual abatement of the nuclear arms race. Yet, even though the doctrine of peaceful coexistence looked very much like the fulfillment of the nonaligned countries' demands, the reality was that the Algerians and many other Third World actors were dismayed by Khrushchev's search for concord with Washington. Fearing a Soviet retreat from Third World issues, Tewfik Bouattoura, head of the MAE political desk, suggested to Bouteflika that he push Ambassador Abramov to explain the extent of his government's commitment to causes such as South Africa and Angola.[176] Writing from the mission in New York in early October, Messaoud Aït-Challal reported his dismay that foreign minister Andrei Gromyko's speech to the UN General Assembly scarcely touched on Third World concerns, which he took as a symptom of a new American-Soviet understanding. He warned that "the delegations [of Third World countries] seem to be anesthetized by the attitude of the Two Superpowers. . . . Faced with the USSR's moderate stance . . . Third World and particularly African delegations' margin for maneuver is proving very limited."[177] While the subsequent intensification of Soviet-Algerian relations did assuage some of these fears, in general Algerian diplomats seemed instinctively wary of detente and even more so of the basic rationale behind peaceful coexistence. For some, Khrushchev's doctrine was reminiscent of what was (in their view) the overly moderate and pacific tone of the Bandung Conference. When Abdelmalek Benhabylès later wrote a report arguing that the post–Moscow Treaty detente helped the Third World, one of his colleagues criticized it as an apologia for peaceful coexistence, and Bouteflika agreed that, even if detente had been beneficial on the whole by encouraging the Soviet Union to strengthen economic ties with countries like Algeria, Khrushchev's desire for rapprochement with Washington had nevertheless "demobilized" anti-imperialist forces in the Third World.[178]

Furthermore, they were not alone in their innate suspicion of great power peacemaking. Yugoslavian officials feared that the Soviets secretly wanted the Third World to remain fragmented and poorly organized and therefore easier to control. At the 1961 Belgrade Conference, which the hosts described as a conference for small countries, Tito had warned that peaceful coexistence should not become a rationalization for maintaining the status quo in international affairs.[179] For the inhabitants of postcolonial countries, "detente" carried the whiff of "spheres of influence" agreements, while agreements such as the Partial Test Ban Treaty were reminiscent of events such as the Berlin Conference of 1884–1885 and the Paris Peace Conference of 1919 that saw Western powers broker peace among themselves by divvying up Africa, the Middle East, and

Asia. Ghana's ambassador in Algiers said the Moscow treaty reminded him of "three big businessmen doing business in a cafe," while an Indonesian diplomat feared a Soviet-Western alliance whereby "white people will turn around and together oppress Eastern and colored peoples."[180] A further, specific objection to the Partial Test Ban Treaty was that many poor countries saw it as targeting a Chinese nuclear weapons program that they tacitly approved of. Of course, the Algerians and other proponents of nonalignment publicly welcomed the Moscow treaty, which Ben Bella signed—a fact that should give pause to those inclined to assess Third Worldism by its rhetoric alone.

As their dispute with the Soviet Union intensified, China's leaders sought to capitalize on these concerns. In 1963, the Sino-Soviet split forcefully spilled into the Third World and into Africa especially, where the two massive communist countries started to compete in earnest for allies and ideological acolytes. Peking also hoped to exclude the Soviet Union from the Third World scene altogether by highlighting its rival's racial, regional, and industrialized character. Algeria was one of the more desirable prizes in this intercommunist contest because of the high profile its socialist experiment enjoyed and because of its influence with anticolonial movements. The Chinese press hailed the Maghribi country as "Africa's rising star," while one MAE report, perhaps produced by the ambassador in Moscow, Mohammed Benyahia, recognized that "Algeria [is] becoming a field of action for the Russians where all the doors are open to them, both internally and in providing the means for projecting influence externally."[181] The Chinese and Soviet governments both offered sizable loans to Algeria in the closing months of 1963, and in that respect, their rivalry rewarded Algeria's ambitious globalism. Yet Ben Bella, Bouteflika, and their colleagues were increasingly alarmed by the escalating acrimony: the communist countries' embassies flooded Algiers with mutually recriminatory propaganda, and when Zhou Enlai visited with great fanfare in December, his hosts were rather dismayed by the undisguised hostility of Soviet and Yugoslavian diplomats.[182] It was becoming clear that the Sino-Soviet split might tear the Third World apart.

China's criticisms of Soviet policies did, in some respects, match those of the Algerians and other Third World elements. In particular, Peking's leaders and representatives fed suspicions that Moscow, in the pursuit of peaceful coexistence, was too timid in its support of controversial anti-imperialist causes, such as the liberation movements of southern Africa. Khrushchev's desire to transform the Cold War into a less dangerous competition of economic philosophies was, Mao's government said, a cowardly betrayal of the global anticolonial struggle. Chinese diplomacy stressed the theme that "old and new colonialism" was the greatest danger to poor countries, and that the decisive dichotomy in world affairs was not the dialectic of communism and capitalism but instead non-Western peoples' continued resistance of Western imperialism.[183] In practical terms, the Chinese continued to be more aggressive in their support for armed movements opposed to both classical imperialism, such as the Portuguese variety, and "neo-imperialist" regimes in nominally independent countries like Congo-Léopoldville. China and Algeria cooperated to some extent in this area; when Major Chadli Benjedid (the future Algerian president) led a military delegation to China in early November, his hosts declared that Algeria was the linchpin of anticolonialism in Africa and the cause of the recent revolutionary upsurge there.[184] Details are sketchy because these exchanges did not go through standard diplomatic channels (and Algeria did not open an embassy in Peking until the following year), but in the ensuing months China reportedly made a financial contribution to the ANP's training camps, and it is clear that the flow of weapons, trainees, and revolutionary militants between China, Algeria, and southern Africa continued to grow.[185] In contrast, Boumedienne had returned from a similar mission to Moscow that summer complaining that the Soviets were placing ideological preconditions on the provision of material assistance, including public criticism of China, acceptance of peaceful coexistence, and the legalization of the PCA.[186] It is notable that he shared this account with the North Korean ambassador, who could be counted on to pass it on to his Chinese comrades.

At the same time, as the communist world's acrimonies became more public, its feuding diplomats were beginning to obstruct the Third Worldist project with their recriminatory diatribes. The representatives of smaller countries complained that communist name-calling and point-scoring spoiled the Afro-Asian Peoples' Solidarity Conferences in Moshi, Tanganyika, in February 1963 and Algiers in March 1964.[187] The French newspaper *Le Monde* captured one African attendee's frustrations at the latter event:

> We are not Marxist-Leninists, and most of us haven't read a line of "The Capital." So what interest can we have in your doctrinaire quarrels? I have had enough of this situation where whenever I eat my sandwich I am accosted by someone who wants to know my opinion on the Soviet stand, and when I drink my coffee, by someone who asks me about the Chinese arguments. I want to be able to eat in peace![188]

In that context, during his December tour of Africa and the Middle East, Zhou Enlai won plaudits for his accomplished presentation of a moderate and accommodating China. He insisted that his government welcomed a diversity of political-economic systems in the Third World (which was a rather ironic stance given the ideological nature of the dispute with the Soviet Union) and also that it supported the proposal for a second Non-Aligned Movement summit, even if China itself would not participate by dint of being unapologetically aligned in

Cold War terms.¹⁸⁹ In reality, though, Zhou's diplomatic aptitude was remarked upon precisely because Chinese representatives already gave the impression of being more rigid and zealous than their Soviet and Yugoslavian rivals, and their reputation deteriorated further still in the new year with the onset of Mao's internal ideological purge, the Cultural Revolution. Peking's hostility to NAM, in preference of the Afro-Asian unifying ideal, was becoming equally apparent.

The Algerian leadership was particularly bothered by Chinese opposition to NAM because, in advocating a racial "Afro-Asian" criterion for membership of the Third World, with the purpose of excluding the USSR and Yugoslavia, Peking jeopardized core tenets of Algeria's engagement with the outside world. Mao told black Africa that white, northern, and industrialized peoples like the Russians and Yugoslavians could never truly share the concerns of the Southern Hemisphere, whereas "[o]ur circumstances are fairly similar.... [S]o when we talk to you, there is no feeling that I bully you or you bully me, nobody has a superiority complex, we are both of a colored race."¹⁹⁰ To give an even blunter example of this line of argument, at the Afro-Asian Writers' Conference in Cairo, in March 1962, Chinese attendees condemned peaceful coexistence on the basis that "sheep and wolves can never co-exist.... These Europeans are all the same [and] we non-whites must hold together."¹⁹¹ Naturally, Yugoslav and Soviet officials railed against this discourse. In an interview with an Algerian newspaper—not coincidentally published the day before Zhou Enlai's December arrival—Khrushchev warned that "geopolitical and even racist slogans" were no substitute for true unity among progressive forces and that "the propagation of racist concepts ... only plays imperialism's game."¹⁹² Unfortunately, despite one Soviet expert's complaint that Chinese propaganda encouraged Africans to "relate to all whites with suspicion [while knowing] very little about the Soviet Union," many of the black and Arab students who spent time there did indeed encounter popular as well as official racism, and most found it to be an oppressive and alienating place.¹⁹³

For the Algerians, this focus on race challenged the rationale of their valuable relationships with the European communist countries, the USSR and Yugoslavia especially, and potentially called into question their involvement in black Africa. After all, the history of Arab-African relations was also troubled by slavery and cultural friction, and the self-appointed Algerian and Egyptian missions to lead the continent to revolution ran the risk of resembling older European and Arab discourses of civilizational superiority. In his treatise *The Philosophy of the Revolution* (1954), Nasser wrote that "[w]e certainly cannot, under any conditions, relinquish our responsibility to help spread the light of knowledge and civilization to the very depth of the virgin jungles of the Continent," while Ben Bella, incarcerated in France, opined one day in February 1961 that "in two or three generations, Arab civilization and the Arabic language could become the *point commun* of all the countries of Africa."[194] Luckily, in practice Algerian and Egyptian diplomacy showed greater awareness of racial dynamics, though the Algerians clearly thought themselves more conscious than their Egyptian colleagues, and patronizing attitudes were not entirely relegated to the past. For example, Ben Bella confided in Tito that "even among the best Africans one can find a complex that always has to be taken into consideration. We understand that very well and we are very careful in our work and measures. We are trying to help them overcome that complex." But the Algerian president then summarized his country's conception of Third World solidarity with deceptive profundity: "The conceptualization has to be political, and not racial."[195] In other words, Chinese propaganda sought to define Third Worldism as the expression of a racial or geographical identity, whereas the Algerians, Yugoslavians, Cubans, and others saw the Third World as a political project open to anyone who shared its goals.

On the whole, looking beyond the contentions of any particular international issue, the early days of independent Algeria's foreign policy reflect a world in which smaller countries battled to defy the established powers' efforts to contain them in manageable regional boxes. Some American officials groused (not without some justification) that the Algerians would not accept that they ought to focus on their domestic problems, and the correspondence of the State Department often seemed premised on the unspoken assumption that international affairs was for the big players, and that small and poor countries should at the very least keep their ambitions modest and stick to commenting on matters close to home. Likewise, the Soviet Union and China, while supportive of Third Worldist aspirations, also wanted to steer them to their own purposes. Whether accurate or not, the elites of small countries often believed that the Soviet Union secretly opposed their efforts to formally organize themselves and create institutions: the Yugoslavians thought so with NAM, and Nasser thought so of the United Arab Republic project, both probably with good reason.[196] China, a major power that was nonetheless strongly opposed to the international status quo at that time, also preferred to see a divided and polarized Third World rather than a more cohesive one that included participants not to Peking's liking. In this light, the ambitious globalist outlook that spurred Algeria to support revolutionary movements in Latin America, spurred Cuba and Yugoslavia to equip rebels in Africa, and inspired efforts to create the developing world's own international institutions, such as the OAU and NAM, stemmed from Third World elites' sense of vulnerability rather than from hubris. The Algerians vaulted continents, the color line, and the Cold War in their determination to avoid the confinements of identity politics, on the one hand, and "great power chauvinism," on the other.

The Sands War, October–November 1963

One purpose of the Algerians' preoccupation with global affairs was to shield them from local contentions. The so-called Sands War was a limited conflict that took place in October–November 1963, when Morocco launched an offensive to seize disputed territory in the Saharan frontier region. This remote and somewhat obscure skirmish entailed significant ramifications for Algeria's domestic politics and foreign relations—ramifications that had, in turn, their own echoes elsewhere in the postcolonial world. With respect to international affairs, a war over territory with a neighboring state challenged the rationale for Algeria's leaders' globalist pretensions, yet it was also the case that many facets of their ambitious foreign policy, such as their embrace of African unity, were motivated in part by a desire to either stave off or better respond to Moroccan aggression. Indeed, Ben Bella's government managed to transform military defeat into diplomatic victory in a manner that vindicated its foreign policy of the previous twelve months, although it failed to prevent Rabat's imposition of Cold War dynamics onto their bilateral relationship. Meanwhile, in domestic affairs, both regimes used the fighting to mobilize nationalist sentiment and discredit internal opposition, with the Algerian authorities accusing rebels in the predominantly Berber region of Kabylia of being in league with foreign powers. On the whole, therefore, the Sands War would encourage a renewed focus on the decidedly nonglobalist concerns of territorial defense and the enforcement of "national unity" among the populace.

The crux of the dispute was that the French and Moroccan authorities had never precisely determined where the border lay between the Sharifian kingdom and the future Algerian Republic, although the governments in Rabat and Algiers would both try to leverage this specific issue in late 1963 in order to assert their authority over the whole of their national territories. The border between the countries was especially uncertain in the vast desert regions because, in the words of a Franco-Moroccan treaty from 1845, "a country which is found without water is uninhabitable and a delimitation thereof would be superfluous," but the situation had very much changed by the 1950s with the discovery of oil, natural gas, iron, and other valuable natural resources.[197] The allegiances of the region's inhabitants were also unclear; during the referendum on Algerian independence in July 1962, the residents of Tindouf, the most significant town in the southwest corner of Algeria, reportedly indicated on their ballots "YES for Algerian Independence, BUT we are Moroccans."[198] Consequently, following Algeria's independence, murky "incidents" repeatedly occurred along this long stretch of poorly controlled, poorly demarcated, and highly prized frontier— sometimes in the form of local protests, sometimes small military operations to occupy some settlement or landmark in the name of one or the other government. High officials in Rabat and Algiers alike condemned and denied responsibility for these incidents, but Hassan II and his advisers were plainly losing patience with the Algerian strategy of constantly deferring any conclusive discussions of the border issue.

A second crucial aspect of the open conflict that broke out in October and November 1963 was that each regime had begun to see the other as an existential, subversive threat in regions far from the frontier. Morocco's conservative monarchical government, where the king was maneuvering to definitively assert his authority over the political parties, feared that Algeria's socialist revolution was gaining influence over its own citizens. By this time, the Algerian authorities had already nationalized most French-owned land in their country, whereas foreign landownership was still deeply entrenched and resented in the Moroccan countryside. Moreover, the Algerians were deliberately blanketing neighboring territories with their propagandistic radio broadcasts and gave shelter to the outlawed Moroccan left-wing party, the Union Nationale des Forces Populaires (National Union of Popular Forces, UNFP), led by Mehdi Ben Barka.[199] Conversely, Ben Bella and his colleagues were convinced that Rabat was supporting the Algerian regime's internal opposition, the most worrisome of which was the Front des Forces Socialistes (Front of Socialist Forces, FFS), led by a previously central figure in the FLN, Hocine Aït Ahmed, that had begun a small-scale rebellion in the mountainous region of Kabylia, east of Algiers. The FFS and other notable critics of the government, such as the similarly ostracized former FLN heavyweight Krim Belkacem, represented Algeria's sizable Berber Kabyle minority that felt culturally and political marginalized in the new order.

Whatever the truth of Moroccan coordination with Ben Bella's foes—which is far less clear than Algiers's involvement with the Moroccan opposition—the timing of Hassan's decision to launch a large military incursion on the western frontier was determined by the sudden and significant expansion of the Kabyle rebellion at the beginning of October, when an ANP colonel, Mohand Ouel Hadj, joined the insurgency along with several thousand ex-mujahideen under his command.[200] The Moroccan offensive began on 9 October. It quickly seized several outposts near Tindouf by dint of tank and air support that outmatched the ANP's lightly armed units. However, even as the two armies met in battle, the more decisive conflict arguably took place over the airwaves and targeted each country's general population. Ben Bella's thunderous accusations of conspiracy with foreign invaders dramatically changed the political calculus for the rebels. With the president leading massive crowds in chants against "Hassan the assassin" and calling on all Algerians to put country first, Ouel Hadj deserted Aït Ahmed to join the fight at the front, while most of the Kabyle public seemed to rally to the government as well.[201] For their part, the Moroccan authorities pressured left-wing elements in their own country to demonstrate their patriotism by repudiating the Algerian regime.[202]

In addition to whipping up nationalist fervor to discredit their domestic foes, the Moroccan and Algerian governments also insisted that their conflict was ideological. The Algerians believed that Rabat's intention was the destruction of their socialist revolution, with Boumedienne asserting that "the battle is not one of frontiers, it is a battle between Republic and Monarchy, a battle between reaction and progress[,] a battle between revolution and imperialism."[203] When Hassan denounced Ben Barka for siding with Morocco's enemy, the latter retorted in the pages of *Révolution Africaine* that he was Algeria's ally in the struggle to create an anti-imperialist, socialist, and united Maghrib. A cartoon in the newspaper depicted the United States, Israel, and capitalist businessmen jointly using the Moroccan king's head as a battering ram against *l'Algérie socialiste*.[204] Ben Bella heeded the advice of his Trotskyite adviser, Mohammed Harbi, to exploit the conflict "in a revolutionary fashion" by re-energizing the populace: as the military situation deteriorated in the west, the Algerian president announced the final nationalization of all remaining French-owned land and finally convened, on 25 October, a long-awaited national congress of self-management farmers that he declared, with great fanfare, to be the beginning of a new era of democratic, consultative socialism.[205]

While the Algerian authorities mostly directed their ideological message inward to mobilize their own public, Hassan and his diplomats were eager to convince Washington that the Maghrib had become a new front in the Cold War. The king told American officials that Algeria was a subversive socialist virus that threatened all of Africa and could only be stopped by the pro-Western virus of "his constitutional system, his democratic ideals and his economic progress." He could get armaments from elsewhere if need be, he said; it was more important that the Kennedy administration recognize the true nature of the totalitarian regime in Algeria and immediately apply the recommendations of the recent "Clay Report" to North Africa.[206] In recommending the cessation of all aid to Latin American countries that criticized American foreign policy or rejected capitalist economics, that congressional report exemplified the growing desire in Washington, in the wake of the Cuban Revolution, to apply Manichaean Cold War logic to the developing world. Kennedy and some of his keys advisers had mostly resisted those calls, with regard to Algeria specifically, and they remained leery of the king's efforts to replicate the Cold War so forcefully and irreversibly in North Africa. "We feel that aid to Hassan just now would simply cause [Ben Bella] to lean even further east," Komer told the president in late October, about two weeks into the fighting in the Sahara. "[The] result would be a new East/West confrontation with [the] UAR and Soviets backing Algeria, while [the] French and ourselves are pressed . . . to back Hassan."[207]

To a sizable degree, Komer's predication came to pass. Despite their strenuous denials and protestations of neutrality, the American and French governments secretly delivered more armaments and munitions to Morocco during the conflict, although the indications are that these deliveries related to preexisting agreements, and Washington, and possibly also Paris, soon turned down Hassan's requests for further aid.[208] Rumors of the American deliveries got out, quite possibly put about by the Moroccans themselves to further polarize the situation, as did still more explosive rumors that American pilots were manning transport aircraft and even bombers on the front lines.[209] Boumedienne insisted to a Cuban journalist that the latter stories were true, citing the precedent of the CIA's use of American mercenary pilots against Castro's regime.[210] Crucially, the Algerians were convinced that Washington's involvement was significant, not least because the Moroccan king seemed to have convinced himself, dubiously, that the French and American governments had given him a green light for the attack on Algeria. "Once again," Komer complained, "... one of our client kings tries a foolish small-time squeeze play, gets in over his head, and then screams for us to bail him out."[211] French involvement is murkier still, though the indications are that de Gaulle sought to appease both sides and not give either reason to jeopardize the Saharan nuclear testing sites, which quietly performed at least one detonation in the midst of the conflict.[212] Awkwardly, the French military was still the most capable force on the Algerian side of the border, but while the Algerians eventually used the French airfield at Colomb Béchar to fly in reinforcements, they did so in civilian planes.[213] Meanwhile, though the Algerian leadership seemed certain that de Gaulle's government was abetting Hassan, it seems that Algiers and Paris had discreetly agreed just days before the Moroccan assault, in the context of the Kabyle rebellion, that the French forces in Algeria should remain there a while longer in order to present an image of stability.[214]

In any case, confronting an army that was better equipped and better organized for conventional warfare, allegedly backed by the United States and France, the ANP turned to Algeria's allies in the East for assistance. Nasser publicly announced his determination to come to Algeria's defense, insisting in a speech at Suez on 23 October that "to attack the Yemeni revolution means to attack the revolution of the UAR [and] to attack the Algerian revolution is to attack the Yemeni revolution."[215] While his intervention on Algeria's behalf was nothing on the scale of Egypt's involvement in the Yemeni civil war, where Cairo now had thousands of troops deployed, Nasser immediately oversaw the dispatch of substantial quantities of Soviet-made armaments—including tanks, MiG aircraft, and naval destroyers—as well as approximately 500 "advisers."[216] When the Moroccans captured four Egyptian officers who were surveying the battlefield by helicopter, it strengthened the impression of a rapidly internationalizing conflict, as did Moscow's quick decision to expedite and expand on its military agreements with Algiers. Toward the end of the month, a Soviet freighter unloaded MiG fighter jets and Hound helicopters in the western city of Oran, accompanied by Soviet technical support crews and Algerian pilots who had been training in the Soviet Union.[217] There is no available evidence to support rumors that Soviet pilots actually flew combat missions, though one scholar's recent revelation that they did man Egyptian planes for combat sorties in Yemen around this time makes the suggestion more credible than previously thought.[218] Either way, the sizable Egyptian and Soviet deliveries were themselves enough to shift the military fortunes back in Algeria's favor. By late October, the ANP had likely suffered greater losses of a few thousand soldiers, but each side had seized some of the other's territory, and the longer-term forecast looked ominous for the Moroccans.

However, probably the most controversial international intervention was that of Cuba, which took the surprising and unprecedented decision, for a relatively small and poor country, to dispatch a tank unit and 200 to 300 troops across the Atlantic to fight for Algeria. By the accounts of both Ben Bella and Sergio Serguera, the Cuban ambassador, this decision was largely taken at the Cuban initiative. Serguera first proposed the idea to Bouteflika at the beginning of the hostilities, after observing that the Algerian armed forces were distinctly disadvantaged by having very few tanks. The Algerian foreign minister then conferred with Ben Bella and Boumedienne, but after responding in the affirmative to Serguera, they were shocked when he came back to them late that same evening to confirm that Havana was dispatching 150 troops by plane in the next twenty-four hours, with tanks and additional personnel to arrive by ship in about ten days' time. The Cubans agreed with Boumedienne that they would be deployed in an upcoming counteroffensive, with the intention of seizing a sizable piece of Moroccan territory to use as a bargaining chip. However, after spending several days training and preparing in the desert, awaiting final confirmation for the attack to come from Serguera in Algiers, the Cubans received word that they were to stand down. This decision seems to have been partly a deliberate political calculation by Ben Bella's government, partly the consequence of miscommunication amid fast-changing events. When Serguera came to Ben Bella's home on the eve of the planned assault, desperate for confirmation, he was surprised to hear that the president was flying to Bamako in the morning to begin negotiations with Hassan, with Haile Selassie and Modibo Keita mediating.[219] Still, when the Cubans were kept well out of sight for the 1 November celebrations, where the Egyptian presence was pushed to the fore, it became evident that the Algerian government feared that overt Cuban involvement would be too geopolitically contentious.[220]

Yet, even without going into battle, the Cuban soldiers affected the outcome of events. First, Havana's intervention may have prompted the much larger-scale

Egyptian and Soviet ones. Nasser told American officials that he had rushed to Ben Bella's aid in order to counteract the dangerous Cuban influence, and the Egyptian ambassador in Algiers claimed that his government had only persuaded the Algerians not to use the Cubans at the last minute by threatening to withdraw all of its own aid.[221] At the same time, the Cubans berated their Soviet counterparts for the lack of revolutionary solidarity, highlighting the embarrassing fact that the Moroccans relied on tanks and jets that the Soviet Union had sold to them several years before. A Cuban officer in the contingent deployed to Algeria reported to Havana that "the situation demands that the entire socialist camp send aid. . . . Some of the Algerian officers are not only worried . . . but indignant. They ask, and rightly so, how can the Soviet comrades help feudal kings like Hassan and not understand that a real revolution, like Cuba's, is taking place here."[222] In this and other aspects of Moscow's gradual embrace of Ben Bella's Algeria in this period, Cuban lobbying and the Cuban leadership's insistence that the Algerians were following in their footsteps seem to have had an appreciable effect on Soviet thinking. Finally, the arrival of Cuban tanks, which rolled off two cargo ships in broad daylight at the port of Oran, certainly contributed to the Kennedy administration's decision to push Hassan toward negotiations before the conflict spiraled out of control. Secretary of State Dean Rusk was, in Komer's words, getting "pretty itchy" and arguing that "if those people take arms from Cuba, we'll just have to back Morocco."[223]

For that very reason Algeria's leaders decided that they needed to reverse the conflict's slide toward Cold War patterns, which after all was what Hassan and the Moroccan command seemed to want. On 29 October, Chérif Guellal, the ambassador in Washington, visited the State Department in order to make the case that "[the] Moroccan effort to paint Algeria [as] pro-Eastern and itself as [a] moderate pro-Western democracy is vicious and manifestly absurd" and to convey his government's concern that the American government seemed to accept the Moroccan line.[224] Aside from being denuded of any Caribbean presence, the speeches and regalia of the 1 November celebrations heavily emphasized Algeria's Arab-Islamic identity and its ties to Egypt, which in addition to reinforcing Hassan's isolation in Arab affairs, situated the conflict in a decidedly regional, non–Cold War context. Most important, Ben Bella sent M'hamed Yazid to Washington a few days later as his personal envoy to President Kennedy. One of Algeria's most accomplished diplomatic operators, Yazid had married an American while acting as the GPRA's minister of information in New York, and he enjoyed a positive reputation in American diplomatic circles. Porter approvingly saw him as being outside of the "revolutionary" circle in Algerian politics, while Komer deemed him as "a shrewd operator and basically pro-US."[225] He was a good choice, in other words, to reassure Kennedy and other senior policymakers in Washington that the Algerian government shared their concern that the confrontation with Morocco had gotten out of hand, that Ben Bella and his team desired a ceasefire and a negotiated solution, and that they were still committed to nonalignment and friendship with the United States.

The Algerians rightly calculated that Yazid's message was one that the White House, though not the State Department, wanted to believe. Komer, in particular, continued to be a forceful advocate of the view that American diplomacy had needlessly alienated Algeria and that it was too important a country to let slide toward the communist bloc. That Kennedy still seemed to be willing at this point to receive Ben Bella in Washington, so long as the latter guaranteed that Fidel Castro would not subsequently appear in Algiers, was remarkable given that Cuban tanks were, at that moment, trundling somewhat purposelessly across the *hammada* (stony desert) of western Algeria. Kennedy's concession testified to his continued special sympathy for Algeria as well as the aptitude of that country's diplomacy. Notably, in tactical terms, Algiers's management of its relations with the United States was similar to its engagement with Paris in this same period: in both cases, Ben Bella and his advisers correctly calculated that his opposite number in the Elysée Palace or the White House could be induced to override the hostility that otherwise prevailed among their officials and staff. The downside of this approach was that Algerian-American relations would rapidly sour following Kennedy's assassination on 22 November.[226]

Algiers's more lasting diplomatic accomplishment, therefore, was to ensure that Selassie and Keita, acting on behalf of the OAU, would monitor the ceasefire with Morocco and arbitrate the dispute between the two North African countries. By the second week of fighting, both sides were looking for a peaceful conclusion before the crisis escalated and internationalized any further, but there were several options for mediation. Hassan pushed first for the United Nations to impose and monitor the ceasefire, believing that his Western allies on the Security Council would protect Morocco's interests.[227] However, neither the American government nor Secretary-General U Thant was eager to get involved, and Guellal informed the State Department that the Algerian government was "unalterably opposed . . . to consideration of [the] conflict by [the] UN" because it would entail the "undesirable introduction of great power involvement."[228] Alternatively, the Arab League held two emergency sessions on 19 and 20 October and formed a mediation committee that included delegates from Tunisia, Libya, the UAR, and Lebanon, but the Moroccans rejected this option because they saw it as one of Nasser's schemes. The Egyptian president published a grandstanding open letter to Hassan in *Al Ahram* a few days later, pleading with the king to put an end to the spectacle of Arabs killing Arabs, in a blunt effort to force him to accept the league's intervention. Given that public campaign, Nasser seems to have been somewhat surprised and irritated, at least initially, when Ben Bella instead invoked the OAU charter's stipulations on the sanctity of existing borders and the impermissibility of territorial revision by force of arms, which prompted Selassie to offer himself as an intermediary.[229] Although it was the Algerian government that initially favored African mediation, the Moroccans could not find a preferable solution, and Hassan was likely reassured by the involvement of his fellow monarch. He was surely less happy that the mediation would take place in the Malian capital, beginning on 29 October, but practicalities and regional diplomacy offered no alternatives.[230]

Ben Bella claimed afterward that, at the last minute, Hassan tried to do a deal directly with him "behind Nasser and Africa's back," but the fact was that he had no incentive to do so because the OAU's mediation was a clear victory for his government.[231] On the one hand, Ben Bella had accrued much greater diplomatic capital than his Moroccan counterpart over the past year. Selassie may have belonged to the conservative wing of African politics, but he was also recognizant of the Algerians' contribution to the Addis Ababa summit's success, while Modibo Keita was an ideological fellow traveler with Algiers's revolutionaries who additionally appreciated their cooperation in enforcing Bamako's sovereignty over the unruly Touareg areas of northern Mali. Rédha Malek confided to the Yugoslavians on 31 October that his government was already quite confident of Selassie and Keita's favorable opinion.[232] At the same time, Hassan's attempt to expand his borders by force of arms was in clear violation of the Addis Ababa resolutions and roundly condemned across the continent. So while the OAU formed a committee to evenhandedly investigated the complex history of the Moroccan-Algerian border, in practice the burden of proof was on Rabat, and Hassan's foreign minister admitted that his government was cooperating despite a prevailing "anti-Moroccan bias."[233] Ultimately, the OAU's investigations did not lead to any conclusive clarification of the frontier, but the organization's mediation did facilitate an improvement in Moroccan-Algerian relations over the course of the following year, if for no other reason than by conveying to Hassan the depth of Rabat's isolation in a nonconfrontational manner. Algeria's diplomats were additionally satisfied at having simultaneously boosted the standing of the African unity organization and defended their own national interests.

In certain respects, then, the Sands War strengthened the Algerian regime's external and internal positions. Morocco was better contained than it had been prior to the conflict, while Ben Bella had used the crisis to splinter and marginalize the Kabyle rebels. Colonel Ouel Hadj had broken with Aït Ahmed to participate in the nation's defense, and the Kabyle public had responded impressively to the president's call for volunteers to fight on the western front.[234] The scale of the rebellion was reduced significantly. A few months later, Ben Bella told Tito that once he had "pointed out the links between the Moroccans and Aït Ahmed," the Algerian people had shown his government extraordinary support, so that "now, neither Aït Ahmed nor the defense of borders represents a problem for us."[235] Yet Ben Bella's administration was also more dependent on the military than ever before. The ANP was engaged in ongoing stability operations in Kabylia, while Boumedienne, smarting from the army's poor performance against the Moroccans, initiated a massive armaments drive and expansion of the armed forces' conventional territorial defense capabilities, principally through Soviet support. In the capital, the international community and those connected with it began to worry that the military's increased influence was shifting the tenor of Algerian politics, away from cosmopolitan internationalism toward a more chauvinistic and intolerant nationalism. Not only were the Kabyle Berbers and other exponents of subnational identities treated as inherently suspect—equated to the treacherous Katangans in Congo and the Kurds in Iraq—some of the foreign participants in the Algerian Revolution were beginning to question their welcome, too. The Moroccan attack had offered a reminder that no state could ignore geographical realities, but the greater challenge to Algerian globalism lay within.

National Chauvinism and Cold War Clientelism

Defying the skeptics, Algeria's leaders demonstrated that Third Worldist ideals could indeed provide the basis for a practical and consistent foreign policy doctrine. If the ultimate objectives of that doctrine were still a very distant prospect—such as restructuring the global economy and the elimination of great power "neocolonial" interference in Third World affairs—it nevertheless yielded several notable early successes. The founding of the OAU proved that elusive concepts of transnational solidarity, in this case pan-Africanism, could indeed take concrete form, and in so doing became the prototype for Algerian diplomacy in the years ahead. Algiers's willingness to pursue proactive and (in the minds of some) provocative initiatives was also rewarded at the Addis Ababa meeting, with Ben Bella's bellicose "blood bank" speech helping to secure a continental consensus on the righteousness of violent anticolonial struggle. The creation of the Committee of Nine, to coordinate African states' support for liberation movements, was the epitome of Algeria's interpretation of Third Worldism: collective defiance institutionalized. Equally successful was the "globalist" strategy of leveraging Algeria's interregional and multifaceted identity. Already acting as a bridge between Africa, Cuba, and Yugoslavia, by 1964 Ben Bella, Bouteflika, and their colleagues were attempting to serve as intermediaries in the rapprochement between France and the Arab world.[236] Additionally, Algeria was one of the most prominent countries striving to harmonize the Afro-Asian and nonaligned trends, which had overlapping but distinct constituencies and priorities. Yet the Sands War crisis provided the clearest vindication of Algiers's diplomacy, as the Third World community overwhelmingly supported the Algerian position, leaving the Moroccan regime virtually isolated. Sympathetic African mediation, Cuban tanks, Egyptian jets: the rewards of globalism were immediate and substantive.

They were also, however, finite. The Sands War was a diplomatic coup for Algeria's leaders, but it also reined in their defiance of geographical constraints by stoking the fires of nationalism and state-centrism. On the one hand, the Moroccan incursion invigorated Algerian militarism. Houari Boumedienne and his commanders pledged to defend the sanctity of the nation's borders and territory, instigating a massive arms buildup and military expansion in response to the Algerian army's poor performance in the field. With the "fraternal" Moroccan and Algerian people locked in an arms race over the most remote possible territorial dispute, the OAU's peace brokering further confirmed the importance and inviolability of the national divisions that decolonization had bequeathed to Africa. That successful mediation was a validation of the newly institutionalized principle of continental unity, yet it also further confirmed that anticolonial solidarity, in the postcolonial era, was a subordinate ideal to that of nation-state sovereignty. That is to say, the Maghreb's deeply rooted, transnational social and cultural bonds had succumbed in emphatic fashion to the prerogatives of the newly constituted postcolonial international order. Among themselves and in conversation with trusted allies, Algerian officials acknowledged that they pursued economic and cultural agreements with Morocco and Tunisia under the mantra of "integration," but they really intended these as inducements for Rabat and Tunis to recognize territorial realities.[237] Foreign minister Bouteflika personified the ironies of the new paradigm, since, as his critics down the years would gleefully remind him, he himself was reputedly born on the Moroccan side of the border. Of course, the ascendance in North Africa of what Kwame Nkrumah had, in a previous era, dismissed as "national chauvinism" was one manifestation of a phenomenon seen throughout the Third World. Just as previous federalist initiatives had failed in French West Africa and then Ghana-Guinea, the project to create an Arab federation joining Egypt, Syria, and Iraq was stumbling through its protracted collapse at this time. Further afield, in Asia, the concurrent territorial conflict between Indonesia and Malaysia (the Konfrontasi) arguably fit the same pattern.

Furthermore, as Ben Bella's adviser Mohammed Harbi complained, the conflict with Morocco encouraged the forces of national chauvinism inside Algeria as well.[238] Like others on the Algerian left, he felt that the army's growing political power exposed a xenophobic streak among the officer corps, often expressed as resentment of the "pieds rouges" and other foreigners, who were especially thick on the ground in the capital. More important in the near term, the national authorities had taken the opportunity to discredit regionalism by accusing

Kabyle elements of conspiring with Morocco. If there was no small degree of cynicism in the way that Ben Bella, Boumedienne, and those around them tried to marginalize and delegitimize subnational identities, their commitment to a homogenizing nationalism was also the product of a sincere fear of division, with the Western-backed Katanga separatists in Congo their oft-invoked nightmare. They shared this fear with many of their opposite numbers in other capitals. For example, at a summit of the Arab League in January 1964, Ben Bella recommended to his Iraqi counterpart that he use the same methods against the Kurds that his government was employing against the Kabyles: though his exact meaning is unclear from the evidence at hand, timing and context suggest he meant exposing regionalists' (supposed) connivance with external enemies to undermine national unity, backed up with the use of force.[239] Both the colonial experience and more recent precedents, such as Congo and Vietnam, lent credence to postcolonial elites' dread of division and secession, but Algeria and Iraq were not the only countries of the Third World in which this concern was used to justify the official intolerance of cultural diversity, frequently enforced in brutal fashion.

The conflict with Morocco also highlighted Algeria's declining maneuverability in the international sphere. The Soviet-Algerian alliance intensified markedly in the following months on the back of Boumedienne's determination to build a capable, conventional military force. From the perspective of Serguera, the Cuban ambassador, this heightened Soviet engagement was one of the Sands War's positive consequences; recalling the Suez Crisis of 1956, he argued that Moscow had once again come to the rescue of a progressive Arab country, in the process disproving Chinese accusations of Soviet indifference to the anti-imperial cause.[240] However, the diverging analysis of his Yugoslavian counterpart, Dizdarević, was more insightful and cognizant of the North African vantage on global affairs. He warned his superiors, "The importance that the USSR wants to give to the Algeria-Cuba analogy has dubious value for relations between Algeria and the Arab and African countries, because it primarily elicits suspicions about Algeria's pretensions to leadership, the vanguard role, and the export of revolution, which the West and the reactionaries [will] use and amplify in order to isolate Algeria."[241] In other words, Dizdarević feared that Ben Bella's government risked making the same error that it had previously identified in Cuba's foreign policy: losing the appearance (let alone reality) of ideological and geopolitical independence. Moreover, as the following chapter elaborates, a stronger Soviet-Algerian relationship could jeopardize the North African country's relations with China as well as the United States. Indeed, the substance of Algeria's communications with its peers in Africa and the Arab world suggests that the Sino-Soviet rivalry was, for at least some developing countries, becoming a more pressing concern in their daily affairs than the contest between

Moscow and Washington. If the increasing multipolarity of international affairs had hitherto benefited the nonaligned states by widening the horizon of possibility, they now faced the worrisome prospect of being hemmed in by several overlapping global Cold Wars.

All told, by 1964 Algeria was fully engaged in an African Cold War in which the interference of multiple outside powers fueled diverse insurgencies and revolutionary movements, yet almost paradoxically, the same process of clientelism also reinforced the continent's fragile new state system. Although the Moroccan-Algerian confrontation would seem to be an example of the instability and arbitrariness of Africa's borders, the manner of that conflict's resolution actually leads to the opposite conclusion. Algeria's leaders began to increase their reliance on the Soviet Union in order to defend their sovereignty and strengthen their state, as Morocco's leaders were doing with the United States, Mali's with China, and so on. Collectively, therefore, Africa's political elites pulled the great powers into their affairs, using Cold War narratives to convince them to invest in the survival of their regimes and, in the process, making their benefactors the guarantors of the postcolonial borders. For all the proxy wars, coups d'état, and guerrilla struggles roiling the continent in the early 1960s, its political map would prove surprisingly durable.

5

Mecca of Impatience and Anxiety

Globalizations and the Third World Order

> Here is the parting of the ways—the new worldview that we can offer to humanity. This worldview and way of life attend to the deepest dimensions of human practical life. This is the resource humankind does not now possess, because it is not among the "products" of Western civilization and European ingenuity, Eastern or Western.
>
> Sayyid Qutb, *Signposts Along the Road*, c.1953–1966

> Perhaps this is what the permanent organizers of the Afro-Asian Conference unconsciously sensed when they chose the location of the second Bandung[;] in the place of that gentle Indonesian city perfumed with jasmine and lulled by soft music, Algiers, dramatic Algiers which, after long years of blood, is seen everywhere as a mecca of impatience or of anxiety.
>
> Arthur Conte, *Bandung: Tournant de l'histoire*, 1965

By the summer of 1965, crews worked night and day at a sprawling building site on the Algerian coast, just twenty kilometers west of the capital. A multinational workforce, with prominent Egyptian and French participation, struggled to complete a new luxury resort and conference center by the end of June, only nine months after first breaking ground. Nadi Snober (the Pine Tree Club) featured of a high-rise hotel, 200 villas, restaurants, shops, and its own bank, post office, and medical center. Purpose-built to host the sequel to the now-mythical Bandung summit of 1955, the conference facilities boasted a massive central hall, multiple secondary meeting rooms, and the latest technology for instant translation, audiovisual presentations, and international communications.[1] Indeed, the Algerian government planned to meet the needs and expectations of about two thousand foreign dignitaries and a comparable number of representatives of the world's press. One minister boasted that the complex would stand as a testament to "Arab ingenuity" and the fact that Algeria had become "an important crossroads in global affairs."[2] The (unofficial) communist daily, *Alger Républicain*, enthusiastically described the construction site as "breathtaking in its immensity and overwhelming activity," and feigned enthusiasm over such supposedly inspirational spectacles as the "superb monotony of a tireless cement mixer that seems to stand in defiance of those who do not believe Algeria will complete this task."[3] This new low in propagandistic bombast hinted to the uncomfortable truth that, despite sizable Chinese financial assistance, this cherished project of Algeria's political elite was a questionable undertaking for a country in which hunger, homelessness, and disease were still rampant, a sizable share of its population reliant on American food donations. *Alger Républicain*'s editors were not really interested in cement; they knew well that the real challenge was laying the human foundations of the new order.

The mid-1960s saw political elites around the world, in the North as well as the South, struggle to channel the converging torrents of technological and economic change. Distance appeared to be shrinking in ways both unsettling and inspiring—especially within the American sphere of influence in Western Europe and East Asia. In November 1963, for example, President Kennedy's shocking death was the subject of the first live trans-Pacific television broadcast, but the same satellites that beamed the assassination news directly into Japanese homes also made it possible, just a few months later, for audiences on the other side of the globe to watch the Tokyo Olympics in "real time." With trade surging on the back of such innovations, the leaders of the major capitalist countries met in May 1964 at the Palais des Nations in Geneva, the former headquarters of the League of Nations whose tranquil gardens offered a respite from the pell-mell transformations that they had gathered to discuss. In his message to the participants, President Lyndon Johnson promised that the US government would spare no effort to ensure the successful conclusion of this new round of negotiations for the General Agreement on Tariffs and Trade (GATT), the framework through which countries accounting for 80 percent of global commerce administered its continued expansion. Trade, vowed Johnson, was the path to a better world.[4] Despite such happy prognostications, this new era brought challenges to even the wealthiest of cities. In January that same year, the architect Minoru Yamasaki unveiled his design for two massive skyscrapers, the tallest ever built, for lower Manhattan in order to reassert New York's centrality and permanence in a world of accelerating competition and reconfiguration. Noting that "the buildings that the World Trade Center would replace are a motley, undistinguished assortment of the 19th century," the local paper of record enthused that "no project has even been more promising for New York."[5] Although it was located at the heart of the wealthy North, the World Trade Center project's grandiosity suggested that its progenitors shared some of the concerns of the postcolonial world's political elites, who were desperate and uncertain in the face of globalization.

From the vantage of the Southern Hemisphere, the steady accumulation of economic treaties between rich countries, above all GATT and the EEC, looked worryingly like the construction of an invisible wall that would permanently exclude the poor nations from Johnson's prosperous future. Seventy-seven developing countries (known thereafter as the Group of Seventy-Seven, or G77, regardless of fluctuations in their actual numbers) passed a motion in the UN General Assembly to create an alternative forum in which the management of the world economy could be discussed with an emphasis on the Third World's concerns. Defying the protests of Western governments, the first United Nations Conference on Trade and Development (UNCTAD) convened a few weeks before the GATT meeting—also in Geneva—where an impressive contingent of delegations from the developing world called for the creation of a different system of global trade, with "fairer" prices for raw materials and agricultural exports, as well as a centralized system for the collection and distribution of economic aid. In comparison to previous Third World meetings, such as Bandung or the Belgrade nonaligned summit, the G77 included many more countries and greater ideological diversity. Speaking from the more rebellious end of the spectrum, Che Guevara warned his fellow attendees to guard against the subtle schemes of the major Western powers lest "the lengthy deliberations at this Conference . . . result in nothing more than innocuous documents and files for international bureaucracy to guard zealously," yet they chose to create a new permanent secretariat for UNCTAD, headed by a respected Argentinian economist with an impressive career in the UN system, Raúl Prebisch. While some of Prebisch's Western colleagues considered him a radical utopian for his statist and protectionist development theories, at Geneva the countries of the Third World chose to penetrate the establishment rather than challenge it. Bestowing his position's imprimatur, U Thant hailed UNCTAD's founding as proof that the division between North and South was just as fundamental to global affairs as that between East and West.[6] Using their greatest asset—numbers—developing countries hoped to take control of international political structures and use them to tame economic globalization.[7]

Eager participants in UNCTAD's founding, Algeria's leaders were typical of the Third World's determination to defend national sovereignty from capitalist integration by giving international political institutions authority over the economic realm. When U Thant visited Algiers in February 1964, just before the UNCTAD conference, Ben Bella urged him to "take initiatives in promoting international conferences which fall indirectly within the framework of the United Nations, and which would strengthen the organization in the long run."[8] Although the UN and its related institutions are often seen as agents of globalization that weaken national sovereignty, Third World elites understood that these institutions were, in fact, the most essential validators and guarantors of sovereignty across much of the Southern Hemisphere. While those elites were suspicious of the Bretton Woods economic institutions, the IMF and World Bank had not yet demonstrated their ability and readiness to dictate policy to desperate governments. In other words, national leaders in the Third World generally believed that by increasing the authority of the UN system, they increased the authority of their own states. Furthermore, although they saw the UN in its present form as a tool of the major Western powers, they also believed that it offered their best opportunity to overcome those powers' self-interested management of the global economy and continued interference in the Southern Hemisphere. "What is vital for [poor countries]," one Algerian foreign ministry report argued, "is to gain access to the international responsibilities at the heart of the United Nations and to ensure that their interests and economic imperatives will no longer be subject to the discretion of a few major powers."[9] Adjusting its own internal bureaucratic hierarchy, the ministry created a new International Organizations Section to complement the existing North America and Western Europe Section, Socialist Countries Section, Arab Countries Section, Africa Section, and Asia and Latin America Section. These high-level analytical and policymaking categories were, in themselves, indicators of the underlying ideological and geographical assumptions of Algerian diplomacy.[10]

Indeed, Bouteflika's reordering of his ministry's operations was a microcosm of a more widespread urge to solidify the Third World order of sovereign states whose leaders were eager to render the logic of their domains, nations, and rule immune to interrogation by either outside actors or their own citizens. The successful institutionalization of the G77 initiative helped achieve that objective: UNCTAD was created to change the global political economy in specific ways, but like the Afro-Asian movement, NAM, the OAU, or the Arab League, this new international entity validated and actualized the postcolonial world's political map just by the fact of its regular operation. That said, while Algeria's brief war with Morocco had highlighted the importance of this facet of diplomacy in the Southern Hemisphere, UNCTAD's impressive geographical and programmatic scope was nevertheless an encouraging indication, for the Algerians and their allies, that the Third World project's boldest and most inspiring aims were still viable.

This psychological boost helped Ben Bella and his foreign policy team to maintain their optimistic pursuit of the Third World agenda despite a deteriorating international climate. The intensification of the Cold War in Africa forced the Algerians to abandon their neutral posture and become one of the most polarizing forces in continental affairs. At the same time, under Johnson, the American government became openly hostile and sought ways to punish Algiers for its subversive activities in Africa and its alliance with the Soviet Union. Most problematic of all were the multiplying conflicts between "progressive" and "anti-imperialist" countries, including the Sino-Soviet split, Sino-Indian antagonism, the Indonesian-Malaysian Konfrontasi (confrontation), and the re-escalation of the Congo Crisis. Algerian diplomacy would have to transcend all of these problems because, in the Geneva conference's afterglow, it was agreed that the time was right for a new Afro-Asian heads of state summit, or "Bandung 2," and Algeria's determined lobbying secured the honor of hosting the momentous event, in June 1965. The Algerian leadership, Ben Bella in particular, anticipated that this *rendez-vous planétaire* would confirm their vanguard role in the affairs of the Third World—so long as they could prevent international tensions from derailing it. "[Algiers's] importance as one of the Third World's great capitals continues to grow," enthused diplomat M'hamed Yazid, " . . . [and] it's no accident that the chosen location of the Second Bandung meeting is the capital of a country, Algeria, whose exploits and sacrifices . . . epitomize . . . the anticolonial struggle."[11] Thus, although the brand new, showpiece complex that the Algerian government rush built expressly for the conference was quite modest in comparison to the World Trade Center project, it too was an edifice to a new world order.

However, just as Ben Bella and his colleagues were on the verge of unprecedented acclaim in the international sphere, objections to Algeria's globalist calling mounted within their own society. While the political elite was obsessed with the threat of capitalist neo-imperialism, many people living away from the capital were more concerned by what might be called "socialist globalization." When the authorities responded to continued economic stagnation by introducing centralizing, command-and-control reforms, it gave the impression that advisers and technicians from the communist countries were on the front line of an unpopular campaign to crush Algeria's experiment in self-management and democratic socialism. At the same time, cultural and religious conservatives were getting bolder and more organized in their condemnation of, in their view, the decadent, corrupting cosmopolitanism that reigned in the capital and the atheistic influence of the president's foreign advisers. More explosive still was the interaction of international events and factional maneuvering at the apex of the political hierarchy, stimulating the latent rivalry between Ben Bella and his defense minister, Boumedienne. As each diplomatic success enhanced their charismatic president's stature, the military chief and his circle concluded that they had to act before Bandung 2 made him too powerful. The vanguard was a dangerous place to be.

Triangular Nonalignment for a Multilateral Cold War

In early 1964, in the context of changing Soviet and American attitudes toward the Third World more generally, the arms race between Morocco and Algeria escalated local Cold War dynamics to a point where the viability of the latter's commitment to nonalignment was questioned. While Moscow's interest in Algeria reflected newfound ideological open-mindedness regarding "unorthodox" socialist revolutions, US foreign policy in the post-Kennedy era conversely showed signs of a less tolerant approach to the Southern Hemisphere. In January 1964, the House Foreign Relations Committee published a report that appraised the Third World along strict Cold War, East versus West lines and rather ominously categorized Algeria, Ghana, and Mali as being "under growing communist influence."[12] Robert Komer warned Ambassador Chérif Guellal that President Johnson did not share his predecessor's special appreciation for the Algerian perspective.[13] Accordingly, the rapid consolidation of a Soviet-Algerian friendship over the following months, capped by Ben Bella's celebratory visit to the communist superpower in April, prompted senior American policymakers to doubt the sincerity of Algerian nonalignment and to deliberate punitive actions, including the withdrawal of food aid. Feeling the pressure of their hostility, Ben Bella protested at the Cairo Non-Aligned Conference that October that neutrality ought not require him to "endeavour to practice, *vis-à-vis* the great powers, a policy involving constant acrobatics."[14]

Although Washington's skepticism was warranted—Ben Bella himself suggested on one occasion to his Yugoslavian confidant, Dizdarević, that he had "chosen a camp"—nonalignment in a more complex and provocative sense was still a fundamental tenet of his government's foreign policy.[15] Indeed, while he publicly protested the need for diplomatic acrobatics, the Algerian president also described his foreign policy to Dizdarević as a multifaceted, global balancing act. For the Algerians continued to perceive a world with multiple great powers that could be played against one another, despite the marked superiority of two of them. Algeria actually pursued a triangular form of nonalignment in this period that used Soviet support as a hedge against the withdrawal of French aid, while simultaneously leveraging Franco-American competition to maintain Paris's interest in its former colony's development.[16] The fact that State Department officials did not perceive the latter dynamic, or at least greatly underestimated its importance, did not preclude its effectiveness. As a result, although it seemed from Washington's perspective that Algerian nonalignment had either failed or been willfully abandoned, Algeria's success in combining French and Soviet assistance suggests that the Cold War might have been more multilateral than its two primary antagonists recognized.

In light of Moscow's caution toward the FLN during the Algerian War and the bad feeling created by the interdiction of the PCA in November 1962, the initial rationale for Soviet-Algerian friendship was very much pragmatic.[17] By late 1963, the Algerians already saw the Soviet Union as a valuable alternative to France for economic assistance and trade, but Soviet military assistance also became a matter of urgency following the clash with Morocco. The ANP was still structured much like a guerrilla force—Ben Bella said that they had initially chosen to keep it as a "popular" army because it was supposed to play a vanguard political role in Algerian society—but it had fared poorly against the Moroccan Royal Army's heavy weapons, aircraft, and conventional maneuvering.[18] Happily, the Kremlin showed it was willing to provide both equipment and training, and it concluded a series of agreements to this effect during three visits by Algerian delegations to Moscow: one led by Boumedienne in October 1963; another headed by the president of the National Assembly, Hadj Ben Alla, in December; and Ben Bella's own trip the following April. As the Egyptian and Cuban "advisers" who had arrived in October drifted away from Algeria, hundreds of Red Army personnel replaced them (some posing as "agrarian advisers") and helped to visibly transform the country's armed forces in a matter of months. By the summer, French and American intelligence judged, Boumedienne's ground forces had received a hundred tanks and fifty armored personnel carriers, as well as artillery, antiaircraft guns, and support vehicles. Likewise, Algeria's nearly nonexistent air and naval capabilities received dozens of MiG fighter jets, bombers, transport aircraft, radar equipment, and combat ships. Hundreds of ANP personnel traveled in the opposite direction to be trained in the use of this equipment and the art of war. Through this massive investment, the Soviet Union became Algeria's primary provider of military hardware and maintenance. Additionally, Soviet influence on the ANP's culture and doctrine was growing: although Boumedienne previously had been an ardent admirer of the Cuban Revolution, his priority was now creating a professional standing army, rather than imitating Castro's ideological shock troops.[19] In short, within a year, the ANP was unrecognizable from the pseudo-guerrilla force, more focused on influencing politics than defending territory, that had fared so poorly in the Sands War.[20]

Consequently, in December, Ben Bella's confidant and president of the National Assembly, Hadj Ben Alla, headed a delegation that spent a fortnight in the Soviet Union to conclude a raft of new agreements. The two sides discussed how Algeria might cash in its $300 million credit and agreed to allocate much of it to big-ticket projects such as a long-proposed steel mill at Arzew (which the French had let lapse), as well as dams, irrigation schemes, and even a football stadium. Mining was an area of special concern for the Algerians, who believed that the sector could provide substantial export revenues to fuel economic modernization elsewhere in the economy, but lacking an external market since independence, production was currently piling up at the port of Algiers without a destination. In fact, Ben Bella had already written to Khrushchev on this subject beforehand, so that when Ben Alla's delegation arrived, the Soviet government pledged to find customers within the socialist bloc for Algerian mercury, lead, zinc, phosphates, and iron ores, and also to buy unsold output itself. Additionally, a team of Soviet geologists would carry out a three-year survey of

Algeria's vast expanses in order to investigate new mining opportunities.[21] Apart from being impressive in financial terms, therefore, Moscow's new economic commitments to Algeria constituted a canny combination of the showy and the substantive, including showpiece construction projects as well as promising commercial agreements that responded to the Algerians' overriding emphasis on industrialization, rapid development, and diversification.[22]

By the Algerians' own reckoning, the Soviet leadership hoped that all this economic and military support would steer their country in a pleasing ideological direction. Though the existing literature generally dismisses the idea that Moscow harbored such hopes for Algeria, as opposed to essentially strategic calculations, there is reason to believe that for a brief period Khrushchev may well have hoped for a Cuba-like progression of events in North Africa. During his last year in power, the Soviet leader embraced Third World radical nationalists with a degree of enthusiasm that was not always to the liking of his more orthodox comrades, and he supported the idea that countries like Algeria, Ghana, or Mali could skip the capitalist stage of development and proceed directly to building socialism.[23] However, Castro himself had vouched for the Algerians, who rarely missed an opportunity to express their reciprocal admiration for the Cuban Revolution, while Khrushchev later admitted to being personally impressed by the nominally banned PCA's prominent influence in Ben Bella's government.[24] On this basis, Soviet analysts claimed to detect the emergence of progressive revolutionary forces in Algerian society, and the Kremlin lauded the Algerian people's "socialist path to development" and their construction of an "independent and democratic state."[25] The Algerian diplomatic team understood that the use of words like "socialist" and "democratic" reflected "a very specific, albeit quite nuanced, understanding of the political situation in our country. This is in fact the first time that Moscow had gone so far in its characterization of a regime outside the socialist bloc."[26] In early 1964, Moscow's Institute of the World Economy formally appended Algeria to the roll of "revolutionary democracies," and Western observers were shocked to hear the new Soviet ambassador, appointed in February, address Ben Bella as "comrade president."[27]

It is notable that the Algerian diplomatic team was quite aware that Moscow had an interest in ratcheting up Cold War tensions in North Africa. The Kremlin, they believed, was determined "by means of revolutionary dynamics and especially the pressure of circumstances" to convince the Algerian government that its national liberation could only be preserved by embracing communism and aligning with the Soviet bloc. "Had it gone on for longer," they noted, "the conflict with Morocco would have greatly benefited this policy."[28] So the dangers to the credibility of Algeria's nonaligned status were not lost on them. They also recognized that Kennedy's death removed the main counterbalance to rising hostility among the American public, Congress, and foreign policy apparatus.[29]

Officials in the United States noted the commencement of a twice-weekly air route between Algiers and Moscow in February, in the expectation that this would lead to flights to Havana, as well as the fact that Ben Bella personally flew on a Soviet Ilyushin plane. In the hands of someone as fond of the international limelight as the Algerian president, the Ilyushin was essentially an aerial advertisement for Soviet friendship; such considerations were treated seriously in Washington, where the integration of developing countries into the Western-oriented and Western-equipped air network had become a priority.[30] Unfortunately, there was a zero-sum logic to that sort of competitive accounting.

As a result, Washington and Algiers were increasingly talking past one another. In January 1964, when the House Foreign Relations Committee categorized Algeria, Ghana, and Mali as countries "under growing communist influence," the Algerian foreign ministry concluded that it proved how out of touch with Third World realities the State Department was.[31] When the American embassy learned that Ben Bella was going to visit the Soviet Union in late April, the majority view in Washington was that he was no longer neutral in the Cold War. Dean Rusk summoned Ambassador Chérif Guellal to ask bluntly, "What kind of country did Algeria wish to be, and what was its orientation?" Pointing to Algeria's deepening ties with the communist world as well as its strident criticism of US policy in Vietnam, Cuba, and Congo, the secretary of state put the ambassador on notice that the American government "did not see much content in the concept of Algerian non-alignment."[32]

However, American policymakers did not properly appreciate that the Algerian leadership was thinking primarily in terms of balancing the Soviet Union against France, rather than the United States. The same blind spot—the insistence on seeing the world in bipolar terms without appreciating that the geopolitical landscape was much more multipolar from the vantage of poor and weak postcolonial countries—lay behind Washington's refusal to compete with the French position in Algeria itself. Consequently, prior to his trip to the Soviet Union, Ben Bella considered it important to improve relations with the French government and to get French economic assistance back on track. He made a surprise visit to de Gaulle's home in Colombey-les-Deux-Églises on 13 March, where the two presidents brokered a rapprochement following the deterioration in bilateral relations as a result of the March Decrees and Ben Bella's public attacks on the Evian Accords.[33] In terms of international strategy, Ben Bella wanted to reassure de Gaulle that the increasing Soviet investment in Algeria was not a threat to French interests, even as he simultaneously leveraged the Soviet threat to ensure that de Gaulle reaffirmed his commitment to Algeria's economic vitality. As the Algerian president explained to his Yugoslavian confidant, Ambassador Dizdarević, he did not want to replace Algeria's dependency on France with a dependency on the Soviet Union, but rather to encourage a hearty sense of competition between Paris and Moscow and open the possibility, in the dire circumstance that de Gaulle really did cut Algeria off, that the Soviets could credibly step in as a replacement.[34] It did not fully dawn on American officials that their French counterparts were more worried by the prospect of being supplanted by American economic power than Soviet, nor that it actually benefited de Gaulle's appeal to nonaligned countries if France's showpiece of economic assistance, Algeria, was also a prominent beneficiary of communist support.

Ben Bella spent two heavily publicized weeks in the Soviet Union, accompanied by a sizable delegation that included governmental, FLN party, and military representatives. The Soviet authorities made it very clear that they saw their relationship as being more than simply businesslike, for the visit culminated in the Algerian president being the guest of honor for the May Day celebrations on Red Square and with his being awarded the Hero of the Soviet Union and Order of Lenin medals. These were rare honors for representatives of the non-communist world, granted only to the likes of Fidel Castro. Both Ben Bella and Khrushchev later testified to the warmth of their personal interactions. "Ben Bella made the very best impression on me," the Soviet premier wrote in his memoirs. "He was a cultured and educated man, well informed on questions of socialist construction and of Marxism. He took a position in favor of scientific socialism. . . . I also liked his domestic policies very much. The Algerian Communist Party, it was true, remained illegal, but that was mostly just a formality."[35] As these comments indicate, Ben Bella's good relations with Algeria's communists made a particularly strong impression on Khrushchev, who mourned the fact that many other African and Arab leaders—even some who benefited from a great deal of Soviet assistance, such as Nasser—had suppressed or even ruthlessly eliminated the communists in their own countries. For his part, Ben Bella described Khrushchev after the trip as "simple and open" and said that he considered the Soviet leader a friend.[36] While Khrushchev was impressed by Ben Bella's appreciation of the merits of communist ideology and communist morality, even without being a communist himself, the Algerian was gratified by the way his counterpart seemed to accept that a poor, Muslim country by necessity did not share the Soviet perspective on all issues.[37]

The Soviets were eager that their aid produce visible results in short order. After all, the American Four Areas project had essentially withered on the vine because the Algerian authorities were unable or unwilling to fund it, so in response to the concern that many of the projects proposed by Soviet experts also required Algiers to invest its own scarce funds, the Soviets announced that they were providing 115 million rubles of credit to cover this shortfall. Ben Bella was taken out to see the ambitious (and ultimately disastrous) effort to create vast new areas of arable land in Uzbekistan. While Khrushchev had long held up Central Asia as a model for developing countries, the Algerians found the climate, geography, and culture of the region to be relevant to their experience.[38] Not only was Central Asia comparably underdeveloped, it also suggested that the Soviet development model was compatible with the Algerians' desire to maintain their Islamic identity. "We wouldn't think of imposing our own path of development on anyone," the Soviet leader said modestly in one speech during Ben Bella's visit. "Although we think it the best, it's up to the Algerian people to decide for themselves which approaches and methods would suit them."[39] Perhaps in time, he suggested, the Algerian agricultural sector might be restructured along lines similar to that of the USSR.[40]

Khrushchev and his colleagues also made more aggressive efforts to pull the Algerians away from France and the United States than has been previously recognized. In her study of Algerian foreign policy, Nicole Grimaud argues that Khrushchev counseled them on the benefits of de Gaulle's friendship, an interpretation perhaps based on the reassurances offered by the Algerian ambassador, Benyahia, to his French counterpart and to Ben Bella's ostentatious paean to *coopération* during a state dinner in Moscow.[41] Paris was particularly bothered by Khrushchev's surprise gift of a petrochemical institute that would be up and running within months, with 300 Soviet instructors training several thousand Algerians in the skills they would need to eventually manage their own oil and natural gas industries.[42] The energy sector, of course, was the most vital issue in the postcolonial relationship between Paris and Algiers, and the new institute, to be built at Boumerdès east of the capital, promised to hasten the day when the Algerians could, as Ben Bella put it, take control "from well to pump." With the two countries about to begin renegotiating the terms of oil and gas exploitation set at Evian in 1962, the Soviet gesture strengthened Algiers's hand. What French officials did not know, however, is that Khrushchev actually instructed the Algerians not to fear French pressure in these talks, for if de Gaulle threatened to stop importing their agricultural products in response to Algerian hydrocarbon nationalization, the Soviet premier promised that his own government would step in to do so instead.[43] The offer suggests that Moscow's aims were not as limited as assumed by observations at the time, or more recently, and had political circumstances in both countries worked out differently over the next year or so, the Algerian-Soviet relationship might have grown closer still.

Meanwhile, Soviet efforts to poison Algerian-American relations were bluntly effective. The Algerians already believed that Washington was backing Morocco's belligerency, although in reality the United States sought to dampen tensions between the two neighbors, and the Soviets purported to confirm Ben Bella's suspicions that the CIA was supporting his internal rivals, apparently by providing forged "evidence" that the agency gave arms or funding to Hocine Aït Ahmed's Front des Forces Socialistes (FFS) rebels in mountainous Kabylia.[44] Though US diplomats and intelligence agents likely did maintain some level of contact with high-profile opposition figures such as Aït Ahmed, Ferhat Abbas, and Belkacem Krim, there is no evidence that the CIA was delivering arms to Ben Bella's internal enemies—not yet at least. However, seemingly riled by the KGB's "proof" of American scheming, Ben Bella went so far as to brand Washington's PL-480 food aid as "poisoned bread" in several widely reported speeches in the USSR, and he returned to Algiers confidently claiming that the Soviet Union would be Algeria's "shield" against neo-imperialism.[45] It is fair to say that the KGB's disinformation campaign found an easy target in the Algerian leader: because he measured himself against the likes of Castro, Guevara, and Lumumba, on some level he wanted to believe that the CIA plotted against him, almost as a point of pride. On the other hand, the paranoid style of Third Worldist politics was not so irrational as Western observers typically claimed. Ben Bella was lucky to escape alive when FFS militants attacked his car with gunfire and hand grenades at the end of May, and later that summer one American diplomat ominously told a British colleague that "the further up the State Department you go, the more you hear the view that [Ben Bella] is 'no better than Castro.' "[46]

For the time being at least, policymakers in Washington were not contemplating anything as severe as the assassination campaign waged against their Cuban foe, but the next twelve months of US-Algerian relations offer valuable insights into the deepening animosity between the United States and radical anticolonial nationalism more generally. Although Algeria was not as central a factor in this story as Cuba and Vietnam were more representative of the broader trend, even if the Algerians' great admiration for Kennedy made the deterioration of their relationship with Washington after his death particularly dramatic. In June, the various US foreign policy bureaucracies began a thorough reappraisal of their policies toward Algeria, searching for ways to either punish Algeria or change the course of its politics.[47] The ensuing discussions among American officials, and their discussions with their Algerian counterparts, reveal some of the fundamental differences of perspective between the leaders of the free world and the would-be leaders of the Third World, but they also demonstrate how even the superpower found its practical options constrained by the way both sides were conscious of performing for an international audience.

The main dilemma for American officials was what to do with the ongoing PL-480 food program. Should they cut back their aid to pressure the Algerians into modifying their policies, leave things as they were for fear of driving Ben Bella further into the Soviet Union's arms, or perhaps even make an effort to win his favor by increasing their aid offerings? Politically, the last option was a nonstarter in Washington in light of widespread antipathy toward the Algerians within the Beltway and in the press, but abandoning whatever leverage America retained in Algiers did not seem prudent: as one State Department official explained concisely, "If [the White House] cut off aid they would be selling out to the Russians, [but] if they increased it they would be assisting a leader who was frankly hostile to the US, as well as having to face American public opinion."[48] In other words, a change of policy in either direction had obvious costs, so even though the status quo was infuriating and wounding to American pride, the Algerians' high profile in international affairs favored a policy of inaction. Thus toward the end of 1964, as some elements of the aid program to Algeria neared their natural point of expiration, US officials convinced themselves that not actively renewing these programs constituted a reasoned policy decision rather than the path of least resistance. The national security adviser, McGeorge Bundy, told President Johnson that "cutting off Algeria would . . . play right into Soviet hands. It's precisely what Moscow would like us to do. On the other hand, food does not buy [Ben Bella's] friendship." Therefore, he concluded optimistically, "What we currently have is a freeze on discussion of new projects with Ben Bella, and I think this is right for the present."[49]

More than being an interesting policy dilemma for the donor government, the food aid question highlighted both sides' aptitude for self-delusion and self-justification. On the one hand, the Americans had reason to be indignant that their charity—which helped at least a million needy Algerians and quite possibly many more—could be pilloried to the point of being called "poisoned bread." More generally, Algiers's brashness in putting aid requests to Western governments had been widely commented on (more than one embassy had received something like a "menu" of development projects from which his government was to select the ones it would fund), and the British ambassador described the country as "a monster child: strident, pushing, ungrateful."[50] Clearly, he did not share the Algerians' belief that the West quite literally owed them such assistance. On the other hand, American generosity was far from being entirely selfless, despite the protestations of one State Department official who asserted that the difference between Soviet and American aid was that communist help was politically motivated while theirs was inspired by the best interests of the recipient country.[51] Not long after, his colleagues were actively debating just how much of their supposedly vital food deliveries they should cut back in order to have the desired effect on Algerian policies, and they only rejected this course of action because it would give Ben Bella the "propaganda coup" of accusing the United States of using hunger as a weapon, not because they were opposed to the idea in principle. During this same period, the Johnson administration actually did proceed with the cynical use of food aid as a cudgel against other wayward Third World governments, most notably India and Egypt.[52]

Moreover, the Algerians did have a point in arguing that the PL-480 program had been designed more on the basis of American domestic political considerations than their needs. For example, some of the surplus agricultural produce delivered through the program undermined Algeria's own farmers, who could not compete with free food. Time and again, representatives of the Algerian government told Washington that they wanted development projects, not food. Guellal told Rusk that "[the] wheat program [was] useful but did not contribute to Algeria's great need for developmental projects. . . . [The] Soviets on [the] other hand promptly selected and studied projects they were interested in and six months later had agreed to begin [a] program."[53] American officials complained that the proposed Four Areas project was delayed on the Algerian side and suspected that leftists in the Agriculture Ministry were deliberately sabotaging them. But in reality the project was unappealing because it envisioned paying rural laborers in food rather than in cash and required Algiers to invest its own funds to get off the ground.[54] Bouteflika told an American delegation in January 1965 that "Algeria needs to solve its economic problems and we want to cooperate with everybody in this effort. To speak frankly, there is another weakness in our relations. The US gives us bread; what we need is work. We need factories that create things and give work to our people."[55] Another basic difference of perspective was that Washington considered Algeria primarily a French concern and limited its own aid accordingly. Yet one of the Algerians' most basic goals was the diversification of their economic relationships, and the American attitude only reinforced their suspicions that the three major capitalist powers (France, Britain, and the United States) had divided the developing world into exclusive spheres of influence to avoid competing with one another in the manner hoped for by the poorer nations.[56] In hindsight, American policy in this regard was fundamentally misguided, since it alienated Algiers for the sake of an illusory Western partnership. In reality, the French were delighted by the deterioration in Algerian-American relations, and Ben Bella later recalled that de Gaulle "was obsessed with the Americans, and in this regard we were objective allies. . . . My relations with de Gaulle were better than those he maintained with [Tunisian President Habib Bourguiba], whom he called 'the American.'"[57] It was not until the spring of 1965 that American officials bitterly realized the full extent to which their Gallic counterparts saw them as competitors rather than allies.[58]

By that time, Algerian-American relations were at their lowest point, bordering on open hostility. Indeed, there is reason to believe that some elements in the US government undertook covert operations to supply weapons to antiregime rebels in Kabylia. When a small cargo plane packed with guns and ammunition landed in Malta early in the morning of 4 February 1965, its American crew told the British authorities that bad weather had prevented them from dropping their payload over Kabylia into the arms of the FFS—a mission that they claimed the CIA had contracted them for in London.[59] Although it is quite possible that the Kabyle rebels had hired them independently, and that they were simply spinning a story so that the British would let them on their way, circumstantial evidence points to official US involvement. The State Department seemed to have no prior knowledge of the affair and made efforts to prevent the crew from flying another mission for fear of the diplomatic fallout should their endeavors come to light, but that fact does not preclude American intelligence or the White House conducting the operation.

The first consideration is the timing, since the incident occurred at a moment when the CIA was actively looking for ways to punish countries like Algeria, Egypt, and Ghana for shipping arms to the leftist Simba rebels in Congo.[60] Significantly, Robert Komer ruled out the now tired idea of cutting back food aid on the basis that it would be counterproductive. "Ben Bella . . . would shout to high heaven about our taking food from hungry mouths for punitive purposes," he told McGeorge Bundy in December. "Those nuts might even *increase* aid to the rebels." On the other hand, he was more willing to confront Algeria than Egypt because "Ben Bella is a fanatic who's never going to play ball with us."[61] So he was already looking around for another way to get back at the Algerians without negative press coverage when the CIA reported in late January that Cuban officers had opened a secret training camp with the Algerian ANP in a remote wooded location in Kabylia—providing another compelling motivation to turn up the heat of the FFS rebellion in that area.[62] Notably, the plane's crew claimed to have been contracted by agents of American intelligence that same day.

Second, the sophistication of the operation strongly suggests the involvement of a capable organization like the CIA. Although Czechoslovakia was a staunch ally of Ben Bella's government, the plane had actually picked up its cargo in Prague thanks to a combination of painting authentic Ghanaian registration numbers on the fuselage and bribery on the ground.[63] In addition to those already impressive preparations, the crew claimed that their contractors had provided maps of Algeria and the specific drop sites in the mountains of Kabylia, and also given reassurances that Algerian radar would not pick them up. That information might have been connected to another curious incident in early January, when two US Navy spotter planes had been forced to land at an airfield in Djelfa, a region to the south of Algiers, after running low on fuel. The two pilots claimed to be searching for a Greek ship (later "clarified" to have been an Italian fishing vessel) foundering at sea, but that model of aircraft, the A1H, was frequently used for surveillance and radar detection, while the landing strip in Djelfa was a good distance inland, so the pilots would likely have flown over more than one more prominent candidate—such as Algiers airport—if they had really being flying from the sea north of the capital, as they claimed. The Algerian military was suspicious enough of their activities to arrest them for several days.[64] Finally, the arms smugglers were confident enough to brush aside the State Department's blandishments and continue with their missions, with the aim of dropping 125 tons of armaments (or $2 million worth) to the FFS before the end of March.⁶⁵ Furthermore, the Algerians knew of at least one such mission. In mid-March, Rédha Malek told Tito that "an American plane loaded with weapons flew over Algerian territory and we assume that it was supposed to drop the weapons with parachutes." Malek said that the airplane was privately owned, but he also observed that "the US government acts indirectly in this way."⁶⁶ In light of all these considerations, it is difficult to believe that the CIA did not have a hand in such a sophisticated and prolonged operation, especially since the American intelligence services had developed the resources and techniques for precisely this style of intervention in Congo and Cuba over the previous years.

In any case, the Algerian leadership was convinced that the United States was actively fomenting subversion, and it was in part for this reason that Ben Bella responded to discreet inquiries from Washington, beginning in April, as to whether Algiers might facilitate a backchannel to Hanoi and to the South Vietnamese National Liberation Front (NLF), also known as the Viet Cong.⁶⁷ Another consideration for the Algerians was their particular identification with the Vietnamese situation and their belief that their powerful Soviet and Chinese supporters might not have Vietnam's best interests at heart. Vociferously critical of US policy in Southeast Asia, the Algerians also believed that ultimately the Vietnamese had to negotiate with the Americans, just as the FLN had negotiated with France, and they also suspected that the Chinese government would have preferred to see the war continue indefinitely.⁶⁸ The initiative began with a meeting between Dean Rusk and Chérif Guellal on 16 April, in which the US secretary of state suggested "not as an official request but merely as a thought passed" that Ben Bella might investigate what the Vietnamese response would be if the Americans halted their bombing campaign.⁶⁹ Separately, Senator Robert Kennedy came to Guellal on behalf of the family of an American captured by the Viet Cong, to see if the Algerian government could facilitate his release.⁷⁰ Replying via Ben Bella several weeks later, the NLF demanded in return the exchange of one of its own officers imprisoned in Saigon, with the suggestion that, if successful, this exchange might be the precursor to a larger-scale prisoner swap in the future.⁷¹ Naturally each side was extremely suspicious of the other, and wary of committing a public relations blunder, but Guellal and Ben Bella at least seemed enthusiastic about playing the role of deniable intermediaries. The Algerian ambassador argued that the debate about the war in Washington was currently finely balanced between doves and hawks, and that the time was right for an initiative that could potentially pave the way for direct negotiations.⁷² The heightened diplomatic activity and prestige that Algeria enjoyed in the weeks before of the second Afro-Asian summit, due to be held in Algiers at the end of June, also made the timing seem propitious.⁷³

The Algerians stood to regain some credit with Washington and enhance their influence in international circles if these initial exchanges led to more substantive communications between the combatants. "It's undeniable," Guellal admitted, "that the success of this operation will result in increased prestige and a larger audience [for Algeria]."[74] Nevertheless, though hearty condemnations of American imperialist aggression gave an impression of fanatical obduracy, the Algerians had long advocated a negotiated settlement to the war in Vietnam. During their own war of independence, the FLN had always maintained its independence from the agendas of the states that supported it, and in the same spirit Ben Bella often insisted to Ambassador Porter and other US officials that they should not mistake the South Vietnamese NLF and Hanoi for mindless puppets of Peking or Moscow. His diplomats believed that China and the USSR desired to see the war in Vietnam go on indefinitely and mourned the fact the North Vietnamese government, which they considered to be fundamentally nationalist rather than communist, was losing control of its own destiny as a result of the Cold War. Direct negotiations with the Americans, however, could reassert North Vietnam's autonomy and the NLF's legitimacy, and hasten the conflict's end (for this reason, in fact, when the Algerians opened their own embassy in Hanoi two years later, they found the Vietnamese as interested in the lessons of Evian as the FLN had once been in Dien Bien Phu).[75] Eventually, the backchannel in Algiers foundered on Ben Bella's downfall in June, although his successors attempted to restart it, but the episode had in any case revealed a sharp distinction between the Third Worldist and communist points of view—a distinction that Washington had frequently denied.

By the summer of 1965, the leaders of Algeria and the United States were separated above all by their different perspectives on international affairs. The secretary of state told Guellal that US-Algerian relations were in a strange state because although there were no direct conflicts between their two countries, their relationship was "seriously tangled in larger issues." Specifically, he said, "Americans did not understand Algeria's motivation in consistently espousing positions antagonistic to ours on issues of vital concern to the United States."[76] In that respect, the Algerians had failed to persuade Washington that it was valid for them to understand international politics primarily in terms of a North-South dynamic rather than the Cold War's East-West one. Ambassador Porter's comment, shortly afterward, that Ben Bella ought to focus on domestic affairs perhaps reflected an arrogant presumption that smaller countries were not entitled even to express opinions about places that the United States saw fit to wage war in, but the greater cognitive clash was that American policymakers could not help but examine Vietnam, Congo, or Cuba through the prism of the Cold War.[77] It was probably unrealistic for Ben Bella and his colleagues to think that they could bring either the North Vietnamese government or the South Vietnamese NLF to the negotiating table with the Americans, but their recognition that Hanoi, China, and the Viet Cong were three distinct entities with differing interests was nevertheless an accurate, sophisticated, and pragmatic analysis of a conflict with the illusion of intractability.

Yet this divergence between the Algerian and American perspectives on international politics was equally applicable to the Northern Hemisphere. Porter and his colleagues had little appreciation for the fact that Algeria's strengthening relationship with the Soviet Union was calculated with France and China in mind as much as the United States. While Ben Bella decried the "capitalist press which is trying to isolate us by pretending that friendship with your country [the United States] and the socialist countries is exclusive," his diplomatic team observed sardonically that they had Western newspapers' fulminations against the "North African Cuba" to thank for the Soviet Union's new generosity.[78] The Algerian strategy, Ben Bella told Dizdarević, owed much to the Yugoslavian example—balancing, on the one hand, opposing views with the Western group (notably the different goals of France and the "Anglo-Saxon" countries) with the conflict between China and the Eastern European communist countries on the other.[79] The Algerian conception of nonalignment was, therefore, very much a multilateral one, reflecting the reality that there were multiple great powers so far as the poorest countries were concerned. Ironically, therefore, France was arguably the biggest beneficiary of the deteriorating Algerian-American relationship, at least so far as de Gaulle assessed the national interest.

Re-escalating the African Cold War

After independence, the new Algerian regime's relations toward its neighbors and Africa as a whole oscillated between the competing objectives of promoting unity and fostering revolution. At first, in light of widespread support for the creation of a new continental unity organization, Ben Bella and his foreign policy team opted to subordinate their revolutionary goals to a broad diplomatic campaign that promoted inter-African cooperation and boosted their standing in some of the more conservative, Western-oriented capitals. From the Algerian perspective, this policy was a major success, in the short term at least. When "neocolonial" leaders like Côte d'Ivoire's Houphouet-Boigny received assurances that Algeria and the other radical countries would not foment subversion among their own populations, they were more willing to condone the armed national liberation movements fighting Portuguese colonialism and white minority rule. As a result, the OAU's charter and liberation committee firmly established the legitimacy of violent anticolonial struggle in decolonizing Africa's nascent international order. In other words, by deprioritizing the overthrow of disagreeable regimes, Algerian diplomats felt that they had helped move the whole continent in a more positive direction on this issue. Nevertheless, even at the time, they considered the OAU's founding the product of an ideological ceasefire that was only temporary. Just a year later, in the wake of encouraging left-wing coups in Congo-Brazzaville and Zanzibar, Ben Bella and his advisers concluded that Africa had arrived at a pivotal moment. He told Tito, "[v]arious political winds are blowing across Africa, some are positive and some are not. A given country can orient itself either toward a positive direction, or towards Congolization." In these circumstances, it was incumbent on Algeria to nudge teetering countries in the right direction, by subversive means if necessary, even at the expense of the hard-won spirit of unity and compromise forged at Addis Ababa. "Our approach was based on that conclusion," Algeria's president said, "and we did not fear that we might lose our political reputation."[80] Believing that they were engaged in a continent-wide battle against American neo-imperialism, the Algerians' renewed focus on exporting revolution exemplified how local actors drove the polarization of developing regions and, as a corollary, the "Third Worldification" of the Cold War.

Defying the rhetoric of Maghrib unity, Algeria's polarizing approach manifested itself first in its own immediate neighborhood. In a wide-ranging survey of the developing world's dilemmas for the foreign ministry, Abdelmalek Benhabylès argued that the Maghrib's modern political evolution was quite different than that of the rest of the Arab world, since he saw North Africa's national identities and nationalist political movements as being more substantive and convincing than those to the east, Egypt excepted. Additionally, the Algerian, Tunisian, and Moroccan governments all placed strong emphasis on social development; even monarchical Morocco, he noted, showed some progressive social inclinations in this regard.[81] Even so, this emphasis on social and economic development highlighted the three regimes' divergent political and ideological characteristics, which Algeria's leaders were determined to "harmonize" as a precondition to regional integration. While they continued to support Bourguiba and Hassan's left-wing opposition financially, materially, and logistically, they also claimed to want their revolution to spread by peaceful means, through the power of its example.[82] "For us," Ben Bella told Tito during his March 1964 visit to Belgrade, "[Hassan's] regime is not acceptable . . . but our experience shows that autogestion is the best weapon against Hassan II." The Yugoslavian leader agreed, predicting that Algeria's socialist accomplishments would "emerge like a mole in neighboring countries and bring about changes because a mole goes under borders."[83] The mole imagery did aptly convey the nocturnal, subversive nature of Algeria's relations with its neighbors—scrabbling in the dark to bring the light of revolution, so to speak.

For their part, declaring that they were "in the process of making a fundamental decision to align [themselves] more closely with the West," the Moroccan authorities sought Washington's assistance to construct a (metaphorical) fence to contain Algeria. Describing their country as a capitalist bulwark assailed by expansive socialism, Hassan's officials pleaded for a significant increase in American military and economic assistance.[84] His foreign minister told Dean Rusk that with adequate aid, his government would "build new industry and prosperous communities along the Algerian border to act as a showcase to the Algerians as West Berlin does to East Germany."[85] Although they tried to assuage Moroccan fears in the hope of arresting the region's polarization, American officials could not help but be stirred, at least a little bit, by such emphatic and unreconstructed Cold War language. As the months passed, Morocco's case was strengthened by the fact that Ben Bella's government was taking many actions that looked hostile from Washington's perspective, elsewhere in Africa and even further afield.

Indeed, while the combination of the Sands War and Kennedy's death initiated the deterioration of US-Algerian relations, the two countries' objectives in the rest of Africa also began to clash more directly. From the Algerian perspective, the problem was that the Johnson administration elected to launch a new imperialist offensive on the continent. "In the past few years," the MAE's Africa desk explained, "we have seen an expansionist push by American [business] interests which function as an expression of both Zionism and imperialism. The activities of US groups are concentrated in two particularly important sectors: banking and oil."[86] This document, like so many others produced by Algerian diplomats, was fully inculcated with a leftist, material determinist interpretation of US foreign policy, arguing that it operated in support of these economic interests. Furthermore, a follow-up elaborated, "Neocolonialism does not result solely from the presence of foreign [business] interests, but also from the establishment of relations between imperialism and national pseudo-bourgeoisies"—that is, American neocolonial interests relied on cooperative self-interested locals.[87] Reporting from Washington that summer, Chérif Guellal supported this analysis by attesting that the State Department was in the process of preparing for a more active role in Africa by solidifying its relations with friendly governments. Although Guellal sometimes appeared less inclined to examine American foreign policy with the rigid, Cuban-style anti-imperialist framework favored by his colleagues on the African desk (as his post required), he warned that Algeria held opposing views to Washington on the African issues that American officials seemed to care most about.[88]

Guellal had in mind recent political developments in Congo-Brazzaville and Zanzibar, which greatly intensified Cold War tensions within Africa. In the former, the reliably pro-French president and Catholic priest, Fulbert Youlou, had lost power amid popular protests the previous August; following a period of uncertainty, in December the leader of the socialist-oriented National Council of the Revolution movement, Alphonse Massemba-Débat, secured the presidency for himself and instituted single-party rule. Almost immediately afterward, and mere weeks after Britain had transferred power to a constitutional monarchy, self-avowed revolutionary forces seized control in Zanzibar. The new leadership groups of both countries had strong contacts with the communist world and were especially effusive in their admiration for Mao's China, which stoked the fears of Western officials and their African allies. In contrast, during a visit to Conakry in late February, Ben Bella admitted to Ahmed Sékou Touré that his government presented a more restrained public persona in order to appease moderate African governments while secretly welcoming coups d'état against the likes of Youlou, and in fact had actually supplied arms to one of the revolutionary factions that instigated the coup in Zanzibar.[89] Yet Algiers immediately recognized the new regimes. To the horror of many of the more conservative African governments that the Algerians had assiduously courted over the past twelve months, one of the FLN's two official organs, *Al Chaab*, enthusiastically greeted these revolutions as a triumph for the nationalist masses over neo-imperialist propertied minorities.[90] "Though economically feeble," an MAE report celebrated, "[Brazzaville's] political orientation constitutes a southern bridgehead for African progressivism."[91]

Certainly, Algerian diplomats were under no illusions that governments such as the Ivory Coast's, with which they had perhaps their most substantive relationship across Africa's ideological divide, did not already fear their socialist rhetoric and deepening alliance with Peking, so they knew that they had little room for ambiguity. However, without abandoning the goal of unity altogether, they were increasingly willing to jeopardize it by pursuing new opportunities and bolder initiatives in support of progressive forces. By their own analysis the OAU had temporarily brought together two differing sets of political and economic orientations, but even they seemed surprised by how quickly that compromise was unraveling.[92] Algiers was very disappointed by the outcome of the OAU foreign ministers' summit in Lagos at the end of February; although the institutional apparatus of the organization was coming together nicely, from the Algerian perspective too many countries were failing to meet the organization's mandate to support the national liberation movements in the south. Despite the call for an embargo, numerous governments not so covertly continued to trade with Portugal and South Africa, while others had not fulfilled their financial contribution to the Liberation Committee's activities. Mohamed Sahnoun, who was essentially the MAE's leading official for African affairs, concluded that the OAU was riddled with neocolonial interests and suggested that "only a new initiative with certain countries that share some of our points of view can relaunch the OAU, and give it a more dynamic character—at the risk of some quite severe shocks, of course."[93] In other words, frustrated with the outcome of the "unity" policy and encouraged by the emergence of like-minded regimes in Brazzaville and Zanzibar, the Algerians were prepared to weather more direct confrontations between Africa's "progressive" and "retrograde" forces.

Southern Africa, the "front line" against imperialism, was the focus of the Algerians' concerns. Throughout the course of the year, they increased their support for the region's nationalist movements, continuing to work with Tanganyika in particular to deliver arms and provide a haven for fighters from Mozambique, Rhodesia, and Congo-Léopoldville. By the end of 1964, for example, the CIA estimated that 200 FRELIMO fighters had received training in Algeria.[94] Noureddine Djoudi, the ambassador in Dar-es-Salaam, therefore continued to have a busy schedule, being the main point of contact for existing and would-be beneficiaries of Algerian assistance.[95] This alliance with Tanganyika and heightening tensions in Rhodesia combined to bring Algeria into conflict with British policy for the first time, for until this point important commercial relations between the two countries had spared London the opprobrium regularly meted out to France, Portugal, and the United States with regard to African affairs. In Tanganyika, after Julius Nyerere requested British troops to protect his government from an army mutiny in January, Algiers lobbied intensively to orchestrate an African solution instead. In March, Nyerere duly replaced the British regiment with a Nigerian one, and the Algerians provided substantial material support in lieu of the forces they could hardly spare. Believing that a battle for Tanganyika's soul was taking place, Algiers then enthusiastically supported its unification with revolutionary Zanzibar in April, in the belief that the new Tanzania would prove a sturdier base of support for the anticolonial struggle in the region.[96] Meanwhile, Algeria stepped up its support for South Rhodesian black nationalist rebels, agreeing to take on nearly a hundred ZAPU fighters in August, and also openly criticized London's approach to dealing with Ian Smith's regime, albeit not quite as harshly as the nationalists would have liked.[97] Nevertheless, by challenging British policy in these areas, Algerian policymakers were making a conscious and noteworthy decision to prioritize Third Worldist revolutionary goals over their own country's economic self-interest.

Indeed, Algeria's overall strategy for Africa was taking a more leftist ideological turn, and it may well be the case that Khrushchev's assurances of Soviet economic support emboldened Ben Bella and the likes of Ahmed Kaïd to challenge Western interests more openly. While still criticizing other more conservative African governments for preferring, say, one Angolan nationalist movement over another, the Algerians began to flout their own dictum that fragmented liberation movements had to unify under a single national front by favoring more radical factions with their diplomatic and material support. Among the Angolans, for example, they established an instant rapport with the leftist MPLA but could not overcome a mutual distrust with Holdern Roberto, who they deemed "a man without conviction, without any fighting spirit, totally submissive to the

Americans, corrupt, [and] tribal." Consequently, he relied on American and anti-Castro Cuban trainers, while Algiers focused its efforts on the MPLA.[98] Around this time, Algerian instructors shifted to a more ideological political program for their charges from the ANC, FRELIMO, MPLA, PAIGC, SWAPO, and ZAPU, stressing the need to form a progressive alliance. They were to be reminded that "the principal enemy is imperialism, and the final objective is to establish democratic and progressive regimes whose program is social revolution."[99] The MAE's Africa desk proposed bringing select candidates to Algeria for political training "above the usual standard" who could then constitute a sort of guerrilla elite cognizant of the theoretical components of popular war.[100] While the success of these initiatives is difficult to assess, the Algerian intent was in itself significant and doubtless contributed to the deepening polarization of the liberation movement scene. For all the early talk of the OAU member governments together supporting unified nationalist fronts, the groups and their patrons were becoming irreversibly fragmented largely along Cold War lines.

Algeria reached out to other like-minded African governments, in addition to liberation movements, in the same fashion. Congo-Brazzaville's revolutionary regime immediately made a good impression, with its leaders proclaiming their own commitment to "scientific socialism" and admiration for Algeria's policies and orientation.[101] In an especially promising sign, at Algiers's request President Massembat-Débat canceled his visit to Israel in the late spring, broke relations with Tel Aviv, and paid a visit to Ben Bella in June instead.[102] The Congolese leaders asked to send sixty of their own civilian cadres to Algeria for "political commissar internships" inside the FLN and on pilot self-managed farms, in addition to training forty military personnel and the president's own son. "Clearly Congo considers Algeria an example," the Algerians concluded. "We have a duty to help our Congolese brothers consolidate their hold on power and develop a socialist economy."[103] Moreover, the Brazza-Congolese leaders shared their commitment to aiding the region's revolutionary movements, opening up a new front just as the situation in the former "Belgian" Congo was turning sour. "We think that this is a great opportunity," the embassy in Brazzaville observed, "to open our country to the [Congolese] elite . . . and ensure the presence of socialism [and] an *avant garde* ready for battle here, thousands of kilometers from Algiers, in a country bordering Congo-Léo, Angola, Gabon, and Cameroon."[104]

Mali was another extremely poor, left-wing francophone country developing ties with China and the USSR, but looking as well to a relatively prosperous and developed Algeria for assistance. Modibo Keita's government and ruling party dispatched numerous personnel for technical and political training, and moved some students from the USSR and Eastern Europe to study in Algeria's more familiar cultural environment (the ambassador in Bamako even started to refer to the *"rayonnement* of our culture" in the manner of French officials discussing their goals for Africa).¹⁰⁵ Although the Malians maintained diplomatic relations with Israel, otherwise they continued to work closely with Algiers in supporting regional revolutionary movements. In particular, the two countries cooperated to clamp down on Touareg rebels in the vast desert between them and abetted Marxist groups opposed to the pro-French governments of Niger and Senegal. Visiting Algiers in August, Keita insisted forcefully to Ben Bella that "either Senghor's regime or ours will fall: coexistence is impossible."¹⁰⁶ The Algerians could easily relate to Mali's rivalry with its Western-backed neighbors, since it was so similar to their own with Morocco: in both cases, each side claimed to be locked in an existential ideological struggle. Believing that France was trying to suffocate their socialist revolution, the Malians desperately pursued alternate avenues of economic assistance in the communist world; one minister wrote odes to communist China, while another pleaded with the Soviet ambassador that his country was so rich that "increasing the amount of aid you give us could not affect you." As neighboring radical regimes amid a sea of neocolonialism, it was inBamako and Algiers's interest to buttress each other ideologically and materially, although there was little realistic scope for the latter.

Ben Bella also added to the continent's tensions by pressing ahead with his determination to link anti-imperialist causes across different regions, thereby bringing some of the most contentious issues in international politics into Africa. First, he and his colleagues continued to drum up support for the Palestinian cause. Having initially kept the Palestinian nationalist movement at arm's length, probably in deference to Egyptian concerns, in early 1964 the Algerians showed their desire to become one of Palestine's most important sources of assistance. In February, several Algerian officers traveled to Lebanon to create a guerrilla recruitment and training center, in cooperation with Syrian intelligence, while the ANP began to receive Fateh fighters in its own camps that summer, with an initial contingent of about 200.¹⁰⁷ The Algerians also counseled Fateh on political and strategic questions, urging them above all to begin their armed struggle as soon as possible, which finally happened on New Year's Day, 1965. Lakhdar Brahimi, the ambassador in Cairo, also hosted reconciliation talks between Arafat's group and the Palestine Liberation Organization (PLO) at his residence in the Egyptian capital.¹⁰⁸

At the same time, Algeria and the other Arab countries vied against Israel's own concerted diplomatic campaign in Africa, where Tel Aviv used trade and development deals to garner a good number of reliably sympathetic voters in the General Assembly.¹⁰⁹ However, at this time, Arab efforts to persuade African states to cut all ties with Israel met with mixed success and caused some friction between Arab and black Africa. The foreign minister of Sierra Leone, Dr. John Karefa Smart, observed sharply in early 1964 that "African members of the League will have to decide soon where they stand. Are they in the Middle East or in Africa?"[110] In fact, the Algerians and Egyptians were not even reliably successful in persuading radical allies like Mali, Ghana, and Guinea to cooperate (for that matter, the Yugoslavians also desisted their entreaties).[111] As of early 1965, Benhabylès conceded, Israel was still winning this battle. Moreover, most Arab governments had yet to show much appreciation for Algeria's interest in African affairs—Iraq alone had recognized the Angolan nationalists' provisional government.[112]

Still, the Algerians persevered in their region-connecting, "interstitial" diplomacy, so that even as they struggled to keep Israel out of Africa, they helped bring Cuba and Yugoslavia in. The two were valuable allies in the international arena and vital accomplices in supporting revolutionary movements, but they suffered from relative isolation in their local environments. American officials noted with suspicion that Havana's ambassador in Algiers, Jorge Serguera, frequently journeyed to places such as revolutionary Zanzibar, while an Algerian diplomat served as a translator for the Cuban ambassador to Ghana during the latter's visit to Brazzaville in May.[113] On the latter occasion, President Massemba-Débat assured Serguera that "in my opinion, the presence at your side of an official from a fraternal country's embassy gives this occasion the sense of a meeting between revolutionary and fraternal countries," before launching into a paean to Algeria's revolutionary example in choosing Cuban friendship over American dollars.[114] At the same time, Cuban-Algerian cooperation in supporting national liberation movements was so close that Serguera hosted meetings with Ben Bella and the movements' representatives at his own residence in Algiers. Struck by the Algerian president's openness and honesty in responding to the Africans' question, Serguera concluded that Algiers had supplanted Cairo as the capital of the continent's anticolonial movement.[115] Then, in the summer, Algeria tried unsuccessfully to rally Africa's condemnation of the US push to have the OAS censure Cuba, yet another example of a steady effort to improve Castro's diplomatic position.[116] Likewise, the Algerians facilitated Yugoslavia's efforts to expand its influence in Africa. In the two cases, Havana and Belgrade abetted Algeria's ambitious policies by supplementing its meager resources in armaments, transport, and funds, while in return the Algerians lent these outsiders their imprimatur and gave them entrée to African circles.

Of course, by the latter half of 1964, the Algerians had more means at their disposal and became more equal partners in bolder revolutionary enterprises. For the Cubans, Algiers was no longer just an entry point to Africa but a bridge to Latin America too. Ben Bella had forged a notably warmer relationship with Che Guevara in particular and supported all of the younger man's projects.[117] An Algerian shell company started delivering material to Cuban-allied left-wing revolutionary groups in Latin America, while a secluded villa on the outskirts of Algiers that had previously served as a notorious torture center for French paratroopers became a discreet base for guerrillas from Argentina, Venezuela, and perhaps elsewhere.[118] The Algerian perspective on Latin America, such as it was, passed entirely through a Cuban prism. The MAE's analyses of the continent described an upsurge of popular resistance and revolutionary protest against US domination and situated Castroism in the stream of anticolonial history. "The revolutionary wind has blown strongly enough from Havana to have shaken up the situation in those countries where the United States' grip is still very strong," argued the Division Asie-Amérique Latine, "and it threatens to substantially change things even more."[119] The next stage in Algeria's Latin American outreach was to open an embassy in Brazil, but this project had to be abandoned following the right-wing coup against the socialist president, João Goulart, on 1 April 1964.[120]

In the second half of 1964, all these developments converged on Congo-Léopoldville, which once again became the central crisis point of African politics. In July the leading secessionist politician from Katanga, Moise Tshombe, assumed the position of prime minister in a coalition government in Léopoldville. Because he was a notorious irredentist, Tshombe's return was greeted warily by a continent whose borders were all the more sacrosanct for their arbitrariness, but his close association with Western interests and Lumumba's execution was especially damning in left-wing circles.[121] Although they hardly needed another reason to loathe him (Ben Bella dubbed Tshombe "a walking museum of colonialism"), the Algerians quickly clashed with the new Congolese prime minister's evident disinterest in supporting the Angolan nationalists.[122] It was bad enough that his predecessor, Cyrille Adoula, had backed Holden in preference to the MPLA (creating a relationship that Mario de Andrade decried in the pages of Algiers's *Révolution Africaine* as "nationalism primarily concerned with the immediate securing of large financial support from Western sources . . . nationalism as business"), but Tshombe seemed to disdain both factions, turning a blind eye to reports of Portuguese aircraft bombarding Holden's camps in Congolese territory.[123] When the Algerian ambassador came to see him in late September, he lambasted the Angolans for depending on the OAU's Liberation Committee and the hospitality of neighboring states. "All these people have to go back to their own country," he said. "I have my own plan [for Angola], and Africa will have to talk to me to solve this problem." Adjali warned that Tshombe boasted great charisma and boundless energy. "He might be the only Congolese leader who knows what he is about and what he is doing. Unfortunately for Africa, he is anti-African, and we must not hope for him to respect any resolution of the OAU, as he only has contempt for [the organization]."[124]

Unsurprisingly, then, Algeria welcomed the re-emergence of a left-wing, Lumumbist rebellion in eastern Congo that summer. Indeed, Algerian instructors had helped train some of the fighters from the Conseil National de Libération

(National Liberation Council, CNL), also known as the Simbas ("lions" in Swahili), in Ghana. Led by former members of Gizenga's cabinet, in August the CNL reignited the Congo Crisis by declaring a new revolutionary government in Stanleyville. In response, Tshombe strengthened the Congolese army's assault on CNL-held territories by relying heavily on white mercenaries (largely South African, French, and British) and an air force of anti-Castroist Cuban exiles managed by the CIA. When the rebels sought to protect themselves by seizing more than a thousand white hostages, including American diplomatic personnel, Washington resorted to a joint military operation with Brussels in November, dropping a regiment of Belgian paratroopers over Stanleyville in order to free the hostages and, tacitly, break the rebellion. Once more, Congo had illuminated a vast gulf between Western perceptions and those on the left wing of African politics, such as the Algerians. Describing the white marble statue of Lumumba, "the wild leftist demagogue," in central Stanleyville as being stained red by the blood of the Simbas' public victims, publications such as *Time* magazine portrayed the revolt essentially as murderous savagery inspired by communist subversion.[125] In contrast, the Algerians branded the US-Belgian intervention as "a criminal action that cost thousands of lives" and saw the rebels as true Congolese patriots battling valiantly against imperialist flunkies and racist guns for hire.[126] "The situation is graver today when Tshombe is imposed from abroad by imperialism," Ben Bella fulminated. "It is no longer Katanga that threatens Congolese unity, it is the whole Congo that has become the Katanga of Africa."[127]

Léopoldville and Algiers were in a state of diplomatic war. The Algerians took a leading role in a campaign to harness African indignation at Tshombe's recourse to South African mercenaries and turn him into an outcast in continental politics.[128] When Modibo Keita visited Algiers in August, Ben Bella recruited him to the cause, which also included Egypt, Ghana, and Congo-Brazzaville. The Malian president was initially conflicted: he valued the principle of nonintervention in another African state's internal affairs, but he recognized that this principle could encourage "the stabilization of unpopular regimes, a foreign presence, and the emergence of centers of subversion."[129] However, this anti-Tshombe alliance failed to have him excluded from an emergency summit of OAU foreign ministers that took place in Addis Ababa in early September. Despite the efforts of Bouteflika and his allies, the majority of African governments voted at that meeting to condemn foreign support for *both* sides of Congo's conflict—the CNL as well as the Léopoldville government.

Instead, the radicals achieved their purpose at the Second Non-Aligned summit that took place in Cairo, 5–10 October. The Algerian delegation helped orchestrate a vote in the conference assembly to forbid the Congolese president's participation, though his country was welcome to send a delegation that did not include him. Tshombe arrived in Cairo determined to call his opponents' bluff, leading to the dramatic—and humiliating—spectacle of the Egyptian authorities physically preventing him from entering the conference building and then confining him to his hotel room.[130] The Senegalese, Nigerian, and Liberian delegations had voted in solidarity with Tshombe, and several Asian countries abstained, but the Algerian diplomatic team believed that, on the whole, they had made an important statement by denying their enemy the legitimacy conferred by participation in the NAM summit.[131] The act of collective condemnation not only was a setback for Tshombe but also helped set the proceedings on a pleasingly radical and confrontational course. Reflecting afterward, Rédha Malek concluded that it was "unquestionably the Tshombe affair that set the tone of the Conference and accentuated its resolutely anti-imperialist character."[132]

Humiliated in Cairo, Tshombe declared himself to be a victim of "Arab colonialism" in an obvious effort to stir up resentments between black Africa and his twin nemeses in the north, Algeria and Egypt. He immediately turned on those countries' diplomatic missions in Léopoldville, which he (justifiably) considered hotbeds of subversion. Unfortunately for the historian, when the Congolese security services surrounded the Algerian embassy, the staff inside frantically incinerated all their sensitive documents, thereby destroying what could have been a treasure trove of information on Congo, neighboring countries, and numerous parties and movements in that period.[133] The ambassador, Abdelhamid Adjali, managed to escape the scene, and he spent the next few nights moving from one friendly embassy to another (likely the Ghanaian, Bulgarian, and Czechoslovak ones, although this is unclear from his reports), the authorities cutting the telephone connection to each in succession in an effort to prevent him from communicating with Algiers. Eventually, on 8 October, he and his team were allowed to cross the river to Brazzaville, where they set about reconstituting the embassy (a move that had been contemplated for some months in any case). Having lost most of their equipment, possessions, and funds, their precarious situation was rather reminiscent of the GPRA days, although the embassy's dramatic relocation from the "neo-imperialist" Congo to the "revolutionary" one also neatly encapsulated Algeria's political trajectory across a polarized Africa during the intervening years.[134]

In any case, with the phony war over, Ben Bella abandoned any equivocation over Algeria's support for the CNL. He publicly declared it a duty for all Africans to aid the Congolese rebels' resistance against white mercenaries, the CIA, and Tshombe's perfidious regime.[135] Though exact figures and details are not available, Algeria did appear to substantially increase its military support to the CNL, delivered by multiple routes. For example, a cargo ship delivered arms to Brazzaville in late September, where the crew had a run-in with French soldiers, while an Algerian plane unloaded three truckloads in western Uganda in mid-November.[136] Tanganyika was probably still the single most important destination, and the CIA believed that Algiers had to ask for surreptitious Soviet assistance in flying munitions down there in greater quantities.[137] In February 1965, the Congolese asked Djoudi in Dar-es-Salaam for equipment for 6,000 fighters, and political commissars to train them.[138] It is impossible to ascertain the exact destination of all these weapons, since once they were in Ugandan, Congo-Brazzavillian, or Tanganyikan hands, they might have gone to any of a number of different rebel groups (Simba, FRELIMO, SWAPO, MPLA, and so on) or have been kept by the recipient country for its own defense.[139] In all likelihood, however, the Algerians did not care greatly, for whether guns went to the army of Congo-Brazzaville, say, or to the Simbas, they aided the anti-imperialist cause in southern Africa. Congo, Angola, Mozambique, Rhodesia—the Algerian instructors told their charges that they faced a common multiheaded foe, and therefore they needed to unite their struggle too.[140] In that spirit, the confrontation with Léopoldville and alliance with Brazzaville seemed to have triggered a generalized escalation of Algeria's revolutionary mission in the region. When the leader of a Gabonese opposition group came to them with a sad story of having been imprisoned by Tshombe on suspicion of being an Algerian agent, the encounter led to the Algerians supporting at least two movements from that country.[141]

Also at this time, Che Guevara consulted closely with Algiers as he formulated his plans for an ill-fated Cuban intervention in Congo, which begs the question of what exactly the Algerians hoped would come of these efforts. Years later, Ben Bella claimed to have cautioned the ardent Argentine about the dim prospects for the revolution there, but at the time Algerian policy seemed more optimistic.[142] That same month, for example, when a Malian diplomat shared his (ultimately vindicated) fear that the Congolese rebels were really a bit of a disorganized shambles and totally unprepared to govern, Algiers's man in Bamako reminded him piously that "as soon as you accept death with a gun in your hand, in the face of foreign intervention and bombardment, then you acquire authority."[143] So much like the Cuban theory of *foco*, the myth of the FLN on 1 November 1954 dictated that courage and commitment mattered far more than numbers, organization, or experience. The Algerians did not believe victory would come quickly or easily, but they urged their numerous revolutionary protégés to commence the armed struggle without delay because they sincerely believed that, with sufficient resolve, victory was inevitable.

In sum, by the first half of 1965, African politics seemed to have returned to the divisiveness of the pre–Addis Ababa era, with Algeria a prominent contributor to the continent's renewed polarization. Opposing camps were coalescing once more, reminiscent of the Casablanca Group and Brazzaville Group that had dissolved in the spirit of unity prior to the OAU's founding. A number of the radical countries—including Algeria, the UAR, Sudan, Ghana, and

Congo-Brazzaville—met in Accra in late January ostensibly to discuss the Congo, but the decision to reconvene as an ideologically coherent group looked very much like an attempt to resurrect the Casablanca Group.[144] The following month, a dozen of the fourteen former members of the Western-oriented Brazzaville Group created the Organisation Commune Africaine et Malgache (African and Malagasy Common Organization, OCAM) in order to check the influence of the radicals. In this light, the MAE's African desk justly reported, "We are far from the coordinated diplomacy envisioned by the Addis Ababa Charter. The Congo situation in particular divides the African countries [and] discordant voices continue to grow amid the members of the OAU, which could jeopardize the future of an already fragile friendship."[145] However, although the Algerians and their allies were quick to blame American neocolonialism for their continent's difficulties, while their more Western-oriented peers likewise blamed Chinese and Soviet subversion, the reality was that Africa's postcolonial elites were at least equally responsible for the further entrenchment of great power clientelism and Cold War polarization.

That said, Ben Bella's government was willing to sacrifice the West's faith in its nonalignment on the altar of anticolonial solidarity. After all, Algiers gave up economically beneficial relationships with Britain, the United States, and West Germany by taking forceful positions on Rhodesia, Congo, and Israel-Palestine, among other issues. Instead, from the Algerian perspective, the greater cost of Africa's polarization was the danger it posed to Third World unity. Alarmingly, the OCAM countries demanded that Ghana expel the national liberation movements it supported.[146] More concerning still, the same group threatened to boycott Bandung 2. What a disaster it would be for Algiers if the Third World project became a casualty of the African Cold War.

The Battle to Define the Third World

The period from early 1964 to June 1965 saw Algeria engage to an even greater degree in the politics of the Southern Hemisphere. The impulse to do so superseded practical constraints or intensifying political intrigues within the country's ruling circles. While it was clear that Ben Bella personally aspired to a global stature comparable to that of Nehru, Nkrumah, or even his idol, Nasser, Algeria's political class was generally united in the belief that theirs was a vanguard nation with a duty to show others the path to revolution in the domestic and international spheres. Therefore, with the initial period of postindependence consolidation completed, they began to broaden the reach of their diplomatic and subversive apparatuses. Desiring greater responsibility and influence over the evolution of the Third World project, they agreed to host a varied sequence of international events, including an AAPSO conference in March 1964, an Afro-Asian economic conference in February 1965, the following summer's World Youth Festival, and, most important of all, the Second Afro-Asian Heads of State Summit, or Bandung 2. At these meetings, Algeria and other smaller countries urged the convergence of mobilizing themes like Afro-Asianism, non-alignment, and the G77, as well as the expansion of the anti-imperialist coalition into Latin America and even Europe. Yet this agenda of harmonization and expansion struggled in the face of worsening antagonisms between powerful states—especially China, India, and the Soviet Union—that threatened to split the Southern Hemisphere into opposing camps and, even more dangerously, provoked a fundamental debate about the very nature and purpose of the Third World. Thus the challenge for Algerian diplomacy, in order that Bandung 2 not become an ignominious disaster, was to somehow reconcile the competing geopolitical interests, ideological conflicts, and cultural tensions of more than half the world.

The Algerian leadership's enthusiasm for hosting conferences in this period had a pragmatic basis. They celebrated the fact that the steady procession of foreign dignitaries through Algiers gave the city the feel of a "global crossroads," and in early 1965, in the run-up to Bandung 2, official media began trumpeting the theme of "Alger: Capitale" as an exercise in Third Worldist branding.[147] But it was real influence they sought, more than just the appearance of it. As conference hosts, they often had greater say over timing and the list of attendees, in addition to being able to steer the agenda through opening and closing speeches and the power of the moderator. At the March 1964 AAPSO meeting, for example, the Algerians pressed their globalist, convergent vision for the Third World. Ben Bella appealed to the participants to simultaneously broaden the horizons of AAPSO and NAM, by committing both organizations to total support for African liberation movements, the UNCTAD economic agenda, and expansion into Latin America.[148] The attendees duly formed a committee to investigate the Latin American question, and an AAPSO-sanctioned economic conference was convened a year later—also in Algiers. At that conference the Algerians once again made the case for bringing Latin America into the Afro-Asian framework and for coordinating with the UNCTAD process.[149] Consequently, they had great ambitions for Bandung 2, which they hoped would finally confirm the Afro-Asian movement's expansion into new regions and convergence with NAM and UNCTAD. In a similar vein, excluding Tshombe from the Cairo NAM summit in October 1964 and the failed attempt to do so in the OAU demonstrated how such conferences provided more opportunities for diplomatic maneuvering.

Moreover, such gatherings helped compensate for the political obstacles and resource constraints that still prevented the construction of a foreign policy apparatus commensurate with Algeria's ambitions. In 1964, the MAE almost doubled the number of embassies it operated around the world, and in January 1965 Bouteflika announced his intent to do so again that year, increasing the number of permanent posts from thirty-four to sixty.[150] However, not only did Algeria still lack representation in a number of capitals important to its foreign relations—only appointing an ambassador to Delhi at the beginning of 1965, for example—but the ministry's internal reports show that its operational effectiveness left much to be desired. In fact, one major examination of the ministry's internal affairs that March argued that "we are practically in Year I of our Ministry." Until recently, it explained,

> the majority of our external services [provided] a presence [but] not representation in any real sense of the term. [T]he reports provided by our Ambassadors [were] veritable cries of alarm. Everywhere, one [saw] a lack of competent personnel [and] the total absence of coordination with other Ministries. Our diplomats live[d] in perpetual uncertainty. The shortage of money [was] felt in every area.[151]

Consequently, the previous months had seen a focus on developing the MAE's central administration, including filing, translation, and archival systems, as well as such basic bureaucratic functions as the recruitment of staff and payment of salaries. As a result, the report noted with satisfaction, "Our missions [abroad] are no longer cut off from the rest of the world and the central administration." Even so, it vowed, these intensive efforts to develop the ministry's central and external functions would continue because "our international obligations, our political choices, our prestige among Third World countries, oblige us [to possess] if not true representation, at least an indispensable presence" in the global arena.[152] In light of the difficulty of establishing that presence, it was extremely useful when events such as the AAPSO summit instead brought the world to Algeria.

Likewise, AAPSO's creation of a committee to pursue ties with Latin America was a boon to the Algerians' efforts to increase their own involvement there.[153] Havana was their sole embassy in the region, while the head of the MAE's small Latin America and Asia Section, Boufeldja Aidi, had never been there.[154] With little firsthand knowledge of their own, Algerian diplomats were very reliant on their Cuban allies' embattled, dialectical perspective. They canceled their plan to open a second diplomatic mission in Brazil after the right-wing coup on 1 April 1964. Algiers immediately blamed Goulart's fall on Washington's neo-imperialist designs; at a reception at the Kremlin a month later, Ben Bella rebuffed the Brazilian ambassador's formulaic pleasantries with the curt observation that "we used to be friends ... [before] the counter-revolution."[155] As a result, Algeria's direct engagement with the region continued to hang almost entirely on its relationship with Castro's government, including increased support for the latter's efforts to export revolution. In a report that could have been taken from the pages of a Cuban newspaper, the Latin America and Asia Section (presumably Aidi) stated optimistically that "a strong wind of revolution blowing from Havana has shaken up the situation in those countries where the United States' grip is still very strong, and it threatens to substantially change things even more."[156] In order to evade Washington's close scrutiny of Cuba itself, an Algerian shell company continued to transport revolutionaries and munitions to the Latin American mainland on Havana's behalf.

The Algerian appraisal of the Middle East was very similar: the region struggled against Western and especially American efforts at domination, with Israel playing a role similar to that of Tshombe's Congo as a neo-imperialist client and source of division. As in Africa and Latin America, in other words, Algerian diplomats tended to portray the United States as the primary opponent of regional unity and true independence. For example, the famous FLN veteran, Ali Kafi, who took over the embassy in Beirut on account of his Arabic language skills, spoke of American officials touring the Arab capitals offering economic assistance as bribes to "defect" to their side.[157] "It is clear, however," Benhabylès argued, "that Arab hopes for the liberation of Palestine can only take concrete form if the Arab countries are prepared to confront Washington and London, even Paris and Moscow, and to accept all the consequences of such a situation."[158] In short, the Algerian analysis of the Middle East region was very consistent with the overarching Third Worldist narrative.

On the other hand, Algeria's involvement in the Middle East continued to be on a smaller scale than its involvement in African affairs. A shortage of Arabic-competent personnel was an even greater impediment to expanding the diplomatic apparatus than in other regions where the Algerians would have been less embarrassed about sending someone with limited linguistic qualifications. Notably, Ben Bella himself could only speak the Algerian dialect incomprehensible in the Mashriq, so surrogates such as Tewfik El Madani tended to accept presidential invitations to Arab capitals in his stead.[159] The other consideration was the fact that Algeria was simply too small and peripheral a player in the Middle East, and the politics of the Arab world already far too divisive to entertain the same kind of ambitions that the Algerian leadership had for Africa. In Benhabylès's assessment, despite the solid cultural and religious foundations underpinning the dream of Arab unity, that goal would take at least a generation. For the time being, only the seemingly solid Algiers-Cairo axis constituted progress in a region of shifting alliances and betrayals. "Since the Algerian experiment dominates the political scene in the Maghreb, while Egypt constitutes the center of political life in the Middle East," he explained, "it was natural that the alliance between these two countries would become the most important feature of the relations among all the Arab states."¹⁶⁰ Therefore, Algeria continued to play something of a supporting role to Egypt in inter-Arab affairs. As noted earlier, Algiers's growing support for the Palestinian nationalists was its only really significant initiative in the region, although even this ostensibly universally supported Arab cause entailed complications. After Jordanian soldiers clashed with Fateh fighters in January 1965, King Hussein complained that the latter had been trained in Algeria and that their activities risked inviting an Israeli attack on his country.¹⁶¹ Simply put, the Middle East was not nearly as conducive to exporting revolution as Africa was.

At the same time, the Algerian government also had strikingly little direct engagement with Asia since independence, but the MAE found it difficult to expand its presence in a region that was so central to Third World affairs. Indeed, in comparison to the foreign ministry's Western Europe and North America Section, Socialist Countries Section, Africa Section, and Arab Countries Section, which all had a clear rationale in terms of Algeria's foreign policy doctrine, the Latin America and Asia Section looked rather like the "everywhere else" department. In fact, it was not until early 1964 that Algeria opened its first two embassies on the continent, in Peking and Tokyo. The prioritization of those two capitals reflected pragmatic national interests. Besides being one of the great powers of the world, China was becoming one of Algeria's most important sources of economic and military aid and was also a key partner supporting national liberation movements. Likewise, the Algerians hoped that Japan could become a valuable source of development assistance and commercial exchange, in the same way that Britain and West Germany were despite belonging to the "neo-imperialist" capitalist bloc. Conveniently, the new embassy in Tokyo was able to quickly hire a familiar local face who had previously served as a translator and secretary for the GPRA mission there.¹⁶² Sympathetic contacts of this kind were extremely useful: not only did the Algerian foreign ministry suffer from a severe shortage of English speakers (let alone Japanese or Chinese speakers), but its limited financial resources meant that it had to carefully consider the start-up costs of a permanent mission on the far side of the world, especially in a city as expensive as Tokyo.

Therefore, despite India's deep association with both Afro-Asianism and nonalignment, the first Algerian ambassador only arrived in New Delhi in January 1965—a full two years after his counterpart had established himself in Algiers. This delay was partly attributable to the coolness of Algerian-Indian relations that dated back to Nehru's refusal to recognize the GPRA but continued after Algeria's independence, since India continued to keep its distance from armed liberation movements and generally uphold a conservative posture in Third World affairs that was irksome to the provocateurs who reigned in Algiers. They also took a dim view of India's deepening military relationship with the

United States, prompted by border disputes with China, while Delhi's similar conflicts with Pakistan alienated several governments in the Muslim world. However, it is doubtful that the Algerians held strong views on the latter subject simply because India did not seem to feature prominently in their thoughts at all—and it is this fact that probably most accounts for the delay in appointing an ambassador. India rarely came up even in lengthy, wide-ranging discussions between the Algerians and other parties active in Third World politics, such as the Yugoslavian, Egyptian, or Ghanaian governments, among others. The evidence indicates that by 1964, if not sooner, India had somewhat isolated itself through a combination of Nehru's reserved approach to Third World affairs, his disinclination to take up more militant anticolonial causes, and his government's antagonistic relations with China, Indonesia (China's ally), and Pakistan. Nasser and Tito seemed to regret that their former partner in the creation of NAM had marginalized itself so: the Egyptian president noted that the nonaligned countries had not only failed to support India in its dispute with China, but many of them actually backed Peking's position.[163]

These disputes between the Asian countries became a major problem for Algerian diplomacy when they threatened to derail Bandung 2. Indeed, in early 1964, Ben Bella had confessed to preferring that a second NAM summit be held before a second Afro-Asian summit because he anticipated that Asia's enmities would make the latter very difficult to organize.[164] When the official preparatory meetings for Bandung 2 began toward the end of the year, procedural discussions became a proxy battleground for two key dilemmas. On the one hand, China wanted to ensure that the Soviet Union would not be invited to attend the Algiers Conference; on the other hand, the Indonesian government insisted on Malaysia's exclusion, since the two countries were locked in the territorial dispute known as Konfrontasi. India was the strongest opponent of both of these campaigns: Delhi's delegates at the preparatory meetings constantly butted heads with their Chinese counterparts, who engaged in increasingly unrestrained denouncements and tirades as the weeks went by. When the Indians proposed that the summit's invitation list be determined by majority voting, thereby denying China and Indonesia a veto over Soviet or Malaysian participation, the head of the Chinese delegation launched into a painfully lengthy diatribe accusing the other of trying to sabotage the Afro-Asian Conference altogether. Ultimately, this hostile atmosphere put the onus on the Algerians to settle seemingly intractable issues; their diplomats were still maneuvering into early summer, mere weeks before the conference was scheduled to begin, to orchestrate compromises that would allow both Indonesia and Malaysia, China, and the Soviet Union to attend.[165]

Most of all, however, the Sino-Soviet split threatened Algeria's hopes for the Third World project. Moscow and Peking's ideological battle produced an unprecedented display of enmity when AAPSO met in Algiers in late March 1964, to the great discomfort and frustration of the other participating countries. The Soviet and Chinese delegates barely let one another speak, hijacking the proceedings with their continual diatribes and counterdiatribes. In addition to claiming that the Partial Test Ban Treaty marked the beginning of a Soviet-American compact, at the expense of the developing countries, one Chinese representative went so far as to accuse the Kremlin of moral culpability for Lumumba's death, with predictable consequences for the tone of the event.[166] M'hamed Yazid, the Algerian diplomat presiding over the meeting, threatened that his government would leave the organization altogether if the communist countries continued to disrupt the proceedings, taking several other African countries with it.[167] He admitted to a journalist afterward that the hostility between Chinese and Soviet delegations had come close to smashing the spirit of Afro-Asian solidarity, but that "the maturity of Asian and African movements enabled us to pull the conference out of the mud."[168] Being more ferocious in their attacks and refusing even to acknowledge that these intercommunist arguments were a disruption, Chinese diplomats probably came off worse than their Soviet rivals in terms of the other Third World countries' attributions of blame. Somewhat unexpected in light of the deft diplomacy that Zhou Enlai had displayed during his recent tour of Africa and the Middle East, the vehemence of the Chinese delegation's assault in Algiers was due to the fact that Peking saw the Afro-Asian movement as its last lever of influence in Third World politics. By dint of its territorial dispute with India and ideological arguments with Moscow and Yugoslavia, China was losing ground to the Soviet message of "peaceful coexistence" and the nonaligned "axis" of New Delhi, Belgrade, and Cairo.

While the Sino-Indian border conflict and Indonesian-Malaysian Konfrontasi were two of the most difficult complications that Algeria's diplomats had to manage, the definitive dilemma at this time was communist China's effort to exclude the Soviet Union and Yugoslavia from the Third World. This goal induced Mao's government to champion Afro-Asianism as the Third World's central organizing theme at the expense of nonalignment. In addition to being a cornerstone of both Yugoslavian and Indian foreign policy, nonalignment provided a rationale for the participation of China's foes from communist Europe because it was a political concept rather than a geographical or racial one like Afro-Asianism. Of course, the Soviet leadership did not claim to be nonaligned, but Moscow's policy of "peaceful coexistence" was similar in spirit and rhetoric—to the point that some in the Algerian foreign ministry wondered how much it had been influenced by the pacific rhetoric of the original Bandung Conference—while from a practical perspective, if one accepted that the Yugoslavians were entitled to attend Third World meetings, it became much more difficult to argue against Soviet participation.[169] Moreover, Soviet policymakers also decided that if China was opposed to NAM, then they were for it, so their propaganda lent support to the idea of a new nonaligned summit on the basis that it would unite anti-imperialist forces "without dividing them on a geographical or any other basis."[170] Consequently, the Sino-Soviet competition for influence with developing countries touched on a basic question about the "Third World": Was it an expression of non-Western identity, or was it programmatic in nature, with no racial or regional boundaries?

From the Algerian perspective, China's insistence on seeing Afro-Asianism and nonalignment as competing themes was unwelcome. In early 1964, Ben Bella and his staff were bothered by the sense that partisans of each concept were racing to hold a summit before the other; "I think that is wrongheaded," he told Tito, "because that question should not be presented as an alternative."[171] His government was strongly in favor of a second NAM heads of state conference as well as a second Afro-Asian one; arguing that nonalignment should be "quite rightly considered an advanced and slightly progressive aspect of Afro-Asianism," Algerian diplomats worked toward bringing the two strands of Third World solidarity together.[172] In that regard, they were pleased by the outcome of the second nonaligned summit, which took place in Cairo on 5 through 10 October. First of all, fifty-seven states sent delegations to Cairo, nearly twice the number at Belgrade in 1961, including nine from Latin America with observer status. Second, the Algerians were satisfied by (and claimed much of the credit for) the conference's strong "anticolonial" spirit, by which they meant Tshombe's exclusion and expressions of support for Palestinian nationalism. Third, they believed that the conference had concluded by finding a satisfying middle ground between two rival tendencies. The presidents of Mali and Congo-Brazzaville had promised Peking that they would, in the words of Zhou Enlai, "oppose every maneuver by Yugoslavia and India—allies of the USA and the USSR—whose representatives everywhere talk solely about disarmament and peaceful coexistence with imperialism."[173] Along with Sukarno, Modibo Keita and Massemba Débat duly criticized the Soviet policy of detente, arguing that it betrayed the anti-imperialist struggle in Vietnam and Cuba, and they tried to ensure that the conference's final joint statement had a confrontational, stridently anti-American flavor. Meanwhile, India and Yugoslavia represented the opposing tendency, which, in the view of Rédha Malek, "insisted that peace and coexistence are equal in importance to the fight against colonialism." In the end, Malek and his colleagues felt that the conference ended with a compromising stance on the subject of peaceful coexistence and the Cold War, while keeping NAM's focus where they felt it should be: on anticolonial issues.[174]

However, it was a concern for smaller countries with a strong investment in the Non-Aligned Movement that the Chinese position hardened further after the Cairo meeting. Peking was already denouncing the Soviet search for detente as an effort to form an anti-Chinese alliance with the United States, but it began to extend this criticism to the concept of nonalignment or neutrality as well. Chen Yi, the Chinese foreign minister, told a Malian diplomat that "to refuse to condemn Khrushchev's positions . . . is to align with the USSR, which has betrayed the cause of Internationalism. A truly neutral government cannot be indifferent to these treacheries." Likewise, he told the Algerian ambassador, M'hamed Hadj Yala, that "Algeria's policy of nonalignment benefits the USSR; it should be grateful to you for it."[175] This argument that neutrality between the Soviet Union and China was impossible, and that those who pursued it were essentially Soviet dupes, was quite reminiscent of earlier American criticisms, expressed most memorably by Secretary of State John Foster Dulles in 1956, that nonalignment in the Cold War was "immoral."

The Algerian government professed its complete neutrality in the Sino-Soviet dispute, with Ben Bella pleading after the disastrous AAPSO meeting that the communist world's ideological differences be excluded from future events. "Debate should be first and foremost be on Africa and Asia," he said, "the next conference should be more positive and its character limited to the Afro-Asian sphere."[176] Yet Soviet and Chinese officials saw Algeria as one of the pivotal battlegrounds in the Third World, alongside Indonesia and Egypt, so both Moscow and Peking contributed significantly more resources to their competition for influence in Algiers than they did in most other countries. In fact, prior to Ben Bella's visit to Moscow in the spring of 1964, Khrushchev admitted to the Algerian ambassador that he considered Algeria to be the key to Africa in the ideological contest with China, rather than with the West.[177] Consequently, assessing the joint communiqué that Khrushchev and Ben Bella published at the conclusion of the trip, a British diplomat noticed that "the Algerians have accepted the Russian line on Russian/Chinese issues," particularly by praising peaceful coexistence and the Partial Test Ban Treaty, but only publicly backed the Soviet position on a portion of contentions between Moscow and the West.[178] In so doing, Ben Bella had likely gone further than he had intended. After all, during his discussions with Khrushchev, he had stressed that Algeria wanted to maintain its neutrality in the Sino-Soviet split and that he intended to visit China himself when the opportunity arose, although he did also say that Algeria considered the Soviet Union a vital ally of the Afro-Asian peoples that deserved to participate in meetings like the sequel to Bandung, should it occur.[179]

Once Algeria was confirmed as the host of Bandung 2 that autumn, both communist powers intensified their efforts to secure Algiers's support on the question of Soviet participation. China's leaders were able to take advantage of the fact that they were already in the Afro-Asian movement. Chen Yi stressed to Ambassador Yala, for example, that his government had supported Algeria's bid to host the conference over the rival bids of Egypt and Indonesia. Moreover,

China provided financing to construct the Club des Pins conference site and to cover the costs of accommodating so many Afro-Asian dignitaries. However, Yala was concerned by the way the Chinese government publicized its assistance. "We know well," he said in a report on his conversations, "that the provision of this credit does not signify that we have aligned with Chinese positions. But we should not lose sight of what African leaders might think of Algeria when they know in advance that for their stay in Algiers . . . their meals will be paid for by Chinese funds."[180] Chinese officials were also quite blatant in linking new offers of development assistance (including several large construction projects as well as credits to buy industrial machinery) to this issue. When the Algerian economics minister, Bachir Boumaza, signed a trade agreement in Peking in September, he was on the verge of boarding his return flight when Mao's foreign minister asked him to remind President Ben Bella of "China's resolute opposition to any Soviet participation in the Afro-Asian Conference."[181]

With the Chinese and Soviet governments both openly linking their aid to Algeria's position on Soviet participation in the Bandung 2 conference, Moscow's advantages in the economic realm came into clear view. Reflecting the USSR's greater financial might in comparison to the PRC, Soviet loans to Algeria in 1963–1964 amounted to approximately $255 million, whereas China's loans to Ben Bella's regime were valued at $100 million.[182] But the Soviet advantage was not simply financial. For example, in May 1964 Ben Bella joined Khrushchev and Nasser for the opening of the massive Aswan Dam project in southern Egypt, a showpiece of the Soviet Union's superior technological, engineering, and logistical resources and a demonstration of Moscow's willingness to take on even the most ambitious development schemes. The Algerian government was very interested in building its own dams for electrical production and to support agriculture, and within two years the Soviets had agreed to construct dozens of them for their North African allies.[183] Similarly, the petrochemical institute and steel mill that Moscow agreed to build, both deemed vital to Algeria's development strategy, were beyond Chinese capacities at that time. In addition to the fact that the Soviets were simply able to offer larger loans and more credit for the purchase of industrial equipment, the Algerians found it difficult to find enough Chinese technology worth buying with the credit that Mao's government did provide. When one Algerian economic delegation visited Peking in September 1964, Yala reported that "in the opinion of the brothers from the Planning Administration . . . Chinese industry is at a very low level."[184]

As a result of the Soviet Union's greater resources, Soviet economic diplomacy outmatched China's through much of Africa and the Middle East; only a small number of countries—such as Mali, Congo-Brazzaville, and Tanzania—were closer to Peking in that regard. Those same countries were among the few that identified more closely with Maoist economic theory, which advocated self-reliance and had greater focus on agriculture, than with the Soviet model embracing international trade and essentially sacrificing agriculture on the altar of industrialization. The Chinese economic message was therefore somewhat out of step with the Third World mainstream and the UNCTAD agenda. At the AAPSO economic meeting in Algiers in February 1965, the Chinese delegate spent a whole evening debating with Boumaza but failed to persuade him on these issues.[185]

On the other hand, China was much more involved than the Soviet Union in supporting armed anticolonial movements, a major source of strength in its relations with countries like Algeria. The former FLN militants who governed Algeria hardly needed reminding that China's support for their struggle for independence was much more extensive than the Soviet Union's had been—though Chinese officials certainly liked to bring it up. Following the PLO's founding in January 1964, Zhou Enlai declared that "we are ready to help the Arab nations to regain Palestine ... we are ready to give you anything and everything," including military and diplomatic support.[186] In contrast, the PLO leader, Ahmed Shukairy, complained that "for two long years (1963–1965) I knocked on the gates of Moscow as though I were Henry IV, standing seven hundred years ago before the gates of Canossa, doing penance before the Pope. ... But the Soviet Union did not agree to the liberation of Palestine and did not want to recognize the Liberation Organization."[187] Consequently, Peking's accusation that peaceful coexistence entailed "betraying" anticolonial causes aroused murmurs of agreement in the Third World's more radical circles.

Algerian-Chinese cooperation in this area grew significantly in the course of the year, beginning with Peking pledging funds to help support Algeria's guerrilla training centers.[188] The Algerians facilitated introductions as well as travel between Peking and many of the groups that they supported. For example, when the Angolan nationalist leader Jonas Savimbi came to visit Ben Bella, the Algerian president instructed his ambassador in Cairo, Lakhdar Brahimi, to furnish him with a passport and abet his transit to China—even though Savimbi was formally disowned at that time by the OAU, Egypt, and Ghana.[189] Likewise, after he opened the Fateh office in Algiers, the Algerian authorities helped Khalid Wazir travel to Peking, Hanoi, and Pyongyong.[190] In return, Chen Yi assured Yala, "Algeria is a revolutionary country and we say this to every African delegation that comes to Peking; we advise everyone we talk to to take their example from Algeria."[191] An Algerian "economic" delegation that visited Peking in December also involved coordinating the two countries' response to the situation in Africa, and the extent to which China could help respond to the "wider American offensive" that both countries' leaders perceived there, in terms of armaments, training, and so on. The Algerians were concerned not only with supporting liberation movements and the Congolese rebels, but also the possibility that Washington might target them directly.[192] In February 1965, the Chinese delivered a shipment of 12,000 tons of military equipment, for the purpose of developing an Algerian militia as well as supplying other movements.[193]

Algeria's leaders also shared Yugoslavian and Soviet displeasure at the Chinese government's use of racial arguments to exclude the Soviets from the Third World movement. Quite simply, Peking insisted, the Soviets and Yugoslavians did not belong in Afro-Asian meetings because they were Europeans. Moreover, Chinese officials suggested on occasion that history had proven that nonwhite peoples simply could not trust Europeans. The Soviet Union offered one of its fiercest rebuttals of Chinese propaganda in February 1964, when Mikhail Suslov, the chief ideological theoretician, gave a public speech to the party leadership accusing Mao's government of abandoning basic Marxist analysis in order to explain anticolonialism with crude nationalist and racist logic.[194] Likewise, when Ben Bella visited Belgrade the following month, Tito insisted that "we should fight the ideas adopted by the Chinese, who say: 'We have had enough of white hegemony, now we the colored people should dominate.'" He proposed that NAM, at its next meeting, formally condemn the rhetoric of racial division and call for greater cooperation between anti-imperialists of every color.[195] The Algerian president agreed with this sentiment emphatically, stating:

> A correction to the idea of nonalignment needs to be brought about, as well as an enlargement of the circle of nonaligned states.... All the countries that signed the charter adopted at the Addis Ababa conference... could participate at the [next NAM] conference. Of course, in addition to Asian countries, Latin American and European countries, among them Finland, would participate at that conference too. We also think that ideas about continents and skin color need to be overcome because progressive forces exist all around the world.[196]

In other words, Ben Bella wholeheartedly advocated a programmatic, expansive concept of Third World solidarity, rather than one based on particularistic identities. His Egyptian ally shared this view. When Zhou Enlai had spoken with Nasser in Cairo the previous December, he argued the need for a second Afro-Asian heads of state summit to demonstrate the unity of non-Western nations but found that Nasser was interested only in political alliances, not race-based unity.[197]

Although this disagreement concerned fundamentally different conceptions of the Third World, in practical terms the Algerian and Egyptian governments were worried that any focus on racial dynamics could become a liability to their diplomacy in sub-Saharan Africa. They were aware of long-standing trans-Saharan sensitivities, especially those relating to the recent history of Arab slave trading. Some Arab representatives made an effort to deny that there was any real racial divide in the continent. For example, the head of the Egyptian delegation to the Conference of Independent African States in Monrovia, in August 1959, told the attendees that Egyptians had historically "freely intermixed with peoples all along the River Nile, up to the innermost heart of Africa, in the Great Lake Region. We have mixed blood in our veins. I shout it to the world and I am proud of it."[198] However, Ben Bella expressed the more common view when he told Tito that "we are white like you, maybe a little more brown."[199]

Therefore, the North Africans put great emphasis on shared political aims and historical experiences. When asked by a Kenyan journalist in 1963 whether he worked primarily "for Arab Unity or for African Unity," Nasser insisted that he saw no contradiction between the two.[200] Likewise, when Sékou Touré visited Algeria in the summer of 1964, Ben Bella and his officials made a concerted effort to overcome the Guinean president's suspicions of Arab intentions by demonstrating to him that "Africanism [was] deeply embedded in the popular consciousness."[201] These efforts clearly satisfied many influential black Africans. For example, the prominent Kenyan nationalist Tom Mboya wrote in 1963, "I have come to believe that the great majority of Arabs in North Africa look on themselves as African ... [and] Nasser, Ben Bella and [Tunisia's Habib] Bourguiba demonstrated fully at the Addis Ababa conference their commitment to Pan-Africanism."[202] Even so, despite the influence they had already accrued in African affairs, Algerian diplomats in particular continued to be conscious of the racial factor in continental relations. "In truth," Abdelmalek Benhabylès conceded in one foreign ministry report, "Arab-African relations continue to be marred by a set of prejudices and misunderstandings, including racism even. This situation is adroitly exploited by Israel and the imperialist countries."[203]

Benhabylès and his colleagues were concerned by several examples of hostile African elements using the racial factor against them. First, they believed that the Israelis played on historic grievances, as well as ongoing intercommunal tensions in countries such as Zanzibar and Sudan, in order to stoke African resentment of the Arab League's campaign to persuade them to reject Tel Aviv's economic diplomacy. The foreign minister of Sierra Leone, Dr. John Karefa Smart, typified a popular view on the subject when he suggested in early 1964 that "African members of the League will have to decide soon where they stand. Are they in the Middle East or in Africa?"[204] In a similar vein, the Algerians suspected that Holden Roberto's FNLA, which had grown increasingly hostile toward them, was exploiting "tribalism" to attack the mixed-race leadership of the MPLA as well as the Arab and communist countries that supported them. Jonas Savimbi told the OAU that summer that Roberto had surrounded himself with mysterious Americans of African heritage, implying a corruption of pan-Africanist sentiment by the CIA.[205] But it was the Congolese president, Tshombe, who used race in the bluntest fashion against his North African foes. Following his humiliating rejection at the NAM summit in Cairo in October 1964, he thundered that Nasser was "motivated only by a feeling of domination vis-à-vis the Congo and black Africa."[206] When he returned home, he staged a "re-enactment" of Arab slave raiders descending ruthlessly on a nineteenth-century Congolese village, before a crowd of 50,000 people in Léopoldville's main stadium.[207] It was, the Algerians noted, a "campaign of hatred and racism against the Arabs" that seemed hypocritical in light of Tshombe's reliance on Belgian paratroopers, South African mercenaries, the CIA, and anti-Castroist Cubans to crush to his domestic enemies.[208]

Meanwhile, Soviet and Chinese pressure on the Algerian government and other African countries steadily mounted as the Afro-Asian Conference in Algiers approached. Although the Soviet leadership had initially promised not to make life awkward for its Third World allies, in the spring of 1965 Moscow began to press heavily for inclusion in the conference, while the Chinese government was determined to outmatch these efforts.[209] Zhou Enlai visited Algiers twice, in April and May, while numerous Algerian delegations traveled to each of the communist rivals to conclude further aid and cooperative agreements: Boumedienne led a military delegation to Moscow, while an FLN party delegation continued the unusual escalation of its relations with the CPSU, with the latter starting to acquire substantial influence over Algerian plans to fully develop its one-party system and strengthen connections between the regime and the populace.[210] Notably, the FLN delegates returned to Algiers convinced that their government should actively lobby for the Soviet Union's participation in the Afro-Asian Conference.[211] In fact, Ben Bella had secretly reached an agreement the previous month with Modibo Keita, Sékou Touré, and Kwame Nkrumah that the four radical African states would collectively support Soviet and Malaysian inclusion, although the Algerians would continue to be circumspect about their stance until the foreign ministers' meeting scheduled for 23 June, a week before the conference, when final decisions would be made.[212] Even so, there was real concern in Algiers that, even if they did manage to secure Soviet participation without incurring a Chinese boycott, the two countries might then hijack the proceedings with their reciprocal tirades and invective.[213]

That agreement between Algeria, Ghana, Guinea, and Mali was due in part to resentment of the Chinese government's increasingly heavy-handed methods of persuasion. Describing one conversation with the Chinese foreign minister, Chen Yi, that veered abruptly from vilification of the Soviet Union to culinary matters, Hadj Yala wrote:

> This is very much the style of Chinese politics, which is a curious amalgam of subtlety, calculated generosity, false modesty, chauvinism, verbal abuse and sometimes crude insults. . . . There is no restraint

anymore with the Chinese, who are trying to drive Third World countries to make a choice and choose sides with regard to the USSR. The Afro-Asian countries' missions in Peking are subjected to intolerable pressures.[214]

Yala complained that the Chinese authorities imposed petty inconveniences on the diplomatic community in Peking, such as impeding interaction between the representatives of Third World countries in Peking and those of the Eastern European countries, and forbidding travel to the Soviet Union even to catch connecting flights to other destinations. His colleagues in Algiers also found Chinese behavior at the Bandung 2 preparatory meetings increasingly unreasonable: at one point, the Chinese and the Indonesians insisted on inspecting the Club des Pins construction site because they suspected the Algerians of concocting false delays in order to gather more support for the Soviet Union and Malaysia.[215] To be fair, Chinese diplomats had complaints of their own. Bemoaning that inordinate flattery was necessary to influence the policies of Ben Bella and his officials, one Chinese report noted that "the Algerian ruling group is very arrogant and conceited, but its tiger's ass can still be petted."[216]

Nevertheless, by 1965 political elites in many of the smaller Third World countries were of the view that the Sino-Soviet rivalry had became an almighty pain in that part of the tiger's anatomy. The Malian leadership, for example, simultaneously resented the Soviet Union's disruptive efforts to attend the Afro-Asian Conference and the Chinese assertion that nonalignment was impossible on this issue.[217] Representing Algeria at one meeting at the AAPSO secretariat in Cairo, M'hamed Yazid suggested that both of the two great communist powers needed to remember that "if the small nations need the large ones, [the latter] are also in need of the small ones."[218] At the AAPSO economic summit in Algiers, Che Guevara launched into a contentious speech that accused both Moscow and Peking of pursuing self-interested economic relations with poor countries; while his hosts could not afford to be as undiplomatic as he was, they did agree with Guevara's basic contention that the Soviet Union and China had the mentality of established powers, not genuine revolutionaries.[219] Behind closed doors, holding a seminar for the Algerian diplomatic corps that May, Bouteflika argued that "when we look at . . . the Third World, we see it divided by China and the USSR, weakening the struggle against colonialism. It is the countries of the Third World that constitute the spear-tip against colonialism, not the doctrinaire states."[220]

All told, by June 1965, the Algerian government was struggling to hold the Third World together. As Bandung 2 approached, its ambitious diplomacy had produced some notable successes: securing the admission of liberation movements to the conference with full status, putting expansion into Latin American on the Afro-Asian agenda, and generally defending the inclusive programmatic conception of the Third World alliance against more divisive, racially themed interpretations. Yet the near impossibility of managing the various contentions that threatened to disrupt the conference also highlighted the limits of the country's power. Algeria's close relations with the communist world, intensified by Sino-Soviet competition, had damaged some of its relationships in the Arab world and Africa, to the point that the OCAM group was threatening to boycott the Algiers conference. Of course, much more damaging absences would occur if the hosts' desperate last efforts, in the final week of preparations, failed to broker compromises over Soviet and Malaysian attendance. The possibility of Bandung 2's ignominious collapse was still very real. Moreover, the strain of mediating intense rivalries between much more powerful countries than Algeria was evident inside the foreign ministry; Bouteflika complained that personnel posted abroad were starting to exhibit the effects of constant ideological and propagandistic bombardment.[221] That complaint also indicated how international pressures were affecting Algeria's domestic affairs, as a consequence in particular of the extension of Moscow and Pekin's competition into that realm. With the Soviet Communist Party advising the development of the FLN and communist influence on Algeria's economic policies more visible by the day, even Yugoslavian observers began to worry about the possibility of alienating the country's "Arabist" and Islamist elements.[222] Perhaps President Ben Bella had staked too much of his own credibility on the potentially impossible task of maintaining the harmony of the Third World.

Algeria's Internal Reaction to Globalism and Globalization

Essentially, the Third Worldist agenda had segmented into three distinct strands since the first Bandung meeting in 1955. Much to the frustration of Algerian diplomats, the first two of those strands—nonalignment and Afro-Asianism—had acquired different meanings and even begun to compete with one another for the loyalty of developing countries, but the prospects of the third, economic component of Third Worldism had never seemed better than in 1964. That year, the first UNCTAD took place in Geneva from March to June, bringing together nearly eighty states from across the developing world to demand fundamental revisions to the structure of the international economy to the benefit of the poor. In notable contrast to the divisive bickering over membership of the nonaligned and Afro-Asian clubs, the continents of Africa, Asia, and Latin America were all ell-represented in UNCTAD, with the well-regarded left-wing Argentinian economist Raúl Prebisch becoming the first secretary-general of the body's new permanent secretariat.[223] Moreover, radical and moderate governments found much common ground on economic matters, agreeing that the rich countries owed more development assistance to the poor ones, and that the latter ought to receive a "fairer" price for their agricultural and mineral exports. Faced with this show of unanimity, Eastern European officials declared their support for Geneva's Group of 77 (G77), while their Western counterparts fretted.[224] Capturing the moment's Third Worldist sense of triumph, Secretary-General U Thant insisted that "North-South tensions are fundamentally as serious as East-West ones" and hailed UNCTAD's creation as proof of the new nations' ability to shape international politics.[225]

Unsurprisingly, the Algerian foreign ministry greeted the Geneva meeting extremely enthusiastically. In the view of the MAE's Economic and Cultural Affairs Section, the conference had "enabled our countries to cross an important threshold in their struggle on a global scale to stand up to the affluent countries of the capitalist world. This was an event without precedent in history."[226] The nationalist leadership had always supported the UNCTAD agenda because, in spite of the promise of oil and natural gas wealth and a near–First World physical infrastructure, Algeria was as dependent on exporting basic commodities as any of its peers, and crushingly overdependent on its economic relations with the former colonial occupier. "Thoughout the colonial period," Ben Bella reminded the FLN cadres in April 1964, "nearly everything that Algeria sold and everything that it bought went to and came from France." After independence, therefore, the goal was to "free ourselves from this narrow economic subjugation that could have quickly assumed the same force as political subjugation."[227] Yet the Algerians also agreed with U Thant when he argued that the solution to underdevelopment was not autarky. "In any society in the world of today," the UN secretary-general reminded the Geneva attendees, "there is a need for ensuring that, somehow, a global outlook is developed."[228] In this spirit, Algiers played host to the Second Economic Seminar of Afro-Asian Solidarity in February 1965, attempting to place as much emphasis on the economic component of Third Worldism as on the political one. Likewise, the Algerian government sought to expand and diversify its sources of trade and assistance, not to substitute French support for another country's, nor to seek some form of self-sufficiency.

Ironically, therefore, the challenges to Algeria's economic goals did not come principally from external factors, as was the case for its pursuit of nonaligned and Afro-Asian solidarity. Instead, with the international environment being relatively promising in this area, the reaction to Algeria's globalist vision came from inside, in the form of local social opposition to the proliferation of foreign interests and foreign advisers. In a sense, Algeria in the mid-1960s reacted against two competing forms of globalization. While the political elite was primarily concerned with containing the "neo-imperialist" capitalist world system, many regular Algerians were more bothered by a sort of "socialist globalization" in the form of the "pieds rouges," advisers from communist countries, and the ideological and cultural influences that they brought with them. In that sense, the Algerian Revolution was becoming too internationalist for many of the country's inhabitants to bear.

Considering first Algeria's ongoing efforts to diversify and expand its sources of trade, a substantial tension persisted between the leadership's revolutionary aspirations and pragmatic concessions. At the beginning of the year the minister of the economy, Bachir Boumaza, outlined what some Western officials interpreted as Algeria's NEP, that is, its efforts to reconcile socialism with the need for Western capitalism. Boumaza explained that his government's mixed approach to trade had pinpointed certain sectors and goods for nationalization, principally in agriculture, while leaving foreign industrial and energy concerns untouched.[229] Consequently, several of the major capitalist economies continued to enjoy a substantial and even growing share of Algeria's trade, relative to the socialist and communist world. Apart from France, therefore, Britain, Italy, Holland, and Belgium were Algiers's principal trading partners in 1964; for example, the total value of trade with Britain (roughly $65 million in 1964 dollars) was six or seven times greater than with the USSR ($9.5 million for the nine months to September).[230] Of course, communist governments such as the Soviet and Chinese ones offered credit to buy their goods, or else imported Algerian agricultural and mineral goods in exchange, but these figures represented precious flows of hard currency. Overwhelmingly, when the Algerian government spent its scarce hard cash, it did so in the West, principally on advanced technology unavailable in the East, and overwhelmingly Algeria's inflows of hard currency came from the same place. Britain and Italy, notably, were the biggest importers of Algerian minerals, and they signed agreements to buy natural gas that soon became cornerstones of the national economy, which spurred substantial investment in the necessary transportation and liquefaction facilities.[231]

Nevertheless, it was widely acknowledged within the foreign ministry that the current state of Algeria's external economic relations was at odds with the country's fundamental principles. "As a country with a genuinely socialist vocation," one report on the subject pondered, "can we integrate with a liberal economic grouping [like the EEC]? There is no precedent for this situation." Moreover, by pursuing opportunities in the West, Algeria was neglecting the much more difficult task of promoting economic relations within the Third World. "Objectively, we are turning our backs on Arab unity and African integration," warned the same report. "This is totally contrary to our [ideological] choices, and let's not pretend that we can integrate ourselves into these three groupings simultaneously, [as] they are totally incompatible. It's pointless to go into the reasons why, which are of a brutally economic nature."[232]

The potential for fruitful economic ties with other developing countries being so meager, the industrialized communist world continued to offer a more palatable alternative to the West. Czechoslovakia, historically a destination for Algerian agricultural and mineral exports before independence, was a good example. Throughout 1963, Algiers failed to conclude a new trade agreement with Prague on account of the latter's insistence on being paid in hard currency, but Algeria's growing importance to Soviet diplomacy evidently overcame this obstacle, and in March 1964 the two countries concluded an exchange agreement worth $9 million. Ben Bella stopped in the Czechoslovak capital on his return from Moscow that spring, when his hosts agreed to provide agricultural advisers and a loan of $15 million to buy modern farming equipment.[233] With such agreements in mind, the MAE's Economic and Cultural Affairs Section observed that "economic cooperation with [the socialist] countries has proven particularly valuable after our socialist vocation drove away many of the French who remained after independence, and began to inspire prudence and reservations among Westerners."[234] Even so, there was a perceptible ambivalence among Algerian officials about the character and value of this type of cooperation. For some, exchange agreements such as the one concluded with Czechoslovakia represented encouraging progress toward a socialist-style trading paradigm, but others would have preferred currency payments for Algerian iron ore, building materials, or fruit. Certainly, some Algerians quietly agreed when Che Guevara undiplomatically lambasted the Soviet Union and China, at the February 1965 Afro-Asian economic seminar, for valuing developing countries' output at international market prices when they negotiated these agreements.[235] There was a widespread sentiment that true socialist solidarity should dictate assigning these goods a "fairer" value, and it became common in later years for Algerian officials to stress the unromantic "businesslike" nature of their relations with the Soviet Union during this period.

In effect, Ben Bella's government was damned if it did and damned if it did not, since it was criticized both for selling out Third Worldist principles by dealing with Western capitalists and for jeopardizing the national economy by scaring away foreign investment. Nowhere was this quandary clearer, or more sensitive, than in Algeria's evolving relationship with France. Criticism of Ben Bella's handling of this issue mounted as Paris retaliated against nationalizations and other revolutionary policies detrimental to French issues by reducing the total amount of aid for 1964 and 1965, and by greatly increasing the proportion of "tied aid" that obligated Algeria to spend those moneys in France itself.[236] As in other areas of the country's international relations, Bouteflika's MAE strove to coordinate policy toward France and bring it more directly under the ministry's authority, with the head of the MAE's French Affairs Section, Djamal Houhou, decrying the "anarchic state" of bilateral relations and warning that "we must apply the brakes hard to this detrimental situation, which is sure in the near term to incur repercussions for the Government's general policies and undermine the national interest."[237] In addition to replicating the old GPRA's turf wars against the other branches of the wartime FLN, by late 1964 and early 1965 the MAE's rationalization efforts might well have taken on the subtext of growing tensions between Ben Bella and his foreign minster, who was one of the key figures in Boumedienne's so-called army clique. A notably frank report by the foreign ministry's economics desk, for example, bemoaned "successive political crises in our relations with France, surmounted each time through laborious negotiations, often at the ministerial level, leading to drastic cuts in French financial assistance as stipulated in the Evian Accords."[238]

Aside from financial aid provisions, the Algerian government's two primary concerns vis-à-vis France were wine and hydrocarbons, which were by far the country's two most important export products.[239] Although Algeria was in fact the world's fourth-largest wine producer by volume, as Houhou noted, its viticulture sector was "essentially a product of colonization," designed entirely toward servicing the needs of the French wine industry. Although it was a usefully labor-intensive industry, local cultural traditions ensured there was almost no domestic demand for the wine industry's output. "Algeria finds itself in an exceptional situation." Houhou warned Bouteflika, "since it must find external markets for a near entirety of its viticultural production." With Paris in a position to dictate how much Algerian wine it would buy each year and at what price, he explained, "a French decree could reduce two million Algerians to famine."[240] Second, the oil and gas sector entailed similar concerns for the substance of Algeria's independence and the viability of the national economy. Although developing the energy sector would require massive investment without directly producing a great deal of employment, the scale of the potential export revenues overshadowed all other considerations in terms of national economic policy. Algiers submitted to Paris a memorandum to this effect in late 1963, arguing that hydrocarbons were not a simple product but of central strategic import to the national economy. Therefore, the Algerian government implied, the country's economic security could not be guaranteed so long as hydrocarbon research, production, and transportation remained entirely in the hands of foreign business interests.[241]

Because the Sahara's oil and gas were almost as important to the French government as to the Algerian one, Ben Bella was able to execute a dramatic reversal in the declining trajectory of Franco-Algerian relations. Returning from a visit to Belgrade in March 1964, he surprised everybody (including most of party traveling with him) by flying to France for a previously unannounced meeting with de Gaulle at the latter's home.[242] The atmosphere of the two presidents' discussions, on 13 March, was perhaps surprisingly warm. Ben Bella recounted the time when de Gaulle, as the leader of the Free French forces, had decorated him for bravery in battle during the Italian campaign in 1944, and at the end of their talk, the French president made a point of walking Ben Bella back to the helicopter that would fly him to the airport. Atmospherics aside, both men had much to gain from an improvement in the bilateral relationship after the previous year's tensions. They each suffered from domestic criticism for the perceived failure of *coopération*—in Ben Bella's case because of Algeria's continued economic woes—and they were also both willing to discreetly deviate from key aspects of their public positions in order to improve the situation.[243] Ben Bella told de Gaulle that he welcomed cooperation as an equal collaboration between two independent countries that also shared an interest in addressing the world's problems. In other words, in return for a healthy resumption of French economic assistance in a manner that suited Algeria's national development strategy, Ben Bella's government would cooperate with de Gaulle's efforts to increase France's influence in the Third World.[244]

In essence, Ben Bella promised to negotiate a new treaty over French access to Algeria's hydrocarbon resources, as the Evian stipulations in this regard were set to expire the following year. Additionally, the Algerian government would continue to turn a blind eye to France's ongoing nuclear tests in the desert until they could be transferred entirely to the Pacific on a similar time frame. In return, de Gaulle would continue to override the mounting objections of his own officials and uphold existing aid programs and would agree to a new treaty that committed France to purchasing Algerian wine for several more years. Moreover, Paris accelerated the withdrawal of its remaining military presence and deprioritized the controversial issue of recompensing French citizens for the properties they had lost in Algeria. All in all, the meeting allowed Ben Bella to return home with his stock enhanced: he could claim to have advanced the country's core economic interests by safeguarding *coopération* and to have extracted further concessions by negotiating with de Gaulle face to face, as the leader of an independent nation meeting with his equal.[245]

As a consequence, trans-Mediterranean relations became very much a function of the personal relationship between the French and Algerian presidents. That summer an official from the Quai d'Orsay told a British colleague that the order had come down to be very lenient in their dealings with Algiers; "under our present monarchical order," he dryly observed, "French policy is much influenced by personal factors . . . and [Ben Bella] greatly impressed the General by the respect he showed toward him during their meeting."[246] The compromise between them rested on the mutual recognition that postcolonial relations were a subject of great sensitivity in both their countries, and the belief that they were both much more reasonable than the alternatives. Just as many French officials despaired at de Gaulle's indulgence toward the Algerians, he seems to have believed that the likes of Boumedienne and Bouteflika were inclined to be much less cooperative than Ben Bella. Revealingly, de Gaulle instructed Ambassador Georges Gorse in March 1965 to tell the Algerian president that although he understood his need to make a show of obduracy for domestic consumption, it was high time for the oil and gas negotiations to reach their conclusion. Recognizing the benefit Ben Bella drew from high-profile sojourns abroad, de Gaulle warned that he would not be welcome again in Paris until a new petrochemical treaty was signed.[247]

In short, Algeria's economic diplomacy was a contentious issue domestically, since each new dealing with the West, the East, or the French could touch different ideological nerves. With the country's generally grim economic situation continuing to refute the revolution's promises, a growing chorus of voices accused the government of sacrificing too many of their principles for the sake of pragmatism, or the inverse. By early 1965, Algerian officials acknowledged that their country's economy had been in a state of tumult since independence, but perhaps slightly defensively argued that falling productivity and organizational chaos were a natural and unfortunate consequence of their socialist reforms. He added that there was no question of submitting to Western "blackmail" by moderating their strident positions on Vietnam or Congo in order to court greater investment and aid.[248] Unfortunately, economic questions were all the more contentious in Ben Bellist Algeria by dint of the government's intentional openness to foreign capital and personnel—a policy that defied the stereotypically hermetic socialist mentality.

Regardless of the tensions between Algiers and Paris, there was a still a massive French presence in the country. In 1964, nearly 5,000 French citizens worked at almost all levels of the Algerian civil service, representing 43 percent of the total at the lowest administrative grade "A," and a striking 77 percent of those at the midlevel grade "B."[249] The embassy official responsible for coordinating the activities of these *coopérants*, Stéphane Hessel, described working with "a strange overlapping of Frenchmen and various backgrounds and Algerians of differing varieties" in reference to the broad political spectrum represented in the state bureaucracies. Among the French were holdovers from the old days— schoolteachers in remote regions and military doctors in the Sahara who had as little contact with the new authorities as they had with the ancien régime— as well as new arrivals in search of salary or adventure, and the true believers, "militants of the *tier-mondiste* revolution, dedicated to serving as the leaven for a people taking their own destiny in hand." On the Algerian side, he encountered a mixture of reactions to the new situation: some resented taking advice and orders from the French, while others were grateful for any assistance in joining the modern era. Many who had studied in France, in Hessel's opinion, "felt almost as disoriented in their own land as the *coopérants* assigned to them."[250]

Complicating this picture was the arrival of growing numbers of advisers, medical staff, and technical experts from the communist world, which obliged the Algerian government to create a dedicated Direction de la Coopération Economique et Technique in September 1964.[251] Although in competition with the French at the level of international politics, the communist visitors shared their relatively comfortable lifestyle with regard to the local context. Paris, Moscow, and Prague, for example, all hashed out an agreement to share responsibility with the Algerian authorities for paying the foreign experts' relatively generous salaries, although even their local counterparts were remunerated at a level closer to that of the industrialized world than the general level of poverty in the country would suggest.[252] As a consequence, astute observers noted, "government payrolls gave downtown Algiers traffic jams and a veneer of prosperity," while regional towns lacked for commerce and employment.[253] Economics minister Bachir Boumaza admitted that Algeria had actually imported $40 million worth of new cars in 1963, but he promised a new era of austerity, and in a bid to combat inflation his ministry opened a dozen Magasins-Pilotes Socialistes (Pilot Socialist Shops) in the capital at the beginning of the new year.[254] Popular resentment of this cosmopolitan technocratic class was already rising, and the confusing mixture of agnostic technocrats, Western capitalists, and Marxist fellow travelers only added to the impression that an essentially opportunist elite was taking hold of the country.[255]

Exacerbating matters was the fact that all of the competing developing paradigms privileged urban society and the industrial sector over the rural world. Less than a year into autogestion's much-hyped indigenous experiment in decentralized socialism, a rich multinational technocratic layer began to impose itself as the true successor to the colonial order. Algiers sought to boost production through national planning apparatuses like the Office National de la Reforme Agraire (National Office for Agrarian Reform, Algeria, ONRA), an entity that inherited much of the staff (French and Algerian) and the institutional habits of a similar late-colonial effort at agricultural development. However, the ONRA also dispatched its personnel on fact-finding missions to countries like Yugoslavia, Egypt, and Cuba, where the persuasive Che Guevara argued emphatically that autogestion was a mistake and preached the virtues of strict central control.[256] At rowdy consultative meetings, local self-management committee leaders strenuously protested the diminishment of their autonomy, but their cries for the "democratization" of autogestion went unheeded. When Mustapha, the manager of a small vineyard, first moved into his former pied noir boss's house, autogestion promised that he would inherit the responsibilities that came with it. By 1964, however, he found himself being ordered about like before, only now by the apparatchiks parachuted in from Algiers to apportion fertilizer and other necessities as they saw fit. He complained that he had become "a cog like any other in the great socialist machine, without any rank and having to prove himself anew."[257] Moreover, contrary to the myth that the Algerian Revolution had been fought in the peasants' name, the efforts of the rural majority went to subsidize urban development. "In the coming years," Ben Bella admitted, "the resources produced by the self-managed lands will be a vital source of finance for industrialization."[258]

The backlash against Algiers also had cultural aspects, most notable in religious and moral conservatives' distaste for the cosmopolitan mores so evident in the streets of the capital. Boasting an almost European urban infrastructure and a sizable stratum of cultured, well-educated French-speaking locals, the Algerian capital was very accessible to sub-Saharan conspirators, Quebecois nationalists, Iberian dissidents, or even CIA officers in search of an agreeable posting.[259] Foreign and local women strolled the sun-bleached avenues in miniskirts, while an American journalist found that "young African exiles, some with beards or goatees, all with plenty of time for all-night talk, give cafes in downtown Algiers a look of the Left Bank in Paris."[260] Even as the diplomatic corps rejoiced in this sense of being a global crossroads, social friction was intensifying. After independence, the flow of migrants from the countryside increased even further, bringing the rural world's popular understanding of Islam and decent behavior onto the city streets. Likewise, the rank-and-file mujahideen who took up thousands of jobs in the administrative apparatus did not always share the attitudes of the FLN's representatives abroad, and the first symptoms of disillusionment gradually set in among some of the leftist women who had been drawn to the Algerian Revolution's progressive reputation but were now often frustrated by their interactions with male officialdom.[261] Then, in January 1964, a new association called al-Qiyam al-Islamiyya (The Islamic Values) rallied a crowd of 3,000 at the University of Algiers, where they enthusiastically applauded speeches calling for the full implementation of sharia (Islamic law), religious teaching in schools, rapid Arabization, and "decent" strictures on women's behavior and the interaction of the sexes.[262]

Of course, the Islamic movement did not focus purely on cultural issues, and at least some of its participants shared elements of the Egyptian Muslim Brotherhood's political-ideological program. Al-Qiyam denounced Ben Bella's close association with Trotskyists and communists, insisting that "no communist, secular, Marxist-socialist, or nationalist party ... can exist in the land of Islam."[263] While the entire history of independent Algeria should not be oversimplified into a predetermined struggle between Islamism and authoritarian secularism, there is no doubt that in Ben Bella's time the corrosive combination of economic stagnation, bureaucratism, and a jarring interaction of the international and domestic domains was already evident.[264] As early as 1964, Sheikh

Bashir Ibrahimi warned the authorities that "our country is sliding nearer and nearer to hopeless civil war,

> [and] an unprecedented moral crisis and insurmountable economic difficulties. Those governing us do not seem to realize that what our people aspire to above all is unity, peace and prosperity and that the theories on which their actions should be founded are to be found not in foreign doctrines but in our Arab-Islamic roots."[265]

In some ways, independent Algeria suffered from its leaders' inveterate internationalism and their globalist outlook. When Mohammed Harbi tasked a French social scientist to investigate the causes of a peasant insurrection in the Aurès, she concluded that it was the result of "the conjunction of inadequate economic integration with an all-too-perfect integration into the ideology of industrial society." Unlike their counterparts in other developing countries, she argued, Algerian peasants had enough acquaintance with the wider world to grasp the extent of their marginalization.[266] In a sense, the Algerian Revolution was a victim of its own success. Its leaders' impatience and desire for rapid socioeconomic transformation stoked resentment and a sense of dislocation among the very people they were trying to help.

Ben Bella later claimed to have experienced a moment of clarity on the road to the ancient city of Souk Ahras, about a month before he expected to open the Bandung 2 conference. The inhabitants of a small town intercepted his convoy in order to berate their president for becoming entrapped in the big city, cutting himself off from the Algerian hinterland. "You shouldn't go back to the capital," he said to himself, "you should stay here amongst your own kind [the peasants]. Why go back to where there's nothing but consuls, ambassadors, politicians, merchants and bureaucrats?"[267] But the allure of the global was too strong, and after enjoying the locals' hospitality for a night Ben Bella was back on the road to Algiers, speeding to an appointment with destiny.

Crossroads

A decade after the original Bandung Conference, the Third World movement was at a turning point. Since that storied 1955 meeting, nearly all of Africa had decolonized, Western Europe had taken major steps toward integration even as the construction of the Berlin Wall had confirmed the stasis of the Cold War on the continent, the superpowers were racing into space, and the communist countries argued while an economic miracle was visibly transforming life in the capitalist sphere. Yet, amid this context of ceaseless change, the political structures of the postcolonial political had cohered and acquired an air of permanence. The basic unit of international society, and the endpoint of decolonization, was indisputably the sovereign state, recognized by the United Nations. Even the territorial borders of those postcolonial states, supposedly so arbitrary and fragile, were already proving surprisingly immutable. Consequently, while a host of specific contentions still animated the Third World (the Vietnam War, white minority rule in southern Africa, Israel, and so on) elites in the Southern Hemisphere were no longer agitating for structural political change. On the contrary, UNCTAD was an important step toward refocusing the Third Worldist agenda on structural change in the economic realm in a manner that actually reinforced the new political status quo. That is, Algeria was in the vanguard of a coalition of smaller, poorer countries that were trying to subject the global economy to the authority of sovereign states through UN mechanisms. By advocating policies such as price stability for commodities and centrally managed wealth redistribution from North to South, this Third Worldist economic agenda would, in time, evolve into something that very much resembled statism, central planning, and socialism writ large. The dilemma for the leaders of the developing world was that they dreaded exclusion from the wealthy capitalist countries' trade regimes yet also feared being crushed by mightier economic forces if they fully submitted to the liberalization of international trade. Their proposed solution was simultaneously globalist and statist.

Still, while the countries of the Third World were reaching toward this new consensus on global economic reform, arguing that the material inequality between North and South transcended the industrialized world's ideological conflict, in other respects their participation in the Cold War was also intensifying in the mid-1960s. In a speech to American academics in April 1964, the Algerian ambassador, Chérif Guellal, nobly claimed that the "nonaligned countries have formed a sort of buffer, a shock absorber between the two [blocs]. . . . [W]e have not the slightest intention to become part of the Cold War."[268] In reality Algerian nonalignment continued to be provocative, aggressive even, in its exploitation of international tensions. Ben Bella's government successfully used the three-sided competition for influence between the United States, Soviet Union, and France to maximize opportunities for economic assistance and trade; in theory, the French and Soviet influences were also supposed to counterbalance one another and minimize the possibility of ideological contagion. At the same time, the Algerians had emphatically adopted a more polarizing posture in African affairs, setting aside the neutrality they had practiced at the Addis Ababa conference in order to side openly with the continent's revolutionary forces. Of course, these decisions came with a clear and serious cost—American hostility—which had proven fatal to numerous governments in the recent past. Nevertheless, Algeria offered an example of how Third World countries fought and, to some degree, shaped the Cold War. In particular, in 1964–1965 the Algerians were combatants in a contest that should be recognized as an African Cold War that drew in the great powers at least as much as it was created by them. As Ben Bella told Tito, "The red telephone between Moscow and Washington should not connect those two countries only. Its wires should pass through Angola and all other countries where people are fighting for freedom."[269]

Conversely, the Chinese government's efforts to reframe the Cold War in racial terms had highlighted a fundamental debate about the nature of the Third World. Was it programmatic—a movement with an agenda that was open to any who shared its political and economic goals? Or was Third Worldism the expression of an innate identity, with its constituency limited to non-Western regions or races? The lofty rhetoric heard at the original Bandung Conference had conveyed both meanings simultaneously, but heated disputes about who could or could not attend Bandung 2 meant that the Algerians, among others closely involved in preparations for the second conference, had to address the issue directly. New sources of evidence, especially the Algerian and the Yugoslavian diplomatic archives, are particularly useful for examining this sort of vital question because, out of diplomatic necessity, the protagonists' public pronouncements were usually guarded, vague, and emollient, doped with inclusive platitudes.

This new evidence shows that Algeria's leaders, like those of Yugoslavia, were firm proponents of a programmatic, more inclusive Third World. On the one hand, it suited their definition of the national interest. The racial theme in Chinese propaganda contradicted Algiers's efforts to build bridges between black Africa, the Arab world, and progressive forces in Europe and Latin America (such as Yugoslavia and Cuba). Moreover, the perception that Algeria was influential in Africa and other regions was an important reason, if not the reason, why the Soviet Union and other European communist countries were so generous in their economic and military support for what was otherwise a marginal Maghribi country with an iconoclastic variant of socialism. For all that Ben Bella and his colleagues insisted on their neutrality in the Sino-Soviet split, Soviet aid plainly influenced their decision to lobby for Moscow's admission to Bandung 2. That said, Algeria's insistence that the Third World was a project, rather than a place, was a principled stance, too. Most of the country's political figures and diplomatic cadres sincerely believed that the broadest possible coalition was necessary in order to achieve Third Worldism's grandest and most important aims, such as restructuring the global economy for the benefit of poor nations. With that perspective, Algerian diplomats lobbied for the Afro-Asian framework to expand to include Latin America, as they also did with regard to the Non-Aligned Movement.

The choice between programmatic politics and identity politics was paramount in the domestic sphere as well. In Algeria's case, Ben Bella and his closest advisers still worried that their revolution lacked sufficient ideological or philosophical content: they had a program (specifically, the Tripoli Program), Ben Bella complained, but no ideology. Prompted initially by the FLN's increased reliance on communist revolutionary praxis in the late 1950s, this concern was now becoming a persistent theme in Algerian political culture. But by 1964–1965, there was mounting criticism in certain socially conservative and staunchly Arabist circles that the Marxist rationale behind the Tripoli Program was gradually filling this ideological void and that foreign leftists had excessive influence in Ben Bellist Algeria, corrupting the nation's culture and identity. These accusations put the president on the defensive; as time passed, he made more and more concessions to religious and ethnocentric sentiment. Whereas he once claimed to have "ceased being a nationalist" in July 1962 because the achievement of independence rendered nationalism "a narrow, chauvinistic vision of our future," by early 1965, he was publicly insisting that "we adopt the Marxist economic analysis . . . but we do not espouse the Marxist ideology because we are Muslims and Arabs," while simultaneously caving to the campaign launched by the ANP's Arabic-language paper, *El Djeich* (The army), that called for pieds rouges elements to be purged from the nation's newsrooms and editorial offices.[270] Naturally, there were religious leaders and intellectuals, such as Malek Bennabi, who defended the regime's claim that its "authentic" socialist revolution was true to Algeria's Islamic and Arab heritage, but Ben Bella himself admitted, in sympathetic capitals, that his government had emphatically rejected making Islam the basis of its ideology.[271] Moreover, foreign policy bore directly on these domestic tensions because of the common postcolonial sentiment that diplomacy was indicative of a nation's identity—too much Africa said some, too much Arab world groused others—as well as the fact that advisers and technicians from friendly communist governments were an increasingly visible presence on Algerian soil. In that respect, Algeria's staunchly anticommunist religious conservatives and peasants aggrieved by changing economic policies constituted the local opposition to the socialist world's version of globalization—leftist internationalism.

In the short term, however, the most pressing interaction of domestic and international politics occurred at the highest levels of Algeria's political hierarchy, in particular the simmering rivalry between Ben Bella and the man who had first put him in power, Boumedienne. As the *Al Djeich* campaign indicates, Boumedienne's "clan" was hostile to the *pieds rouges* phenomenon and had begun to use conservative critiques to attack the president indirectly, although the fact that the defense minister was perhaps the single greatest beneficiary of Soviet support to Algeria ensured that these attacks would never escalate beyond sociocultural issues to touch on relations with communist countries. Ultimately, the most combustible dynamic was not any particular policy of Ben Bella's, but rather the fact that his growing stature in international affairs also strengthened his position at home. Like the ruling circle's perennial sense of ideological inadequacy, the legitimating power of diplomacy was another feature of Algerian political culture that had its origins in the war of independence, when the FLN's diplomatic campaign managed to win the populace's loyalty even as the mujahideen's struggle waned. Consequently, it was Bandung 2 that finally precipitated the resolution of this latent power struggle at the apex of Algerian politics. Ben Bella and Boumedienne both seem to have calculated that the conference would bestow enough domestic capital and international support on the president to make it impossible for the defense minister to move against him. Instead, in mid-June, a week before the long-awaited event, Ben Bella demanded that Bouteflika relinquish the office of foreign minister; as Bouteflika's patron, Boumedienne concluded that his own resignation would be demanded during the conference itself, when the presence of thousands of journalists and dignitaries would deter any of his allies from backing him.[272] After all, just about the entirety of Algeria's new ruling class eagerly anticipated the conference's success—and with it global recognition of their collective accomplishments.

Thus, the foreign dignitaries had already begun to arrive in Algiers when Boumedienne and his entourage carried out their coup d'état, early in the morning of 19 June 1965. The operation was practically flawless. Elite units deployed while the city slumbered, occupying vital intersections and strategic installations such as the airport and the national radio-television broadcaster. They captured the president in the same swift and easy manner, rousing him from bed in his modest residence and leading him away to an unknown fate. In fact, the streets were so calm when morning broke that many people at first assumed that the ANP's soldiers and tanks were serving as extras for the filming of Gillo Pontecorvo's cinematic classic *The Battle of Algiers*. But there was no news on the radio, just a continuous stream of martial music until midday, when the state broadcaster shared the declaration of a new entity called the Revolutionary Council, which announced that it had arrested Ben Bella for the crimes of despotism and high treason, and that it was assuming responsibility for safeguarding the Algerian Revolution.[273] Through some combination of intimidation, confusion, and apathy, the initial public response was muted. Journalists on the scene noted that the cafes downtown filled up with agitated, murmuring customers, but there was little sign of open defiance. In the afternoon, prompt volleys of gunfire sufficed to dissuade a group of university students from the day's only notable attempt at a protest. In short, as was typical of his cautious nature, when Boumedienne finally made his move against the president, he did so with a decisiveness that gave the coup the air of a fait accompli before most people understood what was happening. His relieved coconspirator, Bouteflika, even bragged to the French ambassador the following day that he and the other main orchestrators would have simply executed Ben Bella if they had anticipated just how indifferent the public would be to their president's fate.[274] In reality, they probably spared Ben Bella's life because they feared outrage abroad, for they had deposed one of the Third World's most recognized and popular leaders on the eve of the event that ought to have elevated him to true global prominence. In so doing, the Algerians cast the prospects for the Afro-Asian conference—and those of the entire Third World project—into uncertainty.

Conclusion

and I, Shabine, saw
when these slums of empire was paradise.
        Derek Walcott, "The Schooner *Flight*," 1979

There is such a schism, a gap, between what we thought we could and would accomplish, and what we have, in fact, accomplished.
        Lakhdar Brahimi, 2007

June 1965 was a turning point in the histories of both Algeria and the Third World. Following the coup in Algiers, the leading Afro-Asian governments initially agreed to postpone Bandung 2 until November, but their continued disagreements eventually led to the conference's indefinite postponement, effectively its cancellation. Thus, ten years after the original Bandung Conference had made such a vital contribution to the FLN's survival and eventual victory, Algiers became the place where "Afro-Asianism" died as a relevant organizing theme in international affairs. That said, neither the Algerian nationalist project nor the wider Third World internationalist project died with it. On the contrary, their fates still intertwined, both enterprises went on to enjoy what many observers considered to be their respective golden ages in the early 1970s. With surging oil and gas revenues granting Algerian socialism an impressive luster, President Boumedienne presided over the September 1973 summit of an enlarged, more confident, and more powerful Non-Aligned Movement that championed the notion of a New International Economic Order (NIEO), a revolutionary plan to reshape the global economy for the benefit of poor countries. It was in this latter period that the Polish journalist Ryszard Kapuściński memorably hailed Algeria as "the pivotal Third World state . . . [a] haven for the struggling and oppressed of the world . . . [and an] example for the non-European continents, a model, bright and entrancing."[1] Yet, even if Algeria's and the Third World's best days were still to come, something was lost in June 1965. The coup and Bandung 2's collapse confirmed the end of decolonization's most idealistic and optimistic phase. Out of the diversity of political imaginings and spirit of limitless possibility that had brightened the twilight of empire, a surprisingly homogeneous, constrictive, and even conservative postcolonial order had emerged.

In that respect, the Algerian coup demonstrated the primordial power of diplomacy in shaping the process of decolonization and its structural outcomes. Because traditional, formalized interstate relations had become the most important source of political legitimacy to the Third World's new elites, outweighing even the influence of their own populations, the Afro-Asian conference was the proximate cause of the coup. Bouteflika admitted afterward that the plotters were determined to preempt Ben Bella's attempt to use the conference to empower himself against them—and then to proceed with the conference themselves in order to acquire the Third World's imprimatur for their takeover. Unfortunately, he said, they had misjudged the ideal moment and given their opponents enough time to prevent the meeting from taking place, although given that several dignitaries had already arrived in Algiers and many more were en route, it is hard to see how Bouteflika and his accomplices could have delayed much longer.[2] Their action on 19 June obliged an inbound flight of Chinese diplomats to turn around and return to Cairo, where they engaged in intense discussions with representatives of the Egyptian, Pakistani, and Indonesian governments about whether the conference should go ahead. The foreign ministers of twenty-five countries gathered in Algiers on 23 June to determine the conference's fate.[3] Many of Algeria's allies in the radical wing of Third World politics, including Egypt, feared that they were witnessing a right-wing military putsch and a realignment with Western interests, so they were eager not to bestow the Afro-Asian movement's imprimatur on the usurpers. Fidel Castro and Ahmed Sékou Touré, for example, both openly denounced the coup and declared their opposition to Boumedienne's Revolutionary Council hosting the summit.[4] Others, such as the Indian and Nigerian governments, were understandably wary that the situation in Algiers was unpredictable and liable to tarnish the conference's image; after all, it would be hard to deliver high-minded rhetoric with any credibility while, beyond the walls of the Club des Pins complex, agents of the new regime continued to quell protests and round up its enemies.[5] Therefore, the detonation of a bomb inside the conference venue on 25 June settled the matter—all agreed that the meeting should be postponed until later in the year.

Although the bomb's origins are uncertain and subject to numerous competing rumors, the choice of target was telling. Most likely, Ben Bella loyalists placed it in order to deny Boumedienne and his associates the legitimacy that would come from hosting Bandung 2. While there is speculation that the Egyptian intelligence services could also have been involved, individuals with some familiarity with the events believe that the amateurish design of the device makes this unlikely.[6] An alternative theory posits that the new Algerian authorities planted the bomb themselves because they feared that Ben Bella's many friends abroad could turn the conference against them, denouncing the Revolutionary Council from the podium.[7] Whichever interpretation is closer to the truth, it is clear that both the regime and its enemies attached great importance to the approval of the Third World community.

Moreover, it was most likely a concern for international opinion that spared Ben Bella's life—a decision that, in turn, eased the new regime's acceptance by the Third World. Nasser immediately dispatched Marshal Amer to Algiers to request that the deposed leader be allowed to live in exile in Egypt, though Boumedienne and Bouteflika professed to being insulted by the very idea.[8] Guinea and Mali recalled their ambassadors from Algiers and coordinated with Ghana, Congo-Brazzaville, and Tanzania to demand an investigation into Ben Bella's fate and to prevent Algiers from hosting the Afro-Asian conference in November as well.[9] Moreover, concern for his life transcended Africa's ideological divisions. On the one hand, Yugoslavia officials noted, "Africa has a deep aversion to the political and physical liquidation of heads of state," while on the other, there was widespread appreciation for Ben Bella's status as a nationalist and anticolonial figurehead.[10] On 4 July, Haile Selassie assured the continent that Boumedienne had confirmed that Ben Bella was still alive.[11] In Nigeria, a country whose leaders were very opposed to Algeria's radical policies, there was nevertheless widespread agreement that, despite his flaws, Ben Bella was a nationalist hero and a leader of his people whose life must be spared.[12]

In other words, while there was certainly a great deal of genuine concern for the fallen Algerian president, postcolonial elites also feared the wider ramifications if such a celebrated member of their order were publicly humiliated or eliminated. The Algerian situation was a setback for the radical wing of Third World politics, but it also suggested that no country's leaders could be certain of their position. "We hope that Ben Bella is treated with dignity, not dragged through the mud," one Egyptian diplomat opined, "because throughout recent times, he has been seen as an Arab Leader, not just an Algerian one. . . . [T]he change that has occurred does not only affect Algerians."[13] Castro concurred. "The events in Algeria affect us all," he warned. The coup's instigators "have harmed the revolutionary movement in Africa and in all the world, and the unfortunate introduction of a military coup d'état has caused distrust in other parts of Africa."[14] Fearing that Algiers had now become, in effect, a Mecca of counterrevolution, some of its closest allies began to cut ties between their ruling parties, trade unions, and so on—all in an effort to quarantine a country with a proven ability to export its political ideals.

Ben Bella's fall was, in fact, one of the first manifestations of a systemic convulsion across the Third World. There is evidence to suggest that the Indonesian Community Party leader, Dipa Nusantara Aidit, was at least partly inspired by

Boumedienne's coup when he decided to ally himself with certain factions of the national army in order to take power in Jakarta. He thereby helped precipitate Indonesia's political crisis on 30 September 1965, Suharto's seizure of power, Sukarno's marginalization (and subsequent dismissal), and his own death in the brutal anticommunist purges that claimed hundreds of thousands of lives.[15] Toward the end of the year, Sékou Touré foiled an attempted coup in Guinea, whose orchestrators he accused of trying to imitate "the assassination of Lumumba, [former Togolese President Sylvanus] Olympio and Ben Bella in which they rejoice," and of inciting the army to depose the government "as Ben Bella was deposed."[16] Just two months later, in February 1966, the Ghanaian military took advantage of Kwame Nkrumah's trip to China and North Vietnam to successfully depose him in absentia. Therefore, taking into consideration Nehru's death in 1964, the Third World movement lost many of its key figures in quick succession, some of them to right-wing counterrevolutionary forces. The diminution of Nasser in 1967, following Egypt's disastrous performance in the Six Day War with Israel, further contributed to the sense that an era of militancy was ending and that the radicals were on the defensive. Furthermore, Ben Bella's overthrow was but one of a rash of military seizures of power across Africa: Joseph-Desiré Mobutu (Mobutu Sese Seko) took control in Congo-Léopoldville in November 1965, and the new year brought coups to the Central African Republic, Uganda, Burkina Faso, Nigeria, and Burundi (twice).

All told, the diplomacy of the coup d'état was suddenly a pressing concern for international relations in the Southern Hemisphere. In a March 1966 conversation with the Algerian ambassador, Chen Yi pointed to these recent upheavals and joked that perhaps there might be a coup d'état in China one day that would oblige him to seek asylum in Algiers. When he asked his Algerian guest what he thought of coups himself, the latter replied that it was necessary to refrain from hasty or subjective interpretations; some coups were necessary, he said, legitimate responses to internal problems, as opposed to those that were the consequence of foreign, neo-imperial interference.[17] While insisting that their coup was of the legitimate variety—indeed, with a boldness that many a public relations consultant would surely admire, the Revolutionary Council promptly declared 19 June a national holiday—the new Algerian authorities did not shy away from criticizing other countries' own abrupt political transitions. Ghanaian diplomats were indignant that the Algerians denounced Nkrumah's overthrow as a neocolonial conspiracy. "They've been through it themselves," one of them harrumphed. "You would think they would understand our position better than anyone else."[18] The reality was that, alarming as coups d'état were to postcolonial elites, they were becoming too common to ostracize those government that came to power in that fashion; otherwise, Third Worldist conferences would become increasingly poorly attended events.

Although it would take Algeria some time to convince all its established allies that it was still committed to the same radical anticolonial policies that Ben Bella had personified—visiting Guinea in 1972, for example, Boumedienne was still justifying the coup to Sékou Touré—the new government was quickly accepted by the Third World diplomatic community.[19] Algeria did not participate in the Tricontinental Conference that the Cuban government organized in January 1966, with the goal of connecting Latin America to the Afro-Asian scene, but that was the only noteworthy exclusion. The final cancellation of the delayed Bandung 2, in November 1965, was primarily the result of tensions between China, India, and the Soviet Union, rather than widespread objections to the Algerian hosts. Moreover, Algeria participated in the OAU summit in Accra that October, despite the disquiet of Sékou Touré and Modibo Keita, who saw the situation as similar to the radical countries' efforts to exclude Tshombe from the previous year's summit.[20] The next OAU summit, in November 1966, then recommended that all member states accept the Algerian government's invitation to a conference on trade and development, under the aegis of the G77 movement, which took place in Algiers in October 1967.[21] That meeting proved to be a major step toward effectively mobilizing the majority of developing countries behind a single economic agenda, encapsulated in the so-called Algiers Charter. With more than seventy states participating, the G77 meeting also confirmed not only that Algeria was a still a member in good standing of the Third World project but that the Maghribi country had already regained the pivotal role that it had seemed to squander in June 1965.[22]

In this fashion the Third World order imposed itself, with sovereignty and national authority valued above all other considerations. Its conferences increasingly resembled assemblies of despots who loudly insisted on the principle of noninterference in one another's internal affairs. At the third NAM summit, which took place in Lusaka, Zambia, in September 1970, the participants declared that they "attached special importance" to the rights of "peoples," in the plural, to independence and self-determination, as well as to "the right of all States to equality and active participation in international affairs; the right of all sovereign nations to determine, in full freedom, the paths of their internal political, economic, social, and cultural development."[23] At the same time, the reinforcement of state sovereignty and state authority was the starting point for all policy decisions, whether foreign or domestic, political or economic. "Friends, we must create this State," Bouteflika told Algeria's senior diplomatic personnel. The future belonged to the state, he said, not to high-minded rhetoric. "Yesterday the revolution and its authority guided us, today the principles of a State must enlighten us and guide us in our task."[24] In other words, the state had become not only the sole legitimate manifestation of national liberation or "freedom" but also the irreplaceable instrument of humanity's aspirations, for the wretched of the earth at least.

In other words, Third World internationalism was no longer the subversive phenomenon it had been in the late-colonial period, when anticolonial activists used transnational manifestations of "civil society," such as student groups, labor unions, and religious organizations, to evade and undermine state authority. Like others throughout Africa and Asia in that era, Algerians had celebrated opportunities to escape the prison of colonialism through travel and interactions with the outside world, and the FLN's militants continued to show the same exultation as they traversed the world in search of support, even of the purely symbolic kind such as they found at the Bandung Conference.[25] The influential Algerian intellectual Malek Bennabi (who was not a member of the FLN) enthused after the first Afro-Asian conference that they were witnessing the beginning of "an entirely new era in the evolution of international sociology and civilization . . . a real transfiguration of international relations by the slow, but progressive passage from a 'closed' society of states to an 'open' international society."[26] His exuberance epitomized the feeling of liberation and possibility, of a world opening up, that came with the demise of the colonial police state. Celebrating the diversity of thought represented at Bandung, he spent the next decade trying to formulate a collective philosophy for independent Algeria that reconciled Islam, Marxism, and French republicanism.

But Bennabi's prediction of an open society proved false, since Algeria and most other newly independent countries instead created a society of states that was possibly even more "closed" than the colonial system it replaced. With a mind to preventing exactly the sort of transnational connections that had undermined the colonial order, postcolonial states sought to mediate and manage all interactions between the domestic space and the outside world. In that sense, the profusion of Third Worldist–themed events such as Afro-Asian writers' conferences and Pan-African music festivals reflected a desire to filter every kind of cross-border contact through official international channels, whereas transnational activities that the authorities did not supervise were treated as inherently suspicious. For example, one of the ways that the post-coup Algerian regime tried to win Sékou Touré's favor was to block a conference of North African and West African Islamic leaders, since the Guinean leader shared Algiers's wariness toward regional religious networks "inspired by retrograde forces."[27] By that time, Bennabi himself had grown frustrated with the constrictions of the new reality and became a prominent exponent of Islamic critiques of the predominantly nationalist and socialist rationales for the postcolonial state.

Responding to such criticisms, Algeria was one of several countries that grew increasingly wary of the communist bloc's and the Western bloc's competing efforts to create an "international society" through organizations that brought together trade unions, journalists, youths, and others. By the late 1960s, many Third World regimes were heavily stressing the theme of indigenous authenticity. In much of sub-Saharan Africa, propaganda campaigns oriented around Africanness were accompanied by violence and expropriation against Chinese, Indian, and other minority communities, while religion became a prominent dimension of anticolonial nationalism in places as diverse as Libya, Iran, India, and Israel.[28] However, the discourse of difference and national individuality did not impede the continued expansion of Third Worldist cooperation in the international sphere, which had retained its resolutely programmatic character since the demise of the Afro-Asian movement in 1965.

The national liberation movement phenomenon would seem to contradict this model of a nation-state-centric Third World order, but that is not the case. First, the staunchly anticolonial countries that most actively assisted such movements argued persuasively that the rules of sovereignty simply did not apply to the Portuguese colonies, apartheid South Africa, Rhodesia, or (for some) Israel, largely winning a consensus on this point, at least within the Southern Hemisphere. On the other hand, supporting subversive movements in countries that were already independent, as many radical African states did in the cases of Congo-Léopoldville and Zanzibar, was a more ambiguous and certainly more contentious policy. However, it was, more or less, accepted practice to support movements that aspired to national rule, but a serious contravention of the Third World's norms to support movements with separatist or nonnationalist aims because they rejected the sanctity of postcolonial borders. For this reason, Africa's political boundaries proved stable throughout the second half of the twentieth century, in spite of their seemingly fragile and arbitrary nature, even as the continent became synonymous with proxy wars, violent political transitions, and insurgencies. By and large, the Third World's rebels crossed borders without seeking to redraw them. Finally, there were always tensions between the liberation and revolutionary movements, which were inherently transnational in the operational sense, and the Southern Hemisphere's weak sovereign states, even when the latter were supportive of the former. The Algerian FLN had bristled at India's preference for excluding groups such as theirs from conferences of sovereign states, and the more radical countries made a point of blurring the distinctions between the sovereign and nonstate realms, for approved movements. In the same vein, by late 1965, many African liberation movements were complaining about what they saw as the conservative states' efforts to constrain their activities through the OAU Liberation Committee's heavy-handed oversight.[29] It was always a challenge for such movements to avoid simply degenerating into a tool of another country's foreign policy.

The nature of decolonization and that of the postcolonial order complicate the common narrative that state sovereignty weakened in the post–World War II era. While there is merit to this narrative in the northern, rich world context—though perhaps only so far as Western Europe is concerned—it does not hold true for the majority of the world's population that lived in the developing South. Certainly the processes of globalization and the proliferation of nongovernmental organizations, international organizations, and multinational corporations were real phenomena everywhere. Even when the neoliberal assault on Third World sovereignty in the final decades of the twentieth century is considered, the net outcome was a significant increase in state power and state authority in Africa, the Middle East, and Asia.

In that respect, the Third World's revolutionaries proved to be as conservative in their conception of international relations and political legitimacy as they typically were in their social and cultural policies. This conservatism derived, in turn, from an obsession with order and organization. The Algerian FLN exemplified a pattern by which anticolonial activists identified the supposedly "disordered" or underorganized nature of their societies as the fundamental source of their weakness and subjugation. Their liberation struggle was, therefore, not so much a war to expel a foreign invader as it was akin to a nation- and state-building process that would render the French presence anachronistic and unsustainable. As was true elsewhere, even in countries that achieved sovereignty in peaceful fashion, this nation-state building process continued after independence.

The Third World and perhaps the twentieth-century world as a whole were less the product of ideologies than of methodologies. Strikingly consistent methods of political mobilization and social organization shaped the Southern Hemisphere's hierarchies and rationales of power. This uniformity of praxis therefore accounts for the relative homogeneity of the postcolonial world's political structures, in comparison to its diversity of cultural, social, and historical contexts. The late-colonial order had also been much more heterogeneous, where reassuring swaths of British pink and French blue actually concealed a variety of improvised and muddled systems of control. As one of the key thinkers in the Algerian foreign ministry, Abdelmalek Benhabylès, noted in 1965:

> The presidential regime is spreading even among the member states of the [British] Commonwealth. The single party is replacing dual-party or multiparty [systems], in practice if not in law. . . . [T]he idea of the single party is linked to that of a socialist ideology. . . . Everyone has declared themselves socialist: Nyerere and Léopold Senghor, Hassan II and Massemba Débat. Even his Imperial Majesty Haile Selassie.[30]

While Benhabylès was discussing Africa specifically, this pattern was also generally true of Asia and the Middle East.

In the twenty-first century, the close relationship between Third World internationalism and the legitimacy of postcolonial national elites is still evident. In March 2011, with the major Western powers resorting to military intervention to ensure the success of Muammar Qaddafi's internal opposition, Ugandan president Yoweri Museveni came to defense of his Libyan counterpart. "Qaddafi, whatever his faults," he argued, "is a true nationalist" who had "built Libya." Even his criticisms of Qaddafi hit on the same theme, citing "his involvement with cultural leaders of black Africa — kings, chiefs, etc. . . . Qaddafi, incredibly, thought that he could bypass [the political leaders of Africa] and work with these kings to implement his wishes."[31] The African Union, successor to the OAU, proposed a ceasefire that would leave Qaddafi in power. The Algerian government, whose president was a septuagenarian Abdelaziz Bouteflika, sheltered some surviving members of Qaddafi's family. Whatever its veracity, the Western governments' justification for their intervention—preventing the slaughter and oppression of a regional minority—was precisely the type of action that postcolonial leaders had openly feared in the early 1960s, when Ben Bella treated Kabylia as a potential Katanga.[32]

The Algerian experience also shows that, even as the Cold War shaped decolonization and the postcolonial order, decolonization also changed the nature of the Cold War. Most obviously, while the European and Northeast Asian regions where the Cold War began became frozen in geopolitical terms, with unprecedented military power accumulating, unused, across static front lines, places like Congo and Vietnam became the zones of direct conflict. As the focus of the Soviet-American rivalry shifted from the world's most important industrial regions to places that were, relatively speaking, economically and strategically irrelevant, the Cold War therefore became a more unambiguously ideological affair (with the atypically nonideological nature of the Cold War in the oil-rich Middle East being the exception that proves this rule). At the same time, the Cold War became more multipolar. After all, middle-ranked powers France and China could compete quite effectively against the superpowers in the realms of ideas and economics, given the poverty and weakness of most Third World countries. Thus, although the Sino-Soviet split did not originate in the Third World, these nations' rivalry intensified through competition for influence in Africa and Asia. It is notable that the animosity between those two neighboring countries came closest to escalating into a full-blown military conflict only after their rivalry in the Third World had declined in importance, in the late 1960s. The suspicion is that the Cold War remained "cold" for nearly half a century—at least so far as the northern industrialized countries were concerned—precisely because the Southern Hemisphere provided a comfortably distant arena in which they could express their animosity.

However, if the overwhelming majority of the Cold War's victims lived in the Third World, their leaders were wholly complicit in the expansion and replication of the great powers' rivalries within their own societies and regions. Indeed, contrary to the pacifistic public rhetoric of nonalignment and the original Bandung Conference, the leaders of countries like Algeria feared the abatement of great power tensions. After all, history had taught non-Western peoples that the major Western powers frequently brokered peace by agreeing to divide up Africa, Asia, and Latin America between them. Therefore, in the postcolonial context, the Algerians and their Third World allies dreaded that detente would entail a "spheres of influence" agreement, in the fashion of the 1945 Yalta Conference, that would take away small countries' room to maneuver and their ability to induce the Soviet Union and the United States to compete for influence by offering aid or supporting anticolonial causes. On more than one occasion, Ben Bella expressed concern that the "hotline" installed between the White House and the Kremlin after the Cuban Missile Crisis augured a new era of Soviet-American consultation—to the detriment of the Third World. "For us the bullets that are striking our Angolan and South African brothers are no less murderous today when relations between the great powers seem to be improving," Algeria's first president averred.[33]

In that light, the global history of the 1970s and 1980s is ripe for reinterpretation. It is worth considering, for example, whether the Third World movement's apex in the early 1970s was not so much enabled by superpower detente and a sense of economic crisis in the West, but was instead a reaction against detente and what looked like the communist countries' gradual integration into the Western economic sphere. That is, elites in many developing countries feared that the economic dimensions of detente, which saw the Eastern bloc intensify trade and borrow money from the West, represented the final stage in the construction of a wall of treaties (including GATT and the EEC) that would permanently exclude the Southern Hemisphere from the prosperity enjoyed in the North. In his opening address to the Algiers summit of nonaligned leaders, in September 1973, Boumedienne described detente as a superpower "pretension to reign over the world," while the participant's final declaration complained that detente "has only had limited effects on international co-operation in favor of development" and that the developed countries were "consolidating their economic groupings ... neglecting the major interests of developing countries."[34] Thus, while the NIEO project was an explicit attempt to reconfigure the global economy, theoretically benefiting poor countries, the likes of Algeria also saw the economic warfare of OPEC as a means to reignite a sense of competition and rivalry among the industrialized powers, within the blocs as much as between them. After a decade of attempting to do so, Algiers finally induced the United States to compete openly with France for a stake in Algeria's oil and gas sector.

Meanwhile, in the realm of geopolitics, revolutionary movements in places like Angola, Ethiopia, and Afghanistan compensated for detente by convincing Soviet policymakers that they were proper Marxist-Leninists, thereby creating the conditions for some of the Cold War's costliest and most tragic crises. In short, there are grounds to argue that Third World actors successfully undermined detente and reintensified the Cold War for their own purposes.

That said, the consequences were disastrous for many developing countries. Like many other countries, Algeria's efforts to nationalize its natural resources and jump-start industrialization had necessitated massive investments made possible by heavy borrowing in Western capital markets.[35] Debt rendered these countries vulnerable to the "counterrevolution" in development economics that began in the late 1970s and really gathered pace in the 1980s, when neoliberal economists championing the inviolability of free markets took control of the IMF and the World Bank, in order to wage war on the NIEO, commodities cartels, and Third World socialism.[36] Officials from those two institutions demanded "structural adjustments" as a condition of new loans, obliging scores of poor countries to drastically pare back the state's involvement in the economy as well as social expenditures such as on health care and education.[37] Tanzania's Julius Nyerere, a long-standing ally of Algeria's revolutionary nationalists, decried a Western conspiracy. "When did the IMF become an international Ministry of Finance? When did nations agree to surrender to it their powers of decision making?" he asked. "[The IMF] has an ideology of economic and social development which it is trying to impose on poor countries irrespective of our own clearly stated policies."[38] In 1992, Angolan novelist and former MPLA militant Artur Carlos Maurício Pestana dos Santos captured the post–Cold War mood in (The generation of utopia). This semifictional chronicle followed a group of young revolutionaries from the enthusiasm and danger of 1960s and 1970s through to a dispiriting decade of postcolonial corruption, complacency, and rampant globalization—the "most savage capitalism seen on Earth"—that the author believed threatened the very fabric of the Angolan nation.[39]

At independence, as Algeria's leaders faced the twentieth century's defining dilemma of material and social progress, they opened the doors of their institutions of state to like-minded foreigners who leaped at the opportunity to put their ideas into practice. Fellow travelers like Michel Raptis played a pivotal role in elaborating and implementing *autogestion*, which other foreigners cheered loudest. "In France in June 1935, we were at the threshold of self-management. We had only to take one more step. We did not dare," wrote the French anarchist, Daniel Guérin. "[But] here, in Algeria, the threshold has been crossed. . . . Self-management will survive . . . because it has one advantage: it follows the course of history."[40] Yet, the Cold War did not allow much leeway for such experimentation, and Ben Bella and his colleagues struggled to develop their "own special brand of socialism" in an environment that saddled economic policies with burdensome diplomatic ramifications. Eventually, these pressures and continued disappointments stoked resentment between locals and outsiders. But if economic matters produced the clearest failure of Algerian internationalism, autogestion struck a chord with all those people around the world who desperately wanted to believe in the possibility of a viable Marxism untainted by Stalinism. The fact that Boumedienne threw out most of the pieds rouges after his coup allowed for the myth of a corrupted revolution to flourish (which suits the Trotskyite character) and inspired a substantial literature of disillusionment to supplement their colonial predecessors' nostalgic reminiscences.[41]

Given autogestion's failure, the collapse of the Afro-Asian movement, and the practical limitations of nonalignment that the Algerians encountered even before the end of the Cold War, it might be tempting to look at revolutionary Algeria as a fleeting space for utopianism, to be admired as George Orwell admired Republican Catalonia perhaps, but recognizing that its sudden demise likely averted inevitable disappointment and disillusionment. However, this period's legacies were substantial for international politics as well as for Algeria. First, there were the thousands of would-be revolutionaries who followed the Algerian example. Some, like Yasir Arafat's Fateh, aspired to directly repeat the FLN's precedent (although apparently missing the Algerians' and Mao's central instruction never to cease the armed struggle before victory is achieved). Many more passed through the ANP's camps, making connections and accepting the Third Worldist message to varying degrees, as their Algerian instructors learned from the Chinese and Vietnamese before them. In addition to this ideological impact, over time the groups that most impressed the Algerians with their revolutionary heart (such as MPLA or the Zimbabwe African National Union) tended to prevail over their less-favored rivals, suggesting that Algeria's intermediary role between these movements and great power benefactors could be decisive in picking winners and losers.

Algerian diplomacy also exemplified how the nebulous aspirations and internationalism of "the Global South" could be translated into a practicable foreign policy. In fact, an updated version of the Algerian strategy shows signs of thriving in the early twenty-first century, with the likes of China, Brazil, India, and Iran often cooperating to exert some say on matters of global trade and the management of international society. Crucially, although the Cold War has vanished as a useful source of leverage, these countries are proving more successful than the Algerians could be in convincing the West that the dichotomy between North and South is the defining characteristic of world affairs. When queried on his country's support for Iran's nuclear program in late 2009, for example, the Brazilian foreign minister accounted for the difference between Washington's and Brasilia's perspectives on global affairs with the simple observation that "we are in different latitudes."[42]

Nevertheless, another notable implication of the Algerian story is what it suggests about the nature of revolutionary movements in general, namely, that revolutionary practices can precede revolutionary ideologies, and that revolution can be disseminated as a skill rather than as an idea. Thousands of FLN militants and even larger numbers of youths in Algiers's slums joined the revolution because it told them what to do, not what to think, and "revolutionaries" from different Third World countries typically recognized one other by a shared manner and lifestyle, much less so through debate or sloganeering. As the established order ceased to make sense in the twilight of empire, revolution's vague call placed an appealing emphasis on the how and the what instead of the why—and the FLN's founders explicitly decided not to wait to figure out the last part before setting their struggle in motion. These facts suggest that the internationalist Islamist movement today is not so different from the preceding Marxist-nationalist hybrids it so frequently abhors, and that those denouncing the "deluded" or "nihilistic" tenets of the Islamist worldview should instead focus on the appeal of rigid instructions on how to dress and how to behave, and what its members should be doing *right now* to effect change. Strategic adjustments can lead to new objectives in addition to resulting from them, since the Algerian precedent also indicates that ideologies and ideas can make surprising jumps into quite alien contexts as different revolutionary movements imitate one another's techniques.

Finally, the consequences of the FLN's radicalization for Algeria itself were profound. Within just a few years Boumedienne was beginning to replicate all of his predecessor's policies.[43] Having denounced Ben Bella's "cult of personality" and thirst for personal power, Boumedienne began eliminating his opponents and accepting a more overt leadership role for himself. After capitalizing on local resentment of the cosmopolitan leftist atmosphere that reigned in Ben Bellist Algeria, he moved to ban the Islamist movement, Al-Qiyam, and to reestablish the FLN's relationship with the Communist Party of the Soviet Union. Most striking of all, having accused Ben Bella of neglecting Algeria's domestic concerns in the pursuit of international acclaim, in 1967 the famously reclusive Boumedienne suddenly seized the limelight, profiting from Nasser's humiliating defeat by Israel to declare that Algeria alone would stand by the Palestinians. This dramatic change of course—or resumption of the original course—was a consequence of the inescapable logic of revolution, for in reality Ben Bella and Boumedienne were both products of the FLN's original prioritization of action over reflection, and the ideological insecurity that came from putting practice before theory. In the end, the Algerian nationalist project had become so intertwined with the ideology of Third Worldism that the country's new leaders perhaps secretly feared that without the revolution, there *was* no nation.

NOTES

Introduction

1. "Not Alone Ben Bella," 1966, quoted from the website of the Cheddi Jagan Research Center. www.jagan.org/JanetJagan/JJPoems&Stories/jj_stories_poems.html.
2. For example, see the 2008 interview with Lakhdar Brahimi in Clement Moore Henry, *L'UGEMA: Union Générale des Etudiants Musulmans Algériens (1955–62), Témoignages* (Algiers: Casbah Editions, 2010), 244–247.
3. Stéphane Hessel, *Danse avec le siècle* (Paris: Seuil, 1997), 172–173.
4. Chefik Mesbah, "Entretien avec Lakhdar Brahimi (part 1)," *Le Soir d'Algérie*, 30 June 2007; Chefik Mesbah, "Entretien avec Lakhdar Brahimi (part 2)," *Le Soir d'Algérie*, 1 July 2007.
5. M'hamed Yazid, "De Bandoung à Alger," *Démocratie Nouvelle*, June 1965.
6. Frederick Cooper, "Possibility and Constraint: African Independence in Historical Perspective," *Journal of African History* 49, no. 2 (July 2008): 167–196.
7. Allan Christelow, *Algerians without Borders: The Making of a Global Frontier Society* (Gainesville: University Press of Florida, 2012), 3–4.
8. "Alger: Carrefour du Tiers-Monde," *Révolution Africaine*, 12 June 1965.
9. Frantz Fanon, *Toward the African Revolution: Political Essays* (New York: Grove Press, 1988), 180–181; Arafat quoted in Paul Thomas Chamberlin, *The Global Offensive: The United States, the Palestine Liberation Organization, and the Making of the Post–Cold War Order* (New York: Oxford University Press, 2012), 52; Jean de Broglie quoted in Charles-Robert Ageron, "La cooperation avec l'Algérie indépendante," in *De Gaulle et son siècle* (Paris: La Documentation Française, 1992), 6:216.
10. The Algerian archives contain many duplicates of the passports issued to guerrilla fighters from southern Africa and elsewhere; for example, see boxes 3830 and 3397, Archives nationale d'Algérie (ANA), postindependence FLN party archives (FLN), for material relating to Angola in the late 1960s and 1970s.
11. Martin Lewis and Karen Wigen, *The Myth of Continents: A Critique of Metageography* (Berkeley: University of California Press, 1997).
12. Some of the more successful synthetic studies of Third Worldism include Vijay Prashad, *The Poorer Nations: A Possible History of the Global South* (London: Verso, 2012); Robert A. Mortimer, *The Third World Coalition in International Politics* (Boulder, CO: Westview Press, 1984); Mark Atwood Lawrence, "The Rise and Fall of Nonalignment," in *The Cold War in the Third World: Reinterpreting History*, ed. Robert J. McMahon, 139–155 (New York: Oxford University Press, 2013).
13. Forrest D. Colburn, *The Vogue of Revolution in Poor Countries* (Princeton, NJ: Princeton University Press, 1994).
14. "President Sukarno of Indonesia: Speech at the Opening of the Bandung Conference, April 18, 1955," http://www.fordham.edu/halsall/mod/1955sukarno-bandong.html.

15. A useful collection of essays on Bandung's legacy can be found in Christopher J. Lee, *Making a World after Empire: The Bandung Moment and Its Political Afterlives* (Athens: Ohio University Press, 2010). See also Richard Wright, *The Color Curtain: A Report on the Bandung Conference* (Cleveland, OH: World Publishing, 1956). Also useful are George Kahin, *The Asian-African Conference: Bandung, Indonesia, April 1955* (Ithaca, NY: Cornell University Press, 1956); and Christopher J. Lee, "Conference Report: 'Bandung and Beyond: Rethinking Afro-Asian Connections during the Twentieth Century,'" *African Affairs* 104, no. 417 (2005): 683–684.
16. Vijay Prashad, *The Darker Nations: A People's History of the Third World* (New York: New Press, 2007); Odd Arne Wested, "Epilogue: The Cold War and the Third World," in *The Cold War in the Third World: Reinterpreting History* (New York: Oxford University Press, 2013), 208–219.
17. Claude Liauzu, *Aux origines des tier-monidsmes: Colonisés et anticolonialistes en France (1919–1939)* (Paris: L'Harmattan, 1982).
18. For example, see Jason Parker, "Cold War II: The Eisenhower Administration, the Bandung Conference, and the Reperiodization of the Postwar Era," *Diplomatic History* 30, no. 5 (2006): 873–874; Matthew Jones, "A 'Segregated' Asia? Race, the Bandung Conference, and Pan-Asianist Fears in American Thought and Policy, 1954–1955," *Diplomatic History* 29, no. 5 (2005): 841–868; Salim Yaqub, *Containing Arab Nationalism: The Eisenhower Doctrine and the Middle East* (Chapel Hill: University of North Carolina Press, 2004); Nigel John Ashton, *Eisenhower, Macmillan and the Problem of Nasser: Anglo-American Relations and Arab Nationalism, 1955-59* (London: Palgrave Macmillan, 1996).
19. Quoted in Stewart M. Patrick, "The Nonaligned Movement's Crisis," *The Internationalist* blog, 30 August 2012, website of the Council on Foreign Relations, http://blogs.cfr.org/patrick/2012/08/30/the-non-aligned-movements-crisis.
20. For astute dissections of some of the geopolitical agendas behind the bombast of Bandung, particularly concerning China, see Pang Yang Huei, "The Four Faces of Bandung: Detainees, Soldiers, Revolutionaries and Statesmen," *Journal of Contemporary Asia*, 39, no. 1 (2009): 63–86; Chen Jian, "Bridging Revolution and Decolonization: The 'Bandung Discourse' in China's Early Cold War Experience," *Chinese Historical Review* 15, no. 2 (2008): 207–241; Shu Guang Zhang, "Constructing 'Peaceful Coexistence': China's Diplomacy toward the Geneva and Bandung Conferences, 1954–55," *Cold War History* 7, no. 4 (2007): 509–528.
21. Robert Vitalis, "The Midnight Ride of Kwame Nkrumah and Other Fables of Bandung (Ban-Doong)," *Humanity: An International Journal of Human Rights, Humanitarianism, and Development* 4, no. 2 (2013): 261–288.
22. Recent studies that take advantage of innovative research on the Third World include Pierre Asselin, *Hanoi's Road to the Vietnam War, 1954–1965* (Berkeley: University of California Press, 2013); Lien-Hang T. Nguyen, *Hanoi's War: An International History of the War for Peace in Vietnam* (Chapel Hill: University of North Carolina Press, 2012); Chamberlin, *Global Offensive*; Andy DeRoche, "Non-alignment on the Racial Frontier: Zambia and the USA, 1964–68," *Cold War History* 7, no. 2 (2007): 227–250, doi:10.1080/14682740701284132; Kyle Haddad-Fonda, "An Illusory Alliance: Revolutionary Legitimacy and Sino-Algerian Relations, 1958-1962," *Journal of North African Studies* 19, no. 3 (2014): 338–357, doi:10.1080/13629387.2013.870039; Jeremy Scott Friedman, "Reviving Revolution: The Sino-Soviet Split, the 'Third World,' and the Fate of the Left" (PhD diss., Princeton University, 2011).
23. On the problems of postcolonial archives, see the June 2015 *American Historical Review* roundtable, "The Archives of Decolonization," in particular Todd Shepard, "'Of Sovereignty': Disputed Archives, "Wholly Modern" Archives, and the Post-Decolonization French and Algerian Republics, 1962–2012," *American Historical Review* 120, no. 3 (2015): 869–883; Omnia El Shakry, "'History without Documents': The Vexed Archives of Decolonization in the Middle East," *American Historical Review* 120, no. 3 (2015): 920–934. On the challenges of postcolonial Algerian history, see Malika Rahal, "Comment faire l'histoire de l'Algérie indépendante?," *La Vie des Idées*, 13 March 2012, http://www.laviedesidees.fr/Comment-faire-l-histoire-de-l-Algerie-independante.html.
24. On "decentering" or contextualizing the Cold War, see Tony Smith, "New Bottles for New Wine: A Pericentric Framework for the Study of the Cold War," *Diplomatic History* 24,

no. 4 (2000): 567–591; Matthew Connelly, "Taking Off the Cold War Lens: Visions of North-South Conflict during the Algerian War for Independence," *American Historical Review* 105, no. 3 (2000): 739–769.
25. Geir Lundestad, "'Empire by Invitation' in the American Century," *Diplomatic History* 23, no. 2 (199): 189–217.
26. Excellent examination of US-European tensions over empire can be found in Thomas C. Martin, "Innocent Abroad? Decolonisation and US Engagement with French West Africa, 1945–56," *Journal of Imperial and Commonwealth History* 36, no. 1 (2008): 47–73; and Thomas C. Martin, "Defending a Lost Cause? France and the United States Vision of Imperial Rule in French North Africa," *Diplomatic History* 26, no. 2 (2002): 215–247; Ryo Ikeda, "The Paradox of Independence: The Maintenance of Influence and the French Decision to Transfer Power in Morocco," *Journal of Imperial and Commonwealth History* 35, no. 4 (2007): 569–592; El-Mostefa Azzou, "La propaganda des nationalistes marocains aux Etats-Unies (1945–1956)," *Guerres Mondiales et Conflits Contemporains* 58, no. 230 (2008): 89–98.
27. On the application of state sovereignty to the decolonizing world, see Bertrand Badie, *The Imported State: The Westernization of the Political Order* (Stanford, CA: Stanford University Press, 2000); Robert H. Jackson, *Quasi-States: Sovereignty, International Relations, and the Third World* (Cambridge: Cambridge University Press, 1990); James C. Scott, *Seeing Like a State: How Certain Schemes to Improve the Human Condition Have Failed* (New Haven, CT: Yale University Press, 1998).
28. For alternative examples of Third World state-building through the application of American practices, see Bradley R. Simpson, *Economists with Guns: Authoritarian Development and U.S.-Indonesian Relations, 1960–1968* (Stanford, CA: Stanford University Press, 2008); and Michael E. Latham, *Modernization as Ideology: American Social Science and "Nation Building" in the Kennedy Era* (Chapel Hill: University of North Carolina Press, 2000). On the Marxist influence, see Donald L. Donham, *Marxist Modern: An Ethnographic History of the Ethiopian Revolution* (Berkeley: University of California Press, 1999); Tony Chafer, "Education and Political Socialisation of a National-Colonial Political Elite in French West Africa, 1936–47," *Journal of Imperial and Commonwealth History* 35, no. 3 (2007): 437–458.
29. On the reception of Western and Soviet ideas and practices, see chapter 6 of Geoffrey Barraclough, *An Introduction to Contemporary History* (New York: Basic Books, 1965); Arno J. Mayer, *Wilson vs. Lenin: Political Origins of the New Diplomacy 1917–1918* (New Haven, CT: Yale University Press, 1959).
30. Matthew James Connelly, *A Diplomatic Revolution: Algeria's Fight for Independence and the Origins of the Post–Cold War Era* (Oxford: Oxford University Press, 2002).
31. Malek Bennabi, "L'afro-asiatisme: Conclusion sur la Conference de Bandoeng," *El Djeich*, March 1965; Malek Bennabi, "Les relation internationales à l'heures des fusées," *El Djeich*, March 1965.

Chapter 1

1. ALN and French operational statistics are based on French records, collected in Guy Pervillé, *Atlas de la guerre d'Algérie: De la conquête à l'indépendance* (Paris: Autrement, 2003), 30, 50, 52.
2. "Directives aux Chefs Responsables concernant l'organisation et la hiérarchie de l'ALN," FLN, Commissariat Politique Zone No. 4 [Wilaya unknown], 16 June 1956, Service Historique de l'Armée de Terre, Château de Vincennes (SHAT), 1H 2582.
3. L'aspirant Arnaud, "Réunion H.L.L. à ATTATLA; source: Un informateur non nommé," 25 January 1957, SHAT, 1H 2582.
4. Lakhdar Ben Tobbal quoted in Mohammed Harbi, *Le F.L.N.: Mirage et réalité* (Paris: Editions Jeune Afrique, 1980), 122; Harbi, *F.L.N.*, 122.
5. Gilbert Meynier, *Histoire intérieure du F.L.N., 1954–1962* (Paris: Fayard, 2002), 166–167.
6. "Notes aux militants du FLN," undated, anonymous, SHAT, 1H 2582.
7. Neil MacMaster, "The Roots of Insurrection: The Role of the Algerian Village Assembly (*Djemâa*) in Peasant Resistance, 1863–1962," *Comparative Studies in Society and History* 52, no. 2 (2010): 419–447.

8. Erez Manela, *The Wilsonian Moment: Self-Determination and the International Origins of Anticolonial Nationalism* (Oxford: Oxford University Press, 2007).
9. Manela, *Wilsonian Moment*, 63–73.
10. Manela, *Wilsonian Moment*, 139.
11. Charles-Robert Ageron, *Histoire de l'Algérie contemporaine* (Paris: Presses Universitaires de France, 1979), 2:234.
12. Gilbert Meynier, *L'Algérie révélée* (Geneva: Librairie Droz, 1981), 716–717; Charles-Robert Ageron, "Vérités sur l'émir Khaled," *Algérie Actualité*, nos. 6–12, March 1980.
13. Mahfoud Kaddache, *Histoire du nationalisme algérien* (Algiers: Enterprise Nationale du Livre, 1993), 1:111–113.
14. For Ageron's original interpretation, see Ageron, *Histoire de l'Algérie contemporaine*, 2:296–297; his re-evaluation is found in Ageron, "Vérités sur l'émir Khaled"; see also Kaddache, *Histoire du nationalism algérien*, 1:182–186.
15. Ageron, *Histoire de l'Algérie contemporaine*, 2:296–299; Kaddache, *Histoire du nationalisme algérien*, 1:73–80; John Ruedy, *Modern Algeria: The Origins and Development of a Nation*, 2nd ed. (Bloomington: Indiana University Press, 2005), 129–131.
16. Ageron, *Histoire de l'Algérie contemporaine*, 2:403–411; Jacques Berque, *Le Maghreb entre deux guerres* (Paris: Seuil, 1979), 225; Jonathan K. Gosnell, *The Politics of Frenchness in Colonial Algeria, 1930-1954* (Rochester, NY: University of Rochester Press, 2002), 29–30.
17. Mahfoud Bennoune, *The Making of Contemporary Algeria, 1830-1987: Colonial Upheavals and Post-independence Development* (Cambridge: Cambridge University Press, 1988), 60–82.
18. For example, syndicalist and leftist intellectual currents were particularly noticeable in the Kabyle Berber population, partly on account of the great number of Kabyles who emigrated to find work in France; see Henri Alleg, *La guerre d'Algérie* (Paris: Temps Actuels, 1981), 1:223.
19. René Gallissot, *Maghreb-Algérie: Classe et nation*, vol. 1, *Du Maghreb précolonial à l'indépendance Nationale* (Paris: Arcantère, 1987), 243–250.
20. Ageron, *Histoire de l'Algérie contemporaine*, 2:516–526; Ruedy, *Modern Algeria*, 114–129; Charles Robert Ageron, and Michael Brett, *Modern Algeria: A History from 1830 to the Present* (Trenton, NJ: Africa World Press, 1991), 82–92.
21. Maurice Viollette, *L'Algérie, vivra-t-elle? Notes d'un ancient gouverneur général* (Paris: F. Alcan, 1931).
22. Ageron, *Histoire de l'Algérie contemporaine*, 2:421.
23. Ruedy, *Modern Algeria*, 135; Ageron and Brett, *Modern Algeria*, 94–95.
24. James McDougall, "The Shabiba Islamiyya of Algiers: Education, Authority, and Colonial Control, 1921–57," *Comparative Studies of South Asia, Africa and the Middle East* 24, no. 1 (2004): 147–154.
25. Allan Christelow, "Bashir Ibrahimi and the Islamic Encounter with European Secular and Religious Faiths," *Maghreb Review* 29, nos. 1–4 (2004): 99–122.
26. Quoted in Hassan Remaoun, "La politique coloniale française et la structuration du projet nationalitaire en Algérie: À propos de l'idéologie du FLN, puis de l'etat national," in *La guerre d'Algérie au miroir des décolonisations françaises: En l'honneur de Charles-Robert Ageron: Actes du colloque international, Paris, Sorbonne (23, 24, 25 Novembre 2000)* (Paris: Société Française d'Histoire d'Outre-Mer, Distique, 2000), 281.
27. Ageron, *Histoire de l'Algérie contemporaine*, 2:332–333.
28. Lacheraf quoted in McDougall, "Shabiba Islamiyya of Algiers," 147–154.
29. Manela, *Wilsonian Moment*, 139.
30. Ho Chi Minh, "The Path Led Me to Leninism," April 1960, in *Ho Chi Minh: Selected Articles and Speeches, 1920-1967*, ed. Jack Woddis (New York: International Publishers, 1969), 156–158.
31. The best overview of interwar anticolonialism is found in Odd Arne Westad, *The Global Cold War: Third World Interventions and the Making of Our Times* (Cambridge: Cambridge University Press, 2005), 73–109.
32. Abderrahim Taled Bendiab, "La pénétration des idées et l'implantation communiste en Algérie dans les années 1920," in *Mouvement ouvrier, communisme et nationalismes dans le monde arabe*, ed. René Gallissot (Paris: Editions Ouvrières, 1978), 127–146.

33. Messali Hadj, *Les mémoires de Messali Hadj, 1898–1938*, ed. Renaud de Rochebrune (Paris: JC Lattès, 1982), 151.
34. "Programme de l'Etoile Nord-Africaine Assemblée générale tenue à Paris, mai 1933," in *Messali Hadj par les textes*, ed. Jacques Simon (Paris: Editions Bouchène, 2000), 22.
35. Michele L. Louro, "Rethinking Nehru's Internationalism: The League against Imperialism and Anti-imperial Networks, 1929–1939," *Third Frame: Literature, Culture, Society* 2, no. 3 (2009): 79–94; Vijay Prashad, *Darker Nations: A People's History of the Third World* (New York: New Press, 2007), 16–30.
36. *El Ouma*, no. 29, January 1935.
37. Benjamin Stora, *Le nationalisme algérien avant 1954* (Paris: CNRS Éditions, 2010), 83–85.
38. "Réponse à M. Deloche de *L'Humanité*," February 1937, in *Messali Hadj par les textes*, ed. Jacques Simon (Paris: Editions Bouchène, 2000), 30–31.
39. Messali Hadj, *Mémoires*, 211.
40. Quoted in Ageron, *Histoire de l'Algérie contemporaine*, 2:353. See also Rabah Aissaoui, "Algerian Nationalists in the French Political Arena and Beyond: The Etoile Nord-Africaine and the Parti du Peuple Algérien in Interwar France," *Journal of North African Studies* 15, no. 1 (March 2010): 1–12.
41. L. Carl Brown, "Islam's Role in North Africa," in *Man, State, and Society in the Contemporary Maghrib*, ed. I. William Zartmann (New York: Praeger, 1973), 31–36.
42. Hocine Ait Ahmed, *Memoires d'un combattant, L'esprit de l'indépendance 1942–1952* (Paris: Sylvie Messinger, 1983), 99–100.
43. Jeff Goodwin, *No Other Way Out: States and Revolutionary Movements, 1945–1991* (Cambridge: Cambridge University Press, 2001).
44. Ageron, *Histoire de l'Algérie contemporaine*, 2:558.
45. Murphy is quoted in a catalog of US expression of support for French territorial integrity in a memorandum to Roosevelt, "United States' Position with Respect to French Territory after the War," 7 January 1944, in *Foreign Relations of the United States (FRUS)*, 1944, vol. 3, pp. 770–772.
46. Murphy reported that "the Atlantic Charter has made a profound impression on them, and for months they have hardly spoken of anything else"; see Ageron, *Histoire de l'Algérie contemporaine*, 2:558.
47. Martin C. Thomas, "Innocent Abroad? Decolonisation and US Engagement with French West Africa, 1945–56," *Journal of Imperial and Commonwealth History*, 36, no. 1 (March 2008): 47–73.
48. Waruhiu Itote, *"Mau Mau" General* (Nairobi: East African Institute Press, 1967), 24–25.
49. Quoted in Alistair Horne, *A Savage War of Peace: Algeria, 1954–1962* (New York: Viking, 1978), 28; Ageron, *Histoire de l'Algérie contemporaine*, 2:559–570.
50. "Notes aux militants du FLN," SHAT, 1H 2582.
51. Ahmed, *Mémoires d'un combatant*, 93–94.
52. From a document found by French soldiers titled "Notes aux militants du FLN," SHAT, 1H 2582. Probably written in 1955 or 1956, in accordance with standard FLN practice no author was attributed.
53. Lakhdar Ben Tobbal quoted in Harbi, *F.L.N.*, 122.
54. "Renseignements Fournis par le SLNA du 1er janvier au 31 Octobre 1954 sur les Menaces de Terrorisme," 19 November 1954, SHAT, 1H 2582.
55. Boudiaf quoted in Meynier, *Histoire intérieure du F.L.N.*, 126.
56. Quoted in Horne, *Savage War of Peace*, 141.
57. Quoted in Robert Malley, *The Call from Algeria: Third Worldism, Revolution, and the Turn to Islam* (Berkeley: University of California Press, 1996), 120.
58. French military estimates from Guy Pervillé, *Atlas de la Guerre d'Algérie: De la conquête à l'indépendance* (Paris: Autrement, 2003), 30, 50–53.
59. Matthew Connelly, *A Diplomatic Revolution: Algeria's Fight for Independence and the Origins of the Post–Cold War Era* (Oxford: Oxford University Press, 2002).
60. "L'organisation est la somme de principes régularisant le travail et la vie des homes," found in Bou Derballa, Wilaya IV, 13 November 1957, SHAT, 1H 2582.

61. Zighout Youcef quoted in Charles Robert Ageron, "L'insurrection du 20 août 1955 dans le Nord-Constantinois," in *La Guerre d'Algérie et les Algériens, 1954–1962*, ed. Charles Robert Ageron (Paris: Armand Colin, 1997), 32.
62. Letter from Khider to the counselor of the Saudi embassy in Cairo, 14 December 1954, ANA, archives of the Ministère aux Affaires Extérieures of the Gouvernement Provisoire de la République Algérienne (GPRA-MAE), dossier 1.
63. I am grateful to Matthew Connelly for providing the pamphlet "What Is Algeria: The Algerian Question in Outline," April 1955, ANA, GPRA-MAE, dossier 2.6, April 1955.
64. The event is recounted by Aït Ahmed in Connelly, *Diplomatic Revolution*, 92–93.
65. Bureau de New York, "Rapport d'activité—Propagande et documentation, Octobre 56–Février 57," 18 February 1957, ANA, GPRA-MAE, dossier 4.4.
66. Connelly, *Diplomatic Revolution*, 96–97.
67. Quoted in Westad, *Global Cold War*, 99.
68. "President Sukarno of Indonesia: Speech at the Opening of the Bandung Conference, April 18, 1955," http://www.fordham.edu/halsall/mod/1955sukarno-bandong.html.
69. The Five Principles of Peaceful Coexistence were formally stated in a treaty between India and China in April 1954: mutual respect for territorial sovereignty, nonaggression, noninterference in one another's domestic affairs, equality, and peaceful coexistence.
70. Quoted in Sulmaan Wasif Khan, "Cold War Cooperation: New Chinese Evidence on Jawaharlal Nehru's 1954 Visit to Beijing," *Cold War History* 11, no. 2 (2011): 197–222. See also Gilles Boquérat, "India's Commitment to Peaceful Coexistence and the Settlement of the Indochina War," *Cold War History* 5, no. 2 (2005): 211–234.
71. Jeremy Scott Friedman, "Reviving Revolution: The Sino-Soviet Split, the 'Third World,' and the Fate of the Left" (PhD diss., Princeton University, 2011), 37.
72. Yves Courrière, *La Guerre d'Algérie: Le temps des léopards* (Paris: Fayard, 1969), 77.
73. "L'action internationale du FLN par M'hamed Yazid," August 1957, in *Les archives de la Révolution Algérienne*, ed. Mohammed Harbi (Paris: Editions Jeune Afrique, 1981), 172–174.
74. The former ALN commander and diplomat Ali Kafi credits Bandung with enhancing the FLN's legitimacy; see his memoirs, *Du militant politique au dirigeant militaire: Mémoires 1946–1962* (Algiers: Casbah Editions, 2002), 69.
75. The expression "international 1 November" is in frequent usage in Algeria, but Lakhdar Brahimi attributes it to Abdelaziz, "été le 1er Novembre international pour la lutte du peuple algérien pour son indépendance"; Chefik Mesbah, "Entretien avec Lakhdar Brahimi (part 1)," *Le Soir d'Algérie*, 30 June 2007.
76. A brief summary of these voyages abroad is located in "Tournées effectuées au cours de la période de novembre 54–novembre 56," ANA, GPRA-MAE, dossier 7.1.
77. Clement M. Henry, *L'UGEMA, Union Générale des Étudiants Musulmans Algériens, 1955–1962: Témoignages* (Algiers: Casbah Editions, 2010), 247; author's interview with Lakhdar Brahimi in Princeton, New Jersey, 29 June 2008, and at the London School of Economics and Political Science, 16 March 2009.
78. *Algeria: Unspoken Stories*, directed by. Jean-Pierre Lledo (2007).
79. Abbas quoted in Horne, *Savage War of Peace*, 141.
80. Meynier, *Histoire intérieure du F.L.N.*, 191.
81. Supreme Commander of Tunisian Zone, orders found by French soldiers in April 1956, SHAT 1H 2582, and "Qu'est-ce le 'Djihad'?," *Résistance Algérienne*, no. 9, 1 October 1956.
82. Dr. Lamine Debaghine, "Essay on the definition of the FLN, on its objectives in war and peace," undated, ANA, GPRA-MAE, dossier 29.1.
83. Meynier, *Histoire intérieure du F.L.N.*, 191–193.
84. "Directives aux Chefs Responsables concernant l'organisation et la hiérarchie de l'ALN," FLN, Commissariat Politique Zone No. 4 [Wilaya unknown], 16 June 1956, SHAT 1H 2582.
85. Ageron and Brett, *Modern Algeria*, 109.
86. Figures from Bendiab, "La pénétration des idées," in Gallissot, *Mouvement ouvrier, communisme et nationalisms*.
87. See Martin S. Alexander and John F. V. Keiger, "France and the Algerian War: Strategy, Operations and Diplomacy," special issue, *Journal of Strategic Studies* 25, no. 2 (2002): 5–6, repr. in the authors' edited collection *France and the Algerian War, 1954–62: Strategy,*

Operations and Diplomacy (London: Frank Cass, 2002), 1–34; Mahfoud Kaddace, "Les tournants de la Guerre de libération au niveau des masses populaires," in *La Guerre d'Algérie et les Algériens 1954–1962*, ed. Charles-Robert Ageron (Paris: Armand Colin, 1997), 57–58; Noara Omouri, "Les section administratives spécialisées et les sciences sociales," in *Militaires et guérilla dans la Guerre d'Algérie*, ed. Jean-Charles Jauffret and Maurice Vaïsse (Paris: Editions Complexe, 2001), 383–397.

88. See James C. Scott, *Seeing Like a State: How Certain Schemes to Improve the Human Condition Have Failed* (New Haven, CT: Yale University Press, 1998).
89. Commandant Général de la Wilaya d'Oran, "Décision prises au cours de la réunion du 2 au 7 Octobre 1957," found 19 November 1957, SHAT, 1H 2582.
90. FLN instructions not to cooperate with SAS control practices are reproduced in *Le FLN, documents et histoire: 1954–1962*, ed. Mohammed Harbi and Gilbert Meynier (Paris: Fayard, 2004), 175.
91. "Boycott du tabac, des debits de boissons alcoolisées et des salles de spectacles," FLN tract found May 1956 in Constantine, SHAT, 1H 2587.
92. ALN pamphlet found in schools in Setif on 29 September 1956, "Appel aux algériens pour boycotter les écoles françaises," SHAT, 1H 2587.
93. "Objet: Renseignements," Wilaya d'Oran, from the Captain of Zone 7 to "Brother 25," 23 March 1958, SHAT, 1H 2582.
94. "Directives générales," recovered 17 April 1957 southwest of Port-Gueydon, SHAT 1H 2582. Contrary to the belief that such groups never refer to themselves as terrorists, the FLN seems to have been quite comfortable with the term in its internal communications. The word seems typically to have been used to differentiate an urban operative using the tactics of assassination and bombing from a rural guerrilla.
95. Quoted in Meynier, *Histoire intérieure du F.L.N.*, 201.
96. Quoted in Connelly, *Diplomatic Revolution*, 119.
97. Connelly, *Diplomatic Revolution*, 125.
98. Robert Malley, *The Call from Algeria: Third Worldism, Revolution, and the Turn to Islam* (Berkeley: University of California Press, 1996), 124; quotation from *El Moudjahid*, 1 January 1958.
99. The event is recounted by Aït Ahmed in Connelly, *Diplomatic Revolution*, 92–93.
100. Goal stated in February 1956; see Harbi, *F.L.N.*, 196.
101. A brief summary of these voyages abroad is located in "Tournées effectuées au cours de la période de novembre 54–novembre 56," ANA, GPRA-MAE, dossier 7.1.
102. Yazid to Cairo, 10 June 1956, ANA, GPRA-MAE, dossier 2.4.
103. Minutes of Conseil des ministres, 2 July 1959, ANA, archives of the Gouvernement Provisoire de la République Algérienne (GPRA), microfiche G004. For an overview of FLN diplomacy in its early years, see the summary report by M'hamed Yazid, "L'action internationale du FLN," July 1957, in *Les archives de la Révolution Algérienne*, ed. Mohammed Harbi (Paris: Editions Jeune Afrique, 1981), 172–174.
104. Khider to Benyahia and Brahimi, 10 October 1956, ANA, GPRA-MAE, dossier 1.
105. Bureau de New York, "Rapport d'activité—Propagande et documentation, Octobre 56–Février 57," 18 February 1957, ANA, GPRA-MAE, dossier 4.4.
106. Letter from Abbane to the external delegation, 4 November 1955, reprinted in Mabrouk Belhocine, *Le Courrier Alger–Le Caire, 1954–1962* (Algiers: Casbah Editions, 2000), 108–109.
107. Dahmani Mohamed to Khider, 12 July 1956, ANA, GPRA-MAE, dossier 1. See also Said to Cairo, 24 January 1957, ANA, GPRA-MAE, dossier 3.8.
108. Horne, *Savage War of Peace*, 224.
109. An FLN summary of negotiations with Paris up to August 1957 can be found in "Rapport concernant les contacts qui ont eu lieu entre représentant Français et FLN depuis le debut de la Révolution à nos jours à l'intention de la réunion du CNRA qui doit avoir lieu le 20 Aout 1957 au Caire," ANA, GPRA MAE, dossier 7.2.1.
110. Instructions from Dr. Lamine Debaghine in Cairo to the CNRA, Prefecture of Constantine, Service des Liaison Nord-Africaine, 12 June 1957, information from an informer in the Métropole, SHAT 1H 2582.

111. "Objet: Rensegnements," Wilaya d'Oran, Zone VII, 23 March 1958, from Le Capitaine Chef de la Zone VII to Frère 25, SHAT 1H 2582.
112. "Instructions aux Chefs Responsables de la Presse, de la Radio, de l'Information et de la Propagande en Algerie et a l'Etranger," probably summer 1958, ANA, GPRA-MAE, dossier 17.21.
113. Quotation from General Bigeard's introduction to Erwan Bergot, *Bataillon Bigeard: Indochine 1952–1954, Algérie 1955–1957* (Paris: Presses de la Cité, 1977).
114. See Frédéric Guelton, "The French Army 'Centre for Training and Preparation in Counter-Guerrilla Warfare' (Cipcg) at Arzew," *Journal of Strategic Studies* 25, no. 2 (2002): 35–53; a good overview of the *guerre révolutionnaire* doctrine is found in Peter Paret, *French Revolutionary Warfare* (London: Pall Mall, 1964).
115. "Rappel de Quelques Notions sur la Genèse et l'Evolution du FLN-ALN," Algiers, 22 February 1957, 10th Military Region, 2ème Bureau, SHAT 1H 2582.
116. "Themes de Contact: Idées maitresses," undated document by the 2ème Bureau, SHAT 1H 2582, emphasis in original.
117. For example, see James McDougall's review of Christopher Cradock and M. L. R. Smith, "'No Fixed Values': A Reinterpretation of the Influence of the Theory of Guerre Révolutionnaire and the Battle of Algiers, 1956–1957," *Journal of Cold War Studies* 9, no. 4 (2007): 68–105, published on H-Diplo website, 8 February 2008, www.h-net.org/~diplo/reviews/jcws/jcws2007.html.
118. "Essai sur les inconvénients pour une armée révolutionnaire qui doit livrer une guerre classqiue quand certains conditions ne sont pas remplie," 20 April 1958, ANA, GPRA, dossier 5.9.
119. Krim Belkacem, "Analyse Sommaire: Le combat des unités de l'ALN depuis le 1/11/54—Développement," 26 April 1958, ANA, GPRA-MAE, dossier 26.6.3.
120. Harbi, *F.L.N.*, 218–223.
121. Meynier, *Histoire intérieure du F.L.N.*, 590; see also *El Moudjahid*, 1 and 15 January 1958.
122. Harbi, *F.L.N*, 218–221.
123. Mohieddine Hadhri, *L'URSS et le Maghreb: De la révolution d'octobre à l'indépendance de l'Algérie, 1917–1962* (Paris: L'Harmattan, 1985), 161.
124. Report by Brahim Ghafa in Peking, March 1958, ANA, GPRA-MAE, dossier 132.1.5.
125. Omar Ouamrane, 8 July 1958, in *Les archives de la Révolution Algérienne*, ed. Mohammed Harbi (Paris: Éditions Jeune Afrique, 1981), 189–193.
126. The passage of arms fell from 1,200 per month in 1957 to 200 per month in 1959. Two thousand mujahideen crossed each month in 1957, but 4,000 died in a vain effort to penetrate the frontier defenses the following year. See Jacques Vernet, "Les barrages dans la guerre d'Algérie," in *Militaires et guerrillas dans la Guerre d'Algérie*, ed. Jean-Charles Jauffret and Maurice Vaïsse and (Paris: Editions Complexe, 2001), 253–268.
127. For an account of such a discussion, see L'Aspirant Arnaud, "Réunion H.L.L. à ATTATLA; source: Un informateur non nommé," 25 January 1957, SHAT, 1H 2582.
128. Connelly, *Diplomatic Revolution*, 169.
129. Charles de Gaulle, *Memoirs of Hope: Renewal and Endeavor* (New York: Simon and Schuster, 1971), 46.
130. Report from M'hamed Yazid, "Rapport sur l'attitude Americain," 1 June 1958, ANA, GPRA-MAE, dossier 4.4; Connelly, *Diplomatic Revolution*, 165.
131. Report on the GPRA mission to India in March 1958, ANA, GPRA-MAE, dossier 3.13.
132. Harbi, *F.L.N.*, 211–212.
133. Benyoucef Ben Khedda, "Entrevue avec le President Nkrumah de Ghana au Caire le 17 juin 1958," ANA, GPRA-MAE, dossier 8.11.1
134. Daho Djerbal, "Stratégie gaullienne et stratégie de l'Etat français rupture et continuité: Le cas de l'Algérie," in *De Gaulle et son Siècle*, vol. 6, *Liberté et dignité des peuples*, ed. Fondation Charles de Gaulle (Paris: Fondation Charles de Gaule, 1992), 107–115. For Algeria's role in de Gaulle's African strategy, see "Les etats africains de la Communauté et la guerre d'Algérie (1958–1960)," in *L'Afrique noire française: L'heure des indépendances*, ed. Charles-Robert Ageron and Marc Michel (Paris: CNRS, 1992); also Irwin M. Wall, *France, the United States, and the Algerian War* (Berkeley: University of California Press, 2001), chap. 6.

135. Michael Kettle, *De Gaulle and Algeria 1940-1960: From Mers El-Kébir to the Algiers Barracades* (London: Quartet, 1993), 286-291; Henri Alleg, *La Guerre d'Algérie* (Paris: Temps Actuels, 1981), 3:102-105
136. "Text of the Inaugural Address of General de Gaulle as President of the Republic and of the Community at the Elysée Palace on January 8, 1959," in *Major Addresses, Statements and Press Conferences of General Charles de Gaulle* (New York: Embassy of France, Press and Information Service, 1964), 35.
137. Ahmed Boumendjel, GPRA Provisional Report, August 1959, in *Les archives de la Révolution Algérienne*, ed. Mohammed Harbi (Paris: Éditions Jeune Afrique, 1981), 189-193.
138. Slimane Chikh, *L'Algérie en armes, ou, le temps des certitudes* (Paris: Economica, 1981), 115-116.
139. "La question algérienne à la session 1958 de l'ONU (Addenda à l'étude du 28 Août 1958)," Cairo, 1 December 1958, ANA, GPRA-MAE, dossier 8.5.1/7.
140. Connelly, *Diplomatic Revolution*, 198. The GPRA document cited by Connelly does not seem to be the same as that quoted earlier, despite an identical title and similar reference number. Given the nature of the GPRA's records, such discrepancies do arise, and it is not always clear if one document may be an earlier draft of a similar one, or whether text from one report has been recycled for a new one. Additionally, the numbering system of the Algerian National Archives seems to have changed in the intervening years.
141. The opinion that Ben Khedda and Dahlab were pro-communist is expressed in a Quai d'Orsay report on the new GPRA, 30 August 1961, SEAA, carton 9.
142. Saad Dahlab, *Mission accomplie* (Algiers: Editions Dahlab, 1990), 101-110.
143. "Quelques idées sur les tâches actuelles," 23 December 1958, ANA, GPRA-MAE, dossier 5.8.
144. "L'Algérie et l'actualité international," Cairo, January 1959, ANA, GPRA-MAE, dossier 7.2.5.
145. Ramdane Abbane report from late 1956, "Rapport du CCE au CNRA," 208, reprinted in *NAQD* 12 (Spring/Summer 1999): 191-211.
146. Report by Brahim Ghafa et al., "L'Algérie et l'actualité international," Cairo, January 1959, ANA, GPRA-MAE, dossier 7.2.5: "It must be underlined all the same ... that any aid to the GPRA from a Communist government must have the assent of the UAR, this follows from the division of zones of influence, Algeria being part of the Arab world in which Nasser's leadership is acknowledged."
147. "Le Ministère des Affaires extérieures et ses activités," 19 January 1959, ANA, GPRA-MAE, dossier 6.12.1.
148. "Le Ministère des Affaires extérieures et ses activités," 19 January 1959, ANA, GPRA-MAE, dossier 6.12.1.
149. "Rapport sur le GPRA et ses possibilités politiques dans les Pays de l'est, à l'exception de la Yougoslavie," undated but seemingly from the second half of 1961, ANA, GPRA-MAE, dossier 8.13.7.
150. E. O. Obichkina, "Sovetskoe rukovodstvo i voina v Alzhire, 1954-1962 gg. po materialam arkhiva MID RF" [The Soviet leadership and the war in Algeria, 1954-1962, as seen in material from the archive of the Foreign Ministry of the Russian Federation], *Novaia i Noveishaia Istoriia* 1 (2000): 19-30.
151. "Rapport sur le congrès de Tachkent, 7-13 Octobre 1958," ANA, GPRA-MAE, dossier 7.2.3.
152. Mhamad Yala, "Entretien avec le premier secretaire de l'ambassade de Pologne au Caire, sur sa demande," by Mhamad Yala, 24 December 1958, ANA, GPRA-MAE, dossier 7.2.4.
153. Abdelhamid Boudiaf, Officer of ALN in Wilaya IV, 5 March 1959, in *Les archives de la Révolution Algérienne*, ed. Mohammed Harbi (Paris: Éditions Jeune Afrique, 1981), 189-193.
154. Letter from Abbas to Pham Van Dong, 28 January 1959, ANA, GPRA-MAE, dossier 133.2.
155. Hadhri, *L'URSS et le Maghreb*, 162-163; Meynier, *Histoire intérieure du F.L.N.*, 612-613.
156. Ferhat Abbas, "Rapport de politique générale," 20 June 1959, ANA, GPRA-MAE, dossier 5.8.
157. Connelly, *Diplomatic Revolution*, 198-204.
158. Lamine Debaghine, at a conference in Damascus of GPRA representatives in Arab countries, 8-14 November 1959, in *Les archives de la Révolution Algérienne*, ed. Mohammed Harbi (Paris: Éditions Jeune Afrique, 1981), 189-193.
159. Lamine Debaghine, "Essay on the definition of the FLN, on its objectives in war and peace," ANA, GPRA-MAE, dossier 29.1.

160. See report from Peking, April 1959, for an account of seminars given by PRC generals to the ALN delegation led by Omar Oussedik, ANA, GPRA-MAE, dossier 132.2/4.
161. "Conférence faite par le chef d'état major de l'Armée populaire du Vietnam," 18 April 1959, ANA, GPRA-MAE, dossier 133.5.
162. "Causérie sur le travail politique tel qu'il est concu au Viet Nam," 19 April 1959, ANA, GPRA-MAE, dossier 133.5.
163. Meynier, *Histoire intérieure du F.L.N.*, 314–317.
164. "Rapport de la Commission militaire chargée d'établir une stratégie militaire pour l'ALN," ANA, GPRA, dossier 2.46.
165. "Réunion des dix, session du 6 septembre 1959," ANA, GPRA, dossier 2.19.
166. "Politique intérieure," ANA, GPRA, dossier 5.2. The report is unattributed and undated, but it is atypically long, well-presented, and bound, with the stated intention of producing an analysis of "the general political situation in Algeria" and a "definition of our main political objectives."
167. Boumendjel, GPRA Provisional Report, August 1959, 189–193.
168. Quoted in Thomas Borstelmann, *The Cold War and the Color Line: American Race Relations in the Global Arena* (Cambridge, MA: Harvard University Press, 2001), 113.
169. ALN circular seized in the North Algerois Zone on 13 September 1957, SHAT, 1H 2582.
170. "Address by President Charles de Gaulle on the future of Algeria broadcast over French radio and television on September 16, 1959," in *Major Addresses, Statements and Press Conferences of General Charles de Gaulle* (New York: Embassy of France, Press and Information Service, 1964), 55.
171. Minutes of Council of Ministers, 19 September 1959, ANA, GPRA, microfiche G005.

Chapter 2

1. On Nkrumah bringing African affairs "literally under his nose," see S. E. Quarm, *Reflections of a Pioneer in Ghana's Diplomatic Service* (Accra: Afram Publications, 1995), 14. According to Ras Makonnen, George Padmore advised Nkrumah to isolate African affairs from Ghanaian civil servants whom they believed were being manipulated by London; see Ras Makonnen, *Pan-Africanism from Within*, Kenneth King ed. (Oxford: Oxford University Press, 1973), 258–259.
2. Michael Dei-Anang, *The Administration of Ghana's Foreign Relations, 1957–1965: A Personal Memoir* (London: University of London, The Athlone Press, 1975), 64–67; W. Scott Thompson, *Ghana's Foreign Policy, 1957–1966: Diplomacy, Ideology, and the New State* (Princeton, NJ: Princeton, 1969), 31–41. The final declaration of the 1958 CIAS is reproduced in Colin Legum, *Pan-Africanism: A Short Political Guide* (Westport, CT: Greenwood Press, 1976), 139–148.
3. David Macey, *Frantz Fanon* (New York: Picador, 2000), 366–368; Immanuel Wallerstein, *Africa: The Politics of Unity* (Lincoln: University of Nebraska Press, 2005), 33–34; Jeffrey S. Ahlman, "The Algerian Question in Nkrumah's Ghana, 1958–1960: Debating 'Violence' and 'Nonviolence' in African Decolonization," *Africa Today* 57, no. 2 (2010): 67–84; Thompson, *Ghana's Foreign Policy*, 57–64.
4. Fanon quoted in Ahlman, "The Algerian Question in Nkrumah's Ghana," 67–84.
5. Quoted in Slimane Chikh, "L'Algérie et l'Afrique (1954–1962)," *Revue Algérienne des Sciences Juridiques, Économiques et Politiques* 5, no. 3 (1968): 715; see also Fanon's report on the AAPC in *El Moudjahid*, no. 34, 24 December 1958.
6. See the report on discussions with the FLN by Veljko Micunovic, Under-Secretary of State for Foreign Affairs, 6 November 1959, Archives of Josip Broz Tito (AJBT), Cabinet of the President of the Republic (KPR), I.5.b/2-1; see also "Note sur notre politique maghrébine," 8 March 1960, ANA, GPRA-MAE, dossier 5.10.8.
7. "Rapport sur le déroulement de la conference de Tunis," Chef du Department de Guerre, 4 July 1958, ANA, GPRA-MAE, dossier 26.1.1.
8. Mohammed Harbi, *Le F.L.N.: Mirage et réalité* (Paris: Editions Jeune Afrique, 1980), 253–256; Gilbert Meynier, *Histoire intérieure du F.L.N. 1954–1962* (Paris: Fayard, 2002), 362–364.

9. "New Conception of Our Diplomacy," records of the Tripoli CNRA, 17 December 1959–18 January 1960, ANA, CNRA, dossier 2.14.
10. "Note de politique extérieure," 7 January 1960, ANA, CNRA, dossier 2.18.
11. "Zabeleška o Razgovoru Poslanika I. Topaloskog sa Pretsednikom Privremene Alžirske Vlade Ferhat Abasom i Clanovima Vlade Belkasemom, Bususfom i Serifom," Ilija Topaloski, Yugoslav Legation in Tunis, 30 March 1959, AJBT, KPR, I.5.b/2-1.
12. Chanderli's submission for *El Moudjahid*, 25 March 1960, ANA, GPRA-MAE, dossier 117.1.4.
13. Mohammed Dib, *Qui se souvient de la mer* (Paris: Editions de la Différence, 2007).
14. Saad Dahlab, *Mission accomplie* (Algiers: Editions Dahlab, 1990), 116–117.
15. Memcon of Lakhdari, Rivera and Do Logo, 8 January 1959, 24–25 January 1959, ANA, GPRA-MAE, dossier 117.1.1.
16. Debaghine to Chanderli, 27 January 1959, ANA, GPRA-MAE, dossier 117.1.4.
17. Chanderli report on Cuba, 17 March 1959, ANA, GPRA-MAE, dossier 117.1.4. (emphasis added).
18. Piero Gleijeses, *Conflicting Missions: Havana, Washington, and Africa, 1959–1976* (Chapel Hill: University of North Carolina Press, 2002), 31–32.
19. Simon Reid-Henry, *Fidel and Che: A Revolutionary Friendship* (New York: Walker, 2009), 204–205; Mohamed Heikal, *The Cairo Documents: The Inside Story of Nasser and His Relationship with World Leaders, Rebels, and Statesmen* (Garden City, NY: Doubleday, 1973), 343–344.
20. Jorge I. Domínguez, *To Make a World Safe for Revolution: Cuba's Foreign Policy* (Cambridge, MA: Harvard University Press, 1989), 17–23.
21. "Entretien Mehri-Francis avec Président Délégation Cuba," 24 June 1959, ANA, GPRA-MAE, dossier 117.1.2.
22. "La révolution cubaine," unattributed and likely from autumn 1959, ANA, GPRA-MAE, dossier 117.1.1.
23. Chanderli's report for *El Moudjahid*, "Mission à Cuba," 25 March 1960, ANA, GPRA-MAE, dossier 117.1.4.
24. Chanderli's report for *El Moudjahid*, "Mission à Cuba," 25 March 1960, ANA, GPRA-MAE, dossier 117.1.4.
25. For example, see Michael E. Latham, *Modernization as Ideology: American Social Science and "Nation Building" in the Kennedy Era* (Chapel Hill: University of North Carolina Press, 2000); Nils Gilman, *Mandarins of the Future: Modernization Theory in Cold War America* (Baltimore: Johns Hopkins University Press, 2003); Nick Cullather, *The Hungry World: America's Cold War Battle against Poverty in Asia* (Cambridge, MA: Harvard University Press, 2010); Ragna Boden, "Cold War Economics: Soviet Aid to Indonesia," *Journal of Cold War Studies* 10, no. 3 (2008): 110–128; Odd Arne Westad, *The Global Cold War: Third World Interventions and the Making of Our Times* (Cambridge: Cambridge University Press, 2007). For a good example of Soviet attitudes to peasant society in India, see V. G. Rastiannikov, "Prodovol'stvennaia problema v razvi- vaiushchikhsia stranakh Azii i Afriki," *Narody Azii i Afriki* 1 (1967): 37–38.
26. Harbi, *F.L.N.*, 290; Mohammed Harbi and Gilbert Meynier, eds., *Le FLN, documents et histoire* (Paris: Fayard, 2004), 171.
27. Domínguez, *To Make a World Safe for Revolution*, 118–120.
28. Reid-Henry, *Fidel and Che*.
29. "La politique africaine," Krim to Dahlab, 9 March 1960, ANA, GPRA-MAE, dossier 8.11.3.
30. "Note de politique extérieure," Tripoli, 7 January 1960, ANA, CNRA, dossier 2.18.
31. For a brief history of the game, see the instructions to the Fiftieth Anniversary Edition of RISK, published in 1999.
32. Irwin Wall, *France, the United States, and the Algerian War* (Berkeley: University of California Press, 2001), 158–159, 199–201.
33. Charles de Gaulle, *Discours et messages*, vol. 3 (Paris: Plon, 1970), speech at Federal Assembly of Mali, 13 December 1959, 151–154.
34. Charles-Robert Ageron, *L'Algérie algérienne de Napoléon II à de Gaulle* (Paris: Sinbad, 1980), 247.
35. *El Moudjahid*, no. 29, 17 September 1958.

36. Elizabeth Schmidt, *Cold War and Decolonization in Guinea, 1946–1958* (Athens: Ohio University Press, 2007), 157–179; John Chipman, *French Power in Africa* (Cambridge: Blackwell, 1989), 102–107.
37. Chipman, *French Power in Africa*, 103.
38. "Rapport de Politique Etrangère," report for the August 1961 CNRA, ANA, CNRA, dossier 8.9.
39. Chikh, "L'Algérie et l'Afrique," 718.
40. Telegram from Dahlab to Oussedik, 19 May 1960, ANA, GPRA-MAE, dossier 46.3. Tubman donated $25,000; the Algerians expected little financially from the African nations, and the symbolism of the gesture was more important than the sum.
41. Memcon Eisenhower and de Gaulle, 22 April 1960, National Security Archive, gateway.proquest.com/openurl?url_ver=Z39.88-2004&res_dat=xri:dnsa&rft_dat=xri:dnsa:article:CNP00643.
42. "Rapport de politique étrangère," submitted by MAE for August 1961 CNRA meeting, ANA, CNRA, dossier 8.9. On the reversal in the Ghanaian position, see Thompson, *Ghana's Foreign Policy*, 109–110.
43. "Mémoire au Ministère des Affaires Étrangères du Gouvernement de la République de Guinée," Cairo, 11 June 1960, ANA, GPRA-MAE, dossier 37.1.3.
44. Notes from Krim to the GPRA cabinet, 10 August 1960, ANA, GPRA-MAE, dossier 3.3.
45. "Note sur notre politique maghrebine," Krim to Dahlab, 8 March 1960, ANA, GPRA-MAE, dossier 5.10.8.
46. "Note de politique extérieure," 7 January 1960, ANA, CNRA, dossier 2.1.
47. "La signification de la Crise Marocaine," forwarded by Bouattoura to Chawki, originally produced 31 May 1960, ANA, GPRA-MAE, dossier 238.1.11.
48. "Ministère des Affaires Extérieures: Rapport de politique étrangère," August 1961, ANA, CNRA, dossier 8.9.
49. Recordings of conversations FLN prisoners, no. 255, 1 February 1961, carton 14, Secrétariat d'Etat aux Affaires Algériennes (SEAA), Archives of French Foreign Ministry (French MAE).
50. Fathi Al Dib, *Abdel Nasser et la Révolution algérienne* (Paris: L'Harmattan, 1985), 67, 300–303.
51. Krim to Fanon, 26 May 1960, ANA, GPRA-MAE, dossier 46.5.
52. See Krim's report to GPRA cabinet, 10 August 1960, ANA, GPRA-MAE, dossier 5.8.
53. The letter is preserved in the GPRA's archives, ANA, GPRA-MAE, dossier 25.4.
54. Krim's report to GPRA cabinet, 10 August 1960, ANA, GPRA-MAE, dossier 5.8.
55. Klaas Van Walraven, "From Tamanrasset: The Struggle of Sawaba and the Algerian Connection, 1957–1966," *Journal of North African Studies* 10, nos. 3–4 (2005): 507–528; Meredith Terretta, "Cameroonian Nationalists Go Global: From Forest *Maquis* to a Pan-African Accra," *Journal of African History* 51, no. 2 (2010): 189–212; Finn Fuglestad, "Djibo Bakary, the French, and the Referendum of 1958 in Niger," *Journal of African History* 14, no. 2 (1973): 313–330.
56. *El Moudjahid*, no. 58, 5 January 1960; Edward Mortimer, *France and the Africans, 1944–1960* (New York: Walker, 1969), 364.
57. See also Matthew Connelly, *A Diplomatic Revolution: Algeria's Fight for Independence and the Origins of the Post–Cold War Era* (Oxford: Oxford University Press, 2002), 229.
58. Meynier, *Histoire intérieure du F.L.N.*, 582–583; "Rapport de politique étrangère," submitted by the MAE for the August 1961 CNRA meeting, dossier 8.9, CNRA, ANA.
59. On the FLN's attitudes to the mooted African volunteer force, see "Problème militaire, volontaires," August 1961, ANA, CNRA, dossier 8.11.
60. Frantz Fanon, *Toward the African Revolution: Political Essays* (New York: Grove Press, 1988), 180–181, 208; David Gakunzi, *Abdelaziz Bouteflika, le choix de la paix* (Paris: L'Harmattan, 2003), 40–46.
61. Quoted from Krim's speech in Hanoi, 5 May 1960, reproduced in ANA, GPRA-MAE, dossier 133.4.
62. See message from Brahimi in Jakarta, 15 January 1960, ANA, GPRA-MAE, dossier 8.3; and memcom of Krim, Francis, and Subandrio in Cairo, 25 April 1960, ANA, GPRA-MAE, dossier 46.2.

63. Jeremy Scott Friedman, "Reviving Revolution: The Sino-Soviet Split, the 'Third World,' and the Fate of the Left" (PhD diss., Princeton University, 2011), 65–66.
64. "Notre politique extérieure et la Guerre Froide: Note destinée au Secrétariat général pour elaboration," Belkacem Krim, 13 March 1960, ANA, GPRA-MAE, dossier 8.2.4.
65. For example, on Soviet interests in the Middle East, see Sergei Mazov, "The USSR and the Former Italian Colonies, 1945–50," *Cold War History* 3, no. 3 (2003): 49–78
66. Friedman, "Reviving Revolution," 41–42.
67. *Memoirs of Nikita Khrushchev*, ed. Sergei Khrushchev, trans. George Shriver and Stephen Shenfield, trans. George Shriver and Stephen Shenfield, vol. 3, *Statesman, 1953–1964* (University Park: Pennsylvania State University Press, 2007), 877.
68. Sergei Mazov, "Afrikanskie studenty v Moskve v God Afriki (po arkhivnym materialam)," *Vostok* 3 (1999): 89–103; Julie Hesslier, "Death of an African Student in Moscow: Race, Politics, and the Cold War," *Cahiers du Monde Russe* 47, no. 1 (2006): 33–63.
69. Original quotation in French translation from Constantin Katsakioris, "L'union soviétique et les intellectuels africains: Internationalisme, panafricanisme et négritude pendant les années de la décolonisation, 1954–1964," *Cahiers du Monde Russe* 47, nos. 1–2 (2006): 15–32.
70. E. O. Obichkina, "Sovetskoe rukovodstvo i voina v Alzhire, 1954–1962 gg. po materialam arkhiva MID RF" [The Soviet leadership and the war in Algeria, 1954–1962, as seen in material from the archive of the Foreign Ministry of the Russian Federation], *Novaia i noveishaia istoriia* 2000 (1): 19–30.
71. "Rapport sur l'activité diplomatique du Minist[è]re des Affaires Extérieures (Février 60–Décembre 60)," 19 January 1961, ANA, GPRA-MAE, dossier 7.2.10; quotation from *Blizhnevostochnyi konflikt: Iz dokumentov Arkhiva vneshnei politiki Rossiiskoi Federatsii*, ed. Vitalii Viacheslavovich and and Arkhiv vneshneĭ politiki MID Rossiĭskoĭ Federatsii (Moscow: Mezhdunarodyii fond Demokratiia, 2003), 333–334.
72. "Rapport sur l'activité diplomatique du Ministère des Affaires Extérieures," 19 January 1960, ANA, GPRA-MAE, dossier 7.2.10; Khrushchev quoted in Aleksandr Fursenko and Timothy Naftali, *Khrushchev's Cold War: The Inside Story of an American Adversary* (New York: Norton, 2006), 292–298.
73. "Rapport sur le GPRA et ses possibilités dans les pays de l'Est à l'exception de la Yougoslavie," undated, ANA, GPRA-MAE, dossier 8.13.7.
74. Memcon Bouzide and Menouer at Czechoslovak embassy, Tunis, 25 May 1960, ANA, GPRA-MAE, dossier 128.1.2.
75. Alice Cherki, *Frantz Fanon: A Portrait*, trans. Nadia Benabid (Ithaca, NY: Cornell University Press, 2006), 146.
76. See Lumumba's speech at the University of Ibadan, 22 March 1959, in *La pensée politique de Patrice Lumumba*, ed. Jean van Lierde (Paris: Présence Africaine, 1963), 24–31.
77. On Soviet contacts, see S. Neil MacFarlane, "The Soviet Union and the National Liberation Movements," in *The Soviet Union in the Third World*, ed. Carol Saivetz (Boulder, CO: Westview Press, 1989), 35.
78. Pierre de Vos, *Vie et mort de Lumumba* (Paris: Calmann-Lévy, 1961), 229.
79. Crawford Young, *Politics in the Congo: Decolonization and Independence* (Princeton, NJ: Princeton University Press, 1965), 307–320; John D. Hargreaves, *Decolonization in Africa* (London: Longman, 1996), 194.
80. Westad, *Global Cold War*, 138–139; Madeleine Kalb, *The Congo Cables* (New York: Macmillan, 1982), 24–25. Macmillian quoted in John D. Hargreaves, *Decolonization in Africa* (London: Longman, 1996), 196.
81. Meynier, *Histoire intérieure du F.L.N.*, 584; "The Edge of Anarchy," *Time*, 29 August 1960; see also Achour Cheurfi, *Dictionnaire encyclopédique de l'Algérie* (Algiers: Éditions ANEP, 2007), entry under Djamal Chanderli (pp. 349–350). Already sentenced to death in absentia by the French courts for his collaboration with the FLN, Michel was also suspected of being a Soviet agent by the CIA station chief in Léopoldville; see Larry Devlin, *Chief of Station, Congo: A Memoir of 1960–67* (New York: Public Affairs, 2007), 53.
82. "Affaires politiques. Relations avec le Congo," by Chanderli, 25 July 1960, ANA, GPRA-MAE, dossier 150.5.4.4.
83. *El Moudjahid*, no. 68, 5 August 1960.

84. Letter dated 29 July 1960, ANA, CNRA, dossier 8.26.
85. Report by Fanon, "Rapport sur le Congo," 11 August 1960, ANA, GPRA-MAE, dossier 120.5.3.1.
86. Crawford Young, *Politics in the Congo: Decolonization and Independence* (Princeton, NJ: Princeton University Press, 1965), 324.
87. Madeleine Kalb, *The Congo Cables* (New York: Macmillan, 1982), 68–69, 100–103; Westad, *Global Cold War*, 139; Devlin, *Chief of Station, Congo*, 77–80.
88. See Robert A. Mortimer, "The Algerian Revolution in Search of the African Revolution," *Journal of Modern African Studies* 8, no. 3 (1970): 363–387.
89. Telegram from Krim to missions in Rabat and Tunis, 11 October 1960, dossier 117.5.2, GPRA-MAE, ANA.
90. Wilcox to Merchant, 7 September 1960, FRUS, 1958–1960, vol. 13, document 312, pp. 693–694.
91. *Memoirs of Nikita Khrushchev*, 3:280.
92. On the importance of the UN to Third World governments, see Robert H. Jackson, *Quasi-states: Sovereignty, International Relations, and the Third World* (Cambridge: Cambridge University Press, 1990).
93. For accounts of Khrushchev's trip, see William Taubman, *Khrushchev: The Man and His Era* (New York: Norton, 2003), 477; and Fursenko and Naftali, *Khrushchev's Cold War*, 318–318.
94. The Algerian and Chinese statements are reproduced in Abderrahmane Kiouane, *Les Débuts d'une diplomatie de guerre, 1956–1962: Journal d'un délégué à l'extérieur* (Algiers: Editions Dahlab, 2000), 116–122.
95. Bentobbal quoted in Redha Malek, *L'Algérie à Evian: Histoire des négociations secrètes, 1956–1962* (Algiers: Éditions ANEP, 2001), 72; Mohieddine Hadhri, *L'URSS et le Maghreb: De la Révolution d'octobre à l'indépendance de l'Algérie* (Paris: Harmattan, 1985), 166–167; Connelly, *Diplomatic Revolution*, 229–230; Meynier, *Histoire intérieure du F.L.N.*, 611–612.
96. See the report on discussions with Chinese and Soviet ambassadors in Cairo, September 1960, dossier 9.1, GPRA-MAE, ANA; and memcon Dahlab with Soviet ambassador in Cairo, 18 June 1960, ANA, GPRA-MAE, dossier 8.13.4.
97. For discussions with the Moroccans for the delivery of Soviet and Yugoslav material, see memcon of Krim and Moulay El Hassan, 21 October 1960, ANA, GPRA-MAE, dossier 8.4.
98. Satterthwaite to Merchant, 20 October 1960, FRUS, 1958–1960, vol. 12, document 315, pp. 699–701.
99. "Algerian Implies Reds Offer Arms," *New York Times*, 30 October 1960.
100. Benhabylès, "Rapport de politique générale sur les pays socialistes," 28 February 1961, ANA, GPRA-MAE, dossier 12.1.6.
101. "Politique à l'égard de la Communauté," Dahlab to Oussedik, 19 December 1960, ANA, GPRA-MAE, dossier 37.1.4.
102. "Nehru Calls for a Strong UN," *Christian Science Monitor*, 18 February 1961, 2.
103. "UAR to Withdraw Troops," *New York Times*, 8 December 1960, 4.
104. Saad Dahlab, "Note Politique," 6 January 1961, ANA, GPRA-MAE, dossier 37.7.13.
105. Recordings of conversations FLN prisoners, no. 255, 1 February 1961, carton 14, SEAA.
106. de Gaulle, *Discours et messages*, 3, speech of 4 November 1960.
107. Foreword by Jacques Berque, in Robert Descloitres, Jean Claude Reverdy, and Claudine Descloitres, *L'Algérie des bidonvilles: Le Tiers Monde dans la cité* (Paris: Mouton, 1961), 7–9.
108. Alistair Horne, *A Savage War of Peace: Algeria, 1954–1962* (New York: Viking, 1978), 413.
109. "Relations des communautés en Algérie," Délégation Générale du Gouvernement en Algérie, carton 92, SEAA.
110. Pierre Bourdieu, *The Algerians*, trans. Alan C. M. Ross (Boston: Beacon Press, 1962), 185.
111. Germaine Tillion, *L'Afrique Bascule vers l'avenir: L'Algérie et autres textes* (Paris: Éditions de Minuit, 1961); *L'Algérie surpeuplée: Orientations pour une politique de population* (Algiers: Éditions du Secretariat Social d'Alger, 1958).
112. Jean Claude Vatin, *L'Algérie politique: Histoire et société* (Paris: Presses de la Fondation Nationale des Sciences Politiques, 1983), 290–291.

113. Charles F. Gallagher, "The Other Algeria," October 1960, American University Field Study Reports, North Africa Series, vol. 6, pp. 50–51.
114. "Grandes lignes de notre politique intérieure," 13 March 1960, ANA, GPRA-MAE, dossier 8.2.4.
115. See, for example, the report from Wilaya II by Ali Kafi, 5 August 1959, ANA, GPRA-MAE, dossier 2.5.
116. "Pour une participation plus accrue des populations à la Révolution algérienne," undated, ANA, GPRA-MAE, dossier 29.7.
117. MALG report submitted for the 9–27 August 1961 CNRA meeting, ANA, CNRA, dossier 8.12.
118. Bourdieu, *The Algerians*, 162.
119. Connelly, *Diplomatic Revolution*, 135–136; Albert Fitte, *Spectroscopie d'une propagande révolutionnaire: "El Moudjahid" des temps de guerre* (Montpellier: Université Paul Valery, 1973); circulaire from Dahlab to the missions, 29 May 1960, ANA, GPRA-MAE, dossier 8.2.7.
120. "L'évolution de l'état d'esprit en Algérie depuis les négociations de Melun jusqu'après le referendum," 19 January 1961, carton 92, SEAA.
121. Descloitres, Reverdy, and Descloitres, *L'Algérie des bidonvilles*, 7–9, 12.
122. Foreword by Jacques Berque, in Descloitres, Reverdy, and Descloitres, *L'Algérie des bidonvilles*, 9.
123. Translation of speech reproduced in the *New York Times*, 11 December 1960.
124. Yves Courrière, *La Guerre d'Algérie: 1957–1962* (Paris: Fayard, 2001), 717–719.
125. Fanon, *Toward the African Revolution*, 180–181.
126. *New York Times*, 12 December 1960; Horne, *Savage War of Peace*, 432–433.
127. *El Moudjahid*, no. 86, 1 November 1961.
128. Keith Panter-Brick, "Independence, French Style," in *Decolonization and African Independence: The Transfers of Power, 1960–1980*, ed. Prosser Gifford and William Roger Louis (New Haven, CT: Yale University Press, 1988), 73–104.
129. Charles-Robert Ageron, *La Décolonisation française* (Paris: Armand Colin, 1994), 164.
130. James D. Le Sueur, *Uncivil War: Intellectuals and Identity Politics during the Decolonization of Algeria* (Lincoln: University of Nebraska Press, 2005).
131. Ageron, *La décolonisation française*, 110, 119–124; Guy Pervillé, *De l'empire française à la décolonisation* (Paris: Hachette, 1993), 240–241; Jacques Marseille, *Empire colonial et capitalisme français: Histoire d'un divorce* (Paris: A. Michel, 1984).
132. Alain Peyrefitte, *C'était de Gaulle* (Paris: Editions de Fallois, 1994), 52.
133. See Philippe Dewitte, "L'immigration: L'émergence en métropole d'une élite africaine," 201–211; Pascal Blanchard, Éric Deroo, Driss El Yazami, Pierre Fournié, and Gilles Manceron, "L'immigration: L'installation en métropole des populations du Maghreb," 213–222; and Jean-Luc Einaudi, "Le crime: Violence coloniale en métropole," 225–235, all in Pascal Blanchard, Sandrine Lemaire, and Nicolas Bancel, eds., *Culture impériale: Les colonies au coeur de la République, 1931–1961* (Paris: Autrement, 2004).
134. "Relations des communautés en Algérie," Délégation Générale in Algiers, carton 92, SEAA.
135. See Jean-Bernard Ramon, *L'OAS et ses appuis internationaux: Alliés, influences et manipulations extérieures* (Paris: Atelier Fol'fer, 2008). On Haganah's inspiration, see Jean-Jacques Susini, *Histoire de l'OAS* (Paris: La Table Ronde, 1963), 211.
136. Mouloud Feraoun, *Journal, 1955–1962: Reflections on the French-Algerian War* (Lincoln: University of Nebraska Press, 2000), 287.
137. Draft version of Interior Ministry report, Spring–Summer 1961, ANA, CNRA, dossier 813.
138. Memcom Yazid, Bentobbal, and Tito, 12 April 1961, ANA, GPRA-MAE, dossier 8.13.8.
139. "Zabeleška o Razgovoru Poslanika I. Topaloskog sa Pretsednikom Privremene Alžirske Vlade Ferhat Abasom i Clanovima Vlade Belkasemom, Bususfom i Serifom," Ilija Topaloski, Yugoslav Legation in Tunis, 30 March 1959, AJBP, KPR, I.5.b/2-1; "Aide Yougoslavie," note from Zerdani to Krim Belkacem, 8 November 1960, ANA, GPRA-MAE, dossier 8.13.5.1.
140. Official transcript of Khrushchev speech in *Kommunist*, January 1961, 3–37.

141. "Développement des rapports avec les pays socialistes depuis Mars 1961," ANA, GPRA-MAE, dossier 8.13.7.
142. Walmsley to Rusk, 27 January 1961, Algeria 1A-General 1/20/61–4/23/61, Algeria Country File, National Security Files, John F. Kennedy Presidential Library (JFKL).
143. Rusk to embassies in Paris, Rabat, Tunis, Cairo, and Tripoli, 1 February 1961, Algeria 1A-General 1/20/61–4/23/61, Algeria Country File, National Security Files, JFKL; "Note d'Activites," Ghany to MAE HQ, 19 April 1961, ANA, GPRA-MAE, dossier 6.1.
144. "Note politique," from Dahlab to multiple MAE missions, 6 January 1961, ANA, GPRA-MAE, dossier 37.7.3.
145. "Rapport de politique générale du départment Afrique-Asie," by Ali Lakhdari, 28 February 1961, ANA, GPRA-MAE, dossier 7.3.2.
146. "Rapport d'activité de la section Afrique-Asie," 9 May 1961, ANA, GPRA-MAE, dossier 7.3.3.
147. "Rapport concernant notre mission en Somalie et au Soudan," by Tewfik El Madani, 4 November 1961, ANA, GPRA-MAE, dossier 195.1.2.
148. "Rapport de politique générale du départment Afrique-Asie," by Ali Lakhdari, 28 February 1961, ANA, GPRA-MAE, dossier 7.3.2.
149. "Compte-rendu, Ministre de l'Armement et liaisons générales," August 1961, ANA, CNRA, dossier 8.12.
150. "Développement des rapports avec les pays socialistes depuis Mars 1961," ANA, GPRA-MAE, dossier 7.3.2.8.13.7.
151. Chikh, "L'Algérie et l'Afrique," 703–746; author's interview with Nourredine Djoudi at his home in Algiers, 23 November 2006.
152. John C. Campbell, *Tito's Separate Road: America and Yugoslavia in World Politics* (New York: Council on Foreign Relations, 1967), 76–78; Deva Narayan Mallik, *The Development of Non-alignment in India's Foreign Policy* (Allahabad: Chaitanya Publishing House, 1967), 216–217; Sarvepalli Gopal, *Jawaharlal Nehru: A Biography*, vol. 3, *1956–1964* (London: Jonathan Cape, 1984), 185–186; Robert A. Mortimer, *The Third World Coalition in International Politics* (Boulder, CO: Westview Press, 1984), 12–13.
153. "Note d'information: Communication de l'ambassadeur de Yougoslavie," Tunis 22 May 1961, ANA, GPRA-MAE, dossier 7.3.2.8.13.5.3.
154. "Rapport de politique étrangère," August 1961, ANA, CNRA, dossier 7.3.2.8.9.
155. Rinna Kullaa, *Non-alignment and Its Origins in Cold War Europe: Yugoslavia, Finland, and the Soviet Challenge* (London: I. B. Tauris, 2012), 173–178; Domínguez, *To Make a World Safe for Revolution*, 222.
156. Lalouette to Couve de Murville, 19 February 1962, document 61, *DDF*, 1962, vol. 1, pp. 183–185.
157. Lawrence Ziring, Robert E. Riggs, and Jack C. Plano, *The United Nations: International Organization and World Politics* (Fort Worth: Harcourt, 2000), 312–313.
158. Brian Urquhart, *Hammarksjöld* (New York: Knopf, 1972), 530–541.
159. Gopal, *Jawaharlal Nehru*, 3:199–201; Robert J. McMahon, *The Cold War on the Periphery: The United States, India, and Pakistan* (New York: Columbia University Press, 1994), 281–282.
160. Paul Kennedy, *The Parliament of Man: The Past, Present, and Future of the United Nations* (New York: Random House, 2006), 61–62.
161. "MAGHREB: Rapport bilan de février 1960–février 1961," author unnamed, Cairo, 19 March 1961, ANA, GPRA-MAE, dossier 7.2.14.
162. Paul T. Chamberlin, "Preparing for Dawn: The United States and the Global Politics of Palestinian Resistance, 1967–1975" (PhD diss., Ohio State University, 2009), 47.
163. Ben Turok, *The ANC and the Turn to Armed Struggle, 1950–1970* (Auckland Park, South Africa: Jacana, 2010), 88.
164. Ryan Irwin, "The Gordian Knot: Apartheid and the Unmaking of the Liberal World Order, 1960–1970" (PhD diss., Ohio State University, 2010), 139.
165. Horne, *Savage War of Peace*, 485–489.
166. Recordings of conversations FLN prisoners, no. 255, 1 February 1961, carton 14, SEAA.
167. Recordings of conversations FLN prisoners, no. 255, 1 February 1961, carton 14, SEAA.

Chapter 3

1. See, for example, "Instructions aux Chefs Responsables de la Presse, de la Radio, de l'Information et de la Propagande en Algérie et à l'Etranger," summer 1958, ANA, GPRA-MAE, box 17, dossier 21.
2. The ceremony is described in "Algeria Joins UN as 109th Member," *New York Times*, 9 October 1962.
3. Speech quoted from "Item-in-flag-raising ceremony for Algeria, 9 October 1962," file S-0885-0003-01-00001, UN Archives, Operational Files of the Secretary-General, U Thant.
4. Security Council official records, 17th year, 1020th meeting, 4 October 1962, New York, UN document symbol S/PV.1020, http://daccess-dds-ny.un.org/doc/UNDOC/GEN/N64/257/39/PDF/N6425739.pdf?OpenElement. See also United Nations General Assembly Seventeenth Session Official Records, 8 October 1962, http://www.un.org/en/ga/search/view_doc.asp?symbol=A/PV.1146.
5. See "Ben Bella Pledges in UN to Help Fight Colonialism," *New York Times*, 10 October 1962. For a transcript of Ben Bella's speech, see "Le discours à l'assemblee generale des nation-unies," 9 October 1962, in *Discours du Président Ben Bella du 28 septembre 1962 au 12 décembre 1962* (Algiers: Ministère de l'Information, 1963), 31–36.
6. A. Campbell to FO, 8 November 1962, UK National Archives (UKNA), Foreign Office records (FO), 371/165654.
7. Robert H. Jackson, *Quasi-states: Sovereignty, International Relations, and the Third World* (Cambridge: Cambridge University Press, 1990).
8. "Algeria Joins UN as 109th Member;" "Le discours à l'assemblee generale des nation-unies," 31–36; and Adlai Stevenson's account of a dinner in Ben Bella's honor, Stevenson to Rusk, "Stevenson dinner for Ben Bella," 12 October 1962, JFKL, National Security Files, Algeria Country File, box 111.
9. Quoted in Michael E. Latham, "The Cold War in the Third World, 1963–1975," in *The Cambridge History of the Cold War*, ed. Melvyn P. Leffler and Odd Arne Westad (Cambridge: Cambridge University Press, 2010), 1:480.
10. United Nations Economic and Social Council, Economic Commission for Africa, "Cairo Declaration of Developing Countries (document submitted by the delegation of the UAR), 14 September 1962, http://repository.uneca.org/bitstream/handle/10855/7151/Bib-47253.pdf?sequence=1 (emphasis added).
11. Giuliano Garavini, *After Empires: European Integration, Decolonization, and the Challenge from the Global South 1957–1986* (Oxford: Oxford University Press, 2012), 35–36.
12. *Qu'est ce que le programme de Tripoli* (Algiers: Wizārat al-Akhbār wa-al-Thaqāfah, Direction de la Documentation et des Publications, 1962).
13. Speech by Layashi Yaker to UN General Assembly, 20 October 1962, SEAA, carton 129.
14. Minutes of the Tripoli CNRA, 29 May 1962, pp. 26–29, ANA, CNRA, dossier 12.2.
15. Guy Pervillé, *De l'empire français à la décolonisation* (Paris: Hachette, 1991), 240–241.
16. Philip Chiviges Naylor, *France and Algeria: A History of Decolonization and Transformation* (Gainesville: University Press of Florida, 2000), 52–53.
17. See the introductions to Kristin Ross, *Fast Cars, Clean Bodies: Decolonization and the Reordering of French Culture* (Cambridge, MA: MIT Press, 1995), and Todd Shepard, *The Invention of Decolonization: The Algerian War and the Remaking of France* (Ithaca, NY: Cornell University Press, 2006).
18. Chinese ambassador in Cairo quoted from his conversation with Boussouf on 20 April 1961, ANA, GPRA-MAE, box 15, dossier 5.13.
19. Bernard Tricot, *Les sentiers de la paix, Algérie 1958–1962* (Paris: Plon, 1972), 241–242.
20. Matthew James Connelly, *A Diplomatic Revolution: Algeria's Fight for Independence and the Origins of the Post–Cold War Era* (Oxford: Oxford University Press, 2002), 236–237.
21. MAE's report on the negotiations with France, presented at the CNRA meeting in Tripoli, 9–27 August 1961, ANA, CNRA, dossier 8.10.
22. Note by Mabrouk Belhocine on the Sahara problem, 25 June 1961, in *Les archives de la Révolution Algérienne*, ed. Mohammed Harbi ed. (Paris: Editions Jeunes Afriques, 1981), 393–394.

23. "Compte-rendu militaire du gouvernement," presented at the CNRA meeting in Tripoli, 9–27 August 1961, ANA, CNRA, dossier 8.19.
24. "Compétences des Ministères et Coordination," undated, ANA, GPRA-MAE, box 29, dossier 3.
25. Letter from Bentobbal to Bureau du CNRA, 10 April 1961, ANA, GPRA, dossier 3.8.
26. Mohammed Harbi, *Le F.L.N.: Mirage et réalité* (Paris: Editions Jeune Afrique, 1980), 286–291; Gilbert Meynier, *Histoire intérieure du F.L.N. 1954–1962* (Paris: Fayard, 2002), 372–374.
27. Report on 3rd GPRA, 30 August 1961, SEAA, carton 9.
28. Rédha Malek, *L'Algérie à Evian: Histoire des négociations secrètes, 1956–1962* (Algeria: Éditions ANEP, 2002), 171–173.
29. MAE report to the 9–27 August 1961, CNRA, ANA, CNRA, dossier 8.10.
30. Yves Courrière, *La Guerre d'Algérie*, vol. 2, *1958–1962* (Paris: Fayard, 2001), 1043.
31. On polling in France, see Jean-Pierre Rioux, "Les Français et la guerre des deux Républiques," in *La Guerre d'Algérie: 1954–2004, la fin de l'amnésie*, ed. Mohammed Harbi and Benjamin Stora (Paris: R. Laffont, 2004), 17–26.
32. Jim House and Neil MacMaster, *Paris 1961: Algerians, State Terror, and Memory* (Oxford: Oxford University Press, 2006).
33. De Gaulle quoted in Maurice Vaïsse, *La grandeur: Politique etrangère du Général de Gaulle, 1958–1969* (Paris: Fayard, 1998), 58
34. "Note urgent à faire parvenir aux camarades du GPRA (pour cadres de Paris)," early 1961, ANA, GPRA-MAE, dossier 8.6.
35. On the American attitude to the OCRS, see Berny Sèbe, "In the Shadow of the Algerian War: The United States and the Common Organisation of Saharan Regions (OCRS), 1957–62," *Journal of Imperial and Commonwealth History* 38, no. 2 (2010): 303–322.
36. Connelly, *Diplomatic Revolution,* 254–255.
37. "Le problème algérien vu du Caire III: C'est dans l'expansion que se fera la cohabitation pacifique des communautés," *Journal de Genève*, 28 March 1961, by Georges Vaucher, SEAA 6.
38. James McDougall, *History and the Culture of Nationalism in Algeria* (Cambridge: Cambridge University Press, 2006), 24–25; Achour Cheurfi, *Dictionnaire encyclopedique de l'Algerie* (Algiers: Éditions ANEP, 2007), 747.
39. "Le problème algérien vu du Caire III: C'est dans l'expansion que se fera la cohabitation pacifique des communautés," *Journal de Genève*, 28 March 1961, by Georges Vaucher, SEAA, carton 6.
40. For French reports of the FLN encouraging participation in the Constantine Plan, see Délégation Générale du Gouvernement en Algérie, Affaires Politiques, "La promotion sociale en Algérie," 1961, SEAA, carton 92. Khider quoted in 11 January 1961, recording no. 78, SEAA, carton 14.
41. Délégation Générale du Gouvernement en Algérie, Affaires Politiques, "La promotion sociale en Algérie," SEAA, carton 92.
42. "Entertien avec les sous-préfet de . . . (Constantinois)," 10 October 1961, SEAA, carton 92.
43. Raymond Vallin, "Muslim Society in Algeria," in *Man, State, and Society in the Contemporary Maghrib*, ed. I. William Zartman (New York: Praeger, 1973), 50–64.
44. William B. Quandt, *Revolution and Political Leadership: Algeria, 1954–1968* (Cambridge, MA: MIT Press, 1969), 166–167; Meynier, *Histoire intérieure du F.L.N.*, 647–648.
45. Harbi, *F.L.N.*, 286–291
46. Ben Bella quoted in recording of 26 January 1961, no. 217; see also 28 March 1961, no. 783, and 12 April 1961, no. 928, SEAA, carton 14.
47. Transcript of Ben Bella's telephone call with Khemisti, 16 December 1961, no. 3732, SEAA, carton 14.
48. Transcript of Khemisti's telephone call to Ben Bella, 20 February 1962, no. 0880, SEAA, carton 14.
49. Michel Pablo, *Le Programme de Tripoli: Impressions et problèmes de la Révolution Algérienne* (Paris: Parti Communiste Internationaliste, Section Française de la IVe Internationale, 1962).
50. Harbi, *F.L.N.*, 333–334.
51. *Le Figaro*, 31 May 1962.
52. Minutes of the 28–29 May 1962 CNRA, Tripoli, ANA, CNRA, microfiche no. 12.2, pp. 26–29.

53. "Le problème algérien vu du Caire III: C'est dans l'expansion que se fera la cohabitation pacifique des communautés," *Journal de Genève*, 28 March 1961, by Georges Vaucher, SEAA, carton 6.
54. Minutes of the 28–29 May 1962 CNRA, Tripoli, ANA, CNRA, microfiche no. 12.2, pp. 26–29.
55. Tricot, *Les sentiers de la paix*, 339–340; for the opposite perspective, see Malek, *L'Algérie à Evian*, 124–125.
56. "Rapport du Ministère des Affaires Extérieures," from spring 1962, ANA, GPRA, dossier 5.4.
57. Memcon Ouzegane and Tito, 25 April 1963, AJBP, KPR, I-3-a/2-4.
58. "The Economy of Algeria," 21 April 1964, World Bank Archives (WBA), Department of Operations–Africa, Africa Series, AF18-A; Catherine Simon, *Algérie, les années pieds-rouges: Des rêves de l'indépendance au désenchantement, 1962–1969* (Paris: Découverte, 2009), 31–38.
59. Connelly, Diplomatic Revolution, 279–280; Odd Arne Westad, *The Global Cold War: Third World Interventions and the Making of Our Times* (Cambridge: Cambridge University Press, 2005), 106; author's interview with Lakhdar Brahimi in Princeton, New Jersey, 29 June 2008, and the London School of Economics and Political Science, 16 March 2009.
60. Gorse reporting on Khemisti's discussions with the embassy, 25 January 1963, SEAA, carton 130.
61. Bourguiba interview in *Times of London*, 24 April 1962.
62. Gorse reporting on Khemisti's discussions with the embassy, no. 472/481, 25 January 1963, SEAA, carton 130.
63. Central Intelligence Agency report, "Algerian Army of Liberation Plan to Assassinate Tunisian President Bourguiba," 2 August 1962, JFKL, National Security Files, box 4A.
64. See telegrams from Porter to Rusk on the former's discussion with Harbi of the GPRA-MAE on 4, 5, and 6 July 1962, JFKL, National Security Files, box 4A.
65. Circular Telegram from the Department of State to Certain Diplomatic Posts, 23 March 1962, FRUS, 1961–1963, vol. 21, pp. 93–94; Porter to Rusk, 6 July 1962, JFKL, Algeria Country File, box 4a, 7/1/62–7/15/62; telegrams from embassy Algiers to Paris, 10 and 14 August 1962, SEAA, carton 130.
66. Report on Angeli-Abbas conversation, 9 June 1962, "NOTE au sujet de la situation du FLN," 13 June 1962, SEAA, carton 117.
67. Quoted in *Le Figaro*, 16 July 1962.
68. The KGB station chief in Tunis claimed in his memoirs to have come to an intelligence-sharing and assistance agreement with Boussouf in early 1962; see Vadim Kirpichenko, *Razvedka: Litsa i lichnosti* (Moscow: GEiA, 1998), 78–79.
69. Telegram from Lalovic, 1 August 1962, Diplomatic Archives of the Ministry of Foreign Affairs of Serbia (DASMIP), Political Archives, year 1962, folder (f) 3, document (d) 426136.
70. CIA report on Ben Bella's discussion with Mohamed Laghzaoui, "Comments of Ahmed Ben Bella on US and Moroccan policy toward Algeria," 10 July 1962, JFK Library, National Security Files, Files of William H. Brubeck.
71. Telegram from Lalovic, 1 August 1962, DASMIP, 1962, f3, d426136; for the FLN's similar assurances to the US government, see memcon of Chanderli and McGhee, 30 August 1962, JFK Library, National Security Files, box 4B.
72. Memcon Djerdje and Boukadoum, 20 September 1962, DASMIP, 1962, f3, d430599.
73. Alain Peyrefitte, *C'était de Gaulle* (Paris: Editions de Fallois, 1994), 401–402.
74. Mahfoud Bennoune, *The Making of Contemporary Algeria, 1830–1987: Colonial Upheavals and Post-independence Development* (Cambridge: Cambridge University Press, 1988), 89–90.
75. Memorandum from Komer to Bundy, 22 June 1962, FRUS, 1961–1963, vol. 21, pp. 95–96.
76. As reported in "Cold War Winds Blow in Algeria," *New York Times*, 3 October 1962, 11.
77. "Role of International Agencies in Algerian Assistance Programs," Martin to State, 2 March 1962, JFKL, National Security Files, box 4, 3/1/62–3/9/62.
78. "First Russian Aid for Algeria," *Times of London*, 9 August 1962, 8.
79. Boualem Khalfa, Henri Alleg, and Abdelhamid Benzine, *La grande aventure d'Alger républicain* (Paris: Messidor, 1987), 197–210.
80. "US Gives Algeria 25 Million in Aid," *New York Times*, 31 August 1962, 2.

81. Memorandum from Saunders to Bundy, 17 August 1962, *FRUS*, 1961–1963, vol. 21, pp. 99–100.
82. "Algeria: From War to Peace," by V. Kudryavtsev in *Pravda*, whose articles appeared to represent official opinion on Algeria; *Current Digest of the Post-Soviet Press* 14, no. 34 (19 September 1962): 19–21.
83. "Les relations algéro-soviétiques," 5 January 1967, ANA, MAE, 46/2000, box 19.
84. Figures from the French embassy in Algiers, reproduced in "Les effectifs des français en Algérie par circonscriptions consulaires et par secteurs économiques" as part of a general report on "The Situation in Algeria" for the SEAA's budget proposals for 1966, SEAA, carton 159, item IV.2.1.1.
85. Naylor, *France and Algeria*, 41–43.
86. See "Instructions pour l'ambassadeur de France à Alger," 9 October 1962, *DDF*, 1962, vol. 2, pp. 121–130.
87. Gavin to Rusk, 19 September 1962, JFKL, Algeria Country File, box 4a, 9/1/62–10/15/62; "Instructions pour l'ambassadeur de France à Alger," 9 October 1962, *DDF*, 1962, vol. 2, pp. 121–130; Vaïsse, *La grandeur*, 461.
88. Charles de Gaulle, *Lettres, notes et carnets*, vol. 14 (Paris: Plon, 1980) 380, October 1963.
89. See "Note de la direction des affaires africaines et malgaches: Échanges de vues franco-américains sur l'aide à l'Afrique," by Jean-Marie Soutou, 27 September 1962, *DDF*, 1962, vol. 2, pp. 248–249.
90. Henry Jackson, *The FLN in Algeria: Party Development in a Revolutionary Society* (Westport, CT: Greenwood Press, 1977), 67–68; Nicole Grimaud, *La politique extérieure de l'Algérie (1962–1978)* (Paris: Karthala, 1984), 42–44.
91. Jeanneney to Couve de Murville, *DDF*, 1962, vol. 2, pp. 138–142.
92. "Instructions pour l'ambassadeur de France à Alger," 9 October 1962, *DDF*, 1962, vol. 2, pp. 121–130.
93. Connelly, *Diplomatic Revolution*, 219–220, 235; Edward Kolodziej, *French International Policy under De Gaulle and Pompidou: The Politics of Grandeur* (Ithaca, NY: Cornell University Press, 1974), 447–453.
94. John Ruedy, *Modern Algeria: The Origins and Development of a Nation*, 2nd ed. (Bloomington: Indiana University Press, 2005), 194.
95. The high rate of abstentions reported—36 percent in Algiers, 18 percent nationwide—suggests that the official vote tally was legitimate; see Jackson, *FLN in Algeria*, 77–80.
96. Memcon Chanderli and McGhee, 30 August 1962, JFKL, Algeria Country File, box 4b, Memoranda of Conversations, 4/5/62–11/29/62.
97. See Jeanneney's report of 27 September 1962, SEAA, chrono 5.
98. "Algeria Assembly Meets," *Times of London*, 26 September 1962, 10.
99. Arslan Humbaraci, *Algeria: A Revolution That Failed: A Political History since 1954* (London: Pall Mall, 1966), 91.
100. Bennoune, *Making of Contemporary Algeria*, 98–99.
101. Bennoune, *Making of Contemporary Algeria*, 90.
102. "The Economy of Algeria," 21 April 1964, WBA, Department of Operations–Africa, Africa Series, AF18-A.
103. "Conditions d'exécution des accords d'Evian," report for the 16 November 1962 Conseil des Affaires Algériennes, SEAA, carton 117.
104. See telegrams from Dejean in Moscow to Paris, no. 4081, 29 September 1962, and nos. 4583 &4584, 29 October 1962, SEAA, carton 133.
105. "Cold War Winds Blow in Algeria," *New York Times*, 3 October 1962, 11.
106. Mohamed Heikal, *The Cairo Documents: The Inside Story of Nasser and His Relationship with World Leaders, Rebels, and Statesmen* (Garden City, NY: Doubleday, 1973), 344. When Guevara visited in June 1959, he said that the leaders of the Cuban Revolution were inspired by Nasser's resistance against England, France, and Israel, but was not impressed by the small number of people forced to leave Egypt by Nasser's land reforms. Guevara said he judged the depth of a revolution by the number of refugees it created.
107. Castro speaking to Lakhdar Brahimi in Havana in January 1962, see Mission à Cuba," report by Brahimi, 18 January 1962, ANA, GPRA-MAE, dossier 117.1.5.

108. "Rapport de presentation de texts relatifs aux attributions, à l'organisation et au fonctionnement du Ministère des Affaires Etrangères," date unknown, and "Rapport annuel d'activité" by the Service des Etudes, de la Documentation et des Archives, 17 January 1965, ANA, MAE, 32/2000, box 50.
109. Handwritten note by Shakespeare, 16 November 1962, UKNA, FO, 371/165654.
110. "Le discours à l'assemblee generale des nation-unies," 31–36.
111. Telegram from Lacoste in Brussels reporting conversation with McGhee of State Department, no.1114–1119, 14 November 1962, SEAA, carton 133.
112. "L'Algérie à New York," *Jeune Afrique*, no. 104, 14–20 October 1962, 6–9.
113. "Adlai Stevenson Reports," broadcast on 15 October 1962, ABC TV, New York.
114. "Ben Bella Links Two 'Injustices,'" *New York Times*, 14 October 1962, 20.
115. "Ben Bella Meets Cuban President," *Washington Post*, 8 October 1962, 1; "Ben Bella Greets Cuban," *Washington Post*, 8 October 1962, 8.
116. Rusk to Porter, 17 September 1962, JFKL, National Security Files, box 4A. Boumedienne was quoted in a 16 September 1962 *Washington Post* article by Simon Malley.
117. On Yazid's favorable attitude to the United States, see Komer to Kennedy, 7 November 1963, JFKL, Algeria Country File, box 5; on Ben Bella's pragmatism, see Porter to Rusk, 8 October 1962, JFKL, Algeria Country File, box 111, 1961–1963.
118. Memorandum from Komer to Kennedy, 13 October 1962, FRUS, 1961–1963, vol. 21, pp. 102–104.
119. "Algerian, at UN, Decries Any Effort to Overturn Castro," *New York Times*, 13 October 1962, 1.
120. "Colorful Ceremony Greets Ben Bella at White House," *New York Times*, 16 October 1962, 1.
121. Memcon Ben Bella and JFK, 15 October 1962, JFK, National Security Files, box 4B, 4/5/62–11/29/62.
122. Report by Division Asie/Amérique Latine, "Impérialisme US en Amérique latine," ANA, MAE, 32/2000, box 24.
123. "Algerian, at UN, Decries Any Effort to Overturn Castro," 1
124. Report by Abdallah Khodja, Direction Générale du Plan, to the MAE, 18 May 1965, and by Sellali, Directeur du Commerce Extérieur, 19 May 1965, and undated report by the Direction des Affaires Economiques, Culturelles et Sociales, all from ANA, MAE, 32/2000, box 126.
125. Memcon Ben Bella and JFK, 15 October 1962, JFKL, National Security Files, box 4B, 4/5/62–11/29/62.
126. Rusk to Porter, 22 October 1962, JFKL, National Security Files, box 4A, 10/16/62–12/31/62.
127. A. Dahmouche, Division Europe/Amérique du Nord, "Rapport d'activité 1963," 15 January 1964, ANA, MAE, 32/2000, box 188.
128. Rusk to Porter, 22 October 1962, JFKL, National Security Files, box 4A, 10/16/62–12/31/62.
129. See "Les relations économiques internationales," Direction des Affaires Economiques et Culturelles (stamped "May 1966," but the content suggests it was written in 1964), ANA, MAE, 32/2000, box 24.
130. "National Security Action Memorandum No. 211," 14 December 1962, FRUS, 1961–1963, vol. 21, p. 113.
131. Memcon Ben Bella and JFK, 15 October 1962, JFK, National Security Files, box 4B, 4/5/62–11/29/62; Ernest R. May and Philip D. Zelikow, eds., *The Kennedy Tapes: Inside the White House during the Cuban Missile Crisis* (Cambridge, MA: Belknap Press, 1997), 36–45.
132. *Alger Républicain*, 17 October 1962, 1.
133. Telegram from Gardier in Havana, 17 October 1962, SEAA, chrono 3.
134. Piero Gleijeses, *Conflicting Missions: Havana, Washington, and Africa, 1959–1976* (Chapel Hill: University of North Carolina Press, 2002), 32.
135. Grimaud, *La politique extérieure de l'Algérie*, 146.
136. "Conversation with Ben Bella," 18 October 1962, National Security Archive, Cuban Missile Crisis: 50th Anniversary Update, item CM00010; see also memcon Khemisti and Dizdarević, 28 November 1962, DASMIP, 1962, f3, d439355.

137. See Aleksandr Fursenko and Timothy J. Naftali, *One Hell of a Gamble: Khrushchev, Castro, and Kennedy, 1958–1964* (New York: Norton, 2006), 229–230.
138. "Conversation with Ben Bella," 18 October 1962, National Security Archive, Cuban Missile Crisis: 50th Anniversary Update, item CM00010.
139. Note from the Direction Générale de la Sureté Nationale, 2 November 1962, SEAA, carton 133.
140. David Ottaway and Marina Ottaway, *Algeria: The Politics of a Socialist Revolution* (Berkeley: University of California Press, 1970), 90.
141. Robert Merle, *Ben Bella*, trans. Camilla Sykes (London: Michael Joseph, 1967), 155.
142. "Conversation with Ben Bella," 18 October 1962, National Security Archive, Cuban Missile Crisis: 50th Anniversary Update, item CM00010.
143. Editorial, *Wall Street Journal*, 19 October 1962.
144. Stevenson to Rusk, 19 October 1962, JFKL, Algeria Country File, box 4a, 10/16/62–12/31/62.
145. Stevenson to Rusk, 26 October 1962, JFKL, Algeria Country File, box 4a, 10/26/62–12/31/62; telegram from State Department to embassy Algiers, 23 October 1962, Digital National Security Archive, http://gateway.proquest.com/openurl?url_ver=Z39.88-2004&res_dat=xri:dnsa&rft_dat=xri:dnsa:article:CCC00924. See also telegram from Seydoux de Clausonne, no. 2888-2891, 27 October 1962, and telegram from Hervé Alphand, no. 6056–6059, 29 October 1962, SEAA, chrono 9.
146. Author's interview with Lakhdar Brahimi in Princeton, New Jersey, 29 June 2008.
147. "US Halts Algeria Aid Talks, Ben Bella's Visit to Cuba Cited," *New York Times*, 26 October 1962, 1.
148. Stevenson to Rusk, 26 October 1962, JFKL, Algeria Country File, box 4a, 10/26/62–12/31/62. This stance was also popular at home; see "Ben Bella Cheered for Cuba Stand," *Washington Post*, 21 October 1962, A23.
149. "Summary of Duplicitous Actions Taken by the Soviets with Regard to Cuba," State Department circular, 9 November 1962, Digital National Security Archive, http://gateway.proquest.com/openurl?url_ver=Z39.88-2004&res_dat=xri:dnsa&rft_dat=xri:dnsa:article:CCC02165.
150. Memcon Khemisti and Dizdarević, 28 November 1962, DASMIP, 1962, f3, d439355.
151. Secret telegram from State Department to embassy Algiers, 24 October 1962, Digital National Security Archive, http://gateway.proquest.com/openurl?url_ver=Z39.88-2004&res_dat=xri:dnsa&rft_dat=xri:dnsa:article:CCC01150.
152. Jackson, *FLN in Algeria*, 118–127, 136–137; Edmond Bergheaud, *Le premier quart d'heure* (Paris: Plon, 1964), 124–130.
153. *Alger Républicain*, 10 November 1962, 1–2; *Alger Républicain*, 26 December 1962, 1.
154. *Alger Républicain*, 15 November 1962, 1.
155. Porter to Rusk, 12 November 1962, JKFL, Algeria Country File, box 4a, 11/16/62–12/31/62.
156. "Algeria and the US to Resume Talks," *New York Times*, 27 November 1962, 11; telegram from Bohlen to Rusk, 6 December 1962, *FRUS*, 1961–1963, vol. 12, pp. 111–112; telegram from Alphand to Paris no. 309, 16 January 1963, SEAA, carton 129.
157. CIA information report, "Algerian Prime Minister Ahmed Ben Bella's Visit to Cuba," JFKL, National Security, William H. Brubeck files, Algeria 4/62–10/62.
158. A. Dahmouche, Division Europe/Amérique du Nord, "Rapport d'activité 1963," 15 January 1964, ANA, MAE, 32/2000, box 188.
159. Editorial "La Recontre" by Bechier Ben Yahmed, *Jeune Afrique*, 14–20 October 1962, 9.
160. "Note: Attitude du gouvernement algérien a l'égard des accords d'Evian," 22 October 1962, SEAA, carton 125. This note was probably for the attention of the head of the SEAA, Louis Joxe, who was preparing a briefing for the prime minister, Georges Pompidou.
161. "Attitude du gouvernement algérien a l'égard des accords d'Evian," 22 October 1962, SEAA, carton 125.
162. Quotation from a cover note from Christian Delabelle, charged with compiling the dossier for the Assemblée Nationale, to de Leusse in Rabat, 9 November 1962, SEAA, carton 131.
163. "Aide financière de la France à l'Algérie," 16 November 1962, files for the Conseil des affaires algériennes, SEAA, carton 117.

164. Draft of the instructions for the new ambassador to Algeria, Georges Gorse, 8 January 1963, SEAA, carton 125.
165. Summary conclusion of "Un an après Evian," 13 March 1963, SEAA, carton 125.
166. Gorse to de Broglie, 6 March 1963, *DDF*, 1963, vol. 1, pp. 260–266.
167. "National Security Action Memorandum No. 211," 14 December 1962, *FRUS*, 1961–1963, vol. 21, p. 113; memorandum from Komer to Kennedy, 28 December 1962, *FRUS*, 1961–1963, vol. 21, pp. 114–115.
168. René Dumont, "Des conditions de la réussite de la réforme agraire en Algérie," in *Problemes de l'algérie independante*, ed. François Perroux (Paris: Presses Universitaires de France, 1963), 91.
169. Gorse to de Broglie, 6 March 1963, *DDF*, 1963, vol. 1, pp. 260–266; also Evans's report on 1 November 1962 celebrations, 5 November 1962, UKNA, FO, 371/165678.
170. Peyrefitte, *C'était de Gaulle*, 401–402.
171. "France Resumes Atom Bomb Tests, Algeria Reports," *New York Times*, 20 March 1963, 1.
172. Memcon Ouzegane and Tito, 25 April 1963, AJBP, KPR, I-3-a/2-4.
173. Naylor, *France and Algeria*, 70.
174. "US and Algeria Agree on Terms of Aid Program," *New York Times*, 23 January 1963, 1.
175. "Ben Bella Stresses Food Relief by US," *New York Times*, 5 February 1963, 15.
176. Porter to Rusk, 3 January 1963, and Porter to Rusk, 15 January 1963, both in JFKL, Algerian Country File, box 4b, 1/63–5/63.
177. Ewart-Biggs reporting on Mennon-Williams visit to Scrivener, 12 February 1963, UKNA, FO, 371/173137.
178. Porter to Rusk, 18 January 1963, JFKL, Algerian Country File, box 4b, 1/63–5/63.
179. Ewart-Biggs to Scrivener, 28 May 1963, 2 April 1963, and 15 June 1963, all in UKNA, FO, 371/173137.
180. Memorandum from Mennen Williams to Rusk, "Action Plan for Algeria," 31 January 1963, Digital National Security Archive, http://gateway.proquest.com/openurl?url_ver=Z39.88-2004&res_dat=xri:dnsa&rft_dat=xri:dnsa:article:CPD00953 See also E. Cobbs Hoffman "The Foreign Policy of the Peace Corps," in *Empire and Revolution: The United States and the Third World Since 1945*, ed. Peter L. Hahn and Mary Ann Heiss (Columbus: Ohio State University Press, 2001), 130. According to Hoffman, Sargent Shriver was reluctant to send Peace Corps volunteers to areas considered dangerous such as Algeria or Vietnam.
181. Komer to Kennedy, 4 February 1963, *FRUS*, 1961–1963, vol. 21, 121.
182. National Security Action Memorandum 221, 20 February 1963, *FRUS*, 1961–1963, vol. 21, 122.
183. Memorandum from Mennen Williams to Rusk, "Action Plan for Algeria," 31 January 1963, Digital National Security Archive, http://gateway.proquest.com/openurl?url_ver=Z39.88-2004&res_dat=xri:dnsa&rft_dat=xri:dnsa:article:CPD00953.
184. Yaker to Bouteflika, "Mission de Monsieur le Ministre de l'économie nationale aux Etats-Unis," 20 September 1963, ANA, MAE, 33/2000, box 116.
185. Ben Bella quoted in Porter to Rusk, 27 May 1964, LBJL, National Security File, Algeria Country File, box 94-1, Cables Vol. 1 12/63–7/65
186. A. Dahmouche, Division Europe/Amérique du Nord, "Rapport d'activité 1963," 15 January 1964, ANA, MAE, 32/2000, box 188.
187. Report by the Direction des Affaires Economique et Culturelles, "Les relations économiques internationals," possibly from May 1964, ANA, MAE, 33/2000, box 24.
188. Ricardo René Laremont, *Islam and the Politics of Resistance in Algeria, 1783–1992* (Trenton, NJ: Africa World Press, 2000), 128–131.
189. Vallin, "Muslim Society in Algeria," 51.
190. Ben Bella to 5th National Congress of UGEMA, quoted in *El Moudjahid*, 10 August 1963.
191. *Kommunist*, no.13, September 1962, 92–96, 99–101, 104–109.
192. Memcon Djerdje and Boukadoum, 20 September 1962, DASMIP, 1962, f3, d430599.
193. See Ben Bella's interview with a communist Italian journalist, quoted in *Alger Républicain*, 11 January 1963, 1.
194. For example, see *Pravda*, 14 December 1962.

195. "Les relations algéro-soviétiques: Esquisse de la politique algérienne de l'URSS," report by the Division des Pay Socialistes, undated but seemingly 1964, ANA, GPRA-MAE, 46/2000, box 19.
196. Galia Golan, *The Soviet Involvement in the Middle East* (Jerusalem: Hebrew University, 1971), 55; Yevgeny Primakov, *Russia and the Arabs: Behind the Scenes in the Middle East from the Cold War to the Present* (New York: Basic Books, 2009), 75–86.
197. "Les relations algéro-soviétiques: Esquisse de la politique algérienne de l'URSS," report by the Division des Pay Socialistes, undated but seemingly 1964, ANA, GPRA-MAE, 46/2000, box 19.
198. Telegram from Dejean, no. 670/671, 6 February 1963, SEAA, carton 133.
199. Robert Merle, *Ahmed Ben Bella* (New York: Walker, 1967), 146.
200. Khrushchev later praised Ben Bella's use of such terminology. See *Memoirs of Nikita Khrushchev*, ed. Sergei Khrushchev, trans. George Shriver and Stephen Shenfield, vol. 3, *Statesman, 1953–1964* (University Park: Pennsylvania State University Press, 2007), 833.
201. Ottaway and Ottaway, *Algeria*, 91.
202. See the untitled report by the MAE's Direction des Affaires Economiques, Culturelles et Sociales for a May 1965 conference of the senior diplomatic corps, ANA, MAE, 32/2000, box 126; and also "Les relations économiques internationales," ANA, MAE, 32/2000, box 24.
203. Ben Bella quoted in *Alger Républicain*, 4 April 1963, 1
204. Memcon Ben Bella and Dizdarević, 20 May 1963, DASMIP, 1963, f3, d417268.
205. Fursenko and Naftali, *One Hell of a Gamble*, 331.
206. Carol Saivetz, "Socialism in Egypt and Algeria, 1960–1973: The Soviet Assessment" (PhD diss., Columbia University, 1979), 167–173.
207. "Les relations algéro-soviétiques: Esquisse de la politique algérienne de l'URSS," report by the Division des Pay Socialistes, undated but seemingly 1964, ANA, GPRA-MAE, 46/2000, box 19.
208. Ewart-Biggs to Scrivener, 11 September 1963, UKNA, FO 371, no. 1192.
209. "Les relations algéro-soviétiques: Esquisse de la politique algérienne de l'URSS," report by the Division des Pay Socialistes, undated but seemingly 1964, ANA, GPRA-MAE, 46/2000, box 19.
210. Vallin, "Muslim Society in Algeria," 51.
211. Quoted in Jeremy Scott Friedman, "Reviving Revolution: The Sino-Soviet Split, the 'Third World,' and the Fate of the Left" (PhD diss., Princeton University, 2011), 197.
212. Senior figures within the Algerian presidency and Ministry of Public Works shared these details with inquiring American officials; see the telegram from Root to Rusk of 26 August 1963, JFKL, National Security Files, box 4b.
213. "Les relations algéro-soviétiques: Esquisse de la politique algérienne de l'URSS," report by the Division des Pay Socialistes, undated but seemingly 1964, ANA, GPRA-MAE, 46/2000, box 19.
214. Telegram from embassy Algiers, 22 June 1964, LBJL, National Security File, Algeria Country File.
215. Kyle Haddad-Fonda, "Revolutionary Allies: Sino-Egyptian and Sino-Algerian Relations in the Bandung Decade" (PhD diss., Oxford University, 2013), 279–280.
216. Friedman, "Reviving Revolution," 196.
217. Telegram from embassy Algiers, 22 June 1964, LBJL, National Security File, Algeria Country File.
218. Sergey Radchenko, *Two Suns in the Heavens: The Sino-Soviet Struggle for Supremacy, 1962–1967* (Stanford, CA: Stanford University Press, 2009), 82.
219. Yala, "La mission du Ministre Boumaza à Pékin," 15 September 1964, ANA, MAE, series 33/2000, box 164.
220. Memcon Ben Bella and Dizdarević, 20 May 1963, DASMIP, 1963, f3, d417268.
221. Malek to Ben Bella, "Tour d'horizon sur les relations algéro-yougoslaves," 19 August 1963, ANA, MAE, 33/2000, box 166.
222. See telegrams from French embassy Belgrade, 18 October 1962, and from Amanrich, 14 November 1962, SEAA, chrono 6.

223. The appointment of diplomatic personnel was recorded regularly in the *Journal Officiel de la République Algérienne Démocratique et Populaire*.
224. Malek to Ben Bella, "Tour d'horizon sur les relations algéro-yougoslaves," 19 August 1963, ANA, MAE, 33/2000, box 166.
225. Alvin Z. Rubinstein, *Yugoslavia and the Nonaligned World* (Princeton, NJ: Princeton University Press, 1970) 196–200, 266–282; John C. Campbell, *Tito's Separate Road: American and Yugoslavia in World Politics* (New York: Harper and Row, 1967), 76–78.
226. Quoted in David C. Gordon, *The Passing of French Algeria* (London: Oxford University Press, 1966), 107.
227. In March 1963, one of Dizdareviç's colleagues confirmed to a British counterpart that the Algerian prime minister frequently asked their advice on party and government affairs; see memcon Clive and Komatina, 8 March 1963, UKNA, FO 371/173133; Jean Lacouture, *Nasser*, trans. Daniel Hofstadter (London: Secker and Warburg, 1973), 368.
228. Malek to Ben Bella, "Tour d'horizon sur les relations algéro-yougoslaves," 19 August 1963, ANA, MAE, 33/2000, box 166.
229. Memcon Ahmed Kaid and Tito, 28 March 1963, AJBP, KPR, I-3-a/2-3.
230. BBC Monitor Service B.32 1/9, FO, 371/173134.
231. Kolodziej, *French International Policy under de Gaulle and Pompidou*, 470.
232. Robert A. Mortimer, "Foreign Policy and Its Role in Nation-Building in Algeria" (PhD diss., Columbia University, 1968), 121.
233. Minutes of meetings in the embassy in Algiers, May 1963, SEAA, carton 125.
234. Robert Merle, *Ben Bella*, trans. Camilla Sykes (London: Michael Joseph, 1967), 155.
235. Komer to Bundy, 14 October 1963, *FRUS*, 1961–1963, vol. 21, pp. 128–129.
236. For example, see memorandum from Shoaid to McNamara and the attached overview of the history of the African Development Bank, 29 May 1969, and memcon McNamara and Labidi, 21 September 1970, both in WBA, McNamara Papers, African Development Bank (1968–1980), box 1.
237. Quoted in Rob Konkel, "The Monetization of Global Poverty: The Concept of Poverty in World Bank History, 1944–90," *Journal of Global History* 9, no. 2 (2014): 276–300.
238. "Copie d'une note que j'avais élaborée fin 1963 à l'intention du Président Ben Bella pour la promotion d'une politique pétrolière nationale," Belaïd Abdessalam Papers (BAP), http://www.belaidabdesselam.com/wp-content/uploads/2009/08/documents_cites_dans_le_texte_la_politique_de_developpement_appliquee_par_l_algerie_au_lendemain_de_son_independance.pdf.
239. "Pourquoi le socialisme?" by A.A., *Révolution Africaine*, no. 61, 28 March 1964, 12–13.
240. Peyrefitte, *C'était de Gaulle*, 439.
241. A draft of the letter is included with a report by the Ministère de l'Economie Nationale, 29 November 1963, ANA, MAE, 33/2000, box 116. See also "Mémorandum sur le problème des hydrocarbures remis le 29 novembre 1963 à Monsieur Pierre GUILLAUMAT par le Président BEN BELLA à l'intention du Général DE GAULLE Président de la République Française," BAP.
242. Telegram from Paris, 5 October 1963, UNKA, FO 371/172076.
243. Charles-Robert Ageron, "La cooperation avec l'Algérie indépendante," in *De Gaulle et son siècle* (Paris: La Documentation Française, 1992), 6:208.
244. Jarrod Hayes, "Queer Resistance to (Neo-)colonialism in Algeria," in *Postcolonial, Queer Theoretical Intersections*, ed. John C. Hawley (New York: SUNY Press, 2001), 79–98.
245. "Letter from Sub-officer A.M.," *El Djeich*, August 1963, 8.

Chapter 4

1. "Le discours a l'assemblee generale des nation-unies," 9 October 1962, in *Discours du Président Ben Bella du 28 septembre 1962 au 12 décembre 1962* (Algiers: Ministère de l'Information, 1963), 31–36.
2. "Ben Bella Links Two 'Injustices,'" *New York Times*, 14 October 1962.
3. "Le discours a l'assemblee generale des nation-unies," 31–36.

4. A. Campbell to FO, 8 November 1962, UKNA, FO 371/165654.
5. Robert Mortimer, "The Algerian Revolution in Search of the African Revolution," *Journal of Modern African Studies* 8, no. 3 (1970): 363–387.
6. Mabrouk Belhocine quoted in "Première session de l'Assemblée nationale constituante, séance du Samedi 24 novembre 1962," *Journal Officiel de la République Algérienne Democratique et Populaire* 1, no. 10 (18 March 1963).
7. "Declaration ministrielle a l'assemblee nationale constituante," 28 September 1962, in *Discours du Président Ben Bella du 28 septembre 1962 au 12 décembre 1962* (Algiers: Ministère de l'Information, 1963), 16.
8. Ben Bella quoted in "Discours de son excellence Ahmed Ben Bella prononcé devant l'Assemblée Nationale Constituante," 18 June 1963, Hoover Institution Archives, Library of Social History, box 2.
9. "Le discours de la Place des martyrs," 1 November 1962, in *Discours du Président Ben Bella du 28 septembre 1962 au 12 décembre 1962* (Algiers: Ministère de l'Information, 1963), 45.
10. On Ben Bella's interview by the Middle East News Agency in April, see Brant to Lawrence, 3 May 1962, UKNA, FO, 371/165654.
11. Telegram from Bourdeillette, nos. 727–731, 9 November 1962, SEAA, carton 129.
12. "Décolonisation et lutte contre l'impérialisme, le colonialisme, et le néo-colonialisme," Report on the Arab League, ANA, MAE, 32/2000, box 24.
13. Yazid Sayigh, *Armed Struggle and the Search for State: The Palestinian National Movement, 1949–1993* (Oxford: Clarendon Press, 1997), 91.
14. Alan Hart, *Arafat: A Political Biography* (London: Sidgwick and Jackson, 1994), 102, 111.
15. Embassy in Amman to MAE, "Réunion des ambassadeurs arabes au Palais Royale," 25 January 1965, ANA, MAE, 32/2000, box 121.
16. Sayigh, *Armed Struggle and the Search for State*, 100–102.
17. Author's interview with Lakhdar Brahimi at the London School of Economics and Political Science, 16 and 17 March 2009.
18. "Rapport de présentation de textes rélatifs aux attributions, à l'organisation et au fonctionnement du Ministère des affaires étrangères," undated, ANA, MAE, 32/2000, box 50; Service des Etudes, de la Documentation et des Archives, "Bilan d'activité pour l'année 1964," 19 March 1965, ANA, MAE 32/2000, box 133.
19. Memcon Dizdarević and Ben Bella, 8 March 1963, DASMIP, 1963, f11, d48238.
20. Robert A. Mortimer, "Foreign Policy and Its Role in Nation-Building in Algeria" (PhD diss., Columbia University, 1968), 188.
21. Author's interview with Ahmed Ben Bella, Algiers, 24 August 2007.
22. Quoted in Hart, *Arafat*, 155.
23. Sayigh, *Armed Struggle and the Search for State*, 102–103; Jean-Paul Chagnollaud, "Le Maghreb et le conflit israelo-arabe" (PhD diss., University of Paris I, 1975), 268–269; Paul Thomas Chamberlin, *The Global Offensive: The United States, the Palestine Liberation Organization, and the Making of the Post–Cold War Order* (New York: Oxford University Press, 2012), 52.
24. "Minutes from the Yugoslav-Algerian talks and the meeting between President Tito and Ben Bella," 11 March 1964, AJBT, 837, KPR 1-3-a/2-8.
25. Adeed Dawisha, *Arab Nationalism in the Twentieth Century: From Triumph to Despair* (Princeton, NJ: Princeton University Press, 2003), 219.
26. Dawisha, *Arab Nationalism in the Twentieth Century*, 234; Malcolm H. Kerr, *The Arab Cold War: Gamal 'Abd Al-Nasir and His Rivals* (New York: Oxford University Press, 1971), 95–96; Robert Stephens, *Nasser: A Political Biography* (London: Penguin, 1971), 394–399.
27. Report from Dizdarević, 10 November 1962, DASMIP, 1962, f3, d437502.
28. Telegram from Soulie in Jeddah to Paris on the substance of Moroccan and Tunisian discussions with the Saudi government, 29 December 1962, SEAA, carton 128. As if to emphasis the import of the Algerian-Egyptian relationship, Boumedienne personally saw off officers flying to Cairo; see telegram from Argod in Algiers, 21 June 1963, SEAA, carton 130.
29. Unable to mask his irritation, a Tunisian diplomat in Algiers muttered that such indecent haste "lacked seriousness, like the rest of the comportment of the Algerian leaders." Telegram from Gorse, 11 February 1963, SEAA, carton 128. See also telegram from Gorse, no. 1265/66, 9 March 1963, SEAA, carton 133.

30. See telegram from Evans, 25 March 1963, UKNA, FO 371/173133.
31. Malik Mufti, *Sovereign Creations: Pan-Arabism and Political Order in Syria and Iraq* (Ithaca, NY: Cornell University Press, 1996), 152.
32. Arab Ba'th Socialist Party, *Some Theoretical Principles Approved by the Six National Congress, October 1963* (Beirut: Dar al-Talia, 1974), 38, 43.
33. Telegram from Legourrierec in Baghdad, 1 April 1963, SEAA, carton 129; "Note pour le secrétaire d'etat: Relations algéro-égyptiennes," 18 November 1963, SEAA, carton 130; report from Dizdarević, 22 April 1963, DASMIP, 1963, f3, d414050.
34. Report from Peleš, 25 June 1963, DASMIP, 1963, f3, d421560.
35. Report from Dizdarević, 29 June 1963, DASMIP, 1963, f3, d422308.
36. Report from Dizdarević, 22 April 1963, DASMIP, 1963, f3, d414050.
37. On the collapse of the April 1963 agreement between Syria, Iraq and Egypt, see Fawaz A. Gerges, *The Superpowers and the Middle East: Regional and International Politics, 1955–1967* (Boulder, CO: Westview Press, 1994), 163; Mufti, *Sovereign Creations*, 143–167.
38. Froment-Meurice from Cairo, 30 September 1963, SEAA, chrono 24.
39. Report from Peleš, 25 June 1963, DASMIP, 1963, f3, d421560.
40. "Minutes from the Yugoslav-Algerian talks and the meeting between President Tito and Ben Bella," 11 March 1964, AJBT, 837, KPR 1-3-a/2-8.
41. Telegram from Porter to Rusk, 6 May 1963, JFKL, National Security Files, Algeria Country File, box 4b, 1/63-5/63.
42. On Nasser's disappointment, see Jean Lacouture, *Nasser*, trans. Daniel Hofstadter (London: Secker and Warburg, 1973), 206–207.
43. For Ben Bella's claim that a foreign plot was behind Khemisti's death, see Porter to Rusk, 12 April 1963, JFKL, Algeria Country File, box 4b, 1/63-5/63.
44. "L'Algérie à New York," *Jeune Afrique*, 14–20 October 1962, 6–9; cover story on Khemisti, "man of the week," *Jeune Afrique*, 3–9 December 1962, 8–9.
45. Mortimer, "Foreign Policy and Its Role in Nation-Building in Algeria," 204.
46. Memorandum for McGeorge Bundy, "Algeria and the Prospective UAR Federation," 10 May 1963, JFKL, National Security Files, Algeria Country File, box 4b, 1/63-5/63.
47. Dizdarević, "Nasser's visit," 11 May 1963, DASMIP, 1963, f3, d415998.
48. Jeanneney's report of the consul's discussions with Yacef Saadi (of Battle of Algiers fame) and Commander Moussaoui, 12 September 1962, SEAA, carton 129.
49. "Independence celebrations," report by Evans, 5 November 1962, UKNA, FO, 371/165678.
50. Ben Bella's statements at a press conference quoted in a telegram from Tiné in Rabat, 7 November 1962, SEAA, carton 129.
51. See telegram from Seydoux, 15 June 1962, SEAA, carton 129; telegram from Tiné, 8 September 1962, SEAA, carton 130.
52. Telegram from de Leusse to Algiers, no. 283, 17 January 1963, SEAA, carton 130.
53. Quoted in Clement Henry Moore, *Tunisia since Independence: The Dynamics of One-Party Government* (Berkeley: University of California Press, 1965), 70; telegram from Guiringaud, 19 January 1963, SEAA, carton 130.
54. "Tunis Recalls Envoy from Algeria," *Times of London*, 19 January 1963, 8; Maurice Flory, "Chronique Diplomatique," *Annuaire de l'Afrique du Nord* (Paris: Centre National de la Recherche Scientifique, 1963), 333.
55. Porter to Rusk, 18 January 1963, JFKL, National Security Files, Algeria Country File, Algeria General 1/63-5/63.
56. Telegram from Sauvagnargues in Tunis, 24 January 1963, SEAA, carton 130; telegrams from Gorse, 8 January 1963 and 25 January 1963, SEAA, carton 130.
57. Telegram from Guiringaud, 19 January 1963, SEAA, carton 130.
58. Telegram from de Leusse, 14 February 1963, SEAA, carton 128; telegrams from de Leusse, 16 February 1963 and 19 February 1963, SEAA, carton 128.
59. Memcon Dizdarević and Ben Bella, 8 March 1963, DASMIP, 1963, f3, d48238.
60. "Appréciation de l'attitude marocaine," undated report from early to mid-1963, ANA, MAE, 33/2000, box 166.
61. For example, Bourguiba gave a public speech to this effect in early March; see telegram from Sauvagnargues in Tunis, 4 March 1963, SEAA, carton 128.

62. "Appréciation de l'attitude marocaine," undated report from early to mid-1963, ANA, MAE, 33/2000, box 166.
63. See report by Mouloud Kassim, Division des Pays Arabes, 24 February 1964, ANA, MAE, 33/2000, box 166.
64. Memcom Yazid, Bentobbal, and Tito, 12 April 1961, ANA, GPRA-MAE, dossier 8.13.8.
65. "Appréciation de l'attitude marocaine," undated report from early to mid-1963, ANA, MAE, 33/2000, box 166.
66. Mortimer, "The Algerian Revolution in Search of the African Revolution," 363–387.
67. "Minutes from the Yugoslav-Algerian talks and the meeting between President Tito and Ben Bella," 11 March 1964, AJBT, 837, KPR 1-3-a/2-8.
68. Evans to Earl Home, "Algiers Dispatch No. 6: Algeria's *Vocation africaine*," 5 February 1963, UKNA, FO, 371/173133. The quotation is from comments appended to his document by Scrivener, 20 February 1963.
69. Quoted by Porter, telegram of 5 November 1962, JFKL, National Security Files, Algeria Country File, box 4a, 10/16/62–12/31/62.
70. "Le Discours à l'assemblee generale des nation-unies," 31–36.
71. Quoted by a French diplomatic official in Rabat, 17 October 1962, SEAA, carton 130.
72. Ben Bella quoted in telegram from Porter to Rusk, 28 June 1963, JFKL, National Security Files, Algeria Country File, box 4b, 6/63–9/63.
73. Author's interview with Nourredine Djoudi, Algiers, 23 November 2006.
74. Report from Dizdarević, 15 November 1962, DASMIP, 1962, f3, d437818.
75. Telegram from Deschamps in Dar-es-Salaam, 23 January 1963, SEAA, carton 129.
76. *El Moudjahid*, 19 January 1963.
77. Review No. 22, released on 11 December 1962 by the GRAE, in *The African Liberation Reader*, vol. 2, *The National Liberation Movements*, ed. Aquino de Braganca and Immanuel Wallerstein (London: Zed Press, 1982), 87–88.
78. John A. Marcum, *The Angolan Revolution* (Cambridge, MA: MIT Press, 1969), 2:63
79. *El Moudjahid*, 19 January 1963.
80. Yves Loiseau and Pierre-Guillaume de Roux, *Portrait d'un révolutionnaire en général: Jonas Savimbi* (Paris: La Table Ronde, 1987), 116–117. Before departing to take charge of the Algerian embassy in Cairo that summer, Lakhdar Brahimi was introduced to Savimbi in Ben Bella's home and told to help him make his way to Peking; author's interview with Lakhdar Brahimi in Princeton, New Jersey, 29 June 2008, and at the London School of Economics and Political Science, 16 and 17 March 2009.
81. Interviewed in *El Moudjahid*, 26 January 1963.
82. Author's interview with Lakhdar Brahimi in Princeton, New Jersey, 29 June 2008, and at the London School of Economics and Political Science, 16 March 2009; Marcum, *Angolan Revolution*, 2:64–66; see also the telegrams from the French embassy in Algiers to Paris on 18 and 21 January 1963, SEAA, carton 130.
83. De Andrade's claim is reported in the telegram from Gorse to Paris on 11 May 1963, SEAA, carton 130. On the arms shipment, see Marcum, *Angolan Revolution*, 2:113–114, 115–116; also "Minutes from the Yugoslav-Algerian talks and the meeting between President Tito and Ben Bella," 11 March 1964, AJBT, 837, KPR 1-3-a/2-8.
84. Marcum, *Angolan Revolution*, 2:66.
85. "Décolonisation, lutte contre le colonialisme, le néo-colonialisme et l'impérialisme depuis Bandoeng," report by the Africa desk, likely from early 1964, ANA, MAE, 32/2000, box 24.
86. Author's interview with Nourredine Djoudi, Algiers, 23 November 2006.
87. Klaas van Walraven, "From Tamanrasset: The Struggle of Sawaba and the Algerian Connection, 1957–1966," *Journal of North African Studies* 10, nos. 3–4 (2005): 507–527.
88. Immanuel Wallerstein, *Africa: The Politics of Unity* (Lincoln: University of Nebraska Press, 2005), 60–63; Mortimer, "The Algerian Revolution in Search of the African Revolution," 373. The article is by Bakari Djibo, appearing in *Révolution Africaine*, 23 February 1963.
89. Jean Lacouture, "La diplomatie algérienne demeure orientée en priorité vers l'Afrique," *Le Monde Diplomatique*, October 1963, http://www.monde-diplomatique.fr/1963/10/LACOUTURE/25582.

90. "Minutes from the Yugoslav-Algerian talks and the meeting between President Tito and Ben Bella," 6 March 1964, AJBT, 837, KPR 1-3-a/2-8.
91. "Les relations algéro-ivoiriennes," report from embassy in Abidjan, 13 January 1964, ANA, MAE, 33/2000, box 149.
92. Telegram from Gorse, 30 April 1963, SEAA, carton 129.
93. "Les relations algéro-ivoiriennes," report from embassy in Abidjan, 13 January 1964, ANA, MAE, 33/2000, box 149.
94. Draft copy of an undated letter from Ben Bella to Sékou Touré, probably in March or April 1962, ANA, MAE, 33/2000, box 332.
95. Marcum, *Angolan Revolution*, 2:73.
96. Kwesi Armah, *Peace without Power: Ghana's Foreign Policy 1957–1966* (Accra: Ghana Universities Press, 2004), 106.
97. "Etat des relations Algéro-Ghanéennes avant le 19 juin 1965," report by the Division Afrique, 6 May 1966, ANA, MAE, 33/2000, box 361.
98. Philip E. Muehlenbeck, "Kennedy and Touré: A Success in Personal Diplomacy," *Diplomacy and Statecraft* 19, no. 1 (2008): 69–95.
99. "Les relations de l'Algérie avec les pays africains," presumably a Division Afrique report from late 1965, ANA, MAE, 33/2000, box 275.
100. "Minutes from the Yugoslav-Algerian talks and the meeting between President Tito and Ben Bella," 11 March 1964, AJBT, 837, KPR 1-3-a/2-8.
101. Memcon Tito and Nasser, 12 and 13 May 1963, AJBT, 837, KPR I.3.a/121-30; memcon Dizdarević and Ben Bella, 20 May 1963, DASMIP, 1963, f3, d417268.
102. Slimane Chikh, "L'Algérie et l'Afrique (1954–1962)," *Revue Algérienne des Sciences Juridiques, Économiques et Politiques* 5, no. 3 (1968): 703–746; Mortimer, "The Algerian Revolution in Search of the African Revolution," 363–387.
103. Haile Selassie I, "Towards African Unity," *Journal of Modern African Studies* 1, no. 3 (1963): 281–291.
104. Descriptions taken from Jay Walz, "African Showplace," *New York Times*, 18 May 1963, 10, and Russell Howe, "African Leaders Arrive for Addis Ababa Talks," *Washington Post*, 21 May 1963, A16.
105. Selassie, "Towards African Unity," 285.
106. See also Wallerstein, *Africa*, 64–65.
107. Mortimer, "Foreign Policy and Its Role in Nation-Building in Algeria," 11.
108. Memcon Dizdarević and Ben Bella, 20 May 1963, DASMIP, 1963, f3, d417268.
109. Peter Braestrup, "Ben Bella Seeks Aid for Angolans," *New York Times*, 13 May 1963, 8.
110. R. A. Akindele, "Reflections on the Preoccupation and Conduct of African Diplomacy," *Journal of Modern African Studies* 14, no. 4 (1976): 557–576.
111. Odd Arne Westad, *The Global Cold War: Third World Interventions and the Making of Our Times* (Cambridge: Cambridge University Press, 2005), 106–107.
112. Telegram from Russell to Foreign Office, 27 May 1963, UKNA, PREM, 11/4603.
113. Quoted in Mortimer, "The Algerian Revolution in Search of the African Revolution," 374.
114. John Markakis, "The Organisation of African Unity: A Progress Report," *Journal of Modern African Studies* 4, no. 2 (1966): 135–153.
115. Arianna Lissoni, "Transformations in the ANC External Mission and Umkhonto we Sizwe, c. 1960–1969," *Journal of Southern African Studies* 35, no. 2 (2009): 287–301.
116. Author's interview with Nourredine Djoudi, Algiers, 23 November 2006.
117. "Séance de travail avec nos ambassadeurs en Afrique, Dakar 3 août 1963," report to Bouteflika, 25 September 1963, ANA, MAE, 33/2000, box 166.
118. "Rapport de la mission de bons offices chargée d'aider à la reconciliation des mouvements nationalists de la Guinée dite Portugaise et des Iles du Cap Vert," 31 July 1963, ANA, MAE 33/2000, box 166.
119. Marcum, *Angolan Revolution*, 2:97–99.
120. Armah, *Peace without Power*, 106.
121. Wallerstein, *Africa*, 68.
122. Patricia Berko Wild, "The Organization of African Unity and the Algerian-Moroccan Border Conflict: A Study of New Machinery for Peacekeeping and for the Peaceful Settlement of Disputes among African States," *International Organization* 20, no. 1 (1966): 18–36.

123. "Minutes from the Yugoslav-Algerian talks and the meeting between President Tito and Ben Bella," 11 March 1964, AJBT, 837, KPR 1-3-a/2-8.
124. Marko Nikezić, "Zabaleska o razgovoru sa ambassadorom Alzira u Beogradu R. Malek-om 31.X.63," 31 October 1963, AJBT, 837, KPR I.5.B/2-3, Alžir 27.I.1963-19.XII.1963.
125. Memcon Dizdarević and Ben Bella, 20 May 1963, DASMIP, 1963, f3, d417268.
126. "Rapport general" from the embassy in Dar-es-Salaam, September 1963, ANA, MAE 33/2000, box 166.
127. Letter from Ben Bella to Keita, 28 August 1963, ANA, MAE 33/2000, box 280.
128. "Panorama de la situation en Afrique," report by MAE Africa desk from 1964, ANA, MAE, 33/2000, box 275.
129. "Minutes from the Yugoslav-Algerian talks and the meeting between President Tito and Ben Bella," 6 March 1964, AJBT, 837, KPR 1-3-a/2-8.
130. "Examination of the international situation in light of the first Afro-Asian conference and appreciation of the ten Bandung principles," undated, ANA, RADP, MAE, series 32/2000, box 24.
131. French ambassador, Georges Gorse, reporting on his discussion with Aziz ben Miloud, head of MAE's Arab World desk, 9 April 1963, SEAA, carton 128.
132. Flory, "Chronique Diplomatique," 378; telegram from embassy Algiers, no. 625, 4 Feburary 1963, SEAA, carton 133.
133. Ṣāyigh, *Armed Struggle and the Search for State*, 102–103; Chamberlin, *Global Offensive*, 62.
134. Author's interview with Lakhdar Brahimi at the London School of Economics and Political Science, 16 and 17 March 2009.
135. Jon Lee Anderson, *Che Guevara: A Revolutionary Life* (London: Bantam, 1997), 546–549.
136. Chamberlin, *Global Offensive*, 52.
137. Jorge Serguera, *Che Guevara: La clave africana: Memorias de un comandante cubano, embajador en la Argelia postcolonial* (Jaen: Liberman, 2008), 184–187.
138. "Note: Accord soviéto-algérien," 5 June 1963, SEAA, carton 133; telegram from embassy Algiers, 5 June 1963, SEAA, carton 130.
139. Serguera interviewed in *El Moudjahid*, 23 February 1963; Serguera, *Che Guevara*, 119–120.
140. Telegram from Argod, 24 July 1963, no. 314/19, SEAA, chrono 20.
141. Memcon Kennedy and Guellal, 24 July 1963, JFKL, Algeria Country File, box 4b, Algeria General 6/63–9/63.
142. Briefing Memorandum for Kennedy, "Presentation of Credentials by Algerian Ambassador Guellal," 20 July 1963, JFKL, Algeria Country File, box 111, Algeria Security 1961–1963; Research Memorandum by the State Department Director of Intelligence and Research, "Ben Bella, Castro, and the Algerian Revolution," 15 November 1963, JFKL, Algeria Country File, box 5, Algeria General 11/63.
143. Serguera, *Che Guevara*, 184–187.
144. Piero Gleijeses, *Conflicting Missions: Havana, Washington, and Africa, 1959–1976. Envisioning Cuba* (Chapel Hill: University of North Carolina Press, 2002), 53–56.
145. Alvin Z. Rubinstein, *Yugoslavia and the Nonaligned World* (Princeton, NJ: Princeton University Press, 1970), 246.
146. Ben Bella interview in *Borba* reported on by French embassy in Belgrade by Binoche, 4 December 1962, SEAA, chrono 6.
147. "Tour d'horizon sur les relations algéro-yougoslaves," Malek to MAE, 19 August 1963, ANA, MAE, 33/2000, box 166.
148. "Minutes from the Yugoslav-Algerian talks and the meeting between President Tito and Ben Bella," 11 March 1964, AJBT, 837, KPR 1-3-a/2-8.
149. John C. Campbell, *Tito's Separate Road: America and Yugoslavia in World Politics* (New York: Harper and Row, 1967), 76–78; Rubinstein *Yugoslavia and the Non-aligned World*, 196–206.
150. "Tour d'horizon sur les relations algéro-yougoslaves," Malek to MAE, 19 August 1963, ANA, MAE, 33/2000, box 166.
151. "Minutes from the Yugoslav-Algerian talks and the meeting between President Tito and Ben Bella," 6 March 1964, AJBT, 837, KPR 1-3-a/2-8.
152. Markakis, "Organisation of African Unity," 135–153.

153. "Séance de travail avec nos ambassadeurs en Afrique," Dakar, 3 August 1963, ANA, MAE, 33/2000, box 166.
154. Memcon Tito and Nasser, 12 and 13 May 1963, AJBT, 837, KPR I.3.a/121-30.
155. Boutros Boutros-Ghali, "The Addis Ababa Charter: A Commentary," *International Conciliation*, no. 546 (January 1964): 38.
156. "Les problèmes du Tiers-Monde," draft version of a lengthy report by Benhabylès, May 1965, ANA, MAE, 33/2000, box 177.
157. "Décolonisation, lutte contre le colonialisme, le néo-colonialisme et l'impérialisme depuis Bandoeng," undated report by the Africa desk, probably from early 1964, ANA, MAE, 32/2000, box 24.
158. "Memorandum of Conversation from the Meeting between Premier Zhou Enlai and the Algerian Ambassador to China Mohamed Yala," August 6, 1964, History and Public Policy Program Digital Archive, PRC FMA 106-01448-02, 98-117, translated by Jake Tompkins, http://digitalarchive.wilsoncenter.org/document/118723.
159. Adoula's decision had coincided closely with Mennen Williams's visit; see telegram from Rusk to Porter, 3 July 1963, JFKL, National Security Files, Algeria Country File, box 4b, 6/63–9/63.
160. Root to Rusk, 4 September 1963, JFKL, National Security Files, box 4B, Algeria General 6/63–9/63.
161. "Décolonisation, lutte contre le colonialisme, le néo-colonialisme et l'impérialisme depuis Bandoeng," report by the Africa desk, likely from early 1964, ANA, MAE, 32/2000, box 24.
162. M'hammed Yala, "La visite du Président Ben Bella en Guinée (20–25 février 64)," ANA, MAE, 33/2000, box 332 (contained inside a folder titled "Visite du Président Sékou Touré en Algérie (19–25 mars 1964"). Also available in 33/2000, box 360.
163. "Panorama de la situation en Afrique," report by MAE Africa desk from 1964, ANA, MAE, 33/2000, box 275.
164. A. Dahmouche, Division Europe/Amérique du Nord, "Rapport d'activité 1963," 15 January 1964, ANA, MAE, 32/2000, box 188. General Hemberto Delgado, head of the Portuguese opposition government in exile, decamped from Brazil to Algiers; see telegram from Argod, no. 8379, 13 December 1963, SEAA, carton 130.
165. Telegram from Root to Rusk, 21 September 1963, JFKL, National Security Files, Algeria Country File, box 4b, 6/63–9/63.
166. Flory, "Chronique Diplomatique," 378; telegram from embassy Algiers, no. 625, 4 Februrary 1963, SEAA, carton 133.
167. "Special Comment for Senator Mansfield from Ambassador Porter, 'Where Is Algeria Going and What Should Be the US Role Here?'," briefing from Porter to Senator Mansfield, 5 July 1963, JFKL, Algeria Country File, box 111, Algeria General 1961–1963.
168. Ball to Porter, 19 August 1963, JFKL, Algeria Country File, box 5, Algeria subject: Proposed Prime Minister Ben Bella visit, 1963, 7/3163–10/20/63; Komer to Kennedy, 24 July 1963, JFKL, Algeria Country File, box 4b, Algeria General 6/63–9/63.
169. Memcon Kennedy, Mennen Williams, Porter, Komer, 19 September 1963, JFKL, Algeria Country File, box 4b, Algeria General 6/63–9/63.
170. Memorandum from Komer to Bundy, 14 October 1963, *FRUS*, 1961–1963, vol. 21, Africa, pp. 128–129.
171. Komer memorandum for the president, 5 October 1963, JFKL, President's Office Files, Countries, Algeria, box 111, Algeria Security 1961–1963.
172. Komer memorandum for the president, 8 October 1963, JFKL, Algeria Country File, box 5, Algeria subject: Proposed Prime Minister Ben Bella visit, 1963, 7/31/63–10/20/63.
173. Author's interview with Ahmed Ben Bella, Algiers, 24 August 2007.
174. "Minutes from the Yugoslav-Algerian talks and the meeting between President Tito and Ben Bella," 6 March 1964, AJBT, 837, KPR 1-3-a/2-8.
175. Marcum, *Angolan Revolution*, 2:131–132.
176. Direction des Affaires Politiques (probably Bouattoura) to Bouteflika, Aide-Mémoire, 13 September 1963, ANA, MAE, 33/2000, box 166.
177. Letter from Challal in New York, possibly to Yazid or Ben Bella (or to someone due to accompany him to New York), 5 October 1963, ANA, MAE, 33/2000, box 116.

178. A draft of the report, "L'evolution du camp socialiste et de l'Occident et les rapports Est-Ouest," is found in ANA, MAE, 33/2000, box 177, and minutes of the discussion of it, on 17 May 1965, in ANA, MAE, 32/2000, box 126.
179. Roy Allison, *The Soviet Union and the Strategy of Non-alignment in the Third World* (Cambridge: Cambridge University Press, 1988), 61–62.
180. Jeremy Scott Friedman, "Reviving Revolution: The Sino-Soviet Split, the 'Third World,' and the Fate of the Left" (PhD diss., Princeton University, 2011), 166.
181. Feng Chih-Tan, "Africa's Rising Star," *Peking Review*, no. 28 (12 July 1963): 13–14; "Les relations algéro-soviétiques," dated 5 January 1967 but containing sections written in previous years, ANA, MAE, 46/2000, box 19.
182. Westad, *The Global Cold War*, 165; Jeremy Friedman, "Soviet Policy in the Developing World and the Chinese Challenge in the 1960s" (paper presented at the 2009 Graduate Student Conference on the Cold War, London School of Economics and Political Science, 24–26 April 2009); see also Gorse's telegrams to the SEAA on Zhou's visit, 16, 21, 22, and 28 December 1963, SEAA, carton 133; also Porter to Rusk, 30 December 1963, LBJL, National Security Files, Algeria Country File, box 94-1, Algeria Cables 12/63–7/65.
183. Kyle Haddad-Fonda, "Revolutionary Allies: Sino-Egyptian and Sino-Algerian Relations in the Bandung Decade" (PhD diss., Oxford University, 2013), 243–248.
184. The Algerian delegation supported China's anti-imperialist stance at the AAPSO meeting in February 1963; see "Information on Algeria's current domestic and foreign policy problems, and relations with Yugoslavia," Tito archives, KPR I.5.B/2-3, Alzir 27.I.1963-19.XII.1963; "China Hails Independent Algeria," *Peking Review*, no. 45 (8 November 1963): 17–18.
185. Bruce D. Larkin, *China and Africa, 1949–1970: The Foreign Policy of the People's Republic of China* (Berkeley: University of California Press, 1971), 171.
186. Friedman, "Reviving Revolution," 198.
187. O. A. Amer, "China and the Afro-Asian Peoples' Solidarity Organization, 1958–1967" (Ph.D. diss., University of Geneva, 1972), 120–121.
188. Quoted in David Kimche, *The Afro-Asian Movement: Ideology and Foreign Policy of the Third World* (Jerusalem: Israel Universities Press, 1973), 185–186.
189. Haddad-Fonda, "Revolutionary Allies," 257; see also memcon Tito and Malek, 5 January 1964, AJBT, 837, KPR I.3.a/2-6.
190. Sergey Radchenko, *Two Suns in the Heavens: The Sino-Soviet Struggle for Supremacy, 1962–1967* (Stanford, CA: Stanford University Press, 2009), 82.
191. Quoted in W. A. C. Adie, "China, Russia, and the Third World," *China Quarterly*, no. 11 (1962): 200–213.
192. Secret telegram from Gorse, 20 December 1963, SEAA, chrono 34, folder "déc 63 à fév 64."
193. Friedman, "Reviving Revolution," 78–79; Sergey Mazov, *A Distant Front in the Cold War: The USSR in West Africa and the Congo, 1956–1964* (Stanford, CA: Stanford University Press, 2010), 233–237.
194. Recordings of the conversations of FLN prisoners, 1 February 1961, no. 255, SEAA, carton 14; Gamal Abdel Nasser, *The Philosophy of the Revolution* (Cairo: National Publication House Press, 1960), 69–70.
195. "Minutes from the Yugoslav-Algerian talks and the meeting between President Tito and Ben Bella," 11 March 1964, AJBT, 837, KPR 1-3-a/2-8.
196. Memcon Tito and Nasser, 12 and 13 May 1963, AJBT, 837, KPR I.3.a/121-30.
197. William Zartman, "The Politics of Boundaries in North and West Africa," *Journal of Modern African Studies* 3, no. 2 (1965): 155–173.
198. Wild, "Organization of African Unity and the Algerian-Moroccan Border Conflict," 18–36.
199. See the report on Guellal's visit to the State Department, Ball to Porter, 2 July 1963, JFKL, National Security Files, box 4B; see also the attached dossier by R. S. Scrivener, 8 November 1963, UKNA, FO 371/173802.
200. Nicole Grimaud, *La politique extérieure de l'Algérie (1962–1978)* (Paris: Karthala, 1984), 196. American officials attributed the Kabyle rebellion to Hassan's timing; see "The Algerian Situation," a memorandum for McGeorge Bundy, 14 October 1963, JFKL, National Security Files, Algeria Country File, box 5.
201. Root to Rusk, 15 October 1963, JFKL, box 5, Algeria General 10/63.

202. Statements by Ben Bella and Moroccan minister of information, Abdelhadi Boutaleb, reported in *Alger Républicain*, 2 and 3 October 1963.
203. Quoted in dossier by R. S. Scrivener, 8 November 1963, UKNA, FO 371/173802.
204. *Révolution Africaine*, 24 October 1963, 1; Arslan Humbaraci, *Algeria: A Revolution That Failed: A Political History since 1954* (London: Pall Mall, 1966), 143–144.
205. Humbaraci,*Algeria*, 146; David Ottaway and Marina Ottaway, *Algeria: The Politics of a Socialist Revolution* (Berkeley: University of California Press, 1970), 108–109.
206. Ferguson and King, to McGeorge Bundy from embassy Rabat, 28 October 1963, JFKL, Robert W. Komer files, box 407, Algeria/Morocco folder 2.
207. Memorandum from Komer to Kennedy, 21 October 1963, JFKL, National Security Files, Algeria Country File, box 5, Algeria General 10/63. The French shared American fears; see Lyon to Rusk, 24 October 1963, JFKL, National Security Files, Algeria Country File, box 5, Algeria General 10/63.
208. Komer to Bundy, 1 November 1963, JFKL, National Security Files, box 407
209. Komer to Bundy, 24 October 1963, JFKL, National Security Files, box 407; Saunders to Komer, 15 November 1963, JFKL, National Security Files, box 407.
210. FBIS 51, 26 October 1963, JFKL, National Security Files, box 407.
211. Komer to Kennedy, 25 October 1963, JFKL, National Security Files, box 407; see also Root to Rusk, 15 October 1963 and 17 October 1963, JFKL, box 5, Algeria General 10/63; Komer to Clifton and Kennedy, JFKL, box 5, Algeria General 10/63.
212. Komer to Bundy, 22 October 1963, JFKL, National Security Files, box 407.
213. Bohlen to Rusk, 19 October 1963, JFKL, box 5, Algeria General 10/63.
214. Serbian Foreign Ministry archives, Fejić to Belgrade, 7 October 1963, 1963-432688.
215. Froment-Meurice, no. 735, 23 October 1963, SEAA, chrono 24.
216. Porter to Rusk, 14 November 1963, JFKL, box 5, Algeria General 10/63.
217. Ibid.; and "Bloc Military Assistance to Algeria", Root to State, 31 October 1963, JFKL, National Security Files, Algeria Country File, box 5, Algeria General 10/63; Porter to Rusk, 1 November 1963, JFKL, National Security Files, Algeria Country File, box 5, Algeria General 10/63.
218. Jesse Ferris, "Soviet Support for Egypt's Intervention in Yemen, 1962–1963," *Journal of Cold War Studies* 10, no. 4 (2008): 5–36.
219. Author's interview with Ahmed Ben Bella, Algiers, 24 August 2007; Serguera, *Che Guevara*, 189–199; Gleijeses, *Conflicting Missions*, 41–47.
220. Root to Rusk, 1 November 1963, JFKL, box 5, Algeria General 10/6.
221. Porter to Rusk, 1 November 1963, JFKL, box 5, Algeria General 11/63; "Nasser's Position on Cuban Aid to Algeria," research memorandum by Directorate of Intelligence and Research, Denney to Rusk, 18 November 1963, JFKL, Robert W. Komer files, box 407, Algeria/Morocco folder 2.
222. "Flavio Bravo, Deputy Commander of the Cuban Forces in Algeria, to Raúl Castro, Algiers," October 21, 1963, History and Public Policy Program Digital Archive, Centro de Información de la Defensa de las Fuerza Armadas Revolucionaries (CID-FAR), Havana http://digitalarchive.wilsoncenter.org/document/112126.
223. Komer to MacGeorge Bundy, 1 November 1963, JFKL, Robert W. Komer files, box 407, Algeria/Morocco folder 2.
224. Ball to Porter, 29 October 1963, JFKL, box 5, Algeria General 10/63.
225. Porter to Rusk, 6 November 1963, JFKL, President's Office Files, Algeria Country File, box 111, Algeria Security November 1963.
226. Memcon Yazid and Kennedy, 8 November 1963, JFKL, box 5, Algeria General 11/63; Komer to Kennedy, 7 November 1963, JFKL, box 5, Algeria General 11/63; research memorandum, "Ben Bella, Castro, and the Algerian Revolution," 15 November 1963, JFKL, box 5, Algeria General 11/63; Serbian Foreign Ministry, 1964-03-18 Number 218-Telegram 16.docx.
227. Komer to Kennedy, 24 October 1963, JFKL, Algeria Country File, box 5, Algeria General 10/63.
228. Ball to Porter, 29 October 1963, JFKL, box 5, Algeria General 10/63.
229. Froment-Meurice to Paris, 23 October 1963, SEAA, chrono 23; Froment-Meurice to Paris, 20 November 1963, SEAA, chrono 24.

230. Mortimer, "Foreign Policy and Its Role in Nation-Building in Algeria," 302.
231. Report from Dizdarević, 30 January 1964, DASMIP, 1964, f11, d43498.
232. Marko Nikezić, "Zabaleska o razgovoru sa ambassadorom Alzira u Beogradu R. Malek-om 31.X.63," 31 October 1963, AJBT, 837, KPR I.5.B/2-3, Alžir 27.I.1963-19.XII.1963.
233. Wild, "Organization of African Unity and the Algerian-Moroccan Border Conflict," 18–36.
234. Ottaway and Ottaway, *Algeria*, 98.
235. "Minutes from the Yugoslav-Algerian talks and the meeting between President Tito and Ben Bella," 11 March 1964, AJBT, 837, KPR 1-3-a/2-8.
236. Report from Dizdarević, 18 March 1964, DASMIP, 1964, f11, d49107.
237. Memcon Dizdarević and Ben Bella, 2 June 1964, DASMIP, 1964, f11, d423839.
238. Interview with Mohammed Harbi, "Pour Ben Bella, il y avait plus important que les frontiers," *Jeune Afrique*, 25 November 1977, 70–73.
239. Report from Dizdarević, 30 January 1964, DASMIP, 1964, f11, d43498.
240. Serguera, *Che Guevara*, 200–201.
241. Report from Dizdarević, 22 June 1964, DASMIP, 1964, f11, d427425.

Chapter 5

1. "Minutes of the Permanent Committee of the Second Summit Conference of Afro-Asian States, 20–21 April 1964 and 6 May 1965," 33/2000, box 26, Algerian National Archives (ANA), archives of the Ministère aux Affaires Etrangères (MAE); Robert Merle, *Ahmed Ben Bella*, trans. Camilla Sykes (London: Michael Joseph, 1967), 28.
2. "Alger: Carrefour du Tiers-Monde," *Révolution Africaine*, 12 June 1965.
3. "De Nadi Snober à Zeralda," *Révolution Africaine*, 12 June 1965.
4. "France Refuses to Yield as Tariff Talks Begin," *Times of London*, 5 May 1964, 10.
5. Jameson W. Doig, *Empire on the Hudson: Entrepreneurial Vision and Political Power at the Port of New York Authority* (New York: Columbia University Press, 2001), 382–385; "Biggest Buildings Herald New Era," *New York Times*, editorial, 20 January 1964.
6. "U Thant Addresses Economic and Social Council," in *United Nations Conference on Trade and Development: Geneva, 23 March–16 June 1964* (Geneva: United Nations Office of Public Information, 1964), 28–29.
7. Branislav Gosovic, *UNCTAD Conflict and Compromise: The Third World's Quest for an Equitable World Economic Order through the United Nations* (Leiden: A. W. Sijthoff, 1972), 28.
8. "Items-in-Algeria—meeting with Ahmed Ben Bella," 3 February 1964, UN Archives, S-0878-0001-02-00001, Peace-Keeping Operations, Files of the Secretary-General: U Thant, Other countries; memorandum to Bouteflika from Division Organisations Internationales, 15 January 1964, ANA, MAE, 33/2000, box 116.
9. "Révision de la Charte des Nations Unies," 1965, ANA, MAE, 32/2000, box 24.
10. Memorandum to Bouteflika from Division Organisations Internationales, 15 January 1964, ANA, MAE, 33/2000, box 116; Nicole Grimaud, *La politique extérieure de l'Algérie (1962–1978)* (Paris: Karthala, 1984), 335.
11. M'hamed Yazid, "De Bandoung à Alger," *Démocratie Nouvelle*, June 1965, 153–156.
12. Grimaud, *La politique extérieure de l'Algérie*, 148.
13. Memcon of Komer and Guellal, 15 January 1964, LBJL, National Security Files, Algeria Country File, box 94-1.
14. Quoted in Roy Allison, *The Soviet Union and the Strategy of Non-alignment in the Third World* (Cambridge: Cambridge University Press, 1988) 45.
15. Memcon Dizdarević and Ben Bella, 2 June 1964, DASMIP, 1964, f11, d423839.
16. Report from Dizdarević, 22 June 1964, DASMIP, 1964, f11, d427425.
17. "Les relations algéro-soviétiques: Esquisse de la politique algérienne de l'URSS," report by Division des Pays Socialistes from late 1964 or early 1965, ANA, MAE, 46/2000, box 19.
18. "Minutes from the Yugoslav-Algerian talks and the meeting between President Tito and Ben Bella," 11 March 1964, AJBT, 837, KPR 1-3-a/2-8.
19. Author's interview with Ahmed Laïdi, Algiers, 1 December 2006.

20. Report by Dizdarević, 30 April 1965, DASMIP, 1965, f3, d416030; "Soviet Military Aid to Algeria," a report by the State Department Bureau of Intelligence and Research, 6 August 1964, LBJL, National Security Files, Algeria Country File, box 94-1, Memos and Miscellaneous Volume 1. Similar French estimates are provided in Irina Gridan and Gaëlle Le Boulanger, "Une collaboration pragmatique et circonspecte: Les relations militaires entre l'Algérie et l'URSS, de l'indépendance au début des années 1970," *Outre-Mers* 95, nos. 354–355 (2007): 44.
21. "Compte-rendu sommaire des discussions avec les experts du Comité d'Etat pour les relations extérieures de l'URSS," report by Lakhdari, Directeur des Mines et de la Géologie, Algiers 30 December 1963, ANA, MAE 46/2000, box 27.
22. "Relations soviéto-algériennes depuis l'indépendance de l'Algérie," long overview report by the embassy in Moscow, 7 January 1964, French Diplomatic Archives, Europe 1960–1970, sous-série URSS, carton 1925; see also the telegram from Baudet in Moscow, 25 May 1964, SEAA, chrono 39.
23. Robert Legvold, "Soviet and Chinese Influence in Black Africa," in *Soviet and Chinese Influence in the Third World*, ed. Alvin Z. Rubinstein (New York: Praeger, 1975), 154–175.
24. *Memoirs of Nikita Khrushchev*, ed. Sergei Khrushchev, trans. George Shriver and Stephen Shenfield, vol. 3, *Statesman, 1953–1964* (University Park: Pennsylvania State University Press, 2007), 880–881, 833.
25. See Carol R. Saivetz, "Socialism in Egypt and Algeria, 1960–1973: The Soviet Assessment" (PhD diss., Columbia University, 1979).
26. "Les relations algéro-soviétiques: Esquisse de la politique algérienne de l'URSS," report by Division des Pays Socialistes from late 1964 or early 1965, ANA, MAE, 46/2000, box 19.
27. Telegram from Gorse, 29 February 1964, no. 1438/40, SEAA, carton 133; Grimaud, *La politique extérieure de l'Algérie*, 122–123.
28. "Les relations algéro-soviétiques: Esquisse de la politique algérienne de l'URSS," report by Division des Pays Socialistes from late 1964 or early 1965, ANA, MAE, 46/2000, box 19.
29. Dahmouche, Division Europe/Amérique du Nord, "Rapport d'activité 1963," 15 January 1964, ANA, MAE, 32/2000, box 188; Benhabylès, "Les problèmes du Tiers Monde," ANA, MAE, 32/2000, box 6 (also available in 33/2000, box 177).
30. Jenifer van Vleck, "An Airline at the Crossroads of the World: Ariana Afghan Airlines, Modernization, and the Global Cold War," *History and Technology*, 25, no. 1 (2009): 3–24; telegram from Gorse, 11 January 1964, no. 259, SEAA, carton 133.
31. "Les Etats-Unis et la situation en Afrique," report by Guellal to Bouteflika, 22 June 1964, ANA, MAE, 32/2000, box 197; Grimaud, *La politique extérieure de l'Algérie*, 148.
32. Memcon Rusk and Guellal, 16 April 1964, LBJL, National Security Files, Algeria Country File, box 94-1.
33. Report from Dizdarević, 18 March 1964, DASMIP, 1964, f11, d49107.
34. Report from Dizdarević, 22 June 1964, DASMIP, 1964, f11, d427425.
35. *Memoirs of Nikita Khrushchev*, 880–881, 833.
36. Report from Dizdarević, 22 June 1964, DASMIP, 1964, f11, d427425.
37. Memcon Dizdarević and Ben Bella, 2 June 1964, DASMIP, 1964, f11, d423839.
38. *SSSR i strany afriki, 1946–1962 gg. Dokumenty i materially* (Moscow: Gosudarstvennoe Izdatelsvo Politicheskoi Literatury, 1963), 1:50; Artemy M. Kalinovsky, "Not Some British Colony in Africa: The Politics of Decolonization and Modernization in Soviet Central Asia, 1955–1964," *Ab Imperio* 2013, no. 2 (2013): 191–222.
39. Telegram from Baudet, no. 2326-2332, 2 May 1964, SEAA, chrono 39.
40. According to the Algerian account, Khrushchev told Benyahia that "there was no need to fear French pressure, since the USSR could buy our agricultural surpluses"; "Les relations algéro-soviétiques: Esquisse de la politique algérienne de l'URSS," report by Division des Pays Socialistes from late 1964 or early 1965, ANA, MAE, 46/2000, box 19. Algerian figures for trade with the USSR found in "Tableau des importations algériennes en provenance de l'URSS du 1er janvier au 30 septembre 1964," report from the Ministère de l'Economie Nationale, Direction du Commerce Extérieur, ANA, MAE, 42/2000, box 5.
41. Telegram from Laboulaye in Moscow, reporting on conversations with Ben Yahia, 31 March 1964, SEAA, chrono 39. See also Ben Yahia's account of Ben Bella's visit as reported by de

Laboulaye to Couve de Murville, 13 June 1964, *DDF*, 1964, vol. 1, pp. 588–589; Grimaud, *La politique extérieure de l'Algérie*, 123.
42. See telegram from Baudet to Couve de Murville, no. 2611/2624, 7 May 1964, and no. 2650/60, 8 May 1964, SEAA, chrono 39.
43. Report from Dizdarević, 22 June 1964, DASMIP, 1964, f11, d427425.
44. Christopher Andrew and Vasili Mitrokhin, *The World Was Going Our Way: The KGB and the Battle for the Third World* (New York: Basic Books, 2005), 434. The Algerians alleged that the CIA was working with the Kabyle rebels through nongovernmental organizations; see Rusk to Porter, 20 March 1964, LBJL, National Security Files, Algeria Country File, box 94-1, Algeria cables vol. 1, 12/63–7/65. In late February 1964, Ben Bella told Sékou Touré of Guinea that Aït Ahmed had made contact with the CIA in Zurich, and that Morocco had coordinated its attack with the Kabyle rebellion; see "Visite du president Ben Bella en Guinée (20–25 février 64)," produced by the embassy in Conakry, ANA, MAE, 33/2000, box 332.
45. Ben Bella quoted in Porter to Rusk, 27 May 1964, LBJL, National Security Files, Algeria Country File, box 94-1, Algeria cables vol. 1, 12/63–7/65
46. David Ottaway and Marina Ottaway, *Algeria: The Politics of a Socialist Revolution* (Berkeley: University of California Press, 1970), 99–103; telegram from Owen to London, 3 August 1964, UKNA, FO, 371/178770.
47. Root to Rusk, 29 June 1964, LBJL, Algeria Country File, box 94-1, Algeria cables vol. 1, 12/63–7/65; memo from Saunders to Komer, 16 July 1964, LBJL, Robert W. Komer files, box 111, Algeria December 1963–March 1966; Komer to Porter, 4 September 1964, LBJL, Robert W. Komer files, box 111, Algeria December 1963–March 1966.
48. Telegram from Owen to London, 17 June 1964, UKNA, FO, 371/178770.
49. Memorandum from Bundy to Johnson, 5 January 1965, *FRUS*, 1964–1968, vol. 24, Africa, pp. 36–37.
50. Telegram from Evans to London, 5 December 1963, UKNA, FO, 371/172803.
51. Saunders to Komer, 14 January 1964, LBJL, Robert W. Komer files, box 111, Algeria December 1963–March 1966.
52. Kristin L. Ahlberg, "'Machiavelli with a Heart': The Johnson Administration's Food for Peace Program in India, 1965–1966," *Diplomatic History* 31, no. 4 (2007): 665–701; Robert B. Rakove, *Kennedy, Johnson, and the Nonaligned World* (New York: Cambridge University Press, 2013), 194–197.
53. Rusk to Porter, 17 June 1964, *FRUS*, 1964–1968, vol. 24, Africa, pp. 26–28.
54. See Porter to Rusk, 23 January 1964, LBJL, National Security Files, Algeria Country File, box 94-1, Algeria cables vol. 1, 12/63–7/65; Root to Rusk, 29 June 1964, LBJL, National Security Files, Algeria Country File, box 94-1, Algeria cables, vol. 1, 12/63–7/65.
55. Memcon of Mennen Williams and Bouteflika, 2 January 1965, LBJL, National Security Files, Files of Robert W. Komer, box 111, Algeria December 1963–March 1966.
56. For example, see "Les relation economiques internationals," probably from May 1965, ANA, MAE, 32/2000, box 24.
57. Ahmed Ben Bella, *Ben Bella revient* (Paris: Editions Jean Picollec, 1982), 224.
58. Telegram from Owen, 6 May 1965, UKNA, FO, 371/184106.
59. Howe to Rusk, 11 February 1965, DDRS, fiche R-319H, document 01611.
60. Intelligence memorandum, "US aid to countries aiding Congo rebels," 15 December 1964, Digital DDRS, accessed 17 September 2009. For a firsthand CIA account of the Congo, see Larry Devlin, *Chief of Station, Congo: A Memoir of 1960–67* (New York: Public Affairs, 2007).
61. CIA Intelligence report, "Weekly Cuban Summary," 30 December 1964, Digital DDRS, accessed 17 September 2009; memorandum from Komer to Bundy, 18 December 1964, LBJL, National Security Files, Files of Robert W. Komer, box 111, Algeria December 1963–March 1966.
62. CIA Intelligence Information Cable, "Presence of Cuban technical advisers at secret training camp for Algerian militia," 26 January 1965, Digital DDRS, accessed 17 September 2009; Jorge G. Castañeda, *Compañero: The Life and Death of Che Guevara* (New York: Knopf, 1997), 290.

63. Memcon Mouloud Kassim and Czechoslovak first secretary, 18 March 1964, ANA, MAE, 33/2000, box 116; outgoing telegram no. 565 to The Hague, 11 February 1965, DDRS, document 319G.
64. The two navy pilots supposedly "escaped over the back wall" and made their way to the embassy; see Porter to Rusk, 7, 9, 11, and 12 January 1965, LBJL, National Security Files, Algeria Country File, box 94-1, Algeria cables vol. 1, 12/63–7/65.
65. Howe to Rusk, 11 February 1965, DDRS, fiche R-319H, document 01611.
66. Memcon Malek and Tito, 16 March 1965, Yugoslav archives, KPR I-3-a/2-11.
67. Author's interview with Ahmed Ben Bella at his home in Algiers, 24 August 2007.
68. On Algerian condemnations of US policy at this time, see Peter Willetts, *The Non-aligned Movement: The Origins of a Third World Alliance* (London: Pinter, 1978), 32; Porter to Rusk, 14 April 1965, LBJL, National Security Files, Algeria Country File, box 94-1, folder 2, 12/63–7/65.
69. Memcon Rusk and Guellal, 16 April 1965, LBJL, National Security Files, Files of Robert W. Komer, box 11, Algeria December 1963–March 1966, folder 4.
70. Guellal to Bouteflika, "Project de libération Hertz," 6 August 1965, ANA, MAE, 32/2000, box 124.
71. Rusk to Porter, 26 Amy 1965, LBJL, National Security Files, Algeria Country File, box 94-1, folder 2, 12/63–7/65; memorandum from Berl Herbhard to Bundy, "Message from President Ahmed Ben Bella," 8 May 1965, LBJL, National Security Files, Files of Robert W. Komer, box 11, Algeria December 1963–March 1966, folder 4.
72. Guellal to Bouteflika, "Project de libération Hertz," 6 August 1965, and "Libération Hertz au Vietnam et médiation de l'Algérie," 19 September 1965, ANA, MAE, 32/2000, box 124.
73. See memcon Maiza and Huynh Van Tram (NLF), 8 June 1965, and "Compte-rendu d'entretien avec l'ambassadeur du Viet-Nam Nord," 10 June 1965, ANA, MAE, 33/2000, box 114.
74. Guellal to Bouteflika, "Project de libération Hertz," 6 August 1965, ANA, MAE, 32/2000, box 124.
75. For Algerian views on Vietnam, see "La Crise Vietnamienne," New York embassy, 2 June 1965, ANA, MAE, 32/2000, box 22; "Le problème vietnamien et les Nations Unies," Autumn 1965, ANA, MAE, 32/2000, box 4; "Relations Vietnam-Algérie," report from embassy in Hanoi, 31 July 1968, and "Le Vietnam et les Accords d'Evian" from same, 1 August 1968, ANA, MAE, 32/2000, box 6.
76. Memcon Rusk and Guellal, 16 April 1965, LBJL, National Security Files, Files of Robert W. Komer, box 11, Algeria December 1963–March 1966, folder 4.
77. Bernhard to Bundy, "Message from President Ahmed Ben Bella," 8 May 1965, LBJL, National Security Files, Files of Robert W. Komer, box 11, Algeria December 1963–March 1966, folder 4.
78. Porter to Rusk, 11 May 1964, LBJL, National Security Files, Algeria Country File, box 94-1, Algeria cables vol. 1, 12/63–7/65; "Les relations algéro-soviétiques: esquisse de la politique algérienne de l'URSS," report by Division des Pays Socialistes from late 1964 or early 1965, ANA, MAE, 46/2000, box 19.
79. Report from Dizdarević, 22 June 1964, DASMIP, 1964, f11, d427425.
80. "Minutes from the Yugoslav-Algerian talks and the meeting between President Tito and Ben Bella," 6 and 11 March 1964, AJBT, 837, KPR 1-3-a/2-8.
81. Benhabylès, "Les problèmes du Tiers Monde," ANA, MAE, 32/2000, box 6 (also available in 33/2000, box 177). See also Benjamin Stora, "Algeria/Morocco: The Passions of the Past. Representations of the Nation That Unite and Divide," in *Nation, Society, and Culture in North Africa*, ed. James McDougall (London: Frank Cass, 2003), 14–34.
82. Tron to Rusk, "Conversation with Spanish Consulate Official: Tension with Morocco: Activities of Moroccan Opposition in Algeria," 5 November 1964, NARA, RG59, box 1882, General Records of State Department, Central Foreign Policy Files, 1964–66.
83. "Minutes from the Yugoslav-Algerian talks and the meeting between President Tito and Ben Bella," 11 March 1964, AJBT, 837, KPR 1-3-a/2-8.
84. Memorandum from Harriman to Rusk, 21 January 1965, *FRUS*, 1964–1968, vol. 24, Africa, pp. 167–168; memcon Benhima and Rusk, 18 January 1965, LBJL, National Security Files,

Morocco Country File, Memos and Miscellaneous, vol. 1, 12/63–7/67; "Polarization in North Africa: Implications for the US," a report by the State Department Directorate of Intelligence and Research, 6 January 1965, LBJL, National Security Files, Algeria Country File, 94-1, Memos and Miscellaneous, vol. 1, 12/63–7/65.

85. "Rapport concernant mes premiers visites aux members du gouvernement, au parti de l'USRDA et aux ambassadeurs accredités à Bamako," Aidi to Bouteflika, reached Algiers on 11 January 1965, ANA, MAE, 33/2000, box 280; memcon Benhima and Rusk, 18 January 1965, FRUS, 1964–1968, vol. 24, Africa, pp. 166–167.

86. "Panorame de la situation en Afrique," Division Afrique, 1964, ANA, MAE, 33/2000, box 275.

87. "Décolonisation, lutte contre le colonialisme, le néo-colonialisme et l'impérialisme depuis Bandoeng," Division Afrique, undated but appears to have been written in late 1964, ANA, MAE, 32/2000, box 24.

88. "Les Etats-Unis et la situation en Afrique," Guellal to Bouteflika, 22 June 1964, ANA, MAE, 32/2000, box 197.

89. "La visite du Président Ben Bella en Guinée (20–25 février 1964)," report by M'hamad Yala, ANA, MAE, 33/2000, box 332; "A current appraisal of the Zanzibar situation," intelligence information cable from Zanzibar, 30 March 1964, CIA, FOIA online, accessed 12 October 2009.

90. See Al Chaab, 6 February 1964, and also telegram from Fernand-Laurent, no. 1014/15, 6 February 1964, SEAA, carton 129.

91. "Panorame de la situation en Afrique," Division Afrique, 1964, ANA, MAE, 33/2000, box 275.

92. "Panorame de la situation en Afrique," Division Afrique, 1964, ANA, MAE, 33/2000, box 275.

93. "Rapport: 2éme Session Ordinaire du Conseil des Ministres de l'OUA, Lagos 24–29 février 1964," prepared by Sahnoun as part of a set of preparatory documents for Sékou Touré's visit to Algiers, 19–25 March 1964, ANA, MAE, 33/2000, box 332.

94. Special Memorandum, Sherman Kent, Chairman of Board of National Estimates, "Guerrilla Prospects in Mozambique," 8 December 1964, and Special Report, "Anti-Portuguese Campaign in Africa Shifts to Mozambique," Office of Current Intelligence, 18 December 1964, CIA, FOIA.

95. Author's interview with Nourredine Djoudi, Algiers, 23 November 2006.

96. Immanuel Wallerstein, *Africa: The Politics of Independence and Unity* (Lincoln: University of Nebraska Press, 2005), 74–75.

97. On the agreement to train ZAPU fighters in Algeria, paid for by the Liberation Committee, see "Entrainement des éléments du ZAPU," report by Djoudi in Dar-Es-Salam to Bouteflika, 10 August 1964, ANA, MAE, 33/2000, box 439. On Algeria's condemnation of British policy and role at the UN, see "Comité des 24: Question de la Rhodésie du Sud," report by Algerian mission in New York, 24 June 1964, ANA, MAE, 33/2000, box 439, and "Opportunité d'une declaration condamnant Ian Smith," report by Ougouag, head of the Division Afrique, 24 September 1964, ANA, MAE, 33/2000, box 439.

98. "Rapport de fin d'année," Adjali to Bouteflika, 8 January 1965, ANA, MAE, 33/2000, box 149. John A. Marcum, *The Angolan Revolution* (Cambridge, MA: MIT Press, 1969), 2:141.

99. "La lutte de libération en Afrique australe: Eléments pour une stratégie, document de base," ANA, MAE, 33/2000, box 93.

100. "Le problème rhodésien après la proclamation unilaterale de l'indépendance à la recherche des moyens d'une solution," report by Nekli, head of Division Afrique, ANA, MAE, 33/2000, box 188.

101. Report by the Division Afrique, 29 April 1964, and report from Dahan in Paris to MAE, 6 August 1964, ANA, MAE, 33/2000, box 254.

102. Report from Adjali, "Relations Brazza-Israel," 20 January 1964, ANA, MAE, 33/2000, box 323.

103. "Evolution politique des pays auprès desquels est accredité l'ambassade be Brazzaville," report from the embassy in Brazzaville, 8 January 1965, ANA, MAE, 33/2000, box 149.

104. Report from Adjali, "Stage de Commissaires Politique pour Congolais/Brazzaville," 29 September 1964, ANA, MAE, 32/2000, box 164.
105. "Rapport concernant mes premiers visites aux members du gouvernement, au parti de l'USRDA et aux ambassadeurs accredités à Bamako," Aidi to Bouteflika, reached Algiers on 11 January 1965, ANA, MAE, 33/2000, box 280.
106. "Compte-rendu des entretiens politiques algéro-maliens au niveau presidential et du Bureau Politique," 18 August 1964, ANA, MAE, 33/2000, box 280. Keita supported the Marxist African Independence Party (PAI), while complaining that French bases in Niger provided protection to rebels against his own regime.
107. Yazid Sayigh, *Armed Struggle and the Search for State: The Palestinian National Movement, 1949–1993* (Oxford: Clarendon Press, 1997), 102–103; Jean-Paul Chagnollaud, "Le Maghreb et le conflit israelo-arabe" (PhD diss., University of Paris I, 1975), 268–269.
108. Author's interview with Lakhdar Brahimi at the London School of Economics and Political Science, 16 and 17 March 2009.
109. "Rapport Général" from Djoudi in Dar-Es-Salam, September 1963, ANA, MAE, 33/2000, box 166; Michael M. Laskier, "Israel and Algeria amid French Colonialism and the Arab-Israeli Conflict, 1954–1978," *Israel Studies* 6, no. 2 (2001): 1–32.
110. Quoted in Tareq Y. Ismael, *The U.A.R. in Africa: Egypt's Policy under Nasser* (Evanston, IL: Northwestern University Press, 1971), 70.
111. For example, see the letter from Ben Bella to Sekou Touré, 3 August 1964, ANA, MAE, 33/2000, box 332; "Etat des relations algéro-ghanéennes avant le 19 juin 1965," 6 May 1966, ANA, MAE, 33/2000, box 361.
112. Benhabylès, "Les problèmes du Tiers Monde," ANA, MAE, 32/2000, box 6 (also available in 33/2000, box 177).
113. "Les Etats-Unis et la situation en Afrique," report by Guellal to Bouteflika, 22 June 1964, ANA, MAE, 32/2000, box 197.
114. Ajdali, "Rapport d'entretien entre le president Massemba-Débat et l'ambassadeur de Cuba à Accra," ANA, MAE, 33/2000, box 323.
115. Jorge Serguera, *Che Guevara: La clave africana: Memorias de un comandante cubano, embajador en la Argelia postcolonial* (Jaen: Liberman, 2008), 301–302.
116. "Conférence des Chefs d'Etat et de Gouvernement IIème Session OUA, Situation aux Caraïbes," July 1964, ANA, MAE, 32/2000, box 181.
117. Ben Bella felt much closer to Guevara than Castro; author's interview with Ahmed Ben Bella, Algiers, 24 August 2007.
118. Jon Lee Anderson, *Che Guevara: A Revolutionary Life* (London: Bantam, 1997), 546–549; Castañeda, *Compañero*, 245–246.
119. "Imperialisme US en Amérique Latine," broad overview report by the MAE's Division Asie-Amérique Latine, from around mid-1964, probably for Bouteflika's attention, ANA, MAE, 32/2000, box 24.
120. Tewfik Bouattoura was to have been the ambassador to Brazil, and the Algerian government vociferously denounced the coup; see Gorse's telegram of 20 April 1964, SEAA, carton 133.
121. Odd Arne Westad, *The Global Cold War: Third World Interventions and the Making of Our Times* (Cambridge: Cambridge University Press, 2005), 141–143.
122. Piero Gleijeses, *Conflicting Missions: Havana, Washington, and Africa, 1959–1976* (Chapel Hill: University of North Carolina Press, 2002), 65.
123. Mario de Andrade, "The Origins of the Angolan Insurrection," *Révolution Africaine*, 27 June 1964.
124. Report from Seddikoui, "Voyage au Katanga," 29 September 1964, ANA, MAE, 32/2000, box 164.
125. "The Congo Massacre," *Time*, 4 December 1964, accessed 5 May 2010, http://www.time.com/time/magazine/article/0,9171,830872,00.html.
126. "Sommet Africain d'Accra: Problème congolais," October 1965, ANA, MAE, 33/2000, box 254; "Les problèmes congolais," 14 October 1964, ANA, MAE, 32/2000, box 164.
127. Quoted in Robert A. Mortimer, "The Algerian Revolution in Search of the African Revolution," *Journal of Modern African Studies* 8, no. 3 (1970): 377.

128. "Conférence des Chefs d'Etat et de Gouvernement IIème Session OUA, Le Caire—Juillet 1964, Situation au Congo-Léopoldville," ANA, MAE, 32/2000, box 181.
129. Memcon Ben Bella and Keita, 18 August 1964, ANA, MAE, 33/2000, box 280.
130. "Parley Bars Tshombe as He Stands By," *Washington Post*, 7 October 1964, A1.
131. Grimaud, *La politique extérieure de l'Algérie*, 274; report by Harbi, "Rapport hebdomadaire (semaine du 12/2 au 19/2/1965)," 20 February 1965, ANA, MAE, 33/2000, box 275.
132. Malek, "La Deuxième Conférence des Chefs d'Etat ou de Gouvernement des Pays Non-Alignés," undated, ANA, MAE, 33/2000, box 23.
133. Report from Adjali, "Evolution politique des pays auprès desquels est accredité l'ambassade de Brazzaville," 8 January 1965, ANA, MAE, 33/2000, box 149.
134. Report from Adjali in Brazzaville, 9 October 1964, ANA, MAE, 32/2000, box 164.
135. Peter L. Hahn and Mary Ann Heiss, *Empire and Revolution: The United States and the Third World since 1945* (Columbus: Ohio State University Press, 2001), 80–81, 84; Gleijeses, *Conflicting Missions*, 75
136. "Air Aid to Rebel Units Is Reported in Congo," *New York Times*, 15 November 1964, 35; Robert A. Mortimer, "Foreign Policy and Its Role in Nation-Building in Algeria" (PhD diss., Columbia University, 1968), 268–269.
137. Chase to Rusk, "Current trends in Algerian relations with African liberation movements," 18 November 1965, NARA, RG59, box 1876, General Records of State Department, Central Foreign Policy Files, 1964–66. For the Soviet perspective, see Iurii Vinokurov, "Povstancheskoe dvizhenie 1963–1965gg. v Kongo" [The rebel movement in Congo, 1963–1965], *Narody Azii i Afriki* 5 (1981): 102–109.
138. Note from Rahal to Ben Bella, 4 February 1965, ANA, MAE, 32/2000, box 164.
139. By 1965, the new embassy in Brazzaville alone had established ongoing relations with revolutionary groups from Congo-Léopoldville, Angola, South Africa, Mozambique, South West Africa (Namibia), and Equatorial Guinea; see Adjali's "Rapport de fin d'année," 8 January 1965, ANA, MAE, 33/2000, box 149.
140. For example, see "La lutte de libération en Afrique australe: Eléments pour une stratégie, document de base," ANA, MAE, 33/2000, box 93.
141. Report from Benamar to Bouteflika, "Mouvement National de la Révolution Gabonnaise," 1 June 1965, and report from Belghit, "Compte rendu d'entretien avec Marc Mba Ndong du MNRG," 27 May 1965, and also Belghit, "Le MNRG et le FNRG," 2 June 1965, all in ANA, MAE, 32/2000, box 164.
142. Castañeda, *Compañero*, 276–283.
143. Memcon Aidi and Boubakar Kasse, 16 February 1965, ANA, MAE, 33/2000, box 280.
144. Report by Harbi, "Rapport hebdomadaire (semaine du 12/2 au 19/2/1965)," 20 February 1965, ANA, MAE, 33/2000, box 275.
145. Report by Harbi, "Rapport Hebdomadaire (semaine du 29/11 au 5/12/1966)," 5 December 1964, ANA, MAE, 33/2000, box 275.
146. "Le Ghana et le 19 Juin 1965 (II)," 2 August 1965, ANA, MAE, 33/2000, box 361.
147. Mortimer, "Foreign Policy and Its Role in Nation-Building in Algeria," 342.
148. Telegram from Porter to Rusk, 23 March 1964, NARA, RG 59, Box 1880, General Records of the Department of State, Central FP files 1964–66.
149. "L'homme de la conference," *Révolution Africaine*, 4 April 1964, 17; "Ins and Outs at Algiers," *Economist*, 19 June 1965, 1383.
150. Chase to Rusk, "Ali Lakhdari, Algeria's first ambassador to India," 22 January 1965, NARA, RG 59, Box 1882, General Records of the Department of State, Central FP files 1964–66.
151. Service des Etudes, de la Documentation et des Archives, "Bilan d'activité pour l'année 1964," 19 March 1965, ANA, MAE, 32/2000, box 133.
152. Service des Etudes, de la Documentation et des Archives, "Bilan d'activité pour l'année 1964," 19 March 1965, ANA, MAE, 32/2000, box 133.
153. "L'homme de la conference," 17.
154. "Algerian Policy toward Latin America," telegram from Porter to Rusk, 8 May 1964, NARA, RG 59, Box 1882, General Records of the Department of State, Central FP files 1964–66.
155. Telegram from Kohler to Rusk, 9 May 1964, NARA, RG 59, Box 1883, General Records of the Department of State, Central FP files 1964–66.

156. "Imperialisme US en Amérique Latine," Division Asie-Amérique Latine, circa mid-1964, ANA, MAE, 32/2000, box 24.
157. See "Visite au Moyen Orient de Mr. Philips Talbot," Ali Kafi to Bouteflika, 20 February 1965, and "Phillips Talbot à Amman," from Kabouya to Bouteflika, 11 February 1965, both ANA, MAE, 32/2000, box 6.
158. Benhabylès, "Les problèmes du Tiers Monde," ANA, MAE, 32/2000, box 6 (also available in 33/2000, box 177).
159. Report from embassy in Amman, 12 January 1965, ANA, MAE, 32/2000, box 6.
160. Benhabylès, "Les problèmes du Tiers Monde," ANA, MAE, 32/2000, box 6 (also available in 33/2000, box 177).
161. "Réunion des ambassadeurs arabes au palais royal," report from embassy in Amman, 25 January 1965, ANA, MAE, 32/2000, box 26.
162. "Rapport d'installation," from the embassy in Tokyo, 13 July 1964, ANA, MAE, 33/2000, box 166.
163. Memcon Tito and Nasser, 12 and 13 May 1963, AJBT, 837, KPR I.3.a/121-30.
164. "Minutes from the Yugoslav-Algerian talks and the meeting between President Tito and Ben Bella," 6 March 1964, AJBT, 837, KPR 1-3-a/2-8.
165. "Seconde Conférence Afro-Asiatique, Comité Permanent: Compte-Rendu Analytique," see notes for the first session, 12–13 November 1964, and the fourth session, 8–9 February 1965, ANA, MAE, 32/2000, box 26; report on conversation with Lakhdar Brahimi in Cairo, "Afro-Asian Conference: Round-up no. 3—to 25.3.1965," UKNA, FO, 371/181505; author's interview with Ahmed Laïdi at his home in Algiers, 1 December 2006.
166. Porter to Rusk, 23 March 1964, NARA, RG 59, Box 1880, General Records of the Department of State, Central FP files 1964–66; Porter to Rusk, 1 April 1964, LBJL, National Security Files, Algeria Country File, box 94-1, folder 2, 12/63–7/65; Robert A. Mortimer, *The Third World Coalition in International Politics* (Boulder, CO: Westview Press, 1984), 18–22.
167. Mortimer, "Foreign Policy and Its Role in Nation-Building in Algeria," 351.
168. Yazid quoted in "L'homme de la conference," 17.
169. "Examen de la situation internationale à la lumière de la première conférence Afro-Asiatique et appréciation des dix principes de Bandung," early 1965, ANA, MAE, 32/2000, box 24.
170. G. H. Jansen, *Afro-Asia and Non-alignment* (London: Faber and Faber, 1966), 366–367, 371.
171. "Minutes from the Yugoslav-Algerian talks and the meeting between President Tito and Ben Bella," 6 March 1964, AJBT, 837, KPR 1-3-a/2-8.
172. "Examen de la situation internationale à la lumière de la première conférence Afro-Asiatique et appréciation des dix principes de Bandung," early 1965, ANA, MAE, 32/2000, box 24.
173. Yala, "Les fêtes du quinzième anniversaire de la fondation de la RP de Chine," 1 October 1964, ANA, MAE, 33/2000, box 164.
174. Malek, "La Deuxième Conférence des Chefs d'Etat ou de Gouvernement des Pays Non Alignés," undated, ANA, MAE, 33/2000, box 23; Mortimer, *Third World Coalition in International Politics*, 19–20; Jansen, *Afro-Asia and Non-alignment*, 384–391.
175. Memcon Yala and Chen Yi, 30 October 1964, ANA, MAE, 33/2000, box 164.
176. Alan Hutchison, *China's African Revolution* (Boulder, CO: Westview Press, 1976), 76.
177. Telegram from embassy Moscow, 31 March 1964, French Foreign Ministry archives, Europe 1960–1970, carton 1925.
178. Telegram from Evans, 12 May 1964, UKNA, FO, 371/178769.
179. Dizdarević, "Talks with Ben Bella," 2 June 1964, Serbian FM.
180. Memcon Yala and Chen Yi, 30 October 1964, ANA, MAE, 33/2000, box 164.
181. Report from Yala, "La Mission du Ministre Boumaza à Pékin," 15 September 1964, ANA, MAE, 33/2000, box 164.
182. Jeremy Scott Friedman, "Reviving Revolution: The Sino-Soviet Split, the 'Third World,' and the Fate of the Left" (PhD diss., Princeton University, 2011), 189; telegram from Gorse, 28 December 1963, SEAA, carton 133.
183. On the Aswan opening, see William Taubman, *Khrushchev: The Man and His Era* (New York: Norton, 2003), 609–610. Ben Bella's visit to the USSR described in telegram from Baudet, 8 May 1964, French Foreign Ministry archives, Europe 1960–1970, carton 1925.

184. Telegram from Yala, "La Mission du Ministre Boumaza à Pékin," 15 September 1964, ANA, MAE, 33/2000, box 164.
185. Memcon Malek and Tito, 16 March 1965, AJBT, 837, KPR, I-3-a/2-11.
186. Moshe Ma'oz, "Soviet and Chinese Influence on the Palestinian Guerrilla Movement," in *Soviet and Chinese Influence in the Third World*, ed. Alvin Z. Rubinstein (New York: Praeger, 1975), 109–130.
187. Ahmad Shukairy quoted in Ma'oz, "Soviet and Chinese Influence on the Palestinian Guerrilla Movement," 109–130.
188. Bruce D. Larkin, *China and Africa, 1949–1970: The Foreign Policy of the People's Republic of China* (Berkeley: University of California Press, 1971), 171.
189. Marcum, *Angolan Revolution*, 1:160–161; author's interview with Lakhdar Brahimi at the London School of Economics and Political Science, 16 March 2009.
190. Alan Hart, *Arafat: A Political Biography* (London: Sidgwick and Jackson, 1994), 155–158.
191. Memcon Yala and Chen Yi, 30 October 1964, ANA, MAE, 33/2000, box 164.
192. Report from Gabričević, 12 December 1964, DASMIP, 1964, f11, d448960.
193. Report from Dizdarević, 19 February 1965. DASMIP, 1965, f2, d46887.
194. Friedman, "Reviving Revolution," 153–155.
195. "Minutes from the Yugoslav-Algerian talks and the meeting between President Tito and Ben Bella," 6 and 11 March 1964, AJBT, 837, KPR 1-3-a/2-8.
196. "Minutes from the Yugoslav-Algerian talks and the meeting between President Tito and Ben Bella," 11 March 1964, AJBT, 837, KPR 1-3-a/2-8.
197. Kyle Haddad-Fonda, "Revolutionary Allies: Sino-Egyptian and Sino-Algerian Relations in the Bandung Decade" (PhD diss., Oxford University, 2013), 266–267.
198. Ismael, *U.A.R. in Africa*, 71–72.
199. "Minutes from the Yugoslav-Algerian talks and the meeting between President Tito and Ben Bella," 11 March 1964, AJBT, 837, KPR 1-3-a/2-8.
200. Ismael, *U.A.R. in Africa*, 69.
201. Dizdarević, "Ben Bella on Sékou Touré's visit," 6 April 1964, DASMIP, 1964, f11, d415452.
202. Tom Mboya, *Freedom and After* (London: Andre Deutsch, 1963), 231.
203. Benhabylès, "Les problèmes du Tiers-Monde," draft version of a lengthy report by Benhabylès, May 1965, ANA, MAE, 32/2000, box 6.
204. Quoted in Ismael, *U.A.R. in Africa*, 70.
205. "Evolution politiques des pay auprès desquels est accredité l'ambassade de Brazzaville," January 1965, ANA, MAE, 33/2000, box 149.
206. "Tshombe in Paris: Says Nasser Acts to Weaken Congo," *New York Times*, 10 October 1964, 1.
207. "Tshombe's Villlage Epic," *New York Times*, 20 October 1964, 16.
208. "Evolution politiques des pay auprès desquels est accredité l'ambassade de Brazzaville," January 1965, ANA, MAE, 33/2000, box 149.
209. Odette Guitard, "Alger ou la désunion afro-asiatique," *Annuaire de l'Afrique du Nord*, 1965, 49–61; the Ben Bella–Zhou Enlai discussions are noted in "Compt-rendu d'entretien: Conférence Afro-Asiatique," report by the Division des Pays Socialistes, 13 October 1965, ANA, MAE, 32/2000, box 188.
210. Report by Dizdarević, 30 April 1965, DASMIP, 1965, f3, d416030.
211. Report by Dizdarević, "Poseta delegacije FFLN SSR-u (početkom maja)," 14 June 1965, DASMIP, 1965, f3, d421774.
212. Report by Petrović, 7 April 1965, DASMIP, 1965, f3, d414504.
213. Memcon Malek and Tito, 31 May 1965, AJBT, 837, KPR, I-3-a/2-12.
214. 30 October 1964, Ambassador M. YALA (Peking) to SecGen MAE, "Entretien avec le Maréchal CHEN-YI Premier Vice-Président et Ministre des A.E.," 33/2000, box 164.
215. Memcon Malek and Tito, 16 March 1965, 837, KPR I-3-a/2-11.
216. Friedman, "Reviving Revolution," 200.
217. 30 October 1964, Ambassador M. YALA (Peking) to SecGen MAE, "Entretien avec le Maréchal CHEN-YI Premier Vice-Président et Ministre des A.E.," 33/2000, box 164; Aidi, "Mon entretien avec Monsieur Ousam Ba, Minstre des Affaires Etrangères, 11 février 1965," ANA, MAE, 33/2000, box 280.
218. Mortimer, "Foreign Policy and Its Role in Nation-Building in Algeria," 351.

219. Castañeda, *Companero*, 290–292.
220. "Ordre du Jour: Relations Est-Ouest," 17 May 1965, ANA, MAE, 32/2000, box 126.
221. See the minutes of a large meeting of the MAE senior staff, "Ordre du Jour: Relations Est-Ouest," 17 May 1965, ANA, MAE, 32/2000, box 126.
222. Report from Dizdarević, 22 June 1964, DASMIP, 1964, f11, d427425.
223. Edgar J. Dosman, *The Life and Times of Raúl Prebisch, 1901–1986* (Montreal: McGill-Queen's University Press, 2008), 378–409.
224. Robert M. Cutler, "East-South Relations at UNCTAD: Global Political Economy and the CMEA," *International Organization* 37, no. 1 (1983): 121–142.
225. "U Thant Addresses Economic and Social Council," 28–29.
226. Report by the Direction des Affaires Economiques et Culturelles, "Les relations économiques internationales," ANA, MAE, 32/2000, box 24. The document is stamped "May 1966," but the content suggests that it was drawn up for an important MAE conference in May 1965.
227. Maurice Parodi, "Chronique économique: Algérie," *Annuaire de l'Afrique du Nord*, 1964, 248.
228. "U Thant Addresses Economic and Social Council," 28–29.
229. Parodi, "Chronique économique," 239–240; Henry F. Jackson, *The FLN in Algeria: Party Development in a Revolutionary Society* (Westport, CT: Greenwood Press, 1977), 152.
230. Parodi, "Chronique économique," 275–276. For an Algerian summary of trade with the USSR, see "Tableau des importations algériennes en provenance de l'URSS du 1er Janvier au 30 Septembre 1964," Direction du Commerce Exterieur, Ministère de l'Économie Nationale, ANA, MAE, 46/2000, box 5.
231. Philippe Cabanius-Matraman, "Chronique économique Algérie," *Annuaire de l'Afrique du Nord*, 1965, 279–333.
232. Untitled report by the Direction des Affaires Economiques, Culturelles et Sociales, probably for the May 1965 MAE conference (despite a stamp indicating "Oct 1969," which seems to have been applied later), ANA, MAE, 32/2000, box 126.
233. Division des Affaires Economiques et Financières, "Situation des Relations Economiques Algéro-Tchécoslovaques," 12 September 1964, ANA, MAE, 32/2000, box 48.
234. Untitled report by the Direction des Affaires Economiques, Culturelles et Sociales, probably for the May 1965 MAE conference, ANA, MAE, 32/2000, box 126.
235. "Speech to the Second Economic Seminar of Afro-Asian Solidarity, Algiers, February 1965," in Ernesto Guevara, *Che: Selected Works of Ernesto Guevara* (Cambridge, MA: MIT Press, 1969), 351–352. Raúl Castro was at that moment in Moscow to negotiate a new comprehensive economic treaty that would bind Cuba even more closely to the Soviet model and assistance, and once back in Havana, the Castro brothers excoriated their Argentinian comrade for attacking the Kremlin in such a sensitive forum. For days the Cuban Revolution's famous triumvirate argued with each other, resulting finally in Guevara's self-imposed exile; see Volker Skierka, *Fidel Castro: A Biography* (Cambridge: Polity Press, 2004), 169–174.
236. Jean De Broglie, "Quarante mois de rapports franco-algériens," *Revue de Défense Nationale*, December 1965, 1833–1857; Cabanius-Matraman, "Chronique économique Algérie," 292–296.
237. Note from Houhou (head of MAE Division France) to Bouteflika, 21 September 1963, ANA, MAE, 32/2000, box 155.
238. Untitled report by the Direction des Affaires Economiques, Culturelles et Sociales, probably for the May 1965 MAE conference, ANA, MAE, 32/2000, box 126.
239. Phillip Chiviges Naylor, *France and Algeria: A History of Decolonization and Transformation* (Gainesville: University Press of Florida, 2000), 61–62.
240. Houhou to Bouteflika, "Problème des vins," 24 December 1964, ANA, MAE, 33/2000, box 116.
241. Houhou to Bouteflika, "Négociations économiques et financières tenues à Paris du 29 au 31 octobre 1963," 4 November 1963, ANA, MAE, 33/2000, box116. See also the draft of a letter to the French government, included with a report by the Ministère de l'Economie Nationale, 29 November 1963, ANA, MAE, 33/2000, box 116.
242. Author's interview with Ahmed Laïdi, Algiers, 1 December 2006.
243. Summary of de Gaulle–Ben Bella discussion, 13 March 1964, Archives of the French Foreign Ministry, Correspondances et Messages, carton 377, Entretiens et Messages.

244. Memcon Dizdarević and Ben Bella, 8 March 1963, DASMIP, 1963, f3, d49107.
245. Memcon Dizdarević and Ben Bella, 8 March 1963, DASMIP, 1963, f3, d49107.
246. Telegram from Evans, 16 June 1964, UKNA, FO, 371/178768.
247. Letter from de Gaulle to Gorse, 8 March 1965, SEAA, carton 41.
248. Untitled report by the Direction des Affaires Economiques, Culturelles et Sociales, probably for the May 1965 MAE conference, ANA, MAE, 32/2000, box 126.
249. Arslan Humbaraci, *Algeria: A Revolution That Failed: A Political History since 1954* (London: Pall Mall, 1966), 197–199; *La politique de coopération avec les pays en voie de développement: Rapport de La Commission d'Étude Instituée par le décret du 12 mars 1963, remis au gouvernement le 18 juillet 1963* (Paris: La Documentation Francais, 1964).
250. Stéphane Hessel, *Danse avec le siècle* (Paris: Seuil, 1997), 175–176.
251. Memorandum by Rahal, "Projet de décret portant création d'une Direction de la Coopération Economique et Technique," 22 September 1964, ANA, MAE, 32/2000, box 184.
252. "Echange de lettres du 3 août 1964 concernant le paiement des salaires des experts soviétiques se rendant en Algérie dans le cadre de l'application des accords de coopération économique et technique du 27 decembre 1963 et du 3 juillet 1964," ANA, MAE, 46/2000, box 27; see also Division des Affaires Economiques et Financières, "Situation des Relations Economiques Algéro-Tchécoslovaques," 12 September 1964, ANA, MAE, 32/2000, box 48.
253. Peter Braestrup, "Algerian Road to Socialism Is No Path of Roses," *New York Times*, 25 January 1965.
254. "La politique économique algérienne au début de 1964," *Maghreb: Documents, Algérie, Maroc, Tunisie*, no. 2 (March–April 1964): 16–18.
255. Jeanne Favret, "Le syndicat, les travailleurs et le pouvoir en Algérie," *Annuaire de l'Afrique du Nord* (1964): 44–62; Jackson, *FLN in Algeria*, 144–146.
256. Memcon of Tayebi and Guevara, 21 June 1964, ANA, MAE, 33/2000, box 190.
257. Annie Krieger, "Les prémices d'une réforme agraire en Algérie," in *Essais sur l'économie de l'Algérie nouvelle*, ed. François d'Arcy, Annie Krieger, and Alain Marill (Paris: Presses Universitaires de France, 1965), 97–166; see also Ian Clegg, *Workers' Self-Management in Algeria* (London: Allen Lane, 1971), 113–122.
258. Speaking to the Congrès des Fellahs, 25–27 October 1963, quoted in Krieger, "Les prémices d'une réforme agraire en Algérie," 97–166.
259. Devlin, *Chief of Station, Congo*, 223.
260. "Algiers a Haven for Exile Groups," *New York Times*, 7 March 1965.
261. Annie Leduc and Juliette Minces, "Continuities and Discontinuities in the Algerian Confrontation with Europe," in *Islam and Secularism in North Africa*, ed. John Ruedy (London: Macmillan, 1994), 73–86.
262. Yahia H. Zoubir, "Algerian Islamists' Conception of Democracy," *Arab Studies Quarterly* 18, no. 3 (1996): 65–85; Hugh Roberts, *The Battlefield: Algeria 1988–2002, Studies in a Broken Polity* (London: Verso, 2003), 8–11; Jean Leca and Jean-Claude Vatin, *L'Algerie politique: Institutions et regime* (Paris: Presse de la Fondation Nationale des Sciences Politiques, 1975), 308; and Nourredine Saadi, *La femme et la loi en Algerie* (Algiers: Bouchène, 1991), 45.
263. Quoted in Leca and Vatin, *L'Algerie politique*, 308. See also Ricardo René Laremont, *Islam and the Politics of Resistance in Algeria, 1783–1992* (Trenton, NJ: Africa World Press, 2000), 139–141.
264. Allan Christelow, "Ritual, Culture and Politics of Islamic Reformism in Algeria," *Middle Eastern Studies* 23, no. 3 (1987): 268
265. Humbaraci, *Algeria*, 237.
266. Jeanne Favret-Saada, *Algérie 1962–1964: Essais d'anthropologie politique* (Saint-Denis: Bouchène, 2005), 33–62.
267. Ahmed Ben Bella, *Itinéraire* (Algiers: Editions Maintenant, 1987), 199–200.
268. Chérif Guellal, "Africa vis-à-vis the Western Powers," *Annals of the American Academy of Political and Social Science* 354 (1964): 9–21.
269. "Minutes from the Yugoslav-Algerian talks and the meeting between President Tito and Ben Bella," 6 March 1964, AJBT, 837, KPR 1-3-a/2-8.
270. Quoted in Grimaud, *La politique extérieure de l'Algérie*, 14, and Ottaway and Ottaway, *Algeria*, 181; Root to Rusk, "Ben Bella regime weeds out certain leftists," 25 March 1965, NARA,

RG59, box 1880, General Records of State Department, Central Foreign Policy Files, 1964–66.
271. "Minutes from the Yugoslav-Algerian talks and the meeting between President Tito and Ben Bella," 11 March 1964, AJBT, 837, KPR 1-3-a/2-8.
272. Telegram from Reilly, 21 June 1965, UKNA, PREM, 13/122; Memcon Dizdarević and Bouteflika, 19 June 1965, DASMIP, 1965, f2, d422355.
273. "Proclamation du Conseil de la Révolution du 19 juin 1965," *Annuaire de l'Afrique du Nord*, 1965, 627–629.
274. Telegram from Reilly, 21 June 1965, UKNA, PREM, 13/122.

Conclusion

1. Ryszard Kapuściński, *The Soccer War* (New York: Vintage, 1992), 110.
2. Intelligence Information Cable, "Discussions between members of the Algerian Revolutionary Council, Boumediene and Bouteflika, and African leaders," 9 July 1965, LBJL, National Security Files, Files of Robert Komer, Algeria December 1963–March 1966; telegram from Reilly, 21 June 1965, UKNA, PREM, 13/122.
3. "Record of Conversation between Vice-Foreign Minister Qiao Guanhua and North Korean Ambassador in China Pak Se-chang," July 23, 1965, History and Public Policy Program Digital Archive, PRC FMA 106-00836-13, 95–106, ttrans. Jake Tompkins, http://digitalarchive.wilsoncenter.org/document/118830
4. "Etat des relations algéro-guinéenes," undated (from early 1966), ANA, MAE, 33/2000, box 332.
5. Memcon Uvalić and Dinesh Singh, 24 June 1965, DASMIP, 1965, f2, d423253; report from Topali, 2 July 1965, DASMIP, 1965, f2, d424274.
6. Author's interview with Lakhdar Brahimi at the London School of Economics and Political Science, 16 and 17 March 2009.
7. For example, Dizdarević believed that Bouteflika was leaning toward not holding the conference on 19 June; memcon Dizdarević and Bouteflika, 19 June 1965, DASMIP, 1965, f2, d422355.
8. Intelligence Information Cable, "Discussions between members of the Algerian Revolutionary Council, Boumediene and Bouteflika, and African leaders," 9 July 1965, LBJL, National Security Files, Files of Robert Komer, Algeria December 1963–March 1966.
9. Telegram from Algiers to Washington, "Algeria and the Sub-Saharan Radicals," 10 March 1966, NARA, RG59, box 1882, General Records of State Department, Central Foreign Policy Files, 1964–66; "Etat des relations algéro-guinéenes," undated (from early 1966), ANA, MAE, 33/2000, box 332.
10. Report by Sarajčić, "Preliminarne ocjene o dagadjajima u Alžiru," 23 June 1965, DASMIP, 1965, f2, d424175.
11. "News in Brief, June 11–July 10," *Africa Report* 10, no. 8 (1965): 21.
12. Report from Topali, 2 July 1965, DASMIP, 1965, f2, d424274.
13. El-Kebir, record of meeting with UAR ambassador in Madrid, 5 July 1965, ANA, MAE 32/2000, box 22.
14. Telegram from Algiers to Washington, "Algeria and the Sub-Saharan Radicals," 10 March 1966, NARA, RG59, box 1882, General Records of State Department, Central Foreign Policy Files, 1964–66; "Etat des relations algéro-guinéenes," undated (from early 1966), ANA, MAE, 33/2000, box 332.
15. John Roosa, *Pretext for Mass Murder: The September 30th Movement and Suharto's Coup d'État in Indonesia* (Madison: University of Wisconsin Press, 2006), 161–165.
16. Chase to Rusk, "Algerian-Guinean Relations," 9 December 1965, NARA, RG59, box 1882, General Records of State Department, Central Foreign Policy Files, 1964–66.
17. Sahli, "Entretiens avec Tchen Yi, Chou En Lai et l'Ambassadeur Tsen Tao," 26 March 1966, ANA, MAE, 33/2000, box 164.
18. Jernegan to Rusk, "Algerian-Ghanaian Relations—Continued Cool," 15 November 1966, NARA, RG59, box 1882, General Records of State Department, Central Foreign Policy Files, 1964–66.

19. Memcon Boumedienne and Sékou Touré, 4 June 1972, ANA, MAE, 33/2000, box 275.
20. Immanuel Maurice Wallerstein, *Africa: The Politics of Independence and Unity* (Lincoln: University of Nebraska Press, 2005), 99–101.
21. "Resolution on the World Conference on Trade and Development" (Organization of African Unity, 5 November 1966), website of the African Union, http://au.int/en/sites/default/files/ASSEMBLY_EN_5_9_November_1966_ASSEMBLY_HEADS_STATE_GOVERNMENT_THIRD_ORDINARY_SESSION.pdf.
22. "First Ministerial Meeting of the Group of 77: Charter of Algiers," October 10–25, 1967, website of the Group of 77 at the United Nations, http://www.g77.org/doc/algier~1.htm.
23. "Lusaka Declaration on Peace, Independence, Development, Co-operation and Democratization of International Relations," 10 September 1970, in *The Third World without Superpowers: The Collected Documents of the Non-aligned Countries*, ed. Odette Jankowitsch-Prevor and Karl P. Sauvant (Dobbs Ferry, NY: Oceana Publications, 1978), 2:80–84.
24. "Réunion des chefs de missions diplomatiques: Compte-rendu des travaux," 24–25 avril 1964, ANA, MAE, 32/2000, box 50.
25. Allan Christelow, *Algerians without Borders: The Making of a Global Frontier Society* (Gainesville: University Press of Florida, 2012), 108–140.
26. "Les relations internationales à l'heure des fusées," *El Djeich*, no. 23, March 1965, 22–24.
27. "Etat des relations algéro-guinéennes," first half of 1966, ANA, MAE 33/2000, box 332.
28. For example, see Priya Lal, "Between the Village and the World: Imagining and Practicing Development in Tanzania, 1964–1975" (PhD diss., New York University, 2011), 155–157; Mark Juergensmeyer, *The New Cold War? Religious Nationalism Confronts the Secular State* (Berkeley: University of California Press, 1993).
29. Ryan Irwin, "The Gordian Knot: Apartheid and the Unmaking of the Liberal World Order, 1960–1970," (PhD diss., Ohio State University, 2010), 130–131.
30. Benhabylès, "Les problèmes du Tiers-Monde," May 1965, ANA, MAE, 33/2000, box 177.
31. Yoweri Museveni, "The Qaddafi I Know," *Foreign Policy*, 24 March 2011, http://foreignpolicy.com/2011/03/24/the-qaddafi-i-know-2/.
32. Hugh Roberts, "Who Said Gaddafi Had to Go?" *London Review of Books* 33, no. 22 (17 November 2011): 8–18.
33. Robert A. Mortimer, "Foreign Policy and Its Role in Nation-Building in Algeria" (PhD diss., Columbia University, 1968), 340.
34. Robert A. Mortimer, *The Third World Coalition in International Politics* (Boulder, CO: Westview Press, 1984), 39; "Fourth Conference of Heads of State or Government of Non-aligned Countries: Economic Declaration," 5–9 September 1973, in *Third World without Superpowers*, 2:214–226.
35. Jeff Frieden, "Third World Indebted Industrialization: International Finance and State Capitalism in Mexico, Brazil, Algeria, and South Korea," *International Organization* 35, no. 3 (1981): 407–431.
36. John Toye, *Dilemmas of Development: Reflections on the Counter-revolution in Development Economics*, 2nd ed. (Oxford: Blackwell, 1993).
37. Mahfoud Bennoune, *The Making of Contemporary Algeria, 1830–1987: Colonial Upheavals and Post-independence Development* (Cambridge: Cambridge University Press, 1988), makes an impassioned case that the socialist model could have worked if it were not for liberal reforms in the 1980s. See also J. N. C. Hill, "Challenging the Failed State Thesis: IMF and World Bank Intervention and the Algerian Civil War," *Civil Wars* 11, no. 1 (2009): 39–56, which credits IMF intervention with the Algerian state's survival against insurgency in the 1990s.
38. Quoted in James M. Boughton, *Silent Revolution: The International Monetary Fund, 1979–1989* (Washington, DC: International Monetary Fund, 2001), 598–599. See also Paul J. Kaiser, "Structural Adjustment and the Fragile Nation: The Demise of Social Unity in Tanzania," *Journal of Modern African Studies* 34, no. 2 (1996): 227–237.
39. Phyllis Anne Peres, *Transculturation and Resistance in Lusophone African Narrative*, 84–87 (Gainesville: University Press of Florida, 1997).
40. Quoted in Robert Malley, *The Call from Algeria: Third Worldism, Revolution, and the urn to Islam* (Berkeley: University of California Press, 1996), 139.

41. See, for example, Anne Leduc, *Le chant du lendemain: Alger, 1962–1969* (Saint-Denis: Bouchène, 2004); and Gérard Chaliand and Juliette Minces, *L'Algérie indépendante: Bilan d'une révolution nationale* (Paris: F. Maspero, 1972).
42. "Obama writes to Brazil's Lula about Iran, Honduras," *Earth Times*, 25 November 2009, www.earthtimes.org/articles/show/296368,obama-writes-to-brazils-lula-about-iran-honduras.html.
43. Hugh Roberts, *The Battlefield: Algeria, 1988–2002: Studies in a Broken Polity* (London: Verso, 2003), 17–18.

BIBLIOGRAPHY

Archives and Interviews

ALGERIA

Archives Nationales d'Algérie, Algiers (ANA)
    Conseil National de la Révolution Algérienne, 1956–1962 (CNRA)
    Front de Libération Nationale, 1962– (FLN)
    Gourvernement Provisoire de la République Algeriénne, 1958–1962 (GPRA)
    Ministère aux Affaires Etrangères, 1962– (MAE)
    Ministère aux Affaires Extérieures of the GPRA, 1958–1962 (GPRA-MAE)
Interviews
    Ahmed Ben Bella
    Lakhdar Brahimi
    Slimane Chikh
    Nourredine Djoudi
    Ahmed Laïdi

FRANCE

Archives Nationales, Paris (AN)
    5 AG 1, Papers of the Presidency of Charles de Gaulle
Fondation Nationale des Sciences Politiques, Paris
    Archives d'Histoire Contemporaine
        Couve de Murville Papers
Ministère aux Affaires Etrangères, Paris
    Cabinet du Ministre (CM)
    Mission de Liaison Algérien
    Secrétariat d'Etat aux Affaires Algériennes (SEAA)
    Secrétariat Générale
Service Historique de l'Armée de Terre, Château de Vincennes (SHAT)
    Sous-série 1H, Algérie

GREAT BRITAIN

British Library, London
National Archives of the United Kingdom, Kew (UKNA)
    FO 371, Foreign Office correspondence
    PREM 11, Prime Minister's office files

INTERNATIONAL ORGANIZATIONS

United Nations Archives, New York (UNA)
   Office of the Secretary General, U Thant
      Algeria Country Files
World Bank Archives, Washington, DC (WBA)
   Africa Series
   Algeria Country Files
   Robert S. McNamara Papers

PERSONAL PAPERS

Belaïd Abdessalam Papers (BAP)

SERBIA

Archives of Josip Broz Tito (AJBT)
   Cabinet of the President of the Republic (KPR)
Diplomatic Archives of the Ministry of Foreign Affairs of Serbia (DASMIP)

UNITED STATES

John F. Kennedy Library, Boston (JFKL)
   John F. Kennedy Papers
   National Security Files
   President's Office Files
Lyndon Baines Johnson Library, LBJL
   Lyndon Baines Johnson Papers
   National Security Files
National Archives and Records Administration, College Park, Maryland (NARA)
   Record Group 59, General Records of the Department of State
   CIA Declassified Files Database (CREST)

Newspapers and Magazines

AFRICA REPORT

Al Ahram
Alger Républicain
Christian Science Monitor
Démocratie Nouvelle
El Djeich
Earth Times
Economist
Le Figaro
Isvestiia
Jeune Afrique
Kommunist
Libération
Le Monde
Le Monde Diplomatique
El Moudjahid
Narody Azii i Afriki
New York Times
Newsweek
El Ouma
Le Peuple/Al Chaab
Pravda
Résistance Algérienne
Révolution Africaine

Le Soir d'Algérie
Time
Times of London
Wall Street Journal
Washington Post

Published Memoirs, Interviews, Speeches

Aït Ahmed, Hocine. *Mémoires d'un combattant, L'esprit de l'indépendance 1942–1952*. Paris: Sylvie Messinger, 1983.
Arab Ba'th Socialist Party, *Some Theoretical Principles Approved by the Six National Congress, October 1963*. Beirut: Dar al-Talia, 1974.
Belhocine, Mabrouk. *Le Courrier Alger–Le Caire, 1954–1962*. Algiers: Casbah Editions, 2000.
Ben Bella, Ahmed. "Ainsi était le 'Che.'" *Le Monde Diplomatique*, October 1997, 3.
———. *Ben Bella revient*. Paris: Editions Jean Picollec, 1982.
———. *Itinéraire*. Algiers: Editions Maintenant, 1987.
———. "Pour le développement socialiste: Planification et gestion équilibrée." *Révolution Africaine*, 10 April 1965.
Bennabi, Malek. "L'afro-asiatisme: Conclusion sur la Conference de Bandoeng." *El Djeich*, March 1965.
———. "Les relation internationales à l'heures des fusées." *El Djeich*, March 1965.
Ben Khedda, Benyoucef. *Les Accords d'Evian: La fin de la Guerre d'Algérie*. Algiers: Office des Publications Universitaires, 1987.
———. *Alger, capitale de la résistance, 1956–1957*. Algiers: Houma, 2002.
———. *L'Algérie à l'indépendance: La crise de 1962*. Algiers: Dahlab, 1997.
Bergot, Erwan. *Bataillon Bigeard: Indochine 1952–1954, Algérie 1955–1957*. Paris: Presses de la Cité, 1977.
Boudiaf, Mohamed. *Où va l'Algérie?* Algiers: Rahma, 1992.
Bouhara, Abderrezak. *Du djebel aux rizières: A propos des résistances*. Algiers: Éditions ANEP, 2005.
Bourges, Hervé. *L'Algérie à l'épreuve du pouvoir (1962–1967)*. Paris: B. Grasset, 1967.
———. "Comme Lumumba et Che Guevara." *Jeune Afrique*, 28 June 1978, 56–59.
Boutros-Ghali, Boutros. "The Addis Ababa Charter: A Commentary." *International Conciliation*, no. 546 (January 1964): 5–62.
Broglie, Jean de. "Quarante mois de rapports franco-algériens." *Revue de Défense Nationale*, December 1965, 1835–1857.
Dahlab, Saad. *Mission accomplie*. Algiers: Editions Dahlab, 1990.
De Gaulle, Charles. *Discours et messages*. Paris: Plon, 1970.
———. *Lettres, notes et carnets*. Vol. 14. Paris: Plon, 1980.
———. *Major Addresses, Statements and Press Conferences of General Charles de Gaulle*. New York: Embassy of France, Press and Information Service, 1964.
———. *Memoirs of Hope: Renewal and Endeavor*. New York: Simon and Schuster, 1971.
Devlin, Larry. *Chief of Station, Congo: A Memoir of 1960–67*. New York: Public Affairs, 2007.
Al Dib, Fathi. *Abdel Nasser et la Révolution algérienne*. Paris: L'Harmattan, 1985.
Fanon, Frantz. *Toward the African Revolution: Political Essays*. New York: Grove Press, 1988.
———. *The Wretched of the Earth*. New York: Grove Press, 2004.
Guellal, Chérif. "Africa vis-à-vis the Western Powers." *Annals of the American Academy of Political and Social Science* 354 (July 1964): 9–21.
Guelton, Frédéric. "The French Army 'Centre for Training and Preparation in Counter-Guerrilla Warfare' (Cipcg) at Arzew," *Journal of Strategic Studies* 25, no. 2 (2002): 35–53.
Guevara, Ernesto. *The African Dream: The Diaries of the Revolutionary War in the Congo*. New York: Grove Press, 2000.
———. *Che Guevara on Guerrilla Warfare*. New York: Praeger, 1961.
———. *Che: Selected Works of Ernesto Guevara*. Edited by Rolando E. Bonachea. Cambridge, MA: MIT Press, 1969.
Harbi, Mohammed. "Pour Ben Bella, il y avait plus important que les frontières." *Jeune Afrique*, 25 November 1977, 70–73.

———. *Une vie debout: Mémoires politiques.* Paris: Découverte, 2001.
Henry, Clement Moore. *L'UGEMA: Union Générale des Etudiants Musulmans Algériens (1955–62), Témoignages.* Algiers: Casbah Editions, 2010.
Hessel, Stéphane. *Danse avec le siècle.* Paris: Seuil, 1997.
Ho Chi Minh. *Ho Chi Minh: Selected Articles and Speeches, 1920–1967.* Edited by Jack Woddis. New York: International Publishers, 1969.
Ibrahimi, Ahmed Talbe. *Mémoires d'un Algérien.* Algiers: Casbah Éditions, 2006.
Kafi, Ali *Du militant politique au dirigeant militaire: Mémoires 1946–1962.* Algiers: Casbah Éditions, 2002.
Khalfa, Boualem, Henri Alleg, and Abdelhamid Benzine. *La grande aventure d'Alger républicain.* Paris: Messidor, 1987)
Khrushchev, Nikita Sergeyevich. *Memoirs of Nikita Khrushchev.* Edited by Sergei Khrushchev. Translated by George Shriver and Stephen Shenfield. Vol. 3, *Statesman, 1953–1964.* University Park: Pennsylvania State University Press, 2007.
Kiouane, Abderrahmane. *Les Débuts d'une diplomatie de guerre, 1956–1962: Journal d'un délégué à l'extérieur.* Algiers: Editions Dahlab, 2000.
Makonnen, Ras. *Pan-Africanism from Within.* Edited by Kenneth King. Oxford: Oxford University Press, 1973.
Malek, Rédha. *L'Algérie à Evian: Histoire des négociations secrètes, 1956–1962.* Algiers: Éditions ANEP, 2002.
Mboya, Tom. *Freedom and After.* London: Andre Deutsch, 1963.
Mesbah, Chefik. "Entretien avec Lakhdar Brahimi (part 1)." *Le Soir d'Algérie,* 30 June 2007.
———. "Entretien avec Lakhdar Brahimi (part 2)." *Le Soir d'Algérie,* 1 July 2007.
Messali, Hadj. *Les mémoires de Messali Hadj, 1898–1938.* Edited by Renaud de Rochebrune. Paris: JC Lattès, 1982.
Nasser, Gamal Abdel. *The Philosophy of the Revolution.* Cairo: National Publication House Press, 1960.
Nkrumah, Kwame. *Africa Must Unite.* London: Panaf Books, 2006.
———. *Neo-colonialism: The Last Stage of Imperialism.* London: Nelson, 1965.
Ouzegane, Omar. *Le meilleur combat.* Paris: R. Julliard, 1962.
Paret, Peter. *French Revolutionary Warfare.* London: Pall Mall, 1964.
Peyrefitte, Alain. *C'était de Gaulle.* Paris: Editions de Fallois, 1994.
———. *Faut-Il Partager l'Algérie?* Paris: Plon, 1962.
Saadi, Yacef. *La Bataille d'Alger.* Algiers: Entreprise Nationale du Livre, 1984.
Selassie, Haile. "Towards African Unity." *Journal of Modern African Studies* 1, no. 3 (1963): 281–291.
Serguera, Jorge. *Che Guevara: La clave africana: Memorias de un comandante cubano, embajador en la Argelia postcolonial.* Jaen: Liberman, 2008.
X, Malcom. *The Autobiography of Malcolm X.* New York: Ballantine, 1973.
Yazid, M'hamed. "De Bandoung à Alger." *Démocratie Nouvelle,* June 1965.
Museveni, Yoweri. "The Qaddafi I Know," *Foreign Policy,* 24 March 2011, http://foreignpolicy.com/2011/03/24/the-qaddafi-i-know-2/.

Official Publications

"Address by President Houari Boumediène of Algeria on the Third Anniversary of the Rising of 1 June 1965." *Journal of Modern African Studies* 6, no. 3 (1968): 426–439.
Algerie an II 1962–1964. Algiers: Wizarat al-Irshad al-Watani, 1964.
L'Algérie surpeuplée: Orientations pour une politique de population. Algiers: Éditions du Secretariat Social d'Alger, 1958.
De l'ALN à l'ANP: 20e anniversaire de la lutte de libération. Algiers: Le Ministère, 1974.
Discours du Président Ben Bella, année 1963, 1er trimestre 1964. Algiers: Ministère de l'Orientation Nationale, Direction de la Documentation et des Publications, 1964.
Discours du Président Ben Bella, El Riath 4 avril 1963. Algiers: Ministère de l'Information, 1963.
Discours du Président Ben Bella, du 28 septembre 1962 au 12 décembre 1962. Algiers: Ministère de l'Information, 1963.

Documents diplomatiques français (DDF). Paris: Commission des Archives diplomatiques and Peter Lang, 1961–65.
Foreign Relations of the United States (FRUS). Washington, DC: US Government Printing Office, 1954-65.
"First Ministerial Meeting of the Group of 77: Charter of Algiers." October 10–25, 1967. Website of the Group of 77 at the United Nations. http://www.g77.org/doc/algier~1.htm. Accessed 8 August 2014.
Flory, Maurice. "Chronique Diplomatique," *Annuaire de l'Afrique du Nord*. Paris: Centre National de la Recherche Scientifique, 1963.
Guevara, Ernesto. "Speech to the Second Economic Seminar of Afro-Asian Solidarity, Algiers, February 1965." In *Che: Selected Works of Ernesto Guevara*, edited by Rolando E. Bonachea, 351–352. Cambridge, MA: MIT Press, 1969.
Il'ichev, L.F. ed. *SSSR i strany Afriki, 1963–1970 gg.: Dokumenty i materialy*. Moscow: Politizdat, 1982.
La politique de coopération avec les pays en voie de développement: Rapport de La Commission d'Étude Instituée par le décret du 12 mars 1963, remis au gouvernement le 18 juillet 1963. Paris: La Documentation Francaise, 1964.
"President Sukarno of Indonesia: Speech at the Opening of the Bandung Conference, April 18, 1955." http://www.fordham.edu/halsall/mod/1955sukarno-bandong.html.
"Proclamation du Conseil de la Révolution du 19 juin 1965." *Annuaire de l'Afrique du Nord*, 1965, 627–629.
Projet de programme pour la réalisation de la révolution démocratique populaire. Algiers: Al-Chaab, 1962.
Qu'est ce que le programme de Tripoli. Algiers: Wizārat al-Akhbār wa-al-Thaqāfah, Direction de la Documentation et des Publications, 1962.
Al Raïs Ahmad Bin Billah Yaqul. Algiers: Ministère de l'Information, 1963.
"Resolution on the World Conference on Trade and Development." Organization of African Unity, November 5, 1966. Website of the African Union. http://au.int/en/sites/default/files/ASSEMBLY_EN_5_9_November_1966_ASSEMBLY_HEADS_STATE_GOVERNMENT_THIRD_ORDINARY_SESSION.pdf.
SSSR i strany afriki, 1946–1962 gg: Dokumenty i materialy. Moscow: Gosudarstvennoe Izdatelsvo Politicheskoi Literatury, 1963.
Viacheslavovich, Vitalii, ed. *Blizhnevostochnyi konflikt: Iz dokumentov Arkhiva vneshnei politiki Rossiiskoi Federatsii*. Moscow: Mezhdunarodyii fond Demokratiia, 2003.
"U Thant Addresses Economic and Social Council." *United Nations Conference on Trade and Development: Geneva, 23 March–16 June 1964*, 28–29. Geneva: United Nations Office of Public Information, 1964.

Books, Articles, and Dissertations

Abane, Belaïd. *L'Algérie en guerre: Abane Ramdane et les fusils de la rébellion*. Paris: L'Harmattan, 2008.
Abernethy, David B. *The Dynamics of Global Dominance: European Overseas Empires, 1415–1980*. New Haven, CT: Yale University Press, 2000.
Aburish, Said K. *Nasser: The Last Arab*. New York: St. Martin's Press, 2004.
Adas, Michael. *Dominance by Design: Technological Imperatives and America's Civilizing Mission*. Cambridge, MA: Belknap Press of Harvard University Press, 2006.
———. *Machines as the Measure of Men: Science, Technology, and Ideologies of Western Dominance*. Ithaca, NY: Cornell University Press, 1992.
Adie, W. A. C. "China, Russia, and the Third World." *China Quarterly*, no. 11 (1962): 200–213.
Ageron, Charles-Robert. *L'Algérie algérienne de Napoléon III à de Gaulle*. Paris: Sinbad, 1980.
———. "La cooperation avec l'Algérie indépendante," in *De Gaulle et son siècle* (Paris: La Documentation Française, 1992), 6:216.
———. *La décolonisation française*. Paris: Armand Colin, 1994.
———. ed. *La Guerre d'Algérie et les Algériens, 1954–1962*. Paris: Armand Colin, 1997.
———. *Histoire de l'Algérie contemporaine: 1830–1976*. Vol. 2. Paris: Presses Universitaires de France, 1977.

———. "Vérités sur l'émir Khaled." *Algérie Actualité*, nos. 6–12, March 1980.
Ageron, Charles-Robert, and Marc Michel, eds. *L'Afrique noire française: L'heure des indépendances*. Paris: CNRS, 1992.
Ageron, Charles Robert, and Michael Brett. *Modern Algeria: A History from 1830 to the Present*. Trenton, NJ: Africa World Press, 1991.
Ageron, Charles Robert, and Cécile Thiébault, eds. *La Guerre d'Algérie: Au miroir des décolonisations françaises: En l'honneur de Charles-Robert Ageron: Actes du colloque international, Paris, Sorbonne, 23, 24, 25 Novembre 2000*. Saint-Denis: Société Française d'Histoire d'Outre-Mer, 2000.
Ahlberg, Kristin L. "'Machiavelli with a Heart': The Johnson Administration's Food for Peace Program in India, 1965–1966." *Diplomatic History* 31, no. 4 (2007): 665–701.
Ahlman, Jeffrey S. "The Algerian Question in Nkrumah's Ghana, 1958–1960: Debating 'Violence' and 'Nonviolence' in African Decolonization." *Africa Today* 57, no. 2 (2010): 67–84.
Aissaoui, Rabah. "Algerian Nationalists in the French Political Arena and Beyond: The Etoile Nord-Africaine and the Parti du Peuple Algérien in Interwar France." *Journal of North African Studies* 15, no. 1 (2010): 1–12.
Aït-El-Djoudi, Dalila. *La Guerre d'Algérie vue par l'ALN 1954–1962: L'armée française sous le regard des combattants algériens*. Paris: Autrement, 2007.
Ait Mous, Fadma. "The Moroccan Nationalist Movement: From Local to National Networks." *Journal of North African Studies* 18, no. 5 (2013): 737–752.
Akindele, R. R. "Reflections on the Preoccupation and Conduct of African Diplomacy." *Journal of Modern African Studies* 14, no. 4 (1976): 557–576.
Alexander, Christopher. "Opportunities, Organizations, and Ideas: Islamists and Workers in Tunisia and Algeria." *International Journal of Middle East Studies* 32, no. 4 (2000): 465–490.
Alexander, Martin, and John F. V. Keiger, "France and the Algerian War: Strategy, Operations and Diplomacy," *Journal of Strategic Studies* 25, no. 2 (2002): 1–32. Reprinted in Martin Alexander and John F. V. Keiger, eds., *France and the Algerian War, 1954–62: Strategy, Operations and Diplomacy*, 1–34. London: Frank Cass, 2002.
Alleg, Henri. *La Guerre d'Algérie*. Paris: Temps Actuels, 1981.
Allison, Roy. *The Soviet Union and the Strategy of Non-alignment in the Third World*. Cambridge: Cambridge University Press, 1988.
Amer, O. A. "China and the Afro-Asian Peoples' Solidarity Organization, 1958–1967." PhD diss., University of Geneva, 1972.
Anderson, Jon Lee. *Che Guevara: A Revolutionary Life*. London: Bantam, 1997.
Andrew, Christopher M., and Vasili Mitrokhin. *The World Was Going Our Way: The KGB and the Battle for the Third World*. New York: Basic Books, 2005.
Armah, Kwesi. *Peace without Power: Ghana's Foreign Policy, 1957–1966*. Accra: Ghana Universities Press, 2004.
Ashton, Nigel John. *Eisenhower, Macmillan and the Problem of Nasser: Anglo-American Relations and Arab Nationalism, 1955–59*. London: Palgrave Macmillan, 1996.
Asselin, Pierre. *Hanoi's Road to the Vietnam War, 1954–1965*. Berkeley: University of California Press, 2013.
Aydin, Cemil. *The Politics of Anti-Westernism in Asia: Visions of World Order in Pan-Islamic and Pan-Asian Thought*. New York: Columbia University Press, 2007.
Azevedo, Mario J. "The Organization of African Unity and Afro-Arab Cooperation." *Africa Today* 35, nos. 3/4 (1988): 68–80.
Azzou, El-Mostefa. "La propaganda des nationalistes marocains aux Etats-Unies (1945–1956)," *Guerres Mondiales et Conflits Contemporains* 58, no. 230 (2008): 89-98.
Badie, Bertrand. *The Imported State: The Westernization of the Political Order*. Stanford, CA: Stanford University Press, 2000.
Barraclough, Geoffrey. *An Introduction to Contemporary History*. New York: Basic Books, 1965.
Bendiab, Abderrahim Taled. "La pénétration des idées et l'implantation communiste en Algérie dans les années 1920." In *Mouvement ouvrier, communisme et nationalismes dans le monde arabe*, ed. René Gallissot, 127–146. Paris: Editions Ouvrières, 1978.
Bennoune, Mahfoud. *The Making of Contemporary Algeria, 1830–1987: Colonial Upheavals and Post-independence Development*. Cambridge: Cambridge University Press, 1988.

Berger, Mark T. "After the Third World? History, Destiny and the Fate of Third Worldism." *Third World Quarterly* 25, no. 1 (2004): 9–39.
Bergheaud, Edmond. *Le premier quart d'heure.* Paris: Plon, 1964.
Berque, Jacques. *Le Maghreb entre deux guerres.* Paris: Seuil, 1979.
Berthonnet, Arnaud. "La formation d'une culture économique et technique en Algérie (1830–1962): L'exemple des grandes infrastructures de génie civil." *French Colonial History* 9 (2008): 37–63.
Beshir, Mohamed Omer. *Terramedia: Themes in Afro-Arab Relations.* London: Ithaca, 1982.
Biney, Ama. "The Development of Kwame Nkrumah's Political Thought in Exile, 1966–1972." *Journal of African History* 50, no. 1 (2009): 81.
Bjerk, Paul. "Postcolonial Realism: Tanganyika's Foreign Policy under Nyerere, 1960–1963." *International Journal of African Historical Studies* 44, no. 2 (2011): 215–247.
Blackey, Robert. "Fanon and Cabral: A Contrast in Theories of Revolution for Africa." *Journal of Modern African Studies* 12, no. 2 (1974): 191–209.
Blanchard, Pascal, Sandrine Lemaire, and Nicolas Bancel, eds. *Culture impériale: Les colonies au coeur de la République, 1931–1961.* Paris: Autrement, 2004.
Boden, Ragna. "Cold War Economics: Soviet Aid to Indonesia." *Journal of Cold War Studies* 10, no. 3 (2008): 110–128.
Boquérat, Gilles. "India's Commitment to Peaceful Coexistence and the Settlement of the Indochina War." *Cold War History* 5, no. 2 (2005): 211–234.
Borgwardt, Elizabeth. *A New Deal for the World: America's Vision for Human Rights.* Cambridge, MA: Belknap Press of Harvard University Press, 2005.
Borstelmann, Thomas. *The Cold War and the Color Line: American Race Relations in the Global Arena.* Cambridge, MA: Harvard University Press, 2001.
Bouandel, Youcef. "Political Parties and the Transition from Authoritarianism: The Case of Algeria." *Journal of Modern African Studies* 41, no. 1 (2003): 1–22.
Boughton, James M. *Silent Revolution: The International Monetary Fund, 1979–1989.* Washington, DC: International Monetary Fund, 2001.
Bourdieu, Pierre. *The Algerians.* Translated by Alan C. M. Ross. Boston: Beacon Press, 1962.
Boyer, Christian, and Benjamin Stora. *Bibliographie de l'Algérie Indépendante.* Paris: CNRS, 2011.
Brace, Richard M. *Algerian Voices.* Princeton, NJ: Van Nostrand, 1965.
———. *Ordeal in Algeria.* Princeton, NJ: Van Nostrand, 1960.
Brower, Benjamin Claude. *A Desert Named Peace: The Violence of France's Empire in the Algerian Sahara, 1844–1902.* New York: Columbia University Press, 2009.
Brown, L. Carl. "Islam's Role in North Africa." In *Man, State, and Society in the Contemporary Maghrib,* ed. I. William Zartman, 31–36. New York: Praeger, 1973.
Cabanius-Matraman, Philippe. "Chronique économique Algérie." *Annuaire de l'Afrique du Nord,* 1965, 279–333.
Campbell, John C. *Tito's Separate Road: America and Yugoslavia in World Politics.* New York: Harper and Row, 1967.
Castañeda, Jorge G. *Compañero: The Life and Death of Che Guevara.* New York: Knopf, 1997.
Chafer, Tony. "Education and Political Socialisation of a National-Colonial Political Elite in French West Africa, 1936–47," *Journal of Imperial and Commonwealth History* 35, no. 3 (2007): 437–458.
Chagnollaud, Jean Paul. "Le Maghreb et le conflit israelo-arabe." PhD diss., University of Paris I, 1975.
Chaliand, Gérard, and Juliette Minces. *L'Algérie indépendante: Bilan d'une révolution nationale* Paris: F. Maspero, 1972.
Chamberlin, Paul Thomas. *The Global Offensive: The United States, the Palestine Liberation Organization, and the Making of the Post–Cold War Order.* New York: Oxford University Press, 2012.
———. "Preparing for Dawn: The United States and the Global Politics of Palestinian Resistance, 1967–1975." PhD diss., Ohio State University, 2009.
Chen Jian, "Bridging Revolution and Decolonization: The 'Bandung Discourse' in China's Early Cold War Experience," *Chinese Historical Review* 15, no.2 (2008): 207–241.
———. *Mao's China and the Cold War.* Chapel Hill: University of North Carolina Press, 2001.

Cherki, Alice. *Frantz Fanon: A Portrait*. Translated by Nadia Benabid. Ithaca, NY: Cornell University Press, 2006.
Cheurfi, Achour. *Dictionnaire encyclopedique de l'Algerie*. Algiers: Éditions ANEP, 2007.
Chikh, Slimane. *L'Algérie en armes, ou, le temps des certitudes*. 2nd rev. ed. Algiers: Casbah, 1998.
———. "L'Algérie et l'Afrique (1954–1962)." *Revue Algérienne des Sciences Juridiques, Économiques et Politiques* 5, no. 3 (1968): 703–746.
———. *L'Algérie porte de l'Afrique*, Algiers: Casbah Éditions, 1999.
Chikh, Slimane, and Ḥasan Fatḥ al-Bāb, eds. *Thawrat Al-Jazā'ir Fī Ibdā' Shu'arā' Miṣr*. Algiers: Mu'assasat Mufdī Zakariyā', 2005.
Chikh, Slimane, Hubert Michel, and Centre de Recherches et d'Études sur les Sociétés Méditerranéennes, eds. *Le Maghreb et l'Afrique Subsaharienne*. Paris: Editions du Centre Nationale de la Recherche Scientifique, 1980.
Chipman, John. *French Power in Africa*. Oxford: Blackwell, 1989.
Christelow, Allan. *Algerians without Borders: The Making of a Global Frontier Society*. Gainesville: University Press of Florida, 2012.
———. "Bashir Ibrahimi and the Islamic Encounter with European Secular and Religious Faiths." *Maghreb Review* 29, nos. 1–4 (2004): 99–122.
———. "The Muslim Judge and Municipal Politics in Colonial Algeria and Senegal." *Comparative Studies in Society and History* 24, no. 1 (1982): 3–24.
———. "Ritual, Culture and Politics of Islamic Reformism in Algeria." *Middle Eastern Studies* 23, no. 3 (1987): 255–273.
Citino, Nathan J. "The 'Crush' of Ideologies: The United States, the Arab World, and Cold War Modernisation." *Cold War History* 12, no. 1 (2012): 89–110.
———. "The Ottoman Legacy in Cold War Modernization." *International Journal of Middle East Studies* 40, no. 4 (2008): 579–597.
Clancy-Smith, Julia Ann. *Rebel and Saint: Muslim Notables, Populist Protest, Colonial Encounters (Algeria and Tunisia, 1800–1904)*. Berkeley: University of California Press, 1994.
Clegg, Ian. *Workers' Self-Management in Algeria*. London: Allen Lane, 1971.
Colburn, Forrest D. *The Vogue of Revolution in Poor Countries*. Princeton, NJ: Princeton University Press, 1994.
Colonna, Fanny. "From the Mountain Sanctuary to the Nation." *Journal of North African Studies* 18, no. 5 (2013): 725–736.
———. "The Nation's 'Unknowing Other': Three Intellectuals and the Culture(s) of Being Algerian, or the Impossibility of Subaltern Studies in Algeria." *Journal of North African Studies* 8, no. 1 (2003): 155–170.
———. "Religion, politique et culture(s), quelle problématique de la nation?" *Insaniyat/Revue Algérienne d'Anthropologie et de Sciences Sociales*, nos. 47–48 (2010): 23–33.
Connelly, Matthew. *A Diplomatic Revolution: Algeria's Fight for Independence and the Origins of the Post–Cold War Era*. Oxford: Oxford University Press, 2002.
———. "Taking Off the Cold War Lens: Visions of North-South Conflict during the Algerian War for Independence," *American Historical Review* 105, no.3 (2000): 739–769.
Cooper, Frederick. *Africa since 1940: The Past of the Present*. London: Cambridge University Press, 2002.
———. *Colonialism in Question: Theory, Knowledge, History*. Berkeley: University of California Press, 2005.
———. *Decolonization and African Society: The Labor Question in French and British Africa*. Cambridge: Cambridge University Press, 1996.
———. "Possibility and Constraint: African Independence in Historical Perspective." *Journal of African History* 49, no. 2 (2008): 167–196.
Courrière, Yves. *La Guerre d'Algérie: Le temps des leopards*. Algiers: Casbah Éditions, 2005.
Crenshaw, Martha. *Revolutionary Terrorism: The FLN in Algeria, 1954–1962*. Stanford, CA: Hoover Institution Press, Stanford University, 1978.
Cullather, Nick. "Hunger and Containment: How India Became 'Important' in US Cold War Strategy." *India Review* 6, no. 2 (2007): 59–90.
———. *The Hungry World: America's Cold War Battle against Poverty in Asia*. Cambridge, MA: Harvard University Press, 2010.

Cutler, Robert M. "East-South Relations at UNCTAD: Global Political Economy and the CMEA." *International Organization* 37, no. 1 (1983): 121–142.

Dawisha, Adeed. *Arab Nationalism in the Twentieth Century: From Triumph to Despair*. Princeton, NJ: Princeton University Press, 2003.

De Braganca, Aquino and Immanuel Maurice Wallerstein. *The African Liberation Reader*. Vol. 2, *The National Liberation Movements*. London: Zed Press, 1982.

Dei-Anang, Michael. *The Administration of Ghana's Foreign Relations, 1957–1965: A Personal Memoir*. London: University of London, The Athlone Press, 1975.

Daho Djerbal, "Stratégie gaullienne et stratégie de l'Etat français rupture et continuité: Le cas de l'Algérie." In *De Gaulle et son Siècle*, edited by Fondation Charles de Gaulle, vol. 6, *Liberté et dignité des peuples*, 107–115. Paris: Fondation Charles de Gaulle, 1992.

DeRoche, Andy. "Non-alignment on the Racial Frontier: Zambia and the USA, 1964–68." *Cold War History* 7, no. 2 (2007): 227–250.

Descloitres, Robert, Jean Claude Reverdy, and Claudine Descloitres, *L'Algérie des bidonvilles: Le Tiers Monde dans la cité*. Paris: Mouton, 1961.

Diallo, Abdoulaye. "Sékou Touré et L'indépendance Guinéenne: Déconstruction d'un mythe et retour sur une histoire." *Outre-Mers* 95, no. 358 (2008): 267–288.

Dib, Mohammed. *Qui se souvient de la mer. Roman*. Paris, 1962.

Doig, Jameson W. *Empire on the Hudson: Entrepreneurial Vision and Political Power at the Port of New York Authority*. New York: Columbia University Press, 2001.

Domínguez, Jorge I. *To Make a World Safe for Revolution: Cuba's Foreign Policy*. Cambridge, MA: Harvard University Press, 1989.

Donham, Donald L. *Marxist Modern: An Ethnographic History of the Ethiopian Revolution*. Berkeley: University of California Press, 1999.

Dosman, Edgar J. *The Life and Times of Raúl Prebisch, 1901–1986*. Montreal: McGill-Queen's University Press, 2008.

Engerman, David C. "Learning from the East Soviet Experts and India in the Era of Competitive Coexistence." *Comparative Studies of South Asia, Africa and the Middle East* 33, no. 2 (2013): 227–238.

Escobar, Arturo. *Encountering Development: The Making and Unmaking of the Third World*. Princeton, NJ: Princeton University Press, 1995.

Favret, Jeanne. "Le syndicat, les travailleurs et le pouvoir en Algérie." *Annuaire de l'Afrique du Nord*, 1964, 44–62.

Favret-Saada, Jeanne. *Algérie 1962–1964: Essais d'anthropologie politique*. Saint-Denis: Bouchène, 2005.

Feraoun, Mouloud. *Journal, 1955–1962: Reflections on the French-Algerian War*. Lincoln: University of Nebraska Press, 2000.

Ferris, Jesse. "Soviet Support for Egypt's Intervention in Yemen, 1962–1963." *Journal of Cold War Studies* 10, no. 4 (2008): 5–36.

Fitte, Albert. *Spectroscopie d'une propagande révolutionnaire: "El Moudjahid" des temps de guerre; juin 1956–mars 1962*. Montpellier: Université Paul Valéry, 1973.

Frieden, Jeff. "Third World Indebted Industrialization: International Finance and State Capitalism in Mexico, Brazil, Algeria, and South Korea." *International Organization* 35, no. 3 (1981): 407–431.

Friedman, Jeremy Scott. "Reviving Revolution: The Sino-Soviet Split, the 'Third World,' and the Fate of the Left." PhD diss., Princeton University, 2011.

———. "Soviet Policy in the Developing World and the Chinese Challenge in the 1960s." Paper presented at the 2009 Graduate Student Conference on the Cold War, London School of Economics and Political Science, 24–26 April 2009.

Fuglestad, Finn. "Djibo Bakary, the French, and the Referendum of 1958 in Niger." *Journal of African History* 14, no. 2 (1973): 313–330.

Fursenko, Aleksandr, and Timothy J. Naftali. *Khrushchev's Cold War: The Inside Story of an American Adversary*. New York: Norton, 2006.

———. *One Hell of a Gamble: Khrushchev, Castro, and Kennedy, 1958–1964*. New York: Norton, 1997.

Gakunzi, David. *Abdelaziz Bouteflika, le choix de la paix*. Paris: L'Harmattan, 2003.

Gallissot, René. *Maghreb-Algérie: Classe et nation.* Vol. 1, *Du Maghreb précolonial à l'indépendance.* Paris: Arcantère, 1987.

———, ed. *Mouvement ouvrier, communisme et nationalismes dans le monde arabe: Études.* Paris: Éditions Ouvrières, 1978.

Garavini, Giuliano. *After Empires: European Integration, Decolonization, and the Challenge from the Global South 1957–1986.* Oxford: Oxford University Press, 2012.

Gerges, Fawaz A. *The Superpowers and the Middle East: Regional and International Politics, 1955–1967.* Boulder, CO: Westview Press, 1994.

Gifford, Prosser, and William Roger Louis, eds. *Decolonization and African Independence: The Transfers of Power, 1960–1980.* New Haven, CT: Yale University Press, 1988.

Gillissen, Christophe. "Ireland, France and the Question of Algeria at the United Nations, 1955–62." *Irish Studies in International Affairs* 19 (2008): 151–167.

Gilman, Nils. *Mandarins of the Future: Modernization Theory in Cold War America.* Baltimore: Johns Hopkins University Press, 2003.

Ginat, Rami. "India and the Palestine Question: The Emergence of the Asio-Arab Bloc and India's Quest for Hegemony in the Post-colonial Third World." *Middle Eastern Studies* 40, no. 6 (2004): 189–218.

Gleijeses, Piero. *Conflicting Missions: Havana, Washington, and Africa, 1959–1976.* Chapel Hill: University of North Carolina Press, 2002.

Golan, Galia. *The Soviet Involvement in the Middle East.* Jerusalem: Hebrew University, 1971.

Goodwin, Jeff. *No Other Way Out: States and Revolutionary Movements, 1945–1991.* Cambridge: Cambridge University Press, 2001.

Gopal, Sarvepalli. *Jawaharlal Nehru: A Biography.* Vol. 3. London: Jonathan Cape, 1984.

Gosovic, Branislav. *UNCTAD Conflict and Compromise: The Third World's Quest for an Equitable World Economic Order through the United Nations.* Leiden, A. W. Sijthoff, 1972.

Gosnell, Jonathan K. *The Politics of Frenchness in Colonial Algeria, 1930–1954.* Rochester, NY: University of Rochester Press, 2002.

Griffith, William E. "Sino-Soviet Relations, 1964–1965." *China Quarterly,* no. 25 (1966): 3–143.

Grimaud, Nicole. *La politique extérieure de l'Algérie (1962–1978).* Paris: Karthala, 1984.

Guitard, Odette. "Alger ou la désunion afro-asiatique," *Annuaire de l'Afrique du Nord,* 1965, 49–61.

Haddad-Fonda, Kyle. "An Illusory Alliance: Revolutionary Legitimacy and Sino-Algerian Relations, 1958–1962." *Journal of North African Studies* 19, no. 3 (2014): 338–357.

———. "Revolutionary Allies: Sino-Egyptian and Sino-Algerian Relations in the Bandung Decade." PhD diss., Oxford University, 2013.

Hadhri, Mohieddine. *L'URSS et le Maghreb: De la Révolution d'octobre à l'indépendance de l'Algérie, 1917–1962.* Paris: L'Harmattan, 1985.

Hahn, Peter L., and Mary Ann Heiss, eds. *Empire and Revolution: The United States and the Third World since 1945.* Columbus: Ohio State University Press, 2001.

Harbi, Mohammed. *Le F.L.N.: Mirage et réalité.* Paris: Editions Jeune Afrique, 1980.

———, ed. *Les archives de la Révolution Algérienne.* Paris: Éditions Jeune Afrique, 1981.

Harbi, Mohammed, and Gilbert Meynier, eds. *Le FLN, documents et histoire: 1954–1962.* Paris: Fayard, 2004.

Harbi, Mohammed, and Benjamin Stora, eds. *La Guerre d'Algérie: 1954–2004, la fin de l'amnésie.* Paris: R. Laffont, 2004.

Hargreaves, John D. *Decolonization in Africa.* 2nd ed. London: Longman, 1996.

Harmer, Tanya. *Allende's Chile and the Inter-American Cold War.* Chapel Hill: University of North Carolina Press, 2011.

Harrison, Alexander. *Challenging de Gaulle: The O.A.S. and the Counterrevolution in Algeria, 1954–1962.* New York: Praeger, 1989.

Hart, Alan. *Arafat: A Political Biography.* London: Sidgwick and Jackson, 1994.

Hayes, Jarrod. "Queer Resistance to (Neo-)colonialism in Algeria." In *Postcolonial, Queer: Theoretical Intersections,* ed. John C. Hawley, 79–98. Albany: State Univeristy of New York Press, 2001.

Hazard, John N. "Marxian Socialism in Africa: The Case of Mali." *Comparative Politics* 2, no. 1 (1969): 1–15.

Heikal, Mohamed. *The Cairo Documents: The Inside Story of Nasser and His Relationship with World Leaders, Rebels, and Statesmen.* Garden City, NY: Doubleday, 1973.

Henry, Clement M. *L'UGEMA, Union Générale des Étudiants Musulmans Algériens, 1955–1962: Témoignages*. Algiers: Casbah Editions, 2010.

Hershberg, James G. "'High-Spirited Confusion': Brazil, the 1961 Belgrade Non-aligned Conference, and the Limits of an 'Independent' Foreign Policy during the High Cold War." *Cold War History* 7, no. 3 (2007): 373–388.

Hesslier, Julie. "Death of an African Student in Moscow: Race, Politics, and the Cold War." *Cahiers du Monde Russe* 47, no. 1 (2006): 33–63.

Hill, J. N. C. "Challenging the Failed State Thesis: IMF and World Bank Intervention and the Algerian Civil War," *Civil Wars* 11, no. 1 (2009): 39–56.

Horne, Alistair. *A Savage War of Peace: Algeria, 1954–1962*. New York: Viking, 1978.

House, Jim, and Neil MacMaster. *Paris 1961: Algerians, State Terror, and Memory*. Oxford: Oxford University Press, 2006.

Humbaraci, Arslan. *Algeria: A Revolution That Failed: A Political History since 1954*. London: Pall Mall, 1966.

Hutchison, Alan. *China's African Revolution*. Boulder, CO: Westview Press, 1976.

Iandolo, Alessandro. "Imbalance of Power: The Soviet Union and the Congo Crisis, 1960–1961." *Journal of Cold War Studies* 16, no. 2 (2014): 32–55.

———. "The Rise and Fall of the 'Soviet Model of Development' in West Africa, 1957–64." *Cold War History* 12, no. 4 (2012): 683–704.

Ikeda, Ryo. "The Paradox of Independence: The Maintenance of Influence and the French Decision to Transfer Power in Morocco," *Journal of Imperial and Commonwealth History* 35, no. 4 (2007): 569–592.

Irwin, Ryan. "The Gordian Knot: Apartheid and the Unmaking of the Liberal World Order, 1960–1970." PhD diss., Ohio State University, 2010.

Ismael, Tareq Y. *The U.A.R. in Africa: Egypt's Policy under Nasser*. Evanston, IL: Northwestern University Press, 1971.

Itote, Waruhiu. *"Mau Mau" General*. Nairobi: East African Institute Press, 1967.

Jackson, Henry F. *The FLN in Algeria: Party Development in a Revolutionary Society*. Westport, CT: Greenwood Press, 1977.

Jackson, Robert H. *Quasi-States: Sovereignty, International Relations, and the Third World*. New York: Cambridge University Press, 1990.

Jackson, Steven F. "China's Third World Foreign Policy: The Case of Angola and Mozambique, 1961–93." *China Quarterly*, no. 142 (1995): 388–422.

Jankowitsch-Prevor, Odette, and Karl P. Sauvant, eds. *The Third World without Superpowers: The Collected Documents of the Non-aligned Countries*. Dobbs Ferry, NY: Oceana Publications, 1978.

Jansen, G. H. *Afro-Asia and Non-alignment*. London: Faber and Faber, 1966.

Jauffret, Jean-Charles, and Maurice Vaïsse, eds. *Militaires et guérilla dans la Guerre d'Algérie*. Brussels: Editions Complexe, 2001.

Jones, Matthew. "A 'Segregated' Asia? Race, the Bandung Conference, and Pan-Asianist Fears in American Thought and Policy, 1954–1955," *Diplomatic History* 29, no.5 (2005): 841–868.

Juergensmeyer, Mark. *The New Cold War? Religious Nationalism Confronts the Secular State*. Berkeley: University of California Press, 1993.

Kaddache, Mahfoud. *Histoire du nationalisme algérien*. Algiers: Enterprise Nationale du Livre, 1993.

Kahin, George. *The Asian-African Conference: Bandung, Indonesia, April 1955*. Ithaca, NY: Cornell University Press, 1956.

Kaiser, Paul J. "Structural Adjustment and the Fragile Nation: The Demise of Social Unity in Tanzania." *Journal of Modern African Studies* 34, no. 2 (1996): 227–237.

Kalb, Madeleine G. *The Congo Cables: The Cold War in Africa—from Eisenhower to Kennedy*. New York: Macmillan, 1982.

Kalinovsky, Artemy M. "Not Some British Colony in Africa: The Politics of Decolonization and Modernization in Soviet Central Asia, 1955–1964." *Ab Imperio* 2 (2013): 191–222.

Kalinovsky, Artemy M., and Sergey Radchenko, eds. *The End of the Cold War and the Third World: New Perspectives on Regional Conflict*. New York: Routledge, 2011.

Kapuściński, Ryszard. *The Soccer War*. New York: Vintage, 1992.

Katsakioris, Constantin. "L'union soviétique et les intellectuels africains: Internationalisme, panafricanisme et négritude pendant les années de la décolonisation, 1954–1964." *Cahiers du Monde Russe* 47, no. 1 (2006): 15–32.
Kennedy, Paul M. *The Parliament of Man: The Past, Present, and Future of the United Nations*. New York: Random House, 2006.
Kerr, Malcolm H. *The Arab Cold War: Gamal 'Abd Al-Nasir and His Rivals*. New York: Oxford University Press, 1971.
Kettle, Michael. *De Gaulle and Algeria, 1940–1960: From Mers El-Kébir to the Algiers Barracades*. London: Quartet, 1993.
Khan, Sulmann Wasif. "Cold War Cooperation: New Chinese Evidence on Jawaharlal Nehru's 1954 Visit to Beijing." *Cold War History* 11, no. 2 (2011): 197–222.
Kimche, David. *The Afro-Asian Movement: Ideology and Foreign Policy of the Third World*. Jerusalem: Israel Universities Press, 1973.
Kirasirova, Masha. "'Sons of Muslims' in Moscow: Soviet Central Asian Mediators to the Foreign East, 1955–1962." *Ab Imperio* 4 (2011): 106–132.
Kirpichenko, Vadim. *Razvedka: Litsa i Lichnosti*. Moscow: GEiA, 1998.
Kolodziej, Edward A. *French International Policy under De Gaulle and Pompidou: The Politics of Grandeur*. Ithaca, NY: Cornell University Press, 1974.
Konkel, Rob. "The Monetization of Global Poverty: The Concept of Poverty in World Bank History, 1944–90." *Journal of Global History* 9, no. 2 (2014): 276–300.
Krieger, Annie. "Les prémices d'une réforme agraire en Algérie." In *Essais sur l'économie de l'Algérie nouvelle*, ed. François d'Arcy, Annie Krieger, and Alain Marill, 97–166. Paris: Presses Universitaires de France, 1965.
Kullaa, Rinna. *Non-alignment and Its Origins in Cold War Europe: Yugoslavia, Finland and the Soviet Challenge*. London: I. B. Tauris, 2012.
Lacheraf, Mostefa. *L'Algérie: Nation et société*. Paris: F. Maspero, 1965.
———. *Algérie & Tiers-Monde: Agressions, résistances & solidarités intercontinentales*. Algiers: Bouchêne, 1989.
———. *Histoire, culture et société*. Algiers: Éditions ANEP, 2004.
Lacouture, Jean. *Nasser*. Translated by Daniel Hofstadter. London: Secker and Warburg, 1973.
———. *Le Tiers-Monde de Bandoung à Alger: Conférence . . . 24 Janvier 1974, Université de Yaoundé*. Yaoundé: École Supérieure Internationale de Journalisme de Yaounde, 1974.
Lal, Priya. "Between the Village and the World: Imagining and Practicing Development in Tanzania, 1964–1975." PhD diss., New York University, 2011.
———. "Self-Reliance and the State: The Multiple Meanings of Development in Early Post-Colonial Tanzania." *Africa: The Journal of the International African Institute* 82, no. 2 (2012): 212–234.
"La politique économique algérienne au début de 1964," *Maghreb: Documents, Algérie, Maroc, Tunisie*, no. 2 (March–April 1964): 16–18.
Laremont, Ricardo René. *Islam and the Politics of Resistance in Algeria, 1783–1992*. Trenton, NJ: Africa World Press, 2000.
Larkin, Bruce D. *China and Africa, 1949–1970: The Foreign Policy of the People's Republic of China*. Berkeley: University of California Press, 1971.
Laskier, Michael. "Israel and Algeria amid French Colonialism and the Arab-Israeli Conflict, 1954–1978." *Israel Studies* 6, no. 2 (2001): 1–32.
Latham, Michael E. *Modernization as Ideology: American Social Science and "Nation Building" in the Kennedy Era*. Chapel Hill: University of North Carolina Press, 2000.
Lawrence, Adria "Rethinking Moroccan Nationalism, 1930–44." *Journal of North African Studies* 17, no. 3 (2012): 475–490.
Lawrence, Mark Atwood. "The Rise and Fall of Nonalignment." In *The Cold War in the Third World, Reinterpreting History*, edited by Robert J. McMahon, 139–155. New York: Oxford University Press, 2013.
Leca, Jean, and Jean Claude Vatin, *L'Algérie politique: Institutions et régime*. Paris: Presses de la Fondation Nationale des Sciences Politiques, 1975.
Leduc, Anne. *Le chant du lendemain: Alger, 1962–1969*. Saint-Denis: Bouchêne, 2004.

———. and Juliette Minces, "Continuities and Discontinuities in the Algerian Confrontation with Europe." In *Islam and Secularism in North Africa*, edited by John Ruedy, 73–86. London: Macmillan, 1994.
Lee, Christopher J. "Conference Report: 'Bandung and Beyond: Rethinking Afro-Asian Connections during the Twentieth Century.'" *African Affairs* 104, no. 417 (2005): 683–684.
———. ed. *Making a World after Empire: The Bandung Moment and Its Political Afterlives*. Athens: Ohio University Press, 2010.
Lefebvre, Jeffrey A. "Kennedy's Algerian Dilemma: Containment, Alliance Politics and the 'Rebel Dialogue.'" *Middle Eastern Studies* 35, no. 2 (1999): 61–82.
Leffler, Melvyn P., and Odd Arne Westad, eds. *The Cambridge History of the Cold War*. New York: Cambridge University Press, 2010.
Legum, Colin. *Pan-Africanism: A Short Political Guide*. Special ed. London: Published for the Africa Bureau by Pall Mall Press, 1962.
Le Sueur, James D. *Uncivil War: Intellectuals and Identity Politics during the Decolonization of Algeria*. Lincoln: University of Nebraska Press, 2005.
Lewis, Martin and Karen Wigen. *The Myth of Continents: A Critique of Metageography*. Berkeley: University of California Press, 1997.
Liauzu, Claude. *Aux origines des tier-monidsmes: Colonisés et anticolonialistes en France (1919–1939)*. Paris: L'Harmattan, 1982.
Lissoni, Arianna. "Transformations in the ANC External Mission and Umkhonto we Sizwe, c. 1960–1969." *Journal of Southern African Studies* 35, no. 2 (2009): 287–301.
Lledo, Jean-Pierre, director. *Algeria: Unspoken Stories*. 2007.
Loiseau, Yves, and Pierre-Guillaume de Roux. *Portrait d'un révolutionnaire en général: Jonas Savimbi*. Paris: La Table Ronde, 1987.
Louro, Michele L. "Rethinking Nehru's Internationalism: The League against Imperialism and Anti-imperial Networks, 1929–1939." *Third Frame: Literature, Culture, Society* 2, no. 3 (2009): 79–94.
———. "'Where National Revolutionary Ends and Communist Begins': The League against Imperialism and the Meerut Conspiracy Case." *Comparative Studies of South Asia, Africa and the Middle East* 33, no. 3 (2013): 331–344.
Lumumba, Patrice. *La pensée politique de Patrice Lumumba*. Edited by Jean van Lierde. Paris: Présence Africaine, 1963.
Lundestad, Geir. "'Empire by Invitation' in the American Century," *Diplomatic History* 23, no. 2 (199): 189–217.
Lüthi, Lorenz M. "Rearranging International Relations? How Mao's China and de Gaulle's France Recognized Each Other in 1963–1964." *Journal of Cold War Studies* 16, no. 1 (2014): 111–145.
———. *The Sino-Soviet Split: Cold War in the Communist World*. Princeton, NJ: Princeton University Press, 2008.
Macey, David. *Frantz Fanon: A Biography*. London: Verso Books, 2012.
MacMaster, Neil. "Des révolutionnaires invisibles: Les femmes algériennes et l'organisation de La Section des Femmes du FLN en France métropolitaine." *Revue d'Histoire Moderne et Contemporaine* 59, no. 4 (2013): 164–190.
———. "The Roots of Insurrection: The Role of the Algerian Village Assembly (*Djemâa*) in Peasant Resistance, 1863–1962." *Comparative Studies in Society and History* 55, no. 2 (2013): 419–447.
Malley, Robert. *The Call from Algeria: Third Worldism, Revolution, and the Turn to Islam*. Berkeley: University of California Press, 1996.
Mallik, Deva Narayan. *The Development of Non-alignment in India's Foreign Policy*. Allahabad: Chaitanya Publishing House, 1967.
Manela, Erez. *The Wilsonian Moment: Self-Determination and the International Origins of Anticolonial Nationalism*. Oxford: Oxford University Press, 2007.
Marcum, John A. *The Angolan Revolution*. 2 vols. Cambridge, MA: MIT Press, 1969–1978.
———. "Sékou Touré & Guinea." *Africa Today* 6, no. 5 (1959): 5–8.
Markakis, John. "The Organisation of African Unity: A Progress Report." *Journal of Modern African Studies* 4, no. 2 (1966): 135–153.

Marseille, Jacques. *Empire colonial et capitalisme français: Histoire d'un divorce.* Paris: A. Michel, 1984.
Martin, Guy. "Socialism, Economic Development and Planning in Mali, 1960–1968." *Canadian Journal of African Studies* 10, no. 1 (1976): 23–46.
Mastny, Vojtech. "The Soviet Union's Partnership with India." *Journal of Cold War Studies* 12, no. 3 (2010): 50–90.
May, Ernest R., and Philip D. Zelikow, eds., *The Kennedy Tapes: Inside the White House during the Cuban Missile Crisis.* Cambridge, MA: Belknap Press of Harvard University Press, 1997.
Mayer, Arno J. *Wilson vs. Lenin: Political Origins of the New Diplomacy 1917–1918.* New Haven, CT: Yale University Press, 1959.
Mazov, Sergei. "Afrikanskie studenty v Moskve v God Afriki (po arkhivnym materialam)." *Vostok*, no. 3 (1999): 89–103.
———. *A Distant Front in the Cold War: The USSR in West Africa and the Congo, 1956–1964.* Stanford, CA: Stanford University Press, 2010.
———. "Soviet Aid to the Gizenga Government in the Former Belgian Congo (1960–61) as Reflected in Russian Archives." *Cold War History* 7, no. 3 (2007): 425–437.
———. "The USSR and the Former Italian Colonies, 1945–50." *Cold War History* 3, no. 3 (2003): 49–78.
McDougall, James. "Crisis and Recovery Narratives in Maghrebi Histories of the Ottoman Period (ca. 1870–1970)." *Comparative Studies of South Asia, Africa and the Middle East* 31, no. 1 (2011): 137–148.
———. *History and the Culture of Nationalism in Algeria.* Cambridge: Cambridge University Press, 2006.
———. ed. *Nation, Society and Culture in North Africa.* London: Frank Cass, 2003.
———. "Sacral Suicides, Unpunishable Killings, Rites of Power." *International Journal of Middle East Studies* 45, no. 4 (2013): 810–812.
———. "The Secular State's Islamic Empire: Muslim Spaces and Subjects of Jurisdiction in Paris and Algiers, 1905–1957." *Comparative Studies in Society and History* 52, no. 3 (2010): 553–580.
———. "The Shabiba Islamiyya of Algiers: Education, Authority, and Colonial Control, 1921–57." *Comparative Studies of South Asia, Africa and the Middle East* 24, no. 1 (2004): 149–154.
McDougall, James, and Robert P. Parks. "Locating Social Analysis in the Maghrib." *Journal of North African Studies* 18, no. 5 (2013): 631–638.
McMahon, Robert J., ed. *The Cold War in the Third World.* Oxford: Oxford University Press, 2013.
———. *The Cold War on the Periphery: The United States, India, and Pakistan.* New York: Columbia University Press, 1994.
Merle, Robert. *Ahmed Ben Bella.* Translated by Camilla Sykes. London: Michael Joseph, 1967.
Meynier, Gilbert. *L'Algérie révélée: La guerre de 1914–1918 et le premier quart du XXe siècle.* Geneva: Librairie Droz, 1981.
———. *Histoire intérieure du F.L.N. 1954–1962.* Paris: Fayard, 2002.
Migani, Guia. "Sékou Touré et la contestation de l'ordre colonial en Afrique sub-saharienne, 1958–1963." *Monde(s)* 2, no. 2 (2012): 257–273.
Moore, Clement Henry. *Tunisia since Independence: The Dynamics of One-Party Government.* Berkeley: University of California Press, 1965.
Morin, Jean. *De Gaulle et l'Algérie: Mon témoignage, 1960–1962.* Paris: A. Michel, 1999.
Mortimer, Robert A. "The Algerian Revolution in Search of the African Revolution." *Journal of Modern African Studies* 8, no. 3 (1970): 363–387.
———. "Foreign Policy and Its Role in Nation-Building in Algeria." PhD diss., Columbia University, 1968.
———. *The Third World Coalition in International Politics.* Boulder, CO: Westview Press, 1984.
Muehlenbeck, Philip E. "Kennedy and Touré: A Success in Personal Diplomacy." *Diplomacy and Statecraft* 19, no. 1 (2008): 69–95.
Mufti, Malik. *Sovereign Creations: Pan-Arabism and Political Order in Syria and Iraq.* Ithaca, NY: Cornell University Press, 1996.

Naumkin, Vitaliĭ Viacheslavovich, ed. *Blizhnevostochnyĭ konflikt: iz dokumentov arkhiva vneshneĭ politiki rossiĭskoĭ federatsii*. Moscow: Mezhdunarodnyĭ fond "Demokratiia," 2003.
Naylor, Phillip Chiviges. *France and Algeria: A History of Decolonization and Transformation*. Gainesville: University Press of Florida, 2000.
Nguyen, Lien-Hang T. *Hanoi's War: An International History of the War for Peace in Vietnam*. Chapel Hill: University of North Carolina Press, 2012.
Obichkina, E. O. "Sovetskoe rukovodstvo i voina v Alzhire, 1954–1962 gg. po materialam arkhiva MID RF." *Novaia I Noveishaia Istoriia* 1 (2000): 19–30.
Omouri, Noara. "Les section administratives spécialisées et les sciences sociales." In *Militaires et guérilla dans la Guerre d'Algérie*, ed. Jean-Charles Jauffret and Maurice Vaïsse, 383–397. Paris: Editions Complexe, 2001.
Ottaway, David, and Marina Ottaway. *Algeria: The Politics of a Socialist Revolution*. Berkeley: University of California Press, 1970.
Oulmont, Philippe, Maurice Vaïsse, and Fondation Charles de Gaulle, eds. *De Gaulle et la décolonisation de l'Afrique subsaharienne*. Paris: Éditions Karthala, 2014.
Pablo, Michel. *Le Programme de Tripoli: Impressions et problèmes de la Révolution Algérienne*. Paris: Parti Communiste Internationaliste (Section Française de la IVe Internationale), 1962.
Pang Yang Huei, "The Four Faces of Bandung: Detainees, Soldiers, Revolutionaries and Statesmen," *Journal of Contemporary Asia*, 39, no.1 (2009): 63–86.
Parker, Jason. "Cold War II: The Eisenhower Administration, the Bandung Conference, and the Reperiodization of the Postwar Era," *Diplomatic History* 30, no.5 (2006): 873–874
Parodi, Maurice. "Chronique économique: Algérie." *Annuaire de l'Afrique du Nord*, 1964, 231–283.
Peres, Phyllis Anne. *Transculturation and Resistance in Lusophone African Narrative*. Gainesville: University Press of Florida, 1997.
Perroux, François, ed. *Problèmes de l'algérie indépendante*. Paris: Presses Universitaires de France, 1963.
Pervillé, Guy. *De l'empire français à la décolonisation*. Paris: Hachette, 1991.
———. *Les étudiants Algériens de l'université française, 1880–1962: Populisme et nationalisme chez les étudiants et intellectuels Musulmans algériens de formation française*. Paris: Editions du Centre Nationale de la Recherche Scientifique, 1984.
———. *Atlas de la guerre d'Algérie: De la conquête à l'indépendance*. Paris: Autrement, 2003.
Peyrefitte, Alain. *C'était de Gaulle*. Paris: Editions de Fallois, 1994.
———. *Pour une histoire de la Guerre d'Algérie: 1954–1962*. Paris: Picard, 2002.
Prashad, Vijay. *The Darker Nations: A People's History of the Third World*. New York: New Press, 2007.
———. *The Poorer Nations: A Possible History of the Global South*. London: Verso, 2012.
Primakov, Yevgeny. *Russia and the Arabs: Behind the Scenes in the Middle East from the Cold War to the Present*. New York: Basic Books, 2009.
Quandt, William B. *Revolution and Political Leadership: Algeria, 1954–1968*. Cambridge, MA: MIT Press, 1969.
Quarm, S. E. *Diplomatic Servant: Reflections of a Pioneer in Ghana's Diplomatic Service*. Accra: Afram Publications, 1995.
Radchenko, Sergey. *Two Suns in the Heavens: The Sino-Soviet Struggle for Supremacy, 1962–1967*. Stanford, CA: Stanford University Press, 2009.
Rahal, Malika. "Le camp des oliviers: Parcours d'un communiste algérien." *Journal of North African Studies* 18, no. 4 (2013): 623–625.
———. "A Local Approach to the UDMA: Local-Level Politics during the Decade of Political Parties, 1946–56." *Journal of North African Studies* 18, no. 5 (2013): 703–724.
———. "Comment faire l'histoire de l'Algérie indépendante?", *La Vie des Idées*, 13 March 2012, http://www.laviedesidees.fr/Comment-faire-l-histoire-de-l-Algerie-independante.html.
Rajak, Svetozar. "No Bargaining Chips, No Spheres of Interest: The Yugoslav Origins of Cold War Non-alignment." *Journal of Cold War Studies* 16, no. 1 (2014): 146–179.
Rakove, Robert B. *Kennedy, Johnson, and the Nonaligned World*. New York: Cambridge University Press, 2013.
Ramon, Jean-Bernard. *L'OAS et ses appuis internationaux: Alliés, Influences et manipulations extérieures*. Paris: Atelier Fol'fer, 2008.

Rastiannikov, V. G. "Prodovol'stvennaia problema v razvi- vaiushchikhsia stranakh azii i afriki." *Narody Azii i Afriki* 1 (1967): 37–38.
Reid-Henry, Simon. *Fidel and Che: A Revolutionary Friendship*. New York: Walker, 2009.
Roberts, Hugh. *The Battlefield: Algeria, 1988–2002: Studies in a Broken Polity*. London: Verso, 2003.
——. "Who said Gaddafi Had to Go?" *London Review of Books* 33, no. 22 (17 November 2011): 8–18.
Rochebrune, Renaud de, and Benjamin Stora. *La Guerre d'Algérie vue par les Algériens*. Paris: Denoël, 2011.
Roosa, John. *Pretext for Mass Murder: The September 30th Movement and Suharto's Coup d'État in Indonesia*. Madison: University of Wisconsin Press, 2006.
Ross, Kristin. *Fast Cars, Clean Bodies: Decolonization and the Reordering of French Culture*. Cambridge, MA: MIT Press, 1995.
Rubinstein, Alvin Z., ed. *Soviet and Chinese Influence in the Third World*. New York: Praeger, 1975.
——. *Yugoslavia and the Nonaligned World*. Princeton, NJ: Princeton University Press, 1970.
Ruedy, John. *Modern Algeria: The Origins and Development of a Nation*. 2nd ed. Bloomington: Indiana University Press, 2005.
Saadi, Nourredine. *La femme et la loi en Algérie*. Algiers: Bouchène, 1991.
Saivetz, Carol R. "Socialism in Egypt and Algeria, 1960–1973: The Soviet Assessment." PhD diss., Columbia University, 1979.
——, ed. *The Soviet Union in the Third World*. Boulder, CO: Westview Press, 1989.
Sayigh, Yazid. *Armed Struggle and the Search for State: The Palestinian National Movement, 1949–1993*. Oxford: Clarendon Press, 1997.
Schmidt, Elizabeth. *Cold War and Decolonization in Guinea, 1946–1958*. Athens: Ohio University Press, 2007.
Scott, James C. *Seeing Like a State: How Certain Schemes to Improve the Human Condition Have Failed*. New Haven, CT: Yale University Press, 1998.
Sèbe, Berny. "In the Shadow of the Algerian War: The United States and the Common Organisation of Saharan Regions (OCRS), 1957–62." *Journal of Imperial and Commonwealth History* 38, no. 2 (2010): 303–322.
Sellam, Sadek. "Le FLN vu par l'écrivain Malek Bennabi (1905–1973)." *Guerres Mondiales et Conflits Contemporains* 208, no. 4 (2002): 133–150.
Shakry, Omnia El. "'History without Documents': The Vexed Archives of Decolonization in the Middle East." *American Historical Review* 120, no. 3 (2015): 920–934.
Shepard, Todd. "Algeria, France, Mexico, UNESCO: A Transnational History of Anti-Racism and Decolonization, 1932–1962." *Journal of Global History* 6, no. 2 (2011): 273–297.
——. *The Invention of Decolonization: The Algerian War and the Remaking of France*. Ithaca, NY: Cornell University Press, 2006.
——. "'Of Sovereignty': Disputed Archives, 'Wholly Modern' Archives, and the Post-Decolonization French and Algerian Republics, 1962–2012." *American Historical Review* 120, no. 3 (2015): 869–883.
Shu Guang Zhang, "Constructing 'Peaceful Coexistence': China's Diplomacy toward the Geneva and Bandung Conferences, 1954–55," *Cold War History* 7, no.4 (2007): 509-528.
Simon, Catherine. *Algérie, les années pieds-rouges: Des rêves de l'indépendance au désenchantement, 1962–1969*. Paris: Découverte, 2009.
Simpson, Bradley R. *Economists with Guns: Authoritarian Development and U.S.-Indonesian Relations, 1960–1968*. Stanford: Stanford University Press, 2008.
Skierka, Volker. *Fidel Castro: A Biography*. Cambridge: Polity Press, 2004.
Skocpol, Theda. *States and Social Revolutions: A Comparative Analysis of France, Russia, and China*. Cambridge: Cambridge University Press, 1979.
Slobodian, Quinn. "Bandung in Divided Germany: Managing Non-aligned Politics in East and West, 1955–63." *Journal of Imperial and Commonwealth History* 41, no. 4 (2013): 644–662.
Smith, Tony. "New Bottles for New Wine: A Pericentric Framework for the Study of the Cold War," *Diplomatic History* 24, no.4 (2000): 567–591.
Snyder, Francis G. "The Political Thought of Modibo Keita." *Journal of Modern African Studies* 5, no. 1 (1967): 79–106.

Stephens, Robert. *Nasser: A Political Biography*. London: Penguin, 1971.
Stora, Benjamin. *Algeria, 1830-2000: A Short History*. Revised and updated. Ithaca, NY: Cornell University Press, 2001.
———. *Le nationalisme algérien avant 1954*. (Paris: CNRS Éditions, 2010).
Susini, Jean-Jacques. *Histoire de l'O.A.S*. Paris: La Table Ronde, 1963.
Taubman, William. *Khrushchev: The Man and His Era*. New York: Norton, 2003.
Terretta, Meredith. "Cameroonian Nationalists Go Global: From Forest Maquis to a Pan-African Accra." *Journal of African History* 51 (2010): 189-212.
Thomas, Martin C. "Defending a Lost Cause? France and the United States Vision of Imperial Rule in French North Africa," *Diplomatic History* 26, no.2 (2002): 215-247.
———. "Innocent Abroad? Decolonisation and US Engagement with French West Africa, 1945-56." *Journal of Imperial and Commonwealth History* 36, no. 1 (2008): 47-73.
Thomas, Martin C. and Andrew Thompson. "Empire and Globalisation: From 'High Imperialism' to Decolonisation." *International History Review* 36, no. 1 (2014): 142-170.
Thomas, Scott. *The Diplomacy of Liberation: The Foreign Relations of the African National Congress since 1960*. London: Tauris Academic Studies, 1996.
Thompson, W. Scott. *Ghana's Foreign Policy, 1957-1966: Diplomacy, Ideology, and the New State*. Princeton, NJ: Princeton University Press, 1969.
Tillion, Germaine. *L'Afrique bascule vers l'avenir: L'Algérie et autres textes*. Paris: Éditions de Minuit, 1961.
———. *Algeria: The Realities*. New York: Knopf, 1958.
———. *Les Ennemis Complémentaires: Guerre d'Algérie*. Paris: Tirésias, 2005.
Toye, J. F. J. *Dilemmas of Development: Reflections on the Counter-revolution in Development Economics*. 2nd ed. Oxford: Blackwell, 1993.
Tricot, Bernard. *Les sentiers de la paix, Algérie 1958-1962*. Paris: Plon, 1972.
Turok, Ben. *The ANC and the Turn to Armed Struggle, 1950-1970*. Auckland Park, South Africa: Jacana, 2010.
Urquhart, Brian. *Hammarskjöld*. New York: Knopf, 1972.
Vaïsse, Maurice. *La grandeur: Politique étrangère du Général de Gaulle, 1958-1969*. Paris: Fayard, 1998.
Vaïsse, Maurice, ed. *De Gaulle et l'Algérie: 1943-1969: Actes du colloque tenu à l'amphithéâtre Austerlitz, aux invalides, les vendredi 9 et samedi 10 mars 2012*. Paris: Armand Colin: Ministère de la Défense et des Anciens Combattants, 2012.
van Vleck, Jenifer. "An Airline at the Crossroads of the World: Ariana Afghan Airlines, Modernization, and the Global Cold War." *History and Technology* 25, no. 1 (2009): 3-24.
van Walraven, Klaas. "From Tamanrasset: The Struggle of Sawaba and the Algerian Connection, 1957-1966." *Journal of North African Studies* 10, nos. 3-4 (2005): 507-528.
Vatin, Jean Claude. *L'Algérie Politique: Histoire et Société*. Paris: Presses de la Fondation Nationale des Sciences Politiques, 1983.
Viollette, Maurice. *L'Algérie, vivra-t-elle? Notes d'un ancient gouverneur Général*. Paris: F. Alcan, 1931.
Vitalis, Robert. "The Midnight Ride of Kwame Nkrumah and Other Fables of Bandung (Ban-Doong)." *Humanity: An International Journal of Human Rights, Humanitarianism, and Development* 4, no. 2 (2013): 261-288.
Vos, Pierre de. *Vie et mort de Lumumba*. Paris: Calmann-Lévy, 1961.
Wall, Irwin M. *France, the United States, and the Algerian War*. Berkeley: University of California Press, 2001.
Wallerstein, Immanuel Maurice. *Africa: The Politics of Independence and Unity*. Lincoln: University of Nebraska Press, 2005.
Wauthier, Claude. *Quatre présidents et l'Afrique: De Gaulle, Pompidou, Giscard d'Estaing, Mitterrand: Quarante ans de politique africaine*. Paris: Seuil, 1995.
Westad, Odd Arne. *The Global Cold War: Third World Interventions and the Making of Our Times*. Cambridge: Cambridge University Press, 2005.
Wild, Patricia Berko. "The Organization of African Unity and the Algerian-Moroccan Border Conflict: A Study of New Machinery for Peacekeeping and for the Peaceful Settlement of Disputes among African States." *International Organization* 20, no. 1 (1966): 18-36.
Willetts, Peter. *The Non-aligned Movement: The Origins of a Third World Alliance*. London: Pinter, 1978.

Wright, Richard. *The Color Curtain: A Report on the Bandung Conference.* Cleveland, OH: World Publishing, 1956.
Yacono, Xavier. *De Gaulle et Le F.L.N.: 1958–1962, L'échec d'une politique et ses prolongements.* Versailles: Editions de l'Atlanthrope, 1989.
Yaqub, Salim. *Containing Arab Nationalism: The Eisenhower Doctrine and the Middle East.* Chapel Hill: University of North Carolina Press, 2004.
Young, Crawford. *Politics in the Congo: Decolonization and Independence.* Princeton, NJ: Princeton University Press, 1965.
Zack, Lizabeth. "Early Origins of Islamic Activism in Algeria: The Case of Khaled in Post–World War I Algiers." *Journal of North African Studies* 11, no. 2 (2006): 205–217.
Zartman, William I. *Man, State, and Society in the Contemporary Maghrib.* New York: Praeger, 1973.
———. "The Politics of Boundaries in North and West Africa." *Journal of Modern African Studies* 3, no. 2 (1965): 155–173.
Zhang, Shu Guang. "Constructing 'Peaceful Coexistence': China's Diplomacy toward the Geneva and Bandung Conferences, 1954–55." *Cold War History* 7, no. 4 (2007): 509–528.
Ziring, Lawrence, Robert E. Riggs, and Jack C. Plano. *The United Nations: International Organization and World Politics.* Fort Worth, TX: Harcourt, 2000.
Zoubir, Yahia H. "Algerian Islamists' Conception of Democracy." *Arab Studies Quarterly* 18, no. 3 (1996): 65–85.
———. "The Resurgence of Algeria's Foreign Policy in the Twenty-First Century." *Journal of North African Studies* 9, no. 2 (2004): 169–183.
Zubok, Vladislav. *The Failed Empire: The Soviet Union in the Cold War from Stalin to Gorbachev.* Chapel Hill: University of North Carolina Press, 2007.

INDEX

Abbane, Ramdane
  assassination of, 51
  Ben Bella's rivalry with, 48
  diplomatic strategies of, 42, 51, 58
  Directive Number 9 of, 47
  Easter Uprising as precedent for, 38
  FLN and, 37, 43
  nation-building emphasis of, 45, 63
  Soummam Platform and, 44–45
Abbas, Ferhat
  Atlantic Charter and, 30
  Ben Bella endorsed by, 132
  Ben Khedda resented by, 127, 132
  Chinese mission of, 94
  on Communist bloc aid to Algeria, 95
  on De Gaulle, 55
  diplomatic strategies of, 60
  FLN leadership of, 37, 48
  on FLN's relationship with China, 67
  as GPRA president, 56–57, 121
  initial anti-nationalism and French assimilationism of, 24–25
  Lumumba and, 91
  "Manifesto of the Algerian People" and, 30
  Morocco mission of, 185
  nationalist conversion of, 30
  on need for armed resistance, 35, 43, 51
  as president of National Constituent Assembly, 138
  "self-determination" policies and, 31
  Soviet mission of, 94
  U.S. contact with, 238
'Abd el-Qadir, 19
Abdessalem, Belaïd, 169
Abramov, Aleksandr Nikitich, 163, 210
Adjali, Abdelhamid, 252, 254
Adoula, Cyrille, 190, 192, 197, 252

Aérohabitat building (Algiers), 98
Afghanistan, 89, 296
Aflaq, Michel, 182
African Bank for Development, 168
African Independence Party (Senegal), 83
African National Congress (ANC), 111, 190, 249
African Union, 294
African Volunteer Brigade, 70
Afro-Asianism. *See also* Afro-Asian Peoples' Solidarity Organization (AAPSO)
  Afro-Asian Writers' Conference (1962) and, 213
  Algeria's role in, 12, 213, 257, 263, 267, 269–70
  Bandung Conference and, 6
  decline of, 286, 292, 297
  India's role in, 260
  nonalignment and, 201, 263
  Soviet Union and, 87–88
  students' conference (1956) for, 42
  Third Worldism and, 271, 291
Afro-Asian Peoples' Solidarity Organization (AAPSO). *See also* Afro-Asianism
  Algeria's independence struggle and, 101
  Algeria's participation in, 174
  conference (1964) of, 257, 261–63, 265
  economic conference (1965) of, 257–58, 269
  founding of, 70–71
  Latin America committee of, 258
  Sino-Soviet split and, 163, 212
  Soviet Union criticized by, 87
  Third Worldism and, 109
Ageron, Charles-Robert, 22
Ahidjo, Ahmadou, 84
Aidi, Boufeldja, 258–59
Aidit, Dipa Nusantara, 288

Aït Ahmed, Hocine
  Arabic language skills of, 34
  Bandung Conference and, 41
  diplomatic strategies of, 38–39, 41, 52, 58
  French government negotiations with Algeria (1956) and, 49
  on goals of revolution, 33
  guerrilla warfare and, 32
  imprisonment of, 132
  Kabylia revolt and, 216, 223, 237–38
  on Lumumba, 91–92
  on Messali's popularity, 28–29
  Oran post office plot (1950) and, 33
  PPA and, 32–33
  Sands War and, 222
  U.S. State Department meetings with, 39
Aït-Challal, Messaoud, 210
Alexeev, Aleksandr, 75
"The Algerian Economy: Socialism or Capitalism?" (1963 seminar at Algiers University), 155
Algerian immigrants in France, 104–5, 122–23
Algiers Charter (1967), 290
Algiers Kasbah uprising (1960), 97–99, 102–3, 106
All-African Peoples' Conference (AAPC,1958), 69–70, 85, 101, 109
Alleg, Henri, 43
Alliance for Progress, 143
Amadzadeh, Mas'oud, 68
Amer, Abdel Hakim, 202–3, 288
American Federation of Labor-Congress of Industrial Organizations (AFL-CIO), 54
Angola
  Algerian independence as inspiration for, 3
  Algeria's role in rebellion in, 111, 164, 175, 189–92, 199, 248–49, 255, 266, 295
  All-African People's Conference (1958) and, 70
  armed conflict and factionalism in, 191, 197, 209
  arms shipments from Yugoslavia to, 192, 204
  Ben Bella and, 189, 191, 196, 201, 266, 295
  Cabinda enclave in, 192
  Central Intelligence Agency and, 190, 209, 268
  China and, 191, 201, 209, 266
  Congo-Léopoldville and, 190, 192, 197, 252
  Cuba and, 11
  Organization of African Unity and, 197–98
  Soviet Union and, 210, 296
  United States and, 209
Anti-imperialism Congress (1927), 27, 64
Arab League
  African revolutions and, 175
  Algerian independence struggle and, 35, 89
  Algeria's participation in, 174–75

Israel's Africa diplomacy and, 268
Maghrib countries' relations and, 187
Morocco and Tunisia's admission to, 70
Sands War and, 221
Soviet Union and, 89
Third Worldism and, 109
Arab Revolt (Palestine, 1936), 24–26
Arafat, Yasser
  Algerian independence as inspiration to, 5, 130, 177–78, 297
  Algiers base of, 202
  Ben Bella and, 177–78
  Fateh's reconciliation with the PLO and, 250
  Guevara and, 201
Argentina, 3, 201–2, 252
Armed Struggle (Amadzadeh), 68
Armée de Libération Nationale (ALN)
  Boumedienne's leadership of, 62–63, 77, 82, 85, 108, 120–21, 125–26, 130–31, 136–37, 186
  calls for military aid from communist countries and, 52
  Chinese arms shipments to, 60, 94, 108
  Cuban Revolution and, 11
  Czechoslovakia's arms shipments to, 107–8
  delegation to China of, 61
  delegation to North Vietnam of, 61
  foreign bases of, 47, 55, 62, 71, 84, 97, 108, 120, 130, 189–90
  foreign fighters trained by, 189
  French military actions against, 36, 49, 63, 101
  GPRA's conflict with, 131
  guerrilla tactics of, 14–16, 42, 45–47, 51, 53, 84, 106
  guerrilla training in China and North Vietnam of, 61, 66
  Military Operational Commands (COMs) of, 62
  number of soldiers in, 14, 36
  political commissars and organizational goals of, 14–16, 36, 45, 66, 120
  recruitment of leaders of, 101–2
  Soviet arms shipments to, 59, 88, 95, 108, 162, 218–19, 223, 233
  support bases of, 62–63
Armée Nationale Populaire (ANP, People's National Army)
  Chinese funding of, 212
  coup (1965) and, 284
  Cuban training camp in Kabylia and, 241
  foreign fighters trained by, 180, 201, 250, 297
  Kabylia separatism and, 223
  organizational structure of, 232–33
  Sands War and, 216, 218–19
Arslan, Shakib, 26, 28
Aswan Dam (Egypt), 265
Atatürk, Kemal, 22

Atlantic Charter, 29–30
Attatla (Algeria), 14–16
autogestion (workers' self-management), 149, 153, 171, 245, 278, 296–97

Bachtarzi, Mahieddine, 14
Baghdad Pact, 70
Balewa, Abubakar Tafawa, 205
Bandung Conference (1955)
  Algerian independence statement in communiqué of, 41, 48
  Cold War denounced at, 40, 64
  FLN and, 2, 36, 40–41, 47, 64–65, 286, 291
  Houphouêt-Boigny's critique of, 80
  mythic status of, 3, 7, 40, 109, 227
  national sovereignty affirmed at, 40
  Nkrumah's absence from, 7
  nonalignment strategy and, 86, 201, 209, 295
  relatively pacific nature of, 108, 210, 262, 295
  Third Worldism and, 5–7, 10, 36, 70, 109, 173, 291
"Bandung 2 Conference" (Second Summit of Afro-Asian Heads of State, 1965)
  Algeria as host of, 227, 231, 257, 264, 272, 282
  Ben Bella and, 3–4, 231, 261, 270, 284
  China and, 3, 12, 261, 264–65, 270, 287
  coup against Ben Bella and cancellation of, 3–4, 12, 286–87, 290
  Latin America and, 270, 282
  national liberation movements at, 270
  Organisation Commune Africaine et Malgache countries' threat to boycott, 256, 271
  Soviet Union and, 12, 261, 264–65, 270, 282
  Third Worldism and, 270–71
Ba'th Party (Iraq and Syria), 180–82
Batista, Fulgencio, 74
Battle of Algiers (Pontecorvo film), 49, 98, 284
"Battle of Algiers" (1957), 47–49, 98, 109
Bay of Pigs invasion (Cuba, 1961), 86
Belgian Congo. *See* Congo-Léopoldville
Belgium, 29, 90–91, 97, 253, 273
Belgrade Conference. *See under* Non-Aligned Movement (NAM)
Ben Alla, Hadj, 233
Ben Badis, 'Abd al-Hamid, 25–26, 124
Ben Barka, Mehdi, 83, 185, 216–17
Ben Bella, Ahmed
  Abbane's rivalry with, 48
  African decolonization struggles and, 190, 192–93, 207, 223, 244, 250–51, 256
  Afro-Asianism and, 258, 261, 263–65, 267–69
  Algeria's admission to the United Nations and, 113–14, 140–41, 172–73
  Algeria's transition to independence and, 130–33, 135–44, 152–53
  Angola and, 189, 191, 196, 201, 266, 295

Arabic language skills of, 178–79, 259
Arafat and, 177–78
Aswan Dam opening and, 265
"Bandung 2" Conference (1965) and, 3–4, 231, 261, 270, 284
Ba'th Party and, 182
Boumedienne and, 12, 125–27, 130–32, 183, 185, 231, 283–85, 287, 298
on Brazil, 258
Casablanca Group and, 97, 187
Castro and, 145, 152, 162, 166
China and, 165, 265
Christmas Plot (Tunisia, 1963) and, 186
coup against (1965), 1–4, 12, 243, 284–85, 287–90
Cuba and, 11, 140–42, 144–46, 148, 150, 172, 202, 251
Cuban Missile Crisis and, 11, 144–45, 148
de Gaulle and, 31, 33, 133, 136–37, 141, 235–36, 240, 275–77
diplomatic strategies of, 38–39
economic development issues and, 116–17, 126, 128, 138–39, 169–70, 237, 274–77, 279
on Europeans' economic power in Algeria, 167, 272
Evian Accords and, 125, 155, 235
on FLN preferences in Morocco and Tunis, 82–83
FLN's founding and, 31, 33–34
foreign presence in government of, 12
French assistance to independent Algeria and, 150–51
French government negotiations (1956) and, 49
Islamist criticism of, 279
Israel denounced by, 177, 180
Kennedy and, 207–9
Khider's rivalry with, 178
land redistribution and, 128
left-wing African governments and, 245, 247, 249, 254–55
on Lumumba, 97
on Maghrib unity, 185, 188
March Decrees and, 153–55, 157, 165–66, 169, 235
Nasser and, 131, 142, 166, 176–77, 180–84, 195, 256, 288
nonalignment and, 133, 141, 147, 174, 203, 209, 232, 244, 256–57, 263, 267
Oran post office plot (1950) and, 33
Organization of African Unity and, 195–97, 201, 252
"Oujda Clan" and, 130
on Palestinian cause, 141, 172, 177–78, 250
pan-Africanism and, 97, 172, 175–76, 189, 194–95, 200–201, 213–14, 268

Ben Bella, Ahmed (*Cont.*)
  pan-Arabism and, 175–76, 179, 188
  Partial Test Ban Treaty and, 211
  PCA banned by, 158–60, 165, 212, 234, 236
  Place des Martyrs speech (November 1, 1962) of, 176
  PPA-MTLD and, 33
  premonition at Souk Ahras of, 280
  release from prison (1978) of, 2
  Sands War and, 175, 215–17, 219–22, 224–25
  Sino-Soviet split and, 211, 264, 282
  socialist-inspired ideology of, 2–3, 5, 112–13, 126, 128, 132, 139, 143–44, 150, 153–54, 156, 159–61, 166, 170–71, 236, 245, 283, 297
  Soviet Union and, 149, 159–61, 163, 165, 220, 232–35, 237–38, 244, 248, 264–65, 269, 281–82
  Third Worldism and, 128, 141, 173, 176, 200–201, 214, 223, 230–31, 250, 267, 271, 274, 285, 289, 295
  Tito's relationship with, 166, 180, 199–201, 204, 209, 214, 222–23, 245, 267–68
  training of foreign fighters in Algeria and, 190
  Tripoli Program and, 116–17, 126–28, 130, 133, 137
  Tshombe and, 252–53
  United Arab Republic and, 182, 184
  on the United Nations, 229
  United States and, 39, 133, 140–44, 147–50, 153, 156, 158, 174, 206–7, 221, 232, 238–44, 246, 281
  U.S. back channel in Vietnam and, 242–43
  U.S. delegation to Algeria (1963) and, 156–57
  V-E Day Protests in Algeria and, 31
  West Africa tour (1963) of, 199–200
  western Algerian origins of, 34
  World War II service of, 31, 33
Ben Boulaid, Mostefa, 34, 38
Benhabylès, Abdelmalek
  on Cold War détente, 210
  on diversity of political systems in Africa, 293–94
  on Israel and Africa, 251
  on Maghrib's differences from Arab World, 245
  on Palestinian liberation cause, 259
  on prejudices in Arab-African relations, 268
  Tripoli Program, 126
Benin, 207
Benjedid, Chadli, 212
Ben Khedda, Benyoussef
  Algeria's transition to independence and, 130–33, 135–37
  China missions of, 57, 67
  economic portfolio of, 121
  as GPRA president, 121, 127
  Soviet mission of, 60
  Third Worldism and, 121
  "Tizi Ouzou clan" and, 130
Ben M'Hidi, Mohamed Larbi, 34, 48
Bennabi, Malek, 10, 68, 283, 291
Bentobbal, Lakhdar, 94, 106, 120–21
Benyahia, Mohammed
  Afro-Asian students' conference (1956) and, 42
  as Algerian ambassador in Moscow and, 165, 211, 237
  as FLN representative in Indonesia, 47
  Tripoli Program and, 126
Ben Youssef, Salah, 83, 185
Berber community in Algeria
  Evian Accords and, 120, 123
  separatism and, 198, 215
Berlin Conference (1884–1885), 87, 210
Berlin Crisis (1961), 61
Berque, Jacques, 23, 98–99, 102
Bitat, Rabah, 34, 38
Bitat, Salah al-Din, 182
Bizerte (Tunisia), 110
Blum, Léon, 24, 27
Blum-Viollette reforms (1936), 24, 28
Bolivia, 77
Borgeaud, Henri, 149, 155
Bouattoura, Tewfik, 210
Boudiaf, Mohammed, 34–35, 132
Bouhired, Djamila, 190
Boulahrouf, Tayeb, 41
Boumaza, Bachir, 265–66, 273, 278
Boumedienne, Houari
  aid to poor communities by, 108
  Algeria's transition to independence and, 130–33, 136
  ALN as political force for, 137
  ALN leadership of, 62–63, 77, 82, 85, 108, 120–21, 125–26, 130–31, 136–37, 186
  Arab countries' tour (1963) and, 181–82, 201
  arms buildup supervised by, 223–25, 233
  Ben Bella and, 12, 125–27, 130–32, 183, 185, 231, 283–85, 287, 298
  Bouteflika and, 85, 126, 275, 284
  Bureau Politique proposal of, 120–21, 127, 137
  CNRA's concern about increasing power of, 121
  coup (1965) by, 1, 3, 12, 284–85, 287–90
  cult of personality of, 298
  death of, 2
  de Gaulle and, 277
  on détente, 295
  Egypt and, 183
  Evian Accords opposed by, 122, 125
  FLN's "Arabist" wing and, 176
  foreign fighters trained by, 190, 192, 201

Islamic education and, 176
march on Algiers and Kabylia by, 137
Non-Aligned Movement and, 286
"Oujda Clan" and, 130
Palestinian arms shipments and military training by, 180
Palestinian nationalism and, 298
pieds rouges expelled by, 297
on revolutionary political education of soldiers, 120, 126
Rusk's distrust of, 141–42
Sands War and, 12, 217–19, 223–25
Soviet missions (1960s) of, 212, 233, 269
Third Worldism and, 128
Boumendjel, Ahmed, 70
Bourdieu, Pierre, 99, 101
Bourguiba, Habib
Algeria's independence struggle and, 82
Algeria's Sahara possessions and, 184
Algeria's support for opponents of, 245
Algeria's transition to independence and, 131, 185
ALN's plan to assassinate, 131
Ben Bella and, 131, 240
Ben Youssef assassination and, 83
Christmas Plot assassination attempt against, 185–86
De Gaulle and, 240
distrust of Algerian military in Tunisia and, 55
FLN divisions and, 48, 185
on national cultural identity, 28
oil negotiations with Algeria and, 187
pan-Africanism and, 268
as Tunisian president, 71
United Nations and, 110
Boussouf, Abdelhamid, 62
Bouteflika, Abdelaziz
Algeria's post-independence policies toward France and, 274
Arab countries' tour (1963) and, 181–82
Ben Bella and, 275, 284
Boumedienne and, 85, 126, 275, 284
Congo-Léopoldville conflicts and, 253
coup (1965) and, 285, 287–88
de Gaulle and, 277
embassy expansion coordinated by, 258
Fanon and, 126, 200
as foreign minister, 200, 230, 284
Libya regime change (2011) and, 294
Mali mission of, 85
Sands War and, 219
Sino-Soviet split and, 211, 270–71
on state-building, 290–91
Third Worldism and, 223
United States and, 206–7
on U.S. aid to Algeria, 240
Boutros-Ghali, Boutros, 205

Brahimi, Lakhdar
Afro-Asian students' conference (1956) and, 42
as Algerian ambassador to Egypt, 179
on Algeria's diplomatic visit to United States (1962), 148
on Algeria's relationship with Palestinian nationalists, 178
Angola-China relations and, 201, 266, 326n80
Angola coalition negotiations (1963) and, 191–92
Cuba visit (1962) of, 139
as FLN representative in Indonesia, 42, 47
Palestinian reconciliation talks (1965) and, 250
on schism between Algerian Revolution's ideals and accomplishments, 286
Tripoli Program and, 126
Brazil, 73, 252, 258, 297–98
Brazzaville Group, 255–56
Bretton Woods system, 116, 168, 230. *See also* International Monetary Fund; World Bank
de Broglie, Jean, 154–55, 167, 170, 202
Bugeaud, Thomas-Robert, 19
Bundy, McGeorge, 239
Bureau Politique proposal (Boumedienne), 120–21, 127, 137
Burkina Faso, 289
Burundi, 289

Cabinda enclave (Angola), 192
Cabral, Amilcar, 3, 193, 197, 202
Cameroon
Algeria's independence struggle and, 86, 96
Algeria's support for left-wing revolutionaries in, 189–90, 207
Cuba and, 11
decolonization in, 84
Cape Verde, 193
Cartier, Raymond, 118
Casablanca Group
Algeria's independence struggle and, 101
Ben Bella and, 97, 187
Brazzaville Group and, 255–56
founding meeting (1961) of, 96–97
Morocco and, 185
Castro, Fidel
Algeria coup (1965) and, 1, 287–88
Algerian delegation (1962) and, 145–46, 150
Algeria's international connections and, 202–3
Algeria's post-independence government and, 139, 162, 251
on Algeria's revolutionary potential, 234
Ben Bella and, 145, 152, 162, 166
Boumedienne's admiration of, 141–42, 233
CIA plots against, 218, 238
Cuban Missile Crisis and, 144–45, 147–48

Castro, Fidel (*Cont.*)
  Cuban Revolution (1959) and, 71, 73–74, 78, 111
  Eisenhower on, 75
  FLN's admiration of, 85, 129, 152
  guerrilla warfare and, 77–78
  Kennedy on, 142
  Khrushchev and, 94
  Latin American revolution promoted by, 11, 77
  potential Algeria visit (1963) of, 208–9, 221
  United States denounced by, 75
Castro, Raoul, 89, 145, 341n235
Catalonia, 297
Central African Republic, 289
Central Intelligence Agency (CIA, United States)
  Angola and, 190, 209, 268
  Ben Bella's fears regarding, 237–38
  Congo-Léopoldville and, 91–92, 241, 253, 269
  Cuban Missile Crisis and, 144–45
  Cuba regime change efforts and, 218, 238, 242
  FLN funded by, 54
  Kabylia revolt in Algeria and, 240–42
  Lumumba assassination and, 86, 97
Chanderli, Abdelkader, 41, 74–77, 137, 142
Charles X (king of France), 19
Chen Yi, 264, 266, 289
Al Chihâb (The meteor, ulema journal), 26
China
  African decolonization conflicts and, 175, 211–12, 247
  Afro-Asianism and, 262–67, 269–71, 282
  Algeria as recipient of aid from, 228
  Algerian embassy in, 212, 260
  Algeria's African connections and, 211–12
  Algeria's diplomatic recognition of, 57, 67
  Algeria's independence struggle and, 52, 57–61, 63, 67, 72, 94–96, 101, 107, 111, 266
  Algeria's post-independence government and, 164–66, 170, 225, 228, 244, 247, 260, 263–66, 269, 282
  ALN delegation to, 61
  Angola war and, 191, 201, 209, 266
  arms shipments to Algeria from, 60, 94, 108
  Bandung Conference (1955) and, 40–41
  "Bandung 2" Conference (1965) and, 3, 12, 261, 264–65, 270, 287
  contemporary global diplomacy and, 297
  Cuba and, 75
  Cultural Revolution in, 213
  decolonization and, 8, 87, 266
  détente policies criticized by, 263–64
  FLN and, 94, 164, 209, 266
  Fourteen Points for Peace and, 21
  humanitarian aid to Algeria and, 134
  India and, 175, 261–62, 290, 304n69
  Mali and, 249–50, 264–65, 270
  mass mobilization emphasis in, 68
  Nixon's visit (1972) to, 8
  Non-Aligned Movement and, 212–13, 261–64
  nuclear weapons program of, 211
  revolution (1949) in, 67
  Sino-Soviet split and, 12, 87, 163–65, 175, 188, 201, 211, 225–26, 230, 257, 261–62, 264, 267, 270–71, 282, 290, 294
  Third Worldism and, 164, 211–14, 262–64
  United Nations and, 41, 114, 172
  Vietnam and, 243
  Yugoslavia and, 163–64, 211, 262, 267
Christmas Plot (Tunisia, 1963), 185–86
Churchill, Winston, 29, 87
Clay Report, 217
Clemenceau, Georges, 22
Club Jean Moulin, 125
Code de l'indigénat (Algeria's Native Code, 1881), 20
Cold War
  Africa as a fault line in, 188, 191, 205, 226, 230, 245, 249, 256, 282
  Afro-Asianism and, 212–13
  Algerian independence struggle and, 11, 17, 32, 36–37, 39, 53–54, 57, 59–60, 66–67, 89
  Algeria's economic modernization and, 117
  Algeria's post-independence government and, 131–34, 139–40, 142, 163
  Bandung Conference's repudiation of, 40, 64
  Berlin Wall and, 280
  Congo-Léopoldville Crisis (1960–1961) and, 91, 95–96, 98–99, 294
  decolonization and, 8, 65–66, 294
  détente in, 87, 209–11, 263–64, 295
  end of, 297
  Maghrib as fault line, 217, 220, 231–32, 234, 246
  Middle East as fault line in, 177, 180
  nonalignment and, 86–87, 174, 201, 209, 232, 281
  Third Worldism and, 6–7, 12, 282, 294–96
Collins, Michael, 5
Colonial Exposition (Paris, 1930), 23
Comité de Coordination et d'Éxecution (CCE, Coordinating and Executive Committee), 44
Comité Révolutionnaire pour l'Unité et l'Action (CRUA, Revolutionary Committee for Unity and Action), 35
The Commitments (film), 172
Communist International (Comintern), 26–27
Communist Party of the Soviet Union (CPSU), 88, 162, 269, 298

Community. *See* French Community
  decolonization proposal
Conference of Independent African States
  (CIAS, 1958), 69, 81, 268
Conference on the Problems of Economic
  Development (1962), 115–16
Congo. *See* Congo-Brazzaville;
  Congo-Léopoldville
Congo-Brazzaville (Republic of Congo)
  Algeria coup (1965) and, 288
  Algeria's relationship with, 249
  China and, 265
  Congo-Leópoldville and, 253, 255–56
  left-wing coup (1964) and government in,
    199, 207, 245–49
  Non-Aligned Movement and, 263
Congo-Léopoldville
  Algerian arms shipments to, 254–55, 266–67
  Algerian Embassy removal (1964) and, 254
  Algerian training of militants from, 111
  Algeria's support for armed revolt in, 111, 190,
    207, 248, 253–56, 266–67
  Angola wars and, 190, 192, 197, 252
  Belgium's actions during crisis in, 90–91, 97
  Ben Bella on, 141
  Central Intelligence Agency and, 91–92, 241,
    253, 269
  Cold War framework regarding, 91, 95–96,
    98–99, 294
  Conseil National de Libération in,
    207, 252–54
  coup (1961), 92–93
  coup (1965) in, 289
  crisis (1960–1961) in, 86–87, 90–93, 95–97,
    105, 107–8, 110, 188, 231, 253
  decolonization in, 84, 86
  Katanga region of, 86, 90–92, 96–97, 198,
    223, 225, 252–54
  neo-imperialism in, 212
  Organization of African Unity and, 197
  revolutionary groups in, 175, 192, 199, 207,
    241, 252–56, 292
  Soviet Union and, 86–87, 90–92, 95, 107
  United States and, 235, 242–43
Connelly, Matthew, 9, 36, 54, 119
Conseil National de la Révolution Algérienne
  (CNRA, National Council of the Algerian
  Revolution)
  Evian Accords (1962) and, 120–22
  final meeting of, 127, 130
  as intermittently convening parliament,
    71–72
  Soummam Platform and, 44
Conseil National de Libération (CNL,
  Congo-Léopoldville), 207, 252–54
Constantine Plan (1958), 56, 125, 128
Conte, Arthur, 227

Côte d'Ivoire
  Algeria's assurances to the government
    of, 244
  Algeria's independence struggle and, 80
  Algeria's support for secessionists in, 207
  Algeria state visit of, 193
  decolonization in, 84
  pro-Western orientation of, 189, 193, 247
Couve de Murville, Maurice, 61, 115, 136
Crémieux Decrees (1870), 20
Cuba
  African decolonization conflicts and,
    174–75, 214
  Algeria inspired by revolution in, 11, 72,
    74–79, 85, 98, 111, 139–40, 142–43, 145,
    152–53, 157, 159, 233
  Algeria's independence struggle aided by, 5,
    73–76, 107, 111
  Algeria's international connections and, 202,
    207, 223, 251, 255
  Algeria's post-independence government and,
    145–50, 157, 170, 202–3, 251–52, 282
  Angola and, 11
  Bay of Pigs invasion (1961) and, 86
  Ben Bella and, 140–42, 144–46, 150, 172,
    202, 251
  Cameroon and, 11
  Cold War tensions and, 75, 86, 139, 144–45
  détente policies and, 263
  France and, 75
  guerrilla warfare and, 74, 111
  Kabylia revolt in Algeria and, 241
  Latin American revolutions and, 11, 202–3,
    252, 259
  mass mobilization emphasis in, 68
  medical mission to Algeria from, 202–3
  Missile Crisis (1962) in, 11, 86, 144–45,
    147–48, 150, 202, 295
  Non-Aligned Movement and, 108–9
  Organization of American States and, 205
  revolution (1959) in, 11, 71, 73, 75–76, 78,
    90, 139, 146, 217, 233–34
  Sands War and, 219–21, 224–25
  Soviet Union and, 75, 88, 90, 94, 142, 146,
    149, 158–60, 202, 220, 341n235
  Third Worldism and, 76–77, 146, 214
  Tricontinental Conference (1966) and, 290
  United States and, 74–76, 139–45, 150–51,
    157, 168, 202–3, 217–18, 235, 238,
    242–43, 251–52, 259
Czechoslovakia
  Algeria's economic ties with, 278
  Algeria's independence struggle and, 89–90
  arms shipments to Egypt and, 142
  arms shipments to Kabylia rebels and, 241
  GPRA recognized by, 107
  Soviet arms to Algeria and, 59

Dahlab, Saad
  broader diplomatic strategies of, 71–72
  China mission of, 57
  on December 1960 protests as propaganda point, 107
  as GPRA foreign minister, 121
  Soviet mission of, 60
  Third Worldism of, 121
  on United Nations, 96
Dahomey (Benin), 207
de Andrade, Mario, 192, 252
Debaghine, Mohamed Lamine
  Algerian independence movement and, 32
  Cuba and, 74
  on fears of Cold War détente, 61
  FLN and, 37, 44
  on foreign countries' recognition of the GPRA, 57–59
  nonalignment strategy criticized by, 66
Debray, Régis, 68
De Gaulle, Charles
  African decolonization policies and, 79–80
  Algerian colonial policies of, 54–56, 62, 67, 72, 79–80, 91, 96, 100, 102–3, 115, 122–23
  Algerian hydrocarbon industry and, 237, 276
  Algerian referendum and, 96, 102
  Algeria's post-independence government and, 115, 118–19, 131, 136–37, 151, 155, 161, 167, 170, 275–77
  Algeria tour (1960) of, 102
  autodétermination speech (1959) of, 67
  Ben Bella and, 31, 33, 133, 136–37, 141, 235–36, 240, 275–77
  Brazzaville reform speech (1944) of, 30
  Constantine Plan (1958) and, 56
  counterinsurgency strategies in Algeria and, 100, 103
  coup attempt (1961) against, 105, 122
  Evian Accords and, 118–20, 123–24, 128, 151, 155, 161, 170
  four-power directory proposal of, 87
  Free French government in exile and, 29–30
  French Community decolonization proposal of, 79–80, 83, 103, 194
  French nuclear bomb test in Algeria (1963) and, 155
  French referendum on Algerian negotiations (1961) and, 122
  French withdrawal from NATO command structure and, 60
  GPRA mocked by, 72, 97
  on his doubts regarding assimilation of Algerian Muslims, 104
  Indonesia and, 48
  Khrushchev and, 89
  Mali address (1959) of, 79
  moderate "third force" idea of, 62
  return to French presidency (1958) of, 54–57, 71
  Sands War and, 218
  United Nations' mediation of Tunisia dispute and, 110
  United States and, 240
Descloitres, Claudine, 101
Descloitres, Robert, 101
Dib, Mohammed, 72
al-Dib, Fathi, 126
Didouche, Mourad, 34, 38
Diem, Ngo Dinh, 109
Dien Bien Phu, Battle of (1954), 34, 66, 243
Diori, Hamani, 192
A Diplomatic Revolution (Connelly), 9
Direction de la Coopération Economique et Technique, 278
"Directive Number 9" (Abbane), 47
Dizdarević, Nijaz
  Ben Bella's relationship with, 161–63, 166, 204
  on importance of independence in Algeria's foreign policy, 225
  as Yugoslavian ambassador to Algeria, 166, 204
djema'a (traditional council of elders in North African societies), 15, 19
Djoudi, Noureddine, 197, 199, 248, 255
Dominican Republic, 77
Dorticós, Osvaldo, 114, 141
dos Santos, Artur Carlos Maurício Pestana, 296
dos Santos, Eduardo, 191
Dulles, Allen, 91
Dulles, John Foster, 7, 66, 264

East African Federation proposal, 198
Easter Rising (Ireland, 1916), 38
East Germany, 9, 89, 134, 208
economic development strategy in Algeria
  Bretton Woods institutions and, 168–69
  foreign communist advisors and, 278
  France's role in, 169–70, 275–77
  globalization and international trade in, 169–70, 273–74
  hydrocarbon resources and, 169–70, 237, 275–76, 295
  rural reforms and, 278–79
  wine production and, 275–76
Egypt
  Algeria coup (1965) and, 287–88
  Algeria's independence struggle and, 51–52, 58, 69, 84
  Algeria's post-independence government and, 132, 162, 180–84, 260
  Angola conflict and, 266

Arab League and, 109
arms shipments to Algeria from, 162, 180, 183, 218
Aswan Dam opening and, 265
"Bandung 2" conference and, 3, 287
British rule rejected by, 21
Casablanca Bloc Pact (1961) and, 96
as center of Middle Eastern political life, 259–60
Cold War and, 177
Conference of Independent African States (CIAS, 1958) and, 69, 268
Congo-Léopoldville conflicts and, 241, 253–54, 269
Free Officers Coup (1952) in, 33
Guevara in, 74
Israel and, 180, 289
Non-Aligned Movement and, 108, 204–5, 262
Palestinian nationalism and, 250
pan-Africanism and, 214
pan-Arabism and, 70
revolution (1919) in, 21
Sands War and, 218, 220, 224
Six Day War (1967) and, 289
Soviet Union and, 16, 59, 88, 159–60, 265
Suez Crisis (1956) and, 50, 65, 225
Third Worldism and, 109, 261, 264, 267–68
United Arab Republic and, 70, 177, 181–82, 224
U.S. food aid to, 239
Yemen and, 180
Yugoslavia and, 204
Eisenhower, Dwight D.
Algerian independence struggle and, 39, 81
Castro and, 75
Cold War diplomatic alignments and, 142
Congo-Léopoldville Crisis (1961961) and, 96
United Nations and, 39
Etat Majeur-Général (EMG, General Staff), 77, 85
Ethiopia
Conference of Independent African States (CIAS) and, 69, 81
Italian invasion (1935) of, 27
Organization of African Unity and, 3, 195, 197
Soviet Union and, 296
violent decolonization in, 197
Etoile Nord Africain (ENA, North African Star), 26–28
European Economic Community (EEC), 104, 116, 186–87, 229, 295
Evian Accords (1962)
Algerian independence established by, 11, 115
Algerian national identity and, 118
Algerian opponents of, 125, 155

Ben Bella and, 235
French assistance to Algeria and, 152, 154, 161, 170, 275
French economic and security interests in Algeria and, 118–19, 123–24, 128, 135, 137, 151, 154, 170, 237, 276
French national identity and, 117–18
land redistribution and, 128
nationalization of property as violation of, 166
Saharan issues and, 119
Tripoli Program's incompatibility with, 129, 136

Fanon, Frantz
Algerian foreign policy inspired by, 173, 189
Algerian independence as inspiration to, 2, 4–5
on Algeria's home in Africa, 102
All-African Peoples' Conference (1958) and, 70
Bouteflika and, 126, 200
Congo-Léopoldville Crisis (1960–1961) and, 92
death and immortalization of, 111
FLN radio and, 101
FLN's Ghana office and, 81, 83, 205
Lumumba and, 90, 92
Mali mission of, 85
Palestinian nationalists inspired by, 177
on propaganda and mass violence, 42–43, 70
"Third Worldist" perspective in writings of, 5
West Africa and, 11
fardeau colonial (France's "colonial burden"), 104, 118
Farès, Abderrahmane, 131
Fateh (Palestinian nationalist organization)
Algerian arms shipments to, 180
Algerian military training of, 250
Algiers office of, 179, 266
FLN as inspiration to, 177–78, 297
Jordan's conflict with, 260
Faure, Edgar, 39
Feraoun, Mouloud, 105–6
Fifth Republic (France), 56, 79
Finland, 267
Four Areas development project (Algeria), 156, 235, 240
Fourteen Points for Peace (Wilson), 9, 20–21, 60
Fourth Republic (France), 39
France. *See specific individuals and institutions*
Francis, Ahmed, 121
Free French forces in Algeria, 29–30, 33
Free Officers Coup (Egypt, 1952), 33
French Community decolonization proposal (De Gaulle), 79–81, 83–84, 103, 194

French population in Algeria
  Algerian nationalism as anathema to, 22, 98–99
  Algerian nationalization of abandoned properties of, 149, 151–52, 154–55, 166, 216
  Algeria's civil service staffed by, 277
  Blum-Viollette reforms (1936) and, 24
  centenary celebration (1930) among, 23
  coup attempt (1961) against De Gaulle and, 105, 122
  economic inequality in Algeria and, 23
  emigration from Algeria of, 127, 129, 135–36, 138
  Evian Accords (1962) and, 119, 123–24, 128
  FLN sympathizers among, 43
  growing insecurity of, 106
  jusq'au boutists (bitter-enders) and, 105, 122
  in the nineteenth century, 19–20
  political violence against, 99
  post-World War I reforms and, 22
  protests (1960) by, 102–3
Frente de Libertação de Moçambique (FRELIMO, National Front for the Liberation of Angola), 248–49, 255
Frente Nacional de Libertaçao de Angola (FNLA, National Front for the Liberation of Angola), 190–91, 197–98, 209, 268
Friendship University (Moscow), 88
Front de Libération Nationale (FLN, National Liberation Front)
  African liberation and, 77–78, 80, 82–85, 108, 178
  Algeria's post-independence government and, 130–38, 140, 143
  Algiers Kasbah uprising (1960) and, 97–98
  All-African Peoples' Conference (1958) and, 69–70
  Angola war and, 190–91
  Bandung Conference and, 2, 36, 40–41, 47, 64–65, 286, 291
  Battle of Algiers' losses of, 48–49
  Casablanca Bloc Pact (1961) and, 96
  China and, 94, 164, 209, 266
  collective leadership ethos of, 44–45
  communications and propaganda efforts of, 37, 43, 47, 49–50, 82, 97, 100–101, 103, 113, 119–20, 185
  communist ideological inspirations for, 54, 63, 66, 89, 181, 283
  communist-style organizing techniques of, 37
  Conference of Independent African States (1958) and, 69, 81
  Congo-Léopoldville Crisis (1960–1961) and, 86, 91–93
  Cuba and, 76–78
  decentralized command structure of, 43–45, 120
  diplomatic strategies of, 17–18, 35–42, 47–50, 52–55, 57–61, 63–67, 69–76, 78–85, 87, 90–95, 97, 101, 106–11, 114, 119, 173, 193–94, 243, 284
  diverse constituencies of, 17
  economic development issues and, 116–17, 124–25, 128, 143
  Etoile Nord Africain as inspiration for, 26
  Evian Accords (1962) and, 118–25, 128–29
  foreign fighters trained by, 190
  founding (1954) of, 14, 18–19, 33–35, 124, 255, 298
  in France, 104–5, 122–23
  French government negotiations (1956) and, 49, 242
  French military and police actions against, 36–38, 42–43, 48–52, 63, 71, 97, 100–103, 111–13, 122, 127, 134
  French propaganda against, 50–51, 66, 102
  French schools boycott and, 46
  French sympathizers of, 43, 103–4
  global geopolitics and, 8–9, 11–12
  guerrilla warfare and, 14–18, 35, 42–43, 45–47, 51, 53–54, 66, 72, 74, 78, 106, 111
  "Historic Nine founders" of, 31, 34, 44
  Ho Chi Minh and, 15
  individual rights and, 138
  international delegations of, 41–42, 47–48, 81–82, 84
  on Khaled (imperial era emir of Algeria), 22
  land reform and, 129–30
  Leninism and, 10, 15–16, 19, 53, 66
  Mao as inspiration to, 15–16, 53, 85, 118, 121, 129, 164
  as model for Palestinian cause, 177
  Non-Aligned Movement and, 2, 108–9
  pan-Arabism and, 176
  PCA and, 159–61
  release of prisoners from, 127
  revolutionary rhetoric of, 32–35, 62
  socioeconomic issues emphasized by, 167–68
  Soummam Platform and, 44–45, 50
  Soviet Union and, 16, 87–90, 94–95, 158–59, 161–62, 209, 232, 236, 269, 271, 298
  state formation emphasis of, 10–11, 17, 293
  support bases of, 34, 37–38, 43–44, 62–63
  Third Worldism and, 11, 76–77, 85–86, 98, 101, 110–12, 115, 117, 123, 151, 297
  Tripoli Program and, 126–27, 129
  United Nations and, 16
  U.S. State Department interactions with, 39, 52
  Wilsonianism and, 10, 19, 66
Front des Forces Socialistes (FFS, Front of Socialist Forces), 216, 237–38, 240–41

Gabon, 249, 255
Gandhi, Mohandas, 5–6
Gbenye, Christophe, 192
General Agreement on Tariffs and Trade (GATT), 116, 228–29, 295
Geneva Accords (1954), 34, 40, 66
Germany. See East Germany; West Germany
Ghafa, Ibrahim, 52
Ghana
  African summit (1965) hosted by, 3–4
  Algeria coup (1965) and, 288
  Algeria's independence struggle and, 72–73, 81–82, 84, 111, 114, 194
  Algeria's post-independence government and, 251
  Angola conflict and, 266
  Casablanca Bloc Pact (1961) and, 96
  Conference of Independent African States (1958) hosted by, 69, 81
  Congo-Léopoldville conflicts and, 241, 253, 255–56
  coup (1966) in, 289
  Cuba and, 251
  Guinea and, 224
  independence of, 68, 98
  Niger conflicts and, 192
  Organisation Commune Africaine et Malgache and, 256
  Soviet Union and, 88, 158, 234, 269
  Third Worldism and, 261
  United States and, 232, 235
  Yugoslavia and, 204
Giap, Vo Nguyen, 61–62, 66
Gizenga, Antoine, 108, 141, 192, 253
Gleijeses, Piero, 203
Goa crisis (1961), 110
Gorse, Georges, 152, 154, 277
Goulart, João, 252, 258
Gouvernement Provisoire de la République Algérienne (GPRA, Provisional Government of the Algerian Republic)
  Abbas as first president of, 56–57
  African decolonization and, 84
  Algeria's post-independence government and, 130–33, 140
  ALN's conflict with, 131
  Arab diplomacy and, 182
  Ben Bella and Boumedienne's opposition to, 127
  Congo-Léopoldville crisis (1960–1961) and, 91–92
  Cuba and, 75–76
  De Gaulle's mocking of, 72, 97
  diplomatic strategies of, 12, 175, 205–6, 208
  early cabinet changes in, 121
  economic policy and, 125
  Evian Accords (1962) and, 115, 118–19, 122–24, 130–32
  foreign countries' recognition of, 57–60, 75, 81, 91, 94–95, 106–7, 109, 133
  foreign missions and contacts of, 72, 74, 94, 107
  founding of, 11, 17, 54, 65
  France's attempts to diplomatically isolate, 81
  on the French Community proposal, 80
  humanistic socialism promoted by, 78
  India's refusal to recognize, 260
  Khrushchev and, 93
  Non-Aligned Movement and, 108–9
  political radicalization in, 120, 126
  propaganda efforts and, 82, 100–101
  recruitment of leaders of, 101–2
  Soviet Union courted by, 87
  Third Worldism and, 109–10
Govêrno revolucionário de Angola no exílio (Revolutionary Government of Angola in Exile, GRAE), 190–91
Great Britain. See United Kingdom
Greece, 22, 32
Grimaud, Nicole, 136, 237
Gromyko, Andrei, 61, 89, 210
Group of 77 (G77)
  Algeria's promotion of, 2, 257
  Algiers Charter (1967) and, 290
  creation of, 229–30
  economic development assistance and, 272
  global economic policy and, 6
Guatemala, 77
Guellal, Chérif
  Algerian back channel to Vietnam and, 242–43
  changes between Kennedy and Johnson administrations and, 232
  on larger context of U.S.-Algeria relations, 243
  on nonalignment and the Cold War, 281
  Rusk and, 235, 240, 242
  Sands War and, 220–21
  U.S. food aid program and, 240
  on U.S. foreign policy in Africa, 246
Guérin, Daniel, 296
guerre révolutionnaire doctrine (French military), 50–51
guerrilla warfare
  African independence struggles and, 107–8, 192, 198
  Algeria's nineteenth-century anti-French campaigns and, 19
  Latin America and, 77
  Mao and, 16, 51, 164
  Nkrumah and, 72
  Palestinian struggle and, 250
  western Algeria and, 34

Guevara, Ernesto "Che"
  Algerian delegation to Cuba (1962) and, 145
  Algeria visit (1963) of, 171, 202–3
  Arafat and, 201
  on autogestion in Algeria, 278
  Ben Bella and, 142, 251, 255
  communist ideology and, 75
  Cuban intervention in Congo-Léopoldville and, 255
  G77 remarks of, 229
  guerrilla warfare and, 77–78
  international tour (1959) of, 74–75
  Latin American revolution promoted by, 77
  Palestinian nationalists and, 179
  on revolutions and refugees, 139, 318n106
  Soviet Union and China criticized by, 270, 274
  "Third Worldist" perspective in writings of, 5
Guinea
  Algeria coup (1965) and, 288
  Algeria's independence struggle and, 72, 81–82, 84, 89, 194
  Algeria's post-independence government and, 251
  Casablanca Bloc Pact (1961) and, 96
  Congo-Léopoldville Crisis (1960–1961) and, 92
  coup attempt (1965) in, 289
  decolonization struggle in, 197
  FLN radio and, 100
  French Community referendum (1959) and, 80
  Ghana and, 224
  independence of, 83
  Niger conflicts and, 192
  Organization of African Unity and, 197
  Soviet Union and, 88, 194, 269
Guinea-Bissau
  Algerian independence as inspiration for, 3
  Algeria's support for armed revolt in, 190
  regional diplomacy and, 193

Hadj Ali, Bachir, 161
Haganah militia (Israel), 105
Haiti, 77
Hammarskjöld, Dag, 91, 93, 96, 110
Harbi, Mohammed, 125–26, 161, 217, 224, 280
Hassan II (king of Morocco)
  Algerian independence struggle and, 82
  Algeria's Sahara possessions and, 184, 198
  Algeria's support for opponents of, 245
  Ben Bella and, 187, 245
  Cuban delegation to, 219
  foreign ministers meeting (1963) hosted by, 186
  Organization of African Unity and, 195, 198
  Sands War and, 216–18, 220–22
  United States and, 246

Haykal, Mohammed, 21, 26, 96
Hessel, Stéphane, 277
Ho Chi Minh
  on anti-imperialism's global nature, 14
  Communist initiation of, 26
  FLN inspired by, 15, 85
  North Vietnam independence and, 65
Holden, Roberto
  Algerian criticism of, 248–49, 268
  Algeria visit (1963) of, 191
  All-African Peoples' Conference (1958) and, 70
  ALN training of, 108
  Congo-Léopoldville's support for, 252
  FNLA leadership of, 190
  provisional government of, 197
  Soviet and Chinese assistance to, 209
Houhou, Djamal, 274–75
Houphouêt-Boigny, Félix, 80, 193, 244
House Foreign Relations Committee (United States), 232, 235
al-Husayn, Amin, 26
Hussein (king of Jordan), 260
Hussein Dey, 19

Ibrahimi, Bashir, 25, 280
India
  Algeria's embassy opened in, 258, 260
  Algeria's independence struggle and, 57–59, 111
  Algeria's post-independence government and, 260–61
  Bandung Conference (1955) and, 40–41, 64
  "Bandung 2" Conference and, 261, 287
  China and, 175, 261–62, 290, 304n69
  contemporary global diplomacy and, 297
  Fourteen Points for Peace and, 21
  Goa crisis (1961) and, 110
  Non-Aligned Movement and, 108, 260, 262–63
  religious nationalism in, 292
  Soviet Union and, 158, 175, 230, 257, 290
  United States and, 260–61
  U.S. food aid to, 239
Indochina War (1945–1954), 32, 34, 66
Indonesia
  Algeria's independence struggle and, 57–59, 88–89, 107
  Bandung Conference and, 40
  "Bandung 2" Conference and, 270, 287
  China and, 261
  Communist Party in, 159
  coup (1965) in, 288–89
  FLN delegations to, 42, 47
  India and, 261
  Malaysia's conflict with, 224, 231, 261
  Soviet Union and, 88, 158

Sumatra rebellion in, 48
Third Worldism and, 264
World War II in, 29
International Monetary Fund, 153, 168, 230, 296
International Red Cross, 134
Iran, 292, 297
Iraq
  Algeria's independence struggle and, 89, 181
  Angola and, 251
  Ba'th Party in, 180–81
  coup (1958) in, 70
  Cuba and, 146
  Kurdish separatists in, 223, 225
  Soviet Union and, 88
  United Arab Republic and, 180–82, 224
Ireland, 15, 21, 32, 38, 172
Islamism in Algeria, 279–80
Israel
  African diplomacy and, 268
  Algeria's post-independence government's opposition to, 177, 217, 246, 249–51, 256, 259
  Algeria's struggle for independence and, 177
  Ben Bella's denunciations of, 177, 180
  Congo-Brazzaville and, 249
  Egypt and, 180, 289
  Mali and, 250
  Palestinian nationalism in, 114, 177, 256, 292
  Six-Day War (1967) and, 289, 298
  Third Worldist views of, 177, 281
Italy, 21, 27, 30–31, 41, 273
Itote, Waruhiu, 31
Ivory Coast. *See* Côte d'Ivoire

Jagan, Cheddi, 1
Japan, 29, 260
Jeanneney, Jean-Marcel, 136–37, 152, 167
Jewish community in Algeria
  boycotts against, 24, 26
  Evian Accords and, 120, 123
  FLN and, 43, 63
  Israel's encouragement to emigrate and, 177
  Zionism and, 25
Johnson, Lyndon
  Africa diplomacy and, 246
  Algeria and, 230, 232
  General Agreement on Tariffs and Trade and, 228
Jordan, 260
jusq'au boutists (bitter-enders), 105, 122

Kabylia region
  Berber separatism and conflict in, 215–16, 218, 223, 225, 237, 240–42, 294
  rebellion (1871) in, 19
  Sands War and, 222, 225
  U.S. support to rebels in, 240–42
Kafi, Ali, 259

Kaïd, Ahmed (Si Slimane), 127, 137, 140, 145, 191–92, 248
Kapuściński, Ryszard, 286
Kasavubu, Joseph, 90, 92–93
Katanga region. *See under* Congo-Léopoldville
Keita, Modibo
  Algeria coup (1965) and, 290
  Algerian independence struggle and, 72, 85
  Algeria's post-independence government and, 249–50
  Ben Bella and, 199–200, 250, 253
  Congo-Léopoldville and, 253
  détente criticized by, 263
  Marxist ideology of, 83
  Sands War negotiations and, 219, 221–22
  Soviet Union and, 269
  Sawaba (Niger revolutionary movement) and, 84
Kennedy, John F.
  Algerian delegation's meeting (1962) with, 114, 140, 142–44
  Algeria's independence struggle and, 107
  Algeria's post-independence government and, 114, 138–40, 142–44, 149, 152, 156–57, 168
  assassination of, 221, 228, 234, 238, 246
  Ben Bella's relationship with, 207–9
  Cuba/Cuban Missile Crisis and, 142, 144–45, 147–49, 208, 221
  Foreign Assistance Act (1961) and, 135
  Morocco and, 217
  Peace Corps and, 156
  popularity in Algeria of, 238
  Sands War and, 220–21
  speech supporting Algerian nationalism (1957) by, 58, 142
Kennedy, Robert, 242
Kenya, 31, 86, 198
Khaled (emir of Algeria), 20, 22–23, 30
Khemisti, Mohammed
  as Algeria's foreign minister, 140, 183
  Algeria's policies in Africa and, 189
  on Algeria's post-independence financial problems, 151
  on Algeria's recognition of Ba'th regimes in Syria and Iraq, 181–82
  Arab countries' tour (1963) and, 181, 201
  on Bitat, 182
  Cuban delegation (1962) and, 145
  death of, 183–84
  French assistance to independent Algeria and, 152, 154
  transition to independent Algerian government and, 131
  Tripoli Program and, 126
  United Nations speech (1962) of, 142–43
  U.S. diplomatic visit (1962) of, 147–48
  on U.S. economic aid to Algeria, 144, 150

Khider, Mohamed
　on Algeria's economic modernization, 125
　Algeria's transition to independence and, 137
　Arabic language skills of, 34
　Arab world tour (1962–1963) of, 179
　Bandung Conference and, 41
　Ben Bella's rivalry with, 178–79
　diplomatic strategies of, 38, 41, 48
　FLN's "Arabist" wing and, 176
　French government negotiations (1956) and, 49
　imprisonment of, 132
　Morocco mission of, 185
　Oran post office plot (1950) and, 33
　Palestinian cause and, 178
　PPA-MTLD and, 33
　Tripoli Program and, 126–27
Khrushchev, Nikita
　Afro-Asianism and, 213
　Algeria's independence struggle and, 94–96, 106–7
　Algeria's post-independence government and, 233–34, 237, 248, 264
　on Arab nationalism, 89
　Aswan Dam opening and, 265
　Ben Bella and, 236, 248, 264
　Cold War détente and, 209–11, 264
　Congo-Léopoldville crisis (1960–1961) and, 86, 91–92, 107
　Cuban Missile Crisis and, 86, 145, 148
　De Gaulle and, 89
　FLN received by, 94–95
　Paris Summit (1960) and, 87, 89
　PCA and, 160
　on Soviet foreign aid, 88
　United Nations General Assembly address (1959) of, 88, 93–94
King Jr., Martin Luther, 114, 141, 173
Kitab al Jaza'ir (The book of Algeria, Tewfik al Madani), 25
Komer, Robert
　on Ben Bella, 142
　on changes between Kennedy and Johnson administrations, 232
　on importance of U.S.-Algeria relationship, 208–9, 221
　on Sands War, 217–18
　on Soviet aid to Algeria, 168
　on U.S. aid to Algeria, 134, 157, 168, 241
　on the U.S. role in independent Algeria, 152
　on Yazid, 220
Korea, 21
Korean War, 86
Kosygin, Alexei, 94
Kouyaté, Tiemoko Garan, 27
Krim Belkacem
　on Algeria's leadership in Africa, 77–78, 82, 84

　on Algeria's relations with its neighbors, 71
　Ben Bella denounced by, 137
　Berber minority population and, 216
　on challenges of rebuilding FLN infrastructure, 100
　Congo-Léopoldville Crisis (1960–1961) and, 91, 93
　diplomatic strategies of, 67, 83, 87
　FLN's founding and, 31
　GPRA's removal from cabinet of, 121
　guerrilla warfare and, 51
　Khrushchev and, 94, 96
　MAE leadership of, 101
　on North Vietnam's anti-colonial successes, 85–86
　PPA and, 33–34
　Senegal intrigues of, 83
　Soviet Union and, 87
　"Tizi Ouzou clan" and, 130
　U.S. contact with, 238
　V-E Day Protests in Algeria and, 31
　World War II service and, 31
Kuwait, 179

Lacheraf, Mostefa, 26, 126
L'Algérie, vivra-t-elle? (Viollette), 24
L'Algérie des bidonvilles (Descloitres, Descloitres, and Reverdy), 101
Laos, 107
La Question (Alleg), 43
Larbi, Mohamed, 34, 48
League against Imperialism, 27, 64
Lebanon, 57, 221, 250
Lenin, Vladimir
　on capitalism and imperialism, 27
　FLN inspired by, 10, 15–16, 19, 53, 66
　guerrilla war and, 16
　revolutionary organization theories of, 10, 120
　"Third Worldist" perspective in writings of, 5
　Third World nationalists and, 9–10, 26, 75, 88
les trente glorieuses ("thirty glorious years" of French economic growth), 117
Liberia, 69, 81, 199, 254
Libya
　Conference of Independent African States (CIAS) and, 69
　Maghrib countries' negotiations and, 187
　NATO intervention (2011), 294
　religion and anti-colonial nationalism in, 239
　Sands War and, 221
Ligue de Défense de la Race Nègre (Negro Race Defense League), 27
Lodge, Henry Cabot, 54, 57
Lumumba, Patrice
　Algeria's independence struggle and, 90–91
　assassination of, 86, 92–93, 97, 252, 289

Chinese accusations regarding Soviet
culpability in assassination of, 262
Congo-Léopoldville Crisis (1960–1961)
and, 90–92
election victory (1960) of, 90
pan-Africanism of, 90, 92
Soviet support for, 86, 90–91
Stanleyville statue of, 253

Macmillan, Harold, 91
Magasins-Pilotes Socialistes (Pilot Socialist Shops), 278
Mahsas, Ali, 49
Malaysia, 224, 231, 261, 269–71
Malcolm X, 172
Malek, Rédha
Algeria-Yugoslavia relations and, 165–66, 203–4
on détente and anti-colonialism, 263
Evian Accords and, 122
Sands War negotiations and, 222
on Second Non-Alignmed Movement Summit and Congo-Léopoldville, 254
Tripoli Program and, 126
on Tuareg revolt in Mali, 199
on U.S. intervention in Kabylia revolt, 242
Mali
Algeria coup (1965) and, 288
Algeria's independence struggle and, 83, 85
Algeria's post-independence relations with, 249–51
ALN bases in, 85, 108, 189
Casablanca Bloc Pact (1961) and, 96
China and, 249–50, 264–65, 270
collapse of federation with Senegal and, 83
decolonization in, 84
De Gaulle's address (1959) in, 79
Evian Accords (1962) and, 124
FLN activity in, 83
FLN radio and, 100
Israel and, 250
Non-Aligned Movement and, 263
Soviet Union and, 234, 249–50, 269–70
Sawaba revolutionary movement in, 84
Tuareg separatist movement in, 198–99, 222, 250
United States and, 232, 235
Malley, Robert, 148
Mandela, Nelson, 108, 130, 190
"Manifesto of the Algerian People" (Abbas), 30
Mao Zedong
on achieving victory in armed struggle, 297
African decolonization conflicts and, 211
Afro-Asianism and, 213, 262
Algeria's independence struggle and, 57, 89
Algeria's post-independence government and, 164
Cultural Revolution purges and, 213
on fighting and negotiating, 118
FLN inspired by, 15–16, 53, 85, 118, 121, 129, 164
guerrilla war and, 16, 51, 164
on importance of political unity, 121
Third Worldism and, 5, 262
marabouts, 28
March Decrees (1963)
agricultural collectivization and, 155
autogestion and, 153
French negotiations stalled by, 166, 235
revolutionary fatigue as a motivation for, 154
socialist principles in, 153, 155, 157, 161
Yugoslavia model and, 165–66
Massamba-Débat, Alphonse, 199, 246–47, 249, 251, 263
Massu, Jacques, 49
Mau Mau Uprising (Kenya), 31
Mauritania, 186–87, 198
Mboya, Tom, 70, 268
Meir, Golda, 177
Mendès-France, Pierre, 39, 79
Mennen Williams, George, 156–57
Mers-el-Kébir naval base (Algeria), 151
Messali Hadj
Algerian migrants in France and, 122
cult of personality of, 28–29, 44, 122
Etolie Nord Africain and, 26–28
FLN and, 37, 191
Parti du Peuple Algérien and, 28
PCF condemned by, 28, 58
PPA and, 28, 30–33, 44, 63, 121
self-determination policies and, 31–32
Third Worldism and, 64
ulema (religious scholars) in Algeria and, 28
Michel, Serge, 91, 134–35
Mikoyan, Anastas, 59–60
Ministère des Affaires Etrangères (MAE, Ministry of Foreign Affairs for Algeria)
on African and Asian supporters of Algerian independence, 107
on Africa's ideological divisions, 256
on Arab governments, 72
Arabic language skills as rare in, 178–79, 259
Asian embassies opened by, 260
on Communist bloc countries, 89
Cuba and, 73, 76
diplomatic recognition for GPRA and, 58–59
embassy expansion by, 257–58
Evian Accords (1962) and, 119, 128
FLN radio and, 100
French Affairs Section of, 274–75
on the G77, 272
Krim's leadership of, 71
lack of trained personnel in, 140
on Latin America, 252, 258

Ministère des Affaires Etrangères (MAE, Ministry of Foreign Affairs for Algeria) (*Cont.*)
    leftist interpretation of U.S. foreign policy in, 246
    opening of foreign embassies by, 165
    on Organization of African Unity, 200
    political radicalization in, 120, 126
    propaganda efforts at, 101
    proposal for political training of African leaders by, 249
    on the Soviet Union, 95, 160, 162
    Third Worldism and, 110
    on trade with Eastern Bloc countries, 274
    on U.S. investment in Algeria, 144
    on U.S. policies in Latin America, 143
    U.S. talks with, 147–48
mission civilisatrice (French concept of "civilizing mission"), 18, 118
Mobutu Sese Seko, 92–93, 289
Mohammed V (king of Morocco), 71, 82, 184–85
Mollet, Guy, 39
Monte Cassino, Battle of, 31, 33
Morice Line, 71, 82, 97
Morocco
    Algerian refugees in, 57, 99, 129, 134
    Algeria's arms race with, 231–32
    Algeria's independence struggle and, 47, 51–53, 55, 62–63, 71–72, 79, 82, 110
    Algeria's post-independence relationship with, 8–9, 11–12, 131, 175–76, 181, 184–87, 189, 198, 207, 215–25, 232, 234, 237, 245–46, 250
    Algeria's Saharan holdings and, 185
    ALN bases in, 47, 62, 71, 84, 97, 108, 120, 130, 189–90
    Arab League and, 70
    Bandung Conference and, 41
    Casablanca Bloc Pact (1961) and, 96
    Conference of Independent African States (CIAS) and, 69
    Egypt and, 181
    emigration to France from, 104
    Europe's relations with, 186–87
    Evian Accords (1962) and, 124
    FLN activities in, 82–83
    FLN radio and, 100
    global geopolitics and, 8
    independence of, 47–48, 79, 84
    nationalist movement in, 34, 41
    parliamentary elections (1960) in, 82
    Sands War and, 12, 189, 198, 215–26, 233–34, 237
    social development emphasized in, 245
    United States and, 136, 157, 217–18, 237, 245–46
Mouvement National Algérien, 191

Mouvement National Congolais (MNC, Congolese National Movement), 90
Movimento Popular de Libertação de Angola (MPLA, Popular Movement for the Liberation of Angola)
    Algerian support for, 190–92, 198, 248–49, 255, 297
    Algerian training of fighters in, 192, 249
    Congo-Léopoldville's opposition to, 192, 197
    Marxist influence in, 191
    mixed-race leadership of, 268
    Organization of African Unity and, 197–98
    support bases of, 191
Mozambican Liberation Front, 190
Mozambique, 190, 197, 199, 248, 255
Murphy, Robert, 30
Museveni, Yoweri, 294

Nadi Snober resort (Algeria), 227–28
Namibia, 190
Nasser, Gamal Abdel
    Afro-Asian Peoples' Solidarity Organization and, 70–71
    Algeria coup (1965) and, 1, 288
    Algeria's independence struggle and, 59
    Algeria's post-independence government and, 131–32, 178
    Algeria visit (1963) of, 183–84
    arms shipments to Algeria and, 59, 183
    Aswan Dam opening and, 265
    Bandung Conference (1955) and, 40–41
    Ba'th Party and, 182
    Ben Bella and, 131, 142, 166, 176–77, 180–84, 195, 256, 288
    communists suppressed by, 236
    Cuba and, 74
    détente as source of concern for, 87
    FLN's admiration of, 129
    Free Officers' Coup (1952) and, 33
    mukhabarat intelligence service of, 83
    Nehru and, 261
    Non-Aligned Movement and, 108, 203–5, 261
    pan-Africanism and, 195, 213, 268
    pan-Arabism and, 195, 268
    Sands War and, 218, 220–22
    Six Day War (1967) and, 289, 298
    Soviet Union and, 209, 214, 236, 265
    Suez Crisis (1956) and, 65
    Third Worldism and, 267
    Tito and, 204
    Tshombe's criticism of, 268–69
    Yemen and, 180
National Assembly (Algeria), 173–74, 233
National Assembly (France), 20, 151, 170, 233
National Constituent Assembly (Algeria), 137–38

National Liberation Front (NLF, South Vietnam)
  Algeria as possible U.S. back channel to, 242–44
  Algerian office of, 201, 208
  Palestinian nationalists and, 179
National Union of Populist Forces, 185
Nehru, Jawaharlal
  Afro-Asian Peoples' Solidarity Organization and, 70
  Algeria's independence struggle and, 55, 107
  Anti-imperialism Congress (1927), 27
  Bandung Conference (1955) and, 40, 64
  Ben Bella and, 256
  Congo-Léopoldville Crisis and, 96, 110
  death of, 289
  détente as source of concern for, 87
  Guevara and, 75
  Non-Aligned Movement and, 108, 203, 209, 261
  Panhscheel (five principles of peaceful relations between people) and, 40
  refusal to recognize GPRA by, 260
  on rise of India and China, 41
  Third Worldist perspective of, 5
  United Nations and, 96, 110
The Netherlands, 29, 273
New International Economic Order (NIEO), 286, 295–96
Nguyen Tat Thanh, 26
Niger
  Algerian training of militants from, 111
  Algeria's independence struggle and, 96
  Algeria's support for left-wing revolutionaries in, 84, 189–90, 207
  pro-French government in, 250
  regional diplomacy and, 192
  Tuaregs in, 199
Nigeria
  Algeria coup (1965) and, 288
  "Bandung 2 Conference" and, 287
  coup (1965) in, 289
  FLN and, 81
  GPRA recognized by, 107
  Non-Aligned Movement (NAM) and, 205, 254
  Organization of African Unity and, 197
Nixon, Richard, 8
Nkrumah, Kwame
  African summit (1965) hosted by, 3–4
  Algeria coup (1965) and, 1
  Algerian independence struggle and, 72, 81, 90
  All-African Peoples' Conference (1958), 69–70
  Bandung Conference absence of, 7
  Ben Bella and, 193–95, 256
  Conference of Independent African States (CIAS) and, 69
  Congo-Léopoldville crisis (1960–1961), 92
  coup (1966) against, 289
  on economic modernization, 115
  FLN and, 55, 73
  Ghana's independence and, 68
  guerrilla warfare and, 72
  Khrushchev and, 94
  Lumumba and, 90, 92
  on "national chauvinism," 224
  Non-Aligned Movement and, 108–9
  Organization of African Unity and, 198
  pan-Africanism and, 68–70, 194–95, 198
  socialist and anti-imperialist convictions of, 80, 94
  Soviet Union and, 269
  "Third Worldist" perspective in writings of, 5
Non-Aligned Movement (NAM)
  Afro-Asianism and, 267
  Algeria's participation in, 132, 203, 209, 231–32, 234, 244, 256, 263–64, 282
  Belgrade Conference (1961) and founding of, 2, 71, 108–9, 116, 203, 205, 210
  Cairo Summit (1964) of, 253–54, 257, 269
  Congo-Léopoldville conflicts (1960s) and, 108, 253
  Cuban Missile Crisis and, 148
  decolonization and, 263
  FLN participation in, 2, 108–9
  Latin America and, 282
  Maghrib countries' relations and, 187
  ongoing existence of, 13
  Palestinian nationalism and, 263
  sovereignty of members of, 10, 290
  summit (1964) excluding Tshombe and, 253–54, 257, 263, 269, 290
  summit (1970) of, 290
  Third Worldism and, 109, 201, 204–5, 214, 230, 271
nonalignment
  Dulles's criticism of, 66
  policy implications of, 7–8
  as Third World Cold War strategy, 86–87, 174, 201, 209, 232, 281
North Atlantic Treaty Organization (NATO)
  FLN appeals to members of, 37, 39, 71, 107
  FLN criticism of, 89
  France's disagreements with, 59–60
  Portugal's African colonies and, 205
North Korea, 57, 208
North Vietnam
  Algeria inspired by example of, 85–86
  Algerian embassy in Hanoi and, 243
  Algeria's independence struggle and, 57, 59–61, 63, 111
  Algiers embassy of, 208
  ALN delegation to, 61
  Geneva Accords establishing independence of, 34, 65–66
  Soviet and Chinese support to, 243

nuclear bomb tests in Algeria, 154–55, 276
Nyerere, Julius
  Algeria coup (1965) and, 1
  Ben Bella and, 199
  concerns about coup against, 248
  on the International Monetary Fund, 296

on socialism's international nature, 113
Obichkina, Evgeniia, 59
Office National de la Reforme Agraire (ONRA, National Office for Agrarian Reform), 278
Ouel Hadj, Mohand, 216, 222
Olympio, Sylvanus, 289
Oman, 86
Oran demonstrations (1960), 102–3, 106
Organisation Armée Secrète (OAS, Secret Armed Organization)
  brutal methods of, 111–12, 122, 127
  coup plotters against De Gaulle and, 105, 122
  fight against Algerian independence by, 105–6, 111–12, 122, 127
Organisation Commune Africaine et Malgache (OCAM, African and Malagasy Common Organization), 256, 271
Organisation Commune des Régions Sahariennes (Common Organization of the Saharan Regions, OCRS), 123–24, 256
Organisation Spéciale (OS), 32–33, 37
Organization of African Unity (OAU)
  African Union as successor to, 294
  Algeria-Morocco dispute and, 189
  Algeria's role in founding, 2, 12, 174, 187, 189, 195–96, 245
  Angola conflict and, 198, 266, 268
  armed anti-colonial movements and, 189, 193, 197, 247, 249
  Ben Bella and, 195–97, 201, 252
  charter for, 196–98, 205, 221–22, 244, 256
  compromise as essential at, 200
  Congo-Léopoldville conflicts and, 253, 256–57
  headquarters of, 3, 195
  ideological divisions within, 247, 249, 255–56
  Liberation Committee (Committee of Nine) and, 196–97, 204, 223, 244, 247, 252, 292
  nonalignment and, 205
  obstacles to establishing, 189
  organizational structure of, 196
  pan-African goals of, 195, 201, 223
  Sands War and, 221–22, 224
  state sovereignty and, 10, 198
  summit (1965) after Algerian coup by, 290
  Third Worldism and, 196, 206, 214, 230
  United Nations and, 196
  Yugoslavia and, 204
Organization of American States (OAS), 205, 251

Organization of Petroleum Exporting Countries (OPEC), 295
Orwell, George, 297
Ottoman Empire, 19–20
Ouamrane, Omar, 52–53
Oussedik, Omar, 81, 96
Ouzegane, Omar, 43, 149, 155

Pakistan, 107, 261, 287
Palestine
  Algerian arms shipments and, 180
  Algerian independence as inspiration for, 3, 12
  Algerian support for cause of, 141, 172, 177–78, 250, 260
  Algerian training of fighters from, 260
  Arab Revolt (1936) in, 24–26
  Ben Bella's support to cause of, 141, 172, 177–78, 250
Palestine Liberation Organization (PLO), 250, 266
pan-Africanism
  Algeria's role in, 174, 176–77, 188
  Conference of Independent African States (CIAS) and, 69
  FLN's role in, 85
  Nkrumah and, 68–70, 194–95, 198
  pan-African Congress (1945) and, 68
  pan-African socialism and, 70
  policy implications of, 7
Panama, 77
pan-Arabism
  Algeria and, 25, 176
  FLN and, 18
  Israel and, 177
  policy implications of, 7
  transnationalism *versus* nation-statism in, 180–81
  United Arab Republic and, 70
Panhsheel (Nehru's five principles of peaceful relations between people), 40, 304n69
Paris FLN protests (1961), 123
Paris Peace Conference (1919), 210
Paris Summit (1960), 87, 89
Partial Test Ban Treaty (1963), 210–11, 262, 264
Parti Communiste Algérien (PCA, Algerian Communist Party)
  Ben Bella's banning of, 158–60, 165, 212, 234, 236
  China and, 164
  daily newspaper of, 134
  dissolving of, 43
  Etoile Nord Africain's split with, 27
  "Manifesto of the Algerian People" and, 30
  National Constituent Assembly elections and, 137
  PCF and, 23, 26–27

Soviet Union and, 59, 132, 135, 159–62, 164, 208, 212, 232, 234, 236
Tripoli Program and, 132, 161
Parti Communiste Français (PCF, French Communist Party)
  Etoile Nord Africain and, 27–28
  FLN and, 89
  Messali Hadj and, 28, 58
  PCA and, 23, 26–27
  Popular Front (1930s) and, 27–28
  Soviet Union and, 59
Partido Africano da Independência da Guiné e Cabo Verde (PAIGC, African Party for the Independence of Guinea and Cape Verde), 193–94, 197, 249
Parti du Peuple Algérien (PPA, Algerian People's Party)
  Aït Ahmed's call to reform, 32
  founding of, 28
  French security crackdowns against, 37
  "Manifesto of the Algerian People" and, 30
  Messali's leadership in, 28, 30–33, 44, 63, 121
  MTLD section of, 33, 37, 43–44, 121
  self-determination policies and, 31–32
  support base of, 28–29
Peace Corps (United States), 156–57
People's Democratic Republic of Algeria, 2, 113
Philippeville massacre (1955), 38, 42
pieds noirs. *See* French population in Algeria
pieds rouges ("red feet," nickname for European leftists in Algeria), 5, 224, 273, 283, 297
PL-480 program. *See under* United States
Poland, 20, 60
Ponomarev, Boris, 160
Pontecorvo, Gillo, 49, 98, 284
Popular Front (France, 1930s), 24, 27
Porter, William
  on Algeria's diplomatic visit to United States (1962), 148
  on Ben Bella's international agenda, 243
  on development assistance to Algeria, 150
  on Eastern European embassies in Algiers, 208
  on Yazid, 220
Portugal
  Algeria's training of leftist groups from, 208
  decolonization and armed rebellions against, 110, 189, 205–7, 212, 244, 248, 292 (*See also* Angola; Mozambique)
  Goa Crisis (1961) and, 110
  international embargoes against, 247
  NATO and, 205–6
  Organization of African Unity (OAU), 196
  United Nations and, 110
poverty in Algeria, 23
Prasad, Vijay, 6
Prebisch, Raúl, 116, 229, 271
Progress Club (Algiers), 25

Qaddafi, Muammar, 294
Qassim, Abdelkarim, 70, 89, 181
Qiyam al-Islamiyya (The Islamic Values organization), 279, 298
Qutb, Sayyid, 227

Raptis, Michel, 161, 296
Rassemblement Démocratique Africain (RDA, Democratic African Rally), 80
rayonnement (French maintenance of influence in former colonies), 136, 249–50
regroupement camps, 99–100, 129, 134
Republic of China (Taiwan), 114
Republic of Congo. *See* Congo-Brazzaville
République Algérienne Démocratique et Populaire (RADP, People's Democratic Republic of Algeria), 2, 113, 137, 140
Reverdy, Jean-Claude, 101
Revolutionary Council (Algeria), 284, 287–89
Rhodesia, decolonization revolt in, 196–97, 248, 255–56, 292
Rivera, Armando, 73, 75, 82
Roosevelt, Franklin Delano, 29, 87
Rusk, Dean
  Algerian back channel in Vietnam and, 242
  Algeria's post-independence government and, 141–42, 235
  Boumedienne's influence feared by, 141–42
  Guellal's meetings with, 240, 242, 246
  Sands War and, 220
  U.S. meetings with FLN and GPRA leaders and, 107
  on U.S. NATO commitments and Portuguese African colonies, 206

Sahnoun, Mohammed, 147–48, 247
Sakiet Sidi Youssef (Algeria), French bombardment of, 49, 51
Salafism, 25
Salan, Raoul, 49–50, 112
Sands War
  Algeria's military problems in, 233
  cease-fire in, 221
  Cuba and, 219–21, 224–25
  France and, 218
  Morocco as Algeria's opponent in, 12, 189, 198, 215–26, 233–34, 237
  Organization of African Unity and, 189, 198
  Saharan territory disputed in, 175, 215
  United States and, 217–18, 220–21, 246
  U.S. shipments to Morocco in, 218
San Francisco Charter (United Nations, 1945), 60
Sartre, Jean-Paul, 43, 103–4
Saud (king of Saudi Arabia), 38
Saudi Arabia, 36, 48, 179–80
Sauvey, Alfred, 5

Savimbi, Jonas, 191, 201, 266, 268, 326n80
Scott, James C., 45
Second Economic Seminar of Afro-Asian Solidarity (1965), 272
Secrétariat d'Etat aux Affaires Algériennes (SEAA), 136, 152
Sections Administratives Spécialisées (SAS, Special Administrative Sections), 45–46
Sékou Touré, Ahmed
   Algeria coup (1965) and, 287, 290–91
   Algerian independence struggle and, 72, 80–82, 89
   Ben Bella and, 141, 193–95, 199, 207, 247, 268
   coup attempt (1965) against, 289
   FLN and, 80
   French Community referendum and, 80
   pan-Africanism and, 194–95, 268
   socialist and anti-imperialist convictions of, 80
   Soviet Union and, 194, 269
Selassie, Haile
   Algerian coup (1965) and, 288
   Organization for African Unity and, 195
   Sands War negotiation and, 219, 221–22
Sénac, Jean, 171
Senegal, 83–84, 96, 193, 197, 250, 254
Senghor, Léopold Sédar, 27, 83, 250
Serguera, Jorge, 202–4, 219, 225, 251
Sétif Massacre (1945), 31
Shukairy, Ahmed, 266
Singapore, 29
Sinn Féin, 32
Smart, John Karefa, 250, 268
Smith, Ian, 248
Somalia, 107
Soummam Platform (1956), 44–45, 50
Soustelle, Jacques, 45
South Africa
   Algerian independence struggle as inspiration in, 111
   anti-Apartheid struggle in, 84, 108, 175, 189–90, 197, 292
   Ben Bella on, 189–90, 295
   international attention to, 115, 247, 292
   Lumumba on, 90
   Organization for African Unity and, 196
   Soviet Union and, 210
   United Nations and, 110
South Vietnam
   GPRA recognized by, 109
   National Liberation Front in, 179, 201, 208, 242–43
South West African People's Organization (SWAPO), 249, 255
Soviet Union
   African decolonization conflicts and, 211
   Afro-Asianism and, 212–13, 262, 265, 267, 269–71
   Algerian mining efforts and, 233–34
   Algeria's independence struggle and, 16, 54, 59–61, 72, 87–89, 94–96, 101, 106–7, 114, 266
   Algeria's international connections and, 202
   Algeria's post-independence government and, 132–33, 135–36, 139, 141, 146, 158–66, 168, 170, 208, 213, 226, 232–38, 240, 244, 264–65, 269, 274, 278, 281–84, 333n40
   Algeria's trade with, 273
   arms shipments to Algeria and, 59, 88, 95, 108, 162, 218–19, 223, 233
   "Bandung 2" Conference and, 12, 261, 264–65, 270, 282
   Ben Bella and, 149, 159–61, 163, 165, 220, 232–35, 237–38, 244, 248, 264–65, 269, 281–82
   Berlin Crisis and, 61
   Central Asian development and, 236–37
   Cold War and, 6–7, 53–54, 65, 93, 209–10
   Congo crisis (1960–1961) and, 86–87, 90–92, 95, 107
   Cuba and, 75, 88, 90, 94, 142, 144–46, 149, 158–60, 202, 220, 341n235
   Cuban Missile Crisis and, 144–45
   decolonization and, 8, 266
   détente policies and, 87, 209–11, 263–64, 295
   Eastern bloc hegemony of, 89, 93
   economic development assistance in Algeria and, 163
   economic modernization in, 158, 164
   Evian Accords and, 119
   foreign students in, 88
   France and, 89, 235–37
   humanitarian aid to Algeria and, 134
   India and, 158, 175, 230, 257, 290
   Non-Aligned Movement and, 262–64
   Palestinian nationalism and, 266
   Paris Summit (1960) and, 87, 89
   Partial Test Ban Treaty (1963) and, 210–11, 262, 264
   PCA and, 59, 132, 135, 159–62, 164, 208, 212, 232, 234, 236
   Sands War and, 217–20, 225–26
   Sino-Soviet split and, 12, 87, 163–65, 175, 188, 201, 211, 225–26, 230, 257, 261–62, 264, 267, 270–71, 282, 290, 294
   Third Worldism and, 26, 162–63, 211–14, 262–64, 295
   Vietnam and, 243
   Yemen conflict and, 219
   Yugoslavia and, 163–65, 210, 214
Spain, 207–8
Stalin, Joseph, 27, 87

State Department (United States)
  African decolonization conflicts and, 189
  on Algeria's economic development agenda, 135, 144
  Algeria's post-independence government and, 144, 157
  on Algeria's Third Worldism, 203, 214
  Ben Bella distrusted by, 238
  Boumedienne distrusted by, 141–42
  FLN officials' meetings with, 39, 54
  food aid to Algeria and, 239
  French meetings with, 136
  Kabylia separatism conflict in Algeria and, 241
  Lumumba's meeting with, 91
  MAE's meeting with, 147–48
  Sands War and, 220–21
  on South Africa's Apartheid state, 111–12
  on Soviet aid to Algeria, 95
  Third World blind spots of, 235
Stevenson, Adlai, 115, 141, 147
Sudan, 69, 255, 268
Suez Crisis (1956), 50, 65, 225
Suharto, 289
Sukarno
  Algeria's independence struggle and, 107
  Bandung Conference (1955) and, 5, 40–41
  coup against, 289
  détente as source of concern for, 87, 263
  Non-Aligned Movement and, 109
  Soviet Union and, 209
  Third Worldism as philosophy of, 5
Suslov, Mikhail, 267
Sawaba party (Niger), 84, 192–93
Syria, 21, 70, 180–82, 224. See also United Arab Republic (UAR)
Syrian Revolt (1925), 24

Tanganyika. See also Tanzania
  Algerian arms shipments to Congo-Léopoldville through, 254–55
  Algerian-run training camps in, 192, 197
  Ben Bella's visit to, 199
  decolonization revolts in southern African and, 248
  East African Federation proposal and, 198
Tanzania. See also Tanganyika
  Algeria coup (1965) and, 288
  Algerian Embassy in, 197
  China and, 265
  founding of, 248
  Organization of African Unity and, 197
  socialist ideology and, 113
Tewfik El-Madani, Ahmad
  on Algeria's economic goals, 124–25
  Arab diplomacy and, 259
  correspondence with foreign Muslim scholars and, 25

FLN and, 43
religious reform and nationalism of, 25
on Somalia, 107
Third Republic (France), 20
Third Worldism
  Algeria's support for, 11, 76–77, 85–86, 98, 101, 110–12, 115, 117, 123, 128, 141, 151, 173–76, 200–201, 204, 214, 223, 230–31, 248, 250, 256–57, 259, 263–64, 267–68, 271, 274, 281–82, 285–86, 289, 290, 295, 297–98
  Bandung Conference (1955) and, 5–7, 10, 36, 70, 109, 173, 291
  Ben Bella and, 128, 141, 173, 176, 200–201, 214, 223, 230–31, 250, 267, 271, 274, 285, 289, 295
  coups as threat to, 287–89
  Latin America and, 174 (See also specific countries)
  national sovereignty and, 293
  religion and, 292
  Soviet Union and, 26, 162–63, 211–14, 262–64, 295
Thomas, Martin, 30
Tillion, Germaine, 99
Tindouf (Algeria), 215–16
Tito, Josip Broz
  Afro-Asian Peoples' Solidarity Organization and, 70–71
  Algeria's independence struggle and, 106
  Algeria's transition to independence and, 166
  Ben Bella's relationship with, 166, 180, 199–201, 204, 209, 214, 222–23, 245, 267–68
  FLN delegations to, 71
  Guevara and, 74
  international socialism promoted by, 165
  Nasser and, 204
  Nehru and, 261
  Non-Aligned Movement and, 108, 203–4, 210, 261
Togo, 81, 289
Treaty of Rome (European Economic Community), 104
Tricontinental Conference (1966), 290
Tricot, Bernard, 119, 128
Tripoli Program
  drafting of, 126–28
  economic development goals outlined in, 116, 128, 283
  Evian Accords' incompatibility with, 129, 136
  foreign reactions to, 133, 135, 163
  on France's continued economic hegemony, 117
  Islam discussed in, 159
  PCA's endorsement of, 132, 161
  Third Worldist principles in, 127
Truman Doctrine, 32

Tshombe, Moise
  Ben Bella and, 252–53
  as Congo-Léopoldville's prime minister, 252
  Conseil National de Libération's fight against, 253
  Gabon conflict and, 255
  Katanga region and, 252
  Nasser criticized by, 268–69
  Non-Aligned Summit (1964) and the exclusion of, 253–54, 257, 263, 269, 290
Tuaregs, 199, 222, 250
Tubman, William, 81
Tunisia
  Algerian refugees in, 57, 99, 129, 134, 186
  Algeria's independence struggle and, 47, 51–53, 55, 59, 62–63, 71–72, 79, 82, 110
  Algeria's post-independence relationship with, 11, 176, 181, 184–87, 224
  Algeria's transition to independence and, 131
  ALN bases in, 47, 55, 62, 71, 84, 97, 108, 120, 130, 189
  Arab League and, 70
  arms shipments to Angola by, 192
  Bandung Conference and, 41
  Christmas Plot (1963) in, 185–86
  Conference of Independent African States (CIAS) and, 69
  Egypt and, 181
  emigration to France from, 104
  Etat Majeur-Général in, 77
  Europe's relations with, 186
  Evian Accords (1962) and, 124
  FLN activities in, 82–83
  FLN leaders in exile in, 109
  FLN radio and, 100
  France's clashes with, 110
  French government negotiations with FLN (1956) in, 49
  independence of, 47–48, 79, 84
  nationalist movement in, 34, 41
  Sands War and, 221
  United Nations and, 110
  United States and, 59, 136, 157
Turkey, 20, 22, 32

Uganda, 197–98, 254, 289
ulema (religious scholars) and reform in Algeria, 25–26, 28, 30, 37, 43, 63
Umkhonto we Sizwe (MK, Spear of the Nation, South Africa), 111, 197
Union Démocratique du Manifeste Algérien, 121
Union Démocratique du Manifeste Algérien (UDMA, Democratic Union of the Algerian Manifesto), 43
Union des Populations du Cameroun (UPC, Union of Cameroonian Peoples), 69, 84, 207

Union Générale des Etudiants Musulmans Algériens (UGEMA, General Union of Muslim Algerian Students), 42
Union Nationale des Forces Populaires (UNFP, National Union of Popular Forces), 185, 216
Union Soudanaise-Rassemblement Démocratique Africain (Soudanese Union-African Democratic Rally, US-RDA), 83
United Arab Republic (UAR). *See also* Egypt; Syria
  Algeria's independence struggle and, 89
  Algeria's possible participation in, 181–82, 184
  Algeria's post-independence government and, 160, 182
  Angola conflict and, 266
  collapse of, 198, 224
  Conference of Independent African States (CIAS) and, 69
  Congo-Léopoldville and, 255
  Egyptian-Syrian federation and, 177, 180–82
  founding of, 70, 177, 181
  Organization of African Unity and, 197
  Sands War and, 217–18, 221
  Soviet Union and, 214
  Yemen conflict, 218
United Kingdom
  African military alliances and, 205
  Algeria's foreign policy and, 173
  Algeria's independence struggle and, 81, 96, 114
  Algeria's post-independence government and, 140–41, 157, 239, 256
  Algeria's trade with, 273
  decolonization and, 21, 29, 31, 68, 79, 83, 247–48
  FLN and, 41
  Palestine mandate and, 24–25
  Paris Summit (1960) and, 87
  Partial Test Ban Treaty (1963) and, 210–11, 262, 264
  Suez Crisis (1956) and, 65
  United Nations and, 110
  Versailles Treaty and, 21
  World War II and, 30
United Nations
  Afro-Asian caucus at, 110
  Algeria's admission (1962) to, 113–14, 140–41, 172–73
  Algeria's independence struggle and, 16, 35–36, 38–39, 41, 47–50, 52, 54–55, 57–58, 60, 73, 79, 93, 96, 110
  anti-colonial resolution (1960) at, 110
  Conference on Trade and Development (UNCTAD), 6, 116, 168–69, 229–30, 257, 266, 271–72, 281

Congo-Léopoldville Crisis (1960–1961) and, 86, 91, 110
founding of, 29
General Assembly, 16, 36, 38–39, 41, 47–49, 55, 57, 73, 88, 93, 96, 110, 114, 116, 140, 142, 172–73, 177, 189, 210, 229, 250
humanitarian aid to Algeria and, 134
Israel denounced at, 177
Khrushchev's speech (1959) at, 88, 93–94
national sovereignty and, 281
Organization of African Unity and, 196
Sands War and, 221
San Francisco Charter (1945) of, 60
Third Worldism and, 229–30
"Year of Africa" (1960) and, 73
United States
African decolonization wars and, 192
African military alliances and, 205
Algerian independence struggle and, 16, 39–40, 49, 52–55, 57–60, 78, 81–82, 93, 95–96, 107, 114
Algeria's Africa policies and, 207–8
Algeria's post-independence government and, 132–44, 147–48, 150, 152–53, 156–58, 160–61, 163, 168, 170, 208–9, 214, 217–18, 225–26, 232, 234–35, 237–44, 246, 256, 281
Algeria's Third Worldism and, 202–3
Ben Bella, Ahmed and, 39, 133, 140–44, 147–50, 153, 156, 158, 174, 206–7, 221, 232, 238–44, 246, 281
Cold War and, 6–7, 39, 53–54, 58, 65, 209–10, 295
Congo-Léopoldville and, 86, 91–93, 95, 97, 241, 253, 269
Cuba and, 74–76, 139–45, 150–51, 157, 168, 202–3, 217–18, 235, 238, 242–43, 251–52, 259
Cuban Missile Crisis and, 144–45, 147, 150
decolonization in Africa and, 8, 29–30, 66, 110, 206–7
détente policies and, 263–64
Foreign Assistance Act (1961) and, 135
Four Areas development project in Algeria and, 156, 235, 240
France and, 136–37, 168, 236, 240
France's military aid from, 52
India and, 260–61
Kabylia revolt in Algeria and, 240–42
Morocco and, 136, 157, 217–18, 237, 245–46
NATO commitments of, 206
Non-Aligned Movement and, 263
Paris Summit (1960) and, 87
Partial Test Ban Treaty (1963) and, 210–11, 262, 264

PL-480 program (humanitarian aid to Algeria) and, 134–35, 143, 147, 150, 156, 158, 228, 238–40
racial inequality in, 173
Sands War, 217–18, 220–21, 246
Suez Crisis (1956) and, 65
United Nations and, 57, 60, 93, 110
Versailles Treaty and, 21
Vietnam War and, 242–43
World War II and, 29–30
United States Agency for International Development (USAID), 157
U Thant, 110, 113–14, 221, 229, 272

V-E Day Protests in Algeria (May 8, 1945), 31
Venezuela, 72, 202, 252
Venezuelan National Liberation Front, 201–2
Verges, Jacques, 190
Versailles Conference (1919), 21–22, 26, 87
Vichy regime (World War II France), 29–30
Viet Cong. *See* National Liberation Front (NLF)
Viet Minh, 50
Vietnam. *See also* North Vietnam; South Vietnam
Algerian independence as inspiration for, 3
Algeria's criticism of U.S. policy in, 235, 277
détente policies and, 263
Geneva Accords (1954), 34, 40
guerrilla warfare in, 51
international attention to, 115, 281
mass mobilization emphasis in, 68
Viollette, Maurice, 24, 28

Wafd Party (Egypt), 21
Walcott, Derek, 286
Wested, Odd Arne, 6
Wazir, Khalil, 177, 179–80, 201, 266
West Germany
Algerian independence struggle and, 41, 52
Algeria's post-independence government and, 256, 260
humanitarian aid to Algeria and, 134
Soviet Union and, 89
"What Is Algeria: The Algerian Question in Outline" (FLN publication), 38
Who Remembers the Sea (Dib), 72
Wilson, Woodrow
FLN inspired by example of, 10, 19, 66
Fourteen Points for Peace of, 9, 20–21, 60
Khaled's appeal to, 22, 30
refusal to support anti-colonial causes by, 26
wine production in Algeria, 275–76
Woods, George, 169
World Bank, 130, 138, 168–69, 230, 296
World Peace Council (1961), 107
World Trade Center (New York City), 228, 231
World War I, 20

World War II, 29–31
World Youth Festival (1965), 257
The Wretched of the Earth (Fanon), 71, 85
Wright, Richard, 40

Yaker, Layashi, 147–48, 157–58, 196
Yala, M'hammed Hadj, 60, 206, 264–65, 269–70
Yalta Conference, 295
Yamasaki, Minoru, 228
Yazid, Mohamed
  Afro-Asian Peoples' Solidarity Organization meetings and, 262, 270
  on Algiers' as host of Second Bandung Conference, 231
  Conference of Independent African States (1958), 81
  diplomatic strategies of, 38–39, 48, 54–55
  Sands War negotiations with United States and, 220–21
  State Department evaluation of, 142
  U.S. diplomatic visit of, 147–48
  on U.S. economic aid to Algeria, 144
Yemen, 180–81, 183, 218–19
Youlou, Fulbert, 246–47
Yugoslavia
  African decolonization conflicts and, 175, 214
  Afro-Asianism and, 213, 267
  Algeria coup (1965) and, 288
  Algeria inspired by example of, 166
  Algerian independence as inspiration to, 5
  Algeria's connections in Africa and, 203–4, 207, 223, 251
  Algeria's independence struggle and, 63, 106–7
  Algeria's post-independence government and, 132–33, 165–66, 170, 184, 203–4, 213, 282
  arms shipments to Angola by, 192, 204
  Ben Bella's visit (1964) to, 267
  China and, 163–64, 211, 262, 267
  Egypt and, 132, 183–84
  FLN delegations to, 71–72
  humanitarian aid to Algeria and, 134
  Non-Aligned Movement and, 108–9, 204–5, 214, 244, 262–63
  Soviet Union and, 163–65, 210, 214
  Third Worldism and, 7, 174, 204, 214, 261, 282

Zaghlul, Sa'ad, 21–22
Zanzibar
  African governments' support for coup in, 292
  Algerian arms shipments to, 247
  British transfer of power in, 247
  Cuba and, 251
  FLN newspaper and, 25
  Israel and, 268
  left-wing coup (1964) in, 207, 245–48, 292
  as part of newly independent Tanzania, 248
Zhou Enlai
  Africa and Middle East tour of, 262–63
  Algeria visits (1963 and 1965) of, 211, 269
  Bandung Conference (1955), 40
  FLN received by, 94
  Nasser and, 267
  on need for Second Afro-Asian summit, 267
  on Palestinian cause, 266
  Third Worldism and, 206, 212–13
Zimbabwe, 297. *See also* Rhodesia, decolonization revolt in
Zimbabwe African People's Union (ZAPU), 248–49
Zionism. *See* Israel

www.ingramcontent.com/pod-product-compliance
Ingram Content Group UK Ltd.
Pitfield, Milton Keynes, MK11 3LW, UK
UKHW042005230426
12048UKWH00009B/568